MASTERPLOTS II

WOMEN'S
LITERATURE
SERIES

MASTERPLOTS II

WOMEN'S LITERATURE SERIES

5

Out-Spe

Edited by

FRANK N. MAGILL

SALEM PRESS

Pasadena, California   Englewood Cliffs, New Jersey

Copyright ©1995, by Salem Press, Inc.
All rights in this book are reserved. No part of this
work may be used or reproduced in any manner what-
soever or transmitted in any form or by any means,
electronic or mechanical, including photocopy, recording, or any information storage and retrieval system,
without written permission from the copyright owner
except in the case of brief quotations embodied in
critical articles and reviews. For information address
the publisher, Salem Press, Inc., P. O. Box 50062,
Pasadena, California, 91105.

∞ The paper used in these volumes conforms to the
American National Standard for Permanence of Paper for
Printed Library Materials, Z39.48-1984.

Library of Congress Cataloging-in-Publication Data
Masterplots II. Women's literature series / edited by
Frank N. Magill.
    p.   cm.
Includes bibliographical references (p.) and index.
    1. Literature—Women authors—History and criti-
cism. 2. Literature—Stories, plots, etc. 3. Women in
literature. I. Magill, Frank Northen, 1907-   . II. Ti-
tle: Masterplots 2. III. Title: Masterplots two.
PN471.M37   1995
809′.89287—dc20   94-25180
ISBN 0-89356-898-8 (set)   CIP
ISBN 0-89356-903-8 (volume 5)

LIST OF TITLES IN VOLUME 5

MASTERPLOTS II

WOMEN'S
LITERATURE
SERIES

OUT OF AFRICA

Author: Isak Dinesen (Baroness Karen Blixen-Finecke, 1885-1962)
Type of work: Memoir
Time of work: The 1920's
Locale: Kenya, Africa
First published: Den afrikanske Farm, 1937 (English translation, 1937)

Principal personages:
KAREN BLIXEN, a farm owner in Africa
DENYS FINCH-HATTON, Karen's lover
BERKELY COLE, an English aristocrat
FARAH, Karen's majordomo
KAMANTE, one of Karen's servants
KINANJUI, the Kikuyu chief

Form and Content

Out of Africa, the mythical autobiography of Karen Blixen (who wrote under the name Isak Dinesen), offers an idyll in which humans recover the original unity among themselves, society, and nature. This paradise collapses because of natural and historical interventions. The work is divided into five parts—four acts of idyll, then a fifth describing a swift, unaccountable fall. The dreamlike structure becomes progressively more tangible in its description of the farm's loss. Parts 1 and 2 represent what Dinesen calls Africa's "music."

Part 1, "Kamante and Lulu," tells of a wounded native, Kamante, and of a tiny gazelle, Lulu. Dinesen expresses African music by describing the civilized and wild qualities in each. Kamante's culinary genius makes Dinesen reconsider her own civilization. Elegant Lulu has the air of a wellborn lady. Karen's discovery of civilized traits in nature implies that civilized accomplishments can be judged by their congruence with nature.

"A Shooting Incident on the Farm," the second part, demonstrates the farm's social operation and contrasts European and African justice systems. Because of an accidental shooting, a Kyama (local court) is formed to settle the matter according to native laws. Karen is appointed judge because of her importance to the natives, but because she does not know local laws, she summons Kinanjui, the chief of the Kikuyu, to judge the Kyama.

Part 3, "Visitors to the Farm," describes her European guests and shows that those who frequented the farm were "outcasts," aristocrats such as Denys Finch-Hatton and Berkely Cole who should have lived before the Industrial Revolution or characters with aristocratic viewpoints, such as Knudsen and Emmanuelson. These people get along with Africans because of the orderliness of African society. Although Karen helps Emmanuelson and works with Knudsen, she forms a selective society with Berkely and Denys. When Berkely sulks at having to drink wine from coarse glasses in the jungle, Karen acknowledges his aristocracy by bringing him fine crystal. Denys teaches her how to read Latin and Greek and how to hunt lions. He takes her in his airplane to oversee the land and its animals, a flight so exhilarating that Karen compares Denys to the Archangel Gabriel.

Part 4, "From an Immigrant's Notebook," contains only observations, fables, and reflections. Although it breaks the narrative, it reiterates the book's themes and serves as a transition between idyll and fall. This section contains several animal fables, two about oxen. The first is about a wild ox who eludes capture through a leopard's mutilation, illustrating aristocratic spirit through the animal's energy and pride. The second, about a domesticated ox, illustrates that same pride broken. These animal stories have counterparts in tales about similar human beings. A meditation, "I Will Not Let Thee Go Except Thou Bless Me," implies that in relinquishment of both good and bad experience, people are blessed. This meditation prepares the reader for part 5, "Farewell to the Farm."

"Farewell to the Farm" presents Dinesen's loss of paradise in a series of catastrophes. The first is the collapse of the farm's economy because of grasshoppers and rising coffee prices. The next is Dinesen's failure to grant Chief Kinanjui's deathbed wish. Another betrayal follows when at Chief Kinanjui's funeral, rites are taken over by Christians, who bury the pagan chief in an undersized coffin. Then Denys Finch-Hatton dies in a plane crash. After these disasters, Karen asks for a sign, recognizing it when she sees a white cock biting out the tongue of a chameleon; she concludes that the "Great Powers" are laughing at her.

Analysis

Dinesen's pastoral mourns the loss of the old order of Africa and the similar old order of preindustrial Europe. The story has the structure of the fall of humanity. Its moral is the Lord's answer to Job. Karen's belief that the Great Powers are laughing at her is similar to the answer that Job received from God, that Job had neither the power nor the right to question Him. Karen concludes from her answer that the proper response to life is to experience joy both in beauty and in horror. Having experienced the unbearable, Karen passes through a kind of death, transcends her experiences, and weaves them into a pastoral fable about a paradise lost. This loss is not through choice, but through the outside forces of the modern world and nature.

Out of Africa conveys a common personal experience, the moral growth that occurs after a world is smashed and the resulting adaptation. The book restates this message on a cultural level. It retells, in an African setting, European myths about otherness and a past Golden Age. In order to convey myth, Dinesen is vague. She rarely mentions her name, Karen Blixen. The reader knows only that she is adored by both black and white and that Denys Finch-Hatton is her very close friend. This vagueness sustains the dreamlike nature of the memoir, both as a realized personal dream and as the Golden Age of psychic and cultural childhoods. The mythologizing process achieves the aim of romantic autobiography, illustrating the ideal in the real through individual personal experience.

Dinesen's implicit question, the one answered by the Great Powers is whether life is significant. Emmanuelson, part charlatan and part actor, points to life's significance (although he is not sure what it is) through its grandeur as perceived through the imagination. That Emmanuelson expresses this opinion is apt, for Dinesen considers transcendence to have an element of fakery, since it cannot be justified by facts.

In writing about the rhythms of African life, Dinesen also reconstructs the world of the European romantic past. The coffee plantation's loss to creditors represents the destruction of old European society based on mutual responsibility and affection. The tragedy of the old order's breakup is illustrated by the tribes' desire to stay on the land even after the farm is sold. In a traditional example of noblesse oblige, Karen pesters government offices until she secures the tribes a large reservation. Because of their attachment to nature, the natives' sense of morality is stoic. Their passive strength and endurance of hardships reflect, in their simplicity, the point to which the highest morality returns, at a complete acceptance of God's will.

In the same sense, the natives' primitive Ngomas, or dancing parties, while reminiscent of prehistoric times, also suggest the highest civilization. Karen's description of the people dancing in their appointed places, with intense care for one another's well-being, suggests the essence of social principle. Her description of Ngomas, landscapes, or animals as glorious, primitive, but timeless sights best expresses the message of *Out of Africa*. The glorious sight is Dinesen's perception of otherness, of life apart from human perception, a view articulated by the showman's answer to Count Schimmelmann's question of whether wild animals exist if humans do not see them: The showman answers that God sees them.

This glorious, timeless sight includes recognition that the primitive and the civilized contain elements of each other. If the elements of civilization can be found in primitive nature, then these accomplishments acquire absolute value. Thus a civilization can be judged as to how well it conforms to these absolutes in nature. The central vision of *Out of Africa* is one in which the old order is lauded and the modern one condemned. The right kind of civilization involves recovering those virtues lost in the Fall.

Karen's belief that the Great Powers are laughing at her aids her in her transcendent embrace of all experience. Life, she intimates, is not happy or easy, but sublime. With the right attitude, it can be received with joy. The sublime overview is symbolized in her last airplane flight with Denys. Karen's experience and survival of the lost paradise gives readers the hope that they too can survive such traumas and can even reconstruct through the imagination what has been lost in fact.

Context

Isak Dinesen blazed new trails for women. She farmed an African plantation, hunted lions, doctored native peoples, and judged their Kyamas. Dinesen was also a pioneer in the male province of adventure memoirs, a fact that she acknowledged by assuming a masculine pen name.

Ironically, Dinesen's gender and failure as a farmer began her writing career.

Brought up in a privileged family, she was taught only to marry well. When she returned to Denmark, penniless and divorced, her brother Thomas said that her suggested careers were positions always reserved for men. When Dinesen tentatively suggested writing, Thomas enthusiastically supported her.

Two years later, Dinesen had a short-story collection in manuscript form and several rejection slips. Determined to find a publisher, she wrangled an invitation to a London luncheon where the head of a publishing house was a guest. She broached the subject of her manuscript, but when Mr. Huntington learned that her book contained short stories, he refused to read them—short stories were difficult to sell. Later, Thomas handed the manuscript to writer Dorothy Canfield, who passed it on to publisher Robert Haas. He published the work with no expectation of commercial success, but although criticized for lacking a man's wisdom, *Seven Gothic Tales* was a great American success. As Baroness Blixen, she had gotten nowhere with Huntington, but Huntington wrote a letter full of praise to Isak Dinesen and asked for "his" address. Yet the book was not received well in Denmark. When the public discovered that Isak Dinesen was not a man, criticism of the erotic decadence of *Seven Gothic Tales* increased. One critic accused her of coquetry, shallowness, caprice, and most of all, perversity.

During her first book's success, *Out of Africa* was taking shape. As she wrote, years of subconscious ideas emerged. The work was published in the United States, England, and Denmark. It was well received in America and Denmark, but Huntington reported that only intellectuals liked the book in England. Although she was now lionized and financially independent, Blixen nevertheless received criticism from those dear to her. An old family member believed it almost scandalous for a lady to make money writing books.

Out of Africa places a woman in the center of adventure, instead of as a spectator or supporting figure. Like Job, to whom all was eventually restored, Blixen restored Africa to herself through her imagination.

Sources for Further Study

Gilead, Sarah. "Emigrant Selves: Narrative Strategies in Three Women's Autobiographies." *Criticism* 30, no. 1 (Winter, 1988): 43-62. Perceptively comments on Dinesen's escape into art when her coffee plantation fails. Gilead points out that the self that narrates *Out of Africa* is stable, not changing, as it narrates its chronicle of a lost paradise, and that this stable voice adds to *Out of Africa*'s mythic quality.

Langbaum, Robert. *The Gayety of Vision*. New York: Random House, 1965. Contains an excellent chapter on *Out of Africa* in which its mythical nature is analyzed. Also shows Dinesen's central theme of the unfortunate decay of an old, humane social order. The book also examines Dinesen's claim that the myth-making tradition of Africans is similar to that of Danes centuries ago.

Migel, Parmenia. *Titania*. London: Josef, 1967. A fascinating official biography, notable for its illustrations and quotations. The last chapters chronicle Dinesen's successful lecture tours; her interactions with such famous people as Marilyn

Monroe, Marianne Moore, and Pearl Buck; and her poignant death.

Pelensky, Olga Anastasia. *Isak Dinesen: The Life and Imagination of a Seducer.* Athens: Ohio University Press, 1991. This biography contains previously unpublished information, such as about the influence of Dinesen's father and of Charles Darwin's and Friedrich Nietzsche's works on her imagination. A chapter on *Out of Africa* examines the book as a thematic extension of *Seven Gothic Tales.*

Thurman, Judith. *Isak Dinesen.* New York: St. Martin's Press, 1982. This biography, which stresses Dinesen's literary career, was the first to include letters and family documents. Provides detailed descriptions of important events in Dinesen's life, such as lion hunts, that were later incorporated into *Out of Africa.* Also touches on Dinesen's religious faith.

Mary Hanford Bruce

OUTRAGEOUS ACTS AND EVERYDAY REBELLIONS

Author: Gloria Steinem (1934-   )
Type of work: Essays
First published: 1983

Form and Content

Gloria Steinem, feminist activist and founder of *Ms.* magazine, has been a writer throughout her career. Most of her works have been essay-length magazine articles, and this book is a compendium of selections of those writings. It is a volume of essays that give, in various ways, insights into the experience and character of the author. Some of the essays are comic ("If Men Could Menstruate"), some are sad ("Ruth's Song"), and others evoke horror ("The International Crime of Genital Mutilation"). Some are autobiographical ("I Was a Playboy Bunny") and others are about public figures ("Marilyn Monroe: The Woman Who Died Too Soon"). All are told from a feminist perspective; that is, they flow out of Steinem's conviction that women matter and that women's needs are important. These essays are widely varied in content and focus. What they have in common is that each illustrates an aspect of Steinem's view of the world and her commitment to women's concerns.

The volume begins with an introduction that tells the reader something about Steinem's feminist activism, including her work in founding *Ms.* magazine in 1972, at that time the only magazine editorially controlled solely by women. More than an introduction, however, this initial portion of the book is an essay in itself, whose purpose is to explain the experiences and observations that shaped the author of all the essays that follow.

The narrator of these essays is an unqualified "I." Steinem notes in the introduction that as a young journalist she was taught always to take the "objective" point of view. In these works, however, she unabashedly writes from her own. The essays are personal, self-disclosing, and authoritative. The reader learns what the author thinks and what she has learned.

Steinem divides her offerings into four sections. In the first, "Learning from Experience," the reader learns about some of the events that shaped the author, from growing up with a mentally ill mother during the Depression to going undercover as a Playboy bunny in her years as a reporter. The next section, "Other Basic Discoveries," covers perhaps the widest range of topics, including, for example, insights into the beauty of women's bodies of all shapes and sizes, a discussion of differing male and female styles of communication, and an analysis of the difference between pornography and erotica.

The third section gives Steinem's thoughts about five well-known women. In five separate essays, the reader learns what Steinem has to say about such diverse individuals as Marilyn Monroe, Patricia Nixon, Linda Lovelace, Jackie Kennedy Onassis, and Alice Walker. The final section is called "Transforming Politics," and true to the feminist adage that "the personal is political," it takes the reader from a fantasy on the ramifications of male menstruation to a report from the 1977 National Women's Conference in Houston, Texas.

The unifying factor in this collection is the mind of Gloria Steinem. The whole book is both personal, her perspective on life as she knows it, and political, relating to the world at large and the way it treats women.

Analysis

The title *Outrageous Acts and Everyday Rebellions* deserves analysis. Gloria Steinem means to tell the reader that outrageousness and rebelliousness are positive characteristics for women, who have been trained for many generations to be polite, quiet, and obedient. Although she is not as outrageous and rebellious as some feminist authors, such as Mary Daly, Steinem nevertheless claims the words as the title for her collection of essays.

Steinem grew up in a lower-middle-class home in Toledo, Ohio, during the Depression, and in "Ruth's Song (Because She Could Not Sing It)," Steinem explores her experience living in a fragmented family with a mentally ill mother. The reader learns how it felt for the young girl, who from age ten to age seventeen lived alone with her mother and took on all the adult responsibilities. Steinem writes of her ambivalence about her mother at that time. Yet this essay is not merely a sharing of childhood pain; it takes the reader with Gloria Steinem as she begins to understand her mother's life from her mother's own perspective, to find the person within the woman with whom she had grown up. She finds out about the facts of her mother's life before her illness, the pressures placed on her to conform to societal expectations of womanhood, and the self-limiting choices that eventually led to her mental breakdown. She shares Ruth with the reader so that the reader too can begin to know and appreciate this woman.

"In Praise of Women's Bodies" takes the reader to a women's health spa with the author, to watch with her as her fellow clients slowly come to accept their own bodies in their varieties of shapes, sizes, and types. At first embarrassed because they are not perfect, these women gradually open up, at least in this all-woman environment, becoming willing to appear before one another despite scars, stretch marks, protruding stomachs, wrinkled skin, and other human physical characteristics that women have learned to think of as ugly. As in "Ruth's Song," Steinem offers a feminist analysis of an ordinary event. She asks why it is that men's scars, signs of battle and violence, are emblems of pride, whereas the scars and stretch marks that women earn in the process of giving birth are signs of shame and embarrassment and ugliness. This point of view makes it possible for Steinem and her readers to look at women's scars in a whole new light.

Marilyn Monroe has been analyzed and reanalyzed in the years since her death in 1962, but Gloria Steinem gives the reader a feminist analysis of this woman who epitomizes the very opposite of a feminist role model. Many of the essays in this book explore the subject that would be the topic of Steinem's second book, *Revolution from Within: A Book of Self-Esteem* (1992), and this essay is no exception. Steinem wonders whether Monroe's life might have been different if she had lived long enough to benefit from the women's movement that began only a few years after her death. Specifically, she wonders whether she might have learned to resist the dependency on sexual attractiveness as her only measure of self-worth, her need to define herself totally based on approval and recognition from men. What, Steinem wonders, would have happened if Marilyn Monroe had known the love and friendship of other women?

The book ends with "Far from the Opposite Shore," a look back at the previous ten years or so of the women's movement and a look ahead. In this closing essay, Steinem shares strategies for feminists, including what she calls survival lessons. For example, facing the backlash of the late 1970's and early 1980's, she reminds the reader that serious opposition to feminism is a sign not of failure but of success. It is only because a specter of real equality has faced those who profit from inequality that the backlash has occurred. She ends her book by confessing that she had planned to do feminist activism for only a few years and then go back to her "real life." Now she knows that there is no turning back, that feminists are in it for life.

Context

Outrageous Acts and Everyday Rebellions is not a self-important, scholarly analysis of women's issues, but instead is simply a volume of essays about very ordinary topics. This book has value precisely because it is about topics everyone can relate to, as thought about by a woman who, though famous, sees herself as ordinary, as only one of many feminists in a wide and diverse sisterhood (which also can include men).

The humor and warmth of the essays make them easy to read, yet each packs a punch that stops the reader in her or his tracks with moments of insight—or, in *Ms.*'s language, "clicks." The light goes on—something new must be thought about or something old must be viewed in a new way.

The book is pro-women without being anti-men. It analyzes each subject from an unqualified female perspective, from inside a woman's experience. It looks at women and women's experiences with gentleness, love, and immense understanding. Reading this book could help women accept and love themselves as women, and it could help men see what few men have had the opportunity or have taken the time to see: what things look like from inside a woman's mind.

More even than her later book, *Revolution from Within*, which is more self-consciously introspective and autobiographical, this book helps the reader see who Gloria Steinem is. In the process of writing about a great variety of topics, she discloses herself, and the reader can see inside the mind and heart of this woman who has been so influential in the second wave of the women's movement.

Sources for Further Study

Davis, Flora. *Moving the Mountain: The Women's Movement in America Since 1960.* New York: Simon & Schuster, 1991. This history of thirty years of the feminist movement will help the reader understand the events and issues in which Gloria Steinem has been deeply involved. Steinem is mentioned several times in the book, allowing the reader to see how her journalistic and political work has been woven in with the efforts of others.

Freeman, Jo. *The Politic of Women's Liberation*. New York: David McKay, 1975. This early analysis of the women's movement helps the reader understand how it got started, and the various factions and their emphases. Steinem's work in founding *Ms.* and the National Women's Political Caucus is described.

Henry, Sondra, and Emily Taitz. *One Woman's Power: A Biography of Gloria Steinem*. Minneapolis: Dillon Press, 1987. Written for younger readers, this highly readable biography includes an afterword by Steinem herself. The book takes the reader from Steinem's childhood through her years as a young journalist, the founding of *Ms.*, and her political activism to the publication of *Outrageous Acts and Everyday Rebellions*.

Steinem, Gloria. *Revolution from Within: A Book of Self-Esteem*. Boston: Little, Brown, 1992. Steinem's second book is an examination of the importance of self-esteem in women's lives. Using the language and concepts of the self-help movements of the 1980's and 1990's, this book is self-revealing as well as analytical.

Wandersee, Winifred D. *On the Move: American Women in the 1970's*. Boston: Twayne, 1988. An analysis of the feminist movement in the 1970's from the perspective of a later time. It discusses the controversies between liberal and radical feminists, and the political strategies and events of the seventies, including Steinem's contributions.

Eleanor B. Amico

PALE HORSE, PALE RIDER
Three Short Novels

Author: Katherine Anne Porter (1890-1980)
Type of work: Novellas
First published: 1939

Form and Content

These short novels—"Old Mortality," "Noon Wine," and "Pale Horse, Pale Rider"—vary considerably in form, but all are realistic and are concerned primarily with death and its effects on the living. "Old Mortality" is a kind of family chronicle in which two motherless girls, Miranda and Maria, grow up surrounded by a family which romanticizes some of its members. The chief subject of romantic memory is Aunt Amy, a beautiful and wild young woman who consistently rejected the advances of Gabriel, her chief suitor, and refused to allow illness to limit her activities. Amy finally gave in to Gabriel and died not long after marrying him. In the course of the story, the girls grow up. The most important episode in their maturation is an encounter with Gabriel at a racetrack near New Orleans and a subsequent meeting with the grim woman who is his second wife. Gabriel, present in family legend as slender and handsome, is grossly fat and obsequious, and not even the fact that each girl has won a hundred dollars betting on one of his horses can counteract his unromantic presence. Miranda eventually tries to escape the family by eloping, but an encounter with a relative on a train trip back home for a family funeral shows her that although she will keep rebelling, she will never truly escape the family.

"Noon Wine" deals with another social level. Royal Earl Thompson and his family farm a run-down place in South Texas. His wife is sickly, his sons are unthinking dullards, and he is lazy and selfish. Into their lives comes Olaf Helton, a handyman who sets everything straight on the farm, tames the boys, and through his labor, makes the farm prosper for the first time. This paradise is destroyed when Mr. Hatch arrives, a bounty hunter who brings the news that Helton is in fact an escaped murderer who killed his brother and was committed to an insane asylum. In the minutes that follow, Thompson tries to prevent Hatch from seizing Helton and in doing so somehow kills the bounty hunter with a knife. A posse tracks down Helton and manhandles him so roughly that he dies soon after being put in jail. Thompson is cleared of any wrongdoing, but he cannot come to terms with what has happened to him. He takes his wife with him on increasingly desperate visits to all of his neighbors, trying to explain to them what had happened and why he should not be blamed. The neighbors become increasingly tired of his rationalizing and more and more skeptical about what really happened. Eventually, unable to live with himself and his belief that people think he was guilty of murder, he takes a shotgun, writes an incoherent note trying once more to justify himself, and commits suicide.

"Pale Horse, Pale Rider" returns Miranda to the center of attention. During World War I, she is a reporter on a newspaper in an unnamed city which resembles Denver,

Colorado. Her main job is reporting on bond drives and other war-related activities in the community, and in the course of her work, she meets a handsome young officer named Adam. About to be sent overseas, he has military duties that are almost certain to get him killed. They are beginning to fall in love when Miranda falls ill with the influenza that has become a national epidemic. Adam looks after her, as she becomes more and more delirious, until she can be taken to a hospital. In the next few days, Miranda becomes increasingly subject to hallucinations in which she sees Death as a figure on horseback. She is tended by a doctor named Hildesheim, and his German name evokes in her all the images of anti-German propaganda she has absorbed in her work; she fears and hates him, but he helps her through a near-death experience and she begins to recover. When she is finally able to read her mail, she comes across a note from a buddy of Adam, telling her that Adam had died of influenza. In the end, she is ready to return to the world, but it has become flat, dull, and empty.

Analysis

The manner of "Old Mortality" and "Pale Horse, Pale Rider" is intimate, as if the narrator were almost inside the character of Miranda, which is not surprising in view of the fact that Porter uses the character to present a version of her own experiences. The action of "Old Mortality" is seen in terms of its effect on the two sisters, but chiefly Miranda. The sisters are not at the center of the action until the latter part of the story, but the behavior of Aunt Amy, Gabriel, and the other figures is seen in terms of its impact on them.

In "Pale Horse, Pale Rider," Miranda is the central character, the focus of all the narration, and in several places the narration becomes an internal monologue which conveys the delirium that accompanies her illness. This is especially important because it is in those passages that Miranda imagines death, in terms of a song remembered from her childhood, as a pale rider coming for her on horseback. It is also in one of those passages that the fevered imagery based on wartime hatred of Germans comes to be focused on the doctor in Miranda's own fever. The tragic mood of the ending of the story is made especially moving by the contrast between Miranda's deep depression and the elation of the other characters at the ending of the war.

"Noon Wine," in contrast to the other stories, is told by an omniscient narrator who has no emotional commitment to any of the characters. Helton is in some ways the most sympathetic figure, but that is because he is a helpless victim of the despicable Hatch. On the other hand, he is clearly abnormal, playing the "Noon Wine" tune over and over on the harmonica, which is the only thing he seems to value. Moreover, he has killed his own brother and his handling of the Thompson's sons is harsh, if not brutal. Thompson is feckless and stupid, his wife a weakling, his sons crude and in other ways much like their father. Thompson's suicide, like his fruitless attempts to justify himself to his neighbors, is more an act of weakness than one of remorse or sorrow.

The power of all three novellas is in Porter's use of detail and her depiction of character. The members of Miranda's family are very much individuals, defined by traits of character or dress. In "Pale Horse, Pale Rider," the people Miranda meets in the course of her work are highly individualized, while Adam, a kind of dream lover, is deliberately made a stock romantic figure, too good to be real in the sense that the other characters are real. The wartime atmosphere is especially convincing in its ugly fervor, which is made to seem an infection like the influenza that is rampant in the community and in the country. The details of farm life provide a firmly realistic backdrop for the violent action in "Noon Wine."

Context

Of these three short novels, "Noon Wine" is the least concerned with women's issues. Mrs. Thompson is a slight character, weak physically and personally, unable to control her sons, unable to do anything either to control or to comfort her husband. She is a type character, representing the image of farm wives as a beaten-down group, worn out by childbearing and by the hard physical labor of running a farm, especially if the husband is lazy and improvident.

In the stories about Miranda, however, Porter is presenting female figures who are struggling for independence against the forces of family and society. What happens to Aunt Amy in "Old Mortality" makes her a romantic figure to the young girls, but it is also a warning to Miranda of how strong the bonds of family can be; Miranda's elopement into an unsuccessful marriage is still preferable to allowing herself to be buried in the family's mythology. Whatever becomes of her, she will not be another Amy. Her meeting on the train with Cousin Eva, despised because of her unattractiveness, reinforces her determination. Eva has made a life for herself as a crusader for women's suffrage, and Miranda promises herself that she will be equally independent. She is naïve in her self-confidence, but she will learn.

What she learns in "Pale Horse, Pale Rider" is that life is indeed hard and precarious. As a reporter, she fights to avoid being assigned only to women's interest stories, and she is attacked verbally in the newsroom by a hack performer resentful of one of her reviews. She struggles to avoid the fate of her friend Towney, condemned always to write the women's page. As a person, she finds the beginning of love with the handsome soldier, only to be stricken by influenza and to learn that her lover is dead of the disease. She has gained the independence she wished for in "Old Mortality," but her naïveté is destroyed by the iron facts of life and death.

Sources for Further Study

DeMouy, Jane Krause. *Katherine Anne Porter's Women: The Eye of Her Fiction.* Austin: University of Texas Press, 1983. A feminist reading of Porter's fiction, this book argues that Porter is a precursor of later feminism in her concentration on female characters trying to live independently in a world dominated by men.

Givner, Joan. *Katherine Anne Porter: A Life.* New York: Simon & Schuster, 1982. A detailed and somewhat unsympathetic biography which shows how Porter made use of her experiences, transforming them into fictions that made her early life seem more glamorous and more prosperous than it actually was.

Hilt, Kathryn. *Katherine Anne Porter: An Annotated Bibliography*. New York: Garland, 1990. A listing of all Porter's works and the books and essays written about her through the mid-1980's.

Lopez, Enrique Hank. *Conversations with Katherine Anne Porter: Refugee from Indian Creek*. Boston: Little, Brown, 1981. Stories about Porter's life as she told them to the man who was her companion during the last years of her life.

Unrue, Darlene Harbour. *Truth and Vision in Katherine Anne Porter's Fiction*. Athens: University of Georgia Press, 1985. The best extended critical work on Porter's fiction, this study is distinguished by its focus on an overriding theme in that fiction: the insistence on artistic order in a chaotic world. Also includes close readings of the works.

Warren, Robert Penn, ed. *Katherine Anne Porter*. Englewood Cliffs, N.J.: Prentice Hall, 1979. A collection of essays about Porter's work, by a variety of critics.

John M. Muste

PARALLEL LIVES
Five Victorian Marriages

Author: Phyllis Rose (1942-   )
Type of work: History
Time of work: The nineteenth century
Locale: Great Britain
First published: 1983

> *Principal personages:*
> JANE WELSH, a brilliant salon hostess and correspondent
> THOMAS CARLYLE, a social philosopher
> EFFIE GRAY, the model for several Pre-Raphaelite paintings
> JOHN RUSKIN, an art critic who championed the Pre-Raphaelite
>   Brotherhood
> JOHN EVERETT MILLAIS, a Pre-Raphaelite painter
> HARRIET TAYLOR, the coauthor of *The Subjection of Women*
>   (1869)
> JOHN STUART MILL, a utilitarian and feminist and the official
>   author of *The Subjection of Women*
> CATHERINE HOGARTH, a scotswoman who married Charles
>   Dickens
> CHARLES DICKENS, a prolific and hugely popular novelist
> MARIAN EVANS, a novelist who used the pen name George Eliot
> GEORGE HENRY LEWES, a literary journalist and Evans'
>   unofficial manager

Form and Content

Inspired by *The Mausoleum Book*—Sir Leslie Stephen's marital memoir prompted by James Anthony Froude's biographical portrait of Thomas Carlyle as insensitive husband—*Parallel Lives* explores the relationships of five Victorian writers to their mates. Through these marriages, or parallel lives, Phyllis Rose examines not only the power dynamics between romantic partners but also the way in which each union "seems . . . a subjectivist fiction with two points of view often deeply in conflict, sometimes fortuitously congruent." Her political and literary perspectives fuse into a feminist study of the imaginative patterns shaping Victorian couplehood, and to some extent modern marriages as well.

Rose focuses on a particular period or issue for each couple and arranges the vignettes so as to suggest the progressive stages in a relationship. Opening the book with the courtship of Jane Welsh and Thomas Carlyle, she next explores Effie Gray and John Ruskin's honeymoon and their eventual triangle with John Everett Millais; Harriet Taylor and John Stuart Mill's two-decade companionship during her marriage to another man, the father of her three children; Catherine Hogarth and Charles

Dickens' growing alienation, then publicized separation, in middle age; and Marian Evans and George Henry Lewes' backstreet happiness until his death. Rose distinguishes the Carlyles as the couple who impelled her study by using them as a framing device for the entire text. Thus each of the other narratives follows a Carlylean "prelude"—a brief anecdote thematically linking Jane and Thomas to their contemporaries—while the final pages revisit the pair decades after their courtship, when the balance of power had begun to shift from husband to wife. After two likewise Carlylean postludes that lead into a broader consideration of sexual politics, the book provides a selected bibliography following a chronology of Victorian relationships— in which Charles Darwin and his wife Emma Wedgwood figure prominently as a conventionally happy couple.

The manner in which Rose combines sound scholarship—attested by twenty-one pages of footnotes—with an informal, lively style is consistent with her suggestion that gossip about others' private affairs can be "the beginning of moral inquiry." In pursuing this inquiry, she draws on such diverse cultural critics as Sigmund Freud, Christopher Lasch, Simone de Beauvoir, Leo Tolstoy, Steven Marcus, and Maggie Scarf for fuller interpretation of her couples' interactions, which she describes vividly. As her prologue acknowledges, Victorian scholars will discover no new material in her pages, but Rose's emphasis on the selected marriages as clichéd or innovative constructs within nineteenth century patriarchal conventions of matrimony is original. Similarly new is her respect for the inventiveness and flexibility with which some of her couples accommodated themselves to their age's insistence on the permanence of marriage.

By considering the expectations and failings of both individuals in each couple, Rose avoids a simplistic denunciation of male dominance. Instead, with psychological and political insight, she explores the liabilities incurred by both men and women who allow narrowly traditional marriage plots to define their life partnerships. It is no surprise, therefore, that she regards Marian Evans and George Henry Lewes, who forged their exemplary happiness outside social conventions, as the "heroine and hero of the book."

Analysis

In covering the five years between Jane Welsh and Thomas Carlyle's first meeting and their wedding, Rose investigates female resistance to wifehood as a prescribed role and to marital intimacy with a man who does not inspire passion. Welsh, a young, spunky heiress reminiscent of Jane Austen's Emma and aspiring to be a Scottish Madame de Staël, steadily rebuffed Carlyle's attempts to turn their correspondence into something less platonic: "By a judicious wielding of anger, mockery, and coolness, she . . . won the initial struggle for power between them." Eventually, however, when her need for his intellectual validation combined with her distaste for remaining an unmarried woman in her widowed mother's house, Welsh ignored clues that her poor, lowborn schoolteacher suitor expected a helpmate devoted not to her studies but to "housewife duties." Thus, according to Rose, Carlyle's major achievement as a tutor had been to mold Welsh into a woman who wanted him as her husband.

The theme of sexual disinclination recurs in the story of newlyweds Effie Gray and John Ruskin, but on the husband's side. If the couple's failure to consummate their union in their entire first year together seems peculiar, evidently their honeymoon anxiety and inexperience were only too typical for the age. In recounting the notorious episode of John's "wedding-night trauma," Rose emphasizes Victorian culture's failure to educate its women and to prepare couples for shifting from prenuptial denial of sexual needs to compulsory intimacy. As noteworthy as their virginity, Rose suggests, was the Ruskins' difficulty with the universal newlywed task of cutting apron strings to forge a new identity as a couple. Still attached to his parents, John spared little time and energy for Effie, while demanding greater submission and solicitude from her; she resisted her in-laws' authority and retreated from domestic strife to her parental home. When Effie eventually sued for annulment of the marriage on grounds of nonconsummation, won her case, and wed the Pre-Raphaelite painter John Everett Millais—originally the couple's protégé—John Ruskin felt far more bitter about losing his fellow-artist's company than his wife's.

Whereas John Ruskin clearly undervalued women's worth, John Stuart Mill often seemed painfully uxorious—even before he married his platonic companion of two decades—the bold, passionate Mrs. Harriet Taylor. Impressively, Harriet exerted enough power after four years of marriage to John Taylor, who disappointed her intellectually and imposed on her sexually, to convince him both to tolerate her intimacy with Mill and to give up his conjugal rights. For his part, Mill respected her so much that he made her his collaborator in all he wrote after 1843 and prepared for their wedding (after her husband's death) by renouncing his future legal rights over her property and person. Given Harriet Taylor's dominance on all fronts, what Mill considered a marriage of equals strikes Rose as being more a "domestic case of affirmative action."

By contrast, a far more conventional inequality marked the marriage of Charles Dickens to Catherine Hogarth, whom he initially appreciated as "that dignifying satellite, a wife" only to become disillusioned after her twenty-odd years of subordination, childbirth, and poor housekeeping. Restless at forty-five, Charles denied their early happiness together, concocting a melodramatic fiction of Catherine as a monstrously inadequate wife and mother, and of himself as her victim. When he eventually maneuvered her into requesting a separation, he justified himself to a public steeped in his novelistic images of domestic bliss by publishing a letter in *The Times* to explain their incompatibility—and to deny the accurate rumors about his interest in the young actress Ellen Ternan. Manipulating for power and popularity, deceiving himself and others, Charles Dickens exemplifies the way in which Rose believes one should not end a marriage.

From the frustrations of the traditional Dickens' union, the book moves to the "joint life of exceptional richness" led by Marian Evans and George Henry Lewes, "literary London's most celebrated illicit couple." Faced with unreasonable laws that prevented his divorce from a faithless wife, Lewes committed himself to Evans in an unofficial relationship that lasted twenty-four years and challenged Victorian norms for life partnership. From her fulfillment in this union came her discovery of her creative talents: Thus, the offspring of their union was George Eliot.

To round out the series of marital portraits, Rose returns to the Carlyles, with Thomas as widower agonizing over the diary in which Jane had bitterly chronicled his neglect of her. He chose to expiate his guilt by editing her letters for publication and writing the remorseful *Reminiscences* (1881). If Jane haunted his conscience, however, perhaps he had the last word by shaping her image for posterity.

Context

Parallel Lives is a feminist milestone in a number of ways. First, Rose challenges prevailing misogynist versions of these five relationships. For example, she explores criticism's resistance to Mill's own claim that Harriet Taylor was his collaborator, its emphasis on Marian Evans as a neurotically needy spinster rather than a woman who pursued love assertively, and its assumption that Catherine Hogarth indeed failed Dickens through her middle-aged frumpiness. Second, Rose argues the need to go beyond assigning blame for "bad" behavior in individuals to confronting the deep problems "generated inevitably by the peculiar privileges and stresses of traditional marriage." In fact, merely by introducing the women of the couples first, before their change of status and name, Rose emphasizes the female equality that she considers exceptional, even impossible, in patriarchy's domestic paradigms. With the exception of Catherine Hogarth, her women are clearly role models of female strength in adversity, especially Rose's favorite, the feisty Jane Welsh.

Rose also challenges the facile equation of "Victorian" with "prudish" or "re-pressed" by re-visioning some of the unusual asexual arrangements in her narratives as innovative and inspired. Moreover, she argues convincingly that such irregular pre-Freudian unions as the Carlyles' and the Ruskins' might teach important lessons in flexibility—and that redefining couplehood is still relevant in the late twentieth century, with easy divorce doing little to undermine the monopoly of the marriage plot on people's life choices. Finally, Rose underlines the frequent consistency between familial and national tyranny, by tracing Thomas Carlyle's, John Ruskin's, and Charles Dickens' authoritarianism on the one hand and John Stuart Mill's and George Henry Lewes' liberalism on the other, from their marriages to their political stands on slavery, class, and imperialism.

Parallel Lives found favor with critics as an original, provocative, and witty book. Even Nina Auerbach, whose review in *The New York Times Book Review* faulted Rose for giving her male protagonists the usual lion's share of attention, conceded that the familiar episodes unfold so "compellingly here, they spring to life all over again." Rose's 1978 study *Woman of Letters: A Life of Virginia Woolf* had the same feminist biographical underpinnings.

Sources for Further Study

Basch, Françoise. *Relative Creatures: Victorian Women in Society and the Novel.*

Translated by Rudolf Anthony. New York: Schocken, 1974. Basch opens this impressively documented book with the daily life of actual Victorian women, then considers their fictional counterparts in the works of such writers as Dickens, Eliot, William Makepeace Thackeray and the Brontës. Like Rose, Basch suggests that fulfillment came to Eliot and Lewes, Taylor and Mill—and even Dickens and Ellen Ternan—because they defied Victorian conventions.

Harrison, Fraser. *The Dark Angel: Aspects of Victorian Sexuality.* New York: Universe Books, 1978. Harrison examines social constructions of marriage in the Victorian era, drawing on the ideas and imagery of Ruskin, Dickens, Mill, and Millais, among others, for his first section on "Middle-Class Sexuality." Harrison sensitively explores some of the same issues as Rose: courtship stress, wifely submission, and female education.

Longford, Elizabeth. *Eminent Victorian Women.* New York: Alfred A. Knopf, 1981. Longford introduces her study of family influences and career-romance conflicts in eleven female lives, with a section on Queen Victoria's and John Stuart Mill's dissimilar views on women's rights. Although her only subject in common with Rose is George Eliot, the book—with a wealth of photographs, illustrations, and *Punch* cartoons—resembles *Parallel Lives* in its readability, its feminist perspective, and its period detail.

Lutyens, Mary. *Millais and the Ruskins.* London: John Murray, 1967. A detailed account of the disintegration of the Ruskins' marriage during their friendship with John Everett Millais. Lutyens' chief sources are original letters, on which she draws generously and comments concisely in order to let the principals speak for themselves.

Wohl, Anthony S., ed. *The Victorian Family: Structure and Stresses.* New York: St. Martin's Press, 1978. This book of nine essays explores the Victorian family as a microcosm of its culture, with special attention to the subordination of women and children. The issue of power so central to Rose's study is particularly prominent in David Roberts' "The Paterfamilias of the Victorian Governing Classes" and Michael Brooks's "Love and Possession in a Victorian Household: The Example of the Ruskins."

Margaret Bozenna Goscilo

PARIS JOURNAL, 1944-1965

Author: Janet Flanner (1892-1978)
Type of work: Essays
First published: 1965

Form and Content

Janet Flanner's *Paris Journal, 1944-1965* is a collection of her "Letters from Paris" assembled by her esteemed editor, William Shawn. The two decades of letters in this collection were originally published fortnightly—and with fair regularity—in *The New Yorker*, which for many years was widely regarded as the most literate, sophisticated, and intelligent of America's magazines. The letters here are companions flanking in time those that Flanner collected for her *Paris Was Yesterday, 1925-1939* (1972) and *Paris Journal, 1965-1971* (1971). Together these letters earned "Genêt" (Flanner's pen name) an extraordinary readership not only because of their acute, precise journalism but also for the unique literary qualities that also distinguished her perceptions of a broad swath of French life during the half century of her reportage. In circles where intelligence and style counted, Flanner was easily the most admired woman journalist of her day.

Harold Ross, the energetic young founder of *The New Yorker*, hired Flanner in 1925. She was already living in Paris on a marginal income. At the time, Ross was struggling to launch his fledgling magazine, and Flanner appeared to him as his "great white hope": a bright, experienced writer who knew the Paris scene. Ross had only sketchy notions of what he expected from Flanner. He wanted anecdotal and incidental "stuff" on places and people familiar to Americans, something on the arts and fashion (but not too technical), and chatter about the interesting people gadding about Paris. In short, Ross granted Flanner extensive literary license, clear only that he wanted to receive materials into which "a definite personality" had been injected. Fifty years later, the letters having been interrupted at length only by France's defeat and occupation by Germany, there was abundant evidence that Flanner had skillfully insinuated her own "definite personality" into the hearts and minds of *The New Yorker*'s devotees.

Carefully crafted, Genêt's letters were tart, pithy, and tantalizingly brief. Ross originally asked for commentaries of a thousand words on a weekly basis. When he shortly decided on bimonthly contributions, however, Genêt began sending articles of two thousand words that sometimes stretched to three thousand. When on a score of occasions she was asked to contribute to *The New Yorker*'s soon-to-be-famous "Profiles" column, which she did initially in 1927 by portraying the internationally renowned dancer Isadora Duncan, the length of her contributions rose to 3,600 words.

Vignettes of the personalities whom Genêt profiled more extensively invariably appeared first in her letters, and they included a remarkable array. Among the famous and infamous personalities whom she sketched were novelists and literary lights such as Edith Wharton, André Malraux, and Thomas Mann, along with political figures such as Adolph Hitler, Queen Mary of Great Britain, Léon Blum, Philippe Pétain, Wendell Willkie, and William Bullitt. There were musicians, composers, artists, dramatists, and singers: for example, Igor Stravinsky, Pablo Picasso, Georges Braque, Henri Matisse, Bernard Buffet, and Lily Pons. Society hostess Elsa Maxwell; actress Bette Davis; couturiers Elsa Schiaparelli, Charles Frederick Worth, and Gabrielle (Coco) Chanel; and perfumer and financier François Coty were among those whom Genêt depicted to let readers "in" on the worlds of "stars"—high society, chic, and fashion that added lustre to the Parisian cultural scene.

Genêt's concise reports on the parade of personalities, however, usually were placed in the context of her incisive observations on the grand events shaping the lives of Parisians, and hence of France. Thus, readers who followed the letters regularly were treated to insightful reporting on key features of France's broad, unfolding social history. Ultimately, critics, colleagues, and admirers would characterize her as America's answer to France's Alexis de Tocqueville, one of the greatest nineteenth century observers of American democracy.

Analysis

Flanner began her career with *The New Yorker* as a modestly experienced professional writer, but as she herself recorded, she had much to learn. Her letters therefore trace her progress toward accomplished reporting and, simultaneously, toward the development of a distinctive style. Aware that Ross wanted her writing to reflect what the French thought, not what she thought, she tried from the outset to compose her letters without the inclusion of editorial comment, impressionism, or personal remarks: goals, critics noted, that she did not always reach. Almost immediately, she eschewed the first-person singular, the "I" that involved writer with subject. To garner a basic range of information as well as to grasp opinion, she consistently read a dozen or so French newspapers each day. Because of the precision of the French language— an exactitude that made it the language of international diplomacy for two centuries— she learned to make her sentences athletic, her imagery sharp. Meanwhile, she met everyone and read omnivorously.

Somehow, in the process of disciplining herself and pleasing Ross and his successor, William Shawn (both of whom she greatly admired), the chic, gruff-voiced, chain-smoking Flanner left many readers sensitive to the tone and rhythms of her evocative descriptions and precise, intelligent speech—one reason that she habitually read drafts of her work to companions. Regardless of her subject or its impact on her, the tenor of her work was commonsensical and lively. Shawn commented the year after her death that she was "a stranger to fatigue, boredom, and cynicism," that "she met the world with rapture and wrote about it with pleasure." A brilliant individualist, she nevertheless subordinated her natural vivacity to the essences of her information and to what she believed this hard substance meant.

The twenty-odd years of her postwar letters inevitably differed in tone and content from those that Genêt wrote during the 1920's and 1930's. The changes were partly stylistic, but chiefly they were attributable to the altered character of events. Earlier writings had stressed the whirling color of Paris as an international cultural center, as well as the heart of France. They captured the city's ambience through deft descriptions of its cafés and nightclubs; the openings and closings of its current art shows, plays, and concerts; and even more important, the goings-on about town of newsworthy European and American personalities. Politics certainly were not ignored, but until France was shattered after 1935 by bitter political factionalism, politicians and political activities received less notice than Charles Lindbergh or Mata Hari. This emphasis changed after Genêt resumed her reporting shortly after the Allied liberation of Paris in 1944.

The postwar letters thus began as a chronicle of Parisians' efforts to rehabilitate their lives, their capital, and their nation: chronicles of the moral and physical reconstruction of France as viewed from Paris. Genêt wrote poignant reports of how Parisians ate (badly), how they dressed (poorly), how they went about their work (listlessly), how they dealt with collaborators (harshly), and how tens of thousands of Parisians and hundreds of thousands of former prisoners of war, forced laborers, and concentration camp victims were received after years of captivity abroad (sadly and ineptly).

Flanner's themes during the postwar decade illuminated France's perceived gains and losses. The Marshall Plan, the grudging acceptance of German rearmament, and talks about European Union were positive signs coupled with discernible economic recovery and the renascence of a traditionally critical spirit. Yet noted, too, were the anxieties of the no-longer-powerful. France was caught in the potentially terminal contest between the Soviets and Americans, the two barbaric colossi of the Cold War, and there were rumblings within the anachronistic French colonial empire marked by broken promises and violent, costly revolutions in French Indochina (Vietnam), Morocco, Algeria, and Tunisia. All, to the French, emphasized their lost grandeur. These confusing changes and challenges allowed Genêt to assay a new cast of political players: Pierre Mendès-France, René Pleven, Maurice Thorez, Robert Schuman, and the enigmatic Charles De Gaulle—waiting with destiny, so admirers thought, for the call to revivify France.

If somewhat sublimated in her letters, the writers, painters, composers, musicians, dramatists, films, and cinema stars were hardly forgotten. Literary works by Albert Camus, André Malraux, André Gide, Simone de Beauvoir, Colette, Françoise Sagan, and François Mauriac, for example, as well as criticisms drawn and prizes won, were accompanied by observations on the unconventional plays of Jean Cocteau, Bertolt Brecht, and Samuel Beckett. Even the accolades given to jazzmen "Dizzy" Gillespie and Louis Armstrong were styled around political events. Such was the general balance of her themes and materials.

Context

Genêt's letters rarely touched specifically on feminist issues or women's rights. Rather, Janet Flanner's lifestyle was a sufficient testimonial to her own version of independence. Early in life, she had rebelled against her comfortable, upper-middle-class Indianapolis origins and, via the dissident bohemianism of Greenwich Village, found in Paris the shelter required to nourish her dreams. It was in her novel, *The Cubicle City* (1962), a thinly disguised personal account, that she proclaimed, through the words of her heroine, adherence to her own version of feminine liberation and the precepts of the "New Woman" of the 1920's. This meant, in part, "natural" sexual freedom, of the kind that tradition had vouchsafed to males alone.

All Flanner's abiding lovers were women. With them, she experienced the "healthy eroticism" and "lusty tenderness" embodied in the intimacies of purely feminine relationships. Sometimes without abandoning one companion, she simultaneously loved others, suffering, she recounted, the painful guilt entailed by her inevitable deceptions, for she remained a morally responsible person affected always by traces of her midwestern puritanism. In this context, America represented maleness, although there were aspects of American life that she respected and admired. Paris, on the other hand, was feminine: a city with "an old girl's countenance, shaded by a trollop's gay wig."

While at times she perceived of herself as stereotypically female—passive, easily distracted, lacking willpower, and unable to create anything lasting—and pondered the desirability of a third sex, she recognized these as traps that failed to expose the source of her problems. It was Paris, with its freedom-loving appreciation of the art of living and its civilized tolerance toward creativity, that most warmly nurtured her self-comprehension. Public comprehension earned her the 1966 National Book Award and the undying affection of her readers.

Sources for Further Study

Drutman, Irving, ed. *Janet Flanner's World.* New York: Harcourt Brace Jovanovich, 1979. A splendid assemblage of Flanner's uncollected letters, many of which were datelined London, Berlin, Budapest, Cologne, and Nuremberg and complemented her Paris letters, including her usual analyses of personalities and important political and cultural events. Contains an extensive index and photographs. Informative and characteristically delightful.

Flanner, Janet. *An American in Paris.* New York: Simon & Schuster, 1940. Classic depictions of a wide sampling of French, Parisian, and foreign personalities during the late 1920's and early 1930's. Engaging, with anecdotes and pen-portraits at their best.

——————. *Darlinghissima.* Edited by Natalia Danesi Murray. New York: Random House, 1985. Flanner's intimate letters to her "most darling" friend, the editor of this volume. They are gems of commentary and pithy, relatively unguarded expressions of opinion—something Genêt eschewed in her published works. Well edited and delightful reading. An extensive index is provided, mostly to the scores of personalities to whom she alluded. Many photographs are included.

——————. *Paris Was Yesterday, 1925-1939.* New York: Viking Press, 1972. An essential prologue to *Paris Journal, 1944-1965.* Filled with vivid descriptions of the expatriates' Paris, along with colorful as well as important personalities of the

French version of the Roaring Twenties. Fascinating, and a fine social history. Includes an index.

Wineapple, Brenda. *Genêt: A Biography of Janet Flanner.* New York: Ticknor & Fields, 1989. The author's first book and a solid, well-written, and well-researched study, one unlikely to be replaced for excellence and sensitivity. Offers many photographs, a fine bibliography, and a very extensive index. Particularly strong on evidence of Flanner's constant self-analysis.

Clifton K. Yearley

PASSAGES
Predictable Crises of Adult Life

Author: Gail Sheehy (1937-   )
Type of work: Social criticism
First published: 1976

Form and Content

Gail Sheehy's title *Passages: Predictable Crises of Adult Life* refers to the passages or transitions that people make between years of relative stability in their adult lives. Passages are often painful periods during which women and men are forced to change their assumptions about their relationships, their jobs, and their goals. (Although her subtitle refers to "crises," Sheehy prefers the less threatening word "passages.") These passages are predictable—one way or another, all adults must move from one stage to the next.

Before *Passages* was published, the stages of children's lives (such as "the terrible twos") were well known, but little had been written about how adults develop, and that little was mainly written by men about men. In contrast, Sheehy describes the development of both women and men. She goes on to show that women's lives have different changes from men's and that these changes affect not only the women themselves but also their marriages.

Sheehy began to think about passages one day in her mid-thirties. In her job as a journalist, she was talking to a young boy in Northern Ireland—and his face was shot off. That moment shattered her comfortable assumptions about life and made her confront her own mortality. In her anguish, she wondered if she was unique and alone in what was happening to her at that time in her life. So she set about interviewing other adults about growing older and in time developed a general description of the stages that both men and women live through between the ages of eighteen and about fifty.

Passages is divided into seven parts containing twenty-five chapters and many more subchapters, as well as notes, a bibliography, and an index. It describes more or less chronologically the four predictable passages of adulthood and illustrates them with material drawn from more than one hundred in-depth interviews. Although *Passages* is not wed to theory, Sheehy insists that all adults must navigate the same passages; either they fail and become life's losers, or they succeed and lead more fulfilling lives. Note too that adults cannot skip a passage; they cannot jump directly from disturbed late adolescence to a fulfilled midlife.

Sheehy distinguishes four major times of passage. At about age eighteen, men and women begin their adult lives by "Pulling Up Roots." Then in their "Trying Twenties," they begin to take their place in the world. Turning thirty gives them a new set of problems, and "The Deadline Decade" from thirty-five to forty-five poses even more. If these passages are navigated with some success, Sheehy believes that adults can look forward to happiness and "Renewal."

Analysis

Sheehy has written a popular book which investigates a new subject and informs and entertains the ordinary reader. Her training as a journalist helps her to avoid the jargon of psychologists. *Passages* is divided into short, easy-to-read sections. Although each part is clearly labeled, the book does not proceed with rigorous logic; instead, Sheehy informally accumulates related material: the ideas of psychologists, her own ideas and terms, the stories of people to whom she has talked, and a generous and revealing selection of their own words. Some readers may find it hard to discover exactly what years are covered by which "passage." *Passages* is sometimes inexact because the specific ages when specific passages occur will vary among different people. The author's time frame is general: Adults often experience passages at the ages that Sheehy cites—but not always.

Sheehy begins with the working assumption that adult lives progress in stages about five to ten years long. The first passage occurs between the ages of eighteen and twenty-two, when aspiring adults leave the stability of home. They do not know what they want, except that they do not want to become like their parents. As they establish separate identities, they often seek security in groups, in causes, or in the love of another person. Some women suffer from timidity and look for a mate who is stronger.

The stability that they achieve is disrupted by the problems of Sheehy's second passage. Between the ages of twenty-two and twenty-seven, most men and many women enter the "real world" of work and career. They begin with ideals and illusions; they believe that their choices are binding forever. Here Sheehy's concern with marriage and women's problems becomes more evident. She finds that to a great extent both men and women marry to obtain stability. Their stability is real for a time, even though many men take their new careers more seriously than their marriages and women who have children turn their attention to the home. As husbands become more sure of themselves, some women lose the independence and confidence that they had before they married. The result is tension.

The third time of passage occurs roughly between the ages of twenty-eight and thirty-four. Both men and women discover that they never can achieve all they had dreamed of in their twenties. Problems between husbands and wives begin when they find that they lead different lives and begin to move apart. His career is progressing; she wants to do more than rear children and cook. Sheehy calls this the "Catch-30": If she strikes out on her own, he is jealous of her new interests; if she does not, he feels trapped in a stagnant marriage and thinks that she envies him. Many couples divorce. One product of divorce is the Changed Woman: the divorced wife who enjoys her freedom, makes herself over, and takes on new tasks—much to the dismay of her former husband. Couples can weather this storm, however, and emerge happier and stronger, particularly if the wife is assertive and the husband understanding.

The fourth and last passage that Sheehy discusses is that of the "Deadline Decade," from ages thirty-five to forty-five. About this time, adults realize that life is half over and ask "Is this all there is?" As their own parents grow old and die, they realize (as Sheehy did in Northern Ireland) that sometime they too must die. They realize that they are alone and that their partners are separate individuals as well. A man worries about having time left to do everything; he may believe that he needs to give more attention to his family. A woman without a firm sense of her own identity begins to wonder how to fill the years after her children leave or after she is widowed. Stronger women seize their last chance to achieve something in the world beyond the home. So "Catch-30" is reversed. Now the woman becomes more aggressive and enterprising, just as the man is less satisfied by his career and more interested in the ties of home. His life is made less happy by normal sexual changes and by finding that his children are drawing away into adolescence at about the same time that his wife is asserting herself.

Sheehy sees light at the end of this passage. If both men and women accept the fact that they are alone, if women can transcend their earlier dependence, if men will listen to what women tell them, and if men can avoid stagnation by expanding their interests then both can arrive at a happy mellowing. Through the necessary pain of making their passages, each will have shed illusions and will come to approve of herself or himself. They will have both companionship and sex and will find themselves enjoying the conscious and reciprocal dependence that separate people can achieve.

Some commentators complain that Sheehy's analysis is unsystematic and that its sample is narrow: She interviewed mainly middle-class, college-educated people who seem to have inhabited rather exotic areas of New York City and Southern California in a particular decade. Sheehy's emphasis may be too upbeat for some readers, for although one hears about failure, Sheehy emphasizes winning happiness by facing up to life's problems. Yet many agree that *Passages* addresses important issues worth raising, that it brings together a range of ideas about adult development and applies them intelligently, sympathetically, and evenhandedly to the lives of both men and women. Sheehy's book performs a valuable service by insisting that women's passages are different from men's and that many marriage problems are caused by the differences between husbands' and wives' timetables.

Context

Because Sheehy is not a trained psychologist and because she writes in a popular journalistic style, *Passages* is seldom mentioned in scholarly books. Professionals seem to regard it as a sourcebook, a popular work which has been useful in getting women interested in their own development. Nevertheless, its impact has been great. For one thing, Sheehy was a pioneer. Before her book, few studies differentiated women's development from men's, and few discussed the relations between men and women as they are affected by different personal timetables. She was one of the early writers to focus on one of the most important problems that continue to face contemporary women: how to mix motherhood and a career. All in all, her book has contributed to creating a favorable climate of opinion for discussion of the development of adult women and for more professional and academic studies of them.

Moreover, *Passages* has sold millions of copies, and even if everyone does not find that each aspect of each "passage" is relevant, many readers have discovered insights and perspectives that tally with their own experience and that help them understand their lives. Since many professional books are by necessity limited in scope, the popular and nonprofessional nature of *Passages* allowed Sheehy to be more comprehensive than many books on women's development. Although some readers may say that *Passages* is not really a work of women's literature because it treats men as well as women, Sheehy makes clear that to understand a number of women's problems, it is also necessary to understand men's problems with sympathy. This book led Sheehy to write a sequel entitled *Pathfinders* (1981).

Sources for Further Study
Gilligan, Carol. *In a Different Voice: Psychological Theory and Women's Development*. Cambridge, Mass.: Harvard University Press, 1982. An important and well-written academic study. Gilligan discusses the differences between women and men as revealed by how they talk and write about themselves. Chapter 6, "Visions of Maturity," deals with the problems of women's early adult and midlife years. A bibliography and indexes are included.
Heilbrun, Carolyn G. *Reinventing Womanhood*. New York: W. W. Norton, 1979. In the course of her wise and well-written book, Heilbrun defends Sheehy against critic Christopher Lasch and supports her idea that women's lives follow different patterns from men's. A bibliography and index are provided.
Kaplan, Alexandra G., Nancy Gleason, and Roma Klein. "Women's Self-Development in Late Adolescence." In *Women's Growth in Connection: Writings from the Stone Center*, edited by Judith Jordan et al. New York: Guilford Press, 1991. This article focuses on Sheehy's first passage. It finds that college-age women want both to break away from their mothers and to have close relationships with them. Contains a bibliography and an index.
Lasch, Christopher. "Planned Obsolescence." *New York Review of Books* 23, no. 17 (October 28, 1976): 7. An important negative early review. Lasch thinks that although *Passages* pretends to provide straight talk about growing older, it really gives only the shallow consolations that earlier upbeat books extolled as the power of positive thinking.
Llewelyn, Sue, and Kate Osborne. *Women's Lives*. London: Routledge, 1990. The authors define women's lives not by ages, but by events: marriages, jobs, and motherhood, as well as social, biological, and economic changes. Like Sheehy, they see dangers if a woman fails to make a transition successfully. Offers bibliographies and an index.
Mercer, Ramona T., Elizabeth G. Nichols, and Glen Caspers Doyle. *Transitions in a Woman's Life: Major Life Events in Developmental Context*. New York: Springer, 1989. Even though the "transitions" that the authors investigate are not "passages," this work considers women's lives in a way comparable to Sheehy's. They focus on the influence of mothers and motherhood and conclude that a woman's mother is a greater influence on her than motherhood itself. A bibliography and an index are included.

Sheehy, Gail. *Pathfinders*. New York: William Morrow, 1981. This continuation of *Passages* asks how successful women and men have navigated their passages to achieve well-being. Sheehy adds some new life stages, beginning with the Comeback Decade (ages forty-six to fifty-five). Appendices provide a "Life History Questionnaire" and a key to scoring it. A bibliography and an index are offered.

George Soule

PASSING

Author: Nella Larsen (1891-1964)
Type of work: Novel
Type of plot: Social realism
Time of plot: 1927
Locale: New York City
First published: 1929

> *Principal characters:*
> IRENE REDFIELD, an upper-middle-class, light-skinned African
> American woman
> CLARE KENDRY, Irene's childhood friend, a light-skinned African
> American woman who is "passing" as white
> BRIAN REDFIELD, Irene's husband, a doctor with a lucrative
> Harlem practice
> JOHN (JACK) BELLEW, Clare's wealthy, bigoted white husband,
> who does not know that she is black and who affectionately
> calls her "Nig"
> GERTRUDE MARTIN, a light-skinned African American woman
> happily married to a white man from whom she has no secrets
> HUGH WENTWORTH, a white intellectual who often attends
> Irene's parties

Form and Content

Passing is a conventionally structured novel in which the tale is told from the controlled omniscient perspective. It is a story whose tension emanates from the three main characters and which concludes in a web of ambiguity and mystery. The unmistakable purpose lies in the psychological-social problem area, for the racial dilemmas illuminate intricate personal relationships, all of them possibly doomed.

Nella Larsen, an African American writer and prominent participant in the Harlem Renaissance, explores the consequences of "passing" (a phenomenon sometimes, in social science, called "crossing"; both terms are used to describe a light-skinned African American's choice to live in society as white without revealing his or her true racial history). She also studies potential marital problems precipitated by jealousy and suspicion, dilemmas of child rearing and infidelity, and financial security versus personal fulfillment. There is no doubt, however, that the catalyst propelling the narrative, initiating examination into personal values, and forcing a confrontation with individual racial identity is Clare Kendry, the woman who is, indeed, passing, and whose characterization embodies the theme noted in literary history as "the tragic mulatta."

Larsen's challenging novel focuses on two African American women whose lives have taken radically different paths, it would seem, and who meet after years of separation. In passing, Clare has deliberately distanced herself from the past, but Irene quickly remembers, with more than a touch of uneasiness, her old friend as unpredictable, an aggressive, risk-taking woman who delights in living dangerously. Irene Redfield, proud of her black identity and disapproving of Clare's way of life, instinctively fears the imminent intrusion into her own safe and secure home. Yet, fascinated with the possibilities, she allows it, even encourages it, to happen. The persistent Clare, aided and abetted, however reluctantly, by Irene, makes herself part of the Redfield circle. When her husband, the racist Bellew, goes off on his frequent business trips, Clare and the Redfields are together, for at these moments the passing woman feels that, in a sense, she is openly validating her own identity, reaching out to relate to the people and that part of herself that she had rejected—and that she continues to reject in her life as a white wife. Irene Redfield tolerates the imposition of her old friend, and, in fact, introduces Clare into the sophisticated group of friends, black and white, who gather regularly for art shows, discussions, or parties. It appears that Clare's identity problems and her daily life, poised over the abyss between two disparate worlds, create a riveting, hypnotic aura around Irene. She is repulsed by Clare's passing but must admire her willingness to take the risk that is involved, a risk similar to that of starting a new life, which she is unwilling to take with her husband Brian. A clearly ambivalent Irene Redfield feels the palpable invasion of a new spirit into her home. The bickerings and sometimes harsh arguments between her and her husband are soon exacerbated.

Irene Redfield's understandable contentment with her luxurious home and handsome, articulate children has seemingly created in her a fetish of economic security and marital safety, leading her to oppose Brian's desire that they leave the United States. At the same time, she recognizes that Clare's passing is similarly motivated by the desire for economic survival, safety, and security. The two are, actually, not so different in their overall perception of what is important in life. Thus, suddenly, as if struck by a lightning bolt, Irene, irritated at the domestic turbulence with her husband, realizes that Clare Kendry is a direct threat to her own home and marriage. In response to a question about what she would do if her secret of passing were discovered, Clare asserts that she would move to Harlem to be with her people. Recalling this, Irene becomes suspicious and fearful. If Clare cannot be made to vanish from the earth, at least her secret must be kept and protected at all costs—to keep the Redfields together.

Through an accidental meeting with Irene in the company of a black friend, Bellew is alerted to the possibility that his "Nig" is indeed, passing. Driven by the fury of his hatred, he sets out to discover the truth, first going to the Redfield home and then directly to a sixth-floor apartment where a black cultural soirée is in progress, the couple and Clare in attendance. Unabashed, the racist bolts angrily onto the scene, furiously denouncing his wife as a "nigger." Larsen has set her finale in mystery, one that, nevertheless, dooms all the crucial relationships depicted in her narrative. On Bellew's frantically charged entrance, the frightened Irene rushes to Clare's side, for her passing friend had been calmly standing by an open window. Little of what follows is made perfectly clear, but two things are evident: Clare goes tumbling out the window to her death; her husband did not push her. Many questions, however, remain. Why did Irene rush to Clare? Because the revelation of Clare's passing to Bellew would have ended the union and would have driven her to Harlem, a fear of Irene's? Did Irene push Clare out the window? Accidentally or intentionally, driven by fear, propelled by her psychological desire to have Clare "disappear," did she commit murder? Did Clare, terrified by her husband's fury, accidentally fall? Perhaps Clare committed suicide, realizing that her passing days were over and that her "white" daughter would be lost to her? Amid these questions and possibilities the narrative concludes, leaving evidence for all the interpretations suggested.

Analysis

In *Passing*, Nella Larsen has composed a novel that simultaneously engages several levels of the human experience and, through insightful psychological portraiture, illuminates the often subtle and complex passions roiling about a society whose dilemmas are compounded by racism. She brings about consideration of challenging issues through her penetrating treatment of characters whose emotional dilemmas are highlighted by an intricate series of personal interrelationships.

One valid critical approach is to insist that the major theme in *Passing* is not race at all, but marriage and security. Although Irene Redfield is not passing as white, she is passing as an upper-middle-class American with full access to the opportunities and privileges of any wealthy citizen. Feeling safe and secure, she is even waited on by black servants. Indeed, though Irene does not deny her negritude—as Clare does—she is still, in a sense, passing, all the while trying to ignore her husband's dissatisfaction with life in the United States for a black family. Although Irene Redfield is active in the Negro Welfare League (NWL), she remains apart from her struggling brothers and sisters in the ghetto and in no way wishes to endanger her safety. Irene enjoys material comfort; she will not risk starting a new life in Brazil, although her refusal means sacrificing her husband's happiness.

Thus it is that Irene subconsciously appreciates—though she does not outwardly condone—her friend Clare Kendry's passing, for Kendry, aggressive and impetuous, has taken a risk that has brought her complete access to the upper-middle-class American Dream. From this vantage point, Irene's psychological reaction becomes clear: Her ambivalent attraction toward and repulsion from Clare stems from what she perceives as shortcomings within herself; namely, her inability to take risks, rationalized in the need for safety and security, and her own distancing from less-fortunate black people in Harlem's ghetto. With the dangerous Clare hovering about her secure home, Irene is unable to eliminate her friend's presence even though she begins to live in fear that this "mysterious stranger" will take away her husband and destroy the safety that is her life. It is no wonder, too, that subconsciously Irene wants Clare to disappear, to vanish, to die. Although there is no evidence of an affair between Clare and Dr. Redfield, Irene has become emotionally distraught at the possibility, a turbulent package of nerves fixated on the possible loss of her much-loved material life of leisure, opulence, and exciting friends. Psychologically, if not legally, she is guilty of "eliminating" Clare. Whether she took an active role when the sudden opportunity came will be a matter of conjecture. Nella Larsen's text, concluding in deliberate literary ambiguity, suggests this as a possibility.

Clare Kendry demonstrates the psychological consequences inherent in passing, for in choosing the economic and social safety of the white world, she has repudiated the blood of her ancestors and has destroyed her own identity. Clare must live in a schizophrenic world where her life of deceit now forces the unhappy woman to oscillate between her role as white matron and that of temporary black sojourner. Her days are filled with an atavistic desire to reengage her essential self by associating with negroes, members of the race so bitterly detested by her husband. Clare's sense of isolation and loneliness is compounded by her realization that, should the dark and menacing secret of her passing be revealed, her daughter, who has no knowledge of her mother's true past, will be forever lost to her. Yet it is a subconscious need to be discovered, perhaps, that helps to precipitate Clare's perilous risk-taking adventures with the Redfields, jeopardizing her position each time her husband leaves town. This possible desire to be discovered would then quite naturally deliver her back to her people, without the need to feel that she had abandoned her child. Over the years, Clare Kendry has distorted the essential part of herself and has assumed a disguise that is now odious to her. Yet it is too late for truth; there is too much to be lost. The "passing" woman's consciousness of her emotionally intimidating situation thwarts her ability to make the choice for which her psyche is screaming. The results would be disastrous either way. In the end, does she commit suicide? Does she passively allow herself to be thrown from the window? Has Nella Larsen killed her as punishment for denying her identity or as a possible means to preserve the Redfields' marriage? Curiously enough, at Clare's death scene it is Irene Redfield who is alone and apart, feeling strangely guilty in an all-black group of people.

Dr. Brian Redfield is the third person in this triangle, and although the reader is never privy to Clare's thoughts about him, his own attitudes toward her move from rejection to attention. After a time, it becomes clear that Redfield sees and admires in her the chief virtue that he believes is lacking in his wife: a fearless, risk-taking personality that leads her to choose a means, however onerous, to escape the sting of racism in America. He, too, feels a kinship with Clare Kendry. Although he does not condone passing, Redfield grudgingly recognizes the impulse that prompts it: the desire to escape from the prejudices of racism in everyday American life. He, too, would like to escape these continual pressures by running away—as, in a sense, Kendry has done.

This trio of complicated psychological entities, then, carries Larsen's straightforward fictional narrative. The author fully explores the choices and decisions made by her protagonists: She understands but does not excuse Clare's passing and orchestrates the woman's mysterious death; she empathizes with Dr. Redfield's feelings about racism but leaves him tangled in his conventional, unhappy marriage and superficially fulfilling career; most of all, however, Nella Larsen concentrates on Irene Redfield, who, motivated by traditional concerns for safety and security, makes what she believes are the ethically and appropriately weighed choices for herself and her family, even choosing to remain a black woman in the United States, but who at the end feels isolated, morally ambiguous, and even criminal.

Context

Dedicated to Carl Van Vechten and his actress wife Fania Marinoff, both prominent patrons of black artists during the Harlem Renaissance of the 1920's, *Passing* established Nella Larsen as one of the most promising writers to come from that important aesthetic movement. With this novel, her achievement as an African American woman author is especially notable, for the book examines the psychological divisions and challenges in modern middle-class marriage, emphasizing the women's perspective. The book further explores the limits that society of the mid-1920's imposed on all women, with, naturally, the additional restrictions put upon women of color. *Passing* deals, too, in subtle fashion with female sexuality and its role in the context of racism as well as its power within the emotional drama acted out among Irene, Clare, and Brian, for much of the tension in their unhappy confluence appears to be unleashed by overtones of a suggestive sensual energy. While Larsen has studied the chaotic emotional ambience surrounding the woman who passes, and while her treatment of the tragic mulatta theme is possibly the best in American writing, the social burdens of both women are also demonstrated, with suffering and death finally epitomizing their individual struggles.

Nella Larsen does not sentimentalize women's plight; she approaches the depiction of her women with realism. The limits to a woman's actual freedom in the 1920's were stringent; economic security meant dependence on a husband for support. The freedom of Clare Kendry and Irene Redfield is tied directly to their marriages, Clare's complicated by her "passing" and Irene's threatened by her husband's unhappiness. Here, then, is a portrait of woman as prisoner, a person whose very identity is suspect without acknowledged attachment to a man. Thus, while *Passing* derives its materials profoundly from the experience of the African American woman, it also addresses areas of concern for all women.

Although she was neither a crusader for women's rights nor a modern feminist, Larsen created a quietly powerful portrait of the forces and pressures exerted upon women in America in her time. Perhaps her most important contribution to women's literature lies in her having written *Passing*, a book whose social realism and psychological insight herald an achievement in American letters by a black woman writer whose artistry delineated two vital themes of enduring critical concern: the quest for identity and the struggle of women—both within the dark context of racism.

Sources for Further Study

Davis, Arthur P. *From the Dark Tower: Afro-American Writers, 1900-1960*. Washington, D.C.: Howard University Press, 1981. Takes a historical perspective, focusing on Larsen's fiction and its place in the larger aesthetic ambience of black American writing of the twentieth century.

Fuller, Hoyt. Introduction to *Passing*. New York: Collier Books, 1971. A valuable introduction to Larsen's novel that emphasizes the aesthetic structure of the book and the social dilemmas portrayed through the phenomenon of passing.

Kramer, Victor A., ed. *The Harlem Renaissance Re-examined.* New York: AMS Press, 1987. Especially important in this collection of contemporary background essays updating the critical views on Nella Larsen and her literary associates is Lillie P. Howard's study of the novelist's employment of the themes of crossing and materialism.

Larsen, Nella. *An Intimation of Things Distant: The Collected Fiction of Nella Larsen.* Edited by Charles Larsen. New York: Anchor Books, 1992. A perceptive introduction emphasizing the major motifs and themes embodying the creative energy in *Passing* and, at the same time, relating these themes to the author's life.

Robinson, William H. Introduction to *Passing*. New York: Arno Press, 1969. Introductory remarks focus on the theme of the mulatto as well as on Larsen's expression of the materials within black culture.

Singh, Amritjit. *The Novels of the Harlem Renaissance: Twelve Black Writers, 1923-1933.* University Park: Pennsylvania State University Press, 1976. An analytical survey of prominent contributors to the Harlem Renaissance that includes a study of the psychological and social pressures depicted by Larsen in her text.

Washington, Mary Helen. "Nella Larsen: Mystery Woman of the Harlem Renaissance." *Ms.* 9 (December, 1980): 44-50. This article details the personal saga of Nella Larsen and the concomitant pressures stemming therefrom, all contributing significantly to the materials and the resolution of her novel.

Abe C. Ravitz

PASSING ON

Author: Penelope Lively (1933-   )
Type of work: Novel
Type of plot: Domestic realism
Time of plot: The 1980's
Locale: Long Sydenham, a village in the Cotswolds, England
First published: 1989

> *Principal characters:*
> HELEN GLOVER, a part-time librarian in her early fifties
> EDWARD GLOVER, Helen's younger brother
> LOUISE GLOVER DYSON, Helen's younger sister
> PHIL DYSON, Helen's nephew and the inheritor of Dorothy's
> house
> GILES CARNABY, the Glovers' solicitor
> RON PAGET, an unscrupulous builder and developer
> DOROTHY GLOVER, mother of Helen, Edward, and Louise

Form and Content

Passing On is the story of two middle-aged children who are struggling to free themselves of their dead mother's malicious influence. In their attempt to understand current circumstances, Helen and Edward, who are almost fifty when the novel opens, recall many earlier events in their lives. The constant juxtaposition of contemporary action with memory emphasizes how isolated Helen and Edward have become. They have lapsed into dependency on their mother and each other, and they have ignored the changes and demands of the outside world.

Helen, who is working as a part-time librarian, has become immersed in books. As a child, she viewed reading as a way to escape any confrontation with her mother, but the habit developed into a genuine love of all types of literature. Only after her mother's death does Helen recognize that her fascination with books has been a way of defying Dorothy, who is hostile to education in any form. Ignorant and opinionated, Dorothy sees reading as a waste of time and an excuse for inaction.

Edward retreats from conflict by maintaining vigilant observation of the Britches. An amateur naturalist, he keeps detailed records of the changes that occur over the years in the woods. Reviewing his notes, Edward finds little that is truly meaningful because he refuses to write anything personal. His indignation about the exploitation of the natural world and his deep sympathy for endangered species are genuinely felt, but they also indicate the extent to which he has misplaced his own emotional life. His habit of avoiding close relationships takes a huge toll by the end of the novel; he has nightmares, experiences periods of insomnia, and behaves spitefully toward Helen, who has always protected him. Finally, his unnecessary struggle to repress his sexuality and need for intimacy erupts into a crisis that could threaten both his and Helen's future.

The novel is about many of the practical matters that follow a death. Inheriting the Britches, Helen and Edward must decide whether to sell the property or to continue to resist the pressure of Ron Paget, an unscrupulous builder who wants to develop the site for new housing. They must face, for the first time, their financial state. Neither makes enough money to live elsewhere or to remodel the aging family home to contemporary standards. Unless they sell the Britches, they will be trapped in the same circumstances that have immobilized them for years, a plight, Helen and Edward realize, that their mother has intended.

Necessary legal considerations bring together Helen and Giles Carnaby, a smooth, glib solicitor with a reputation for womanizing. Helen recognizes his flaws and tells herself—in Dorothy's voice—that Giles is simply toying with her. Nevertheless, she falls in love with him and finds herself eagerly waiting for his next phone call, postcard, or chance visit. Giles is a master of flirtation who enjoys his effect on women but never intends to develop any relationship seriously. When Helen at last challenges his behavior, she recovers a large measure of self-respect and no longer hears her mother's voice. By refusing to let herself be manipulated, Helen begins to move beyond her mother's dominance.

Two incidents bring home to Helen the full extent of her mother's control. While cleaning out an oak chest of Dorothy's, Helen finds a dress of her own which Dorothy had hidden. Helen remembers the honey-colored muslin as her only attractive dress and remembers, too, Dorothy's offhand explanation that the dress had been destroyed at the cleaners. This was devastating to Helen at eighteen; at fifty-two, she is almost sick at this revelation of her mother's mean-spiritedness. Her next discovery is even worse: In an old jacket of Dorothy's, Helen finds a letter addressed to herself. Written nearly twenty-five years earlier, the letter is from a former beau of Helen's who seeks to be reconciled after a foolish argument. Helen realizes that this goodwill gesture would have made all the difference in their relationship and that her mother undermined the possibility of Helen's marriage by keeping the letter. While Helen blames her mother's evil nature, she is also forced to acknowledge her own passivity. Helen's self-honesty is a refreshing antidote to Dorothy's deceptive manipulations.

Edward finds his mother's influence harder to come to terms with than does Helen. With less direct cause to rage at Dorothy, he turns much of his anger against himself or his sisters. He mocks Helen's relationship with Giles, fusses at her attempts to cook new foods, and resists all attempts to improve the house. Inwardly, he howls over his wasted life. Forced by his mother's death to face his own mortality, Edward is propelled to the edge of a breakdown that culminates in an act that nearly destroys him: He makes sexual overtures to Ron Paget's son, who has come to do gardening for Helen. Horrified by what he has done, Edward tries to kill himself, but he is saved by Helen and Phil. Recovering from an overdose, Edward feels drained but prepared to get on with his life, freed from his mother's oppressive presence and the sexual taboos of her generation.

In contrast to Helen and Edward's passivity is the ceaseless activity and worry of Louise, their younger sister. Louise has also been scarred by her mother's brutal attempts at control, but she rebelled in adolescence and escaped to London, never to return home. Her life, however, is defined by a series of emotional upheavals that threaten her marriage and her relationship with her children. Like her mother, Louise can be blunt and tactless with Helen and Edward, but her remarks are never calculated or uttered with malicious intent. By the end of the novel, she too escapes her mother's legacy by mending her relationship with Phil, who decides to go back to London and return to school.

Analysis

Passing On begins with a death, but the title is more than a euphemistic reference to that event. With its suggestions of movement and change, *Passing On* proves to be a careful examination of what human beings inherit from one another and what they leave behind as they pass through formative relationships. By focusing on the emotional and psychological damage that Dorothy Glover has done to her children, Penelope Lively explores the consequences of one generation's intangible legacy to another. There is also the literal passing on of one's goods: In this case, Dorothy bequeaths her house to her great-nephew, though she grants her children a lifetime tenency, and her wooded property, the Britches, to Helen and Edward.

The novel unfolds as a straightforward, chronological narration interspersed with apposite memories of Helen and Edward. This method of storytelling emphasizes the passage of thirty years, but ironically, it is time in which little or no change has occurred. Much more happens in the real time the book covers, the few months after Dorothy's death. It is almost as if Helen and Edward have been caught in a time-warp and have an enormous amount of catching up to do. This is exemplified by a trip they take to London, their first trip in years. They recognize few buildings and landmarks, and have no idea how long it takes to cross London by Tube. A restaurant they search for is gone, replaced by an expensive wine bar. They meet stockbrokers in an enormous glass office building that had not existed on their last visit. Their disorientation makes them dependent and childlike, as if their adulthood has been stripped away.

Perhaps the most ingenious device of the novel is that the character who has the most influence dies before the story begins. Dorothy Glover speaks to the reader only through her children's memories, and despite her abuse of them, they are trustworthy conveyers of Dorothy's character. Helen and Edward, in fact, seem to be recognizing for the first time how awful their mother was. Oppressed by her for years, they take for granted her superiority and their inferiority. Despite their diffidence, they are portrayed sympathetically, and the slow emergence of their personalities from their mother's shadow is a matter of celebration.

Dorothy's sole motivation in life seems to be to control others. Helen and Edward can remember their father only in vague, shadowy ways. When Helen finds some old family photographs, she sees none of her father, and she realizes that his impact on her life has been equally inconsequential. Dorothy has dominated not only the home but also the surrounding village. She is perceived by her neighbors as loud and unlikable, someone with vehement opinions but little ability to present a rational argument. Helen realizes that her mother was not a nice woman and can think of no one her mother would call a friend. The novel, which begins with the physical absence of Dorothy, documents her lingering influence. For some months after death, Dorothy's imagined presence is a real obstacle to her children. Only when they begin to experiment with new relationships does she disappear from their landscape.

That some of Helen and Edward's experimentation is in the realm of sexuality is an appropriate response to their release from Dorothy's oppression. Both have repressed their need for intimacy for years—Helen because she believes herself unattractive and uninteresting, Edward because he has internalized social taboos against homosexuality. Neither has come to grips with his or her sexual needs as adults, and both live in a state of enforced childhood while Dorothy is alive. Yet it is a childhood without warmth; Dorothy discouraged hugging and other physical displays in her children, and Helen cannot remember any gesture of affection passing between her mother and father. Deprived of such elemental nurturing, Helen and Edward find themselves practically overcome by the strength of their physical responses to others after their mother's death. Part of their emotional recovery involves finding the balance between succumbing to physical desire and retaining self-respect.

Context

Penelope Lively is a brilliant practitioner of the domestic novel. A literary genre well established by Jane Austen and practiced by twentieth century writers such as Barbara Pym, domestic realism focuses on the lives of women at home. Often exposing the economic and social inequities facing women, the domestic novel attempts to recognize the realistic hardships and accomplishments of characters who typify the times in which they live but are not represented in the public sphere.

In most of her novels for adults, Lively, who has also written extensively for children, addresses the concerns of women in middle-class circumstances who are going through a period of change. The heroines of nineteenth century novels would often work to achieve marriage proposals, but Lively's characters have different aspirations, reflecting the wider choices available to today's women. In *Passing On*, Helen develops a greater sense of self-worth by withdrawing from a demeaning relationship. In Lively's novel *Cleopatra's Sister* (1993), the most developed female character recognizes the importance of trying to balance a career with an intimate relationship.

Although her work is not overtly feminist, Lively demonstrates great sensitivity to the roles women play in twentieth century society, and she is one of the few contemporary writers to examine the complexities of parenting from both a female and a male perspective. She demonstrates great skill at revealing the emotional background to human action, as well as delineating its historical context. A historian by academic training, Lively often uses her novels to explore the relationship between individuals and the historical moment. Her most experimental treatment of history occurs in *City of the Mind* (1991), which uses London's architecture as a device to recount episodes from different periods of the city's development.

Despite having won Britain's most prestigious annual literary award, the Booker Prize, for *Moon Tiger* (1987) and having received high praise from book reviewers, Lively has been the subject of little critical analysis. Because of her emphasis on realism, she may not invite as much scholarly attention as do writers who challenge familiar novelistic devices and structures. By choosing to write about subjects that are within ordinary experience, however, and by doing so with talent and insight, Lively is contributing to the rich tradition of literature by and about women in a new way.

Sources for Further Study

Bausch, Richard. *The New York Times Book Review*, February 11, 1990, 12. A review that focuses on Lively's scathing portrayal of Dorothy Glover, typing her as a nearly Dickensian villain. Bausch praises Lively's gift of capturing what takes place in the most private moments, especially the small nuances of emotion.

Birch, Dinah. *The London Review of Books* 11 (April 29, 1989): 20. A review that praises the particularity with which the characters of Helen and Edward are drawn but suggests that the conclusion of the novel is unconvincing.

Le Mesurier, Nicholas. "A Lesson in History: The Presence of the Past in the Novels of Penelope Lively." *The New Welsh Review* 2 (Spring, 1990): 36-38. A brief discussion of the relationship between the individual and the past in Lively's novels. Mentions also the changing historical perception of children.

Moran, Mary Hurley. "Penelope Lively's *Moon Tiger*: A feminist 'History of the World.'" *Frontiers* 11 (1990): 89-95. An article that notes the lack of scholarly interest in Lively and identifies Lively's place in the developing tradition of the feminist novel. Calling the novel a "subversive attack on established assumptions about reality," Moran demonstrates how the heroine attacks linear notions of history and challenges male expectations of female behavior.

Walker, J. K. L. *The Times Literary Supplement*, April 7, 1989, 363. A review that assesses Lively's ability to write about apparently dull characters and make them interesting and sympathetic.

Gweneth A. Dunleavy

PASTORS AND MASTERS

Author: Ivy Compton-Burnett (1884-1969)
Type of work: Novel
Type of plot: Satire
Time of plot: Around 1920
Locale: An English university town
First published: 1925

> *Principal characters:*
> EMILY HERRICK, the novel's heroine, who has great intellectual
>   powers and moral sensitivity
> NICHOLAS HERRICK, her brother, the owner of a boys' school
> WILLIAM MASSON, a tall and lanky don at Herrick's old college
> RICHARD BUMPUS, William's companion, also a don
> MR. MERRY, Herrick's partner, who serves as head of the school
> MRS. MERRY, his wife
> MISS BASDEN, a middle-aged teacher and school matron
> REVEREND PETER FLETCHER, a frail, elderly pastor with a
>   patronizing attitude toward women
> THERESA, Peter's wife
> REVEREND FRANCIS FLETCHER, Peter's nephew
> LYDIA FLETCHER, Peter's sister
> HENRY BENTLEY, the father of two of the children who attend
>   Herrick's school

Form and Content

Pastors and Masters is the first of Ivy Compton-Burnett's novels to establish her characteristic style and subject matter. This novel introduces her distinctive use of dialogue and her satiric depiction of Victorian institutions. Her heroine, Emily Herrick, is singled out for her perspicacity, which brings with it a loss of innocence and trust.

One of the goals of this slender novel is to satirize the institutions of church, school, and family. The novel begins in a school for boys run by Mr. Merry, who manages to both bully and neglect the forty boys in his charge. These boys are largely nameless, faceless victims of incompetence and arbitrary power. The questioning of masculine authority in the person of Mr. Merry is broadened to include Henry Bentley, father of two of the schoolboys and domestic tyrant. The church is also depicted as an imperfect and narrowly patriarchal institution. The values of the Reverend Fletcher and his family ratify masculine authority and require endless sacrifice on the part of their women.

The main purpose and plot of the novel, however, concerns the raising of Emily Herrick's consciousness. This aspect of the novel leads the reader to her brother

Nicholas, who is the absentee owner of the school run by Mr. Merry. Nicholas and his friends Richard Bumpus and William Masson shared a tutor in college referred to as old Crabbe. Nicholas has told his two friends, who are now dons at the university, that, at the age of seventy, he has at last produced the book that will cap his career as an educator. At the same time, Richard announces that he has finally completed a book on which he has been working for many years. Before Nicholas begins to read his book aloud, Richard mentions that the original version of his book was accidentally left at the deathbed of old Crabbe. Nicholas at once undergoes a change of heart and elects not to read his manuscript. In fact, he declares that he will not publish it at all. It is the observant Emily who puts all this cross talk together. She sees that Nicholas, thinking it was his moribund tutor's, has stolen Richard's manuscript and has claimed it for his own. As the conversation continues, it is also apparent that Richard's new book is little different from the one left with old Crabbe; he has essentially been writing the same book his entire life. Neither of the men sees through the other's deception. It is only Emily who detects not only their pompous duplicity but also their lack of innovation—there is only one old manuscript, and neither of them has written anything new. The arrogance and hypocrisy of her brother and his friends come as a revelation to Emily. She sees that their need for recognition and prestige is greater than their ability to do any meaningful work. They take credit where credit is not due. Emily's new knowledge shocks her into a sudden maturity; her fifty-first birthday is used as a symbol for this new level of consciousness. It is almost a rebirth for her, as she sees her life in a new and truer way. Nevertheless, Emily, like the other women in the novel, continues to support men; Mr. Merry will continue to dominate the schoolboys; and the husbands and fathers will continue to wield their heavy-handed authority. Yet the women in the novel, and Emily in particular, have begun to assimilate a deep knowledge of their situation that reflects a more modern and liberated perspective.

Analysis

Pastors and Masters signals the reemergence of a talent that had lain dormant for fourteen years. Stunned by the tragedies that beset her family, including the suicide of two sisters, the death of two brothers in World War I, and the fragmentation of her large Victorian family, Ivy Compton-Burnett underwent a period of recuperation and reassessment that brought about a transformation of her style and values. *Pastors and Masters* liberated her from her major precursor, George Eliot, whose earnest Victorian values influenced Compton-Burnett's first novel *Dolores* (1911). *Pastors and Masters*, however, reaches back for inspiration to the lively and comic approach of Jane Austen, who is singled out for tribute during one of *Pastors and Masters'* many conversations. The novel's interest in authorship and in those who copy or repeat the past suggests that, on one level, Compton-Burnett was asserting her own claims to originality. Although Austen is an important influence on her work, Compton-Burnett's work is her own. *Pastors and Masters* is the first of her unique "dialogue" novels, which feature virtually disembodied voices whose talk constitutes the narrative. Because there is little exposition, the reader must draw his or her own inferences, much as Emily does when she silently observes the behavior and the talk of her brother and his friends. Although this novel remains more of a sketch than her other novels do, it contains within its slender plot all of her important themes and narrative strategies.

The title *Pastors and Masters* reflects the novel's theme—masculine authority. In short order, Compton-Burnett questions the masculine power structure in religion, education, and the family. The pastors of the title are portrayed as intensely conservative men whose God is a father-figure with several serious character flaws. Emily describes him as not only arrogant, vindictive, and overindulgent but also, in one of the book's memorable lines, as "one of the best drawn characters in fiction." The values of Christian charity which the men espouse seem to turn women into martyrs whose lives are spent serving the selfish interests of others.

The Victorian institution of the family is similarly questioned. The representative father in the novel, Henry Bentley, is the first in a series of domineering and destructive parents in the work of Compton-Burnett. The men who supply the intellectual backbone of this educational world, the university-educated masters, are exposed as essentially incompetent. Richard Bumpus appears to have written the same book all of his life. Nicholas Herrick is unable to write a book at all, and he simply plagiarizes the work of his old tutor. The reader sees, along with Emily, that Richard and Nicholas are more concerned with their own prestige and power than with devoting themselves to good work or the welfare of others. When one learns that Nicholas will allow himself to take credit for work done by someone else, one comes to understand the depths of his self-aggrandizing nature.

Pastors and Masters also introduces the reader to Compton-Burnett's moral philosophy, an original deployment of her father's pioneering work in homeopathic medicine. Just as homeopathic medicine intertwines health and illness as a therapeutic strategy, so Compton-Burnett suggests that people's moral and psychological lives are at their healthiest when they understand the dark side of human nature. Emily describes this, in a witty metaphor, as a process by which virtue "condenses" vice. Good cannot purify itself of evil but instead must cope with its constant presence. This reflects Emily's new sophistication with regard to the moral character of her brother Nicholas. Although she still loves Nicholas, she sees that he is not divine, but all too human; he has within him the potential for wrongdoing. The propensity for criminality within erstwhile respectable families becomes one of Compton-Burnett's great themes in subsequent novels.

All the men in the novel are engaged in a holding action against the disempowered members of their society—the women, servants, and children who are beginning to question their authority. It is significant that this is the only novel written by Compton-Burnett that is set after World War I. This novel strongly reflects both the devastation of the war and the social changes created in its wake. Compton-Burnett carefully darkened the texture of her last chapter by referring to the loss of the two Fletcher sons in the war. Her questioning of her society's leadership comes as a consequence of the war, which disillusioned an entire generation. Compton-Burnett's satiric novel reflects this loss of faith in leaders who seemed less like trusted elders than impervious old men. Although her other novels are set at the turn of the century, all of them take their cue from the detached and critical spirit of modernity that Ivy Compton-Burnett establishes in *Pastors and Masters*.

Context

The "Woman Question" is central to *Pastors and Masters*. The novel's title, which refers to male authority, suggests the systematic exclusion of women from society's power structures. In spite of this exclusion, however, the reader sees that the various reverends and teachers in the novel are in the process of being challenged by the women and children around them. Within the narrow context of a small boys' school, Compton-Burnett is tracking the liberalizing process of modernity, through which women and other disenfranchised groups have gained recognition. In *Pastors and Masters*, women are portrayed as equaling or surpassing men in matters of both mind and heart. Compton-Burnett extends Emily's capacity for insight to a sisterhood that includes her confidante Theresa and the schoolteacher Miss Basden. Together, they conclude the novel with a lively disquisition on the situation of women. Miss Basden speaks for Compton-Burnett when she notes that until their recent enfranchisement as voters, the women in her society were classed with paupers, idiots, and children, and that as a result they are still required to establish their credentials as competent adults. Miss Basden also takes issue with the Victorian idea of putting women on a pedestal, holding the very contemporary view that the sentimental exaltation of women is in reality a form of contempt. Emily is particularly scathing when it comes to women and marriage. Objecting to a society in which women are confined within the institution of marriage and family, Emily prefers to assign value to women independent of their relationship to men. She suggests, however, that if a woman does not establish herself as a wife and mother, she is considered a liability, and that a patriarchal solution to women such as herself would be to expose them at birth. When the objection is made that one cannot tell which will be the single women when they are born, Emily slyly replies that all children are born single; that is, as individuals and not as part of a couple, a family, or a larger whole. The sanctity of the individual is at the heart of Compton-Burnett's work, and she eventually extends her concern with the preservation of women's singularity and individuality to humanity in general.

Sources for Further Study

Baldanza, Frank. *Ivy Compton-Burnett*. New York: Twayne, 1964. An excellent general introduction researched with the help of Ivy Compton-Burnett herself. Includes biographical material, a brief chronology up to 1964, a treatment of technique, and a survey of English, American, and French criticism.

Burkhart, Charles, ed. *The Art of I. Compton-Burnett*. London: Victor Gollancz, 1972. A compilation of critical essays and interviews, including an essay on Compton-Burnett's dialogue by the French novelist Nathalie Sarraute.

Gentile, Kathy Justice. *Ivy Compton-Burnett*. New York: St. Martin's Press, 1991. Part of a series on women writers, this study establishes Compton-Burnett as a feminist and adds new and important perspectives to her work. Has an excellent bibliography.

Greenfield, Stanley. *"Pastors and Masters*: The Spoils of Genius." *Criticism* 2, no. 1 (Winter, 1960): 66-80. Seminal analysis of *Pastors and Masters*. A detailed discussion of the novel that perceives the depth of what appears to be a slender novel.

Liddell, Robert. *The Novels of Ivy Compton-Burnett*. London: Victor Gollancz, 1955. The first important interpretation of Compton-Burnett, this work remains the standard critical book. Includes a detailed and appreciative analysis of each work, with particular reference to the theme of "domestic tyranny."

Nevius, Blake. *Ivy Compton-Burnett*. New York: Columbia University Press, 1970. A short, general discussion of the work of Compton-Burnett. Serves as a lively introduction for those who find her work difficult and inaccessible.

Spurling, Hilary. *Ivy: The Life of I. Compton-Burnett*. New York: Alfred A. Knopf, 1984. This definitive and indispensable biography of Compton-Burnett includes much useful information about her crucial early years. Details also her later, happy, highly creative years with her companion, author Margaret Jourdain.

Margaret Boe Birns

PATRIARCHAL ATTITUDES

Author: Eva Figes (1932-   )
Type of work: Social criticism
First published: 1970

Form and Content

Eva Figes's 1970 publication *Patriarchal Attitudes* was one of a group of three books that came out that year explicating the history and root causes of women's oppression by men. It was a banner year for women; as Figes's book hit the stores, along with Kate Millett's *Sexual Politics* and Germaine Greer's *The Female Eunuch* the next year, the women's liberation movement was born into a world already at a fever-pitch of political excitement over the Vietnam War and the Civil Rights movement. Women who had learned how to organize working for other issues were ready to challenge the basic tenets that ruled their own lives and enforced their oppression.

Figes offered the analysis women needed in their quest for equality. Taking up the age-old question "What makes a woman a woman?" she reviewed centuries of teaching, economics, and social science. Figes concludes that the way in which people are nurtured, not their innate nature, determines their values and actions. People become what culture teaches them to be, and the mainstream cultural works that Figes had just reviewed were extraordinarily hostile to women.

Figes uses the words of some of Western civilization's most renowned speakers to show the widespread fear of women that permeates Western society. She quotes Moses, Giovanni Boccaccio, Jean-Jacques Rousseau, Sigmund Freud, and others, marching through the canon of written works that contain Western culture's most revered ideas. Ancient Hebrew myth, John Milton, and the poetic tradition all add their voices to the cultural chorus. Figes unearths a society that idealizes woman when she identifies completely with a man's desires and demonizes her whenever she opposes him.

Chapter by chapter, Figes shows that Westerners live in a world in which man controls woman to elevate himself. In Western religion, in economics, in philosophy, science, and psychology, male needs are presumed to be universal human needs, while women are forced into a mold that denies their most basic personal goals and aspirations.

It is the breadth of Figes's analysis that makes her position difficult to dispute. By allowing her argument to grow out of the words of culture's most revered icons, she uses their presumptive brilliance to prove her points. The work is short, not quite two hundred pages including notes, bibliography, and index, but it presents a comprehensive view of Western society and women's lives within it. *Patriarchal Attitudes* provides readers a context within which to place current pronouncements upon the nature of women, along with enough information to deconstruct the assumptions underlying contemporary culture.

Analysis

Figes phrases her arguments in universal terms, speaking categorically of "A Man's World" and "A Man's God," but it is important for the careful reader to note that she examines only Western culture, Judeo-Christian religion, and literature that was written in or translated into English. Thus, while she makes no note of the cultural biases of her study, some generalizations may not apply to cultures that are based in different texts and traditions.

Figes begins her examination of the question, "What makes a woman a woman?" by acknowledging the basic biological differences between the sexes. Most women can bear children; men categorically cannot. Women tend to live longer than men, their blood carries a different mixture of hormones, and generally their muscles are less well developed. The first two differences appear to be unalterable; the last depends very much upon the activity in which the individual engages, as Figes proves by quoting anthropologists who have studied many cultures. If musculature is alterable by usage and custom, what other supposedly innate characteristics can be similarly affected? Boys and girls enjoy largely the same hormone balance prior to puberty, yet behavioral differences emerge far earlier in their lives. Education is responsible for these differences, Figes demonstrates; in fact, it is responsible for virtually all human responses—physical, emotional, and intellectual—to the world of stimuli.

In her chapter "A Man's World," Figes asserts that the cultural environment has been defined by male eyes. Language, mathematics, music, and art have all been delineated by male scholars. The world they have mapped excludes women's perceptions. In fact, woman's identity is entirely a male construct; women are taught to want and to be the things man wants in a woman, not the things that would fill their own lives with meaning. Through art, history, and literature, men perpetuate the image of themselves as the doers of all heroic deeds, as the embodiment of all greatness, as the face of God, and as the defenders of a self-created moral code. They impose this worldview by sheer physical power, by economic exclusion, and by granting themselves unequal rights under the law.

The concept of God may once have included women, Figes notes in "A Man's God," but if people once believed it was Eurynome who laid the world egg, they have now converted to a religion that is almost exclusively male in both its icons and its aims. Childbirth appeared to ancient humanity, she argues, as an incontrovertible sign of women's divinity. Once man realized the connection between sex and childbirth, however, he understood how to co-opt woman's power for himself. By claiming ownership of a woman and ensuring that the only man who touched her was himself, he could guarantee the legitimacy of his offspring. Man then began to construct his own immortality based on long lines of descendants; the endless genealogies of the Old Testament give witness to this preoccupation.

Man's religion proclaimed his control over women essential. Men fear being manipulated by sexuality, a fear that Figes finds throughout literature. They fear being emasculated, as Samson was, and they fear women's supposedly endless sexual appetite, which threatens to suck men dry. Therefore, religion portrayed woman as responsible for humankind's fall from grace. Celibacy was promoted, and woman was depicted as an evil temptress who would lure man into sin, but lust repressed does not disappear, it merely changes form. Figes cites the witch burnings of the fourteenth and fifteenth centuries, which annihilated up to one-quarter of the population in certain areas, as an example of male lust projected onto women. Just as God controls man, so man must control woman, even if that control takes the form of mass murder.

It has been a slower process for men to dominate women's economic status, yet Figes claims that here, too, women have gradually lost their equality. Until recent decades, mere survival depended upon the labor of both sexes. In sixteenth century England, there was very little division between the worlds of home and work. Marriage was a partnership in which a woman's work truly mattered; as a result, not only were women permitted to inherit their husbands' businesses but also they were admitted to guilds and allowed to engage in independent trade. With the rise of capitalism, the consolidation of capital, and the separation of home and work, however, women were increasingly excluded from the economic world. By Victorian times, upper-class women were forbidden to work by strict social mores. In addition, because industry and thrift were considered prime virtues in a capitalistic society, man's role as the sole breadwinner bolstered his convictions of superiority and simultaneously gave him complete control over his household's every need.

This autocratic rule was oddly incongruent in a world whose political climate focused more and more clearly upon the inalienable rights of man. Eighteenth century philosophers proclaimed that man was born free; revolutions were fought to achieve that freedom. Yet woman was not liberated. Figes points to the Romantic movement as the intellectual sleight-of-hand that allowed men to exclude women from the rights of mankind. Woman was both idealized and marginalized, regarded as morally superior but intellectually incapable. Thus, woman, with her tender sympathy, was given the job of taming man's aggressions, of being the ideal mother whose power lay in her complete selflessness.

Nineteenth century scientists also tried to prove the fundamental rightness of man's domination. Charles Darwin's theory of survival of the fittest was said to demonstrate that man's rule was a matter of scientific law. Philosophers used intricate logic to demonstrate that man was spirit and woman was material; he was reason and she was emotion. Figes proposes that precisely such divisive, bipolar thinking allowed Nazi Germany to annihilate millions of Jews in the gas chamber. If one pole represents perfection, the other must embody all that is loathsome and must therefore be dominated or destroyed.

Women did not always accept their subordination meekly. Toward the end of the nineteenth century, many women actively sought greater equality and participation in the exclusively male professional world. Religion, economics, and philosophy alone were not enough to stall their drive toward productive lives. Into this threatening situation stepped Sigmund Freud, whose theories of psychoanalysis had a profound effect upon modern thinking. Women, Freud pronounced, were inherently inimical to the aims of civilization. Their innate drives were too strong for them to fully repress; therefore, men must exert control in the interests of preserving all that is of value in an orderly world. Women who objected to this control were merely demonstrating their neurotic desire to possess what they could never have: a penis. Ambition in women was a sickness, a reason for pity and sympathy, but not a desire that should ever be gratified.

Even women who have realized their own ambitions have discriminated against other women throughout history. Frequently, successful women look at their sisters and find them despicable. Powerful women must understand that their own success does not disprove the oppression of millions or demonstrate that the oppressed deserve their condition.

Finally, Figes offers some suggestions for human evolution. They seem thin in the light of the weight of custom she has laid before the reader so convincingly, but perhaps the changes in family law, the easing of divorce laws, the provision of state support for children that she suggests would make some practical difference. Economic independence, she admits, is not a guarantee of emotional independence, but it is a necessary condition.

Context

Eva Figes is only one in a long line of women philosophers who have attempted to delineate the causes and history of female oppression. Mary Wollestonecraft first posited the notion that women's upbringing rather than their inherent nature was responsible for their seeming inferiority. Simone de Beauvoir, Virginia Woolf, and countless other theorists have made the same arguments that Figes worked out. Even in the face of such history, Figes believed that she worked in isolation. Perhaps that feeling of isolation is the key to the significance of her work, for while the ideas that she outlines are not new, they are ideas that are continually being forgotten. Figes's work marks the beginning of a great period of female scholarship that took as its primary task the rediscovery of women's cultural heritage. *Patriarchal Attitudes* demonstrates the great need for women to seek their image and identity in the words and works of their sisters. It teaches that male perceptions exclude much that women find valuable in the world.

Figes's subsequent works are largely fictional and seek to provide precisely that feminist viewpoint that she taught her readers to value. Highly experimental both stylistically and philosophically, they examine issues of identity and history through the eyes and interests of women.

Sources for Further Study

Beauvoir, Simone de. *The Second Sex*. Translated by H. M. Parshley. New York: Alfred A. Knopf, 1953. Figes read this classic volume of feminist theory, and although in various articles she claims it offered too little analysis of women as sexual beings, many arguments made by Beauvoir appear in Figes's work.

Friedan, Betty. *The Feminine Mystique*. New York: W. W. Norton, 1963. Friedan attacks cultural views of women that keep them in the home. In doing so, she takes on Freud and a host of anthropologists, including Margaret Mead.

Tomalin, Claire. "What Does a Woman Want?" *New Statesman* 26 (June, 1970): 917-918. Tomalin agrees with much of Figes's analysis but argues that the importance of family was not given enough weight in her work.

Vidal, Gore. "In Another Country." *New York Review of Books* 22 (July, 1971): 8-10. Vidal points out the similarities between *Patriarchal Attitudes*, *Sexual Politics*, and *The Female Eunuch*. He elevates Figes's work above the others, especially endorsing her argument that social conditioning produces human behavior. This is true not only for women, Vidal notes, but also for men.

Woolf, Virginia. *The Three Guineas*. London: Harcourt, Brace, 1938. Woolf was the first to suggest the connection between sexual oppression and political oppression, a connection that Figes stresses even more strongly in regard to Nazi Germany.

Susan E. Keegan

PATTERNS OF CULTURE

Author: Ruth Benedict (1887-1948)
Type of work: Social criticism
First published: 1934

Form and Content

At the age of thirty-two, having struggled for years to discover herself in poetry and in an unsatisfactory marriage, Ruth Benedict took her first course in anthropology, studying with Franz Boas, whose work is the cornerstone of American anthropology. During the next fifteen years, she became an extremely influential anthropologist in her own right and published *Patterns of Culture*, which can be considered the key statement of the culture-and-personality school of anthropology, the tenets of which are as ingrained in modern thinking as are the theories of evolution and psychoanalysis.

Benedict argues that every culture is organized around specific beliefs that can be seen in the range of behaviors considered acceptable within that culture. These beliefs constitute the culture's fundamental conceptions of reality and what it means to be human. Behaviors that are not consistent with these beliefs are not recognized as being natural to humans. Implicit, then, is the suggestion that the range of possible human behavior is much wider than that provided within any one cultural context; an "outsider" in one milieu may be an "insider" in another.

Indeed, this suggestion is central to *Patterns of Culture*, and it explains the interest this book has inspired among many feminists, for the freeing of "human nature" from its cultural constraints extends equally to women and men. Although Benedict never referred to herself as a feminist, the most passionately argued moments of *Patterns of Culture* arise in defense of what she calls "a more realistic social faith"—namely, cultural relativism, a premise central to much of the feminist critique and to late twentieth century progressive thought in general.

The book can be divided into three sections. The first introduces the concept of patterning, evidence for which is provided in the section that follows—an in-depth examination of three disparate cultures. This examination leads in turn to a discussion of "abnormal" behavior—what it means within a particular culture and what it could mean were one able to view behavior objectively, unblinded by one's own cultural preconceptions. It is this last section that builds the argument for cultural relativism and that makes *Patterns of Culture* more a work of social criticism than an unimpassioned anthropological text.

Analysis

At the outset, Benedict makes a case for the careful study of primitive cultures. The arguments she presents seem unremarkable now, but at the time she was writing, many Western academicians could see no point in examining cultures far less developed than their own. Benedict addresses this short-sightedness, faulting "the white man" (her words) for not realizing that customs and cultural institutions determine the individual's perception, and that more of human behavior is socially ingrained than is biologically determined. The principal reason for studying primitive societies, then, is that they provide case material, in a form far simpler than that offered by Western cultures, for the differentiation between culturally determined and biologically determined behavior.

The diversity of cultures, each with institutions and behaviors that often seem diametrically opposed to those of other cultures, in itself offers evidence for the weighting of the equation toward social determination. Benedict argues that there is a great arc of possible human interests and behaviors of which each culture embodies but a fraction. Indeed, a culture that included too much material would be as unintelligible and as unmanageable as a language that employed every sound possible to the human vocal apparatus. The necessity for the selection of specific behaviors and the rejection of others explains the diversity of cultures, each of which is an example of the endless combinations that are possible.

These combinations are not arbitrary. Each exhibits "a more or less consistent pattern of thought and action" with "characteristic purposes not necessarily shared by other types of society." This fact leads Benedict to argue against the mere cataloging of behavior, which many anthropologists engage in instead of attempting to portray the culture as an articulated whole.

Benedict's own attempts to portray the patterns of three very different cultures occupy more than half of the book. She chooses two tribes of North America, the Pueblo and the Kwakiutl, and one of New Guinea, the Dobu. She discovers in each a "consistent pattern of thought and action" founded in a generalized attitude toward the world and toward others which permeates the consciousness of the individual members of the tribe. She finds that the Pueblos, for example, distrust all forms of excess. In consequence, all their institutions, from their marriage arrangements to their religious ceremonies, exhibit a startling lack of intensity. Ceremonies are entirely formulaic, with the stress laid on strict adherence to each movement and word prescribed by tradition, and with no provisions for religious ecstasy or trance. A good person is considered one who fits in, is friendly, and causes no problems.

For the Dobu, however, goodness—or, more correctly, success—is associated with treachery and ill will. Everyone, even one's wife or husband, is a potential enemy against whom one must exercise a guileful sorcery, both to protect oneself and to attack the other. The Dobuan blames every bad happening, from minor aggravations to real catastrophes, on the machinations of an enemy. Dobuan institutions reflect this paranoia and are essentially prescriptions for revenge and for the prevention of the enemy's attacks.

An entirely different set of assumptions governs the behavior of the Kwakiutl of the Pacific Northwest, a tribe already extinct in Benedict's time. In many ways, the Kwakiutl operated at the opposite pole from that of the Pueblo; the greater the display of excess, the more worthy the individual. Excess for them meant a self-glorifying exhibition of wealth; exorbitant sums were paid for brides and in rituals of exchange called potlatches. Often a Kwakiutl would destroy incredible amounts of material possessions; such wantonness was held as evidence of great wealth indeed.

What becomes clear from these examples is that the various institutions common to human society—such as mourning, marriage, coming-of-age, and economics—do not indicate "generic drives and motivations" that determine the range of behaviors associated with them. Rather, they provide "certain occasions which any society may seize upon to express its important cultural intentions." Marriage for the Zuni, for example, does not serve the same cultural function that it does for the Dobu or the Kwakiutl. The biological function served by marriage—procreation—is eclipsed by the accretions of content that are purely local and cultural. This is as true for "the white man" as it is for the "primitive." Western institutions, Benedict states, are just as "compulsive," not "basic and essential in human behavior," as Westerners might like to believe.

This assertion leads Benedict to a consideration of "abnormality." What a culture excludes from the immense range of possible human interests is labeled abnormal. A culture that provides a rich field for the exercise of these interests, however, also provides for the satisfaction of its members. A culture that narrows its focus—that, for example, subsumes all interests, from sex to death, under the will to power, as does Western culture—creates a situation in which the natural tendencies of many of its individual members are thwarted. In support of this idea, Benedict compares the acceptance of homosexuality in many cultures with its nonacceptance in the West. Those whom a culture considers normal, however, "have a license which they may almost endlessly exploit," often to the detriment of the society itself.

Context

It is with these concluding arguments that Benedict has most influenced feminist thought. The "white man" as defined by his culture takes the opportunity to "endlessly exploit" not only foreign cultures and the environment but also members of his own culture, male and female. Benedict's plea for the necessity of cultural relativism has taken root under the banner of multiculturalism. Benedict's arguments served as the harbinger of the backlash, which became evident in the 1960's, against cultural exploitation. For this reason, Margaret Mead, herself a student of Benedict and an important voice in the women's movement, in 1974 reassembled her 1959 collection of Benedict's papers in order to conform to contemporary interests.

Sources for Further Study

Caffrey, Margaret M. *Ruth Benedict: Stranger in This Land.* Austin: University of Texas Press, 1989. Caffrey examines Benedict's life and work from a feminist perspective, revealing her to have held beliefs not common until twenty years after her death. This book is valuable for the light it sheds on Benedict's last years, which she spent conducting an ambitious federal project, and it also provides an unflinching portrait of her childhood and her sexuality.

Mead, Margaret. *An Anthropologist at Work: The Writings of Ruth Benedict.* Boston:

Houghton Mifflin, 1959. This is the most complete collection of Benedict's papers, ranging from her poetry to scholarly work. It is chronologically arranged in sections, and each section is prefaced by a biographical sketch by Mead. The portrait that emerges is slanted toward Mead's own interests and is perhaps clouded by Mead's emotional closeness to her subject.

——————— . *Coming of Age in Samoa*. New York: William Morrow, 1964. One of the precursors to Benedict's *Patterns of Culture*, this book offers a detailed examination of adolescence in Samoa and demonstrates that children in Samoa go through none of the turmoil associated with pubescence in Western cultures. The conclusion, then, is that the way in which a culture patterns its members accounts for much behavior. This constitutes a refutation of arguments based on "human nature."

——————— . *Ruth Benedict*. New York: Columbia University Press, 1974. Mead revised her earlier collection of Benedict's writings for more contemporary audiences, widening her scope to include references to Benedict's feminism. She also provides a short biography that is somewhat more objective than her first effort was. This is a good introductory volume for students who are new to Benedict's writings and life story. Includes a good bibliography.

Modell, Judith Schachter. *Ruth Benedict: Patterns of a Life*. Philadelphia: University of Pennsylvania Press, 1983. Modell attempts to discern the pattern of Benedict's life by locating its recurrent themes. She includes a wealth of quotations from journals and letters. Because Modell takes a more traditional biographical stance than Caffrey does, leaving certain topics off limits, some readers may find her book less interesting than Caffrey's.

Peter Crawford

PENTIMENTO

Author: Lillian Hellman (1905-1984)
Type of work: Memoir
Time of work: The first half of the twentieth century
Locale: The United States and Europe
First published: 1973

> *Principal personages:*
> LILLIAN HELLMAN, a playwright
> BERTHE BRUNO KOSHLAND, a young German relative of the
> Bowman family, a distant cousin of Hellman
> UNCLE WILLY, the husband of Hellman's Great-Aunt Lily, her
> mother's relative
> JULIA, a girlhood friend of Hellman
> DASHIELL HAMMETT, a writer and the most significant man in
> Hellman's life for more than thirty years
> ARTHUR W. A. COWAN, a quixotic millionaire

Form and Content

Written after her autobiography *An Unfinished Woman* (1969) and before her castigation of the McCarthy era entitled *Scoundrel Time* (1976), *Pentimento* lives up to its title. Hellman explains this artistic term at the beginning of the book thus:

> Old paint on canvas, as it ages, sometimes becomes transparent. When that happens it is possible, in some pictures, to see the original lines: a tree will show through a woman's dress, a child makes way for a dog, a large boat is no longer on an open sea. That is called pentimento because the painter "repented," changed his mind. Perhaps it would be as well to say that the old conception, replaced by a later choice, is a way of seeing and then seeing again.

This is a memoir, organized by devoting a chapter to Hellman's cousin Berthe Bruno Koshland, her Uncle Willy, her childhood friend Julia, and her friend Arthur W. A. Cowan; her longtime companion Dashiell Hammett appears throughout, and the one nonhuman "character" is a turtle. There is also a chapter entitled "Theatre," which deals with Hellman's memories of many people involved with her during her years as a playwright. There is also a last, very brief chapter called "Pentimento" in which the author speaks of an experience that she had while teaching a writing seminar at Harvard University just after Hammett's death.

True to her explanation of the book's title, Hellman looks at both the original "paintings" and the same incidents and people years later. This technique lends credence to the criticism that some of the stories may have been altered to the point that they approach fiction. Yet her interaction with these compelling characters (including the turtle) results in a fascinating and readable book. It also gives a complete picture of a woman who saw herself clearly, faults and all, and who remained true to her feminist ideas throughout her life.

As Doris Falk makes clear in her 1978 biography of Hellman, however, she herself never felt the need of being "liberated from the male put-down," although she resented being called "a woman playwright—even America's greatest." Rather, she believed that the goal of the feminist movement should be economic equality for women. This viewpoint is entirely compatible with Hellman's general stance regarding the connection between money and power, delineated so forcefully in all of her work.

Some of the people appearing in *Pentimento* were sketched in *An Unfinished Woman*, and Hellman has modeled many of the characters in her plays on friends and members of her family mentioned in both books. This is a common practice of writers in all genres, but some have wondered whether a character such as Julia, represented by Hellman as a "real" person in *Pentimento*, actually lived or was a complete fabrication, as the author Mary McCarthy charged publicly on *The Dick Cavett Show*. This accusation and other derogatory remarks by McCarthy resulted in a libel suit brought by Hellman. She and her attorney, Ephraim London, felt confident of success, but the suit never came to trial because of Hellman's death.

One of Hellman's themes throughout her work is love in its many forms. When she first discusses some of the personages as she remembers them from her own adolescence, she does not recognize the sexual undertones that she sees quite clearly as a mature adult. For example, Berthe, a distant cousin who is brought to the United States for an arranged marriage and then deserted, seems at first only an occasional visitor to the boarding house run by Hellman's aunts, Hannah and Jenny. When Berthe becomes involved with a small-time member of the mafia who is murdered, however, young Lillian recognizes sexual attraction as one form of love. Later, she accuses her aunts of having deserted Berthe but learns that they have secretly supported the "fallen woman" for years out of another kind of love.

Also on the theme of love, in the chapter entitled "Willy" Hellman first sees this handsome husband of her Great-Aunt Lily from the perspective of a child. He seems a swashbuckling adventurer, not a merchant of illegal guns shipped to quell "trouble-making natives" in Central America. Willy, treating her like a child, takes the young girl fishing, but on the overnight stay in a bayou, she comes to realize that Willy has a Cajun mistress. The mature Hellman recognizes that she was indeed sexually attracted to Willy and jealous in a very adult way. When she sees him one last time, years later in New Orleans, she finds some of his charisma is still there for her, but she wisely returns to Hollywood and Hammett after spending one day with Willy.

Her deep love for a girlhood friend, who is called Julia in *Pentimento*, is quite probably an accurate account of her feelings in adulthood when she realizes that such love calls for involvement, even at the risk of personal danger. Whether, as Carl Rollyson suggests in *Lillian Hellman: Her Legend and Her Legacy* (1988), she based the character on Muriel Gardener's activity in the anti-Nazi Resistance and whether she exaggerated details of her own part in smuggling money for the Resistance are moot. What this chapter illustrates is Hellman's love not only on a personal level but also in a broader social sense—it is her love of justice in the world.

In recounting her thirty-one-year relationship with Dashiell Hammett, another facet of love becomes clear. Both he and Hellman had problems with alcohol, and there were a number of partings and reconciliations through the years. Nevertheless, she appreciated his role as unrelenting critic of her work and gives credit for much of her success to his encouragement. Furthermore, they truly loved, understood, and respected each other, despite disagreements from time to time.

"Theatre" describes Hellman's first success with the play *The Children's Hour*, which was an important landmark work in 1934 because it dealt with lesbianism. She also tells of her second play, *Days to Come*, which was a failure so devastating that it was two years before the playwright tried again, this time rewriting *The Little Foxes* nine times to ensure its success. In *Pentimento*, she credits Hammett with working hard for her on this play because after *Days to Come* he was "scared for her future."

In this chapter she also tells of her Hollywood days, working as a writer for Samuel Goldwyn, and of her relationship with Tallulah Bankhead, who starred in *The Little Foxes*. She tells too of *Watch on the Rhine* and a visit to the White House when it played there for President Franklin D. Roosevelt and Eleanor Roosevelt. Her memories of *The Searching Wind* include anecdotes of Dudley Digges and his conversations with a brilliant newcomer, Montgomery Clift.

Next, in typically frank fashion, Hellman discusses her clumsy attempt to direct her play *Another Part of the Forest*, admitting that the only positive result of that experience was her discovery of the young Patricia Neal, who became a lifelong friend. Most significant of her other plays and adaptations perhaps is one of her later works, *Toys in the Attic* (1960), in which she began to tell the story from the viewpoint of its protagonist, Julian Bernier, but found that she had to rewrite it so that the play focuses on the women who control and ultimately ruin his life: his sisters, Carrie and Anna; his young wife, Lily; his mother-in-law, Albertine Price; and a former lover, Mrs. Charlotte Warkins. Hellman discussed her concern with Hammett, tore up the original script, and revised the play emphasizing the women. It was a huge success.

The chapter in *Pentimento* entitled "Arthur W. A. Cowan" is episodic, going back and forth through time, but it never really explains Hellman's friendship with Cowan. Perhaps this is because his peculiar, mercurial personality defies labeling. The only consistent fact is that Cowan, a millionaire, was able to take care of Hellman's money and did so successfully. In all other respects, their relationship seems strange simply because Cowan was strange. Several biographers believe that they were lovers, but Hellman does not admit this in *Pentimento*. This man lies about everything: his age, his nationality, his politics, even his occupation. Hellman's friend Molly Howe, also a friend of Cowan, characterizes him as "a game of true or false, a James Bond character," which seems an accurate assessment.

"Turtle" is on the surface merely a retelling of how a large snapping turtle injured Hammett's favorite dog, in reprisal for which Hammett shot the turtle. The animal, however, survived both the bullet and the axe blow which severed its head, not succumbing until the following day.

The final short piece entitled "Pentimento" recounts Hellman's time at Harvard, shortly after Hammett's death. Here she talks of her companion Helen (who replaced her "childhood mammy, Sophronia") and of Helen's young friend Jimsie, a brilliant but impoverished student.

Analysis

Lillian Hellman admitted to being a strong-willed and often difficult person from childhood on. In *Pentimento*, she herself becomes a "character" in her own life story, and her skill in dramatizing herself and those with whom she interacts helps to substantiate the claims of her detractors that the book may be more fiction than truth.

She is quoted by Rollyson as "refusing to be a bookkeeper of [her] life" when faced with accusations that dates and places cited are inaccurate. As William Wright admits, however, the people in *Pentimento* figure so strongly in the playwright's life (as well as providing models for characters in her plays) that minute veracity becomes a relatively unimportant issue when evaluating the book.

In a number of instances throughout *Pentimento*, Hellman adopts a high moral tone, which she recognizes as somewhat false. She does it in "Berthe" when she accuses her aunts of deserting the woman; she does it again in "Willy" when what she really feels is rage at her uncle's lustful relationship with the Cajun mistress; and she repeats this pose when, after Cowan has "cracked up," she dismisses him as "a man of unnecessary things." Helen, however, constantly reminds Hellman that everyone is "getting ready for the summons" (death), so nonjudgmental understanding is preferable to false piety.

The chapter "Julia" is the high point of *Pentimento*, the one most often the focus of critical attention, both favorable and negative. Peter Feibleman in *Lilly* (1988) tells how Hellman had told him a story years earlier about a girlhood friend whose life paralleled Julia's experience, although he admits that the details, such as the wallpaper in the little German restaurant, were certainly added. What may be most important about "Julia" is not whether it is fact or fiction but that it illustrates a very deep friendship between young girls who grow into committed women, illustrating Hellman's brand of feminism and her disdain for people who simply stand by in the face of evil and do nothing. The latter idea became the major theme of *Watch on the Rhine*.

Toward the end of the 1930's, politics became important to Hellman, and in "Theatre" she tells of becoming increasingly aware of the political inquisition that would peak with Hammett being jailed and her own appearance in front of the House Un-American Activities Committee. She explains the basis for her feelings about injustice, which many liberals of the period believed would be eliminated by Marxism. As she admits, "I am, in fact, bewildered by all injustice, at first certain it cannot be, then shocked into rigidity, then obsessed, and finally as certain as the Grand Inquisitor that God wishes me to move ahead, correct and holy." This insight into her way of thinking does much to explain her so-called pro-Communist position, vis-à-vis Nazism. It was not until the nonaggression pact between Adolf Hitler and Joseph Stalin was signed in August, 1939, that she began to look more objectively at communism as practiced in the Soviet Union.

Another theme that runs through *Pentimento* is Hellman's love of nature. She believed that the happiest years of her life were those spent at Hardscrabble Farm in Westchester, which she and Hammett bought in June, 1939. It was a peaceful time in their relationship, and Hellman loved, according to Rollyson, "to work herself to weariness, to feel good-tired from writing, or spring planting, or cleaning chicken houses, or autumn hunting." It is here that "Turtle" is set, here that Hellman begins to ask what Hammett considers theological questions (which he refuses to answer) when the turtle survives the bullet and the axe. She asks "What is life?" After she has buried the animal, he puts a little tombstone over the grave, painted "My first turtle is buried here. Miss Religious L. H."

Throughout *Pentimento* runs the thread of money and its power. Hellman is aware of the link and thoroughly enjoys the life and extravagances that a good income allowed. She is also aware, however, of what greed can lead to, as she dramatizes in *The Little Foxes* and *Another Part of the Forest*, plays about the Hubbards (representing her mother's family). On the other hand, a disappointment repeatedly voiced by the playwright is that reviewers missed the ironic humor with which she drew these characters. For example, she says she had meant to "half-mock my own youthful high-class innocence in Alexandra, the young girl in the play," and later, "I had meant the audience to recognize some part of themselves in the money-dominated Hubbards; I had not meant people to think of them as villains to whom they had no connection." It is love that she is expressing—a love of family—even though she delineates their faults very clearly. The combination of regard for people and anger at their behavior, including sometimes her own, is a feature of *Pentimento*, as is the theme of survival.

Context

As Hellman would probably have admitted, her impact on women's literature was not dependent on *Pentimento*, or even on its autobiographical companion pieces, but on her plays. As an important dramatist, she made her foremost contribution in that area. Yet *Pentimento* did assure her place in a second genre—as a literary figure—and this no doubt pleased her. Her candor about her life, even if it is sometimes viewed through a veil of memory (and embellished, her detractors claim), paints a picture of a strong, somewhat angry personality, but one capable of great love. She was undoubtedly opinionated and seemed somewhat egotistical to those who did not like her, but above all, she had a keen desire to sample all that life offered. It is therefore no surprise to read in all the books written about Hellman that even when she was almost blind and very ill during the last months of her life, she insisted passionately on continuing her activities. She was indeed, like the turtle, a survivor.

Sources for Further Study

Falk, Doris V. *Lillian Hellman*. New York: Frederick Ungar, 1978. A well-written biography of Hellman covering her life and her work, with many references to *Pentimento*. A bibliography is included.

Feibleman, Peter. *Lilly: Reminiscences of Lillian Hellman*. New York: William Morrow, 1988. An affectionate portrait which defends the way in which Hellman wrote *Pentimento*, particularly the chapter "Julia." Hellman carefully researched details that would later, in Feibleman's view, be "examined thread by thread, picked bare by all those nimble writers whose finest tools are a magnifying glass and a pair of tweezers."

Gould, Jean. *Modern American Playwrights*. New York: Dodd, Mead, 1966. Published years before any of Hellman's memoirs, the chapter entitled "Lillian Hellman" illuminates the playwright's position on social issues and feminism.

Harriman, Margaret Case. *Take Them Up Tenderly*. New York: Alfred A. Knopf, 1944. In her chapter "Miss Lilly of New Orleans," Harriman focuses on Hellman's life from childhood through the first plays and makes clear the playwright's feelings about "the little people" in society.

Lederer, Katherine. *Lillian Hellman*. Boston: Twayne, 1979. Devoting only one short chapter to "Life and Times," Lederer concentrates instead on a critical view of Hellman as an ironic voice in both her plays and her memoirs. Offers a section devoted to *Pentimento* and a selected bibliography.

Riordan, Mary Marguerite. *Lillian Hellman: A Bibliography, 1926-1978*. Metuchen, N.J.: Scarecrow Press, 1980. An extraordinary book listing in easy-to-find form everything that Hellman wrote, all the speeches she made, and all the books and articles written about her and about her work through 1978.

Rollyson, Carl. *Lillian Hellman: Her Legend and Her Legacy*. New York: St. Martin's Press, 1988. With copious notes, a bibliography, and a carefully done index, Rollyson's picture of Hellman (and *Pentimento*) seeks a well-balanced analysis of the woman and her work.

Wright, William. *Lillian Hellman: The Image, the Woman*. New York: Simon & Schuster, 1986. A well-written, unauthorized biography which makes claim to an inordinate amount of research in the attempt to show "a more human portrait of Hellman" than she painted of herself. Contains notes to each chapter and an index, but no bibliography.

Edythe M. McGovern

PERSUASION

Author: Jane Austen (1775-1817)
Type of work: Novel
Type of plot: Domestic realism
Time of plot: The early nineteenth century
Locale: Southern England
First published: 1818

> *Principal characters:*
> ANNE ELLIOT, the novel's protagonist, who was once in love
>   with Frederick Wentworth but chose not to marry him
> FREDERICK WENTWORTH, a naval officer who has made his
>   fortune at sea
> SIR WALTER ELLIOT, Anne's father, a vain country gentleman
> ELIZABETH ELLIOT, Sir Walter's eldest daughter, who serves as
>   matron of the Elliot household
> MARY MUSGROVE, the youngest of the Elliot daughters, married
>   into a sensible family
> CHARLES MUSGROVE, Mary's husband
> LADY RUSSELL, Anne's longtime friend
> WILLIAM ELLIOT, the nephew of Sir Walter and the heir apparent
>   to the Elliot title and property

Form and Content

Like most of her novels, *Persuasion* affords Jane Austen an opportunity to explore social relationships among middle-class men and women living in what is usually considered a refined, country environment away from the commercial and political centers of England. Unlike other Austen novels, however, *Persuasion* features a heroine who is not a young ingenue first learning the customs and taboos of polite society. Anne Elliot, second daughter of a minor country baronet, is nearing thirty when the action of the novel begins. Readers learn early that she was once engaged to Frederick Wentworth but gave up her lover when friends and relatives convinced her that he was not worthy of her. The action of the novel concentrates on her becoming reacquainted with Wentworth, now a naval captain, and overcoming the objections of others and the connivances of rivals for Wentworth's affection.

Austen centers the action in various locales: Kellynch Hall, the ancestral home of the Elliots; the country village of Uppercross; and the resort city of Bath. Rising debts cause Anne's father to rent out Kellynch Hall and move to less expensive lodgings in Bath; Anne visits relatives in Uppercross, where she first learns that Wentworth has returned to the region after rising to distinction and amassing a comfortable fortune through service in the Navy. In a series of connected episodes, Anne and her circle of family and friends travel freely in a series of visits and excursions that give the young men and women ample opportunity to discuss important social issues and establish amorous attachments. Their conversations give readers a glimpse into the values held most sacred by the middle class of English society at the turn of the nineteenth century. It is clear that the young women spend most of their time plotting to snare an eligible bachelor; those who are married focus their attention on their families, taking time to assist in advancing the courtships of their unmarried associates. Although the young men pursue a variety of professions, they are as interested in social repartee as the women are. The novel is filled with parties, dinners, and trips to see local sights of interest.

Throughout the novel, Anne vacillates in her feelings about Wentworth, wondering whether she should renew her ardent love for him. She struggles to overcome the social prejudices that led her to reject Wentworth eight years earlier, all the while being concerned that others, especially her friend and confidante Lady Russell, might object to a reprise of a relationship of which they had been critical in the past. She is alternately persuaded to pursue him or to relinquish the idea that they might rekindle the affection they once felt for each other. Meanwhile, other women younger than Anne set their sights on Wentworth; Louisa Musgrove, sister to Anne's brother-in-law, makes a particularly demonstrative play for his affections. A freak accident in which Louisa is seriously injured appears to drive Wentworth forward in his attentions toward her, and Anne can do nothing but be patient and let events take their natural course.

Because Austen tells the story almost exclusively from the point of view of her heroine, readers are led to wonder along with Anne whether Wentworth is serious in his attentions toward other women. Only when her cousin William Elliot appears as a suitor on the scene to seek Anne's hand does Wentworth finally reveal that he is still smitten with her, at which point the two put aside their fears about what others might say and restore their engagement—this time as a prelude to marriage.

Analysis

As she does in her other novels, in *Persuasion* Jane Austen focuses her attention on the subjects that concern her most: love and marriage. Anne Elliot's story is but a variation on the theme that consumed Austen's creative energies all of her life. She is interested in the proper relationships between the sexes; her exploration of Anne's trials in overcoming the prejudices of her contemporaries gives her ample opportunity to probe deeply into the conventions of a social world seemingly secure in its understanding of the proper role of men and women at every level in a highly structured society.

In more than a half dozen major male-female relationships, Austen examines the ways in which men and women accommodate to courtship and married life. She offers readers an idea of the ideal marriage in her portrait of Admiral and Mrs. Croft; she displays the tribulations of family life in her description of the home of Charles Musgrove and his wife Mary, Anne's youngest sister. She explores the insidious nature of marriages made for social gain in episodes involving Sir Walter and Mrs. Clay, the

Musgrove sisters, and Anne herself when she is pursued by her cousin William Walter Elliot, presumptive heir to Sir Walter's title and estates.

The social circle of the Elliots, the Musgroves, and their friends is but a small slice of the larger English nation; often described as a miniaturist, Austen focuses her attention on a stratum of the middle class tightly bordered by the petty nobility at one extreme and the working-class gentlefolk at the other. No kings or dukes inhabit the novel, and the servant class, though mentioned, gets scarcely a nod. Nevertheless, within this limited scope, Austen employs her extensive understanding of human nature and human feelings to show how society's prescriptions and expectations often inhibit personal growth and crush genuine feelings beneath the weight of convention and false propriety.

Austen portrays Anne Elliot as a quiet rebel within this world. She is a woman who comes to recognize her personal dignity and worth in a society that has little use for women as people. She is sensitive to her own feelings and to the feelings that others have. She questions and ultimately rejects the social order represented by her family, seeing aristocratic values as bankrupt. She is equally repulsed by the crass manipulations of people such as her cousin William, whose quest for financial security motivates his pursuit of marriage partners, and Mrs. Clay, who schemes throughout to marry Anne's widower father for the same reason.

Viewed from a twentieth century perspective, Anne may be seen as a quiet feminist. She is unwilling to accept without comment the social restrictions placed on women. Whenever possible, she spends her time with men so that she can converse with them about issues of importance; she is not willing to be limited to discussions of domestic matters. She is unwilling, too, to accept the notions that men are more rational than women, and that they are better suited for certain forms of responsibility. At the moment of the only real crisis in the novel, when Louisa Musgrove is injured in a fall and thought to be near death, Anne remains calm and lends assistance while the other women dash about frantically. Austen wants readers to see that, emotionally and intellectually, if not economically, Anne Elliot is able to be self-sufficient.

Through Anne, Austen provides a stern critique of the country aristocracy who believe that their bloodlines make them exempt from rules of courtesy or from acknowledging the personal worth of individuals outside their class. Anne's father, her older sister, and several other characters come under fire from the author for their craven self-interest or for their unfounded belief that appearances are more important than honest expressions of opinion and feeling. The professional classes are presented as a worthwhile alternative to the nobility. Especially noteworthy is Austen's presentation of the Navy; virtually all the admirable male characters in the novel are associated in some way with naval service.

Context

Unlike many women novelists before the twentieth century, Jane Austen has always enjoyed a good reputation among writers (both men and women), and from the initial publication of her work in the first decades of the nineteenth century she has been considered a standard toward which aspiring novelists—especially women novelists—were to reach. Although most male novelists and critics writing prior to the 1960's have been somewhat patronizing toward Austen because she focuses her attention on domestic and social issues, women writers have long looked to her as one of the earliest feminist novelists. Her heroines usually emerge above the conventional roles expected of women in Austen's day, although the author's critique of gender relationships remains a muted strain in works that seem conservative to casual readers. Her work was known and respected by the Brontës and by George Eliot; she is the subject of commentary by the earliest critics now associated with the twentieth century women's movement, including Virginia Woolf.

Because it was her final novel and was published in what most critics consider an unfinished state, *Persuasion* has not enjoyed the reputation and influence accorded to other works in the Austen canon, especially *Emma* and *Pride and Prejudice*. Nevertheless, in the later decades of the twentieth century, the novel has received increasing attention from critics, especially those interested in women's issues. Chapters in scholarly studies are devoted to detailed examinations of the work's characters, themes, and techniques. A number of critics find the novel an advance over earlier Austen works, noting that the writer is able to provide extensive background through brief synopsis so that attention may be concentrated on the climactic scenes in which Anne asserts her independence from the patriarchal society that has denied her the opportunity to make her own choices regarding marriage and lifestyle. The novel is often cited as a mature critique of the social system that treats women as objects and trivializes their intellectual abilities. The union of Anne and Captain Wentworth as equal partners in marriage is hailed as a goal that Austen was promoting despite her apparent acquiescence to traditional social and moral values.

Sources for Further Study
Dwyer, June. *Jane Austen*. New York: Continuum, 1989. Dwyer offers readings of each of Austen's major novels, including *Persuasion*, and in separate chapters discusses the writer's life and her literary techniques and concerns.
Gard, Robert. *Jane Austen's Novels: The Art of Clarity*. New Haven, Conn.: Yale University Press, 1992. Gard writes what he calls a corrective to criticism that has moved readers too far away from the texts of Austen's novels into theoretical concerns. His chapter on *Persuasion* discusses Austen's mature ability as a novelist.
Johnson, Claudia. *Jane Austen: Women, Politics, and the Novel*. New Haven, Conn.: Yale University Press, 1988. Johnson considers the political dimension of all Austen's novels, showing how the writer integrates her own voice and views subtly within texts that seem conservative on casual reading.
Kirkham, Margaret. *Jane Austen, Feminism, and Fiction*. Totowa, N.J.: Barnes & Noble Books, 1983. Kirkham places Austen's work within the feminist tradition, showing that the writer's concerns are those of her feminist contemporaries. She includes a chapter on eighteenth century feminism. The chapter on *Persuasion* shows how Austen uses the novel as a feminist critique of society.

Tanner, Tony. *Jane Austen.* Cambridge, Mass.: Harvard University Press, 1986. Tanner's thorough study of Austen's six novels focuses on the author's concern with society, education, and language. A chapter on *Persuasion* stresses the skepticism that Austen exhibits toward society and the positive attitude she has toward the Navy.

Todd, Janet, ed. *Jane Austen: New Perspectives.* New York: Holmes & Meier, 1983. Nineteen essayists explore Austen's novels from varying perspectives, most of them inspired by poststructuralist theory or feminist ideology. Recurring themes are highlighted; each of the major novels is discussed in at least one essay.

Williams, Michael. *Jane Austen: Six Novels and Their Methods.* Houndsmills, England: MacMillan, 1986. Williams examines Austen's means of shaping her novels; a chapter is included on each of the six major works, including *Persuasion*; Williams believes that its complex plotting and characterization give the novel a richer texture than those of earlier works by the novelist.

Laurence W. Mazzeno

PICTURE BRIDE

Author: Cathy Song (1955-   )
Type of work: Poetry
First published: 1983

Form and Content

The content and form of this first book of poems reflect intimately the personal background and interests of its author. Therefore, many of these poems have their locations in Hawaii, where Cathy Song was born and reared, and the continental United States, where she attended university and married. Song is the daughter of a Korean American father and a Chinese American mother, and her poems are valuable repositories of an Asian American woman's sensibilities experiencing the intricate varieties of familial and personal relationships—as daughter, wife, mother, lover, and friend. Art, too, is an informing interest of Song's, especially that of the Japanese ukiyo-e master Utamaro and that of the American feminist painter Georgia O'Keeffe, whose life and works lend inspiration and shape to this book of poems.

Picture Bride is organized into five sections, each section deriving its title from a painting by Georgia O'Keeffe. Thus, the book begins with an initial statement of themes and an imagistic setting of scenes in "Black Iris" (familial relationships and home), continues with the development of these themes and scenes in "Sunflower," moves into a contemplation of the effort and achievement of art in the central "Orchids," renders scenes suggesting a darker, perhaps Dionysian, side to art and life in "Red Poppy," and proceeds to a final affirmation of the validity and variety of human creativity and productivity in "The White Trumpet Flower." The central section of the book also contains the key poem "Blue and White Lines After O'Keeffe," whose speaker is Song's imaginative re-creation of Georgia O'Keeffe and which is itself divided into five subsections with subtitles that replicate exactly the titles of the five sections of the book itself.

The title poem of this book, "Picture Bride," is a young Korean American woman's meditation on the feelings, experience, and mentality of her immigrant grandmother, who came to Hawaii to be married to a sugar-cane-field worker. This poem strikes the chord that forms the basis of many of the book's poems: woman's (and especially the ethnic woman's) experience of family. Because Song's feminism is so imbued with ethnicity, some readers may prefer to call her work "womanist," the term coined by African American author Alice Walker in *In Search of Our Mothers' Gardens* (1983). That Song should choose to meditate on her grandmother in "Picture Bride" would seem natural enough to the majority of contemporary American readers, but in terms of traditional Confucian and Asian hierarchy the ancestor Song should have memorialized and venerated was her male ancestor. Instead, the grandfather is devalorized into a mere "stranger." Therefore, Song's choice of subject in this poem is itself a break from traditional Asian patriarchy and a declaration of allegiance to a feminist hierarchy of family history, a privileging of women's experience.

It has been reported on good authority that the prepublication title of Song's book in manuscript form was "From the White Place," and the poem with that title bears a dedicatory epigraph: "for Georgia O'Keeffe." It is fair to surmise, then, that Georgia O'Keeffe's embodiment of sexual independence and creative power is as strong an element in this book as is the ethnic woman's experience embodied by Song's grandmother. Indeed, Georgia O'Keeffe, an exemplar of modern feminist painting, strikes the keynote of creativity and art by and about women.

Women's experience, ethnicity, and art are therefore the main spheres of interest in *Picture Bride*, while the works of feminist artist Georgia O'Keeffe provide it with an encompassing structure and indwelling spirit.

Analysis

Most of the poems in Song's book deal with the various spheres of women's familial experience. These range from mother-daughter relationships (in, for example, "The Youngest Daughter," and "A Pale Arrangement of Hands"), to father-daughter relationships ("Father and Daughter"), to sibling relationships ("For My Brother," "Tribe," "Lost Sister"), to the numerous poems dealing with spousal relationships ("Birthmarks," "The White Porch," "Seed," "Stray Animals," "A Dream of Small Children," and "January"). Apart from these poems of women's familial experience, some pieces concentrate mainly on an ethnic topic; for example, "Untouched Photograph of Passenger" focuses on a fresh-off-the-boat immigrant, and "Chinatown" attempts to capture the spirit of a place and a people through a collage of images of several Chinatowns. Several other poems focus on art or artists: music and musicians in "Blue Lantern" and "The Violin Teacher"; Utamaro, the Japanese artist who painted women, in "Beauty and Sadness" and "Girl Powdering Her Neck"; a woman writer (probably Song herself) in "Hotel Genève"; and, most important, the American feminist artist Georgia O'Keeffe in "Blue and White Lines After O'Keeffe" and "From the White Place."

As one might expect, however, many of Song's poems elude a rigid thematic categorization that would separate, for example, poems of women's experience from those about ethnicity or from those about art. In fact, these themes are sometimes organically and inextricably intertwined. For example, one will happen on poems about ethnic women's experience and about women artists/artisans, such as "The Seamstress," whose speaker is a Japanese American woman who makes dolls and creates wedding gowns but who seems condemned to remain in the background, a silent spinster (and spinner), or "For A. J.: On Finding That She's on Her Boat to China," which addresses an Asian ballerina manquée returning to Asia to become a materfamilias.

In exploring these themes, Song uses with dazzling skill many of the tools and devices of the poet's craft. Employing a colloquial diction in the open form of subtly cadenced free verse, Song is equally adept at narrative, monologue (be it lyrical-meditative, conversational, or dramatic), and evocation (of a place, time, or person). Yet everywhere it is Song's brilliant use of imagery that makes her poetry shine forth.

Indeed, many readers have noted and lauded the clarity and originality of Song's imagery. As well as being lucid and unique, Song's imagery is also richly meaningful and allusive. For example, in the poem that is at the umbilical center of the book, "Blue and White Lines After O'Keeffe," the very title conjures up pictures of O'Keeffe's paintings as well as the image of blue-inked lines of poetry written on a white page. The poem then begins as a dramatic monologue spoken through the persona of the painter Georgia O'Keeffe, who is describing her feelings in New York City: "I climb the stairs/ in this skull hotel./ Voices beat at the walls,/ railings/ fan out like fishbones." The hard, ungiving, and treacherous qualities of New York are caught in Song's choice of the images of skulls, walls, railings, and fishbones to express her experience. "Skull hotel" is a brilliantly macabre and unique image, infusing connotations of death and intellectual sterility into one's dwelling place, effectively turning one's lodgings into a charnel house. Moreover, this image appears in combination with the kinesthetic image of climbing the stairs, an allusion to Christ's climbing the hill of Calvary or Golgotha toward his crucifixion (*golgotha* is the Aramaic word for "skull"). The synesthetic image of the phrase "voices beat at the walls," combining the auditory and tactile senses, further extends the pervading sense of frustration and claustrophobia. "Railings," too, is an image with double meaning: not only is it a physical image of a cold metallic structure, but it also denotes arguing and quarreling—an eloquent description of a thoroughly unfriendly neighborhood. A final synesthetic image in this stanza that likens the neighbors' voices to "fishbones" vividly combines the audible quality of treachery in the neighbors' talk with the visceral sensation of pain in the gullet. By deftly deploying such richly suggestive and allusive imagery, the opening stanza of this poem conveys the sense of malaise felt by a woman artist starting out in New York.

Song also uses imagery to make effective contrasts. For example, the initial New York section of "Blue and White Lines After O'Keeffe" contrasts imagistically with the third section of this poem, which moves to a Hawaiian setting (Makena Beach, Maui). Whereas in the New York section the Christian images are painful memento mori, in the Hawaii section the Christian images become positive: "I wear hats . . . like halos," "I cross myself/ with ti leaves" (reminiscent of Christ's triumphant Palm Sunday), and "the eyes of old fishermen" (echoing Christ's calling of his first disciples). New York was a cold, mean place bereft of greenery; and in the following passage about New York, the double meaning of "palette" synthesizes a gustatory image with a visual one to suggest a deadening unavailability of green freshness in physical food as well as in food for the creative appetite: "I . . . dine alone./ I stare into the palette,/ imagine green in my diet,/ Peeling back the tins of sardines,/ these tubes of paint,/ lined like slender bullets:/ my ammunition." Hawaii, however, is a place of plenitude; it is provident and nourishing, physically and creatively. Instead of the fishbone-like railings of her New York neighbors, the "bird language" of the Hawaiians beautifully "spirals up in the blue air." In contrast to the lethal and destructive images of bullet-like tubes of paint in New York, the speaker says that, in Hawaii, "I have all the colors I need." Instead of the unappetizing tinned sardines and merely imaginary greens of New York food, the speaker says of Hawaii's lush plenty: "What tropical plants/ I cannot eat,/ I can use for dyes." In this manner, then, Cathy Song uses imagery to its peak of effectiveness.

Context

Cathy Song was one of the first Asian American women poets to win a major literary prize—the 1982 Yale Younger Poets prize, an award that numbers among its laureates such distinguished women as Adrienne Rich (1950) and Carolyn Forché (1975). Only a very few Asian American women poets have received awards and recognition that might be equivalent to Song's; those who come to mind are Ai, the Japanese African American Indian winner of the Lamont Poetry prize for *Killing Floor* (1978), and Shirley Geok-lin Lim, the Chinese American from Malaysia who won the Commonwealth Poetry Prize for *Crossing the Peninsula* (1980). Song is certainly the only Korean American woman to achieve her literary stature in the United States, the only other Korean American woman who approaches Song in literary accomplishment being Theresa Hak Kyung Cha (*Dictée*, 1982), whose promising career was terminated by her brutal murder.

Many of the poems in Song's *Picture Bride* explore feminist themes of woman's experience and the world of womanist culture. Many of Song's most effective poems explore the relationships between women as mothers, daughters, sisters, and friends. For example, the interior monologue of "The Youngest Daughter" captures the painful and constricting symbiosis of a migraine-stricken daughter and an insulin-dependent mother: As the daughter distastefully bathes her mother, she notices her "breasts/ floating in the milky water/ like two walruses,/ flaccid and whiskered around the nipples" and thinks "with a sour taste" that "six children and an old man/ have sucked from these brown nipples." Similarly, as the mother prepares their afternoon meal, the daughter (whose skin is as friable as "pale . . . rice paper") compares her own unfulfilled "white body" to "a slice of pickled turnip" about to be eaten, symbolically cannibalized by their relationship. In "Tribe," the speaker of the poem recalls her elder sister's childhood assertiveness with males via an image associating the sister with the huntress-goddess Diana/Artemis: The elder sister "disappeared like a huntress/ into the bushes, the only girl/ in a gang of boys," boys who would lose their marbles to this girl as later she "returned triumphant, . . . with all their marbles/ bulging in the pockets/ of [her] leopard-spotted pedal pushers."

Female sensuality and reproductive ability endow Song's women with sensual force and creative self-awareness. A woman awaiting her man's return home is vibrantly alive to her own sensuality in "The White Porch"; the speaker's sexuality pervades the women's chores of shampooing her hair ("like a bridal veil"), of preparing dinner ("the sponge cake rising in the oven" whose crumbs her man will "lick clean"), of stretching to hang out laundry ("the small buttons of my cotton blouse/ are pulling away from my body"), and of shelling beans ("the mountain of beans/ in my lap" suggests a feast of seed and sexuality). Each of these mundane acts leads the speaker through a "slow arousal" of her sensuality which climaxes in the urgent, empowering, apostrophized memory of how she used to smuggle this man into her parents' home, into her bedroom, to her person: "I would let the rope down/ at night, strips of sheets,/ knotted and tied, . . . / my hair freshly washed/ . . . like a bridal veil. . . . Cloth, hair and hands,/ smuggling you in." There are also moving poems about conception and pregnancy, such as "Seed," a yearning lyric spoken by a mother-to-be, and "Stray Animals," which subtly uses a road-killed stray cat as an objective correlative for a pregnant woman's fear of miscarriage, while the subject of contraception and/or abortion is suggested in "A Dream of Small children" by powerfully visceral images such as "The sky is bandaged with white gauze./ A jet slits open the belly of clouds. . . . Eskimos who skin whales/ . . . Eat the ripe ovaries like fruit,/ while I mourn/ and dream of small children."

In addition to exploring and celebrating female sexuality, Song also presents the possibilities of female empowerment through a vision of the woman as artist, (for example, the O'Keeffe poems) and the woman as art object (the Utamaro poems). In several of Song's poems, woman's work becomes her art, as it does in the quiet creativity of "The Seamstress" or the imaginative infectiousness of the mother in "A Pale Arrangement of Hands," who infuses her children with poetic awareness when she makes them see rain as "Liquid sunshine." Finally, in Song's poetry, the exploration of the female subculture is enriched by her awareness of an ethnic subculture, an awareness that speaks feelingly of the generational differences between Asian American immigrant mothers and their daughters and granddaughters; thus, in poems such as "Lost Sister" and "Picture Bride," Song deals explicitly with matrilineal inheritance within the Asian American subculture.

In sum, then, Song is a pioneering Asian American woman poet of the very first order. Sensitive and complex in her perception of the world, powerful and accomplished in wielding the tools of her poetic craft, Cathy Song is a writer whose work rewards those who read and study it.

Sources for Further Study
Fujita-Sato, Gayle K. " 'Third World' as Place and Paradigm in Cathy Song's *Picture Bride." MELUS* 15, no. 1 (Spring, 1988): 49-72. This intricate and meticulous essay proposes an innovative framework for reading both Song's work and ethnic writing in general. Fujita-Sato sees places and people as points from which to view ethnic experience and cultural synthesis. She pays special attention to "Picture Bride," "Blue and White Lines After O'Keeffe," "Blue Lantern," "Hotel Genève," "The White Porch," "From the White Place," "Easter Wahiawa, 1959," and "Leaving."
Lim, Shirley. "Reconstructing Asian-American Poetry: A Case for Ethnopoetics." *MELUS* 14, no. 2 (Summer, 1987): 51-63. Lim makes a case for an ethno-centered reading of Asian American poetry, outlining three levels at which ethnopoetics functions—stylistic traits of diction or figurative language, linguistic inclusions of Asian languages, and use of ethnic background and allusions. Lim refers to Song's use of imagery that is specifically Asian American in *Picture Bride*.
_____ . Review of *Picture Bride. MELUS* 10, no. 3 (Fall, 1983): 95-99. Lim

notes that kinship is the primary theme of the collection. Lim sees Song's ability to merge organic imagery with emotion and form as her major strength. The only weakness that Lim describes is an overuse of linguistic conventions to present Asian American culture, rendering a few of Song's metaphors strained and unbelievable.

Sumida, Stephen H. "Pictures of Art and Life." *Contact II* 7, nos. 38-40 (1986): 52-55. A highly informed and penetrating analysis of Song's imagery, narrative element, and dramatic monologue. Sumida is a leading authority on Hawaiian American literature, and he brings his expertise and sensibility to bear in his analysis of the book, especially of the poems "Picture Bride," "The Youngest Daughter," "The Seamstress," and "Blue and White Lines After O'Keeffe" (to which Sumida devotes half of his article).

Wallace, Patricia. "Divided Loyalties: Literal and Literary in the Poetry of Lorna Dee Cervantes, Cathy Song, and Rita Dove." *MELUS* 18, no. 3 (Fall, 1993): 3-19. Wallace distinguishes the literary from the literal in the works of minority women poets, "literary" being the poet's ability to manipulate language to express, and "literal" being the poet's attempt to reflect knowledge from experience. She examines how these two impulses function independently even as they appear together in a work. Although Wallace's discussion of Song centers on Song's second book, *Frameless Windows, Squares of Light*, Wallace does specifically refer to the poem "Picture Bride."

C. L. Chua
Laura Mitchell

PICTURING WILL

Author: Ann Beattie (1947-   )
Type of work: Novel
Type of plot: Social realism
Time of plot: An unspecified present and twenty years later
Locale: Charlottesville, Virginia; New York; Florida; and Connecticut
First published: 1989

> *Principal characters:*
> WILL, the son of Jody and Wayne
> JODY, Will's mother
> WAYNE, Jody's former husband
> MEL ANTHIS, Will's stepfather
> D. B. HAVERFORD, an art gallery owner whom Jody refers to as
>   "Haveabud"
> CORKY, Wayne's third wife

Form and Content

In form, *Picturing Will* resembles chronologically arranged snapshots of a post-modern family. Divided into three sections entitled "Mother," "Father," and "Child," the novel often focuses on the characters' external environments, exhibiting Beattie's trademark use of telling details, including references to consumer goods and fashionable trends. While Beattie has often been praised for the photographic accuracy of her descriptions and her realistic portrayal of disjointed lives, *Picturing Will* deals more with the emotional complexity of relationships than her previous work does, demonstrating that people are not simply the roles they are assigned, such as the role of "mother." The complicated, fragile, and enduring love between a parent and child has more to do with commitment than with biology. Interspersed throughout each section are italicized passages that attempt to deal with the frustrations and terror, the joy and wonder of rearing a child.

In part 1, "Mother," Jody is forging a new life for herself and Will after having been abandoned by Wayne four years earlier. She cannot really remember why she married Wayne, but her life and ambition had been thwarted by the experience. In her new life as an in-demand wedding photographer and Will's caretaker, she knows that she has the luxury of suspension, to be "neither the harried mother nor the beleaguered artist." While Mel is waiting for her to decide whether she will marry him, Jody seems to relish her work (she often returns to the scene of a wedding to experiment with lighting, texture, and subject) and her life with Will (they go to the park and have meals of "color"—a strip of avocado, a hot dog, a tomato). She periodically sends manila folders to Wayne, day-to-day reminders of the facts of their existence—clearly not a passive gesture on her part. Obviously talented, she is always ready with a camera to record an elusive scene.

This section also introduces Mel, who often travels from New York to Charlottesville to visit Jody and Will. He helps to care for Will, even editing the endings of frightening bedtime stories. He is, perhaps, overcautious, but life seems to have rewarded him. He has inherited a house and money from a grandfather and has a successful job at an art gallery. When Haverford wants Mel to come and work at his gallery, Mel does so on the condition that Haverford view Jody's pictures. Haverford does, and Jody's international career has begun.

Part 2, entitled "Father," begins two years later with Mel taking Will to Florida to visit Wayne. "Haveabud" has invited himself and a former protégé's child, Spencer, along for the ride. While Mel is sleeping in the next room, Will witnesses a homoerotic scene between Haveabud and the boy, a scene that haunts and confuses him. Wayne, as the biological father of Will, is too preoccupied with having affairs to pay much attention to Will. Instead, Corky, Wayne's third wife, entertains Will, trying also to prove to Wayne that they should have a child. Because of one of his affairs, Wayne is falsely accused of cocaine possession. The final image that Will has of him is of a handcuffed Wayne being led to a police car.

The final italicized chapter of this section turns all the reader's assumptions and expectations around. These passages are the works and thoughts of Mel, who has been keeping a journal for Will, a journal that documents his disappointment in a marriage to a withdrawn, preoccupied, and famous photographer and a journal that details his love and hope for Will. The final six-page section, "Child," deals with Will's point of view twenty years later. Now an art historian, married, and the father of a son, Will reads the journal that Mel gives to him, recognizing that Mel has been his most devoted parent.

Analysis

Beattie has often been labeled as a chronicler of her generation, a label with which she does not agree. She has also written often about characters who came of age in the 1960's and 1970's, characters who lack permanent emotional ties and commitments while feeling a vague malaise and incomprehension at the direction that their lives have taken. While Wayne does fall into this category of characterization, and while *Picturing Will*, like Beattie's other works, does use episodic style and short, intensified moments that are captured and framed like photographs, this novel deals fully with the emotional complexity of adult relationships and the parent/child bond.

This novel haunts the reader as Beattie's use of telling details escalates. During part 1, "Mother," a reader might first believe that *Picturing Will* is another "woman's" story about single parenting; however, there are too many unanswered questions about Jody. She married Wayne without even knowing that he had been married once before, and her habit of sending Wayne manila envelopes stuffed with grocery receipts, teachers' notes, parking tickets, and junk mail is disquieting. Jody admits that she is withholding part of herself from Mel, and this detachment is part of her personality and part of her profession. She is, after all, an artist, with all the difficulties that her personal quest and vision necessitate. She views aspects of life in terms of events being wide-angle shots or close-ups. Will is her buffer from the world as she recovers from Wayne's abandonment, but a camera also offers protection from the inconstancy and indeterminacy of life.

Although Jody could be accused of not being a "good" mother according to conventional standards, Beattie certainly does not indict her characters for the choices, or lack of choices, that they make. Even Wayne, a character who refuses to grow up and who has a vague premonition that the world somehow "owes" him something, is not condemned in Beattie's neorealistic world. He is too busy having an affair with a woman he has just met on the beach to be at home to greet Will's arrival to Florida. Even when he is around Will, he cannot quite find sufficient emotional resources to communicate with him in a meaningful way. Other characters come in and out of focus in the work, and the pictures are constantly being shuffled and rearranged as point of view changes, just as the events of life constantly call for a reinterpretation of their meanings.

Mel's true importance to the novel and to Will is not revealed until immediately before the final short section, and the realization that it is Mel who has been responsible for the italicized passages on the terror and joy of rearing a child again calls for the reader to reevaluate the events that have gone before. Mel and Jody did not live happily ever after, and the more famous Jody became, the more she withdrew. As Mel states, "She pursued fame, and left it to you to pursue baby-sitters." What is clear from this final entry in Mel's journal is that, despite the fact that life did not turn out as he expected, he loved Will and still thinks of himself as the person who knelt so many times to tie Will's shoes, the person on whom a trusting Will depended. Mel seems to prove that neither biology nor gender guarantees parentage; instead, the ability to make a lasting commitment that can survive life's surprises is the necessary role of a parent.

Will's final section acknowledges that "Mel never misled him," and despite the subtle feeling of apprehension about Will's upbringing throughout the novel, Will does survive his childhood and even becomes a father himself. Although Beattie's novels most often have unresolved endings, *Picturing Will*, although it does not give any answers, does offer a possibility of a synergistic picture. The final image of the novel has Will imagining a photograph of himself and his son on a green lawn. Mel has given the baby a ball, and Will's final words of the novel are for the baby to let go and throw the ball. In this final image, there is a sense of continuity and, perhaps, of fragile hope.

Context

Some critics view Ann Beattie as writing about a new "lost generation," a generation of people who came of age in the late 1960's and early 1970's and who wander through a landscape of postmodern disappointment and general dissatisfaction. In *Picturing Will*, however, Beattie seems to have gone more deeply into the psychological ravines of the characters than she has in previous novels (*Chilly Scenes of Winter*, 1976; *Falling in Place*, 1980; and *Love Always*, 1985). She has acknowledged in interviews that this novel took three years to write and that this work contains more of her personal vision of the world than her previous work does. While *Picturing Will* still does not offer any preconceived answers to the perplexing questions and disappointments of life, love, and rearing children, the powerful images presented to the reader like a shifting collage of photographs leave the reader with a shock of recognition. Some of the most mundane events in life are, in fact, the most illuminating.

Beattie forces the reader to examine experience and the fact that experience may not be what it seems. In this novel, conventional roles are turned upside down. While Jody is not a conventional mother, Beattie never lets the reader forget that she is an artist, and as an artist, she is on a personal quest. The roles that people play in the lives of others are not strictly defined by biology and gender. If that were the case, life might easily be framed in a photograph. As Beattie points out, however, life is not that easy, not that resolute. Some people make better choices, have better luck, or gain more from experience.

As a minimalist writer, Beattie has been grouped with such writers as Raymond Carver, Mary Robison, Tobias Wolff, and Alice Munro. *Picturing Will*, however, seems to take this pointillistic approach to style one step farther. She has captured the ethos of her age and has shown once again fiction's ability to hold up a mirror to life and reveal the foibles and pathos of a given era. As bleak as life may seem, the object, as Mel says, is to proceed. A character in "Learning to Fall" (from *The Burning House*, 1979) expands upon Mel's advice and perhaps sums up the ideal, if not the reality, of Beattie's vision: "What Ruth had known all along: what will happen can't be stopped. Aim for grace."

Sources for Further Study

Gerlach, John. "Through 'The Octascope': A View of Ann Beattie." *Studies in Short Fiction* 17, no. 4 (Fall, 1980): 489-494. This is a comprehensive analysis of Beattie's short story "The Octascope." Gerlach also views Beattie's work as a whole as a kind of octascope that lets the reader see the reversals and distortions in human love.

Gilder, Joshua. "Down and Out: The Stories of Ann Beattie." *New Criterion* 1, no. 2 (October, 1982): 51-56. This essay criticizes Beattie's fiction for failing to offer viable moral solutions to the philosophical problems that her fiction raises.

Griffith, Thomas. "Rejoice If You Can." *Atlantic Monthly*, September, 1980, 28-29. Griffith thinks that there is a "defiant purity" in Beattie's refusal to give answers to complaints about modern life. He points out that it is important to Beattie to describe her world and get it "right."

Iyer, Pico. "The World According to Beattie." *Partisan Review* 50, no. 4 (1983): 548-553. This essay compares Beattie's work to the writings of J. D. Salinger, John Cheever, and John Updike, pointing out how she speaks for a displaced generation. While admiring Beattie's style and photographic realism, Iyer sees her short stories as producing torpor.

Murphy, Christina. *Ann Beattie*. Boston: Twayne, 1986. This full-length study of

Beattie's work includes discussion of her works up to *Love Always*. It includes a short biography of Beattie as well as useful discussions of minimalism and the redefinition of the mimetic tradition. This work favorably assesses Beattie's contribution to contemporary literature and contains a selected bibliography.

Laurie Lisa

PILGRIM AT TINKER CREEK

Author: Annie Dillard (1945-   )
Type of work: Essays
First published: 1974

Form and Content

The fifteen interconnected yet surprisingly independent chapters of *Pilgrim at Tinker Creek* chronicle the cycle of seasons in and around the place the author identifies as "a creek, Tinker Creek, in a valley in Virginia's Blue Ridge." This place will not be found on any map, yet no reader would accuse the writer of creating an imaginary stream. Tinker Creek is real and holy to the writer, and Dillard aims to leave the reader believing in Tinker Creek's existence, continuance, and, ultimately, its importance.

In chronicling the year, *Pilgrim at Tinker Creek* presents the reader early on with "one of those excellent January partly cloudies." The book ends at a similar point approximately twelve months later when, in the last chapter, the reader learns, "Today is the winter solstice," and "Another year has twined away, unrolled and dropped across nowhere."

In taking the reader through the seasons of this sacred spot, the "pilgrim" narrator reveals little about herself. The reader learns that she smokes, that she reads astonishingly widely, and that she has a cat who jumps in through the bedroom window at night and leaves her covered in bloody paw prints. Except for these few incidental personal details, the reader's gaze is rarely fixed on the viewer, focusing instead on the viewer's world, on what is seen. Dillard would have the reader see not herself, but what she sees. Perhaps the most important thing that the reader learns about Dillard is that she has an infinite capacity for wonder and surprise—twin capacities that she uses to reawaken the same responses in her readers.

Dillard initially set her book in Maine and made the narrator a young man, but her editors eventually convinced her to do otherwise. In a taped interview with Kay Bonetti in 1989, she recounts living in a tent one fall in Maine and doing little else but reading. Among the books she was reading was one in which the writer referred to lightning bugs and to his ignorance of how they worked. Realizing that she knew how lightning bugs worked and that she knew much more about the natural world and writing than this writer did, Dillard concluded, "I should be writing this book."

Dillard wrote *Pilgrim at Tinker Creek* while she was in her late twenties. She completed the book in less than a year, working from her collection of about nineteen journals. She wrote from December to August, and she recalls of that time, "I was not living then, I was just writing. I would never do it again. It was like fighting a war."

The book has been labeled a collection of essays, a designation that displeases Dillard. She insists that *Pilgrim at Tinker Creek* is a sustained narrative. Another designation that Dillard finds particularly distasteful is meditation. She believes that the term "meditation" suggests randomness and passiveness and ignores *Pil-*

grim at Tinker Creek's muscularity.

Throughout her book, which is inscribed simply "For Richard," Dillard offers an account of what she sees, and she presents the reader with an eye and a voice that, while never mistaken for masculine, resist overtly proclaiming themselves feminine. It is perhaps in its uncompromising validation of personal vision—anyone's vision— that the book makes its greatest contribution.

Dillard refuses to present a sanitized, airbrushed view of nature to the reader. In addition to the beauties of a mockingbird's free fall and the tree with the lights in it, the reader also witnesses the giant water beetle that sucks the life from its victim and the praying mantis that beheads and devours its partner during mating. "It's rough out there," Dillard reminds the reader repeatedly.

Dillard writes seemingly with no set agenda. She frankly admits, "We don't know what's going on here." She adds that

> Our life is a faint tracing on the surface of mystery. . . . We must somehow take a wider view, look at the whole landscape, really see it, and describe what's going on here. Then we can at least wail the right question into the swaddling band of darkness, or, if it comes to that, choir the proper praise.

Analysis

Dillard never lets the reader lose track of the season under consideration, but much more than a calendar year binds *Pilgrim at Tinker Creek* together. The book presents the reader with a view of the outer world as it is reconstructed indoors—filtered, sorted, and sifted through the writer's own inner world. "I bloom indoors in the winter like a forced forsythia; I come in to come out. At night I read and write, and things I have never understood become clear; I reap the harvest of the rest of the year's planting," Dillard writes. At one point, Dillard calls her book "a mental ramble" and refers to her mind as a "trivia machine." "Like the bear who went over the mountain," she says, I wanted to "see what I could see."

What Dillard sees and records includes what she has read. Her book includes references to philosophy, religion, insects, Arctic exploration, medicine, poetry, and various other subjects. She devotes several pages to a summary of a book about newly sighted persons and their experience of the world. The pattern of the entire text could perhaps best be described as following the formula "I went here, I saw this, it made me think of this, I saw something else, and then I came home."

In many ways, Dillard's text reads like a travelogue. One finds many of that genre's typical markers: "I set out," "I go," "I sit," "I cross," "West of the house," and "north of me." Yet the book is no more a travelogue than it is a psalm, a field book, a reflection, a diary, a poem, an eyewitness account. The book defies classification in any of the traditional genres. Dillard's voyage is at once physical and spiritual. The sense of self and the sense of place are inextricably intertwined. Speaking of the creek, Dillard says, "I come to it as to an oracle; I return to it as a man years later will seek out the battlefield where he lost a leg or an arm."

Dillard has been compared with a number of writers, including Emily Dickinson, William Wordsworth, Gerard Manley Hopkins, W. B. Yeats, Rainer Maria Rilke, and Paul Valéry. It is to the Jesuit poet-priest Hopkins that Dillard pays most homage in her work. One hears echoes of "God's Grandeur" when Dillard maintains that "the whole world sparks and flames." Dillard evokes "The Windhover" when she speaks of "the most beautiful day of the year," which leaves her with "a dizzying, drawn sensation." She quotes several lines from one of Hopkins' lesser-known works, "As Kingfishers Catch Fire." Her closing lines of the book also evoke Hopkins as she returns to the opening image of her book—the cat that makes the bloody paw prints. The encounter leaves her, as does her encounter with the larger world, "bloodied and mauled, wrung, dazzled, drawn." *Pilgrim at Tinker Creek* also contains references to Andrew Marvell, William Blake, Robert Burns, and Dylan Thomas.

Dillard's tonal ranges include the sober, the philosophical, the flippant, and the celebratory. She can be exacting in her observations, yet she can also be carefree, as can be seen in this early statement: "I was walking along the edge of the island to see what I could see in the water, and mainly to scare frogs." She frequently uses a light-hearted tone to offset her serious and, at times, terrifying subject matter. This lighter tone can be heard in such statements as "Fish gotta swim and bird gotta fly; insects, it seems, gotta do one horrible thing after another." Dillard sees around her both the horrible and the humorous. She chooses to share both in *Pilgrim at Tinker Creek*. At times the reader gets both in one breath. Speaking of the endless variety in nature, she observes, "No form is too gruesome, no behavior too grotesque," and she counters with, "you ain't so handsome yourself."

Context

Dillard is often likened to Henry David Thoreau, to whom she refers frequently in her book. Her experience at Tinker Creek is often compared with Thoreau's self-imposed isolation at Walden Pond. Dillard has resisted seeing herself as a feminist writer, and she said in an interview, "I want to divorce myself from the notion of the female writer right away and then not elaborate." Despite any protests or disclaimers by the author, *Pilgrim at Tinker Creek* continues to be considered a feminist text by many readers. It refuses to confine woman to home and hearth, to an inner world. It refuses to define woman in terms of relationships with others. The book also staunchly refuses to privilege one sex as designated explorers of the natural world. Although Dillard's femaleness, her femininity, are not in the foreground in the text, *Pilgrim at Tinker Creek* can be seen, on the one hand, as transcending issues of gender, and, on the other hand, as inscribing a place for the solitary woman in the unbounded out-of-doors.

Sources for Further Study

Chénetier, Marc. "Tinkering, Extravagance: Thoreau, Melville, and Annie Dillard." *Critique* 31, no. 3 (Spring, 1990): 157-172. Chénetier stresses that "Dillard's work amply feeds upon classical texts" and notes that Dillard's readers engage "in a sort of symphonic reading" inasmuch as hearing Dillard's voice, unmistakable and distinctive as it is, involves hearing numerous other voices.

Clark, Suzanne. "The Woman in Nature and the Subject of Nonfiction." In *Literary Nonfiction: Theory, Criticism, Pedagogy*, edited by Chris Anderson. Carbondale: Southern Illinois University Press, 1989. Clark explores the apparent "lack of self" in Dillard's prose, the writer's refusal to emphasize her female identity, and the overlapping voices of "woman, poet, madman and mystic."

Dillard, Annie. "A Face Aflame: An Interview with Annie Dillard." Interview by Philip Yancey. *Christianity Today* 22 (May 5, 1978): 14-19. Dillard identifies her audience as "the unbeliever" yet acknowledges a large readership among people of many religious persuasions. She discusses readers' reactions to her work and describes herself as someone "grounded strongly in art and weakly in theology."

——————. *Teaching a Stone to Talk: Expeditions and Encounters*. New York: Harper & Row, 1982. In fourteen essays, many of which have been anthologized, Dillard explores themes introduced earlier in *Pilgrim at Tinker Creek*.

Dunn, Robert Paul. "The Artist as Nun: Theme, Tone, and Vision in the Writings of Annie Dillard." *Studia Mystica* 1, no. 4 (1978): 17-31. Dunn suggests that Dillard's works "are important because they suggest the possibility and value of recapturing in our materialistic age the beauty and pain of mystical vision." He explores Dillard's remarkable ability to speak convincingly to agnostics and believers alike, and her adoption of the dual role of artist and nun.

McIlroy, Gary. "*Pilgrim at Tinker Creek* and the Social Legacy of *Walden*." *The South Atlantic Quarterly* 85, no. 2 (Spring, 1986): 111-122. McIlroy describes the immediate environment around Tinker Creek and demonstrates that the boundaries between nature and society are anything but fixed. He addresses Dillard's detachment or "social isolation" and the critics who fault Dillard for not writing a political text. He finds in Dillard a "detachment from society as well as [an] acknowledgement of the common bond of all living things." He notes, "Like a prophet, she travels alone."

Maddocks, Melvin. "Terror and Celebration." *Time* 117 (March 18, 1974): 78. Maddocks warns: "Reader, beware of this deceptive girl, mouthing her piety. . . . Here is no gentle romantic twirling a buttercup." He adds that "Miss Dillard is stalking the reader as surely as any predator stalks its game." Maddocks concludes that what Dillard achieves in *Pilgrim at Tinker Creek* is "a remarkable psalm of terror and celebration."

Scheick, William J. "Annie Dillard: Narrative Fringe." In *Contemporary American Women Writers: Narrative Strategies*, edited by Catherine Rainwater and William J. Scheick. Lexington: University Press of Kentucky, 1985. Scheick proposes that Dillard's statement "We wake, if we ever wake at all, to mystery" forms the thesis of *Pilgrim at Tinker Creek* and other of her works. Includes a bibliography of Dillard's writings.

Beverly J. Matiko

PITCH DARK

Author: Renata Adler (1938-   )
Type of work: Novel
Type of plot: Romance
Time of plot: The 1960's to the 1980's
Locale: The United States, Ireland, London, and the fictional Orcas Island
First published: 1983

> *Principal characters:*
> KATE ENNIS, the narrator and protagonist who becomes "Adler"
>   in the second of the novel's three parts
> JAKE, Kate's married lover, a successful lawyer

Form and Content

Pitch Dark is an odd variant of a familiar literary type, the love story, told entirely from the woman's point of view but in a decidedly postromantic, postmodern manner. The novel comprises three linked yet very nearly self-contained parts of approximately equal length that are comparable to Greek tragedies as Kate's friend Diana defines the form. "What I understand about Greek tragedies is this: the Athenians went to three dramas a day, and at the end they were so exhausted, that was the catharsis. The exhaustion itself was the catharsis." Clearly, if *Pitch Dark* is at all tragic, it is tragedy written in a contemporary mode, particularly in Adler's use of a plot that is both minimal and disjointed.

"Orcas Island," the first of the novel's three parts, introduces the various themes upon which *Pitch Dark* plays its several variations. One is Kate's breakup with her lover, Jake. Another, equally important, concerns Kate's uncertainty regarding how to tell the story of that breakup. This uncertainty manifests itself quite early in a series of tentative beginnings: variants self-consciously tried and found wanting but never quite discarded. A third theme centers on a related aspect of Kate's uncertainty—her indecisiveness about whether she should "stylize it" or "tell it as it was." This, in turn, leads to the reader's uncertainty about which of the novel's parts (granting a certain suspension of disbelief) are fact and which are fiction, as well as to Kate's doubts about whether her reader will understand and "care" about her narrative.

Although it is short on plot, Adler's narrative is long on details, non sequiturs, repeated refrain-like passages, and tautologies, one of which, "I know I've lost him because I have," reads like a postmodern version of the conventional wisdom concerning "woman's intuition." Above all, "Orcas Island" is full of inserted narratives that either echo the main story (as does the longest, a five-page account about an ailing raccoon that Kate unsuccessfully tries to befriend) or deliberately turn away from it, and of dialogues involving Kate and Jake (either recalled or imagined) or Kate and a part of herself that she calls "the anti-claque," which, instead of applauding her efforts, disparages them.

When read one way, "Orcas Island" moves freely, if randomly, through time and space; when read another way, it oscillates between two poles, two narrative impulses. One is Kate's ability to write confidently about certain specific though seemingly tangential, trivial events. "Here is exactly how it was" is the way she prefaces a passage dealing with a Chinese hypnotist. At the other pole is her inability, or perhaps her unwillingness, to confront the absence that lies at the heart of both her life and her narrative. Indeed, at the novel's exact center Kate places what amounts to by far the longest of its many inserted (and conventionally plotted) stories. "Pitch Dark," the second section, does not deal with Kate's love affair; it does not even deal with Kate. It deals, instead, with a narrator-protagonist whose name appears to be "Adler" (although the reader only learns this quite late, assuming until then that the narrator-protagonist is still Kate). More specifically, this "Pitch Dark" takes the form of a mystery-thriller, via Sigmund Freud, Franz Kafka, and Samuel Beckett, and concerns "Adler's" trip to Ireland, the odd staff of the ambassador's country house where she stays alone, and her various misadventures (a minor accident, running out of petrol, the difficulties she experiences finding her way around the island and, in the end, leaving it). "Pitch Dark" teasingly duplicates Kate's efforts to narrate her story and her reader's efforts to follow it through what amounts to a narrative "pitch dark."

In "Home," Kate, now not at home at all but instead in London (Adler's destination at the end of part 2), resumes the story and style of "Orcas Island." Here, her telephone conversations with Jake (including his brief comments on reading "Orcas Island") alternate with her descriptions of getting not out of Ireland but to Orcas Island, a version of the island to which Jake took his family each Christmas but never quite got around to taking Kate. The novel ends with one of their conversations. Neither novel nor narrator, however, ever makes it clear whether this conversation actually takes place in the present or is being recollected by Kate or is imagined by Kate, who only wishes that there had been such a call. All that can be said with certainty is that someone, presumably Jake, asks, "But you won't go?" and that someone, presumably Kate, answers, "no," and that someone, this time presumably Kate, asks, "Do you sometimes wish it was me?" and that someone, presumably Jake, answers, "Always," adding, after a "pause," "It is you." The reader of a novel in which "Adler" may be as much Kate's creation as Kate is Adler's wishes that he or she could say the same thing and say so with as much confidence.

Analysis

The disjunctiveness of this text written for and about "the century of dislocation" underscores Adler's preoccupation with various kinds of relations, from the syntactic and narrative at one extreme to the social and personal at the other. Kate's relationships are of paramount importance. These are her relationships to her former lover, to the other characters, to Adler (in both her roles: that of the novel's author and that of the character who figures in the novel's second part), to her tale and to her telling, and to the various ways in which women have been depicted in the literary tradition in which Kate is, by virtue of her education, well versed. In this regard, Kate is the other woman, the damsel in distress, the woman scorned (in her Medea mask), and "the Blue Angel . . . in reverse." She is also the faithful Penelope of Homer's *Odyssey*, weaving and unweaving her tapestry/narrative, keeping the suitors at bay while she awaits the return of her husband, Odysseus, whose wanderings are reflected in Kate's narrative peregrinations. (It is significant that Kate retells, or reweaves, Penelope's story from a feminist perspective in one of the many brief sections/episodes/narrative threads that make up "Orcas Island.") Kate is equally, and perhaps most intriguingly, the wily Scheherazade of *The Arabian Nights' Entertainments*, who uses her gift for storytelling to escape death, the fate of her powerful husband's former wives. Scheherazade would certainly understand what Kate at one point states outright and what *Pitch Dark* everywhere implies: that her yearning for her lover is mixed with dread.

> I long for you to be here, miss you when you are gone, but sometimes to [sic] wonder whether I can amuse you, or whether you will not be bored, tired, called away for bridge, or work, or tennis, or because one of your daughters has had a whim, well, sometimes I dread what will follow such a visit, and so I've come to dread a bit the visit too.

Given the variety of her roles, including the variety of her literary forebears, Kate doubts not only whether the versions she gives of events are accurate but also whether the voice in which she speaks is actually hers. "Wait a minute. Whose voice is this? Not mine. Not mine," she points out on more than one occasion. In the "Introduction" to *Toward a Radical Middle* (1969), a collection of essays originally published in *The New Yorker*, Adler considers one consequence of belonging to "an age group that [never had its own] generational voice": "Lacking an idiom entirely our own, we cannot adopt any single voice without a note of irony." It is precisely this "note of irony" that is so pronounced in *Pitch Dark*, but only in counterpoint, as it were, to an equally strong and equally compelling note of regret, as in Kate's referring to her narrative as her "torts song." A tort is a wrongful act that, although it does not involve breach of contract, does involve liability for which a civil suit can be brought. A torch song is a sentimental piece in which the singer laments a lost lover. Combining elements of both, *Pitch Dark* is narrated to an audience that also serves as jury and lover whom Kate, like a lawyer, must convince and, like Scheherazade, must please. If, on two occasions late in the novel, this reader is identified as Jake, on others it clearly is Kate herself, forced by circumstances to play both parts, narrator and narratee, lawyer and jury, plaintiff and defendant. Moreover, no matter how strong her case against Jake may be, Kate at times feels that she is the guilty (rather than the injured) party, at fault either for what she did or for what she did not do.

"Did I throw the most important thing, perhaps, by accident, away?" Adler is especially successful in the way in which she incorporates Kate's uncertainty, the epistemological equivalent of her emotional insecurity, into her bleak yet at times bleakly funny novel about a woman who is too well educated, too intelligent, too cosmopolitan, and too wised-up not to detach herself from the sense of loss she so obviously feels—something, that is, as retrograde as unrequited love. Once upon a time, novels could pretend to be histories, biographies, autobiographies, but *Pitch*

Dark does not follow and cannot pretend to follow any one model (unless that model is quantum physics). In typically postmodern fashion, Adler's novel internalizes the vast array of possible models upon which it can be structured: weaving and unweaving, spinning yarns, an Arabian night's entertainment, a striptease, film, the absurdist plays of Samuel Beckett and Harold Pinter (with their gaping pauses), telephone conversations, Ovid's metamorphoses, and Ludwig Wittgenstein's language games, among others. It is this superfluity of possible structures that helps to make Adler's novel seem so provisional, so unfinished, and, paradoxically, so compelling.

Context

Renata Adler writes what reviewers like to call "quintessentially New York" fiction, yet the author whose work most resembles her own is Joan Didion, who is generally thought of as a quintessentially California writer. Although they are intimately connected to quite different geographical myths and sensibilities, Adler and Didion are connected to each other by virtue of their parallel interests in fiction writing, journalism, and film, and more especially because they write novels that are at once so contemporary and so inextricably bound up with the experience of women in that world. *Pitch Dark* retells a conventional female subgenre, the love story, from the decidedly contemporary and unconventional perspective of an educated, intelligent, and financially independent woman.

Pitch Dark is thus situated at the point at which the conventional and the contemporary intersect, which is also the point at which so many modern women find that their lives, caught between old plots and new, often involve problematic possibilities. Strangely, however, Adler's two novels, though acclaimed by many reviewers, have attracted no critical attention. There have been no book-length studies, no articles in academic journals, extraordinarily few mentions and only one brief discussion in the standard literary histories, and no anthologizing of her work. Oddest of all is the silence on the part of feminist critics, who are interested in Luce Irigaray's and Helene Cixous' theories of a distinctly different female language, or in strategies of reticence and silence in women's fiction (for example, Janis P. Stout), or in the ways in which women writers metafictionally retell familiar stories (for example, Gayle Greene). Adler's fiction invites these approaches. Finally, feminist critics who are interested in reception theory would do well to address the ways in which *Pitch Dark* has been read along largely masculinist lines that fail to consider Kate's dilemma: having to make both herself and her story interesting, seductive, and accessible.

Sources for Further Study

Adler, Renata. *Toward a Radical Middle: Fourteen Pieces of Reporting and Criticism.* New York: Random House, 1970. The essays collected here and, more especially, Adler's introduction provide useful background to understanding Adler's politics and her and Kate's generation.

Epstein, Joseph. "The Sunshine Girls." *Commentary* 77 (June, 1984): 62-67. This review of *Pitch Dark* and Didion's *Democracy* offers a critical overview of two writers whom Epstein faults for their fragmented narrative structure and their unearned pessimism.

Greene, Gayle. *Changing the Story: Feminist Fiction and the Tradition.* Bloomington: Indiana University Press, 1991. Although Greene does not even mention Adler directly, her study offers an excellent theoretical and practical model for reading *Pitch Dark* in terms of innovative women's fiction.

Kornbluth, Jesse. "The Quirky Brilliance of Renata Adler." *New York* 16 (December 12, 1983): 34-40. An invaluable profile of a writer about whose life little is known outside the New York cultural circle. In his remarks on *Pitch Dark*, Kornbluth commends Adler for transforming "eccentricities into assets" and for finding "a voice that is right for these times."

Prescott, Peter S. "Age of Angst and Anxiety." *Newsweek* 102 (December 19, 1983): 82. Considers *Pitch Dark* "anorexic" and inferior to *Speedboat*; calls its repetitions annoying and its fragmented structure ineffective.

Shattuck, Roger. "Quanta." *New York Review of Books* 31 (March 15, 1984): 3. Shattuck finds *Pitch Dark* less novelistic than autobiographical or confessional. This "inwardly impassioned work" shows little interest in outward events yet offers nevertheless a sense of its times through Adler's two "astutely shuffled" narratives.

Robert A. Morace

PLAIN PLEASURES

Author: Jane Bowles (1917-1973)
Type of work: Short stories
First published: 1966

Form and Content

Jane Bowles's stories often focus on women who are loners. Some are steel-willed and independent; those who are not await whatever force will spring them from marriage, domesticity, or the boredom of middle-class life. Bowles's characters are quirky, even disturbing, in ways she devised to challenge stereotypical notions of what women are or should be in the twentieth century. Some of her women are conservative (to the extent that they ape socially acceptable ideologies of their class); others are radical in their behavior and distinctly amoral.

Often their lives seem ordinary at first. These "ordinary" women, however, become candidates for testing social codes of behavior. Many are middle-aged, unmarried women who travel or live alone. Often a character will seek intimacy but will for some reason find herself unable to tolerate emotional proximity to anyone. Bowles's unconventional characters roam outside the mainstream toward uncharted territories, underworlds, and strange affairs.

"Plain Pleasures," the title piece in this slim volume of stories, is about an affair between a man and a woman that never gets off the ground. Mrs. Perry, a middle-aged widow living in a run-down New England apartment house, meets her neighbor John Drake in the backyard during a cookout. Having offered to share her potato-bake with this "equally reserved" man, she embarrasses him by asking, "Don't you think that plain pleasures are closer to the heart of God?" Their fragile conversation survives long enough for him to invite Mrs. Perry to dinner at the restaurant the next evening. It is her first invitation in years.

Dinner with Mr. Drake does not go well. The more intimacy the shy man musters, the more unreasonable and inimical she becomes toward him. Finally, she leaves the table angrily, stumbles upstairs to a bedroom, and falls asleep, distraught and tipsy. In the morning, she awakens undressed, presumably having been raped by the restaurant owner, who followed her upstairs. Downstairs, she looks for the table she and Drake had occupied the night before but cannot recognize it. Oddly, this anonymity and the violation she has endured make her feel great tenderness for her neighbor: " 'John Drake,' she whispered. 'My sweet John Drake.' "

"Everything Is Nice" was originally a nonfiction travel piece called "East Side: North Africa" that Bowles wrote for *Mademoiselle*. The fictionalized version recounts a Western woman's visit to a Moslem woman's home in a small seaside town in Morocco. Perhaps seeking friendship, the visitor finds her efforts thwarted by a cultural chasm. Her notions of family and female independence clash with the Moslem women's beliefs. The matriarch of the house offers the guest tea and inedible cookies. The women quiz her relentlessly. Why is she not living in her own country?

Where is her mother? "Why don't you go and sit with your mother in her own house?" they scold her. She resists trying to explain. From porcupines to husbands to trucks, the conversation ricochets back and forth past any hope of connection or sharing. Finally, Zodelia (who brought the Western woman home), her mother, and the protagonist are frustrated and annoyed. The departure is gracious but sour. Outside, a distant memory surfaces when the woman brushes her fingers along some fresh blue wash on the wall. The image calls up in her "some longing" in a poignant and mysterious closing.

Strange characters, mysterious developments, and an unsettling tone make "Camp Cataract" a challenging story. Like Bowles's other stories, it mixes the tragic and comic, the compassionate and sardonic. Harriet and Sadie, two wacky middle-aged sisters, live quietly with their sister Evelyn and her husband, Bert Hoffer. One day, Harriet, having suffered nervous fits, decides to go away to a resort camp. She says she will put down roots there in imitation of "the natural family roots of childhood" and then make "sallies into the outside world almost unnoticed." Sadie, who passionately loves Harriet and guards this terrible secret, decides to defy her sister's wish for solitude by going to Camp Cataract to persuade her to come home. In the unfamiliar atmosphere of the camp, Sadie hallucinates. She imagines that she meets with Harriet and begs her, "Let's you and me go out in the world . . . just the two of us." She imagines that her sister responds with hatred. In agony, Sadie commits suicide by jumping into the falls.

"A Guatemalan Idyll" and "A Day in the Open" have Latin American settings. These stories explore the mysterious and sometimes idiotic behavior of men and women who come together in romantic or sexual pursuits. Señora Ramirez, a wealthy, overweight widow, stays at Señora Espinoza's cheap pensión with her spoiled daughters Consuelo and Lilina. She seduces a young American salesman who finds himself terrified of her passion. Afterward, in a buoyant mood, she walks through the countryside to daydream about love. Even though "her eyes glowed with the pleasure of being in love," she is not thinking of the traveler at all—as if being in love were unrelated to another person. During her walk, she seduces a young boy. Meanwhile, her daughter Lilina is with a boy who is pained because Lilina purposely allows her beautiful snake, which he admires, to be run over by buses. At the pensión, Consuelo also professes love for the traveler, who is scared and remorseful because of his experience with Señora Ramirez.

In "A Day in the Open," two prostitutes, Inez and Julia, agree to accompany rich Señor Ramirez and his friend Alfredo on an outing in the country. Julia is forlorn and uncertain about the arrangement, but Inez is efficient and entertaining. Ramirez is boisterous. He claims to be the richest businessman in the country and "the craziest. Like an American." At the picnic spot all four get drunk. Then Julia cuts her head when Señor Ramirez slips and drops her on the rocks while carrying her over a stream. Suddenly spent and irritable, Ramirez hurries the women back to the bar and pays them. Later, alone, each dwells on the day's proposals and adventures. Inez reviews their spoils (including Ramirez's abandoned dinnerware), while Julia deals with the memory of his promises and his abrupt departure.

"A Quarreling Pair" is a short skit whose puppet players are sisters, Harriet and Rhoda. Harriet, who is domineering, berates Rhoda for her sloppy homemaking, for not minding her own business, and for being preoccupied with the world's problems. Harriet is practical and insistent; Rhoda is dreamy and dependent on Harriet. The two quarrel in a battle of wills but seem to be unable to resolve their differences, if indeed they want to.

"A Stick of Green Candy" has a child protagonist, Mary, who avoids the other children at the playground, preferring to play alone in an isolated claypit. She imagines that she is the benevolent commander of a regiment of soldiers. One day her orderly, predictable world is invaded by a strange boy named Franklin. Gradually, Mary realizes that she has fallen in love with Franklin, a "real-life" event that invades and endangers her imaginary world. In the end, she betrays her imaginary men, as well as the value system she had devised to control them, and leaves the claypit behind. Bowles's last finished work, "A Stick of Green Candy" explores the world of childhood imagination and values, which the young forsake with difficulty when they accept their roles in adult society.

Analysis

"I must try to find a nest in this outlandish place," declares Mrs. Copperfield in Jane Bowles's novel *Two Serious Ladies* (1943). Bowles's short-story characters are often engaged in the same search, seeking shelter for their confused emotions or some structure to guide their offbeat lives that does not rely on societal codes they have rejected: that women must marry, be mothers, be monogamous, stay home, or be polite in male company.

Bowles's stories have a biting wit and can be comic, although a tragic view of life is central to her vision. Most of her characters live outside society's mainstream and seem to suffer for it. Their quirks are riveting and comical, although their yearnings are common enough. Misfits looking for human contact, they often find themselves unable to forge new relationships and unable to protect the precarious ones they have. Sometimes they nurture their own isolation; sometimes they become trapped by it. Often their intelligence reveals social hypocrisy; at other times, they are thematically united in their choice to be independent, most notably from men.

Bowles's observations about human relationships can seem disarming in their directness and deeply puzzling at the same time. Most difficult of all, perhaps, is the fact that Bowles makes no moral judgments about her characters' appetites and predicaments. A fat rich widow lures men and boys into ferocious sex; an unmarried sister prefers to leave home and lapse into madness rather than accept the domestic company of her sisters; a lonely tourist wanders through a foreign city uncertain what she is seeking. The traditional female roles of mother, nurturer, gentle seductress, reassuring lover, and friend are not present. Bowles's women are hungry nomads, late-life call girls, escapees from repressive marriages trapped in a world of one-night stands—in lives they have chosen. Whether it is tragic or liberating, they have their autonomy, and Bowles typically describes their self-possession without making judgmental asides.

Context

Jane Bowles may be best known for her short fiction, and many consider it her most successful work. *Plain Pleasures* consists of six stories and a short skit. Three of the stories were originally published in 1946, 1949, and 1957 in *Harper's Bazaar* and *Vogue*. The stories "A Guatemalan Idyll" and "A Day in the Open" were originally part of her novel *Two Serious Ladies*. A play, *In the Summer House* (first performed in 1953), and a few other fictional pieces and fragments since collected in *My Sister's Hand in Mine* (1978) make up the balance of her small but influential canon.

The novelist Alan Sillitoe called Bowles's novel *Two Serious Ladies* "a landmark in contemporary literature," and the poet John Ashbery hailed her in a review of *The Collected Works of Jane Bowles* (1966) as "one of the finest modern writers of fiction, in any language." Yet her work, as Ashbery and other critics suggest, stands outside the mainstream of contemporary American literature. She is indeed "a neglected genius," as she was called in an early review of *The Collected Works*. Aside from the previously mentioned critical acclaim, her work did not receive much attention in the decades following its publication.

The novelist and essayist Francine du Plessix Gray believes that the mainstream reading public has resisted Jane Bowles's redefinition of female freedom. Bowles, Gray has written, is "one of the twentieth century novelists who have written most poignantly about modern women's independence from men," placing her work alongside that of Colette, Kate Chopin, Doris Lessing, and Jean Rhys. Moreover, in exploring her vision "of women who are truly independent from men—spiritual, nomadic, asexual women"—she creates a cast of complex heroines who are mysterious and disturbing. Their worlds separate them from the mainstream, and their preoccupations with sin and salvation do not allow readers to place them easily alongside the predictably "female"—that is, romantic—heroines of Western literary tradition.

Since the publication of Bowles's biography in 1981 and that of her collected letters in 1985, her work has become better known. The number of critical essays published since 1985 suggests that her work will continue to gain attention. In 1993, her play *In the Summer House* was revived at New York City's Lincoln Center on Broadway, giving her work the kind of exposure that will gain her a permanent place in the American literary canon.

Sources for Further Study

Bassett, Mark T. "Imagination, Control, and Betrayal in Jane Bowles' 'A Stick of Green Candy.'" *Studies in Short Fiction* 24 (Winter, 1987): 25-29. Bassett studies the story in terms of possible influences the desert environment might have had on Bowles while she finished it. He suggests that the story pits the order and control exerted by the childhood imagination against the chaos and uncertainty of the real world, or adult society.

Bowles, Jane. *Out in the World: Selected Letters of Jane Bowles, 1935-1970.* Edited by Millicent Dillon. Santa Barbara, Calif.: Black Sparrow Press, 1985. Jane Bowles's letters constitute the most complete record of her struggles with her work, her fear of writer's block, and her obsession with words and exactness of expression. The letters paint a picture of her travels, relationships, and final illness. Essential reading for an understanding of one whose life and work were so closely related.

Dillon, Millicent. "Jane Bowles: Experiment as Character." In *Breaking the Sequence: Women's Experimental Fiction.* New York: Princeton University Press, 1989. Dillon revises her thinking on Bowles's inability to complete her later work. Her uncompleted fragments were not from writer's block, but from an impulse to express herself in a fragmented style that reflected her sense of experience. Discusses the story "Camp Cataract."

_____ . *A Little Original Sin: The Life and Work of Jane Bowles.* New York: Holt, Rinehart and Winston, 1981. Dillon's biography is meticulously researched and passionately written. Includes thorough discussion of the genesis of Bowles's stories and other writings. Contains a chronology, a bibliography, an index, and notes.

Gray, Francine du Plessix. "Jane Bowles Reconsidered." In *Adam and Eve and the City: Selected Nonfiction.* New York: Simon & Schuster, 1987. A short, useful introduction to Bowles's work, mostly through discussion of her novel *Two Serious Ladies.* Gray considers the theme of women's independence central to Bowles's fiction. She compares Bowles's work with the work of other twentieth century novelists, especially Jean Rhys.

Roditi, Edouard. "The Fiction of Jane Bowles as a Form of Self-Exorcism." *The Review of Contemporary Fiction* 12 (Summer, 1992): 182-194. Roditi speculates that Jane Bowles relieved herself of her own insanity by giving it to her characters. When Paul Bowles took her to Tangier, however, away from suburban America, she became disoriented, collapsed into insanity, and died. An interesting premise by a friend and literary acquaintance of the Bowleses.

JoAnn Balingit

PLAY IT AS IT LAYS

Author: Joan Didion (1934-   )
Type of work: Novel
Type of plot: Psychological realism
Time of plot: The late 1960's
Locale: Los Angeles, Las Vegas, and the Mojave desert
First published: 1970

Principal characters:

MARIA WYETH, a model and actress who courts destruction with
   sex, alcohol, and drugs
CARTER LANG, Maria's estranged husband, the father of Kate,
   and a successful film director
KATE, Maria and Carter's four-year-old, brain-damaged daughter
BZ, a promiscuous homosexual Hollywood producer
HELENE, BZ's wife, who has an affair with Carter
LES GOODWIN, a married screenwriter with whom Maria has an
   affair
FRANCINE WYETH, Maria's mother
HARRY WYETH, Maria's father
IVAN COSTELLO, Maria's former boyfriend, an alcoholic
JOHNNY WATERS, an actor with whom Maria has a one-night
   stand

Form and Content

Play It as It Lays is an episodic novel that focuses on Maria Wyeth's loss and
regaining of identity in a patriarchal society where she has been labeled as her father's
daughter, as sex object, and as "wife."

Set in the late 1960's among the jet-set crowd in Beverly Hills, Maria's story begins
and ends with her voice—in a mental hospital. The first three chapters, set off from
the eighty-four numbered chapters and entitled "Maria," "Carter," and "Helene," are
told from the viewpoints of these three characters and give the reader their accounts
of Maria and what went wrong in her life. Most of the subsequent numbered
chapters—from one to eighty-four—are told in the third person from Maria's point of
view and are, collectively, a flashback. This flashback constitutes the bulk of the novel
and chronicles, in a series of nonlinear and fragmented episodes, the parameters of
Maria's exterior and interior life in the year preceding her breakdown.

The events of the novel are not as important as the setting in which Maria plays out
her story, for it is the setting—a wasteland motif operating in a patriarchal framework—that is ultimately making Maria sick. Joan Didion uses the California setting
as a metaphor for the exhausted possibilities of wealth, industry, and the "good" life.
In *Play It as It Lays*, Maria's associates are people whose main concerns are sex and

appearances. Maria lives in an artificial environment in which the water in the pool is always 85 degrees and in which a labyrinth of freeway systems leads ultimately to nowhere. It is a sterile setting in which human connections have been severed.

The events of the story—Maria putting more than seven thousand miles on her Corvette the summer she and Carter separated; Maria lying by the pool, sleeping late into the afternoon; Maria numbing herself with sex, alcohol, and barbiturates; Maria going to parties she does not want to go to; Maria fighting with Carter; Maria going to visit her institutionalized daughter, Kate; Maria having an unwanted abortion; Maria crying for her mother; Maria engaging in sadomasochism with BZ and Helene; Maria holding BZ's hand while he swallows "20 or 30" Seconal tablets—are significant mainly because it is this series of disconnected events that leads Maria to the heart of nothingness and to her present crisis. It is only by finding the meaninglessness inherent in her existence that Maria can rename her own experience and find the "truth" of her own identity.

As her father's daughter, Maria has been taught two lessons: "It goes as it lays, don't do it the hard way"; and "Overturning a rock was apt to reveal a rattlesnake." Although these two maxims seem to "hold up" for Maria, they give her neither values to live by nor clues to her unique identity. In the end, Maria redefines her father's advice into an existential meaning for herself. She chooses to live, to concentrate on the present, and to reaffirm the uniquely feminine values that have to do with motherhood, life, and family.

Analysis

Didion is a moralist, but her vision of morality is never sentimental, only clearly and rigidly stark. *Play It as It Lays* is an existential novel (and essentially a moral tale) about Maria Wyeth's search for meaning, but in this novel meaning is found only by confronting its absence and, for Maria, by battling with the primordial fathers (the male world), who in this novel are associated with the desert and with spiritual disintegration. When one examines the fragmented episodes and the colored pages that make up Maria's life through Maria's eyes, it becomes clear how this hero's descent into what might be called insanity (like the classical hero's descent into the underworld) is both Maria's means to salvation and a somewhat sane response to an insane world.

Throughout this novel, Maria is used and named as a sex object. Maria becomes a model because her parents encourage it and because in a male-dominated society there is a market for attractiveness. Maria is called a "whore" by the woman in Ralph's Market whom she tries to help, and she is assumed to be a prostitute by the desk clerk in the Sands. In the film called *Angel Beach*, Maria is cast by her husband, Carter, in the starring role—she gets to "be" a woman raped by twelve bikers.

Like her role as a sex object, Maria's role as "wife" is largely handed down to her by a society that often views married women as their husbands' wives rather than as unique and separate individuals. (Maria's quest begins when she becomes separated from Carter.) A man in an elevator gives Maria the look "dutifully charged with sexual appreciation, meant not for Maria herself but for Carter Lang's wife"; Maria is not seen for herself but only as the property of a well-known film director. Even the nurse in the hospital refers to Maria as "Mrs. Lang," although Maria tells the reader on page 2 of this novel that she herself "never did."

Although Maria is somewhat defined by the male world because of the roles that have been given her, Didion also gives the reader glimpses of another Maria. After telling Carter of her pregnancy, Maria is frustrated and sorry at not being able to penetrate Carter's world. Throughout the novel, Maria is associated with water, which is symbolic of life and feelings. She feels guilty because of her mother's death and the abortion; in several places, Maria cries and tries to hide her tears. She tries to suppress herself in this artificial environment where "failure, illness, fear, they were seen as infectious, contagious blights on glossy plants."

In her dreams, Maria imagines herself as the mother in a family. She dreams at one point that she has the baby (instead of the abortion) and that she and Kate are living with Ivan Costello. In another dream, she and Les Goodwin and Kate live by the sea. Although Ivan Costello tells her, "there's not going to be any baby makes three," and Carter threatens to take Kate if she does not go through with the abortion, Maria's identity as a female and mother is apparent in these passages.

Maria's separation from the male world and her identification with the female world seem to be a necessary step in her heroic struggle. Early in the novel, Maria looks in the mirror and sees "Carter's reflection"; a little later on, Maria deliberately stands before a hand mirror "picking out her mother's features."

Maria's abortion is what leads to her complete breakdown; it is also what saves her. After the abortion, Maria wants to see her mother; however, in the absence of such comfort, she is forced to confront herself and her world and to cut away that which does "not apply." Toward the end of the novel, Maria tells Carter and his group that they are all making her sick (as indeed they are). After BZ's death, Maria experiences the "nothingness" that is perhaps a prerequisite for all truly modern heroes and begins to affirm and assert that "feminine" and somewhat traditional self that is "Mar-eye-ah." She tells the reader at the end of the novel that she will "get Kate, live with Kate alone, do some canning." She says, "After everything I remain Harry and Francine Wyeth's daughter." She tells the reader, as that agent of life that all heroes must be, that she knows what "nothing" means and keeps on playing.

Context

Unlike Didion's novels *Run River* (1963) and *A Book of Common Prayer* (1977), *Play It as It Lays* exists apart from a definite historical context (although it is set in the late 1960's, her story is interior and timeless) and in a nonpolitical one (discounting the sexual politics). It is existential in nature but examines "madness" from a uniquely feminist perspective, although male critics have not drawn this connection, one calling it "a triumph not of insight as such but of style," and another a "parody of the novel of despair."

Maria is a quester/hero whose journey is to find what Adrienne Rich has called "the thing itself and not the myth." Like Margaret Atwood's protagonist in *Surfacing* (1972), like Oedipa Maas in Thomas Pynchon's *The Crying of Lot 49* (1966), like Doris Lessing's Martha Quest in *The Four-Gated City* (1969), Maria must search to find herself amid the ruins of a culture that has given her few clues to her ancestry and identity.

The journey motif is certainly not new in women's literature—the most famous quester/hero is probably Charlotte Brontë's Jane Eyre in the novel by the same name (1847)—however, a woman's quest is often and uniquely associated with madness. It is only quite recently that feminist critics have begun to analyze this madness in such books as Sandra M. Gilbert and Susan Gubar's *The Madwoman in the Attic* (1979) and Barbara Hill Rigney's *Madness and Sexual Politics in the Feminist Novel* (1978).

Like the narrator in Charlotte Perkins Gilman's *The Yellow Wallpaper* (1899), Maria's withdrawal is from an insane world that has predefined acceptable female roles. It is the world R. D. Laing speaks of in *The Divided Self* (1959), which is translated for Maria into one in which language and connections are broken and which denies her guilty and feeling nature. In order to escape that world, Maria must, like any true hero, withdraw inward. Yet unlike the male hero, who must first separate his ego from the mother who gave birth to it, Maria must struggle against the primordial father rather than the mother, with whom she can identify.

Play It as It Lays became a best-seller, was nominated for a National Book Award, and was made into a movie. It is, however, generally seen by critics from an existential perspective rather than from a feminist one. Didion herself has been skeptical of the women's movement, yet she does believe that women are unique in experiencing what she calls that "dark involvement with blood and birth and death"; Maria Wyeth is a testament to that particular kind of involvement.

Sources for Further Study

Didion, Joan. *Slouching Towards Bethlehem*. New York: Farrar, Straus & Giroux, 1968. A collection of essays that preceded *Play It as It Lays*. Three of the essays in this collection have particular significance to that novel: "On Morality," "Los Angeles Notebook," and "Goodbye to All That." Each is an indispensable aid in understanding Didion's sensibility and worldview. Similarities between the text of the novel and Didion's own life are readily apparent.

Friedman, Ellen G., ed. *Joan Didion: Essays and Conversations*. Princeton, N.J.: Ontario Review Press, 1984. A collection of essays including three interviews, Didion's nonfiction essay "Why I Write," and several critical interpretations of her prose through *Salvador* (1983). This volume contains three important essays on *Play It as It Lays*.

Henderson, Katherine U. *Joan Didion*. New York: Frederick Ungar, 1981. A monograph that includes a biographical essay on Didion and one essay each on her books through *The White Album*, this book stresses the importance of the frontier experience in Didion's writing and shows how traditional American experience and values collide with the "new order." A brief but good introduction to Didion.

Rigney, Barbara Hill. *Madness and Sexual Politics in the Feminist Novel*. Madison: University of Wisconsin Press, 1978. Although this book does not discuss Joan Didion's novel in particular, the introduction serves as a useful general preface to women and "madness" in literature.

Winchell, Mark Royden. *Joan Didion*. Rev. ed. Boston: Twayne, 1989. An update of a book that appeared in 1980, this work is a part of Twayne's United States Authors Series and a most important reference. Includes a chronology through 1987, a selected bibliography of both primary and secondary sources, and an examination of Didion's works through *Democracy* (1984).

Candace E. Andrews

PLAYS BY SUSAN GLASPELL

Author: Susan Glaspell (1882-1948)
Type of work: Dramas
First published: 1987

Form and Content

Susan Glaspell's thirteen plays, treating mostly feminist themes, were produced by the to-become-renowned Provincetown Playhouse and in New York City between 1915 and 1922. Four of her works are found in the 1987 collection entitled *Plays by Susan Glaspell: Trifles, Inheritors, The Verge,* and *The Outside.*

From 1915 to 1919, Glaspell wrote six one-act plays. Several were satiric comedies, but some were less amusing. *The Outside* (1917) focuses on two recluses, a young grass widow and her widowed servant, dwelling in a remote former seacoast lifesaving station. They leave self-imposed isolation after realizing that abandonment by men, through either desertion or death, need not require burial from life.

Glaspell's most outstanding, popular, and durable work is *Trifles* (1916), a short play whose genesis stemmed from a trial, attended by Glaspell, of an Iowa woman accused of murdering her husband. The play, set in a rural midwestern farmhouse kitchen and taking place on one day, centers on the fate of the accused offstage character, Minnie Wright. Two women are patronizingly relegated to the kitchen by their husbands, a sheriff and a farmer, while the men with the county attorney search elsewhere for evidence. As the women examine Mrs. Wright's belongings, "trifles" attesting the life of a once-cheerful woman married to an abusively hard man who had forbidden her even a telephone, they discover incriminating evidence revealing motivation for murder, particularly a wrecked birdcage and a strangled songbird. They conceal the evidence that they are legally obligated to reveal to the men, feeling compassion and also guilt at having been unheeding neighbors, acquitting her on humane grounds. The central conflict lies between the men's world of insensitive legality and the women's world of compassionate justice. *Trifles* also demonstrates its author's effective technique of centering a play on an offstage character.

Glaspell also wrote strong full-length plays. In a realistic mode, the three acts of *Inheritors* (1921) cover three generations—past, present, and future. Extending from 1879 to 1921, the action centers on a midwestern college affected by prejudice. Act 1 discloses founder Silas Morton, with the collaboration of a Hungarian refugee, envisioning a college dedicated to the American ideals of freedom and hope for the oppressed. Act 2 discovers the college at its fortieth anniversary attacked by postwar jingoists for harboring liberal thought and freedoms, as exemplified by a professor's defense of wartime conscientious objectors and by Hindu students' protesting for a homeland. In act 3, college authorities insist on conformity, attempting to compromise liberal and conservative factions to appease an influential senator, but they are opposed by protagonist Madeline Morton, the founder's granddaughter. Despite the threat of jail, she staunchly defies attempts to muzzle freedom of thought. The drama deals with important issues of the time and calls for rededication to the virtues of the past.

The Verge (1921) introduces protagonist Claire Archer, who tests the limits of anticonventional, independent behavior by disturbing the balance between unlimited freedom and conformity. Refusing the responsibilities of her station as wife and mother, she rejects her family, abhors being graciously feminine, and compares her rebellion against locked-in convention to the total independence of the mutating plants that she grows as an experimental horticulturist. The drama mixes realism, symbolism, and expressionism, and comedy with melodrama. Each act ends with a climax pushing Claire to the verge of irrationality. Finding no one to join her on her quest for "otherness," she ultimately attacks the persons around her, moving uncompromisingly from passion to madness, destroying even her plants for not developing a new form. At the final curtain, she strangles her lover.

Analysis

Glaspell's moralistic midwestern origins and her acquaintance with radical thought both served to foster the themes of her major plays. Coupled with a dedication to the traditional values of integrity and social responsibility are such issues as the freedom of individuals (especially women) to self-expression or to experience life fully and experimentally, the right of true feeling over prescriptive morality, the compassionate justice of women versus instituted male laws, and the constriction of women's achievement in a man's world. In *Trifles*, the women realize in examining Minnie Wright's effects that she was caged and strangled like the songbird, choked to death by her hard, insensitive husband. The symbol of Minnie as songbird, although unmistakably obvious, is telling: A cheerful, lively woman has been stifled. Male condescension motivates the women to ally with Minnie, conceal the incriminating clues ironically found in what the men consider trifles, and reject male justice. It is significant that the sheriff's wife takes the decisive step of concealing the evidence. Within the context of a short play in which the author's exposition masterfully reconstructs a whole life through a series of trifles, from broken fruit jars to a dead bird, Glaspell clearly articulates issues of justice and the deserved fulfillment of women confronting a male-controlled world.

Inheritors is Glaspell's most serious comment on the American Dream, with its early promise of freedom and hope and its diminishment before the forces of extreme nationalism. A college founded on the ideals of freedom must survive in an uncertain postwar era (following World War I). Each major character represents a different approach to the problem. To win support for state funds from a jingoistic senator who thinks that the college is a radical hotbed, the founder's second generation (who are also the college's administrators and supporters) attempt compromise and repression; a liberal professor compromises his ideals to keep his position; and a third-generation student attacks foreign-student protests with hooligan tactics. Protagonist Madeline Morton, despite such pressures as her isolationist father's admonition to stay clear of others' struggles, refuses to forgo humanistic causes and freedom of thought. Although the play fails to answer the question that it raises, its young heroine adheres to her ancestors' initial vision of freedom and brotherhood. The dialogue and characters insufficiently illustrate differences in period and personae, yet a significant theme and a lively "new woman" heroine are presented.

The *Verge* critically dissects the actions of radical feminist protagonist Claire Archer. Influenced by Swedish dramatist August Strindberg and German philosopher Friederich Neitzsche, Glaspell advances a heroine who skillfully explores the limits of radical anarchism through transmutation, rejecting all conventional obligations. Immense, exotic plants in Claire's greenhouse become the play's symbolic center, asserting a parallel between motivation in the world of plants and of humans. Claire wishes the plants to transform themselves, just as she wishes herself to do. When by act 3 she finds both goals impossible, she is driven to madness and murder. The drama posits a warning that radical interference with nature leads to disaster. Although eclectic and inventive in exposing the issue, the action of *The Verge* is overdependent on lengthy discussion by underdeveloped characters and lacking in sufficient transitions between incidents.

Overall, in Glaspell's dramas intellect prevails over lyricism, with dramatic language inexpressive of the characters' thoughts. Two of her plays, however, can be considered successful by contemporary dramaturgical standards: *Alison's House* (1930), which is now outdated, and *Trifles*, which remains a one-act masterpiece both structurally and thematically.

Context

Glaspell brought her background as a novelist acquainted with important writers and ideas of her day to her plays, and the issues contained therein became influential sources for feminist scholars and playwrights of the final decades of the twentieth century. Modern for their time, her dramas introduce a panorama of rebellious heroines in extreme situations, struggling to articulate their needs to men whose lives revolve around other priorities. The onstage women in *Trifles* support a victimized member of their sex by valuing humane justice over man-made law that is insensitive to a woman's complexity and needs. The student heroine of *Inheritors* is on the cutting edge of liberality: She risks imprisonment by uncompromisingly championing freedom of thought and expression, deemed inseparable from the American Dream. Claire Archer of *The Verge* represents the dangers of excessive individualism and antisocial behavior in exploring the frontiers of experience beyond human scope. Glaspell brought to the American stage a procession of memorable women, from repressed midwestern wives to radical feminists. She did so while advancing the issues and women of a new age without abandoning the more cherished traditional aspects of American culture. The coexistence of modern themes and characters with such traditional beliefs, which she often integrates into harmonious dramatic unity, stands as her major achievement.

Critical reviews of Glaspell's published plays cite her success as a dramatist of ideas. For example, Ludwig Lewisohn, in *Expressions in America* (1932), describes her as an artist harboring the composite of the Puritan schoolteacher espousing pioneer virtues and a modern radical whose plays for their time were second only to those of Eugene O'Neill in contributing to serious American dramatic literature. The awarding of the 1930 Pulitzer Prize for *Alison's House* afforded her recognition as a serious dramatist. Her work at the Provincetown certainly led to the appearance in the 1920's of other serious realistic plays, particularly ones by or about women: Zona Gale's *Miss Lulu Betts*, dealing with a repressed midwestern woman who is similar to Minnie Wright in *Trifles*, or Rachel Crothers' plays on the position of the modern woman, reaching conclusions found in *The Verge*. Although Glaspell published no plays after *Alison's House*, she retained an active interest in the theater. As director of the Midwest Play Bureau for the Federal Theater in 1934-1945, she offered further inspiration to others in the writing of plays.

Sources for Further Study

Ben-Zvi, Linda. "Susan Glaspell's Contributions to Contemporary Women Playwrights." In *Feminine Focus: The New Women Playwrights*, edited by Enoch Brater. New York: Oxford University Press, 1989. Discusses Glaspell's importance as a feminist playwright, for introducing a new type of female character and employing structure and dramatic language to express feminist sensibility.

Bigsby, C. W. E. Introduction to *Plays by Susan Glaspell*. Cambridge, England: Cambridge University Press, 1987. An invaluable thirty-one-page introduction to the collection. Encompasses a chronology, biographical information, and perceptive analysis of the four plays.

Chinoy, Helen Kroch, and Linda Walsh Jenkins, eds. *Women in the American Theatre*. Rev. ed. New York: Theatre Communications Group, 1987. Glaspell is discussed in several collected essays. Chinoy's introduction cites Glaspell's avant-garde qualities, focusing on *The Verge*. Rachel Frances and Karen Stein discuss *Trifles* in two separate essays as an intensely feminist work. Judith Louise Stephens records the contribution of *Alison's House* to women characters in Pulitzer Prize-winning plays.

Malpede, Karen, ed. "Susan Glaspell." In *Women in Theatre: Compassion and Hope*. New York: Drama Book, 1983. Includes a chapter on Glaspell's dramatic work and stresses her commitment to women and to humanistic social movements.

Papke, Mary E. *Susan Glaspell: A Research and Production Sourcebook*. Westport, Conn.: Greenwood Press, 1993. A detailed, definitive sourcebook giving summaries, production history, and criticism of all Glaspell's plays. Includes a chronology, a bibliography of primary sources, and annotated secondary sources such as reviews and author and general indexes.

Waterman, Arthur E. *Susan Glaspell*. New York: Twayne, 1966. A comprehensive description of Glaspell's life and work, including analyses of her plays and novels. A chronology and a bibliography with annotated secondary sources are provided.

Christian H. Moe

PLUM BUN

Author: Jessie Redmon Fauset (1882-1964)
Type of work: Novel
Type of plot: Social realism
Time of plot: The beginning of the twentieth century to the 1920's
Locale: Philadelphia and New York City (Greenwich Village and Harlem)
First published: 1929

> *Principal characters:*
> ANGELA MURRAY (ANGÈLE MORY), a young black woman who
>   wants to escape the narrow confines of her life in Philadelphia
> VIRGINIA (JINNY) MURRAY, Angela's younger sister
> ROGER FIELDING, a wealthy white man who is enamored of
>   Angela
> ANTHONY CROSS, a mulatto artist who, like Angela, is "passing"
> RACHAEL POWELL, a talented art student

Form and Content

    Plum Bun is divided into five sections that recount the physical and psychological journeys that Angela Murray takes as she attempts to reconcile her racial identity as an African American with her personal identification as a woman. Racial discrimination and gender bias make this sort of reconciliation difficult. Angela wants to enjoy the material possessions and the social influence that money can buy. Believing that life as a black person will deny her this happiness, Angela tries to free herself from the limitations that being black forces upon her.

    As a girl growing up, Angela spent Saturday afternoons with her mother, frequenting stores and restaurants where black people were not welcome. They were so light-skinned that they could "pass" for white. This apparently harmless activity gave them the opportunity to amuse themselves and see how the other half lived. One Saturday while Angela and her mother were on one of their outings, they encountered Virginia and Mr. Murray, Angela's dark-skinned sister and father, who usually spent their Saturday afternoons together. The two couples passed each other without acknowledging the other's presence. This public denial of familial connections repeats itself when Angela does not acknowledge her sister publicly after they move to New York.

    Ironically, although she aspires to be an accomplished artist, Angela cannot comprehend the advantage of being a colored woman. She does not realize that "colour may really be a very beautiful thing." After moving to Greenwich Village and enrolling in an art class as Angèle Mory, Angela ignores her African American blood ties and re-creates herself simply as a young woman who is developing her artistic talent. She meets people who she thinks are color-blind. She is especially attracted to Roger Fielding, who is similarly attracted to her.

Angela thinks of marrying Roger because his wealth and social position could be translated into the protection and power she is seeking. She daydreams about living in a home large enough for a drawing room where liberal-minded men and women can meet and discuss all sorts of topics. Angela concludes, "Marriage is the easiest way for a woman to get those things, and white men have them." She plots to snare Roger and goes into debt to "dress to keep herself dainty and desirable." Angela keeps Roger interested in her, but contrary to her expectations, Roger does not propose marriage. His attraction is purely sexual. He wants her "to be my girl; to keep a love-nest where I and only I may come."

Angela resists this proposition, but Roger's frequent visits to her apartment eventually result in the loss of her innocence and a decline in his interest. Although Roger does not know that she is black, the realization that their relationship follows the pattern of similar liaisons between white men and black women troubles Angela. She understands Jinny's criticism that passing for white occurs because being black is inconvenient.

Angela stops playing the marriage game by ignoring advice to "give a little" so that her bills will be paid and her poverty will be relieved. Instead, she thinks of relieving her loneliness by marrying Anthony Cross. Obviously, she has not abandoned the notion that marriage will solve any problems a woman might have. Cross, who does not know that Angela is black, tells her that they cannot be married because he is black. He has been passing, and he feels uncomfortable about himself, especially since his complicated family history includes his father's lynching. Angela tries to tell him who she really is, but Anthony does not give her a chance to reveal herself to him. They separate, only to be reunited after a series of fateful events.

Angela focuses her attention on her work and art, which improves so much that she is awarded a scholarship to study in France. Miss Powell is awarded a comparable prize, but the passage money is revoked because the scholarship committee believes that Miss Powell's artistic abilities will not overcome racial prejudice. Incensed by this news, Angela publicly reveals that she is also black. Finally, Angela realizes that her skin color is not an inconvenience. When she and Anthony are reunited, they know that their marriage will be an equal partnership because of what they can give to each other and what they can contribute to their race.

Analysis

Jessie Redmon Fauset's use of the nursery rhyme "To market to market/ To buy a plum bun;/ Home again, home again,/ Market is done" characterizes the compromises that women make in order to be suitable marriage material. Although Angela Murray transforms herself into the perfect woman, her efforts go unrewarded because she assumes that passing for white will destroy the restrictions of racial discrimination. The subplots regarding her mother, Mattie, and Anthony Cross contribute to an understanding of the depth and complexity of Angela's anxieties regarding her status as a black person and as a woman.

Mattie Murray, a mulatta, married a dark-skinned man because his color meant that she could enjoy the protection and privilege of middle-class black life in Philadelphia. Still, Mattie cannot divorce herself from a psychological need to pass for white. Her seemingly harmless trips into the white world with Angela point to the discomfort that blacks feel even though they have achieved a certain level of financial security and social prestige. An aura of mainstream respectability that includes hard work and religious devotion surrounds the Murray family, but they are constantly aware that their lives are defined by skin color. Angela's discomfort is magnified by her move to New York, where she chooses to change her name to Angèle Mory and live not in Harlem, with most black New Yorkers, but in Greenwich Village, where broad-minded white artists and liberals reside.

Mattie's notion that marriage is a refuge also influences Angela to think that marriage can solve any woman's problems, particularly when she cannot or does not want to contend with everyday worries. Mattie believes that her husband is God, and Junius thinks that Mattie must be protected and cared for. Consequently, Mattie does not think that she can live without her husband. When Junius dies from a heart attack shortly after pretending to be his wife's chauffeur, Mattie sits and waits for her death, which comes a few weeks later. Angela's dependence on marriage is not exactly like her mother's, but she does believe that marriage will provide wealth and power.

Initially, Angela lacks the self-confidence to establish a set of standards that will define her existence. Angela is intelligent and talented, but her ultimate goal is to make herself physically attractive to a man.

In addition, Angela cannot forget that she is black. If she wants to make the "best" marriage possible, she must seriously consider marrying a white man. She looks white, and a wealthy white man such as Roger can provide her with anything she might want. Roger rejects Angela because he could never explain her to his class-conscious father, who holds the purse strings to his inheritance. Roger's rejection is so complete that Angela refers to it as "Roger's passing," as though he had died.

Pretending characterizes Anthony Cross, whose name symbolizes the psychological burdens that people must carry when they deny a portion of their racial identity. Anthony feels guilty because he has denied his connection to his black father, who was lynched and dismembered. Eventually, Anthony reveals to Angela and then publicly that he is black. Angela does the same thing, first to Anthony, and then to newspaper reporters. Acknowledging who they are affirms their abilities to survive as people and to work in behalf of that survival in a marriage based on love and companionship, not wealth and power.

Context

Plum Bun is part of a feminist literary tradition that reached back to Kate Chopin's *The Awakening* (1899) and "The Storm" (wr. 1898, pub. 1969). Chopin's novel and short story treat the issue of a woman's sexuality that does not mirror accepted social notions of how a woman should conduct herself. As is *Plum Bun*, *The Awakening* is concerned with a young woman's artistic urgings for self-re-creation. Zora Neale Hurston's *Their Eyes Were Watching God* (1937) treats the conflicts between communal and personal interpretations of a woman's status and behavior relative to marriage. The institution encourages women to maintain a standard of beauty and decorum that often does not satisfy their needs and expectations. Along with class and gender issues, black women must think about race as they attempt to define their place in society. Nella Larsen's *Quicksand* (1928) and *Passing* (1929) also treat these three issues. Written during the Harlem Renaissance, *Plum Bun* is also characterized by sentimental situations that underscore the dual artistic concerns of black female authors who want to depict the realism of their experiences without offending the aesthetic sensibilities of a mainstream readership.

Sources for Further Study
Ammons, Elizabeth. "New Literary History: Edith Wharton and Jessie Redmon Fauset." *College Literature* 14 (Fall, 1987): 207-218. Despite comparisons between Edith Wharton and Jessie Fauset, Ammons contends that Fauset's writing makes sharp distinctions between white female issues and black female issues.
Ducille, Ann. "Blues Notes on Black Sexuality: Sex and the Texts of Jessie Fauset and Nella Larsen." *Journal of the History of Black Sexuality* 3, no. 3 (1993): 418-444. Complex novels about urban, northern, and bourgeois black women subtly did two things. They critiqued black middle-class and lower-class extremes of bourgeois pretense and primitive exoticism, and they focused on themes of the classic blues: love, lust, and longing.
Feeney, Joseph J. "Black Childhood as Ironic: A Nursery Rhyme Transformed in Jessie Fauset's Novel *Plum Bun*." *Minority Voices* 4, no. 2 (1980): 65-69. There is a marked disparity between the joy and hope of the nursery rhyme that gives the novel its title and the despair and disillusionment of the reality of the lives of black children who grew up reciting its lines.
McDowell, Deborah E. "The Neglected Demension of Jessie Redmon Fauset." In *Conjuring: Black Women, Fiction, and Literary Tradition*, edited by Marjorie Pryse and Hortense Spillers. Bloomington: Indiana University Press, 1985. Imitating the novel of manners gave Fauset the opportunity to write about controversial subjects such as black female sexuality without offending readers during the 1920's.
_____ . "Regulating Midwives." Introduction to *Plum Bun*. Boston: Beacon Press, 1990. McDowell emphasizes the novel's focus on power relationships in American society that impinge on the development of a black female who is ensnared in fantasies about passing and marriage.

Judith E. B. Harmon

POEMS AND FRAGMENTS

Author: Sappho (c. 615 B.C. - c. 550 B.C.)
Type of work: Poetry
First published: Written third century B.C.; published 1560 (English translation, 1735)

Form and Content

In classical antiquity, the standard edition of Sappho appears to have been arranged into nine books. The first book included 330 Sapphic stanzas, a total of 1,320 lines in the meter invented by her and named for her. The length of a book averaged 1,000 to 1,500 lines; the extent of Sappho's lost works can be gauged by the fact that only about 1,700 lines have survived, most of which are fragmentary and some amounting to no more than a letter. Books 2 and 3 consisted, respectively, of poems in dactylic hexameters and poems in the Asclepiadean meter. The fourth book seems also to have been metrically consistent. Books 4 through 8 were apparently compiled on bases other than meter, although there is scant mention of any of them by ancient commentators, and on the sixth book there is no information of any kind. The ninth book, the only one given a title instead of a number, was called "Epithalamia" (wedding songs). The classical scholar Denys Page summarizes this editorial information and elucidates the contents of Sappho's poetry as "Epithalamians," "Aphrodite," "Divine and Heroic Legend," and "Political and Domestic Allusions."

Some translators arrange Sappho's poems and fragments in thematic groups. Paul Roche, for example, entitles his groupings "Overtures of Loving," "Petitions and Observations," "Converse," "Epithalamia," "The Taut Tongue," and "Memory-and-Malediction." Josephine Balmer has nine groupings: "Love," "Desire," "Despair," "Marriage," "Mother-and-Daughter," "The Goddess of Love," "Religion," "Poetry-and-the-Muses," and "Nature-and-Wisdom." The two representative lists have in common only the themes of love and marriage, but all the titles are variously descriptive of the content of the poetry.

The formal character of Sappho's poetry is to be discerned in its intricate metrical compositions and in the Aeolic dialect of Lesbos, neither of which can be more than distantly reflected in English translations of her works. Sappho and her contemporary compatriot Alcaeus, with whom an invalid tradition links her in romance, shared the Aeolic dialect, which is free of aspirated consonants, that is, of the equivalent of the letter *h*. It is consequently smooth in sound and conducive to melodious phrasing. Aeolian poetry is generally intended for solo performance as opposed to choral rendition; that is, it is monodic as opposed to choric. Smooth consonance (*psilosis*) and monodicism both lend themselves effectively to the intimacy and subjectivity that Sappho's poetry generates.

The formal content of Sappho's poetry can be illustrated by brief passages from her severely fragmented canon. An example of her mastery of pure lyric is the following stanza: "and through the branches of the trees there is/ a rustling sound of cool water;/ roses lend/ their shadows to the grove, and sleep pours down from/ whispering tree leaves." Translation can suggest, but not reproduce, the Sapphic meter and the fluid soughing of softly guttural and sustained sibilant music. An example of her dedication to love as the preeminent human value is the following opening of a poem: "According to some, the best thing on this/ dark earth is the cavalry, to others/ the infantry, to others the navy, to me it/ is one's beloved." Another feature of her poetry is her preoccupation with the divine personifications of human impulsions, notably the goddess of love, whom she invokes, in the one poem of all her works that has survived in virtual entirety, as "Colorfully-throned Aphrodite." Finally, her sense of her worth as a poet is frankly and prophetically expressed in these lines: "The golden Muses have truly blessed me;/ I shall not be forgotten after death."

Analysis

Discussion of Sappho's poetry necessarily entails what has come to be identified as her primary motif; namely, female homoeroticism. The term "lesbian" in its late nineteenth and twentieth century English usage is referentially derived from the reputation of Sappho of Lesbos. The grounds for diagnosing Sappho as homosexual involve two assumptions: that Sappho's expressions of emotion are subjectively her own and that her use of her own name in homoerotic context is self-identical and not generic. In most studies of Sappho, these assumptions are both unstated and understood.

That not all Sappho's poems express homoeroticism and that Sappho, even in self-identical context, is not exclusively homosexual are suppositions that any reader of her work in translations published during the latter half of the twentieth century will recognize. Earlier translations, commentaries, and scholarly articles presented a Sappho varying from an almost deranged homosexual to a paragon of heterosexual chastity or moral purity. In her hymn to Aphrodite, the single poem that has been preserved in full, Sappho presents herself, or her generic namesake, as being addressed by name by Aphrodite, to whom she has prayed for the renewed affection of her beloved and by whom she is told that the now indifferent beloved will soon be courting Sappho's favor. A single letter, missing from some codices but included in others, is the determinant that the indifferent beloved is a woman. In the absence of that letter (an *alpha*, denoting feminine gender), Sappho's, or her namesake's, beloved may be either male or female. A translation published in 1902 by John Philip Merivale makes the beloved a male; but almost all later translations, even those by scholars who prefer a chaste Sappho and consider homosexuality, in Denys Pages's word, a "perversion," adhere to the supposition of a female beloved.

Sappho's attention to heterosexuality is attested in lines such as "svelte Aphrodite has melted my will away/ and filled me with longing for a boy," as well as in the epithalamia, which celebrate the formalizing of conjugal heterosexual love. Sappho's own conjugal heterosexuality is made explicit in two fragments in which she refers to her daughter Kleis.

There is nothing in Sappho's poetry to support the legend that she loved a man named Phaon; there is no historical evidence that she, having abandoned her homosexuality in his interests, leaped to her death from a cliff when he subsequently deserted her. The legend was propagated by the Greek dramatist Menander (second century B.C.) in a line from one of his plays that is quoted by Strabo (c. 64 B.C.-A.D. 24); it is also the subject of a long Latin poem questionably ascribed to Ovid (43 B.C.-A.D. 18).]

Legend and biographical fictions inhibit the analysis of Sappho's work, likewise the conjectures of editors and translators that add to her extant text words and passages. For example, the fragment ". . . ēr' a . . . dērat . . . Gongyla . . . " appears in Paul Roche's translation as "Then Gongyla spoke." In Josephine Balmer's translation, it is "[I tell you I am miserable,] /Gongyla. . . ." Most translators settle for "Gongyla . . . to retain the only intelligible word in the sequence. Some translators, and for that matter some editors, expunge the entire sequence in preference to interpolation or emendation. Guy Davenport offers as his translation "Spring/ Too long/ Gongyla," insisting that "the misreading, if misreading it be, is by this time too resonant to change." He is perhaps referring to the popularity of Ezra Pound's poem "Papyrus," published in *Lustra* (1916) and reading "Spring . . ./ Too long . . ./ Gongula . . ."

The most cogent analysis of Sappho's lyricism is found in the essay on sublimity written, according to most estimates, in the first century A.D. by a critic called "Longinus." The author exemplifies sublimity by quoting, and thereby preserving for posterity, four stanzas of a poem in the meter named for Sappho. The stanzas describe an observer, presumably Sappho, reacting to the sight of a man seated next to a woman whom the observer adores. The man impresses the observer as virtually godlike both because he is favored by the woman's presence and because he can retain his equanimity when the very sight of the woman sends the observer into emotional excess. Longinus writes that Sappho always selects the precise, the greatest, and the most intense symptoms of love and combines them into an illustrious whole. The symptoms in the poem include loss of voice, sight, and hearing; fever, with cold sweat and spasms; pallor; and a sense of death. Longinus explains that the paradox of being both hot and cold and both rational and unhinged is expressed as a synthesized emotional integer. Sappho's rationality, or *noesis*, is found in her observer's logical diagnosis as she simultaneously suffers emotion and disciplines her rendition of the event with precise metric.

Context

The opening lines of the poem preserved by Longinus achieved key status in one area of twentieth century feminist criticism. In literal translation they read: "He seems to me to be on a par with the gods, that man who sits facing you." A feminist preference is to eliminate an actual male presence in favor of a hypothetical one; this is done by changing "that man who" to "whatever man" or "whoever." Although K. J. Dover rightly pointed out, in *Greek Homosexuality* (1978), that Greek grammar precludes such a reading, the change was effected in many later twentieth century English translations, attesting the success with which Sappho's canon was enlisted in the support of women's issues.

Two factors in Sappho's verse that gained new emphasis during the twentieth century, and in turn helped to determine the direction of modern feminism, are Sappho's independence as an artistic genius and the frank sexuality to which her art gives unabashed expression. As the feminist movement gained momentum, Sappho received proportionately more attention. Every decade of the twentieth century had its Sappho publications: translations, editions, or articles. The preoccupation with Sappho's "moral purity" or with the minimalizing of her homoeroticism, carried over from the nineteenth century into the beginning of the twentieth, gradually gave way to the picture of Sappho as a consummate lyricist forthright in her projection of sexuality, whatever its turn; Sappho became a picture of a feminist for feminists.

It is significant that in the twentieth century Sappho received attention from more women translators, scholars, editors, and hermeneucists than in virtually all previous centuries combined. Eva-Maria Voigt's masterly edition of Sappho and Alcaeus in 1971 superseded the standard edition by Edgar Lobel and Denys Page in 1955. Translations by women became commonplace: Olga Marx in 1945, Mary Barnard in 1958, Suzy Q. Groden in 1966, Anne Pippin Burnett in 1983, Sherri Williams in 1990, Diane Rayor in 1991, Josephine Balmer in 1992, and Sasha Newborn in 1993. The renditions by Barnard, Groden, Burnett, and Balmer set new standards for reliability. In addition, the feminist scholar Mary R. Lefkowitz reeducated the modern reader by repudiating the tradition that Sappho's erotic lyrics were self-referential and by cautioning against deriving from the poetry autobiographical elements that would then become the means of interpreting it.

Sources for Further Study
Bowra, C. M. *Greek Lyric Poetry: From Alcman to Simonides.* 2d ed. London: Oxford University Press, 1961. Chapter 5 remains the prime introduction to the poetry of Sappho in its temporal setting. All but a few quotations in the original Greek are translated or paraphrased.
Burnett, Anne Pippin. *Three Archaic Poets: Archilochus, Alcaeus, Sappho.* Cambridge, Mass.: Harvard University Press, 1983. "Part Three: Sappho" is a searching and informative essay on the poet and includes accurate translations of the poems and fragments, with occasional rhyme that is both efficacious and unobtrusive.
Campbell, David A. ed and trans. *Sappho, Alcaeus.* Vol. 1 in *Greek Lyric.* Loeb Classical Library 142. Cambridge, Mass.: Harvard University Press, 1982. Superbly supersedes the 1928 Loeb Library edition by J. M. Edmonds; incorporates a half century of valuable scholarship. Campbell's prose translations adhere meticulously to the Greek text, which is included on facing pages.
DeJean, Joan. *Fictions of Sappho, 1546-1937.* Chicago: University of Chicago Press, 1989. Exceptionally informative scholarship. DeJean makes it clear that translations of Sappho and speculation regarding her sexuality reflect the mores of the times and countries in which her work is published.
Duban, Jeffrey M., ed. *Ancient and Modern Images of Sappho: Translations and*

Studies in Archaic Greek Love Lyric. Lanham, Md.: University Press of America, 1983. Contains the first-rate summary "Sappho in Recent Criticism," as well as a less satisfactory comparison of various translations of Sappho's poems and fragments favoring Duban's own thirty-eight rhymed translations.

Lefkowitz, Mary R. "Critical Stereotypes and the Poetry of Sappho." *Greek, Roman, and Byzantine Studies* 14 (1973): 113-123. Cogently questions the validity of Sappho's work as inherently self-referential.

Page, Denys. *Sappho and Alcaeus: An Introduction to the Study of Ancient Lesbian Poetry*. London: Oxford University Press, 1955. Staid but requisite orientation in the study of Sappho. Page claims that while Sappho was not averse to homoeroticism, there is no evidence in her extant work of her taking part in it.

Rayor, Diane. *Sappho's Lyre: Archaic Lyric and Women Poets of Ancient Greece*. Berkeley: University of California Press, 1991. Information about and translations of seven male lyric poets and (including Sappho) ten female lyric poets. With helpful notes and bibliographical references.

Roy Arthur Swanson

POEMS ON VARIOUS SUBJECTS, RELIGIOUS AND MORAL

Author: Phillis Wheatley (1753?-1784)
Type of work: Poetry
First published: 1773

Form and Content

Poems on Various Subjects, Religious and Moral is the collection of poems produced by a nineteen-year-old Colonial American slave, Phillis Wheatley, the first African American woman ever to be published. The significance of this publication can be understood best in terms of the author's identity and social position, and less by the poetry itself, which is largely imitative of the style and material that were popular at the time. Wheatley was brought as a captive from Senegambia (now Senegal and Gambia) to New England when she was approximately seven years old and was educated by the family who bought her. She was considered a prodigy, since she learned the English language within less than two years of her arrival and successfully studied Latin, the Bible, and English poetry—especially the work of Alexander Pope and John Milton. At age thirteen, she wrote her first religious verse, which was published. Her work became widely known after her elegy on the death of the popular preacher George Whitefield was published in 1770.

Wheatley's collection is written almost entirely in the popular neoclassical form. Neoclassicism is an emulation of what the English believed to have been the Greek ideals of reason and restraint in art. Most of the thirty-nine poems are elegies, which are formal poems wherein the author meditates on a solemn occasion or theme, such as death. Wheatley is best known for her elegies, and she was often commissioned to write them. Her subjects include widows, widowers, parents who had lost children, and numerous popular male figures who were usually respected members of the clergy. Besides elegies, Wheatley's collection contains two stories from the Bible transformed into couplets (pairs of rhyming lines), one Latin translation, several patriotic praises (one to George Washington), and tributes to morning, evening, the imagination, and African American Bostonian artist Scipio Moorhead.

Wheatley lived in an age when there was a great debate among the white slave-owning population over the humanity of African Americans. Her education and poetry demonstrated that African Americans were indeed intellectually capable of engaging in the "arts and sciences," even if her work was limited and was censored by her audience, which acted as both patron and oppressor. Before her poems could be published, Wheatley had to be "examined" by eighteen of Boston's most prestigious male minds, who signed a document attesting the authenticity of her work. This document was appended to the book before it was published, since the work otherwise would not have been believed to be hers. Wheatley's membership in the church, even though it, too, was segregated into black and white, provided the only possibility for freedom and equality in her life and in her art, and the theme of spiritual salvation is prevalent throughout her writing.

Analysis

As neoclassicism demands, Wheatley's poetry recognizes the human being as a limited, imperfect creature in need of instruction, order, and harmony; imagination is highly regarded, but it is never an alternative to the harsh realities of life. Neoclassical poems were valued for their instruction, and they avoided both the adverse and the highly imaginative aspects of nature. This restrictive form suited Wheatley's social status as a slave and conformed to the Christian idea of an individual as an imperfect being whose only hope of salvation rests in the figure of Christ.

Wheatley's poems often begin with the neoclassical appeal to the Muses and often employ Greek deities and legends, remaining mindful of the structured Greek universe; in her poetry, however, God is the highest deity. Wheatley's focus is on salvation and resurrection, as is apparent in her numerous elegies, in which the idea of the well-ordered universe extends to human suffering; even the death of an infant is the will of God and should be looked on as such. Wheatley constructs her elegies (which frequently resemble one another and which were often written in only a few days) of several components that do not always occur in the same order. First, she stresses that death itself comes from the hand of God: "His fatal sceptre rules the spacious whole" ("To a Lady on the Death of Three Relations"). Second, she graciously acknowledges and pictures the mourners' suffering: "Thy sisters, too, fair mourner, feel the dart/ Of death, and with fresh torture rend thine heart." Third, she includes an appeal to mourners to transform their sorrow to joy: "Smile on the tomb, and soothe the raging pain." Often, the dead themselves speak to the mourners from above. (In some elegies to male figures who were prominent in the church, Wheatley emphasizes their earthly deeds, as if petitioning for their entry into the state of bliss.) Finally, a new vision of the deceased is offered to the onlooker: "From bondage freed, the exulting spirit flies."

With few exceptions, the lines of Wheatley's poems are predictably structured in iambic pentameter, each line consisting of ten syllables, five of which are stressed. Wheatley often contracts words, such as "watery" to "wat'ry" in order to conform to the required pattern, using the customary neoclassical rhymed couplet, or pair of rhyming lines. She was skilled in the use of metaphor (identifying one object with another), as the young biblical hero David demonstrates in "Goliath of Gath": "Jehovah's name—no other arms I bear." Her transformative images are also memorable, such as the trees that turn into ships in "To a Gentleman in the Navy": "Where willing forests leave their native plain,/ Descend, and instant, plough the wat'ry main."

Wheatley often uses personification, attributing human qualities to objects or ideas. "On Imagination" is an example of personification, celebrating that faculty (imagination) and its marvelous transforming power; sadly, but true to the neoclassic tenets, the poem ends by acknowledging the limits of the imagination, conceding that the reality of "winter" and "northern tempests" must win over the mind in the end: "They chill the tides of Fancy's flowing sea,/ Cease then, my song, cease the unequal lay."

Wheatley's poems abound in skillfully rendered alliteration, the repetition of consonant or vowel sounds in lines, as in the opening of her elegy for the Reverend George Whitefield: "Hail, happy saint, on thine immortal throne,/ Possest of glory, life and bliss unknown." She also effectively employed the technique of repeating the same word at the start of sentences or clauses (anaphora).

Some critics see Wheatley as having waged an invisible war against slavery in her poetry, mostly in biblical allusions that ultimately admonish Christian slave-holders. Her poem "On Being Brought from Africa to America" is an example of this. In it, she refers to her "benighted soul," acknowledging the widely held theory of her time that equated dark skin with sinfulness, and quotes Christians who would say of African Americans, "'Their color is a diabolic die.'" At the same time, Wheatley refutes the connection between skin color and sinfulness, since the reference is to her "soul" before she knew the "light of Christ" and not to her skin color. She also reminds Christians in the same poem that even Cain, who was "black," could be assured of the salvation of Christ.

Wheatley consistently refers to the dark skin of the African American as "sable" in her poems, and she often alludes to Africa as "Eden," a reminder to Christian audiences that Eden was thought to have been located in Africa. Additionally, Wheatley also uses the term "Ethiope" to designate African Americans, connecting her race with ancient Ethiopians who are mentioned throughout the Bible, thus elevating the status of the African American through the perspective of Christianity. Many of Wheatley's poems are didactic and at the same time signal her racial identity, such as "To the University of Cambridge, in New England": ". . . Ye blooming planets of human race divine,/An Ethiop tells you 'tis [sin] your greatest foe." Other poems tell of her pride in her African heritage and of her love and admiration for fellow African Americans; "An Ode/On the Birthday of Pompey Stockenridge" praises a fellow African American Christian man, and the poem to Scipio Moorhead is a tribute to African American artists.

Context

Wheatley's poetry was well received as an example of superior African intellect. Her work was used as an evangelical tool among slave-holders who wished to convert their slaves to Christianity. Her poems were also held up by the abolitionists as proof of the humanity of African Americans. In other words, she was well received to the extent that she served the purpose of others, as her role as an African American, woman, slave, and Christian patriot in Colonial America dictated.

Wheatley was censored by her audience, and she was unable to publish without approval and verification; her situation was comparable to that of black writers in South Africa under the system of apartheid, which was rendered untenable by the laws of censorship, banning, and exile. Wheatley was further censored by her obligation to the Wheatley family for her privileged position in their household. It must be recognized that even her skill as a writer was "owned" by someone else, and that it was the only survival skill available to Wheatley.

Critics have complained about, ignored, and indicted Wheatley's poetry on the ground that it lacks feeling, racial identity, and warmth. One must consider what she was allowed, however, and that her privileged status did not make her any less a slave or any less censored—perhaps it made her even more so, judging by the poetry of the more outspoken (and less privileged) George Moses Horton, which was published with hers by abolitionists in 1838. Wheatley can also be viewed as more isolated than other African Americans because she was cut off from other slaves. Her greatest friend and lifelong correspondent, Obour Tanner, mirrored rather than ameliorated this isolation, since she, too, was a domestic slave who was literate and was a member of the church.

There is much irony in the fact that the material produced by the first published African American woman does not make explicit her achievement or reveal the significance of that achievement to African American and female writers who followed her. Perhaps proving the fundamental fact that African Americans were human and literate was the only public achievement that could have been allowed Wheatley during her lifetime; she was forced to imitate the white culture in order to gain ground and hold a place for the more diverse and authentic African American expression that was to follow.

Wheatley's life after her publication demonstrates further irony; her own attempts to continue selling her work in America were cut short by the Boston Tea Party in 1773 (in one of her poems, Wheatley admonishes England as a harsh mother, unduly taxing her overburdened son), and then made impossible by her unexpected acquisition of freedom in 1778 (two years after the United States declared its independence) when the elder Mr. Wheatley died, at which time she married, cutting herself off from the remaining Wheatley family. Wheatley spent the end of her short life working with her hands; she and her three infants died soon after she gained her freedom, in poverty and obscurity.

Sources for Further Study
O'Neale, Sondra. "A Slave's Subtle War: Phillis Wheatley's Use of Biblical Myth and Symbol." *Early American Literature* 21 (Fall, 1986): 144-165. In this article, O'Neale examines Wheatley's careful use of words to describe color and her use of words to describe sin, arguing that Wheatley both admonished Christians and attempted to change their perceptions of African Americans through her word choice. She also shows how Wheatley used biblical allusions to elevate the status of the African American in the eyes of white Christians.
Richmond, M. A. *Bid the Vassal Soar: Interpretive Essays on the Life and Poetry of Phillis Wheatley and George Moses Horton*. Washington, D.C.: Howard University Press, 1974. This book examines the poetry of two African American slaves in order to discover what impact the institution of slavery has had on African American identity; what is left unsaid in their poetry is more important to this discovery than what remains in print.
Robinson, William H. *Phillis Wheatley and Her Writings*. New York: Garland, 1984. This book is so far the most complete collection of Phillis Wheatley's writings,

including extant poems and letters, a facsimile of her published volume, annotations, a sketch of her life and of Boston during her times, and an examination of her poetry. A selected bibliography is included.

_____ . *Phillis Wheatley in the Black American Beginnings*. Detroit: Broadside Press, 1975. This book offers a new perspective of Wheatley's poetry, considering it from the social, religious, and literary standpoints of Colonial America. It argues that Wheatley was conscientiously aware of her racial identity and African roots.

Wheatley, Phillis. *Life and Works of Phillis Wheatley*, edited by G. Herbert Renfro. Freeport, N.Y.: Books for Libraries Press, 1970. Written in the late 1800's, this book is significant in that it provides the contemporary reader with an account of Wheatley's life written by a sympathetic and well-educated man who lived just after her times. It is both interesting and ironic in that it is a positive account of her life yet is laced with inherent sexism. For example, Renfro claims: "Nature had designed Phillis for a queen, not for a slave."

Jennifer McLeod

POLITICAL WOMAN

Author: Jeane Kirkpatrick (1926-   )
Type of work: Social criticism
First published: 1974

Form and Content

In the early 1970's, the growing women's movement led to the establishment of numerous groups that set out to study the status of women in American society. Among the early organizations was the Center for the American Woman and Politics, established as part of the Eagleton Institute of Politics at Rutgers University in New Jersey. That group took as one of its earliest tasks an investigation of the status of women in American politics, and to spearhead their study they chose Georgetown University professor of political science Jeane Kirkpatrick.

Understanding the background to Kirkpatrick's investigation of American women in various political offices is important, for the aims of the study in large part determined both the form and the methodology of her work. The center was established to determine why so few women had participated actively in American politics and to recommend ways in which women could increase their involvement. As the author of the study that would eventually be published as *Political Woman*, Kirkpatrick was given access to the data collected from fifty influential women politicians who attended a conference in 1972; there, these women debated among themselves the qualities they thought necessary for success in politics, and they completed confidential interviews during which they gave additional personal testimony about their struggles to be successful in an environment traditionally dominated by men.

Kirkpatrick's study is a distillation of information garnered from these women, who had already demonstrated their ability to be effective at the local, state, or national level. To these comments, Kirkpatrick adds her own insights, bringing to bear her wide range of information on the political process. A chapter is devoted to exploring the relationship between gender and power, showing how women have traditionally been excluded from political decision making on the basis of sexual stereotypes. Succeeding chapters describe in detail how women who have ignored these stereotypes and have entered the political arena have exerted their influence on local, regional, and national political assemblies. Kirkpatrick explains why certain women choose to run for office, how they become involved (usually starting as volunteers who transfer an enthusiasm for service first nurtured in civic and community organizations to the political arena), and how they conduct their business in what was, at the time of the study, an almost exclusively male preserve.

A central chapter provides a detailed analysis of the legislative styles women in politics use to achieve their goals. Kirkpatrick identifies four types of political women: leaders, moralizers, problem solvers, and personalizers. Her study reveals that each type can be successful, but each approach has its drawbacks, and women who are not constantly aware of their own biases may be patronized or ignored.

In her concluding chapter, Kirkpatrick speculates on the future of women in politics. She sees that future as bright, noting that more and more women have begun to take seriously the idea promulgated in the 1960's that gender need not be a barrier to careers in any field. In an appendix, she provides readers with a copy of the interview questionnaire that was used to collect information from the lawmakers. While some questions are designed to force choices from among a limited number of alternatives, many are open ended, allowing respondents to provide elaborate explanations of what made them successful and what obstacles they found particularly challenging.

Analysis

The dominant characteristic of *Political Woman* is its moderate, scholarly tone. Eschewing the more radical and polemical stances being taken by contemporaries writing on women's issues, Kirkpatrick retains throughout a sense of disinterestedness toward her topic. She often lets her interview subjects speak for themselves, summarizing astutely their feelings about their struggles and accomplishments. Only in her conclusion does she move away from her more conservative role as a documentary expert to issue what might be considered a challenge to American society to give women a greater voice in the political process than they had hitherto been accorded.

As a consequence, the work may be more accurately described as a portrait of "what is" rather than as a declaration of "what ought to be." The women interviewed for Kirkpatrick's study had all achieved some level of success in the predominantly male world of politics; it should not be surprising, therefore, to find that many of them had accepted the norms of the society that gave precedence to men in these roles. The result is that many seem to exhibit characteristics of behavior that could be described as accommodating. A majority of these female politicians attributed their success to their ability to remain feminine and to accept the roles assigned to them within the system; they believed that they were serving best by first doing what they were allowed, then advancing, when permitted, into more responsible positions within their parties and legislative assemblies. The underlying message of the book is that gradualism is the preferred method for breaking down the traditional barriers that have limited women's participation in politics at all levels in American society.

Like most products of social science research, *Political Woman* exhibits a strong debt to the methodology common to the discipline. The evidence upon which Kirkpatrick's conclusions are based is gathered from surveys, and often the forced-choice responses to the questions asked of participants in the study lead to more absolute conclusions than might be expected or desired. It is difficult to determine subtle differences from Likert-scale responses to direct, objective questions. Fortunately, Kirkpatrick supplements her quantitative analysis with substantial qualitative data; a number of the questions she posed to the women politicians were open ended, and she is able to integrate many personal anecdotes into the work. The voices of these women—none of whom feel silenced by society or intimidated by the dominance of men in the sphere in which they have chosen to work—speak out clearly about their successes and failures. They join together in denouncing the notion that women must be agents for radical change; they are equally insistent that if a woman is to be successful in politics, she must maintain the highest standards of personal integrity— perhaps even higher than those of her male counterparts.

Because the status quo in 1970 has not remained so for future generations of politicians, some of the advice offered by these women has become quickly dated. Surprisingly, however, their predictions that the growth of women in legislatures would not necessarily lead to a more proportionate number of women being elected to the highest administrative offices (governor, president) in the near future has proved to be true. One gets a sense that, as a group, these women, who achieved success at considerable personal sacrifice, were realists in their expectations. Kirkpatrick shares that view. She advocates the gradual integration of women into more responsible positions in politics, and she confirms the observations of those whom she surveys that it is imperative for a woman politician to retain her femininity and her sense of self-worth even when the circumstances suggest that unorthodox compromise might bring short-term political gain. Throughout *Political Woman*, Kirkpatrick exhibits the beliefs that women have a legitimate place in politics, that their role should expand, and that moderation is the best course to pursue if women wish to achieve long-term success beside their male counterparts.

Context

Despite its place of prominence among studies of women in American political life, Kirkpatrick's *Political Woman* has not been acknowledged in the ways that one might expect for a pioneering study. Although it is cited politely on occasion by scholars who have conducted similar examinations, the book has not received the acclaim of other groundbreaking studies such as Betty Friedan's *The Feminine Mystique* (1963).

Although there is no definitive evidence to indicate why such a seminal work has not been more frequently alluded to, several possible reasons may be posited. First, the study is highly scholarly and therefore is most attractive to political scientists and sociologists. Kirkpatrick's organization of her material and her academic style make the book's appeal to the general public understandably limited. More significant, however, is that the conclusions Kirkpatrick reaches and the path she advocates for women in politics are not attractive to more ardent feminists, whose subsequent work has dominated the literature about women in society. Kirkpatrick believes that women can survive in a world dominated by men through accommodation in little things; she suggests that women retain their traditional femininity, focus on issues about which they have significant interest, and do what they can to influence the political process. For her, gradualism is the most appropriate course of action. Although such a position may have been acceptable in the early 1970's to many women (and men) as an alternative to the more strident feminist pronouncements being made at the same time by other women writers, this approach has simply not proved to be palatable to radicals who have wished to revamp the political process immediately and give women significant power within the system.

Another possible reason that Kirkpatrick's work may have had only limited influence is that its author has pursued a career counter to that of many women politicians. Although she was an active member of the national Democratic Party when she composed her study, Kirkpatrick soon switched her political allegiance and became an influential figure among Republicans. As a reward for her work in the more conservative party, she was appointed ambassador to the United Nations by President Ronald Reagan. Because most sociological and political writing during the period since Kirkpatrick published her work has been done by women with more liberal ideologies, it is not surprising to see that *Political Woman* has been set aside in favor of calls for more immediate and sweeping change. Kirkpatrick herself has become marginalized by women pursuing careers in a profession long dominated by men. This is certainly an ironic twist of fate, since *Political Woman* is the first study to demonstrate the limited influence women had exerted on politics before its publication, and among the first to examine the ramifications of unwritten policies of exclusion, which Kirkpatrick argues are wrong and must be changed.

Sources for Further Study
Centre for Social Development and Humanitarian Affairs. *Women in Politics and Decision-Making in the Twentieth Century: A United Nations Study.* Boston: Martinus Nijhoff, 1992. This study commissioned by the United Nations explores the obstacles to women's participation in political decision making. Chapters examine women's roles in elected political bodies and their participation as appointed officials. A final chapter suggests ways in which women can be given greater roles in the political process.
Klatch, Rebecca. *Women of the Right.* Philadelphia: Temple University Press, 1987. This study analyzes the beliefs and activities of women who align themselves with conservative political causes in America. Klatch shows the wide range of opinion among members of this political group. She includes Kirkpatrick among her subjects and frequently cites Kirkpatrick's writings, especially those on communism.
Phillips, Anne. *Engendering Democracy.* University Park: Pennsylvania State University Press, 1991. A feminist scholar uses the tools of feminist political theory to examine the democratic process. A chapter on women's participation reveals that, despite formal provisions guaranteeing equal opportunities, women are underrepresented in both local and national political bodies.
Sunstein, Cass R., ed. *Feminism and Political Theory.* Chicago: University of Chicago Press, 1990. This collection of fifteen essays examines a variety of political issues from a feminist perspective. Writers investigate topics such as women's rights and responsibilities within the political system, differing perspectives on politics held by men and women, and women's reactions to moral dilemmas arising from political decisions.
Tinker, Irene, ed. *Women in Washington: Advocates for Public Policy.* Beverly Hills, Calif.: Sage Publications, 1983. The editor brings together a collection of eighteen

essays outlining the accomplishments of women in national politics. Several essays update the findings of Kirkpatrick's earlier study.

Laurence W. Mazzeno

POPCORN VENUS
Women, Movies, and the American Dream

Author: Marjorie Rosen (1944-   )
Type of work: Social criticism
First published: 1973

Form and Content

Films came into existence in the closing years of the nineteenth century and were thus born in an atmosphere of Victorian morality, but Marjorie Rosen points out that their birth also coincided with, and hastened, the genesis of the modern woman. In *Popcorn Venus: Women, Movies, and the American Dream*, the question Rosen explores is: To what extent has the modern woman found adequate images of herself on the screen? The answer, Rosen suggests, is less than encouraging.

The first two decades of the century constitute the formative years of the cinema. Those years saw the rise of a new phenomenon: the film star. Women stars were not all cut from the same cloth. Theda Bara's vamp figure was a grotesque variation on the venerable theme of the woman as temptress and destroyer. Mary Pickford, "America's Sweetheart," specialized in playing children and adolescent girls whose combination of pluck and innocence won the hearts of audiences. Bara's vogue was shortlived, however, and audiences refused to let their sweetheart Mary grow up. She was still playing little girls well into her thirties. What both Bara and Pickford may represent, then, is the early cinema's reluctance to deal honestly with the experience of women. Even the greatest filmmaker of that era, D. W. Griffith, saw women largely in terms of Victorian conventions of sentimentality and idealization.

The 1920's and the 1940's represent for Rosen periods of relative, though finally compromised, liberation. The flapper of the 1920's, most eloquently captured in the performances of Clara Bow, spoke for a woman's right to enjoy freedoms comparable to those taken for granted by men. Yet the films assured their audiences that the flapper would ultimately find fulfillment in marriage to the right man, who might turn out to be the flapper's millionaire employer. One value the flapper surely symbolized was social mobility; she might finally respect moral boundaries, but she was undaunted by the boundaries of class.

The relative emancipation of the 1940's arose largely out of the necessities of wartime. Women were required to step out of their stereotypical roles and to assume responsibilities long regarded as masculine. While this period saw the emergence of the pinup girl (Betty Grable, Rita Hayworth) and the bobby soxer, it also paid significant attention to the theme of women living without men. Love might remain the central point of conflict, but the films of stars such as Rosalind Russell and Katharine Hepburn, especially when Hepburn teamed with Spencer Tracy, suggest that self-awareness and professional élan may exist side by side with romance.

The 1930's and 1950's, however, were periods of relative regression and repression. Women suffered disproportionately from the effects of the Great Depression of the

1930's, but neither the reality of their lives nor the generosity of their aspirations found more than intermittent expression on the screen. The period had its share of powerful female stars. Greta Garbo and Marlene Dietrich found new complexity and depth in the figure of the mysterious woman, and Jean Harlow and Mae West embodied in their different ways the woman as subject, rather than object, of desire. Too often, however, the women of Depression-era films appear as sacrificial lambs, willingly denying their own needs for the sake of their men, or as profligate socialites in the social fantasies that were among Hollywood's favorite strategies of denial.

By the 1950's, women had become the numerical majority in American society, but the films of the era reveal a shift away from the relatively autonomous heroine of the 1940's. Whereas in the real world the national divorce rate was climbing precipitately, films were asserting the value of marriage over a career. The woes of the "woman alone" became a common subject, and not even Katharine Hepburn, in such "spinster films" as *The African Queen* and *Summertime*, managed to depart from the premise that the middle-aged unmarried female was merely half a person. One of the great stars of the period was Marilyn Monroe, who is viewed with sympathy by Rosen but is ultimately classified with her many imitators under the heading of "Mammary Madness."

From the perspective of 1973, Rosen's view of what the 1960's and after represent, while not without hope, remains tentative at best. She can, in speaking of this period, use words such as "revolution" and "renaissance," but she follows them with a question mark. Finally, she is uncertain whether the future holds the promise of breakthrough or the threat of backlash.

Analysis

Proceeding for the most part in chronological order, and organizing her book decade by decade, Rosen tells the story of the changing images of women projected by motion pictures over the years. She works from two assumptions. The first is that art reflects life. To some extent, then, films function as a mirror held up to the face of society. They reflect society's changing images of women over the years under consideration. According to her second assumption, however, life also reflects art. Specifically, people derive from motion pictures perceptions, values, and attitudes that they apply to everyday life. No one should be surprised, she argues, that American women have often been expected, and have themselves often aspired, to live up to the glittering images of women projected on the motion-picture screen.

From one point of view, *Popcorn Venus* is a history of those images, but it is a critical history, not a mere chronicle. The story involves the constant conflict of repression and emancipation. What one sees on the screen also forms complex patterns of interaction with the world beyond the cinema. Rosen juxtaposes her observations about the films of each decade with a sociological and historical analysis of the situation of women. This material is too closely interwoven with her analysis of films to be dismissed as "background." The films and the sociohistorical conditions are meant to be mutually illuminating and, together, to realize the author's purpose:

to define woman's position in the decade being examined and to explore the ways in which films reflect and reinforce that position.

The actual content of the book, however, is only in part determined by the author's dominant purpose. Rosen seems compelled to provide, as far as possible, an exhaustive account of the images of women and the careers of important actresses in each of the decades she considers. It is thus not advisable to read the book as a systematic development of organizing ideas. Such ideas serve Rosen primarily as points of departure. If a film or film artist interests her, she will pursue that interest, even if to do so compromises the formal integrity of her argument.

The organization by decades presents problems of its own. It may seem arbitrary, for example, to chop a long and impressive career such as that of Katharine Hepburn up into ten-year segments; one result is that little sense of the continuity of the career, and of what the career in its continuity might suggest about the portrayal of women in the cinema, can emerge. Rosen could certainly reply that some principle of organization is necessary, and all have their limitations. Still, a greater flexibility might have been attempted.

It is always possible to argue with an author's approach to her material, and often the argument is in essence the wish that the author had written a different book. There are different books to be written on the subject of *Popcorn Venus*. In fact, some of those books have already been written. Rosen's is perhaps best understood as an informal critical history of its subject, covering a range of material that others will examine more selectively and developing in broad terms themes that others will refine. When it appeared in 1973, *Popcorn Venus* was a pioneer study. It remains a lively introduction to its subject, and that is perhaps its most important function.

Context

Marjorie Rosen's subject in *Popcorn Venus* is the portrayal of women in motion pictures from the beginnings to early in the 1970's. The subject had not received extended consideration before 1973. Ironically, in that same year, Molly Haskell's *From Reverence to Rape: The Treatment of Women in the Movies*, which covered much of the same material, also appeared.

It is not surprising—although it must have surprised both authors—that these two books appeared in 1973. The women's liberation movement, which had emerged in the 1960's, had reached by 1973 a point of maturity and influence that made it inevitable that attention would turn to the treatment of women in popular culture and in art, and films belong to both categories.

In its exploration of images of women, including such topics as film characters as role models for women in society, *Popcorn Venus* represents a relatively early stage of feminist criticism. Some later feminist critics would look more closely at how masculine values are embedded in basic film structures and strategies. The emergence of a number of woman directors in the years following the publication of *Popcorn Venus* has provided others with their subject, leading to attempts to define what a woman's cinema might be. In addition, some feminist critics have found in the very films Rosen considers more liberating qualities than she acknowledges. Rosen herself has been criticized by some feminists for letting ideological categories narrow her perceptions.

Yet Rosen's belief that life imitates art remains justified. As long as films continue to affect how people perceive reality and how they process their perceptions, what Marjorie Rosen has to say will remain relevant.

Sources for Further Study
Basinger, Jeanine. *A Woman's View: How Hollywood Spoke to Women 1930-1960.* New York: Alfred A. Knopf, 1993. In the "woman's film" the author locates a dialectic of repressions and hidden liberations. Basinger places in a later perspective many of the materials examined by Rosen.
Byars, Jackie. *All That Hollywood Allows: Reading Gender in 1950s Melodrama.* Chapel Hill: University of North Carolina Press, 1991. Byars, like Brandon French, finds in the American films of the 1950's more complexity than Rosen does; many films of the period, Byars argues, challenged sacrosanct gender roles.
Doane, Mary Ann. *The Desire to Desire: The Woman's Film of the 1940s.* Bloomington: Indiana University Press, 1987. Focusing on one of the three decades covered by Basinger, this is an academic, theory-driven, difficult book. It may provide a useful and suggestive alternative to the more empirical approaches of Basinger and Rosen.
French, Brandon. *On the Verge of Revolt: Women in American Films of the Fifties.* New York: Frederick Ungar, 1978. Examining the films of a decade that was, for Rosen, especially depressing from a feminist point of view, French sees things differently: Many films of the decade explore critically the malaise of domesticity and the untenably narrow boundaries of the female role, foreshadowing the feminism of the 1960's.
Haskell, Molly. *From Reverence to Rape: The Treatment of Women in the Movies.* 2d ed. Chicago: University of Chicago Press, 1987. Published almost simultaneously with *Popcorn Venus*, Haskell's book was perceived by a majority of critics as the more psychologically astute and critically sensitive of the two, although some later critics have been disturbed by what they regard as Haskell's cultural conservatism. The second edition brings the story forward to 1987, finding evidence of progress and of unfinished business.
Lesser, Wendy. *His Other Half: Men Looking at Women Through Art.* Cambridge, Mass.: Harvard University Press, 1991. Several essays in this stimulating collection discuss cinema. Lesser challenges what she regards as the "orthodox feminist" treatment of filmmakers such as Alfred Hitchcock and film stars such as Marilyn Monroe and Barbara Stanwyck. Her interests intersect provocatively with those of Rosen.
McCreadie, Marsha. "The Feminists." In *Women on Film: The Critical Eye.* New York: Praeger, 1983. Compares Rosen's work to that of Molly Haskell, who is, in McCreadie's view, more stylistically and referentially sophisticated. Rosen, says

McCreadie, has absorbed the standards of the women's liberation movement
uncritically and has applied them mechanically.

Modleski, Tania. *The Women Who Knew Too Much: Hitchcock and Feminist Theory.*
New York: Methuen, 1988. A close feminist analysis of the work of one of the major
filmmakers discussed by Rosen. Modleski's flexible and sophisticated approach
illuminates nuances invisible to Rosen.

W. P. Kenney

PORNOGRAPHY AND SILENCE
Culture's Revenge Against Nature

Author: Susan Griffin (1943-   )
Type of work: Social criticism
First published: 1981

Form and Content

   Pornography and Silence: Culture's Revenge Against Nature is a provocative and poetic study of the chauvinist mind. Susan Griffin argues that "the other," whether woman, black, or Jew, has been excluded from society by the split between nature and culture. Pornography is the mythology of this chauvinist mind, which sees in opposites. Through her focus on six lives damaged by pornographic culture, Griffin examines the results of misogyny and racism. The historical figures she spotlights are the American novelist Kate Chopin; Franz Marc, a German painter; the Marquis de Sade, a French pornographer; actress Marilyn Monroe; convicted rapist Laurence Singleton; and Holocaust victim and diarist Anne Frank.

   Griffin uses each of these lives as an "emblem" to illustrate some aspect of the chauvinist mind. In "Sacred Images," her first chapter, she examines the lives of Marc and Chopin—two artists who censored themselves because of society's outraged reactions to their honest depictions of sensuality. She regards the female body and sensuality as victims in both pornography and religion, which demand a deadening of feeling. The necessity for exerting control over feeling is explained further in "The Death of the Heart," in which Griffin examines ancient mythology, popular culture, and modern novels that focus on women's death as the price paid for male vitality and freedom. Men's fear that women will trap them, Griffin argues, leads to attempts to silence women through rape, violence, and murder (as she demonstrates through her analysis of the Singleton case).

   "The Sacrificial Lamb," which focuses generally on racism and specifically on anti-Semitism, analyzes the ways in which hateful racial caricatures (such as those of evil, materialistic Jews and ignorant, sexually powerful blacks) parallel sexist caricatures. To Griffin, the racist mind and the pornographic mind are identical. Both separate "the other" (nonwhites, women) from prevalent culture and assign them secondary status as part of nature. Although nature is relegated to inferior status, the chauvinist mind fears its power and presence in every human being. Such hatred and fear is woven into every aspect of life, from pornographic images to racist jokes. In "Silence," the necessity of altering one's self so as to be "seen and not heard" for the sake of social, economic, or physical survival is graphically illustrated through stories about fashion models, actresses, and concentration camp victims.

   Through her exploration of images from the pornographic mind, Griffin shows how the severe split between male and female, eros and pornography, "the other" and the chauvinist dominate culture in history, film, religion, literature, and art. Her vision is not, however, entirely negative. In her epilogue, she offers hope that those such as

Franz Marc and Kate Chopin—those who tried to heal the split self and reconcile nature with culture—will leave records for the world to emulate.

Analysis

Griffin's book is a fine example of a trend in recent feminist writing: She combines academic research with personal reaction and passionate feeling for her subject, as does Rachel Blau DuPlessis in *The Pink Guitar* (1990). Her examples are far-reaching and eclectic. Compassionate analysis of six lives damaged by pornographic culture illustrates her points; she also studies the chauvinist mind in examples as diverse as the classics, films from the Hollywood mainstream and underground, mythology, religion, high fashion, punk rock, and traditional writers such as Alfred, Lord Tennyson, Algernon Swinburne, William Faulkner, and Edgar Allan Poe. Here she relates the victimization of the subject and of the pornographer, examining the psychological and social—as well as sexual—dynamics of the situation. An important aspect of these dynamics is the degradation of innocence: Through cynicism and "the death of the heart," pornography turns a human being with a soul into an object.

Griffin acknowledges the immense power that pornographic images and thinking have in Western culture, but she does not pose her work as an argument for censorship. Instead, she challenges the basic assumptions people make about erotica, about sexism, and about racism. She equates pornography not with any one legalistic definition, but with a fear of bodily knowledge and the desire to silence eros. Pornography is not about erotic desire or the life of the body, but about fear and control of that fear. Her definition of pornography draws considerably from sexual psychology and from close analysis of actual pornographic writings and films. Griffin's approach is broadly interdisciplinary, crossing boundaries between traditional divisions of "academic" and "popular." She uses not only the analyses of psychologists such as Sigmund Freud, Carl Gustav Jung and R. D. Laing but also first-person accounts and quotations from Holocaust survivors, pornographic actors, and commentary on excerpts from Adolf Hitler's *Mein Kampf.*

This work does not fit neatly into a particular category; it balances research with powerful poetic writing and commentary. As a poet, Griffin discusses the fact that women's bodies in pornography are used as symbols, analyzing the "madonna/whore" dichotomy demanded of women by religion as one example. She finds symbols of her own to represent her major categories of discussion: the heart (love and desire), the triangle (Judaism), the circle (inclusiveness), and the rose (beauty).

"Sacred Images" delineates the difference between the erotic and the pornographic. Marc's early paintings and Chopin's *The Awakening* (1899) show the influence of two strains of the Romantic movement. The former refuses to acknowledge the existence of eros and the importance of nature; nature becomes feared (as in Lord Byron and Friedrich von Schiller) as "darkness" or "the other." The other strain of Romanticism desired political and sexual freedom and a celebration of nature (as in William Blake and Elizabeth Barrett Browning). Griffin shows how women came to be equated with nature and to be seen as threatening to their "opposite"—culture.

Women's sexuality affords only the negative power of seductively destroying a man's soul (particularly in Griffin's reading of biblical and mythological themes). Sexual knowledge brings men down to earth; they are made aware of and vulnerable to the true inseparability of culture and nature, spirit and matter. Control of emotion and impulse—represented by nature—has become increasingly important. Such falsity is expressed, Griffin writes, in the designs of high fashion, in punk rock's nihilism, in stereotypical religious images, and in pornography itself. Like many feminist texts, such as Margaret Atwood's *Surfacing* (1972) and Marilyn French's *The Women's Room* (1977), Griffin's work shows how both sexes have been terribly damaged by the elevation of culture over nature.

In "The Death of the Heart," Griffin uses Euripides' *Iphigenia* and the Marquis de Sade's *Justine* to show the difference between a great tragedy and pornography: feeling. Each work focuses on the sacrifice of a young woman, yet *Justine* kills emotion and numbs the reader to brutality. Pornography, Griffin writes, is essentially cruel and lacking in soul. Culture outside pornography has demanded "tough" heroes such as Norman Mailer and Marlon Brando. She discusses how arguments defending pornography are merely a reflection of the pornographic mind, decrying the idea that males' need for catharsis must be met because violence is a "natural" instinct.

Griffin examines the power of images, arguing that because pornography's link to violence has not been indisputably proved, it still cannot be discounted. She points out that pornography is a sadistic art, an act of degradation, using graphic accounts from former pornographic actress Linda Lovelace's autobiography as examples of female submissiveness taken one step further. The last section in this chapter examines the transformative power of illusion on culture, and its role in creating the violence and fear felt by many women and children: schoolyard humiliation, sexist jokes, sexual harassment, battering.

The Third Reich's official racism and sexism is described in "The Sacrificial Lamb." Racism and pornographic sensibility are equated as similar "mass delusional forms." These delusions force the chauvinist to be trapped inside his fears. Such fears about "the other"—in this case, the Jew—leads to dehumanization of both victor and victim. The fascist persona demands "hardness" and brutality, a more extreme manifestation of the "toughness" required of men in dominant culture.

Griffin notes, in "Silence," that a terrible danger lies in women's belief in the pornographer's message. She shows the self's split between the false, socially acceptable one and the lost true one. The schism leads to a numbness, a sleepwalking quality shown by damaged women such as Marilyn Monroe. The horrific and pornographic *The Story of O* is used to show a woman's transformation into first a symbol of conquered nature and then a symbol of nothingness.

The twisted fruits of oppositional thinking—racism, sexism, pornography, and violence—are brilliantly and passionately depicted in this book. Although it analyzes and criticizes aspects of society and the literature it produces, *Pornography and Silence* is deeply personal. Its style is passionate and poetic, sometimes repeating a word or phrase as an incantation. Griffin's vision is of a world in which people choose beauty over silence, in which knowledge of eros gives back to people their capacity for culture, for expression, and for joy.

Context

Pornography and Silence is unusual in its treatment of a subject long debated by women's rights advocates. Feminists disagree on the question of censoring pornography because of its negative effects on women and because of the idea of freedom of speech. Griffin puts these questions in a larger context, believing that if people work for a more egalitarian society, pornography will no longer be seen as a necessary evil by so many people.

The work's unique style is one of its most important strengths. It is an early example of feminist criticism that links poetic writing and personal approach with academic research. Although it conveys a protest against the horrific price paid for "culture's revenge against nature," Griffin's tone is elegiac rather than angry or bitter. She attempts to get inside the mind of the chauvinist and to see his fears and humiliations with compassion and understanding. Griffin also calls readers to rethink their most basic assumptions about beauty, fashion, classic literature, and film. Seeing these genres as productions of a pornographic and deeply fearful society explains the hateful messages against women that they spread.

The book is sometimes difficult to read—not because of its style, which is deeply poetic and moving—but because of the graphic descriptions of dehumanizing pornographic images. Griffin ends with a hopeful image of a "seventh life," a life that transcends narrow and hurtful stereotypes and lives forever. Her breadth of vision and originality make *Pornography and Silence* essential reading for those who are interested in feminist analyses of pornography.

Sources for Further Study

Faludi, Susan. *Backlash: The Undeclared War Against American Women.* New York: Crown, 1991. A thorough and readable study of how feminism came to be seen as a scapegoat for a broad spectrum of problems in American society. Faludi examines popular culture, including fashion, film, magazines, television, and the men's movement, to trace the backlash against the movement for women's equality.

Greer, Germaine. *The Female Eunuch.* London: Paladin Books, 1971. Greer examines ways in which women can find motives and causes for political and social action through reassessing themselves and through questioning basic elements of education and socialization. The provocative quotations inserted into the main text and the thorough footnotes are helpful.

Griffin, Susan. *Woman and Nature: The Roaring Inside Her.* New York: Harper & Row, 1980. Written in a style similar to that of *Pornography and Silence*, this "long prose poem" focuses on the oppression of women. Griffin links the exploitation of women with the victimization of the earth; both are sustaining forces and are often victims of male revenge.

Showalter, Elaine, ed. *The New Feminist Criticism: Essays on Women, Literature, and*

Theory. New York: Pantheon Books, 1985. Sections on feminism and the academy, feminist criticism of literature and society, and women's writing make this essential reading for those interested in understanding feminism and its influence on reading and writing. Very thorough bibliography.

Steinem, Gloria. *Revolution from Within: A Book of Self-Esteem*. Boston: Little, Brown, 1992. Research on factors that affect self-esteem, combined with personal stories from Steinem and other women. Steinem examines education, the family, the body, and ways of working for positive change.

Michelle L. Jones

THE PORTABLE DOROTHY PARKER

Author: Dorothy Parker (1893-1967)
Type of work: Essays, short stories, and poetry
First published: Dorothy Parker, 1944

Form and Content

   The Portable Dorothy Parker, originally published in 1944, contained verse and stories composed by Parker that had been published in the 1920's and 1930's. Parker, known for her caustic comments and witticisms, had her first collection of poetry published in 1926. Called *Enough Rope,* it not only sold its entire first printing but also became a national best-seller. Most poetry anthologies were expected to be meager sellers; however, because of Dorothy Parker's reputation, the book enjoyed enormous success, surprising her publisher, her friends, and, most of all, Parker, who always had great trouble with her own talent.

   As a magazine caption writer, Parker learned that brevity must be the soul of wit. From that position at *Vogue* magazine, she was promoted to temporary theater critic at *Vanity Fair* magazine, where she established lifelong friendships with Robert Benchley and Robert Sherwood. These three, along with Alex Woollcott, George S. Kaufman, Heywood Broun, Charles MacArthur, and other notable writers of the day, dined together at the Algonquin Hotel at a round table and established what became known as "The Round Table" group, which exerted tremendous influence on the direction of American letters between the wars.

   The group's members quoted one another in print. They were quoted by others in print. They were fictionalized in novels. They were dramatized in plays. No one was more quoted, copied, and admired for humor than the only female member of the club—Dorothy Parker. Yet, for all of her apparent effervescence, she was a woman in great pain. She had one alcoholic husband and one homosexual one and a very tragic, although comfortable, childhood. She was expected to be perennially witty, and indeed she was, but her poetry and stories reveal the sorrow behind the outward appearance of gaiety.

   The "Roaring Twenties" was an era of both progressive ideas and repressive attitudes. Women had gotten the vote, but liquor was illegal. Dorothy Parker experimented with extramarital affairs and alcohol, which took a heavy toll on her personal life. She wrote about contemporary relationships based on her own experiences, exposing the wounds of her own life to her public, who accepted both the gay and the poignant Parker.

   In keeping with the modern, Parker's work included stories about drug overdoses, abortions, golddiggers, and gigolos. The stories are meant to be read in one sitting, almost as if Parker were recounting a tale over lunch. Her poetry does not break any formal ground and is, in fact, quite ordinary in structure. Her message is usually about the inability of love to thrive in the modern world, and it is through irony that Parker affects the reader.

It is common knowledge that poets such as Ezra Pound, T. S. Eliot, and others made great strides in modernizing poetry between the wars. Parker, however, was not so much involved in experimenting with form as she was with content. The greeting card rhymes that serve as the structure of her poetry belie the punch, the sting that Parker delivers with her themes. Parker was writing her poetry for the readers of magazines, and she knew their familiarity with and appreciation for Edna St. Vincent Millay. She patterned her verses after Millay's, hoping to draw the reader's attention with something that seemed comfortable but was, in fact, sophisticated. She endeared herself to her readers with witty phrases such as "Men seldom make passes/ At girls who wear glasses," many of which have become American slogans. A poem called "Comment" states:

> Oh, life is a glorious cycle of song,
> A medley of extemporanea
> And love is a thing that can never go wrong;
> And I am Marie of Roumania.

Her readers understand that behind the wit is a wise and knowing woman who has lived. Her own attempts at suicide do not engender long, sad, self-pitying verse; rather, she says in "Résumé":

> Razors pain you;
> Rivers are damp;
> Acids stain you;
> And drugs cause cramp.
> Guns aren't lawful;
> Nooses give;
> Gas smells awful;
> You might as well live.

Again, the form is banal, but the title, "Résumé," if it serves to list the methods and experience, the past of this writer, is a shocking look at desperation—the failure to perform the act itself and the resignation to survive. Parker's work is riddled with this kind of ambivalence—she will try to love again and again yet she has little faith in the perfect romance. Her stories relay this same constant and simultaneous hope and doubt.

Analysis

Arthur F. Kinney, in his superb analysis of Parker's works, points out the author's familiarity with Horace's *Satires*. Kinney believes that through her studies of Horace, Parker learned about "compression" in verse and the point of view of studying human follies. Like Horace, Parker was writing for an inner circle, and her puns, use of irony, and twists and turns, so similar to the great classic writer's technique, confirm Kinney's theory as essential in understanding Parker's creative process. The poems are carefully carved, however flip and casual they may seem. Her stories are anything but lighthearted, and it is in her short stories that Parker is at her finest.

She admitted that it could take her six months to write a story. She worshipped Hemingway and tried, as he did, to bring an economy of words into these stories. Because she was known for her verbiage, this seems inconsistent with her persona, but Parker viewed her stories as her serious efforts and put her ego aside in order to reveal even her own hypocrisies.

Although she kept up a pretense that she was blissfully married to the young soldier Ed Parker, Dorothy in fact found that their brief times together were awkward and was happier when he was away. He, too, could be found avoiding their apartment on a drinking binge during the furlough time he had to visit his wife. Dorothy, an emotionally demanding woman, was often too intense for Ed, who wanted to maintain superficial conversations and drink liquor.

"The Lovely Leave" recounts the story of a couple in just such a situation. Both characters emerge as simultaneously sympathetic and irritating. Parker focuses on each character's expectations. The woman, Mimi, has carefully planned a special romantic weekend that goes sour because she is not aware that her husband's leave will be for only a few hours. She has purchased lingerie and flowers. He arrives and wants to take a bottle of scotch into the bathroom and take a hot bath—simple luxuries for one living in army camps. Intimacy is revealed with such verisimilitude of dialogue that the reader feels voyeuristic in the middle of this scene. Endearments and insults reveal the couple's frustration with each other and their untenable predicament of having only moments together every now and then. Instead of focusing on romance, the soldier asks for brass polish so that he can shine his belt buckle. Mimi is devastated that her plans are dashed. Parker's modern woman, who has set the stage for seduction, has failed. This story is about the risks one takes when falling in love. All through the story, Mimi reminds herself not to become too emotional, because he doesn't like it. The repetition of this self-censorship causes the reader to realize that these are two very different people who, in fact, are strangers. This is a sad love affair. These people, who seem to communicate effortlessly, repeat and repeat and repeat behavioral patterns that cause each other pain.

Parker delineated many of her unhappy experiences with men in her stories. Although she seemed very unlike the uneducated protagonist in "Big Blonde," she was, in fact, a kindred spirit. She herself became an alcoholic. The young secretary in "Mr. Durant" may seem unlike the urbane and fashionable Dorothy Parker, but her experience as a young woman who becomes pregnant by a man who will never marry her was the same one that Parker experienced when she, too, decided to have an abortion. The techniques of colloquial dialogue, repetition, and attention to tiny details are used in these two stories to cover the same themes Parker chose to explore in "The Lovely Leave." The search for love, the impossibility of, yet the constant hope for, love is made all the more impossible and painful by the inability of two people to communicate. They speak intimately to each other yet cannot convey their innermost feelings. Like Parker and her group, her characters often hide behind quips, drugs, and alcohol to conceal their true natures.

Context

It has been noted in the biographies of Parker that she had a terrible relationship with her father and with successive lovers. In fact—except for men with whom she shared professional interests—she viewed men as incomplete and withholding human beings. Her male characters, such as Hazel's husband in the "Big Blonde" and Mr. Durant, embody the cold and shallow man with whom Parker's female characters were continually involved and by whom they were perennially hurt. The theme of women hurt by love is a constant issue in the stories and poetry of Dorothy Parker.

Who, then, is the modern woman in Parker's story? She is passionate, assertive, and solitary. Mimi, in "The Lovely Leave," has a career and lives alone while her husband is off at war. Hazel lives alone after her husband leaves her. She goes to bars to meet men and is tolerated only when she is amusing. Her suffering must be done in private. The young secretary, Rose, in "Mr. Durant," works in a city where she has no family. She is forced to abort her pregnancy, pay for part of it, and make no demands on her lover. These women jump into love affairs without thinking about the consequences, like Parker herself and her "flapper" contemporaries in the 1920's. These women are sad because their passions meet no counterpart. They are also worthy of respect because somehow they manage to survive.

Sources for Further Study

Frewin, Leslie. *The Late Mrs. Dorothy Parker*. New York: Macmillan, 1986. This book makes an interesting study of the role of Round Table members in bringing wit and sophisticated culture to the masses, much as their counterpart Bloomsbury and Fonquet groups did in London and Paris. There is a very useful bibliography of works by and about leading intellectuals and artists of modernism. The author is British and is very interesting in tracing Parker's travels and her interest, in general, in becoming an international figure.

Keats, John. *You Might as Well Live*. New York: Simon & Schuster, 1970. The biographer has researched his subject well, but he often creates little atmospheric meanderings. These "imaginings" cause the reader to doubt Keats's accuracy in some cases. A competent if not comprehensive bibliography is included.

Kinney, Arthur F. *Dorothy Parker*. Boston: Twayne, 1978. The definitive study of the life and work of Parker. Kinney's critical analysis is perceptive, and his study of literary influences on Parker's poetry and stories is essential to understanding her methodology. An intelligently compiled bibliography is provided.

Meade, Marion. *Dorothy Parker: What Fresh Hell Is This?* New York: Villard Books, 1988. This biography is a collage pieced together through the letters, photographs, and recollections of Parker's friend. Some of the episodes recounted are suppositions, and they lend an element of fictionality to this less-than-accurate biography. A tabloid-style piece of writing rather than a scholarly effort.

Woollcott, Alexander. "Our Mrs. Parker." In *The Portable Woollcott*. New York: Viking Press, 1946. As her colleague and friend, Woollcott presents biographical information about Parker and her role as a member of the Round Table. He notes her talent and assumes that she will be read a hundred years to come. He sees her as a great feminine talent in a sea of male voices.

Susan Nagel

POSSESSING THE SECRET OF JOY

Author: Alice Walker (1944-   )
Type of work: Novel
Type of plot: Social realism
Time of plot: The last half of the twentieth century
Locale: California and a village in Africa
First published: 1992

> *Principal characters:*
> TASHI, an Olinkan woman who undergoes the genital and facial
>   mutilation traditional to her people
> ADAM, Tashi's American husband
> OLIVIA, Adam's sister
> LISETTE, a refined French woman who becomes Adam's lover
> BENNY (BENTU MORAGA), Tashi's partially retarded son
> PIERRE, Lisette and Adam's son
> M'LISSA, the old woman who brought Tashi into the world
> MBATI, a young woman who becomes Tashi's spiritual daughter
> RAYA, an American therapist
> MZEE (OLD MAN), Lisette's uncle, a therapist
> DURA, Tashi's older sister

Form and Content

   Possessing the Secret of Joy, which Alice Walker dedicates "with tenderness and respect to the blameless Vulva," is divided into twenty-one parts; each is the reflection of one of the characters. The story is prefaced by a quote from Walker's novel *The Color Purple* (1982), and the last section is told by Tashi's soul after she has been shot by the firing squad. The sections are not in chronological order, and many relate African legends and myths that the characters are learning and that help them to explain genital mutilation and the ancient, ancestral tribal practices that are the heritage of the Olinkans. Tashi finally understands and identifies with her people, who are simple and natural and actually possess the secret of joy, which enables them to survive the suffering and humiliation inflicted upon them.

   Although the story is told by Tashi, Adam, and Olivia when they are well-advanced in middle age and are quite white-headed, the narrative goes back to the time when the missionaries arrived from America. When Adam and Olivia first see Tashi, she is still crying inwardly and outwardly because of the death that morning of her sister Dura, who has bled to death following the female initiation ceremony. The implications and circumstances of Dura's death and Tashi's own circumcision are gradually remembered by Tashi with the help of Olivia, who remains the sister of her heart; Adam; and her therapists.

   As a young adult, Tashi has run away to go to M'Lissa and submit herself to the cutting of tribal marks on her face and to the female initiation ceremony, which is usually done at age eleven. In spite of the protests of the missionaries, Tashi wants to demonstrate her loyalty to the practices of the Olinkan people. Adam, who is in love with her, follows her to the distant Mbele camp and brings her home to the Olinkan village. He demonstrates his support by having his own face cut with tribal marks on the day before their wedding and return to America for the reunion with Celie and Shug, which takes place in the final scenes of *The Color Purple*.

Prior to this, Tashi and Adam have defied the Olinkan customs and have made love in the fields, loving in the way that is the greatest taboo of all—but that brings the most pleasure—in which Adam caresses her clitoris with his tongue. Tashi receives as much pleasure as Adam does and thus experiences the secret joy of total but forbidden sexual pleasure.

Living in California, Tashi frequently checks herself into the Waverly Psychiatric Hospital. She suffers from the odor of her mutilation, the difficulty of urination and menstruation, and the impossibility of sexual intercourse. She has undergone the removal of her entire genital area; the remaining sides of her vulva have been stitched together, leaving only a very small opening. The tendons in her upper legs have also been harmed, so she walks with a shuffle, as do the other Olinkan women. Because of her humiliation and suffering, Tashi constantly wants to mutilate herself, and once she cuts rings about her own ankles.

Her first breakthrough in therapy comes when she and Adam are in Switzerland visiting Lisette's uncle. In the security of his villa, she responds to this old man's love and sympathy. One day, Tashi passes out while watching some films of his trips to Africa. The scene that disturbs her shows young girls lying on the ground waiting to be circumcised while a large fighting cock walks proudly about. For hours after she is revived, Tashi paints a large rooster again and again until she is able to recall that at Dura's death M'Lissa had thrown her severed clitoris to the chickens. For the first time, Tashi is able to acknowledge to herself that Dura was, in effect, murdered as she finally remembers the circumstances that she observed as a young child hiding in the grass outside the hut where the mutilation took place.

Back in California, Tashi is able to express to her therapist, Raya, her new understanding of Dura's death and of what has been done to her. Raya relates to Tashi's pain, and she attempts to show her sympathy by having her gums mutilated to help her understand pain and by coming to Olinka to be present at her execution.

Lisette's presence in Adam's life also causes her pain, yet after Lisette has died of stomach cancer, Tashi begins to recognize that she had been sincere in wanting to understand and to help Tashi as well as Adam. Lisette and Adam met in the Olinkan village in the hut of an old man who was refused care by everyone in the village because he lost control of his young wife, who ran away and drowned herself after he cut her open with a hunting knife so that they could have intercourse. His act was acceptable behavior, and her rebellion threatened the web of society, of life itself. Lisette has grown up in a different culture and is profoundly affected by this story. Much later, she confesses to her son Pierre that her refusal to marry is the result of having actually known a young woman who ran away from her husband and was forced to return.

When Pierre first attempts to visit Tashi, she stones him and he runs away. His gentle persistence and his extensive knowledge of the history of genital mutilation and of the ancient traditions of her people finally convince Tashi to accept his love and support.

Tashi goes to the Olinkan village to confront M'Lissa, the woman who has killed her sister. She finds the old woman, now greatly revered by the Olinkan people, in bed. Tashi bathes her body and listens to her tell of her life and of her own suffering; Tashi actually learns to relate to her suffering and to realize that she can forgive even this woman whom she has hated and resented for so long. M'Lissa tells her that it is traditional for a well-appreciated *tsunga* to be murdered and then burned by someone whom she has circumcised. In placing a pillow over her face, Tashi is simply carrying out what the old woman expects of her.

The penultimate section of the novel is a letter signed "Tashi Evelyn Johnson, Reborn soon to be Deceased," to Lisette. In it, Tashi explains that she is now ready to face the firing squad and looks forward to being Lisette's friend in heaven. She explains that she has already come to be her friend through knowing her son.

In the last section, Tashi's spirit recalls the moment when she was shot and the fact that Adam, Olivia, Benny, Pierre, Raya, and Mbati were all holding a huge banner that said *RESISTANCE* IS THE SECRET OF JOY!

Analysis

Walker's novel is about love, forgiveness, and self-acceptance. Tashi experiences physical and emotional pain so intense that it is almost inconceivable, yet she resists self-destruction and finds inner peace.

Tashi explains in her letter to Lisette that even though he was more progressive than most preachers of color, Adam's sermons always focused on the suffering of Jesus and thus tended to exclude the suffering of others. She wanted her own suffering to be recognized and acknowledged. Ironically, it is Pierre, the son of Adam and Lisette, who has submerged himself into the mystery of her suffering and whose life is dedicated to destroying the suffering caused by torture. He has helped her to understand herself, her mother, M'Lissa, and all the women who have been crucified as well as those who are still cringing before the overpowering might and weapons of torturers. In having found this self-knowledge, she is able to recognize and acknowledge suffering and to accept death without anxiety.

Pierre also has been kind enough to befriend and patient enough to teach Benny, his retarded half brother. With his help, Benny will be able to survive in a cruel and indifferent world. He is also able to help Benny find a way to deal with what is happening to his mother on a level that he can understand in his own simple terms.

Both boys work with Adam in caring for the many AIDS patients who are crowded into one floor of the Olinkan prison where Tashi has been held throughout her trial. Working with these suffering men, women, and children who patiently wait for death with animal-like acceptance helps Adam to understand Tashi's suffering and his own. One young man thinks Adam is a priest and, as he dies a miserable and painful death, confesses to Adam that he has killed the monkeys whose kidneys were to be used to grow the cultures that had produced the vaccines that spread the AIDS virus. Adam learns from his suffering, the suffering of the girls whose infection was spread by the unclean knife when they were circumcised, and Tashi's suffering that there is no greater hell for humans to fear than the one on Earth. He accepts himself as a man of God and as a human man who has been a loving friend to Tashi. At last, he also realizes that he has always depended on his sister Olivia to be his feeling side and that he is now able to feel and to suffer as himself.

Context

In an interview with Pratibha Parmar, the coauthor of her book *Warrior Marks: Female Genital Mutilation and the Sexual Blinding of Women* (1993), Alice Walker makes it very clear that *Possessing the Secret of Joy* is a protest novel. She wants to enlighten women to ways in which women in all parts of the world are rather routinely mutilated and to the fact that pain that is done to women is often overlooked because women can accept pain. Walker uses as an example her own visual mutilation, which occurred when she was eight. She was blinded in one eye when her brother shot her, causing her pain, humiliation, and serious medical problems. Yet her parents always dismissed the incident and referred to it as "Alice's accident."

Alice Walker uses a portion of the proceeds from her novel to support projects designed to educate women about various types of mutilation, and she travels to all parts of the world to encourage women to take a political and moral stand against such practices.

In the novel, Pierre is a sensitive, well-informed, and dedicated feminist who possesses the secret of joy in making his life's work the resistance of such harmful practices. He studies the traditional patriarchal attitudes that have created the practices and have kept them alive, and even more important, he lovingly shares the lessons he learns with Tashi and intends to continue to share them with other women.

The novel also makes an important statement about the spread of AIDS and the suffering that AIDS brings to women and children as well as to men. The compassionate care that Adam, Pierre, Benny, and Olivia give to those who are dying from AIDS also encourages women to take a political and moral stand.

The bonding between women and the mutual support and encouragement that women provide for one another is clearly shown not only between Tashi and Olivia but also in the relationships that Raya, Mbati, and Lisette have with Tashi.

Lisette is a wonderful example of a strong and independent woman who values sexual pleasure even in childbirth and who follows the example of her grandmother in refusing to be intimidated by traditional social expectations. She educates her son by precept and example to be strong in his resistance against traditional masculine beliefs and practices that do not value and respect women and women's right to education, information, and independence.

Sources for Further Study

Barker-Benfield, G. J. *The Horrors of the Half-Known Life: Male Attitudes Toward Women and Sexuality in Nineteenth-Century America.* New York: Harper & Row, 1976. Explains the practice of female circumcision in the United States and the circumstances that allowed it to occur.

El Dareer, Asma. *Woman, Why Do You Weep?* London: Zed Press, 1982. The author is one of the women Alice Walker quotes frequently in *Warrior Marks*, and this work is recommended at the end of *Possessing the Secret of Joy.*

Kemp, Yakini. Review of *Warrior Marks*, by Alice Walker and Pratibha Parmar. *Belles Lettres* 8 (Fall, 1992): 57. This insightful review describes the novel as a poetic and powerful condemnation of the practice of female genital mutilation.

Lightfoot-Klein, Hanny. *Prisoners of Ritual: An Odyssey into Female Genital Circumcision in Africa.* New York: Haworth Press, 1989. This book explains that those who practice female genital circumcision are, generally speaking, kept ignorant of its real dangers, which include the breakdown of the spirit and the body as well as the spread of disease.

Walker, Alice. *In Search of Our Mothers' Gardens: Womanist Prose.* San Diego: Harcourt Brace Jovanovich, 1983.

———. *Living By the Word: Selected Writings, 1973-1987.* San Diego: Harcourt Brace Jovanovich, 1988. These essays enable the reader to get to know Alice Walker as a person, to learn more about her own visual mutilation, and to follow her interest in fighting all practices that undervalue women.

Walker, Alice, and Pratibha Parmar. *Warrior Marks: Female Genital Mutilation and the Sexual Blinding of Women.* New York: Harcourt Brace, 1993. Records the story of Walker and Parmar's collaboration in making a film about female genital mutilation and about women they interviewed in Africa who have been circumcised, who have had their daughters circumcised, and who actually perform the circumcisions. Contains many photographs and an excellent bibliography.

Constance M. Fulmer

1866

POSSESSION
A Romance

Author: A[ntonia] S[usan] Byatt (1936-   )
Type of work: Novel
Type of plot: Romance
Time of plot: The 1980's, alternating with the 1870's and 1880's
Locale: London, Lincolnshire, and North Yorkshire, England, and the Breton coast in France
First published: 1990

Principal characters:
RANDOLPH HENRY ASH, a famous Victorian poet
CHRISTABEL LAMOTTE, a single Victorian woman
ELLEN ASH, Randolph's wife
BLANCHE GLOVER, Christabel's companion
ROLAND MITCHELL, the protagonist, a research assistant who discovers correspondence between Ash and LaMotte
MAUD BAILEY, a university lecturer and a direct descendant of Christabel LaMotte
JAMES BLACKADDER, the scholar who employs Roland
BEATRICE NEST, a diligent researcher who preserves the story of Ellen
LEONORA STERN, an American scholar
MORTIMER CROPPER, an American who wants relics for his museum

Form and Content

Possession: A Romance opens with an epitaph from "The Garden of Proserpina" by the Victorian poet Randolph Henry Ash which describes how Hercules will "Come to his dispossession and the theft." Proserpina is the Greek queen of death, so the hero is stealing life from death when he "dispossesses" her garden of its golden apples. So too will Ash's contemporary double, Roland Mitchell, find a "golden apple" in the London Library and "dispossess" that institution of two rough drafts of a love letter written by Ash a century earlier.

This pattern of character doubles, the relationships between literature and actions, and the meanings of "possession" continue to form and inform the novel. By claiming possession of these "living words," Roland has initiated a romantic quest that will unite contemporary actions with words from the Victorian lovers, Ash and Christabel LaMotte. This heritage of love transforms the future as it is relived by Roland and Maud Bailey, Christabel's contemporary double.

Roland and Maud follow a paper trail of letters, poetry, diaries, tales, and journals to discover the secret meetings and subsequent parting of the Victorians. Their journey takes them to Christabel's last home in Lincolnshire, now held by Sir George and Lady Joan Bailey; near the North Sea to Whitby, where the lovers spend a month; and to Breton in France, where her cousin Sabine's journal records the birth and subsequent disappearance of Christabel's child.

As Roland and Maud begin their romantic quest, other characters will turn it into a race, a chase, and a detective story, all forms of the romance. Most will find more than they bargained for as the quest for knowledge is revealed to be a quest for love. They will learn more about themselves and about one another in the process of learning about love.

Women particularly need to be opened to love, the novel reveals, because their stories often remain hidden in a patriarchal society. For example, Christabel's passion creates a hybrid art, captured in the symbol of Melusina, half woman and half monster. In her life, it results from suffering, isolation, and the suicide of her friend Blanche Glover. Christabel herself will end her days as a "witch" in the family attic, while her attempts at direct communication will be buried with another woman's secrets.

Each character learns from the others. James Blackadder will join the race to save the relics of Ash for his "Ash Factory," while Leonora Stern sternly demands the feminist appreciation of Christabel's art. When the two begin to appreciate each other, their English and American, male and female differences can be embraced in the marriage of their ideas. Beatrice Nest joins the quest to protect the secrets of Ellen Ash, whose journals record her hidden story in cryptic riddles. Beatrice, too, will learn that when books are shared and graves are opened to the air, only the dead past crumbles away.

Only Mortimer Cropper remains opposed to the living past, as his deathly name suggests. Wanting only to possess relics to bury in his museum, Cropper enlists the aid of Ash's descendant Hildebrand Ash in his attempt to claim legal possession. After surviving a gothic night of storms and grave-robbing, the questers find themselves together in the Rowan Tree Inn. Cropper opens the relics, within which the others find the end of one love story and the beginning of their own, their living heritage. Yet even they do not know the whole story, for the past keeps some secrets, and Byatt suggests that the marriage of true minds might sometimes survive body and soul.

Analysis

By alternating the story of the past with the actions of the future, A. S. Byatt reminds the reader that literature preserves that part of the living past that can be communicated, whereas history can record only the known actions of dead bodies. Even actual genetic heritage may remain unrecorded in a patriarchy, in which a man knows he is a father because a woman tells him so. At the same time, the idea or romance captured in literature lives on cyclically, however dead the people imagining or experiencing it may be. The literary present can inspire present actions, a contemporary expression of the ongoing human story, as the stories of Ash and Christabel inspire those researchers whose quests open them to new ideas.

Encouraging her reader to let go of things, Byatt resurrects the hope that can help balance fear, the romance or idea that can be made real once again in one's own time and place, enabling one to enjoy Proserpina's garden of life married to death. From the past, Byatt recalls the passion that creates both art and life itself. This unique document novel lets its reader recapture the Victorian period in representative poetry and composite characters that resemble known literary figures of the time. The more clues one recognizes, the more the novel can offer one. So too does an earlier literature emerge in the allusions to myths and symbols of Celtic goddess lore that Byatt borrows from Robert Graves's *The White Goddess*.

Yet literature is not the only language that Byatt re-creates. Ash tells his story of love in his *Ask to Embla* poems, the title of which easily translates to refer to the *ash* and *ember* of his and Christabel's passion. It also suggests, however, that one should *ask* the *emblems* of the text for clues. Pictorial emblems explained in the text are common in English literature. Each of Byatt's twenty-eight chapters and the postscript begin with an emblem of two woodcut flowers, with a single smaller woodcut flower indicating breaks within chapters. Marching in twos above the chapter headings, however fragmented the lone flowers may reveal the chapters to be within themselves, the emblems promise a series of pairings and sharings, correspondences and marriages.

The many languages of nature also speak forth in the novel. Graves writes of the runic alphabet and the language of trees in his study, and Byatt offers some examples in her names: from Ash himself to the Rowan Tree Inn. The language of flowers is mentioned more than once as well. Retracing the steps of the Victorian lovers, Maud and Roland visit a jewelry store run by an old woman who shows them brooches carved in this language: "clematis and gorse and heartsease—which is to say Mental Beauty and Enduring Affection and 'I am always thinking of you.' You should buy *that* for the young lady. Better than old hair."

While they visit the location of the past lovers' tryst, the potential lovers of now are reminded that the most enduring aspect of love is in memories, the love of the spirit. Furthermore, the natural image of flowers, a recurring metaphor for love, is to be preferred to the dead relic of the loved one's hair. Love is not an object that deteriorates and decays. Why possess things from the past when nature and art offer recurrent life and living passion?

Physical love and beauty remain in their brief moment, while their memory endures to transform the future. Thus, Christabel will write in her final letter to Ash that she no longer regrets losing their moments of passion as much as she misses their shared writings and their "trusting *minds* which recognized each other."

The emblem further reminds the reader that the flowering of nature is always new, always recurring, unique to each flower yet common to the natural world—a promise that such is equally true of human nature. When Ash realizes his love for Christabel, he finds words for everyone, and she observes that he is in love with the world. In the particular love, then, universal love may be discovered.

Context

The winner of England's coveted Booker Prize, *Possession* is the best known of Byatt's novels. Her empathy for the hidden, cryptic, and silenced stories of women fills it with insights into private lives and understanding of the wordless stories of nature. Christabel has been compared to Emily Dickinson and also resembles Christina Rossetti, not only in her sisterly attachment to Blanche Glover, which recalls "Goblin Market," but also to the suggestive love poems of that other "spinster" poet.

In *Possession*, as in life, most women accept the comfort of small houses or the protective silences within a patriarchal marriage in order to avoid exposure. The unmarried woman is vulnerable; to feel safe, even the contemporary professor Maud Bailey must hide her beautiful hair and surround herself with icy perfection.

Even sisters are not always supportive; after love draws Christabel out into the open, Blanche considers herself "superfluous" and commits suicide. Later, Christabel will put herself into Ellen Ash's hands to reach out to a dying Ash, but Ellen decides to take that truth to her grave.

Gothic elements explore demonic possession when women are tempted to betray social definitions or rational desires. In Ash's poem "Mummy Possess't," he takes on a female voice to explain that "we Women have no Power/ in the cold world of objects Reason rules" and presents spiritualism as the way women can gain knowledge, a threshold to a "negative world" of the "Unseen/ Unheard, Impalpable, and Uncon-fined." Only in such a world do women find the power to possess, briefly, the objects of their love. Christabel compares herself to a worm kept in a jar to be studied; it too is "Possessed of a Restless Demon—or hatred of Jar-panopticons," much as her own passion will not remain confined in the safe imprisonment of a small house or the social roles allowed women.

Even in the supposed immortality of art, Christabel receives little attention until she is rediscovered by Byatt's contemporary feminists. The balance Ash could achieve did not come easily to Christabel, as he himself suggests when she will not respond to his letters and he guesses that it might be "out of sudden hatred, at the injustice of the different fates of men and women."

Despite these depressing realities, *Possession* remains a comedy, precisely because of its allegiance to the cyclical story of nature, the story of continuous rebirth and the possibilities of love even from the ashes and embers of a seemingly dead past. Women's literature has often been written from the communal perspective of this neglected and devalued mode, reminding one that the whole of life is greater than any fragmentation of its rich diversity and that therefore love can still outweigh fear.

Sources for Further Study

Bradbury, Malcolm, and David Palmer, eds. *The Contemporary English Novel.* New York: Holmes & Meier, 1980. The preface addresses Byatt's importance among her contemporaries.

Campbell, Jane. "The Hunger of the Imagination in A. S. Byatt's *The Game.*" *Critique* 29, no. 3 (Spring, 1988): 147-162. Although the article discusses an earlier novel,

it addresses Byatt's emblematic style and concern with failures in communication.
_____ . "'The Somehow May be Thishow': Fact, Fiction, and Intertextuality in Antonia Byatt's 'Precipice-Encurled.'" *Studies in Short Fiction* 28, no. 2 (Spring, 1991): 115-123. Discusses connections between this short story in *Sugar* and *Possession* in their use of Victorian poetry, a mix of fact and fiction, and thematic relationships of art and life.

Cosslett, Tess. "Childbirth from the Woman's Point of View in British Women's Fiction: Enid Bagnold's *The Squire* and A. S. Byatt's *Still Life*." *Tulsa Studies in Women's Literature* 8 (Fall, 1989): 263-286. Discussion of motherhood as metaphor in women's fiction suggests similarities to Christabel's experience in *Possession*.

Giobbi, Giuliana. "Sisters Beware of Sisters: Sisterhood as a Literary Motif in Jane Austen, A. S. Byatt, and I. Bossi Fedrigotti." *Journal of European Studies* 22 (September, 1992): 241-258. Provides a larger context for the sisterhood motif in *Possession*.

Jenkyns, Richard. "Disinterring Buried Lives." *The Times Literary Supplement*, March 2, 1990, 213-214. This unusually detailed review praises the many styles and voices in *Possession* and compares it with Alison Lurie's *The Truth About Lorin Jones*.

Karlin, Danny. "Prolonging Her Absence." *London Review of Books* 12 (March 8, 1990): 17-18. This review tries to identify the Victorian models for the poetry in *Possession*.

Miles, Rosalind. *The Female Form: Women Writers and the Conquest of the Novel*. London: Routledge & Kegan Paul, 1987. In her discussion of "Lady Novelists and Honorary Men," Miles traces the degeneration of romance and refers to Byatt's description in *Degrees of Freedom* (1965) of modern romances as providing consolation. An important formal context for the history of the romance by women writers.

Showalter, Elaine. *A Literature of Their Own: British Women Novelists from Brontë to Lessing*. Princeton, N.J.: Princeton University Press, 1977. Showalter associates Byatt with other women novelists, including Charlotte Brontë, Iris Murdoch, and Byatt's sister Margaret Drabble, who share a concern with the ethical considerations of writing novels.

Thelma J. Shinn

PRAISESONG FOR THE WIDOW

Author: Paule Marshall (1929-   )
Type of work: Novel
Type of plot: Psychological realism
Time of plot: 1976
Locale: The Caribbean islands of Grenada and Carriacou, Tatem Island (off the South Carolina coast), and Brooklyn
First published: 1983

Principal characters:
AVATARA (AVEY) JOHNSON, a sixty-four-year-old widow who has lost touch with her African cultural roots
GREAT-AUNT CUNEY, an old woman who rejects institutions that enslave black people with empty standards of behavior and expression
LEBERT JOSEPH, the proprietor of a rum shop in Grenada
MARION JOHNSON, Avey's youngest daughter

Form and Content
    When Avey was a girl, her Aunt Cuney called her to pass the cultural heritage from one generation to the next. Aunt Cuney would take Avey to the Landing and tell the story about the arrival of a shipload of Ibo slaves. At first, Avey answered her calling and told her brothers, but once her trips to Tatem Island stopped and after her adult attention shifted to achieving the American Dream, Avey sublimated what she had learned. The breach between Avey and her cultural heritage widened, and Avey stopped identifying with the struggles and concerns of other African Americans. She, along with her husband Jay, focused attention on material possessions and social status. Avey wrapped herself in her mink stole, attended social functions with her husband, and after his fatal stroke took Caribbean cruises with her friends. Voyages on a luxury liner and then on a flimsy schooner finally take Avey on a difficult yet successful journey back to her cultural origins.
    During one voyage, aboard the *Bianca Pride*, Avey begins having troubling dreams about Aunt Cuney, and she remembers the early years of her marriage when she and her husband, though poor, were happy. She cannot recognize her image in mirrors, and the rich foods that are served, especially a peach parfait à la Versailles, are nauseating. Avey tries to regain her composure by seeking solitude. Despite her efforts, she cannot escape the crass materialism of the shipboard environment, which becomes overwhelmingly repulsive. She is horrified and outraged by one symbol of American society, a skeletal old man wearing red and white striped trunks and a blue visor who tugs at her skirt and invites her to have a seat beside him. Neither her friends' protests nor the loss of the $1,500 fare for the cruise are enough to dissuade Avey from her decision to leave the ship and return to New York.

Avey thinks that she will be able to return to the comfort and familiarity of life in North White Plains. Her return is delayed because she arrives in Grenada too late to catch a plane that leaves once a day for New York City. While determining where she will spend the night, Avey notices a crowd of people along a wharf waiting for boats to take them to a place about which she knows nothing. Avey does not want to be among these strangers, who speak a patois she cannot understand. Although Avey feels out of place, a man mistakes her for a woman named Ida. She is like these people even though she does not recognize her relationship to them. The people are Carriacou out-islanders who are participating in the annual Carriacou Excursion. This tradition foreshadows Avey's communal and personal journey back to her cultural origins.

Avey spends a restless night in a hotel dreaming about her husband's preoccupation with working long hours to make enough money to provide for his family and her suspicions that he was having affairs with the white women who worked with him. The next day, Avey awakes feeling as though her mind has become a tabula rasa. After showering, she puts on a wrinkled dress, half combs her hair, does not wear makeup, and leaves her watch in the bathroom. Gradually, Avey is shedding her concern about possessions and outward appearances.

Avey leaves the hotel and walks aimlessly until she enters a seedy but pleasant rum shop, where she meets the shop's ancient proprietor, Lebert Joseph. Initially, he is uncomfortable with Avey's strangeness; however, after some faltering attempts at communication, his attitude softens, and Lebert shares his family history with Avey. He tells her that people participate in the excursion because they need to relax, celebrate, and, most important, give remembrance to the "Long-time People." Avey tries to leave, but she is tired from her long walk and her troubling dreams. She begins to tell Lebert about her recent experiences, but she cannot tell him everything. The pain is too recent. Somehow, Lebert understands her unspoken words, and he invites Avey to accompany him to Carriacou that day.

The boat ride makes Avey ill. The vessel is not sturdy; people are packed on board, and the motion of the sea makes Avey lean with her head over the railing so that she can disgorge whatever is making her nauseated. Old women soothe Avey. At Carriacou, other women bathe and feed Avey until she senses physical renewal. When she witnesses the dancing, the songs, and the rituals of the Big Drum and the Beg Pardon, Avey remembers her cultural past. She recognizes the lamentations of the sorrow songs whose "source had to be the heart, the bruised still-bleeding innermost chamber of the collective heart."

Avey returns to America, but not to New York. She goes back to Tatem Island. She has been called to remember her past that had been lost in a quest for material possessions and social status. After her trip to Carriacou, Avey determines that "at least twice a week . . . she would lead them, grandchildren and visitors alike, in a troop over to the Landing," and she would tell them about the Ibos who came in slave ships.

Analysis
Avatara is the name Avey's Aunt Cuney chose for her. Avatara has been called to

pass along the culture from one generation to the next by Cuney, who has performed that role. Cuney appears in Avatara's dreams to call her back to a remembrance of her ancestors. Marshall writes the story of Avatara's movement away from and back to her cultural roots by using several techniques. She divides the novel into four parts to describe the stages of Avatara's journey, and she uses images and symbols that are peculiar to the feminine creative experience. While Avatara progresses from one stage to the next, Marshall recounts Avatara's dreams, which are often detailed memories of past experiences that may have been either personal or communal. These memories have relevance to the present when Avatara notices the resemblances between the ceremonial rituals she witnessed as a child and those she observes at Carriacou. Marshall's references to literary selections written by black writers from the United States are apt expressions of black experiences that occurred on slave ships in the Caribbean and in the collective consciousness of black people regardless of their geographical location.

In the first section, "Runagate," Avatara is escaping her bondage to the materialism represented by the luxury liner, the *Bianca Pride* (*bianca* is Italian for "white"). She has been dreaming of her trips to the Landing with Cuney. There was a serious ceremonial air about the journeys past the woods, the church, and the homes that held the histories of black people in America, and Cuney would take Avatara to the place where the stories begins. Cuney wore two belts, as the other old women did when they went out. One belt cinched the waist of their skirts, and the other belt was "strapped low around the hips like the belt for a sword or a gun holster." People believed that this belt gave the women strength.

"Sleeper's Awake" and "Lave Tete" are the second and third sections of the novel. The Ibos knew that black people would suffer in America, so they returned to Africa. For thirty years, Avatara has avoided thinking about the connections between her life and those of black people who suffered during civil rights demonstrations or those of women who endured abusive marital relationships. Avatara's acceptance of middle-class American life has separated her from her people, and that separation has manifested itself in psychological discomfiture and physical illness. She must awaken from an anesthetized existence, but before she can be reborn, Avatara's body, soul, and mind must be cleansed.

The voyage to Carriacou upsets Avatara, and she begins vomiting. More than a reaction to the schooner's movements, Avatara is suffering from the pains of her new self's birth. Avatara's body is racked with waves of nausea. "She might have fallen overboard were it not for the old women. They tried cushioning her as much as possible from the repeated shocks of the turbulence." After a while, Avatara is left alone in the schooner's small deckhouse, where she is reminded of the accommodations slaves had during the Middle Passage. Her suffering pales by comparison.

The setting in this novel is dominated by an image of water that functions in several ways. Water is the vehicle for Avatara's journey aboard the cruise ship and later on the schooner that takes her to Carriacou. Water and boat transportation are central to the experiences of black people. Ibos came to America on a slave ship. Out-islanders traveled to Carriacou on boats. Blacks in New York took an annual excursion up the Hudson River. Water is also the symbol of spiritual renewal. The Ibos walked the water to return to their homeland, and Avatara's experience on the schooner is the sign that a new life is coming into the world.

The fourth section of the novel, "The Beg Pardon," brings Avatara to an understanding of how the past and the present relate to each other. Just as she remembered going on the excursion up the Hudson River when she was a girl, Avatara recognizes furniture and table settings that remind her of ceremonial rituals that defined her past. The Carriacou Tramp reminded her of the Ring Shout that took place in the black church on Tatem Island. Furnishings, food, physical movement, and the act of remembering form a link between past and present that completes Avatara's sense of self and brings her into a community that is complex in its relationships between past and present and different geographical locations but simple in the symbol of a circle that encompasses all.

Marshall's story is about the creative process of birth, renewal, and remembrance. Black women are singularly significant in this process because they fulfill the role of passing the cultural heritage from one generation to another. Although men such as Lebert Joseph influence this process, the strength to perform this task is generated in a community of women. Even though Lebert invites Avatara on the excursion, when she begins to suffer agonizing and massive contractions, he can only wait anxiously by the door while the old women make her comfortable. Marshall's emphasis on Avatara's calling and on the help she gets from black women points to the importance of black women to the black cultural heritage.

Context

The feminist movement of the 1970's and its demands for social equality increased an awareness of and interest in novels written by women. Coming after the civil rights and black power movements, this increased feminism led to the publication of novels that focused on the experiences of African American women. In the 1980's, several novels written by black women demonstrated that islands of black feminine existence were not separate from an understanding of the communal African American experience. Female-centered novels such as Alice Walker's *The Color Purple* (1982), Gloria Naylor's *The Women of Brewster Place* (1982), and Toni Morrison's *Beloved* (1987) underscore the significance of women to the black community. These novels also show that there is a community of women who understand one another, who protect one another, and who, like Avey, assume the responsibility of teaching black children about their cultural heritage. These authors are models for other African American women, such as Bebe Moore Campbell (*Your Blues Ain't Like Mine*, 1992), Thulani Davis (*1959*, 1992), and Rita Dove (*Through the Ivory Gate*, 1992).

Sources for Further Study

Christian, Barbara T. "Ritualistic Process and the Structure of Paule Marshall's *Praisesong for the Widow.*" *Callaloo* 6 (Spring/Summer, 1983): 74-84. The article focuses on the rituals of naming and "tribal" ceremonies that recall Avey Johnson to reaffirm the essential connection between the individual and the community.

Pettis, Joyce. "Self Definition and Redefinition in Paule Marshall's *Praisesong for the Widow*." In *Perspectives of Black Popular Culture*, edited by Harry B. Shaw. Bowling Green, Ohio: Bowling Green State University Popular Press, 1990. Through a literal and a metaphorical journey, Avey Johnson becomes a "new woman" in the canon of African American literature, who rejects materialistic values and replaces them with a renewed sense of her connection to her African past.

Scarpa, Giulia. " 'Couldn't They Have Done Differently?' Caught in the Web of Race, Gender, and Class: Paule Marshall's *Praisesong for the Widow*." *World Literature Written in English* 29 (Fall, 1989): 94-104. Points out that reminiscences allow Avey Johnson to revive a past that had been overshadowed by cultural and personal sacrifices she had made while imitating the living standards of a homogenized American society.

Waxman, Barbara Frey. "The Widow's Journey to Self and Roots: Aging and Society in Paule Marshall's *Praisesong for the Widow*." *Frontiers* 9, no. 3 (1987): 94-99. A "young-old" widow completes a self-purification ritual through which she integrates body and soul and identifies with her ethnic heritage.

Wilentz, Gay. "Towards a Spiritual Middle Passage Back: Paule Marshall's Diasporic Vision in *Praisesong for the Widow*." *Obsidian II* 5, no. 3 (Winter, 1990): 1-21. A varied treatment of the effect of females, particularly female ancestors, who motivate Avey Johnson to reconcile her African and American selves and assume the woman's role of passing on stories and cultural traditions to her daughter and a wide community of African American children.

Judith E. B. Harmon

PRIDE AND PREJUDICE

Author: Jane Austen (1775-1817)
Type of work: Novel
Type of plot: Domestic realism
Time of plot: The early nineteenth century
Locale: Hertfordshire, Derbyshire, Kent, and London, England
First published: 1813

Principal characters:
ELIZABETH BENNET, the protagonist
FITZWILLIAM DARCY, an aristocrat and one of the most eligible
men in English society
MR. BENNET, Elizabeth's father
MRS. BENNET, his wife, who embarrasses the more intelligent
members of her family
JANE BENNET, Elizabeth's older sister
CHARLES BINGLEY, Darcy's friend
CHARLOTTE LUCAS, Elizabeth's best friend
WILLIAM COLLINS, a clergyman who marries Charlotte Lucas
GEORGE WICKHAM, a military officer who runs away with
Elizabeth's youngest sister, Lydia

Form and Content

Pride and Prejudice is a novel about marriage. The author's purpose is to make it possible for her two most interesting characters, Elizabeth Bennet and Fitzwilliam Darcy, to be united. In order to accomplish the author's purpose, they must overcome both external obstacles and the personal flaws suggested in the title of the book. Although he is attracted to Elizabeth, the proud aristocrat Darcy is prejudiced against her family because of their social inferiority, which is evident to him in the folly of Mrs. Bennet and her younger daughters, as well as in the fact that the family has a kinsman in trade. Elizabeth's own pride is injured when she overhears Darcy's slighting comment about her; her resulting prejudice is confirmed by George Wickham's lies and by her own discovery that Darcy had advised Charles Bingley not to proceed with his courtship of Jane Bennet. If the lovers are finally to come together, not only must Wickham be exposed and Jane be reunited with Bingley, but also both Elizabeth and Darcy must become wiser, so that in the future their judgments will be based not on pride or on prejudice, but on reason.

In form, it has been noted, *Pride and Prejudice* is highly dramatic. Each character is introduced with a short summary much like those found in playscripts. The story proceeds through dialogue, with Austen herself functioning as an onstage commentator, summing up what has happened since the last scene or adding stage directions; for example, exits, entrances, or displays of grief or anger. *Pride and Prejudice* even falls into five segments, or acts, as do the witty comedies of manners by William Congreve, Oliver Goldsmith, and Richard Brinsley Sheridan on which it is probably modeled.

The first dozen or so chapters of the work, like the first act of a play, are devoted to exposition. The Bennets are introduced; it is established that the five girls of the family, as well as their friend Charlotte Lucas, need husbands; and two eligible single men, Darcy and Bingley, appear on the scene.

In the second segment of the novel, two more unmarried men, William Collins and George Wickham, enter the lives of the Bennets. Wickham tells Elizabeth that Darcy has behaved villainously toward him. Collins, who would have married either of the two older Bennet girls, finds himself a wife in the person of Charlotte Lucas.

In the third act, while visiting Charlotte at her new home, Elizabeth once again encounters Darcy, whose aunt is Collins' patron. To Elizabeth's surprise, Darcy proposes; after she has haughtily turned him down, Elizabeth discovers that she has wronged her suitor and admits to herself that she does indeed love him.

The proof of Darcy's character comes in the final two sections of the novel. When Lydia Bennet elopes with Wickham, Darcy chooses to help the Bennet family avoid disgrace. He finds the couple and forces Wickham to marry Lydia. In the process, he befriend's Elizabeth's tradesman uncle and revises his assumption that merit can be found only in the landed gentry. Like all traditional comedies, the novel ends with appropriate marriages. Jane weds Bingley, and Elizabeth is at last united with Darcy.

Analysis

It has often been pointed out that Jane Austen's novels deal only with the world of which she had firsthand knowledge. They are set in the ballrooms, the drawing rooms, the bedrooms, and the gardens where, like the ladies in her books, she spent her life. Her books do not reflect the political turmoil of her time, revolution and conquest on the Continent, fears of revolution in Great Britain. If her works are limited in scope, however, they are not without serious import. Austen's methods are those of the satirist, her subject is society, and her preoccupation is the creation of an effective family unit through marriage.

As Austen shows so clearly in *Pride and Prejudice*, unsuitable marriages lead only to unhappiness and social instability. After discovering that his wife is incapable of comprehending anything he says, Mr. Bennet has stopped trying to communicate with her. A man of his reserved and scholarly nature can adjust easily to isolation from his family, and Mrs. Bennet is too scatterbrained to suspect that something may be missing from her relationship with her husband. It is the Bennet children who suffer most from the ill-conceived marriage of their parents. Left to their mother, three of the five Bennet daughters turn out badly. Mary Bennet is a pedant without intellectual gifts; Kitty Bennet, a flirtatious fool; and Lydia, a girl so unthinking that she runs off with the first plausible man who comes along, thereby disgracing her family and destroying the possibility of any other marriage or even, if she remains unmarried, her acceptance in respectable society. As Mr. Bennet admits, Lydia's actions are in part the consequence of his paternal neglect, but that in turn is the result of his marrying unwisely, without regard for his future wife's suitability in temperament, character, and intelligence.

Austen supports her argument that a bad marriage is worse than no marriage at all with two additional examples. Collins marries Charlotte only because, as a clergyman, he needs a respectable wife; she marries him because, at twenty-seven, she is becoming desperate. The result is not surprising. When Elizabeth goes to visit the newlyweds, she finds that Charlotte has developed a daily routine that places her as far away from her husband as possible. If Charlotte's situation proves how miserable a marriage of convenience can be, what happens to Lydia and Wickham shows the folly of allowing mere sexual attraction to govern one's decision about a partner for life. Forced to marry Lydia, Wickham soon tires of her, and before long her affection for him has also died. Moreover, since neither of them is capable of planning for the future, Lydia and Wickham live unsettled lives, frequently moving, constantly plagued by financial difficulties, surviving only through the aid of their prosperous relatives.

Thus, the author shows the unhappy consequences of unwise marriages. Nevertheless, what Austen sees as essential for a happy union is not equality of either fortune or caste. Although they live comfortably, the Bennets do not have the wealth that both Bingley and Darcy possess, and while Mr. Bennet is a member of the gentry, he ranks well below the aristocracy. Jane and Bingley are both easy-going and tolerant people, however, while Elizabeth and Darcy share the same incisive intelligence and strength of will. What Austen seems to be saying is surprisingly modern: that the best basis for marriage is a love based on mutual respect and shown in an easy, comfortable companionship.

Context

Jane Austen's heroines have long been admired. Like Elizabeth, they are all intelligent, independent, and strong-willed. Nevertheless, all of them have flaws. The imaginative young Catherine Morland of *Northanger Abbey* (1817) tries to make a Gothic novel out of ordinary life, while in *Emma* (1815), the forceful title character, Emma Woodhouse, is so determined to do good that she ignores the wishes of others, with unfortunate results. The deficiencies of Austen's heroines, however, are defects not of character, but of judgment. When, in the course of the novels, they come to know themselves better and to see others more clearly, their inherent virtues are strengthened by wisdom.

With the growth of feminist criticism, however, have come new questions about Austen's intentions, especially where her heroines are concerned. While there is still general agreement that Elizabeth Bennet is the most admirable, as well as the most appealing, of her female characters, some critics argue that Elizabeth's marriage to Darcy represents a sacrifice of her selfhood. Even in a patriarchal society such as Austen's, a girl whose father is as passive as Mr. Bennet can rule her own life unless, like Lydia, she blatantly defies society. Darcy, however, is quite a different kind of person from Mr. Bennet. It is questioned whether Elizabeth can maintain her independence as the wife of a man who is her equal in will and intellect and her superior in rank and wealth, especially since she will be moving in his social circle. Since Austen wrote no sequel to *Pride and Prejudice* which could settle the issue, however, most critics continue to believe that the novel ends happily. They see Elizabeth as a woman who will assert herself, no matter what her situation, and Darcy as a man who would never attempt to destroy the very qualities in Elizabeth that initially elicited his admiration. Perhaps the significance of these questions is not merely that they emphasize how repressive Jane Austen's environment actually was, but also that they underline her amazing achievement. In a society dominated by males, she managed to bring to life a number of strong-willed female characters and to produce some of the finest literary works of her era.

Sources for Further Study

Gillie, Christopher. *A Preface to Jane Austen*. London: Longman, 1974. An invaluable guide that includes useful background material and brief discussions of Austen's novels. A reference section contains notes on people and places of importance, maps, and explanations of numerous words used in the works. Amply illustrated. Annotated bibliography.

Halperin, John, ed. *Jane Austen: Bicentenary Essays*. New York: Cambridge University Press, 1975. A collection of essays on various aspects of Austen's work. An excellent chapter by Robert B. Heilman explains how the title *Pride and Prejudice* defines the theme and the structure of the novel. In another essay, Karl Kroeber suggests some reasons for the work's lasting popularity.

—————————. *The Life of Jane Austen*. Baltimore: The Johns Hopkins University Press, 1984. A thorough and highly readable critical biography, written with the stated purpose of making Jane Austen "come alive." Argues that neither Elizabeth Bennet nor any other character in the novels should be taken as representing so complex a person as Austen. Has perhaps the best summary available of the theories about the genesis of *Pride and Prejudice*. The book also includes a family tree, copious notes, and numerous illustrations.

Howe, Florence, ed. *Tradition and the Talents of Women*. Urbana: University of Illinois Press, 1991. Feminist criticism of various writers. An essay by Jen Ferguson Carr notes that although both Mrs. Bennet and Elizabeth are excluded from power in a male-dominated society, only the daughter is intelligent enough to use language to "dissociate herself from her devalued position."

Kirkham, Margaret. *Jane Austen, Feminism, and Fiction*. Brighton, Sussex, England: Harvester Press, 1983. Although Elizabeth Bennet is the most appealing of Austen's heroines, the novelist herself had misgivings about *Pride and Prejudice*, probably because its light-hearted ending depends upon Elizabeth's losing her integrity. Concludes with a helpful summary of the critical tradition.

McMaster, Juliet, ed. *Jane Austen's Achievement*. New York: Barnes & Noble, 1976. A collection of six papers delivered at the Jane Austen Bicentennial Conference at the University of Alberta. Lloyd W. Brown's chapter "The Business of Marrying and Mothering" and A. Walton Litz's "'A Development of Self': Character and Personality in Jane Austen's Fiction" both deal with *Pride and Prejudice*.

Moler, Kenneth L. *Pride and Prejudice: A Study in Artistic Economy*. Boston: Twayne, 1989. Places the novel in its historical and critical context and then proceeds to comment on theme, symbolism, style, and literary allusions. Includes also a chronology and an annotated bibliography. Well-organized and lucid.

Smith, LeRoy W. *Jane Austen and the Drama of Woman*. New York: St. Martin's Press, 1983. In *Pride and Prejudice*, Austen shows the ideal marriage as depending upon overcoming the institution's "threat to selfhood." Unlike most women of her period, Elizabeth Bennet insists both on choosing her own husband and on retaining her intellectual and emotional independence.

Sulloway, Alison G. *Jane Austen and the Province of Womanhood*. Philadelphia: University of Pennsylvania Press, 1989. Pointing out that in nineteenth century society men had "rights" and women had "duties," this author examines the various areas in which women function in Austen's novels, including the "Ballroom," the "Drawing Room," and the "Garden." Sulloway's approach is original and perceptive.

Yaeger, Patricia, and Beth Kowaleski-Wallace, eds. *Refiguring the Father: New Feminist Readings of Patriarchy*. Carbondale: Southern Illinois University Press, 1989. A collection of essays on various writers. In "The Humiliation of Elizabeth Bennet," Susan Fraiman argues that when Elizabeth Bennet marries Darcy, she is exchanging a passive, permissive father for a father figure who, as a strong-willed male of lofty social status, may give her ease but will certainly take away her independence.

Rosemary M. Canfield Reisman

THE PRIME OF LIFE

Author: Simone de Beauvoir (1908-1986)
Type of work: Autobiography
Time of work: 1929-1944
Locale: France, Spain, Italy, and Greece
First published: La Force de l'âge, 1960 (English translation, 1962)

> *Principal personages:*
> SIMONE DE BEAUVOIR, a writer, philosopher, and feminist
> JEAN-PAUL SARTRE, a writer, philosopher, and Beauvoir's
> lifelong companion
> OLGA KOSAKIEVICZ, a student and a close friend to Beauvoir and
> Sartre
> PAUL NIZAN, a philosopher and friend to Beauvoir and Sartre
> JACQUES-LAURENT BOST, a journalist and Beauvoir's close friend
> MICHEL LEIRIS, RAYMOND QUENEAU, and ALBERT CAMUS,
> writers and friends to Beauvoir and Sartre

Form and Content

Beyond Simone de Beauvoir's now-classic study of the subordinate role that women have played throughout history, *Le Deuxième sexe* (1949; *The Second Sex,* 1952), her self-exploratory series of autobiographies may well constitute her most lasting achievement. The initial volume, *Memoires d'une jeune fille rangée* (1958; *Memoirs of a Dutiful Daughter,* 1959), describes her first twenty-one years and focuses on her steady but painful movement away from her parents' rigid, petit bourgeois values. The second installment, *The Prime of Life,* spans the fullness of her years, from the summer of 1929 to the liberation of Paris in August, 1944. It begins on a note of relief at her emancipation from her family and closes on an even higher note of joy at France's deliverance from the Germans. Beauvoir's subsequent memoirs include *La Force des choses* (1963; *The Force of Circumstance,* 1965), *Une mort très douce* (1964; *A Very Easy Death,* 1966), and *Tout compte fait* (1972; *All Said and Done,* 1974). Her book on Jean-Paul Sartre's declining years, *La Cérémonie des adieux* (1981; *Adieux: A Farewell to Sartre,* 1984), is also deeply self-revealing.

In July, 1929, Beauvoir was a philosophy student at France's most distinguished university, the École Normale Supérieure. Studying for her comprehensive orals, she was invited to join a small circle of male fellow-students who were also preparing for them; one of them was the intellectually dazzling Sartre. By the fall, they had begun a friendship and companionship that was to become a lifelong union. They agreed that, while theirs was an "essential" love, it should not be allowed to degenerate into constraint or mere habit; nor should their partnership prevent them from experiencing "contingent" liaisons with others. Moreover, they promised neither to lie to each other nor to conceal anything from each other. They considered theirs an enduring alliance "of the mind, the imagination and the senses." After all, they shared a passionate commitment to thinking, to writing, to individual freedom, to words, words, words. "One single aim fired us," states Beauvoir, "the urge to embrace all experience, and to bear witness concerning it."

Sartre and Beauvoir initially decided on a "two-year lease" for their relationship, then renewed it for their lives. Since they intended to pursue their respective careers and anticipated long periods of separation, and since neither desired children, they saw no need to marry. By the spring of 1934, however, when Sartre was offered a position at a lycée in Le Havre and Beauvoir a similar posting in Marseilles, at the opposite end of France, he did offer to marry her so that they could both teach in the same preparatory school. She declined his proposal, to safeguard their independence. By 1936, both she and Sartre were teaching in Paris. They became the reigning couple of a group they termed "the Family." The unchanging core of this unit consisted of the Kosakievicz sisters, Olga and Wanda (both of whom Sartre bedded), and Jacques-Laurent Bost, a brilliant journalist who married the moody Olga and was also an occasional bed-partner of Beauvoir. She and Sartre would congratulate themselves for having originated a new social network, a chosen rather than genetic family.

Beauvoir's association with Olga Kosakievicz, who had originally been her nine-years-younger pupil, was particularly close. She found the Russian girl to be an intelligent and sensitive companion with whom she could talk intimately about everything. Yet the Sartre-Beauvoir-Kosakievicz-Bost quartet never attained the equilibrium and harmony in fact that Sartre and Beauvoir considered attainable in theory, since Olga's shifting moods kept the others continually off balance. Olga's intrusion into the intimacy Beauvoir and Sartre were enjoying provided Beauvoir with the plot for her acclaimed novel *l'Invitée* (1943; *She Came to Stay*, 1954).

The 1930's were extremely active years for Beauvoir. She read voraciously, discovering Ernest Hemingway, William Faulkner, John Dos Passos, Martin Heidegger, and Edmund Husserl, among others. She frequented, usually with Sartre, cafés, theaters, cinemas, art galleries, grubby pubs, jazz dives, and lively, long-lasting parties, strolling, scribbling, and talking with enormous energy. To the urban Sartre's discomfort, she loved to clamber up steep and stony hillsides in search of ancient ruins, to conquer rock walls, to hike through not only France but also Spain, Italy, and Greece, seeking mountain peaks to conquer.

As World War II approached, Beauvoir and Sartre finally abandoned their apolitical, self-interested individualism, which excluded meaningful concern for others. They were, to be sure, broadly in favor of social justice, but they remained indifferent to the day-to-day occurrences of domestic and world politics. The atrocities committed by the Nazis at last convinced Beauvoir and Sartre, in mid-1939, that war was inevitable and that they needed to commit themselves to political action. After some unsuccessful Resistance work, however, they concentrated on their writing, and they made their literary reputations during the German Occupation. With the Allied entry into Paris, Beauvoir ends her book with an ardent appetite for further challenges:

". . . the more I saw of the world, the more I realized that it was brimming over with all I could ever hope to experience, understand, and put into words."

Analysis

At its best, *The Prime of Life* is a hymn to individual freedom and to the importance of the intellect, an invaluable description of the French intelligentsia's way of life in the 1930's and during World War II. It lacks the unity of *Memoirs of a Dutiful Daughter*, which succeeded in rendering the maturation of a sensitive and brilliant young girl struggling for self-definition in a repressive household. Instead, Beauvoir here uses a wide range of techniques to describe the beginnings of her career as a teacher and writer, her alliance with Sartre, the *vie de Bohème* the pair lived until the war, and their conversion from romantic individualism to political commitment.

Beauvoir divides her narrative into chronological periods that vary from whole school years to weeks-long holidays to weekends with Sartre. She frequently summarizes her latest conclusions about life at either a chapter's beginning or end. These are, more often than not, views that are jointly held with Sartre. Occasionally, however, she does distinguish between their temperaments: He was more at home with abstractions than she, more detached than she in expressing feelings, more devoted to literature, and indifferent to external nature.

Both agreed that, absent a God, they trusted only themselves. As for the world at large, "We counted [until World War II] on events turning out according to our wishes without any need for us to mix in them personally." They accepted no external limitations, no overriding authority, no imposed pattern of existence. They rejected not only religion but also the secular disciplines of Marxism and psychoanalysis. The myth that Beauvoir believed in was that of romantic spontaneity. She moved from one exuberant emotion to another, exulting in what Sartre was to term "perfect moments" of insight. In *The Prime of Life*, she pays tribute to the tumultuousness, rebelliousness, and vitality of youth and seeks to postpone adult responsibilities as long as she can, refusing to admit that her life need recognize any will but hers, and disdaining such bourgeois habits as marriage, family life, and the acquisition of material possessions.

The dominant note in Beauvoir's book is her uncompromising honesty about herself. She invites the reader to share her extraordinary clarity of self-perception about both her virtues (a splendid mind, an acute sensibility, high moral principles, integrity, and courage and gusto for experience) and her faults (a lack of humor or wit, a drive to intellectualize all behavior, a brusque rudeness to persons she considers mistaken or inferior, and a tendency to sermonize). Altogether, the book is an admirable testimony to crucial stages in the life of one of the century's great women, who lived to test her mind.

Context

Simone de Beauvoir occupies a deservedly central place in the history of feminism. In *The Second Sex*, she uses existential notions of people's need to establish their freedom in a purposeless, absurd universe to encourage women no longer to resign themselves to the role of the weaker and inferior person in relation to a man. In much of her fiction, such as the novel *Les Mandarins* (1954; *The Mandarins*, 1956), she describes women whose dependency on men has hobbled their ability to construct satisfying lives for themselves. As much as any writer, she is responsible for inspiring women's movements throughout the world.

In *The Prime of Life*, however, Beauvoir's influence on women's issues, and hence women's literature, is a mixed one. She frequently asserts her claim that highly charged emotional relationships are amenable to rational control, that people can rigidly compartmentalize their emotional and intellectual needs. Yet her autobiography testifies otherwise. She admits that ". . . my body had its own whims, and I was powerless to control them; their violence overrode all my defenses." Her sexual appetites, she discovers, "were greater than I wanted them to be" and greater than she cared to avow to Sartre, despite their pact of absolute candor with each other. "By driving me to such secrecy my body became a stumbling block rather than a bond of union between us." Yet she provides the reader with no advice on how sexual relationships are to be conducted or what role physical affection is to play in one's personal life. In Beauvoir's fiction, most affairs bring humiliation and destruction to women.

In *The Second Sex*, Beauvoir argues that much of woman's psychological self is socially constructed, with few physiologically rooted feminine qualities or values. One assumes that she would question much of the American feminist concern for "women's culture" and "feminist studies." In *The Prime of Life*, she describes marriage and family life in generally negative terms, with coolness toward relatives and no interest in children. She has achieved autonomy from parental control, barely mentions her mother, and devotes only one paragraph to her father's death in 1941.

Beauvoir carefully explains her rejection of motherhood:

> [Sartre] was sufficient both for himself and me. I too was self-sufficient. I never once dreamed of rediscovering myself in the child I might bear. . . . Maternity itself seemed incompatible with the way of life upon which I was embarking. . . . By remaining childless I was fulfilling my proper function.

It can be argued, however, that both she and Sartre acted out parental roles in their relationships with students and other young people whom they admitted to their circle. In this regard, their ultimately failed friendship with Olga Kosakievicz provides a provocative example, since Beauvoir depicted the pains of the Beauvoir-Sartre-Kosakievicz triangle in *She Came to Stay*, whose publication justified her claim to be a writer—and not to be a mother. In *The Prime of Life*, Simone de Beauvoir gives birth not to children but to her career. Surely, a number of other talented women have been encouraged by her work to do likewise.

Sources for Further Study

Brée, Germaine. *Women Writers in France.* New Brunswick, N.J.: Rutgers University Press, 1973. Professor Brée, a leading authority on contemporary French literature, discusses Beauvoir's writings with sensitive understanding.

Leighton, Jean. *Simone de Beauvoir on Woman*. Rutherford, N.J.: Fairleigh Dickinson University Press, 1975. This is a luminous interpretation of feminism in Beauvoir's work.

Marks, Elaine, ed. *Critical Essays on Simone de Beauvoir*. Boston: G. K. Hall, 1987. An assemblage of nearly thirty articles, essays, and reviews by such scholars and critics as Mary McCarthy, Elizabeth Hardwick, Rene Girard, Francis Jeanson, and Terry Keefe.

—————— . *Simone de Beauvoir: Encounters with Death*. New Brunswick, N.J.: Rutgers University Press, 1973. By far the leading book-length interpretation of Beauvoir's career, this work is both learned and lucidly written.

Winegarten, Renée. *Simone de Beauvoir: A Critical View*. New York: St. Martin's Press, 1988. Winegarten's study is compact, incisive, and often sharply skeptical of Beauvoir's behavior, such as her slow awakening to political responsibility. A ten-page chronology of Beauvoir's life is included.

Gerhard Brand

THE PRIME OF MISS JEAN BRODIE

Author: Muriel Spark (1918-   )
Type of work: Novel
Type of plot: Psychological realism
Time of plot: The 1930's
Locale: Edinburgh, Scotland
First published: 1961

Principal characters:
MISS JEAN BRODIE, a teacher at the Marcia Blaine School for
Girls
SANDY STRANGER, a member of Miss Brodie's set at the school
JENNY GRAY, Sandy's closest friend
EUNICE GARDNER, the athletic girl in the set
ROSE STANLEY, a member of the set who eventually forgets Miss
Brodie's influence
MONICA DOUGLAS, a girl with great mathematical ability
MARY MACGREGOR, the scapegoat of the set
TEDDY LLOYD, a married art teacher at Marcia Blaine
GORDON LOWTHER, a music teacher at Marcia Blaine and Miss
Brodie's lover

Form and Content

Miss Brodie lives life on a grander scale than the typical unmarried schoolteacher does, and she believes that her students should have the benefit of her experiences, which she considers more valuable than the lessons within their texts. Her students are told to hold their history books open when they are really hearing about Miss Brodie's travels in Italy, her dead fiancé, or her views on art.

The six girls who make up the Brodie set are selected at age ten, when they are in her junior school class. They are chosen not so much for their special abilities as for what Miss Brodie will be able to do with them—each has parents who will not question the teacher's departures from traditional educational patterns.

In addition to vicariously experiencing Miss Brodie's youthful affair with a soldier who was killed in World War I and her travels in Europe, the members of the set are educated in other ways that Miss Brodie finds most appropriate. They accompany her to concerts, to ballet performances, and on walks through derelict sections of Edinburgh, where they see historic buildings and learn about unemployment.

The girls remain Miss Brodie's students for two years but continue to be the "Brodie set" through all their years at Marcia Blaine. They take tea and excursions with their former teacher as they grow older, telling her what they are learning in senior school and continuing to hear of her vacations and opinions. Their behavior is shaped by Brodie's ideas; none joins the Girl Guides or is actively a team player because Miss

Brodie does not believe in conformist behavior. This contrasts strangely with the teacher's vocal admiration for the order in Italy under Benito Mussolini and his fascists. Only Sandy picks up on and ponders this puzzle.

Joyce Emily Hammond, a girl who desires to join the set when she transfers to Marcia Blaine, is never quite accepted, but she does fall under Miss Brodie's influence. She runs away from the school and is killed in a train wreck on her way to Spain to fight in the revolution.

The set is privy to Miss Brodie's ongoing battle with the more conservative elements within the school, especially the headmistress, Miss McKay. Miss McKay disapproves of Miss Brodie's methods and continually tries to find enough evidence of wrongdoing to fire her. As the girls get older, Miss McKay pumps them for what she hopes will be incriminating information.

After Miss Brodie takes up with Mr. Lowther, the girls still take tea with her, two each weekend, in his home. While Mr. Lowther plays the piano or sits quietly with them, Miss Brodie interrogates the girls about their art lessons with Teddy Lloyd, with whom she is still in love. She conceives the scheme of having Rose act as her surrogate and become Mr. Lloyd's lover while Sandy will become her informant. She tries subtly to push the girls in this direction. Sandy, whose insight Miss Brodie has recognized and praised, sees through this plan and ends up as Lloyd's lover herself for a brief time. After she has become a nun, Sandy attributes her exposure to Catholicism to Lloyd.

Some time after the girls have left the school, Miss Brodie is forced into early retirement because she is suspected of being a fascist and because of her role in encouraging Joyce Emily Hammond to go to Spain. Miss McKay takes pleasure in telling Miss Brodie that one of her own girls has betrayed her. In her visits with girls from the set for the remainder of her life, she repeatedly wonders which of them it was, but she does not learn the answer before she dies of cancer.

Sandy's betrayal of Miss Brodie is mentioned fairly early in the novel; she feels that Miss Brodie's influence is too strong and that she must be stopped, yet at the end of the story, it is perhaps she who has been most influenced by Miss Brodie. She has joined an enclosed order, become Sister Helena, and has written a surprisingly popular psychological treatise, *The Transformation of the Commonplace*. When visitors to her convent ask about the influences in her life, expecting her to name famous writers and thinkers, she is forced to admit the powerful effect that Miss Brodie had on her.

Analysis

Rather than employing a traditional chronological plot, *The Prime of Miss Jean Brodie* works through flashbacks and glimpses into the future. The secrets of the story are all calmly revealed before they are set in a chronological context. This defeats a typical pattern of building, climax, and falling action, thus focusing attention not on what happens, but on why it happens. While suspense is eliminated, character motivation is highlighted. Spark can manipulate her readers' responses because she controls the timing. The author likewise manipulates responses to the title character, because readers see her first through the eyes of those who worship her and interpret all of her actions positively.

Another unusual aspect of the novel's construction is its multivoiced style. Juxtapositions of various levels of language add texture to the novel. Miss Brodie's lofty speeches on arts or aesthetics are interrupted by her briskly chiding a girl to sit up straight or to stop fidgeting. The narrative voice is fairly uniform throughout, but tone in the girls' fantasy letters and stories provides humor and an alternate narrative texture through parody. The hilarious imaginary letter that Sandy and Jenny write from Miss Brodie to Mr. Lowther, for example, is a polyvocal combination of adolescent girls' ideas about sex, legal terms they have read in the newspaper, language from books such as *Kidnapped* and *Jane Eyre*, ideas gained from Miss Brodie herself, and formal letter-writing phrases.

It is through such letters that Miss Brodie's effect on her set is revealed. Although the letters and stories introduce a comic element, the powerful influence of the teacher over her students manifests itself in ways that are more serious. As her girls grow older, Miss Brodie wants them to do things that she would not do herself—Rose's predicted affair with Teddy Lloyd, for example, reflects a projection of her own unfulfilled dreams. She has started to live vicariously through them, whereas earlier, they had lived vicariously through her.

Miss Brodie's influence over the girls raises many questions. Why are her companions little girls instead of friends her own age? Why must she be the controlling, dictating element of a group rather than an equal member? Is her need for power based on her own dimly perceived weaknesses?

Although she never thinks to question the morality of her own actions, Miss Brodie attempts to turn her weaknesses into strengths by interpreting them as such in her own mind. She downplays the significance of senior school subjects such as geometry that she is unable to teach her girls; she is trying to prevent her girls from moving beyond her. Her paranoia at being observed by other teachers is converted to a feeling of kinship among her students—they stand united against the intruders.

In the end, it is Miss Brodie's sense that her power is absolute that brings about her downfall. Mr. Lowther's marriage to another teacher reveals perhaps the first chink in her armor. Her influence weakens as the girls grow older and do not follow her plans for them. Finally, she is defeated not by her enemies, but by the betrayal of one of her own girls.

Despite her defeat and betrayal, Miss Brodie remains a paradox. Although Sandy believes that Miss Brodie must be stopped, she recognizes that her teacher's innocence—her inability to view herself critically—is the reason for her manipulative behavior. Readers are encouraged to think highly of Miss Brodie through Spark's characterization methods, which show her in the most positive light, even while readers are beginning to question her need for absolute power. Much of her behavior is contradictory: She keeps the Sabbath by worshipping at a different church each week and refusing to allow Eunice to turn handsprings on Sunday, but she carries on her affair with Mr. Lowther on Sundays. Similarly, she refers to Miss McKay as her enemy, but she will not let the girls criticize her. Further ambiguity surrounds the end result of Miss Brodie's life: She is the one most harmed by her controlling, manipulative behavior; her girls have escaped any negative influences. She truly believes that she has dedicated her life to her girls, and she dies under the power of this delusion.

This ambiguity influences even Sandy, who self-righteously betrays Miss Brodie but needs to justify her behavior by claiming that Miss Brodie first betrayed her girls.

Context

The Prime of Miss Jean Brodie powerfully evokes a women's world. All the major characters are female, and their views and voices dominate the text. The Marcia Blaine School is a female universe and functions as a microcosm in which women play almost all the roles. This novel was one of the first to portray sophisticated girls unsentimentally. The Brodie set members are not the "sugar and spice" young women of stereotype.

The Prime of Miss Jean Brodie also functions as a study of female social patterns. The girls' school setting provides a comparison with the many works that focus on the interactions of boys and men in schools and other closed groups.

Because the story is so woman-oriented, the male characters almost become objects. Certainly, the passive Mr. Lowther, who allows Miss Brodie to control his kitchen and his bedroom, seems more acted upon than active. Even Mr. Lloyd is under the power of women: All the portraits he paints resemble Miss Brodie because he is obsessed with her, and Sandy is able to make him kiss her simply by manipulating the way she looks at him. This female-male pattern is unusual in literature.

More subtle woman-related issues involve Miss Brodie's role as a spinster. She never reproduces herself literally. It may be that she is trying to reproduce herself through her girls. Perhaps Miss Brodie's power becomes warped because her position as a junior school teacher only allows her to exercise that power in a limited arena. If this aging, unmarried woman had possessed more options for power in her life, perhaps her need to control would not appear so manipulative.

Spark's novel was received enthusiastically, and it remains her most popular work. Film and stage adaptations have proved to be extremely popular; Maggie Smith won an Oscar for best actress for her portrayal of Miss Brodie. The concept of a Miss Brodie—a controlling but inspiring teacher—has even entered popular discourse as a sort of cultural archetype.

Sources for Further Study

Bold, Alan. *Muriel Spark*. London: Methuen, 1986. A treatment of Spark's poetry and fiction, with an excellent bibliography.

_____ , ed. *Muriel Spark: An Odd Capacity for Vision*. Totowa, N.J.: Barnes & Noble Books, 1984. A series of nine essays dealing with various themes and techniques in Spark's work. Two of the essays contain extended treatments of *The Prime of Miss Jean Brodie*.

Hynes, Joseph. *The Art of the Real: Muriel Spark's Novels*. Cranbury, N.J.: Associated

University Presses, 1988. An analysis and explication of seventeen of Spark's novels, especially in terms of their comedy, ironic social criticism, and religious elements.

Richmond, Velma Bourgeois. *Muriel Spark.* New York: Frederick Ungar, 1984. Contains background material on Spark and discussion of her work in terms of its major themes.

Sproxton, Judy. *The Women of Muriel Spark.* New York: St. Martin's Press, 1992. Studies three primary types of female characters in Spark's work. The chapter on Miss Jean Brodie labels her a "woman of power" and shows how she manipulates and deludes others but is ultimately deluded herself.

Rebecca L. Wheeler

THE PRINCESS OF CLÈVES

Author: Madame de La Fayette (Marie-Madeleine Pioche de la Vergne, 1634-1693)
Type of work: Novel
Type of plot: Psychological realism
Time of plot: 1558-1559
Locale: Paris, France
First published: La Princesse de Clèves, 1678 (English translation, 1679)

Principal characters:
THE PRINCESS OF CLÈVES, a beautiful heiress from one of the most important families in France
JACQUES DE SAVOIE, the Duc de Nemours, an eligible bachelor who falls in love with the Princess of Clèves
THE PRINCE OF CLÈVES, the husband of the Princess
MADAME DE CHARTRES, the mother of the Princess
KING HENRY II, the reigning king of France and the son of the notable king François I
DIANE DE POITIERS, the Duchesse de Valentinois and the mistress of both François I and Henry II
CATHERINE DE MÈDICIS, the queen of France as the wife of Henry II
MARY STUART, Queen of Scots and the "Queen Dauphine" as the wife of the king's oldest son

Form and Content

The Princess of Clèves presents a new twist on an age-old dilemma, the conflict between love and duty. As the title of the novel suggests, the main focus is on the Princess of Clèves and her predicament. On the one hand, she has a duty toward her husband, but on the other, she seeks gratification through her love for Nemours. The novel explores the competing demands of duty toward others and toward oneself; it does this by presenting a sympathetic and complex heroine, one of the first such female characters in literature and one with enduring importance. The psychology of other characters is important insofar as it contributes to this dilemma, but otherwise remains undeveloped.

The core of the drama is whether the Princess should follow love or duty. When she marries, she is honest with her husband—an honesty consistent with her open disposition—and tells him that although she respects and honors him, she does not love him. At the time, the Prince of Clèves is satisfied with unrequited love, hoping that someday their affection will be mutual, but as he becomes aware of his wife's feelings for Nemours, the challenge of keeping his word becomes increasingly difficult. His death leaves the Princess free to fulfill her desire and remarry, this time to her true love, the bachelor Nemours, but her controversial decision at the end of the novel to remain a widow and retire from society appears to place duty before love.

The novel is set principally during the reign of Henry II, particularly in the years 1558 and 1559, and it draws considerably on historical events. Thus, when the novel opens, Elizabeth of England has just succeeded to the throne of England and Mary Stuart has just married the heir to the throne of France, the dauphine, events that took place in 1558. Toward the end of the novel, Henry II is killed in a tournament and peace for France is achieved through a series of arranged marriages alluded to in the novel, events that took place in 1559.

The author, Madame de La Fayette, scrupulously observes the historical record for the most part, but within this framework she invents the conversations and details of intrigue that occupy her novel. The major departure from history is the character of the Princess herself. This is not to say that the character of the Princess is without historical basis: She may have been modeled on Anne d'Este, who married first the Duke of Guise (who also figures in Madame de La Fayette's novel) and then the Duc de Nemours.

The novel is divided into four "books" of approximately equal length. Each book leads the reader up to a new crisis in the plot, increasing the tension until the final resolution. Thus, the first book ends with the death of Madame de Chartres, the Princess' mother. This leaves the Princess vulnerable and without an ally, for Madame de Chartres had been her confidante and counselor. Madame de Chartres recognized the difficulty of the ordeal that her daughter faced and in her dying words encouraged her to do her duty and to leave the court to avoid temptation.

When the Princess tries to do the right thing, circumstances thwart her good intentions. Thus, she attempts to follow her mother's advice to leave court, but ironically it is her husband's wish that she remain, and in obeying him she is exposed to greater temptation. Such psychological twists add to the dramatic irony of the novel by making the Prince complicit in his own eventual unhappiness.

At other times, the Princess is betrayed by her own feelings in spite of her attempt to control and conceal them. She also learns that love does not bring only happiness; when she believes she has a rival for Nemours' affection, she experiences the pain of jealousy, a factor that will be important in her final decision.

The Prince of Clèves is also trapped in a similar dilemma. He cannot reproach his wife with dishonesty, but his emotions get the better of him at times. Thus, he proclaims that, because of the value he places on sincerity, he would not react bitterly if his wife confessed she loved another, but when the Princess heeds his words, he finds that he is unable to maintain his equanimity. Although the Princess achieves some peace of mind through her confession (another important factor in her final decision), the shared knowledge drives a wedge between the couple. The Prince is increasingly tormented by jealousy, and he sends spies to watch his wife. As further evidence of his tragically flawed nature, he erroneously concludes from these reports that his wife has been unfaithful, and he falls fatally ill.

The court setting of the novel offers several advantages. Court life constantly combines love and politics, showing at every turn how love and power are interrelated. This background highlights the value of the pure disinterested love felt by the Princess. The contrast between the hypocritical life at court and her sincerity adds to the interest of the main character. The court setting also means that the Princess is constantly exposed to scrutiny and that virtually no action can remain private or secret, which heightens the psychological pressure.

Analysis

The Princess of Clèves is generally considered to be the first psychological novel in French and one of the best examples of the emerging novel genre in any language. Although many of the secondary characters are not developed, the behavior and decisions of the Princess of Clèves are given thorough psychological underpinning and treatment.

This is not to say that everyone agrees on the degree of realism; indeed, this very problem of "verisimilitude" has been much discussed. In particular, Madame de La Fayette's contemporaries cited two scenes they found especially unbelievable: the confession scene (when the Princess tells her husband that she loves another) and the renunciation (when the Princess decides not to marry Nemours even though she is free to do so). Close attention to the text shows that Madame de La Fayette prepares and defends these choices on the part of her heroine. The Prince practically invites such a confession, and when the Princess makes it, she reiterates that she is aware of how unusual it is. In addition, the "frank and open disposition" of the character is stressed. In the case of her decision not to marry Nemours, this is prepared carefully in the text (by the emphasis on duty, by the moral weight of death-bed promises, by the Princess' experiences of the pain of jealousy and the value she places on peace of mind).

An important formal aspect of the novel is the use of embedded narratives (subplots or secondary stories narrated or "nested" within the framework of the main story). There are four of these in the novel. Although they have sometimes been viewed as digressions that distract the reader from the main plot, a comparison between the themes of the main plot and the embedded narratives reveals that they are closely linked. The four embedded narratives occur in the first two books and at the beginning of book 3. Occasionally, they serve to form a bridge between one chapter and the next. Each of the four narratives concerns the love life of a female character and contains a lesson for either the Princess of Clèves or Nemours. The first narrative, told by Madame de Chartres, answers the question (posed by the Princess) of what attracts Henry II to his older mistress, Diane de Poitiers, by telling the story of Diane's political triumph. It illustrates the point frequently articulated by Madame de Chartres that anyone who judges people at court by appearances will be deceived. The second embedded narrative concerns the deception of Madame de Tournon, the mistress of one of the Prince's friends. This story also illustrates the deceptiveness of appearances, but its main importance is that it provides the occasion for the Prince to tell his wife that he would be sympathetic if she were in love with someone else. The third narrative concerns Anne Boleyn, the wife of Henry VIII of England. It suggests that love does not survive marriage: In the story, Anne Boleyn is Henry's mistress for nine years, but after they are married, he suddenly becomes jealous and has her executed. One of the factors that the Princess weighs when she decides not to marry Nemours is her belief that he will not remain faithful once she marries him. The final narrative tells the story of the Vidame's friendship with Queen Catherine and highlights the dangers of deception.

From an examination of the psychological motivations of the characters and the structural composition of the novel, *The Princess of Clèves* appears to be a carefully composed and expertly written novel.

Context

The significance of this novel for women's literature is twofold. It provides an unusual example of a woman writer whose eminent place in the canon has never been questioned. Although *The Princess of Clèves* was first published anonymously, the identity of the author was quickly discovered. Because she was the author of the first psychological novel, Madame de La Fayette's name has not been forgotten. (It is true, however, that her authorship of the novel has been questioned.) There has been a tendency to consider Madame de La Fayette as an exception to the generalization that women of her period did not write, but the trend in contemporary scholarship (in the work of Joan DeJean, for example) is to see her as part of a larger movement of women writers rather than as the token exception.

The second point of significance concerns the central character and the theme of the novel. *The Princess of Clèves* features a central female character who may be viewed as a role model and focuses on issues of concern to women—love and marriage, and the circumstances in which a woman might reject them. Although the ending has been read as traditional female sacrifice and renunciation, some critics (such as Nancy K. Miller) have also argued that the Princess offers an example of female empowerment by depicting a woman who refuses the traditional marriage plot in favor of less tangible but more important advantages.

Sources for Further Study

Danahy, Michael. *The Feminization of the Novel*. Gainesville: University of Florida Press, 1991. A long chapter on *The Princess of Clèves* in this book focuses on gendered spatial archetypes and patterns of communication.

DeJean, Joan. *Tender Geographies: Women and the Origins of the Novel in France*. New York: Columbia University Press, 1991. The extensive chapter "Lafayette and the Generation of 1660-1689" places *The Princess of Clèves* in a broad historical context and situates it with regard to politics and to other French women writers of the period.

Kamuf, Peggy. *Fictions of Feminine Desire: Disclosures of Heloise*. Lincoln: University of Nebraska Press, 1982. Analyzes a number of novels, including *The Princess of Clèves*, in which the author focuses on the role of Madame de Chartres in "constructing" her daughter.

Lyons, John D. "1678: The Emergence of the Novel." In *A New History of French*

Literature, edited by Denis Hollier et al. Cambridge, Mass.: Harvard University Press, 1989. A brief but useful article that situates the novel in its historical literary context.

Miller, Nancy K. *Subject to Change: Reading Feminist Writing*. New York: Columbia University Press, 1988. This book reprints Miller's seminal article "Emphasis Added: Plots and Plausibilities in Women's Fiction." Miller takes up the question of verisimilitude ("plausibility") to offer a new interpretation of the Princess' choice as an act of desire rather than renunciation.

Stanton, Domna C. "The Ideal of 'Repos' in Seventeenth-Century French Literature." *L'Esprit Créateur* 15 (Spring/Summer, 1975): 79-104. Stanton traces the origins and meaning of the term "repos," one of the key values in the Princess' moral code.

Melanie C. Hawthorne

THE PROGRESS OF LOVE

Author: Alice Munro (1931-   )
Type of work: Short stories
First published: 1986

Form and Content

   The Progress of Love collects eleven of Alice Munro's short stories. As the title suggests, the stories tend to focus on the progress—or lack of progress—in family and love relationships. Many of the major characters are women in their forties and fifties who are looking back at life events, momentous or trivial, that changed or illuminated a moment in time: A girl believes that her mother is about to commit suicide, a man visits his former wife with the girlfriend he no longer desires, a schoolgirl imagines an affair with an older man.

   Although the stories are, on the surface, unrelated, a common thread binds the collection: A character experiences some sort of self-illumination. Munro's characters, young or old, male or female, show a baffled puzzlement at the complexity of love and a courageous (if sometimes doomed) willingness to keep seeking happiness, equality, and free communication. Different kinds of love and bonds, from romantic to familial, are explored: men in mid-life crisis seek reassurance with younger lovers, a woman in a trance of devotion tolerates an ugly and possibly abusive relationship, a husband allows his wife to do an outwardly foolish thing that will give her peace.

   In several stories, a young, newly awakened girl is paired with an older woman—an aunt, a mother, or even an older self. Munro shows the similarities in the younger, sexually aware female preoccupied with her "new" body and concerns about aging, deterioration, and death in her older counterpart. The twenty-two-year-old punkish Dina of "Lichen," the "trollop" of the middle-aged and insecure David, is paralleled and contrasted by his earthy former wife Stella, who gleefully allows her body to run out of bounds, unconstrained.

   Munro habitually writes on women's issues and about women's lives: the double standard of appearance and sexual behavior for women and men, the temptation of surrendering one's "self" for others, the struggle for independence and integrity. In "White Dump," a daughter, mother, and grandmother see the same event from the standpoint of their "places" in time: youth, middle age, and old age. In other stories, such as "A Queer Streak," the point of view is that of an omniscient narrator who relates events in the lives of successive generations. Parents, or their surrogates, and their roles in shaping their children's futures are an important theme.

   Munro's style is delicate and complicated. Through her careful control of pacing and point of view, she is able to "freeze" a moment so that it seems utterly realistic. She has an unswerving grasp on the details that are intrinsic to character: Andrew's insistence on lettuce in his sandwich ("Miles City, Montana") speaks volumes about his fussiness; Peg's measured and deliberate response to her discovery of a murder-suicide indicates her craving for control after leaving a violent marriage. Munro's ability to sketch complicated characters with a few words or a tiny scene is stunning.

Analysis

Munro's fiction is lovingly crafted and artfully constructed, yet there is no feeling of artificiality or manipulation of the reader. This effect, which is so difficult to achieve, comes about partly because Munro's voice is so often ironic. Never bitter but sometimes rueful, this irony is important in maintaining equilibrium in her stories. After the near-drowning in "Miles City, Montana," the mother imagines what the family's life would be if Meg had not been rescued, but she tells herself that this is a shameful and "trashy" thing to do, which saves the story from becoming highly emotional speculation and therefore much less effective. Similarly, in "Eskimo," Mary Jo seems to experience a sort of enlightenment about her long-standing affair with her employer after she sees the slavish devotion of a young girl to a much older man. Munro's ironic voice can also take the form of juxtaposition of a young, innocent character who is observing events and a worldly or more cynical version of that character who is explaining them.

Because her stories, though brief, are very complex, Munro often uses two characters' points of view or a "limited omniscient" narrator. This technique also allows revelation of another of her important themes: the "editing" of memory, its inaccuracy, and its sudden surprising power to illuminate present events. In the title story, a woman recounts two versions of a family event: one as she has told it to others (to illustrate to them her definition of love) and one as she remembers it. Both versions are necessary for the reader's full understanding of this chapter. Munro achieves a strong sense of the complexity of everyday life by such sure employment of various points of view and little reliance on chronological time. "White Dump," "A Queer Streak," and "The Progress of Love" all span five or six decades and center on family relationships between the generations. All stress the simultaneous hurtfulness and irresistibility of maintaining family ties. In "White Dump," the characters related by blood are shown to have similar obsessions (stubbornness and "managing" others), yet they are not cookie-cutter copies of one another. Like other Canadian writers such as Margaret Laurence and Margaret Atwood, Munro often takes "the sins of the fathers" (and mothers) as a theme, showing how the flaws and strengths of an individual can manifest themselves in successive generations.

As a feminist, Munro often uses control—of emotion, of one's body, of another person, of nature—as a theme. Breakdowns in tightly wielded control often occur; violence and murderous hatred can erupt in the most mundane situations. These eruptions show the abyss of fear that most characters manage to cover up in everyday life. Most notably in "A Queer Streak," imagined and threatened brutality and ugliness are just as damaging as real violence. In "Fits," an apparently ordinary couple die in a murder-suicide; in "Circle of Prayer," a seemingly happy marriage slowly dissolves. Although tragedy can lurk beneath life's surfaces, so can great joy and revelation: Just as a woman sees that her life has been tragically wasted in an attempt to save her sister, she finds love; deserted by her husband, a woman finds unexpected wisdom and humor from a disabled man. In "The Moon in the Orange Street Skating Rink," the male narrator wonders whether everyone has a life of happiness with which he or she only occasionally catches up.

Such hope or despair emerging from commonplace situations is mirrored in Munro's use of everyday objects as metaphors. In the title story, a house's many layers of wallpaper and paint suggest the accretion of experiences in the lives of its inhabitants. "White Dump," referring to discarded candy from a factory, comes to symbolize the unexpected richness and bounty that can be found in an ordinary day. In "Monsieur les Deux Chapeaux," Colin and Glenna's desire to renovate their house and have a stable family is contrasted by the irresponsible younger brother's attempts to restore a flashy, dangerous classic car.

Possibly the most prevalent theme in this collection is the inevitability of death: The title story begins when the narrator hears the news of her mother's death, and nearly every story contains references to old age or real or imagined death. Aging and the mind's and body's deterioration is a related theme: Violet, in "A Queer Streak," begins to have hallucinations about the past; the father-in-law in "Lichen" is so old that David thinks of him as an artifact. Setting and changes in landscape are also used to mirror changes and encroachment of the new upon the familiar: The glaring new developments in "White Dump" and the influx of hippies into the town suggest the encroachment of new ideals and lifestyles on the old. The destruction of the marriage in "Circle of Prayer" is shown through the destruction and chaos on the street on which the family lives. Munro has often been described as a regionalist writer; her strong sense of place allows her to use landscape at times as another fully realized character. Munro's work in this collection is strong, sure-handed, and emotionally powerful. She shows that love can "progress" through unexpected means.

Context

The Progress of Love was critically acclaimed for its portraits of family life and its strong characterization. Winner of the Governor-General's Award for fiction, the collection was chosen by *The New York Times Book Review* as one of the top ten fiction books of 1986. These accolades add to the stature Munro has achieved as a short-story writer; she writes regularly for *The New Yorker* and has found great popularity in the United States as well as Canada.

Munro has been deservedly praised for her accurate portraits of the hopes and fears of women of various ages: From Del Jordan's coming-of-age in *Lives of Girls and Women* (1971) to the women in *The Progress of Love*, her characters struggle toward self-realization, toward equilibrium in their relationships with others, and toward an understanding of their pasts. Here her female characters, who range from young and impressionable girls to divorced and single older women, show the alternatives that are open to women and the various ways in which women strive toward independence. A crucial feminist theme here is the relationship between women, whether mothers and daughters, schoolgirl "best friends," or a mother- and daughter-in-law; Munro carefully documents the tension and rivalry and, sometimes, lightning-like flashes of sympathy or understanding that are possible between women. She also creates sympathetic, fully realized male characters. Some of them are childishly fighting against the realization of their age and responsibilities, but others hopefully, clumsily, and precariously climb toward knowledge. Munro makes these experiences seem not exclusively male or female, but universal.

The Progress of Love reflects a maturation and extension of some of Munro's prevalent themes. Her characters and themes here are far more complex than they are in previous works, her use of symbolism and metaphor relaxed and unrestrained. As she mentioned in an interview, her stories' endings seem to flow as natural results or culminations of characters' actions, and not as contrivances. Although she denies being an intellectual writer or one who is conscious of writing with a message, Munro's stories give powerful new insight into everyday life and an appreciation of the textures beneath the most commonplace experiences.

Sources for Further Study
Carrington, Ildiko de Papp. *Controlling the Uncontrollable: The Fiction of Alice Munro*. DeKalb: Northern Illinois University Press, 1989. Examines Munro's major themes, metaphors, and uses of points of view. Interprets *The Progress of Love*'s major theme as characters attempting to control humiliating situations and examines alter egos in several stories. Includes excellent primary and secondary bibliographies.
MacKendrick, Louis K., ed. *Probably Fictions: Alice Munro's Narrative Acts*. Downsview, Ontario: ECW Press, 1983. Includes a lengthy and informative interview with Munro about her inspirations, work habits, and background as well as critical analyses of her narrative techniques, her presentation of the ordinary as extraordinary, and her sense of the absurd.
Martin, W. R. *Alice Munro: Paradox and Parallel*. Edmonton: University of Alberta Press, 1987. A close and careful critical study of Munro's body of work, including uncollected stories. Argues that, like Coleridge, Munro makes the strange familiar and that, like Wordsworth, she makes the familiar wonderful. The stories in *The Progress of Love*, Martin claims, end in wisdom and moral insight. Includes a useful index and a bibliography.
Miller, Judith, ed. *The Art of Alice Munro: Saying the Unsayable*. Waterloo, Ontario: University of Waterloo Press, 1984. Collects papers from a conference on Munro among which are articles on Munro's female aesthetic, the quest in her work, and "writing as self-defense." Includes a helpful interview with Munro.
Rasporich, Beverly J. *Dance of the Sexes: Art and Gender in the Fiction of Alice Munro*. Edmonton: University of Alberta Press, 1990. Incorporates extensive interviews with Munro which illuminate texts later discussed in analyses of her works as feminist, ironic, regionalist, and female. A section on *The Progress of Love* closely studies Munro's technical inventiveness.

Michelle L. Jones

QUARTET IN AUTUMN

Author: Barbara Pym (1913-1980)
Type of work: Novel
Type of plot: Psychological realism
Time of plot: The 1970's
Locale: England
First published: 1977

Principal characters:

LETTY CROWE, an unmarried woman in her sixties who is
approaching retirement

MARCIA IVORY, an unmarried woman in her sixties who works in
the same office as Letty

EDWIN BRAITHWAITE, their coworker, a widower with a married
daughter who lives some distance away

NORMAN, the fourth of the office workers, who is single and lives
alone

MRS. POPE, an independent, rather haughty woman in her
eightieth year

JANICE BRABNER, a young volunteer social worker

Form and Content

Quartet in Autumn follows the lonely lives of four single people in their sixties who work together in a London office as they approach retirement. The novel covers a period of approximately eighteen months, during which the two women (who are the novel's most developed characters) retire and one of them, Marcia, dies. The novel is episodic in structure, and its point of view moves from individual to individual as each goes about his or her daily round of activity. The four are not friends, although they make conversation in an agreeable enough way during office hours. They never see one another at any other time.

The novel begins in spring, and in an early chapter the four take vacations. Letty stays with her old friend, Marjorie, in the country, but she finds that Marjorie is romantically involved with David Lydell, the local vicar, and she feels left out. Marcia's holiday treats are strange: a medical checkup, which brings her closer to the orbit of Dr. Strong, the surgeon who performed her mastectomy; and a bus trip to Strong's house, which she admiringly views from a distance. Norman has no idea of what to do with himself when he is not working and just loafs about his bed-sitting-room. Edwin has a more normal vacation, visiting his daughter and son-in-law, but there are hints that in the future the young couple may take their vacations abroad and Edwin may not be wanted.

Letty had planned to share a cottage with Marjorie after her retirement, but her plans are scuttled when Marjorie and David become engaged. Letty's life is further disrupted when the house in which she lives is sold. The new owner is a Nigerian priest of a religious sect who has noisy meetings in the house. Letty decides to leave, and Edwin finds her a room in Mrs. Pope's house.

Christmas is a difficult time, the general aim being to get through it as quickly as possible. Only Edwin spends a traditional Christmas with his immediate family. Norman has Christmas dinner with his brother-in-law; both think they are doing the other a favor. Marcia's young neighbors invite her in for a meal, but Marcia is uncommunicative and it is an awkward occasion. Letty eats with Mrs. Pope, but only because Mrs. Pope thinks it is silly for two women in the same house to eat Christmas dinner separately.

When the women retire, the company gives them a mean-spirited retirement party. In retirement, Marcia goes rapidly downhill. She does not bother to eat properly, convincing herself that she had never been a big eater. Her behavior becomes increasingly strange, exasperating Janice Brabner, the social worker who believes that it is her duty to help the aged, even if they do not wish to be helped. Letty attempts to spend her time constructively but soon abandons her attempt at "serious reading" in social studies. Norman and Edwin wonder vaguely how the women are, and out of a sense of duty Edwin suggests that the four of them go out to lunch. The men ensure that the occasion costs them as little as possible.

These small lives continue in this way until a crisis erupts in early autumn, when Marcia is found semiconscious on her kitchen table. She is taken to the hospital and dies shortly afterward. Marcia's death brings the remaining three closer together.

Everyone is astonished when it transpires that Marcia has left her house to Norman. Another shock follows when Letty learns that David has broken off his engagement to Marjorie, having decided that Betty Doughty, the warden of the old people's home in Marjorie's village, is a better prospect. The novel ends as Letty, Norman, and Edwin accept Marjorie's invitation for a day in the country, and Letty optimistically concludes that "life still held infinite possibilities for change."

Analysis

"Far/ From the exchange of love . . . / Unreachable in a room," a passage from Philip Larkin's poem "Ambulances," was certainly on Barbara Pym's mind—she quotes part of it—as she wrote her bleak story of unfulfilled, isolated lives. Marcia, Letty, Norman, and Edwin have lost the ability to form close relationships with others; even to attempt it would threaten the self-protective walls they have built little by little over the years. So many years of refusing to reach out beyond themselves make each thought or act that reinforces their isolation easily justifiable. Edwin does not visit Marcia even though he does not live far away and occasionally passes the road where she lives. He assumes that someone from the church will be keeping an eye on her, and anyway she likes to keep to herself. He is vaguely troubled by the parable of the Good Samaritan, but he does not pursue the matter. Marcia easily justifies not wanting to invite Letty to live with her (two women could not possibly share the same kitchen, among other reasons); Norman and Edwin justify not giving the women a retirement present because they do not expect one and "it would only embarrass them." Even when a helping hand is offered, the narrator quietly undercuts the character's motive, as when Edwin takes it on himself to find Letty new accommodations, but perhaps only, the narrator suggests, because "he see[s] himself as a person wanting to help ladies."

What these characters seem to lack most is a sense of achievement. Their work, as they well know, lacks any purpose at all. In fact, it is so unimportant that the reader is never told what it is. When the women retire, they are not replaced, and the company plans to phase out the department completely when the men retire. This contributes to the feelings expressed by Marcia and Letty—Pym does not bestow on her male characters the same power of self-reflection—that their lives do not make a difference in any way. When Marcia is in the hospital for her mastectomy, she asks herself whether it would matter if she were to die. She is unable to answer that it would. Letty experiences this sense of nothingness even more acutely, especially when she visits the office after her retirement and finds that the men have spread out to occupy the place that was formerly hers, leaving no trace that she had ever been there. In these lives, small achievements take on large significance. Toward the end of the novel, Letty is invigorated when she realizes that others will be interested in whether she decides to move to the country. Norman, too, feels a sense of achievement when his efforts to persuade the police to remove an abandoned car from outside the house where he lives finally bear fruit. Like Letty, he gets a boost from knowing that he can influence people's lives by deciding whether to live in the house that Marcia left him.

In chronicling these lives, Pym never loses the gentle, understated wit that is so characteristic of her fiction. Even death, which haunts the novel, is not immune from comic touches. After the funeral service for Marcia, Mrs. Pope offers Letty some refreshment, but Letty says, " 'I think just a cup of tea.' There was something to be said for tea and a comfortable chat about crematoria." At the cremation, an irreverent couplet, "Dust to dust, ashes to ashes,/ Into the grave the great Queen dashes," pops uninvited into Norman's mind, displacing the twinge of emotion he might otherwise have felt. This is one of many hints in the novel that there might at one time have been the possibility of some feelings between Norman and Marcia. The human yearning for love and closeness cannot wholly be extinguished, even in lives buried under so many layers of isolation and suspicion.

Although *Quartet in Autumn* is a novel about loneliness, it is not about despair. Deprived these people may be, but they are not, for the most part, depressed; they accept the limitations of their lives as normal, and make the best of it. Philip Larkin commented in a letter to Pym on the "*courage* that all your characters can call on and have to call on." To others the four may appear joyless, but they will eke out what pleasures they can from their small routines.

Context

Quartet in Autumn occupies a key position in Pym's career. She worked on it for a period of three years, from 1973 to 1976, but she did not expect ever to see it published. Several publishers rejected it in 1976, continuing the pattern of rejection of Pym's work that had begun in the 1960's. Although Pym had had six moderately successful novels published between 1950 and 1961, the publishing mood of the 1960's demanded more sensational topics than those of the commonplace, gently comic world of Barbara Pym.

The breakthrough came in January, 1977, when *The Times Literary Supplement* published a list, compiled by notable literary figures, of the most underrated writers of the century. Pym was the only writer to be listed twice, by poet Philip Larkin and critic Lord David Cecil, both of whom were longtime admirers of her work. (Larkin had read *Quartet in Autumn* in manuscript and had written to Pym, "It's so strange to find the tender irony of your style unchanged but dealing with the awful end of life: I admire you enormously for tackling it, and for bringing it off so well.") Within a month, Macmillan had accepted *Quartet in Autumn*, and it was published to universally appreciative reviews, as well as being shortlisted for the Booker Prize, Britain's most prestigious literary award.

This was the beginning of the revival of Pym's literary reputation on both sides of the Atlantic. In 1978, *Excellent Women* (1952) and *Quartet in Autumn* became the first Pym novels to be published in the United States. By 1980, all of her novels were either published or in the process of being published in the United States.

Because of its taut, sparse structure and its serious exploration of a tragic theme, *Quartet in Autumn* is often regarded as Pym's finest novel. It marked a new stage in Pym's lifelong observation of the nature and experience of women (disproving the comment made by Letty that "the position of an unmarried, unattached ageing woman is of no interest whatever to the writer of modern fiction"). Yet also, with its accurate representation of changing social patterns and its evocation of the disconnectedness and fragmentation of contemporary life, *Quartet in Autumn* struck a more universal note.

Sources for Further Study
Benet, Diana. *Something to Love: Barbara Pym's Novels*. Columbia: University of Missouri Press, 1986. Traces the evolution of Pym's work from a comic, predominantly feminine vision to a tragic, universal vision. Includes one of the fullest scholarly analyses of *Quartet in Autumn*, which shows the significance of the concept of community and how desperately the characters need it.
Cotsell, Michael. *Barbara Pym*. New York: St. Martin's Press, 1989. Discusses Pym's novels in relation to contemporary literary theory, showing how they differ from their realist predecessors. Uses Pym's notes to show how *Quartet in Autumn* evolved, and shows that the novel is not only about age but also about the failure of civilization.
Holt, Hazel. *A Lot to Ask: A Life of Barbara Pym*. London: Macmillan, 1990. An authorized biography by a close friend and colleague of Pym's. Describes the progress of *Quartet in Autumn* through notebooks, manuscript, and correspondence, and the remarkable events of 1977, which launched Pym's revival.

Nardin, Jane. *Barbara Pym*. Boston: Twayne, 1985. An introductory survey of Pym's work, describing her characteristic themes and their evolution during the course of her work. The section on *Quartet in Autumn* is mainly paraphrase and plot summary.

Rossen, Janice, ed. *Independent Women: The Function of Gender in the Novels of Barbara Pym*. New York: St. Martin's Press, 1988. A collection of ten essays that use biographical, historical, and feminist approaches to Pym's work. *Quartet in Autumn* is discussed most extensively by Laura L. Doan in "Text and the Single Man," an examination of the role that bachelors play in Pym's novels. Doan shows how Pym's "sexual ideology informs her narrative structure."

_____. *The World of Barbara Pym*. New York: St. Martin's Press, 1987. Focuses on the elements of Pym's fiction that have roots in Pym's personal life, as well as her fundamental ideas and perspective, such as English literature, spinsterhood, the Anglican church, and anthropology. Concludes that Pym's work is colored by a provincial British view.

Bryan Aubrey

THE QUEST FOR CHRISTA T.

Author: Christa Wolf (1929-   )
Type of work: Novel
Type of plot: Social criticism
Time of plot: 1933-1962
Locale: The former German Democratic Republic (East Germany)
First published: Nachdenken über Christa T., 1968 (English translation, 1970)

> *Principal characters:*
> CHRISTA T., the protagonist, who dies of leukemia at the age of
>   thirty-five
> THE NARRATOR, Christa T.'s childhood friend
> JUSTUS, a veterinary surgeon and Christa T.'s husband
> KOSTIA, Christa T.'s lover during her years at the university
> GÜNTER, another friend from Christa T.'s years as a student

Form and Content

The novel, which chronicles the years 1933 to 1962, starts with the narrator's attempt to rescue her dead friend Christa T. from oblivion. While randomly sifting through a box of writings left behind by Christa T., the narrator remembers her friend's life and passion. Already at school, where Christa T. and the narrator meet in 1944, it is apparent that Christa T. is different from the other pupils, and even though the narrator is unwilling to admit it, it is this difference—or Christa T.'s indifference to her surroundings—that fascinates the narrator. Soon, however, the two girls lose sight of each other in the turbulence of the war. It is not until 1951 that they, now both students in Leipzig, meet again by accident. In the course of their reunion, the narrator hears about Christa T.'s last seven years: cutting out uniforms on a Mecklenburg farm, working in the fields, and finally, after a nervous breakdown, deciding to do her part for the state by becoming a teacher. In her eagerness to participate, however, Christa T. is ill prepared for the reality of her students, who less than ever resemble the picture of the new socialist citizen painted by the Party and the enthusiasm of the "Aufbau" years. What she is confronted with instead is the likes of Hammarubi, a student who, prompted by a bet, bites off the head of a toad—just for sport; another pupil who climbs a poplar tree and willfully smashes a bird's eggs against a boulder; and, finally, those students who have learned quickly how to get by in the new system without having to believe in any of the doctrines and who mock their teacher's morality.

In the meantime, the people around Christa T., including the narrator, are swept up by the promises of a new beginning. Studying, discussing, and arguing, they adjust to the new world and make it their own, quickly replacing their disillusionment of the past with illusions of a new utopia. Although Christa T., too, at first eagerly embraces the hope of this new, socialist state, she quickly realizes that she cannot adjust as readily as her friends do. With her "difficulty of saying 'I'" and her wish that nothing should ever be finished but rather in a constant process of "coming to be," she begins to drift and starts to feel alienated. What she sees developing around her is neither the paradise of her dreams nor the new human being, but the beginning of a tightly controlled state apparatus that calls for "factual people" and "up-and-doing people," not dreamers and hopers such as herself. At this point, she is almost ready to give up, but when she meets Justus and subsequently marries him, she decides to give her life one more chance. Since she was unable to contribute to the socialist state in the public realm, she decides to contribute by becoming a housewife and mother. It seems that with her plans to build her own house by the lake, she, too, has finally arrived in everyday life and is willing to adjust. Yet she never manages to settle down and accept life as it is. Her passion for constant renewal, for fantasy and consciousness—the two things she names as absolutely essential for the survival of the human species—do not allow her to adjust to the new mentality around her. She dies of leukemia shortly after the birth of another child, just after the building of the Berlin Wall.

Analysis

The story line of *The Quest for Christa T.* does not develop in a linear fashion but follows the narrator's rummaging through the box of papers left behind by Christa T. In this way, the reader gets a glimpse of Christa T. as a sixteen-year-old, a glimpse of her as a child in her native village, writing prose. There is a flash forward to her last days before she dies, then a reconstruction of her life as a student. Each memory is triggered by a piece of writing—a poem, a diary entry in Christa T.'s little brown notebook, notes on receipts and household accounts—and is fleshed out by the narrator's own memory as well as imaginary conversations with people. The novel's multilayered structure is not readily accessible. A purposeful vagueness about narrative time and a constant interchanging of narrative perspective further underscore the novel's complexity. Yet it is these dramatic devices that make for the richness of the novel.

The novel begins with the epitaph "This coming to oneself—what is it?," a quotation from Johannes R. Becher, cultural minister of the German Democratic Republic (GDR) that summarizes the theme of the novel: the question of individual self-actualization (realization) within a socialist state or "the difficulty in saying 'I'" in a society insisting upon a collective "we." Although on one level the novel serves as a personal elegy for a childhood friend, *The Quest for Christa T.* can be read on another level as a critical development of early GDR history, of the kind that cannot be found in official textbooks. The author not only tells the tale of the friendship of two women but also chronicles the life of the generation born in the 1930's, Wolf's own generation. She addresses those who, liberated from fascism after the war, immediately and enthusiastically began building the socialist state without coming to terms with the past. With *The Quest for Christa T.*, Wolf issues a plea for learning from one's mistakes by remembering instead of ignoring one's history.

That the GDR has not dealt adequately with its past is exemplified throughout the novel through key episodes in which Christa T.'s own sensitivity and struggle to come to terms with reality confront the coldness and violence of her surroundings. Increasingly, she finds that personal feelings and considerations are no longer important to the development of the new socialist state. This is especially evident in the case of Günter, who, during his test class in front of his peers and the headmistress Frau Mrosow, was to "demonstrate the superiority of social motives over personal ones as exemplified by Ferdinand's conduct in Schiller's play *Love and Intrigue*." After passionately advocating the sanctity of love in front of his bewildered students, he is punished as "an example of what happens to a man who falls under the spell of subjectivism."

Against this tendency away from subjectivity and consciousness, toward reason and technical progress, Wolf sets a heroine who, through her individuality and skepticism, quietly rebels. Christa T. rebels in the choice of her thesis topic, "The narrator Theodor Storm," which she approaches not scientifically but in order to find the premises for her own artistic ability and to decide "how, if at all, one can realize oneself in a work of art," a position clearly opposed to the demands upon a writer to help stimulate and further the material production process within the socialist state. Here again, she defies the unwritten rules of behavior of the new socialist citizen. In 1955, Christa T. arrives at a costume party dressed as Sophie La Roche (with Justus dressed as Lord Seymour), a highly romantic and sentimental writer of the eighteenth century, and insists on portraying La Roche's character Fräulein von Sternheim, who leads a loving yet utterly boring bourgeois country life with her lover Lord Seymour. Then Christa T. shocks her friends by announcing her plans to build her own house and is accused of wanting to become a "property owner." All these acts depict her difficulty in conforming to the demands of her times. The true message of what it takes to be a citizen in this new world is delivered to her in 1960 by one of her former students—now a doctor—who explains that he has made a discovery that has finally put his mind to rest: "The essence of health is adaptation or conformity. . . . This means that at all times conformity is the means of survival: adaptation, conformity at any price." Clearly, Christa T. has never learned to be healthy in this sense, and it is this illness of nonconformity that eventually causes her death.

Context

With the quest for Christa T., the narrator engages in a quest not only for the identity of her childhood friend but also for the identity of the socialist state—a quest that serves as a warning against the dangers of a rigidly defined political structure that gives little concern to its individual citizens. In contrast to the "arrival" literature of the 1960's (a term based on the title of a book by Brigitte Reimann, *Ankunft im Alltag*, published in 1961), *The Quest for Christa T.* already exposes the dangers of such an "arrival" or rigidification of political structures that forecloses on the possibility of future developments. Therefore, as the narrator states at the beginning of the novel, Christa T.'s life needs to be remembered not for Christa T.'s sake but "for our sake. Because it seems that we need her."

Wolf's novel arrived at a time when literature in the socialist state had a clear political agenda: to establish and solidify a GDR identity and to inspire the individual to social activism. Thus, the publication of the novel immediately sparked a heated discussion. In the East, *The Quest for Christa T.* was severely criticized for being too personal, too pessimistic, and too unproductive as a literary model. In the West, the novel was welcomed because it was one of the first to criticize the German Democratic Republic. Although the references to real political events in the novel are rather vague, they always coincide with emotionally troubling times in Christa T.'s life, thus leaving no doubt that the historical developments within the GDR directly affected the lives of its citizens.

With the figure of Christa T. as heroine of the novel, a woman who is passionate, creative, and caring, Wolf purposefully sets a contrast to a society that she sees as increasingly dominated by a patriarchal and objectifying mind-set. The ideas that society, in its hunger for technology and industrialization, has taken a wrong path and that values such as caring and nurturing are no longer appreciated are themes that run throughout all of Wolf's works. Increasingly, Wolf looks to women for answers to the survival of the human species, and her critique of patriarchy and out-of-control technology intensifies from novel to novel, making its sharpest claim perhaps in *Kassandra* (1983; *Cassandra: A Novel and Four Essays*, 1984) and culminating in *Störfall: Nachrichten eines Tages* (1987; *Accident. A Day's News*, 1989), a novel in which she attempts to discover the reasons behind the nuclear catastrophe at Chernobyl in 1986. Long before "subjectivity" and "female authenticity" became terms that were used to describe the experience of women's lives in a patriarchally defined society, Wolf concerned herself with these issues and put them at the center of her writing.

Although Christa Wolf's works were usually met with resistance when first published, they have since been reprinted numerous times and translated into many different languages. Her novels not only give an invaluable insight into GDR life but also raise important issues relating to women's roles and the balance of responsibility between the individual and society.

Sources for Further Study
Fries, Marilyn Sibley, ed. *Responses to Christa Wolf: Critical Essays*. Detroit: Wayne State University, 1989. This collection of twenty essays deals with different aspects of Christa Wolf's writing, from a psychological perspective to a political analysis to a feminist account of her characters.
Huyssen, Andreas. "Trace of Ernst Bloch: Reflections on Christa Wolf." In *Responses to Christa Wolf: Critical Essays*, edited by Marilyn Sibley Fries. Detroit: Wayne State University Press, 1989. Huyssen's analysis traces the impact of Ernst Bloch's *The Principle of Hope*, a philosophical account of Marxism, on Christa Wolf's *Quest for Christa T.* and explores the importance of "remembering" as a literary device.
Kuhn, Anna. *Christa Wolf's Utopian Vision*. Cambridge, England: Cambridge University Press, 1988. This book offers a thorough Marxist feminist analysis of Christa

Wolf's novels from her beginnings as a writer with *Divided Heaven* to *Accident. News of a Day*, with a separate chapter devoted to *The Quest for Christa T.*

Probst, Gerhard F. "Thematization of Alterity in Christa Wolf's *Nachdenken über Christa T.*" *The University of Dayton Review* 13 (1976): 25-35. This essay examines Wolf's technique of using a narrator to tell Christa T.'s story and the distancing this literary device allows. It also explores the different narrative voices and their relationship to one another and to the author.

Wolf, Christa. *The Fourth Dimension: Interviews with Christa Wolf.* Translated by Hilary Pilkington. London: Verso, 1988. This invaluable work contains essays, lectures, and interviews covering the years 1959 to 1985.

Karin U. Herrmann

QUICKSAND

Author: Nella Larsen (1891-1964)
Type of work: Novel
Type of plot: Tragedy
Time of plot: The 1920's
Locale: The South, Harlem, and Denmark
First published: 1928

Principal characters:
HELGA CRANE, a cultured and refined woman, the daughter of a
black father and a white, Danish mother
MRS. HELEN HAYES-RORE, a wealthy widow who employs Helga
as a traveling companion and editor
JAMES VAYLE, Helga's colleague and former fiancée
ANNE GREY, a widow and political activist in Harlem
DR. ANDERSON, Anne's husband
PETER NILSSEN, Helga's wealthy maternal uncle
KATRINA DAHL, Helga's maternal aunt
AXEL OLSEN, a pompous Danish artist
THE REVEREND MR. PLEASANT GREEN, Helga's husband
MRS. HARTLEY, Helga's nurse when she falls ill
AUDREY DENNEY, a personable woman who embodies the
qualities that Helga aspires to cultivate in herself

Form and Content

Divided into twenty-five chapters, this autobiographical novel traces Helga's—
and, by extension, fictionalizes Larsen's—futile and endless search for identity and
happiness. Its relentless social realism recalls Larsen's own delicate and unstable
personality as the daughter of a Danish mother and black Indian father who died when
Larsen was young. Like Helga, Larsen went from post to post and was involved in an
unsatisfying marriage to a physicist. Larsen is thus able to voice the unique dilemmas
of a mulatta woman writer of the male-dominated Harlem Renaissance.

Among the themes her plot progression raises is the tension between sexual
repression and sexual expression for women who desire, simultaneously, sexual
fulfillment and social respectability in a culture that has made these mutually exclusive options for black females. This psychic division compounds, for black women,
the double consciousness that W. E. B. Du Bois described; it also serves as a
structuring device, as the narrative vacillates between these extremes as well as
between other dualities (urban/rural).

The beginning locus for this fluctuation is Naxos, which is most likely a composite
of Tuskegee Institute and Fisk University. Although she enjoys teaching, Helga finds
the blacks' passive acceptance and efforts to appease whites increasingly intolerable.
Because she can neither conform nor be content in her difference, she leaves her

pretentious fiancé, James Vayle, and the loathsome and self-deluded Naxos community in search of a less hypocritical path in Chicago, where she pursues her Uncle Peter only to be brutally rejected and disowned by his racist new wife.

Helga's homeless and rootless migrancy, established early in the novel, accompany her sense of dual alienation to frame the "tragic mulatta" narrative. Her first employer, Mrs. Hayes-Rore, at once assuages and compounds Helga's struggle, for while she offers Helga a way out of gray Chicago and a job and home in New York, she also advises her to keep her dismal history to herself. This repression makes her defensive during encounters with people from her past, as is shown in her ambivalence and anger after meeting with Dr. Anderson in New York. Her uncle's subsequent termination of ties with her and the internalized racism that rejection evokes make life seem "an excruciating agony." Her related conflict with Anne over Audrey Denney, whom Helga admires and Anne despises, solidifies her resolve to travel to Denmark.

Unfortunately, here, too, Helga "didn't at all count," except insofar as the Dahls were able to use her exotic "other" status for their own social-climbing ends. She refuses, to their chagrin, to marry the egotistic artist Axel Olsen, realizing that his unflattering portrait of her bespeaks his distorted regard for her sensuality. In her consequent desire to return to her black heritage, in part as an escape from her too-prolonged dissatisfaction among European whites, Helga is finally able to empathize with and forgive her father's abandonment.

After rejecting yet another proposal—the second from James Vayle, now assistant principal at Naxos—Helga suffers rejection, this time by Dr. Anderson, whose illicit kiss upon her return from Denmark she mistakenly assumes reciprocates her own dawning awareness of desire. Seeking shelter from the tumultuous storm that both figuratively and literally engulfs her, she wanders, hysterical, into a fateful revival in which participants assume she is a repentant Jezebel. After convincing herself of God's benevolence, she assents to the illusory stability that marriage to the Reverend Pleasant Green provides. Serial pregnancies bring her three babies in twenty months, a stillborn, exhaustion, and depression. Because her own grievous past will not allow her to desert her children, she continues to inhabit this downward spiral; she is pregnant with her fifth child as the novel closes.

Analysis

Sterling Brown, a cultural critic and one of the last living poets of the Harlem Renaissance, delineated the negative and positive qualities of the mulatta, which it is Larsen's goal to expose. Among these are a sense of alienation and isolation, the futility of searching for a concrete and stable identity, internalized ambivalence and hatred, and the constant pursuit of a continuously elusive and deceptive happiness. To the tragic mulatta's credit, however, is the keen ability to see the world from dual perspectives—one, for example, that witnesses the racism of both whites and blacks. This dual vision is precisely what enables Helga to see through superficial interaction—be it at Naxos among snobbish blacks or in Denmark among self-important whites. Larsen also deploys this point of view to illustrate the paradox of Du Bois' double consciousness when it simultaneously breeds self-contempt and disdain for the outside world of exploitative forces.

Larsen also suggests that miscegenation is a powerful and apt metaphor for confusion. Helga's "two-ness" is compounded because she is the offspring of Danish and black parents, rejected by both communities into which she desperately tries to fit, to her own eventual detriment. Larsen adds another dimension in making the protagonist a woman: Patriarchy exacts its own brand of double consciousness, which more richly complicates Helga's dilemma, for she is not accepted by women or men. Each wants her to repress or alter some integral aspect of her identity: Mrs. Hayes-Rore, her partially white background; Anne Grey, her nonjudgmental stance; James Vayle and Axel Olsen, her critical mind and astute scrutiny; her Aunt Katrina, her principles and autonomy; the Reverend Green, her self, her own desires and needs; Uncle Peter, her relation to and memory of him. Each wishes to construct a useful Helga, one who will solidify his or her own perception of the world and his or her inflated place in it. Thus it is that not only in Denmark—where she is exoticized in order to detonate her potency—but also in Naxos, Chicago, Harlem, and the South she is objectified and, thereby, disempowered.

Helga was fifteen when her mother died and her uncle placed her in a "school for Negroes," where Helga discovered that she "was not necessarily loathsome" and that in fact she could consider herself "without repulsion"; her internalized racism, thus, is deep-rooted and habitual. The reader wonders, along with the narrator, whether this capacity for self-contempt precludes her happiness, which, on some fundamental or unconscious level, she does not believe she merits or deserves. The fact that she understands and sympathizes with the racist viewpoint of her stepfather, his children, Mrs. Nilssen, and, to a degree, her mother demonstrates the breadth and depth of the disdain she absorbs. Similarly, she duplicates the white and black cultures' massive denial mechanisms regarding miscegenation by denying various parts of herself, depending on where and with whom she is. On this insidiously self-flagellating course, she incriminates herself on the basis of this fraudulence. Furthermore, she perceives Anne's ambivalence as hypocritical: Anne despises whites and their materialism and deems blacks superior, even while she dismisses the songs, dances, dialect, and attire of her own people. Thus does Helga's tragic mulatta status reap benefits as well; namely, the capacity to see clearly others' inconsistencies.

Indeed, one could argue that it is not so much her mulatta status that makes Helga tragic as it is her internalized disgust, which sets her to looking relentlessly outside herself for approval and validation. This constant seeking for others' valuation, in fact, moves the plot and action forward. Not until she travels inward during her stupor of exhausted withdrawal and rebellious isolation does she realize that she has run into a dead end. She has resigned herself to her suspicion that in America, "Negroes were allowed to be beggars only, of life, of happiness"; unlike whites, by and for whom the Constitution was written, they were not entitled to these pursuits.

Ironically, Helga is abroad when she realizes this during a disquieting ragtime performance by black dancers, whose cavorting shames and betrays her in its perpetuation of the spectacle and stereotype that Axel and his cohorts are all too eager to view. This epiphany solidifies her resolve not to bring more negro or mulatto children into the world to endure what she has suffered. She cannot replicate the pattern that makes death seem a viable alternative. Significantly, it is when she can no longer entertain death as a possibility because it would reduce her to nothingness that she enters her self-imposed death sentence. Larsen clearly equates marriage and motherhood with the deaths of women's spirits, the degeneration of their health, and the depletion of their bodies and emotional and mental resources.

Heterosexual marriage may constitute the quagmire to which these institutions and the societal and religious sanction of them relegates her. Helga laughs at the latter when Miss Hartley reads Anatole France's "The Procurator of Judea," anti-Christian and blasphemous sentiments now paralleling her own because of the recognition of institutionalized religion's role in her oppression. The more she struggles to extricate herself, the deeper she sinks into the notches that sociocultural expectations carve for those who are at once suppressed, oppressed, repressed, and depressed by the consuming quagmire of race, class, gender, and religion. Larsen allows the reader this comprehensive view through the omniscient character of Miss Hartley, introduced at the novel's end, the only "all-seeing" or caretaking person who, even though—and perhaps because—she is aware, tends to and prioritizes Helga's needs. Like the title, the closing pages of the novel, through Larsen's poignant diction, reiterate the "asphyxiation" and "suffocation" that inform this mulatta woman's tragedy.

Context

Larsen's work recasts the genre of racial uplift novels by focusing on the costs to women of this alleged, male-dominated uplift. One such cost is the dividing of women, which is evident in Anne's assumption that Audrey is passing for white and is therefore a despicable traitor to her race and her sex. This drives a wedge between Anne and Helga at the same time that it inhibits Helga from approaching Audrey, whom she admires. Similarly, the novel subtly alludes to the divergent perceptions regarding the role of marriage and parenthood in racial uplift. After Helga returns from Denmark, she confesses to James Vayle her belief that it is sinful to bring more negro children into the world to endure pain and prejudice. He is "aghast" and declares his elitist stance that it is precisely the upper-class educated who are obligated to reproduce. This male prerogative reinforces a dualism surrounding women and their sexuality which Larsen also scrutinizes. When Helga is not contributing "to the cause" in this way, she, like Audrey, is deemed a prostitute or a Jezebel, which both Axel Olsen and the revival congregation call her.

The delusion that her only salvation is to submit to the opposite of this mistaken designation within the sanctioned reproductive sexuality of marriage exacts an extreme toll upon Helga's psyche. She shuts down her reasoning skills and closes her inquisitive mind in order to maintain a blind faith in God's marvel and in the marriage, upon which she refuses to reflect for fear that it will necessitate greater denial. Thus does she—in typical submissive-wife fashion—rationalize and deny her husband's offensive hygiene and slovenly habits. She even numbs herself to these disgusting traits: "she was even able to be unaware" and to ignore his suffocating, asphyxiating self-satisfaction (which "pour from him like gas from a leaking pipe") and his neglect. Only in illness is Helga able to secure any quiet or tender care and protection, which is, significantly, proffered by a woman nurse. Although her only road to recovery is to leave this exploitative institution, the burden of her abandonment and its grave consequences for her entire life do not permit her to desert the children, even to save herself. Yet her severe depression—more of a breakthrough than a breakdown—clarifies the travesty of religion's oppressiveness to women, and this confrontation suggests that time will continue to reveal to her the truths that will genuinely retrieve her from the quagmires, just as her pivotal understanding and forgiveness of her father had earlier enabled her to extricate herself from the quicksand of appeasing relatives by marrying a conceited white bore.

Larsen's novel also critiques the travesty of determining one's worth in binarism, which unequally values different races, sexes, and classes. In Denmark, "she didn't at all count," because she was a black middle-class rather than upper-class woman who, because she was on display as a curio, peacock, decoration, or otherwise exoticized object, was not fully human.

For all these reasons, *Quicksand* was a critical success and won Larsen both the Harmon Foundation Bronze Medal and a Guggenheim Fellowship. Unfortunately, a false accusation of plagiarism and the breakdown of her own marriage after fourteen years prompted her own withdrawal from the literary scene and into nursing. Her retrieval from the quagmire of obscurity by Deborah McDowell and others involved in the American Women Writers Series assures her a rightful place as a prominent figure of the Harlem Renaissance, one who suffers a variation on the black female *Bildungsroman* and thereby influences many contemporary writers, such as Alice Walker, whose novel *Meridian* (1976) is clearly influenced by *Quicksand*.

Sources for Further Study

Ammons, Elizabeth. *Conflicting Stories: American Women Writers at the Turn into the Twentieth Century*. New York: Oxford University Press, 1991. Ammons places Larsen's novels in the context of the artist's rebellion—in *Quicksand*, against the standard options available to middle-class African American women. Because of the era's intense emphasis on individualism, Larsen's was a solitary struggle that could have benefited from a community of women writers. Classism within the Harlem Renaissance exacerbated this tension.

Beemyn, Brett. "A Bibliography of Works by and About Nella Larsen." *African American Review* 26, no. 1 (Spring, 1992): 183. In this bibliography, novels and periodical works as well as criticism, bibliographic works, and biographical studies are listed chronologically and alphabetically in six sections. The first two concern *Quicksand* and *Passing* editions and reviews from 1928 to 1989 and periodical publications from 1920 to 1930.

Kramer, Victor, ed. *The Harlem Renaissance Re-examined*. New York: AMS Press,

1987. In the chapter "'A Lack Somewhere': Nella Larsen's *Quicksand* and the Harlem Renaissance," Lillie Howard argues that Helga's quests for materialism, the proper family, and acceptable expression of sexuality bespeak a fragmented self and a perpetual ambiguity about race which preclude her ability to take advantage of various alternatives. The mulatta need not be tragic, according to Howard.

Kubitschek, Missy Dehn. *Claiming the Heritage: African-American Women Novelists and History*. Jackson: University Press of Mississippi, 1991. Kubitschek contends that as an immigrant white woman, Helga's mother Karen's guidance of Helga's black American woman's experiences would have been limited. Reaffirming the need for a socioculturally contextualized critical approach to Helga's development and demise, she claims that Larsen inverts the trope of miscegenation to emphasize the isolation of the resulting daughter and the inability of the mother to assist or protect Helga. She demonstrates Helga's internalization of racism and sexism and highlights her multiple modes of repression.

Lay, Mary. "Parallels: Henry James's *The Portrait of a Lady* and Nella Larsen's *Quicksand*." *CLA Journal* 20, no. 4 (1977): 475-486. Lay faults Helga's poor judgment, rather than her environment or difficult context as a mulatto, as the reason for her downfall.

McDowell, Deborah. Introduction to *"Quicksand" and "Passing."* New Brunswick, N.J.: Rutgers University Press, 1986. In this introduction to the American Women Writers Series edition, McDowell argues that Helga Crane's primary dilemma is between sexual repression and expression. She cites Larsen as a pioneer in the African American female literary tradition in her treatment of black female sexuality within conventional morality.

Morgan, Janice, and Colette Hall, eds. *Refining Autobiography in Twentieth Century Women's Fiction: An Essay Collection*. Vol. 3. In *Gender and Genre in Literature*. New York: Garland, 1991. In the chapter "Self-Representation as Art in the Novels of Nella Larsen," Jacquelyn McLendon cites Larsen's title as self-revelatory of narrative intent regarding Helga's struggle and fate. Helga's sacrifice does not weaken the book, but instead forces the reader to face the questions Larsen raises about various oppressive social institutions and the unresolved tension between personal desire and societal expectation.

O'Neale, Sondra. "Race, Sex, and Self: Aspects of *Bildung* in Select Novels by Black American Women Novelists." *MELUS* 9, no. 4 (1982): 25-37. O'Neale delineates seven criteria for African American female *Bildungsroman*: the mulatta preoccupied with communal acceptance, procreation's disastrous results, death as an alternative, thwarted mother-daughter relationships, and three others. She illustrates the various ways in which *Quicksand* fits into this genre.

Thornton, Hortense. "Sexism as Quagmire: Nella Larsen's *Quicksand*." *CLAJ* 16, no. 3 (March, 1973): 285-301. Thornton contends that society, the world, and the irreconcilable facts of being negro and American and a woman are to blame for Helga's situation.

Roseanne L. Hoefel

A QUIET LIFE

Author: Beryl Bainbridge (1933-   )
Type of work: Novel
Type of plot: Domestic realism
Time of plot: Post-World War II
Locale: Southport, England
First published: 1976

>*Principal characters:*
>ALAN, a seventeen-year-old who must cope with his
>   dysfunctional family
>MADGE, Alan's fifteen-year-old sister, whose unconventional
>   behavior causes Alan embarrassment and concern
>ALAN'S FATHER, a sickly perfectionist who dislikes his wife and
>   children
>ALAN'S MOTHER, a dramatic and prim woman who believes in
>   the importance of appearances
>JANET LEYLAND, Alan's shallow girlfriend
>AUNT NORA, Alan's father's sister

Form and Content

Beryl Bainbridge's novel *A Quiet Life* begins with middle-aged Alan waiting for his sister Madge to meet him to discuss their mother's recent death and to take their mother's ring. Madge refuses this momento of her mother, and Alan slips into a dramatic flashback of his adolescence, which makes up the bulk of the novel.

Alan's flashback, which takes up eight chapters, portrays his selective memory about his family. Although he reveals the painful slights and emotional injuries incurred and endured by the four family members, there seems to be an unconscious suspension of the deeper realities at home. Perhaps an element of self-pity enters into the picture; Alan's memories are believable, however, and readers can sense that his inability to dig deeper into his past shields him from greater misery.

The novel's title—*A Quiet Life*—seems to be ironic in that the family's situation does not allow for quietude. In fact, Alan's home life is disquieting. His memories of his seventeenth year begin with random vignettes of his day-to-day life: He recalls his mother's constant rearranging of the furniture, the family's typical tea-time crises, and his sister Madge's lies about her time away from home. When his maternal grandparents and his paternal aunt arrive for a family gathering, Alan's flashback becomes more focused. The family's behaviors exhibited with these extended family members allow the reader to appreciate more fully the emotional damage that Alan continually allows for in his memory.

A Quiet Life goes on to recount the ups and downs of Alan's tempestuous and confining family life. Much of the novel centers on Alan's disgust for the behavior of his father, who so often gives in to tantrums and vicious acts of destruction about the house, but the flashback also characterizes the father as a quiet, contemplative man who putters in his garden. This conflicting characterization parallels Alan's conflicting emotions for his parent. In his flashback, Alan wants to remember the father as a nurturer, yet the terrifying realities of his father's temperament intrude throughout his narrative.

Perhaps most worrisome to Alan is his sister's erratic behavior with the German convicts housed in nearby barracks. It bothers Alan that Madge sneaks out of the house; he vaguely recognizes that it might be dangerous. Yet he is unable to reason with her. Madge challenges Alan's illusion of stability: "She influenced them all without their knowing; she peeled back the layers. She had only to hint . . . that they weren't a close family."

Whereas Madge defies her family's tyranny and dysfunction by flaunting her behavior, Alan withdraws. Rejecting his sister's bold actions, Alan broods over his family's problems and his embarrassment. Late in the book, Madge tries to explain to Janet about Alan: "He keeps everything bottled up. . . . Anything for a quiet life."

Analysis

Bainbridge's main focus in *A Quiet Life* is to portray the dissonance and dissolution of a middle-class English family that appears to be happy. Yet the story goes much deeper than that: Bainbridge portrays four members of this family who require their own illusions in order to survive the relationships that exist within the family structure. Her exploration is always presented from Alan's point of view. Although the story is not presented as a first-person account, the plot is revealed via Alan's consciousness, thus offering a very personal and far-from-objective treatment.

Early in the book, Alan confronts his sister about her running through the woods to meet the German prisoner-of-war. He points out: "There's unexploded bombs. . . . You should stay in the house." Madge replies, "There's worse things than bombs, you know." The brother and sister must live carefully at home where so many unexploded emotional bombs are hidden. They are never safe from their parents' explosive and vindictive actions.

Throughout the narrative, Alan's relationships with his family and his friends are explored within an aura of guarded detachment. Bainbridge's text is filled with details that seem to compete with Alan's pain and longing; the details offer a sharp edge that tends to blunt the reader's total grasp of Alan's emotional state. Bainbridge's choice of detail produces a spare seriocomic effect, underscoring the story's grotesque quality: "They were having their tea, silent under the hanging flypaper."

Bainbridge addresses a disquieting silence in this family. For all the carping and sniggering, there is a silence that isolates each family member. That is not to say that there is no conversation, no arguing, no accusations, but there is an element of isolation, of a silence that hangs over the family and paradoxically echoes louder than spoken words: "Someone would retaliate—Madge would interfere, Father would chuck the sugar bowl at the wall, the three of them would lapse into a silence more brutal than words."

A Quiet Life is also a novel about physical space. Madge seems to require release from the space within her home; she runs through the woods and on the beach. The freedom of open spaces outdoors signifies Madge's recklessness. It is the confined and cramped house that seems to signify Alan's predicament: "It can get on your nerves." When Alan says to his girlfriend Janet Leyland, "You see, it's very cramped at home, very confined," he is not referring only to a lack of space and privacy. His comment represents the claustrophobia that his parents impose upon him and his sister as well as the constant shifting of loyalties within the family—not unlike his mother's constant rearrangement of the furniture. It is for these reasons that Madge and Alan take every opportunity to go out. Their father, too, flees his home to mope at his sister's home, and their mother cannot bear to be at home in the evening, so she goes to the train station to read.

Essentially, the novel is about pretense—the family's simulation of a harmonious home life. Bainbridge is able to assemble the four family members and present them in their smug self-deception for the reader: "They sat for a little while drinking tea by the fire; they were a happy family." Yet within one page, she has scraped away the family's protective coating to reveal their reality: "You make me sick," Madge pushes at Alan, "You keep everything bottled up. You won't face facts." The fact is that the family—especially Alan—cannot confront reality. He must quietly live his life in pretense as a method of survival. It is the survival instinct that motivates virtually all the family members' actions in the book—all of them are fleeing from home.

There is one character, however, who does not seem to function under pretense. That character is the father. Bainbridge has drawn his character as grotesque and menacing, at the center of the family's dysfunction. At one point, Bainbridge describes him as "a demented saboteur." Alan cringes in embarrassment and pain whenever his father is present: "What right had he, thought Alan, to fume and bluster, to fill the house with anxiety?" The father's actions are frantic and uncontrollable— totally without pretense—from throwing a handful of pennies across the room when a parlor game does not go his way to chopping down the family's favorite tree outside their home.

A Quiet Life is an exhibition of adolescent anguish. Bainbridge allows Alan to remember only so much of his troubled seventeenth year, a turning point for his family. The author's restrained yet searing detail and the obscured point of view produce a muted realism. Although the novel lays bare Alan's family's stunted nature, it does not allow Alan to recognize his own self-deceptions—even from the vantage point of looking back at his childhood.

Context

A Quiet Life is a departure from the majority of Bainbridge's work in that she features a male voice as its central consciousness. Seventeen-year-old Alan observes his emotionally damaged family and recognizes his younger sister Madge as the pivotal family member in this domestic novel. Perhaps by means of this device Bainbridge forces a more hard-edged portrayal of this young woman, tinged with certain elements of sibling rivalry.

The novel grapples with a woman's sense of worth, her sense of emotional entrapment in a hopelessly dysfunctional setting. Both Madge and her mother initiate escapes, yet each contributes to the damaging climate in the home. Bainbridge does not let them off the hook; they are not drawn as heroic, but as realistic and flawed characters.

In many respects, *A Quiet Life* continues a tradition in modern literature written by English women that portrays twentieth century angst. Bainbridge captures much of the despair of cramped lives and dependence that characterizes Shelagh Delaney's play *A Taste of Honey* (1959) and Jeanette Winterson's novel *Oranges Are Not the Only Fruit* (1985). A notable contemporary American counterpart to Bainbridge is Anne Taylor; both authors create characters from families in which the grotesque and seriocomic are the norms.

Sources for Further Study

Bannon, Barbara A. "Beryl Bainbridge." *Publishers Weekly* 209 (March 15, 1976): 6-7. In this interview, Bainbridge discusses her family and her writing process. She states that she is attracted to the Victorian period because "women knew where they were then." Her theatrical background is noted, and her developing talent as a painter is mentioned.

Perez, Gilberto. "Narrative Voices." *The Hudson Review* 30 (Winter, 1977-1978): 610-620. This review of several novels addresses *A Quiet Life* in passing, complaining that Alan is boring and that the limited point of view is unsuitable, holding that the first person would be more effective stylistically. The reviewer says that Madge is the more intriguing character.

Pickering, Jean. "Drabble, Byatt, Dunn, and Bainbridge: Their Lives and Their Books." *Albion* 11 (1979): 197. This abstract of a paper presented at a scholarly conference describes the similarities of the four contemporary women writers. The short report notes the favorable publishing market in England for women's fiction. In interviews, the four authors explain how they have had to juggle their careers and family lives, and they note that, as contemporaries living in London, they share a supportive literary environment.

Punter, David. "Beryl Bainbridge: The New Psychopathia." In *The Hidden Script: Writing and the Unconscious*. London: Routledge & Kegan Paul, 1985. Bainbridge's novels are explained as "fables of psychosis" and her characters are described as stunted and bizarre. A theme of rebellion runs throughout Bainbridge's novels, yet in *A Quiet Life* Alan's rebellion results in regression and cautious claustrophobia. Alan and Madge's relationship is worrisome to Alan throughout his adolescence and in his middle age because he senses that she has a story to tell about him and that it is potentially damaging.

Wenno, Elisabeth. *Ironic Formula in the Novels of Beryl Bainbridge*. Göteborg, Sweden: Acta Universitatis Gothoburgensis, 1993. Bainbridge's fiction exhibits a "realistic simplicity" that relies on irony, the effect of which is ambiguity. These textual dimensions underscore the author's "ethical stance." Wenno's study includes an extensive bibliography of newspaper reviews of Bainbridge's novels in addition to many interviews with Bainbridge and introductory articles about her.

Douglas A. Jones

THE RADIANT WAY

Author: Margaret Drabble (1939-   )
Type of work: Novel
Type of plot: Satire
Time of plot: 1980-1985
Locale: London and the town of Northam in northern England
First published: 1987

Principal characters:
 LIZ HEADLEAND, a psychoanalyst who learns that her husband is
  leaving her for the boring Lady Henrietta Latchett
 ALIX BOWEN, Liz's friend from college
 ESTHER BREUER, a close friend of Liz and Alix at college
 CHARLES HEADLEAND, Liz's second husband, a television
  executive
 BRIAN BOWEN, Alix's husband
 SHIRLEY HARPER, Liz's younger sister
 JILLY FOX, Alix's brilliant but ill-fated student
 RITA ABLEWHITE, the mother of Liz and Shirley

Form and Content
 The Radiant Way, which has no chapter breaks, switches back and forth from one character to another and has an omniscient narrator who intrudes occasionally in a neighborly way to comment on the course of events. The narrative voice beguiles in its wit, allusiveness, and erudition. Symbols and myths pop up, and the clamor of public affairs and politics rumbles in the background, but the unfolding lives of Liz Headleand, Alix Bowen, and Esther Breuer evolve into a loose structure around which details fall into place.
 Most of the action takes place in London, but Northam provides structural and thematic contrasts. The novel opens with the Headleand's splashy New Year's Eve party for two hundred guests from London's professional circles, and the scene shifts abruptly to Northam, where Shirley Harper is grimly entertaining her husband Cliff's brother and his wife, Cliff's parents, and Brian Bowen's father. Brian's kind and likable father contrasts with Cliff's disagreeable mother, whose every sly complaint grates on Shirley exactly as the old harridan intends. Such comic scenes recall the novels of Jane Austen, whom Drabble invokes at one point with the observation that "Jane Austen recommended three or four families in a country village as the thing to work on when planning a novel."
 No beginning, middle, and end shape Drabble's account of five years in the England of the Margaret Thatcher era. Liz Headleand endures Charles's abandonment of her in divorce and a wrenching removal from her fashionable Harley Street address. Her mother dies, and in rummaging through her mother's closet she finds newspaper

clippings that clear up the mystery of her fatherless upbringing and her mother's long withdrawal from the world: Her father had apparently killed himself after committing a sex offense.

Alix Bowen suffers no painful divorce and discovers no skeletons in the family closet, but her worries about Jilly Fox climax in a visit to Jilly's awful flat, or "squat," as the homeless call a lodging in a dilapidated, unused building. Obscene and nightmarish murals cover Jilly's walls, and she dismisses Alix, insisting that her life is over. When Alix leaves the squat, she discovers that neighborhood delinquents have let the air out of her tires. Returning the next day, Alix comes upon a crowd around her car and finds Jilly's severed head on the front seat. She has become the latest victim of a serial killer known as the Harrow Road Horror.

Esther Breuer lives in the dangerous neighborhood of the murders, but is indifferent to the mean streets all around her; the discovery that the murderer lives in the flat above her stuns her. Her independent ways encourage alliances with unconventional people, none of whom is more unconventional than the Italian anthropologist Claudio Volpe, who serves for years as her platonic consort. Claudio studies werewolves, an eccentric preoccupation, perhaps, but a harmless one until he gives a scholarly lecture in which he describes straightforwardly his meeting in the Bulgarian forest with a werewolf who led him to his village. Esther and Claudio's sister have been good friends for years, and after the Harrow Road murders and Claudio's death soon after, Esther goes to Italy, where she spends most of her time engrossed in her studies of art history.

After leaving Liz, Charles Headleand settles in New York with Henrietta Latchett, but something goes awry with his television production plans among the Yanks, because Christmas of 1985 finds him at Liz's new house in St. John's Wood with all of their children. The hope that he had invested in *The Radiant Way*, his television production of twenty years earlier, has come to nothing. Strikes plague the country, and Charles has swung to the political Right. The Left has failed, and a new mood has arisen.

Analysis

The depiction of a long-running sisterhood, augmented by the pleasure of watching the children grow up with their own independent visions of life, gives *The Radiant Way* immense appeal. Alix swells with gratitude to the gods for her son Nicholas and his beautiful, talented companion, Ilse. They are both talented artists, generous and open to life, and the fortune that Deborah Manning, Nicholas' grandmother, bestows on them gives a storybook happy closure to their affairs.

Liz's children and stepchildren appear less prominently, but they all seem to be coping successfully with youth's vicissitudes and are finding their own places. They have so far sidestepped the great traps laid for young people by drugs, alcohol, and sex, and clearly Liz has had much to do with their success. She has loved her stepsons as she has loved her own daughters, and she is loved by them in return. The successes of the Headleand children contrast with the collapse into madness and death of the unfortunate Jilly Fox, whose parents are vacationing in foreign lands when Jilly is beheaded. With so much urban madness everywhere around them, the children of Liz and Alix keep level heads.

Celia Harper, daughter of Shirley and Cliff, is every bit her Aunt Liz's niece. Although she has not realized it yet, Shirley is incubating another Cambridge intellectual from Northam. Celia reads about the Brigantes, she watches the fuddled domesticity around her, and she waits. She is nurturing her wits and gathering the strength to leap. No early sex with awkward blue-collar Romeos for her; her eye is on Oxbridge and a life amid richer sensibilities.

The mainly unproblematic sex lives of Liz, Alix, and Esther offer little to titillate the voyeur. Liz's first marriage, to Edgar Lintot, was a disappointment, but Charles's sexuality complemented hers in a gratifying way—at least until the years had diminished its infinite variety. Liz had a number of extramarital misadventures—including one with a Dutchman on a boat that she still remembers—but with Charles's departure she decides it is time to say goodbye to all that. She has warm feelings for a roving journalist named Stephen Cox, but he does not notice.

Alix's first marriage lacked the brutality of Liz's, but Sebastian Manning's carnal feelings were either stunted or turned in another direction. His early death by accident freed Alix from what would have soon become a life in death and left her with a great gift in her son, Nicholas. Brian Bowen provides the sexual companionship she had missed in Sebastian, and they remain well attuned to each other in a generally contented union. When Brian's oldest friend falls in love with Alix and kisses her impulsively in an unguarded moment, Alix is stirred but is resolute in passing this milestone of married life.

Esther Breuer appears to lead a fully satisfying life without the gratifications of sex. Her fastidiousness about physical contact allows her to maintain her long, apparently platonic, problem-free relationship with her werewolf authority, Claudio Volpe. Speculation that she is a lesbian seems to be confounded by the picture presented of her in bed with Claudio's sister, both of them lying there chastely, like two virgins awaiting their lovers on St. Agnes Eve. Esther and Claudio enjoy a close relationship that is rooted in mutual interests, and this closeness is deepened by their heterosexuality, but that is it. Not all relationships are founded on carnality.

Context

Margaret Drabble has written a dozen novels chronicling the lives of modern women, works that are always closely observed and sincerely felt. One of her earliest novels, *Thank You All Very Much* (in America, *The Millstone*), presents the plight of a highly educated young woman who finds herself pregnant by a man she has no interest in marrying. Indeed, he does not even know that she is pregnant. Drabble's sympathetic treatment of this theme is fixed in a larger context: As the unwed mother-to-be makes her way through the British system of socialized medicine, she realizes the many day-to-day obstacles faced by people of lesser education and resources. As an account of a young woman's loss of innocence, *The Millstone* typifies

Drabble's concern with a human predicament that always overlaps with other people's struggles to get on in the world.

This all-important social context in which Drabble situates her characters puts her more in the "great tradition" of F. R. Leavis than in any variety of feminism. In fact, Liz studied under Leavis at Cambridge and looks back with great pleasure on his dating classes, which involve taking an unidentified scrap of quotation and homing in on its date and author. Drabble studied at Cambridge and must have excelled at dating exercises.

Alix Bowen, in December of 1983, questions herself about her feelings on the state of affairs in London. Her answers are perhaps Drabble's answers also: Although London is a more dangerous place than it was in 1979, it is probably not the Tories' fault; although Brian thinks that a Labour government would have improved things, Alix has changed her mind from five years ago and no longer thinks so. Although the Metropolitan Police are probably corrupt, a Labour government would be able to do little to halt a largely inevitable decay. Although the left-wing groups mean well, they may be "positively encouraging the growing inequality of the society they claim to wish to redeem." Despite all these doubts, Alix still calls herself a socialist.

Two later novels continue the characters of *The Radiant Way*: *A Natural Curiosity* (1989) finds Liz and Shirley learning more about their family background, and Alix caught in a familiar liberal dilemma; *The Gates of Ivory* (1991) takes Liz on a harrowing search for Stephen Cox in Kampuchea (Cambodia).

Sources for Further Study

Duguid, Lindsay. Review of *The Radiant Way*. *The Times Literary Supplement*, May 1, 1987, 458-459. Praises the honesty and social consciousness of *The Radiant Way* but says that the "highly wrought prose" renders the political concerns "strained and unconvincing."

Gray, Paul. Review of *The Radiant Way*. *Time* 130 (November 16, 1987): 87. Stresses the depiction of Thatcher-era England in this "odd hybrid, soap opera grafted onto newsreel," that "engrosses" and actually "works."

Hulbert, Ann. "Maggiemarch." *The New Republic* 197 (December 14, 1987): 38-42. Sneers at Drabble's "version of the emerging Social Democratic sensibility" and her "portentously detached and cliquish" style. The novel reveals no empathy, only smugness, and it revels in a "hackneyed symbolism."

Stuewe, Paul. Review of *The Radiant Way*. *Quill & Quire* 53 (April, 1987): 33. A sour judgment on *The Radiant Way* as a feminist's delight but "a pretty dismal trip" for other readers.

Updike, John. Review of *The Radiant Way*. *The New Yorker* 63 (November 16, 1987): 153-154. Rousing applause from another master novelist. Notes Drabble's "chummy" way with her readers and praises "her lively mind showing its incidental erudition, its epigrammatic flair, its quick-witted impatience and impudence." Mostly, however, Updike praises "her earthiness—her love of our species and its habitat—and her ability to focus on the small, sweaty intersections of mind and body, past and present." These qualities make *The Radiant Way* "a rare thing—a novel we would wish longer."

Frank Day

A RAISIN IN THE SUN

Author: Lorraine Hansberry (1930-1965)
Type of work: Drama
Type of plot: Problem play
Time of plot: Post-World War II
Locale: Chicago's South Side
First produced: 1959, at the Ethel Barrymore Theatre, New York City, New York
First published: 1959

> *Principal characters:*
> WALTER LEE YOUNGER, an intense young African American man
> LENA YOUNGER, Walter Lee's mother, a hardworking, devout widow
> RUTH YOUNGER, Walter Lee's wife
> BENEATHA YOUNGER, Walter Lee's sister, a college student
> GEORGE MURCHISON, Beneatha's college friend
> JOSEPH ASAGAI, a young African who wants Beneatha to return to Africa with him
> TRAVIS YOUNGER, the ten-year-old son of Walter Lee and Ruth
> CARL LINDNER, a representative of the Clybourne Park Association who tries to persuade the Younger family to move to "a Negro community"
> BOBO, Walter Lee's friend

Form and Content

Written just as the Civil Rights movement began to get underway, this play (and the motion picture made from it in 1960) made an important statement regarding race relations. Lorraine Hansberry, coming as she did from an affluent African American family, had experienced discrimination in her own childhood when her father moved the family out of the Chicago ghetto to a home in Englewood, Illinois. She also had strong opinions about the position of black women in American society, who are represented to a great extent by the character of Beneatha in this play.

Additionally, Langston Hughes's poem "A Dream Deferred" must be considered seminal in understanding the play. In it the poet asks, "What happens to a dream deferred? Does it dry up like a raisin in the sun?. . . or does it explode?" and Hansberry has successfully dramatized various human reactions to such deferment. The time in the play spans only a few weeks, but the dreams held by each of the characters have roots that reach far back. As the play begins, Lena is expecting a check of $10,000 as beneficiary of her husband's life insurance, and each character sees that money as the key that will unlock the future.

Most volatile about getting control of the money is Walter Lee, who wants to invest (with two other men) in a liquor store and become an independent businessman. He represents the dream that is ready to explode. In the first scene, he makes his attitude very clear when he asks his wife Ruth to persuade his mother to give him the money, and he becomes very upset with her when she insists that it is Lena's money to do with as she likes.

Walter Lee's frustration with his life causes him to project his predicament on his wife, as a representative of all black women. As he puts it, "Man say I got to change my life. I'm choking to death, baby! And his woman say—your eggs is getting cold!"

Lena Younger, knowing that she and her husband never realized their dreams, has accepted life as God has willed it. In the words of the poem, she has "crusted and sugared over—like a syrupy sweet." Because of the insurance money, however, she believes that she has been given a second chance at her dream of improving the lives of everyone in her family by moving out of the ghetto. Furthermore, because she is very religious, she disapproves of the idea of a liquor store for her son. Representing the older black woman who heads the family, Lena is a loving but quietly controlling matriarch.

The early-morning scene that opens the play illustrates clearly the physical conditions in which the Youngers live. The apartment is clean but very crowded; Travis sleeps on a couch in the living room, and the family shares a bathroom with other tenants in the building. Quite soon, Ruth reveals that she is pregnant, and her consideration of an abortion strengthens Lena's resolve regarding the use of the money.

Beneatha's dream of becoming a doctor is quite concrete; she has had it since adolescence. Unlike her brother, she does not solicit her mother's financial assistance. Representing the newly emancipated black woman (in the image of the playwright), Beneatha gives the impression that she will not marry for security or surrender her free-thinking ideas. At one point, Lena actually slaps Beneatha and insists that she affirm her belief in God, but it is clear that the young woman acquiesces only out of respect for her mother. She will march to the beat of her own drummer.

A three-act play, *A Raisin in the Sun* follows the typical dramatic format. The stage setting cues the audience regarding the milieu in which the Younger family lives, and in the first act the characters are established and the major conflict is made clear. In the second act, the situation becomes more complex when Lena Younger announces that she has purchased a house in a "white" neighborhood and tries to justify her decision to her son, who refuses to be placated. In this act, too, the young men who are interested in Beneatha are introduced. The audience then sees her reactions to both the upper-middle-class George Murchison, who is a fool in Beneatha's eyes, and Joseph Asagai, whose idea of her future in Africa does not appeal to her either.

After realizing Walter Lee's deep bitterness because she has acted as head of the family by buying the new house, Lena Younger changes her mind and decides to trust Walter Lee with all of the money that is left after she has made the $3,500 down payment on the house. She gives him instructions to put half away for Beneatha's medical school, with the understanding that the third that remains is his to invest as he wishes.

In the second act, the family is packing to move, and even Walter Lee seems happy now that Lena has abdicated her role as ruling matriarch and has given him his position as "head of the family." At this juncture, however, Karl Lindner interrupts their newfound harmony with his proposal to pay the Youngers rather handsomely if they will agree not to move to lily-white Clybourne Park. During this encounter, Beneatha has a chance to assert her assimilationist point of view, one undoubtedly held by the playwright, while in his newfound position of power, Walter Lee unceremoniously shows Lindner the door.

At this point, Lena returns and is made to understand what the "Clybourne Park Welcoming Committee" really signifies. She graciously accepts, however, the gardening set her children have bought for her and the too-fancy gardening hat, which Travis has selected for his grandmother to wear as she gardens in their new yard.

Bobo, the visitor who arrives after Lindner has left, represents the messenger who brings word of the classic reversal of fortune for the protagonist. Bobo reports that Willy Harris did not meet him at the railroad station to go to Springfield to get the license for the liquor store. Instead, he simply disappeared with Bobo's money and with the entire amount that Lena had entrusted to Walter Lee, including Beneatha's portion.

How each character reacts to this crisis initially is no surprise. After Lena has momentarily lost her temper, she prays for strength, castigates herself for "aiming too high," and begins to think in terms of "fixing up the apartment." Beneatha seems to have given up her idea of becoming a doctor. Practical Ruth says that the family could still make the new house payments if everybody worked. Walter Lee, however, who is completely devastated, has decided to telephone Lindner and accept his offer.

In the final scene, Lena insists that Travis witness his father's degradation in accepting payment from "the Man" under these circumstances, which causes another reversal for Walter Lee. He cannot bear to see his son present as he exchanges his manhood for money, so he tells Lindner that they are a plain but proud family who will try to be good neighbors. As the moving men arrive, the Youngers begin their move to Clybourne Park.

Analysis

Hansberry, using the physical move from the ghetto as the fulcrum for the discussion of the African American place in the world of the 1950's, has carefully avoided a number of pitfalls. Most important, although the white Lindner is far from an admirable character, it is a black man, Willy Harris, who is the real villain of the piece. In addition, it is Walter Lee's overeagerness to move into a world he sees as the white man's world which makes him such easy prey for Willy.

Furthermore, even Beneatha, who seems to be free from the restraints that the segregated society attempts to impose, has been lured into some imitative behavior, such as "expressing herself" through expensive hobbies that she drops in quick succession. Near the end of the play, Asagai accuses her of using her brother's loss of her tuition money as an excuse for giving up her dream.

A major theme of *A Raisin in the Sun* is love, particularly love of children in African American families. Lena speaks of a child she and Big Walter had "lost to poverty," and she appeals to Walter Lee to persuade Ruth that there is no need to abort her baby. Actually, everything Lena does she does out of love for her children, even if she is oblivious to the fact that exercising her rights as matriarch is not the best way to do so, particularly because of her son. After Walter Lee's defeat, it is Lena who admonishes Beneatha that the time to love a person is "when he's at his lowest and can't believe in hisself 'cause the world done whipped him so."

In the scenes between Asagai and Beneatha, there is a sense of what Hansberry said in her play *Les Blancs* (posthumously produced in 1970) about black revolutions in Africa not always being beneficial to the natives in those countries, so this too may be considered a theme of *A Raisin in the Sun*. Yet, it is the playwright's conviction that any variety of racism is evil that certainly dominates.

In addition to using Langston Hughes's poem as a metaphor for the characters in the play, Hansberry uses a plant as a symbol. The poor straggly thing struggles to get enough sunlight in the tenement flat, and it barely survives with loving care from Lena. When the family is about to move, Lena insists on taking the plant with them. Presumably, it will flourish in the new environment, just as the Younger family will.

Realistically, the family will probably have the same problems that the Hansberrys encountered after their move to Englewood, but the playwright leaves the audience with a note of hope for a future that has, in the years following her death, been partially fulfilled.

Context

Hansberry's influence in the theater in terms of black performers and black audiences—who saw themselves truthfully presented onstage for the first time in *A Raisin in the Sun*—was far greater than might seem to be the case. By 1959, Hansberry had attained fame as the youngest American and the only black dramatist to win the Best Play of the Year award. *A Raisin in the Sun* ran for 530 performances, toured extensively, and has been published and produced in more than thirty countries. In it, she raised the issues of racism and segregation, showing their negative influence on all of American society. She also illustrated the stereotypical hierarchy common in African American families that lack a father-figure, and she represented fairly those whom Walter Lee characterizes as "takers"—those of all colors who exploit others.

The feminist point of view is best represented by Beneatha, but Hansberry shows her three-dimensionally, not as a perfect woman, but as one probably on her way to growing into a warmer, less egocentric person, one who can combine social and political awareness with more tolerance for the foibles of her fellow human beings.

A Raisin in the Sun certainly represents Hansberry's personal philosophy, which she summed up in an address to young black writers when she said:

> What I write is not based on the assumption of idyllic possibilities or innocent assessments of the true nature of life, but, rather, on my own personal view that the human race does command its own destiny and that that destiny can eventually embrace the stars.

Sources for Further Study

Cheney, Anne. *Lorraine Hansberry*. Boston: Twayne, 1984. In this generally compli-
mentary biography, Cheney cites both Paul Robeson (as political radical) and
Langston Hughes (as poet of his people) as major influences on Hansberry. She also
defends Hansberry's assimilationist views, which some African Americans criticized harshly.

Chinoy, Helen Krich, and Linda Walsh Jenkins, eds. *Women and American Theatre*.
New York: Theatre Communications Group, 1987. In "Lorraine Hansberry: Artist,
Activist, Feminist," Margaret Wilkerson stresses Hansberry's early awareness of
the connection that exists between racism and sexism. She also makes the point that
Hansberry understood and tried to dramatize the difference between Lena's notion
of material advance for the family and Walter Lee's crass materialism. Furthermore,
she asserts that the playwright had come to terms with her lesbianism, but she gives
no concrete evidence for this assumption.

Cruse, Harold. *The Crisis of the Negro Intellectual*. London: W. H. Allen, 1969.
Ignoring completely the feminist value of *A Raisin in the Sun* and the fact that
Hansberry was the youngest dramatist to win the Best Play award, Cruse is
vehement in his criticism of the dramatist simply because she represents assimilation and integration as a solution for racial difficulties. Cruse is a separatist who
believes that all black acceptance of middle-class [white] values is a "sell-out" and
that therefore *A Raisin in the Sun* should be considered a "soap opera."

Hansberry, Lorraine. *To Be Young, Gifted, and Black*. Edited by Robert Nemiroff.
Englewood Cliffs, N.J.: Prentice Hall, 1969. Hansberry's husband and executor of
her estate has put together bits and pieces of her work—published and unpublished—letters, autobiographical statements, and speeches—which give a clear
picture of this extraordinary woman. As a work for the stage, it had a long run at
the Cherry Lane, off-Broadway in 1968 and 1969, and it has been done in a number
of university and regional theatres since that time. The introduction, the affectionate essay "Sweet Lorraine," by James Baldwin, poignantly describes the playwright
from 1957 until her untimely death in 1965.

Scheader, Catherine. *Lorraine Hansberry*. Chicago: Campus, 1978. Part of a series
subtitled "They Found a Way," this biography written for young readers stresses
events in the playwright's life which show her determination to succeed. Many
photographs embellish the work.

Edythe M. McGovern

RAMEAU'S NIECE

Author: Cathleen Schine (1953-   )
Type of work: Novel
Type of plot: Bildungsroman
Time of plot: The early 1990's
Locale: Manhattan, New York
First published: 1993

> *Principal characters:*
> MARGARET NATHAN, the protagonist, who enters upon a failed
>   intellectual and sexual quest
> EDWARD EHRENWERTH, Margaret's husband, who teaches
>   American literature
> LILY, Margaret's friend from college, a feminist art critic
> MARTIN COURT, a Belgian tourist whom Margaret attempts to
>   seduce
> SAMUEL LIPI, Margaret's dentist, who does not resist her sexual
>   advances
> RICHARD, Margaret's editor

Form and Content

Rameau's Niece is the title of both Cathleen Schine's novel and the parodic philosophical tract contained within it. The outer framework, the novel, is the story of Margaret Nathan, a renowned scholar of eighteenth century intellectual history who lacks confidence in her intellectual abilities and seeks sexual conquests as a means of proving them. The inner framework, the philosophical tract, is the impetus for the progression of the novel's plot. While conducting research for her Ph.D. dissertation on Madame de Montigny, a forgotten eighteenth century anatomist, Margaret discovers a pornographic French manuscript entitled *Rameau's Niece*, which appears to be a contemporary parody of the Enlightenment philosophy of Claude-Adrien Helvetius, Immanuel Kant, and Denis Diderot, among others. As Margaret begins to translate *Rameau's Niece*, its slick logic seduces her into believing that sexual experience is the means to knowledge, and she begins to conduct her own life accordingly.

The influence of *Rameau's Niece* suddenly brings Margaret's world alive with sexual significance. She travels to Prague to deliver a paper on the underground literature of the eighteenth century and finds herself gazing luridly at naked statues in the architecture. On the flight home, she fantasizes about Martin Court, the man in the seat next to her, and dreams of her own naked body next to his green-and-white-striped shirt. Once home, she invents sexual fantasies involving her editor, Richard; her friend, a feminist art critic, Lily; and her dentist, Dr. Lipi. In fact, the only person she does not desire sexually is her husband, Edward.

In an attempt to judge her feelings for Edward, Margaret decides to separate from him and to act on her sexual desires. She tries to seduce Martin, she attempts to kiss Lily, and she actually succeeds in her pursuit of Dr. Lipi. She finds, however, that the actual experience of adultery is unequal to what she imagined. Lipi is handsome and a perfect performer, but she longs for the intellectual attachment to Edward that had once deepened her desire for him. Shortly thereafter, Margaret returns to Edward and recognizes—in the words of the teacher in *Rameau's Niece*—that "our truest opinions are not the ones we have never changed, but those to which we have most often returned."

Analysis

Rameau's Niece is a good-natured parody of the contemporary intellectual elite and of the empiricist tradition against which they have reacted. Deconstructionists, feminists, and Marxists reveal themselves at their most absurd in Schine's novel. Dinner-party conversation reflects on the liberation of the signifier. A French student of American popular culture pontificates that literature is merely the acquisition and distribution of cultural capitalism. An art critic, Lily, explains that restaurant menus are a sign of male domination and that the Gulf War was a patriarchal invasion into the vaginal gulf. These highly educated, middle-aged people are still comparing their SAT scores and have nothing more to say to one another than "What is your field?" and "What are you working on?"

In its swipe at academicians, *Rameau's Niece* takes its place alongside David Lodge's *Small World* and A. S. Byatt's *Possession*. In addition to parodying those who purport to possess truth in contemporary culture, however, *Rameau's Niece* also questions, in good postmodernist fashion, whether truth is attainable at all. Margaret Nathan, the novel's protagonist, discovers an eighteenth century pornographic parody of Enlightenment philosophy entitled *Rameau's Niece*, which she determines to have been based on Denis Diderot's dialogue *Rameau's Nephew*. When Margaret's analysis of *Rameau's Niece* is finally published, critics point out that the parody actually predates the publication of *Rameau's Nephew* and therefore could not be based on it. After several weeks of mortification over her error, Margaret comes to the conclusion that it may be her job only to seek the truth, not to find it.

Even when the novel does suggest that truth is attainable, it parodies the means of attaining that truth, the empirical method. The philosophical tract that is embedded within the novel is itself a parody of that method. Like Diderot's *Rameau's Nephew*, after which it is patterned, the manuscript that Margaret translates is, at least superficially, a philosophical dialogue on the subject of epistemology. A male teacher and his female pupil discourse on the Enlightenment proposition that truth is obtainable only by sensory perception. On another level, however, the dialogue is an elaborate double entendre. The teacher uses the language of rationalist empiricism to seduce his student, and she learns her lesson at least well enough to teach it to the gardener.

Like the dialogue, the novel is a parody of empiricism. While translating *Rameau's Niece* from French to English, Margaret begins to shape her own life according to its principles. The dialogue posits that truth can be determined only by comparing and judging various sense perceptions. As she reads, Margaret begins to fear that her own poor memory prevents her from making comparisons and that perhaps the most important judgment she ever made in her life, the choice to marry Edward Ehrenwerth, was based on inadequate comparison. Consequently, she sets out to gather more data.

The problem, however, is that her test subjects are unwilling to participate in the experiment. Margaret tells her gay editor that she is in love with him, but he grants her permission only to worship him from afar. In a drunken stupor, she tries to seduce her Belgian friend Martin, but he only laughs and puts her to bed in the spare room. Finally, when she passionately kisses her friend Lily, whom she believes to be a lesbian, Margaret is again rebuffed. Essentially, the unpredictable, irrational side of human personalities prevents her rationalist project from succeeding.

Furthermore, Margaret's own irrationality subverts her experiment. When Margaret attempts to kiss Lily, they are interrupted by the sight of Margaret's husband Edward in the doorway of Lily's bathroom. Despite her own adulterous intentions, Margaret becomes furious at the thought that Edward and Lily are having an affair. She stomps out of Lily's apartment and falls into the arms of her dentist, Dr. Lipi. By this time, however, thoughts of jealousy and revenge have supplanted her original desire for comparison and judgment; in a sense, her experiment is completed before it ever begins. Margaret knows before she spends the night with Samuel Lipi that Edward is the man with whom she wants to spend her life. Her jealousy and anger, rather than her comparison and judgment, tell her so. Emotionality, not rationality, proves to be the means to truth. Margaret's original intuitive knowledge of Edward proves to be correct, and the sexual comparisons she seeks in the name of rationalist judgment turn out to be merely redundant.

Context

Rameau's Niece is an example of the female *Bildungsroman* and a debunking of the myth of the male *Bildungsroman*. Margaret Nathan, the novel's protagonist, goes through a female rite of passage toward self-awareness. At the opening of *Rameau's Niece*, she is on the brink of an intellectual crisis that spawns a sexual quest. Margaret is a scholar of eighteenth century intellectual history whose biography of the anatomist Madame de Montigny has brought her international fame. Nevertheless, Margaret believes she is inadequate because of her poor memory. Her inability to remember names and faces makes her feel socially inept, and she worries that her research method (she masters material just long enough to write about it and then promptly forgets it all) reveals her to be an intellectual sham.

Once Margaret discovers and translates an underground philosophical dialogue entitled *Rameau's Niece*, however, she begins to imitate its heroine's epistemology and transforms her career-related fears into a sexual quest for personal knowledge. The dialogue that she translates affects Margaret so dramatically because it echoes her own intellectual crisis and seems to offer a satisfactory means to solving it. The dialogue particularly appeals to her as a woman because its philosophy promises to unite both spheres of her life, the public and the private. As she reads, Margaret begins to worry that her poor memory might have affected more than her career. According to the dialogue's logic, truth results from judgment and judgment results from comparison. Margaret reasons that her deficient memory prevents her from making comparisons and therefore from arriving at truth. Perhaps, she thinks, the most important decision of her personal life, the choice to marry Edward Ehrenwerth, was based on insufficient comparison.

In an attempt to discover truth, Margaret imitates Rameau's niece and embarks upon sexual conquests. She attempts to seduce her gay editor, a female art critic, an acquaintance from Belgium, and even her dentist, in order to compare and judge the choice she made in marrying Edward. Her external quest for knowledge, however, one more often associated with the male than with the female *Bildungsroman*, fails to reveal truth to Margaret. In the end, her jealousy (emotionality rather than rational comparison and judgment) makes her realize the truth of her feelings for Edward. By the time she finally sleeps with Dr. Lipi, Margaret has already found the answers she sought.

Margaret's sexual quest suggests that a male-oriented, rational approach to knowledge may be merely redundant for women, who often come to truth through intuition. Actually, Margaret's quest is not to gain empirical knowledge at all but to learn to appreciate the intuitive knowledge she already possesses. Margaret's self-criticism results from her tendency to contrast herself with her husband Edward, whom she believes to be more knowledgeable because he never forgets things. Her discovery of truth in spite of, even because of, the failure of her empirical experiment reveals to Margaret that intuition is an equally valid means to knowledge.

At first glance, Schine's novel may seem antifeminist. Margaret's sexual quest leads her not to independence but back to her husband. Margaret's story differs from a novel such as Erica Jong's *Fear of Flying* or Judith Rossner's *Looking for Mr. Goodbar* in that sexual exploration is not a means to self-knowledge. In fact, *Rameau's Niece* depicts Margaret's attempt to re-create the plot of the Enlightenment version of *Looking for Mr. Goodbar* in her own life as comedy, not revelation.

The feminist significance of *Rameau's Niece*, however, is that it differentiates the female and male quests, and honestly portrays women's struggle for self-knowledge at the turn of the twenty-first century. For Margaret, as for many women, the goal is to unite the public and private spheres, to balance career and love relationships, and to make a place for herself as an individual while remaining connected to family and society.

Sources for Further Study

Annan, Gabriele. "La Femme Savante." *The New York Review of Books* (April 22, 1993): 29. Annan's review compares Margaret Nathan to her prototype in Hollywood movies, the attractive bluestocking, and notes a "cheerful antifeminism" in the novel.

Coates, Joseph. "A Zestful Satire Smites the Chic of the New Academics." *Chicago*

Tribune, April 15, 1993, sec. 5, p. 3. Coates focuses on the novel's parody of the new intellectual elite.

Goodrich, Chris. "A Novel of Ideas Is Cloaked as Comedy." *Los Angeles Times*, March 23, 1993, p. E3. Goodrich praises the novel for its combination of comedy and Enlightenment philosophy.

Goreau, Angeline. "How Do You Know You're Happy?" *The New York Times Book Review*, March 21, 1993, 13-14. Goreau discusses the novel as a parody of the postmodernist literary genre it imitates.

See, Carolyn. "Philosopher in the Bedroom." *The Washington Post*, May 9, 1993, p. C5. See praises the novel and discusses its combination of sexuality and philosophy.

Apryl Lea Denny

REBECCA

Author: Daphne du Maurier (1907-1989)
Type of work: Novel
Type of plot: Romance
Time of plot: The 1930's
Locale: Rural Cornwall, England
First published: 1938

Principal characters:

THE NARRATOR, a woman who becomes obsessed with her
husband's first wife, Rebecca

MAXIM (MAX) DE WINTER, her husband, the owner of Manderley

MRS. DANVERS, the housekeeper at Manderley

JACK FAVELL, Rebecca's cousin

FRANK CRAWLEY, Max's agent and the narrator's confidant

COLONEL JULWIN, the magistrate for Kerrith

Form and Content

   Rebecca is a gothic romance of the kind that has been popular since the genre was invented in the late eighteenth century. The plot is conventional: The protagonist, a young woman, finds herself in an unfamiliar and sinister setting, where she must solve a mystery and win the heart of a handsome man. This novel, which is considered one of the finest of its type, continues to be popular in the late twentieth century, despite the fact that the central character accepts a subservient role in society and in marriage.

   Rebecca begins, "Last night I dreamt I went to Manderley again." This often-quoted line sets the story in motion, not only establishing the narrative voice but also indicating that what follows will be an account of past events, ending sadly. In the pages that follow, however, the narrator explains that although they must live far from home, she and her husband are devoted to each other. After further arousing the curiosity of her readers with tantalizing references to the title character and to a Mrs. Danvers, Daphne du Maurier begins her story.

   Although from this point on the novel moves chronologically, the narrator frequently uses similar hints to foreshadow future events, thus maintaining a high level of suspense. For example, in chapter 3 she muses, "I wonder what my life would be today, if Mrs. Van Hopper had not been a snob." It soon becomes clear that the social aspirations of this rich American woman vacationing in Monte Carlo have resulted in the introduction of the narrator, who is Mrs. Van Hopper's hired companion, to the aristocratic Maxim de Winter, and eventually in their marriage. When Mrs. Van Hopper decides to leave immediately for New York, the recently widowed Max does not want to lose his young companion, and to the older woman's astonishment, he proposes. The result of Mrs. Van Hopper's snobbery is now clear; what is still to be explained is the rest of the sentence, which recalls the narrator's statements about suffering in the introductory chapters. For those answers, one must read on.

After this brief beginning, the novel moves to England and Manderley, Max's country house by the sea. From the moment she sees the staff waiting for her, the narrator feels insecure. Ill at ease in British upper-class society, the shy, inexperienced girl fears that she cannot live up to the standards set by Max's late wife Rebecca, a woman of great sophistication and legendary beauty. The narrator's sense of inadequacy is carefully nurtured by the housekeeper Mrs. Danvers, who adored Rebecca and who takes every opportunity to make her successor feel like an intruder. Unfortunately, Max goes on with his own life, minimizing his wife's concerns and refusing to talk about Rebecca. Thus isolated, the narrator is sustained only by the kindness of Max's sister Beatrice Lacy and by the evident approval of his agent Frank Crawley.

Without any facts at her disposal, the protagonist proceeds blindly, with no way of knowing what will please or displease her husband. When she breaks a valuable ornament, horrifying Mrs. Danvers, Max treats the matter as trivial. Yet he disapproves of his wife's going into a boathouse used by Rebecca, and he becomes livid after learning that Rebecca's cousin Jack Favell has put in an appearance. The protagonist does not feel Max's full fury, however, until the ball. When he sees her in the costume that Mrs. Danvers had suggested, he becomes enraged. Without explaining that Rebecca had previously worn an identical costume, he simply tells his wife to change and throughout the evening treats her like a stranger. Taking advantage of this breach between husband and wife, Mrs. Danvers has begun hypnotizing the broken-hearted girl into jumping to her death when, providentially, the explosion of rockets, signaling a shipwreck, shocks the narrator into sanity.

Ironically, it is the shipwreck that reunites the couple, even though it also results in Max's having to defend himself against a suspicion of murder. When he hears that divers have found Rebecca's body on her sunken boat, Max finally takes the narrator into his confidence. Throughout their marriage, he says, Rebecca had been malicious and promiscuous; when she indicated that she was to have a bastard child, who would inherit Manderley, Max shot her, put her body in the boat, and sank it. Now, he says, Rebecca has won. When the narrator assures him that she has no intention of deserting him, however, it is evident that, in fact, Rebecca has lost. Whatever follows, love has triumphed.

The final segment of the book describes the inquest and its aftermath. Despite the efforts of Jack Favell and Mrs. Danvers, Max is officially cleared of suspicion. Even though he has guessed the truth, the magistrate, Colonel Julwin, is so sympathetic with Max's sufferings and so repelled by Favell's attempts at blackmail that when he discovers Rebecca had been terminally ill, he chooses to call the drowning a suicide. On their way back from London, however, Max and his wife see a glow in the sky and realize that Rebecca's two friends have taken revenge by setting Manderley on fire.

Analysis

Even though she is writing in the well-worn gothic pattern, Daphne du Maurier incorporates elements from other literary traditions into her novels. Both thematically and symbolically, her works are much richer than most others of their kind.

For example, *Rebecca* reflects one of the central motifs in literature: the expulsion from paradise. Significantly, when in the first chapters of the novel the protagonist mentions her grief, the focus is not on Manderley, the house, but instead on that area of the grounds called the Happy Valley. The house was a showplace, created by Rebecca and imbued with her evil spirit. Her presence dominated the west wing, overlooking the ocean, and it was almost as evident in the east wing, where the newly wedded couple had been placed, for their rooms had been prepared by Rebecca's second self, Mrs. Danvers. Rebecca seemed to haunt the oceanside cottage, where she had met her lovers, and the ocean itself, whose deceptive beauty and destructive force mirrored her own being.

While in her dream the narrator does return briefly to the library at Manderley, where she and Max had some companionable moments, it is the Happy Valley that must be seen as their paradise. At Monte Carlo, when he first describes his home to his future wife, Max dwells not on the house, but on that particular area of the grounds. Even without his comments, however, the protagonist would have recognized the importance of the Happy Valley. When Max takes her there, she sees his joy, she finds herself freed from the oppression that grips her elsewhere on the estate, and somehow she knows that the Happy Valley is the heart, the central reality, of Manderley.

The fact that the Happy Valley still exists after the house has been destroyed represents the triumph of good over evil, which is central to du Maurier's story. Although Max, and the protagonist along with him, must pay the price of murder by being expelled from Manderley and turned away from the paradise at the heart of it, in their love for each other, which the forces of evil could not destroy, the pair carry with them into exile the goodness that they sensed resided in the Happy Valley.

Closely associated with the theme of the lost paradise in *Rebecca* is that of the loss of innocence. In her choice of a female protagonist as the character who moves from innocence to experience during the course of the story, du Maurier is merely following a convention of gothic romance. By having her narrator play the role of her earlier self as she relates the story, however, the author can show how closely innocence is allied with ignorance and even with potentially deadly error. Admittedly, initially Max finds the protagonist appealing because, unlike Rebecca, she is so innocent. Admittedly, he does send her into danger by evading her questions about the past. It is as much her own imagination as Max's silence, however, which very nearly results in the protagonist's suicide. In a sense, while she lives at Manderley, the narrator is writing her own novel. She busies herself inventing scenes in which the gentry criticize her and pity Max—scenes in which she is unfavorably compared to Rebecca. At one point, to Max's horror, she even acts the part of the Rebecca she imagines. After Max confides in her, it becomes clear how erroneous all the narrator's assumptions have been. The world she has created does not exist except in her imagination. What du Maurier seems to be suggesting is that in the real world, innocence can be dangerous, even fatal. It is experience, not innocence, knowledge, not ignorance, which enable the narrator to survive.

Context

When *Rebecca* appeared in 1938, it was dismissed as a romance written to fit a familiar formula, designed purely for entertainment. Critics admired du Maurier's technical skill, but they did not look in the novel for thematic or symbolic subtleties. The fact that since its publication *Rebecca* has continually remained in print, selling steadily over the years, must be attributed primarily to its still holding the same appeal for readers which made it such a commercial success a half century ago. The book is exciting and suspenseful, it has the kind of setting that lends itself to ghost stories, and it is essentially a love story with a happy ending.

Although many women readers evidently can still identify with heroines as subservient as the protagonist of *Rebecca*, contemporary critics are taking a new look at the novel. It is difficult to reconcile its seeming acceptance of a patriarchal system of male dominance with what, in her authorized biography, Margaret Forster has shown about the author herself. Not only was du Maurier convinced from childhood that she was a male in a female body, but, though a wife and mother, she felt free to have affairs with other people of both sexes. In other words, although she was not selfish and spiteful, in many ways du Maurier resembled Rebecca more than she did the virtuous protagonist of her novel.

Evidently, *Rebecca* is a more complex work than it was once thought to be. While it can hardly be argued that Rebecca is a sympathetic character or that her minions, Favell and Mrs. Danvers, are anything but revolting, du Maurier does show how dangerous not only innocence but also a system based on female subservience can be for both partners in a relationship. As she finally realizes, the narrator is of little use either to herself or to Max until she has developed an identity of her own. It is not the shy and helpless girl, but a woman—strong, self-confident, and independent—who chooses to support her husband in his ordeal and, in their exile, to make his life worth living.

Sources for Further Study

Bakerman, Jane S., ed. *And Then There Were Nine . . . More Women of Mystery*. Bowling Green, Ohio: Bowling Green State University Popular Press, 1985. A collection of essays. Bakerman's chapter on Daphne du Maurier argues that in her six "romantic suspense novels," including *Rebecca*, can be seen not only new uses of the gothic "formula" but also reflections of other literary traditions. Sees du Maurier as preeminent in her genre.

Beauman, Sally. "Rereading Rebecca." *The New Yorker* 69, no. 37 (November 8, 1993): 127-138. Points out that the publication in 1993 of Forster's biography of du Maurier and of Susan Hill's *Mrs. de Winter*, a sequel to the novel, indicate the lasting importance of *Rebecca* in literary history. Beauman voices her surprise that feminist critics have not turned their attention to a work in which the narrator so clearly equates love with submission. A balanced and perceptive analysis.

Conroy, Sarah Booth. "Daphne du Maurier's Legacy of Dreams." *The Washington Post*, April 23, 1989, pp. F1, F8. Accounts for du Maurier's continuing appeal by placing her in the oral tradition. The deep-seated "universal fears" that are experienced by her characters and the rhythms of her prose are reminiscent of fireside storytelling. Of all of her well-developed characters, the most convincing is Manderley itself.

Forster, Margaret. *Daphne du Maurier: The Secret Life of the Renowned Storyteller.* New York: Doubleday, 1993. The first authorized biography of du Maurier. With the aid of previously unavailable source materials, Forster reveals du Maurier's lifelong ambivalence as to her sexual identity. She concludes that the novels permitted du Maurier to be psychologically, as well as financially, independent. Although it contains little critical analysis of the works, the volume is a useful addition to du Maurier scholarship.

"Novel of the Week: Survival." *The Times Literary Supplement*, August 6, 1938, 517. A contemporary review of *Rebecca*, "a low-brow story with a middle-brow finish." Of the characters, only the narrator is believable; however, the work is well crafted and readable, one of the few in its genre which can be considered an unqualified success.

Rosemary M. Canfield Reisman

RED EMMA SPEAKS
An Emma Goldman Reader

Author: Emma Goldman (1869-1940)
Type of work: Essays
First published: 1972

Form and Content

Combining essays and lectures from various published and unpublished sources, *Red Emma Speaks* contains the best of Emma Goldman's writings on political and social issues. Emma Goldman was a national figure—if not a household word—in the two decades preceding World War I, and she was considered by many, including the young J. Edgar Hoover, the most dangerous woman in America when she was deported during the "Red Scare" of 1919. Though not a Communist, she was for nearly fifty years misunderstood by the American public as "Red Emma," the implacable enemy of polite society, a woman whose only goal was the destruction of the institutions that make America strong and, ultimately, America itself. Goldman did target such institutions as marriage, the family, government, and religion, but her contention was always that these institutions weakened and enslaved humankind. *Red Emma Speaks* focuses on Goldman's wide-ranging thought on the events and issues of her time and on her vision of anarchism (the absence of government) as the single truth that she hoped would reshape the world.

The importance of Emma Goldman's life and work to women's issues and concerns should not be underestimated. Although she disagreed with many of the leading feminists of her day on major issues confronting women, she was a more innovative, more radical, and certainly more militant advocate for the emancipation of women than were the acknowledged leaders of the mainstream women's movement. For Goldman, anarchism and feminism were intertwined, and unlike many radicals before or since, she lived an emancipated life. Emigrating from Russia to Rochester, New York, in 1886 at the age of seventeen, Goldman married later that year, but she soon divorced her husband and moved to New York, the center of the anarchist movement. She entered the movement as the protégée of Johann Most, but she was too independent to remain a mere protégée, and she broke with Most over ideological differences two years after meeting him. She soon became a noted lecturer and writer who advocated anarchism; atheism; the emancipation of all from economic, religious, and social constraints; and the emancipation of women through equal economic opportunity, equal sexual freedom, and open access to contraception. For half a century, Emma Goldman was a very visible model of the emancipated woman.

Red Emma Speaks is organized in four sections. Part 1, "Organization of Society," includes six essays on Goldman's own personal credo, her explanation of the widely misunderstood—and perhaps as widely hated—anarchist movement, her comments on other radical movements, and an elucidation of the relationship between the individual and the state. Part 2, "Social Institutions," contains twelve essays, five of which discuss the plight of woman in the early twentieth century. Part 3, "Violence," consists of six essays on political violence and Goldman's address to the jury at her 1917 trial, in which she and codefendant Alexander Berkman were convicted of conspiring to persuade young men not to register for the military draft. Part 4, "Two Revolutions and a Summary," includes four selections on Goldman's disillusionment with the revolutions in Russia and Spain and concludes with the retrospective "Was My Life Worth Living?" (1934). Most of the material comes from three sources: Goldman's own anthology *Anarchism and Other Essays* (1911); the monthly radical magazine *Mother Earth* (1906-1918), which Goldman founded and edited; and Goldman's two-volume autobiography *Living My Life* (1931). Editor Alix Kates Shulman supplies an even-handed reappraisal of Goldman's feminism, a brief biographical introduction, and thematic introductions to each of the four groups of essays.

Analysis

Contemporary accounts portray Emma Goldman as an impassioned, forceful speaker, but the essays in *Red Emma Speaks* also reveal a clear thinker whose words cut to the heart of an issue with the precision of a scalpel and the power of a sword. Without resorting to histrionics or overblown rhetoric, Goldman shines her own bright light unerringly and unflinchingly on the modern society that humankind has created. For example, though the American myth exalts capitalism and democracy, Goldman examines the effects these systems have on the individual spirit. Capitalism, she points out, does not provide limitless opportunity, but instead forces men into demeaning, dehumanizing jobs in which they serve as little more than machines, and forces women into dull, loveless marriages in which they serve only as servants and breeders. Democracy, Goldman insists, does not provide for the pursuit of happiness, but instead imposes the will of the majority, with all its emotional and intellectual limitations, on the minority, and thus provides inevitably for the frustration of the individual.

Perhaps the essence of *Red Emma Speaks* is to be found in two of the essays from part 1, "What I Believe" (*New York World*, 1908) and "Anarchism: What It Really Stands For" (*Anarchism and Other Essays*, 1911), along with the five essays in part 2 that discuss women's issues. Other essays discuss the failure of the modern educational system, which Goldman sees as a system of factories; the tyranny of Christianity, which Goldman sees as another in a long line of institutionalized "superstitions"; and political assassination, which Goldman sees less as a crime than as the predictable response to the "crimes" committed by governments. Underlying all her political and social thinking, however, is an overriding devotion to individual liberty. Anarchism is the political ideology of that concern, and feminism is the primary social ideology.

"What I Believe" attempts to explain Goldman's personal credo to an American public still angry over the assassination of President McKinley in 1901 by Leon Czolgosz, a young anarchist who claimed to have been inspired by Goldman. (Goldman had no connection with the assassination, but she and her movement were so badly misunderstood that she was jailed briefly and forced underground for five years, resurfacing in 1906 as the editor and publisher of *Mother Earth*.) In this essay, Goldman claims that the productivity of modern labor produces plenty for all, but that capitalism allows only a favored few to accrue property, which they then withhold from others. Government exists solely to protect this property and the "rights" of its owners, not to ensure equal rights for all. Goldman attacks the military because it robs individuals of their will and criticizes organized religion because it insists that all accept the same "superstitions" as truth and therefore stifles free thinking and freedom of expression. She also attacks other institutions, such as marriage, but for Goldman the common crime of them all is their subjugation of the individual will and their denial of individual liberty. Under these legal and social institutions, the human spirit is twisted and crushed, much like the spirit of an animal in a cage.

"Anarchism: What It Really Stands For" explains that faith in the human spirit is the rock upon which Goldman's political philosophy is built. Progress, Goldman says, results always from the struggle of the individual against society, never from submission to society. Predicated on human liberty, anarchism asks people to take part in that struggle; it demands that people act as individuals, that they think for themselves, that they analyze and question all that they read or hear. It will ultimately succeed, Goldman believes, because it is the only political philosophy that exalts humankind rather than subjugates individuals to the state, the church, or the majority.

This faith in the individual has led to fundamental misunderstandings concerning Goldman's feminism. Goldman has often been criticized because she did not support woman suffrage and was not a member of the mainstream women's movement. Goldman insists throughout her writings that women are fully as capable as men, but because she believes democracy to be essentially harmful and government of any kind unnecessary, she considers the right to vote irrelevant. Women are neither worse nor better than men, and they will not succeed in purifying any political system because political systems cannot be purified. Furthermore, Goldman sees the mainstream women's movement as hopelessly bourgeois, fettered by religion and conventional morality.

Emma Goldman's anarchism urges the emancipation of all, which cannot be achieved without the emancipation of women, whom Goldman sees as enslaved not only by the same economic, moral, and religious forces that enslave men, but also by their sex. Freeing women of legal and social restrictions associated with gender, however, would only elevate them to equal status with men, who are themselves, in Goldman's opinion, still enslaved. For Goldman, women's emancipation had to begin in the soul of each individual. Without feminism, there could be no anarchism. Without anarchism, feminism would be pointless.

Context

Emma Goldman's impact on the women's movement in her own era is difficult to measure. Though she was a superb—and world-famous—speaker and writer, she was so closely identified with the anarchist movement, which most Americans perceived as a foreign threat, that she was often judged by her notoriety rather than by her beliefs. Her insistence on sexual and reproductive autonomy for women and her advocacy of contraception even offended many anarchists. Her frequent lecture tours, during which she typically spoke in small but packed halls, sometimes reached as many as twenty thousand listeners, and there are numerous accounts of people who went to hear her out of curiosity but left the hall converted to anarchism and committed to the liberation of women. Neglected by history in the years following her death, Goldman's writings have, since the late 1960's, enjoyed a resurgence in popularity and influence as part of the ongoing feminist recovery of women writers. As Alix Kates Shulman points out in her introductory essay on Goldman's feminism, her works are now widely available, her face has become a familiar symbol of liberation, and she is now accepted as a hero of the women's movement.

In addition to the essays and lectures compiled in *Red Emma Speaks*, Emma Goldman produced two other collections of essays, *Anarchism and Other Essays* (1910) and *The Social Significance of the Modern Drama* (1914). A number of her speeches appear in *Anarchism on Trial: Speeches of Alexander Berkman and Emma Goldman Before the United States District Court in the City of New York, July 1917* (1917), and many of her letters were compiled in *Nowhere at Home: Letters from Exile of Alexander Berkman and Emma Goldman* (1975, edited by Richard and Anna Maria Drinnon). *My Disillusionment in Russia* (1922) chronicles Goldman's disenchantment with the workers' revolution in the Soviet Union, and *Living My Life* (1931) is a two-volume autobiography.

Sources for Further Study

Chalberg, John. *Emma Goldman: An American Individualist*. New York: HarperCollins, 1991. This brief, popular biography of Goldman focuses on her refusal and/or inability to maintain permanent alliances, either politically or personally.

Drinnon, Richard. *Rebel in Paradise: A Biography of Emma Goldman*. Chicago: University of Chicago Press, 1961. Perhaps the definitive Goldman biography, this work places Goldman's work in context with other political and social movements of her day. Its thorough bibliographic essay is indispensable for students of Goldman's life and work.

Falk, Candace. *Love, Anarchy, and Emma Goldman*. New York: Holt, Rinehart and Winston, 1984. Quoting liberally from many intimate—and carefully edited— letters, Falk examines Goldman's free and open attitudes toward sex, love, and marriage as revealed in her numerous love affairs, particularly those with Alexander Berkman, Edward Brady (1859-1904), and Ben Reitman.

Morton, Marian J. *Emma Goldman and the American Left: "Nowhere at Home."* New York: Twayne, 1992. This political biography examines the relations between Goldman's anarchism and other popular left-wing movements of the early twentieth century.

Wexler, Alice. *Emma Goldman: An Intimate Life*. New York: Pantheon Books, 1984. A study of Goldman's personal life from childhood to 1919, when she was deported to Russia. Especially interesting is the clash between Goldman's belief in free love and her intense jealousy over Ben Reitman, the great love of her life, who was a compulsive womanizer.

Craig A. Milliman

REENA AND OTHER STORIES

Author: Paule Marshall (1929-   )
Type of work: Short stories
First published: 1983

Form and Content

Paule Marshall is the daughter of Barbadian immigrants who came to the United States after World War I. Marshall was born in Brooklyn, New York, in the tightly knit, hard-working community of Bajans and has spent most of her life in the New York area. Problems of acculturation and racism that she experienced as a black woman and as the child of immigrants became parts of her stories. Many of these stories were based on those she heard in her mother's kitchen. The language used there became an integral part of her writing, particularly in *Reena and Other Stories*.

Reena and Other Stories consists of six short stories: "The Valley Between," "Brooklyn," "Barbados," "Reena," "To Da-duh, in Memoriam," and "Merle," which is adapted from Marshall's novel, *The Chosen Place, the Timeless People*. Included also is an essay, "The Making of a Writer: From the Poets in the Kitchen," which was first published in *The New York Times*. In several stories, Marshall introduces the reader to an infrequently encountered area of African American literature: the immigrant experience. The major themes in this collection of short stories are a search for identity in an oppressive environment and the importance of history and tradition for African Americans, especially women.

The stories deal not only with West Indian immigrant women but also with African American women and women in a Caribbean setting. These women are in varying stages of maturity and self-awareness. Although they must deal with a world that is hostile to blacks, women, and immigrants, they cope and survive. They manage to persevere because they have the audacity to make their own decisions. Most of Marshall's characters are women because she believes that black women have been neglected in literature. She more than compensates for their omission in this slim volume of short stories.

In "Brooklyn" and "Barbados," the male characters come to self-understanding through two young women. The semi-retired Watford in "Barbados" returns to his Caribbean home affluent after a half-century of working in New England. When dealing with his own people, he assumes an air of superiority and distance that he has copied from the dominant culture. He extends this manner to his relationship with his young female servant, who remains unnamed throughout the narrative, thus rendering her invisible and marginal. Watford maintains a "master-slave" relationship with her, revealing that he has internalized the warped lesson of colonialism—to hate the oppressed rather than the oppressor. He is patronizing and condescending, as befits a member of the master class. Eventually, Watford realizes that love has been lacking in his life and turns to his servant, who coldly rejects him. With her rejection of Watford, she ceases being invisible and marginal and shows her self-awareness and self-assuredness.

Both characters in "Barbados" are of African extraction, but in "Brooklyn" only the female character is black. Ms. Williams, an "amber-colored" woman, has come to an institution of higher learning to perfect her French. Max Berman, a teacher of French literature, believes that he can regain not only his joie de vivre but also his virility if he can exploit her sexually. His seduction attempt, colored with antebellum visions of European American owners and enslaved African women, fails. The unsuccessful effort allows Ms. Williams to come to terms with her parentally imposed isolation from other African Americans.

These women are two examples of self-assured, complex women characters who grapple successfully with their gender, race, and history. They believe that "the only way you begin to know what you are and how much you are capable of is by daring to try something, by doing something which tests you."

Analysis

A mature, middle-aged Selina, the protagonist of Marshall's novel *Brown Girl, Brownstones* (1959), can possibly be found in the short story "Reena." The story has been described by critic Barbara Christian, in *Black Feminist Criticism* (1985), as "one of the first pieces of Afro-American fiction to delve into the complex choices confronting the contemporary, educated African-American woman." Reena is self-exploratory; she knows what she wants from life. As a woman who has fought her way from working-class to middle-class status, she has had experiences that are similar to those of other African American women: rejection by African American men, single parenthood, and underemployment. A sophisticated and intelligent woman, Reena is aware of the inequities that are inherent in American society and are reproduced in different forms in African American communities.

After two unsuccessful love affairs, she is understandably reticent in beginning new relationships. Her first lover rejects her because his family considers her too dark. The second, a European American, represents not only a part of her involvement in radical politics but also an escape from her "self." As she evolves, she must discard him. She must, however, find an acceptable partner. African American men of a suitable status prefer European American women, are homosexual, or are resolutely yoked to their parents. Not only has Reena been subjected to the racism and sexism of U.S. society, but she has also experienced the "colorism" that exists in many African American communities.

Reena eventually marries an African American and begins the life of the typical American homemaker, but her husband's career as a photographer is not immediately successful, and he frequently takes out his frustrations on her. In this relationship, as in others, Reena, powerless, is the subordinate member. Sensing the power base of these relationships, she leaves. There is a divorce, and she is left to rear her children alone. Reena blames many of her marital problems on her absent husband and, in a sense, blames all African American men for the problems of African American women.

After the divorce, however, Reena's sense of independence emerges, and she begins to plan a husbandless, fatherless life for herself and her children, a life that includes possibly living and working in Africa. She tells her friend Paulie that she has everything she needs: her children and her career. Having suffered the constraints of an American marriage, she feels that she must live her life alone. Yet neither she nor Paulie will spare herself the brutal truth that she feels rejected by African American men.

In her fiction, Marshall explores the racism that permeates American society, but the racism gives way to the sexism and colorism of the African American community. In order to avoid the racism and sexism that are seemingly endemic in Western societies, many of her characters journey to other places. Reena and Merle Kinbona ("Merle" and *The Chosen Place, the Timeless People*) go to some unnamed African destination. Avey Johnson (*Praisesong for the Widow*), however, goes to Tatum Island in search of her "self." These women leave the United States or their Caribbean islands in search of a place to find themselves instead of looking inside themselves for answers. This search for truth is an effect of the diaspora on the lives of these women. In order to understand their position in contemporary society, they have to understand from where they came.

In order to achieve a sense of self, they usually journey to Africa, which, for Marshall, symbolizes the Pan-African consciousness that is important in the development of black identity. With her concentration on African American women and their search for identity and history, Marshall links her racial themes to the feminist movement. Yet, with their racial and gender crises and their wandering, these women are not defeated. They make radical choices that make them self-liberated. The women in these stories not only discover their natural powers and reinforce them but also represent the independence that has been a constant in the lives of many African American women.

Context

"Reena," "To Da-duh, in Memoriam," and "Merle" are unusual stories. These are among the few literary works that examine the black woman's experiences as an immigrant. The dominant culture views these women, because they are blacks and immigrants, as marginal and powerless. For this reason, another of Marshall's themes is the acquisition of power. Not only does Marshall stress obtaining power and the female immigrant experience, but she also underscores female relationships and the need for women to define themselves. In their search for self, her women characters insist on not being defined by men or by European American society. Additionally, stereotypical depictions of the black woman appeared frequently in earlier literature: the mammy, the loose woman, or the tragic mulatta. Marshall is primary among contemporary writers who eliminate the stereotype and create fully developed black female characters.

Moreover, with her tripartite vision of African, African American, and Afro-Caribbean women, Marshall connects all black people worldwide. This international bond illustrates that black people share a common history and must share a common future. Marshall, who has been described as an "unfortunately better kept secret," has, with her emphasis on fully developed black female characters and the importance of history, become an important twentieth century writer. Nevertheless, much of her work was ignored when it was first published, although her artistic vision has earned for her the Guggenheim Fellowship, the Rosenthal Award, Ford Foundation and National Endowment for the Arts grants, and the MacArthur Fellowship. Some of the stories in *Reena and Other Stories* were published at a time when African Americans were beginning to question and to understand their unique place in American history. Marshall's perspective as a first-generation American was distinctive and thus was overlooked.

Sources for Further Study

Brown, Lloyd W. "The Rhythms of Power in Paule Marshall's Fiction." *Novel: A Forum on Fiction* 7, no. 2 (Winter, 1974): 159-167. Brown suggests that Marshall's primary interest is power. Her analysis of power is complex and imaginative not only because it is the political goal of ethnic and feminist groups but also because it shapes racial and sexual roles.

Christol, Helene. "Paule Marshall's Bajan Women in *Brown Girl, Brownstones*." In *Women and War: The Changing Status of American Women from the 1930s to the 1940s*, edited by Maria Diedrich and Dorothea Fischer-Hornung. New York: St. Martin's Press, 1990. Christol asserts that Marshall's insistence on women as complete individuals and as part of the black community prefigured such themes in the works of Toni Morrison, Alice Walker, and Ntozake Shange.

Cook, John. "Whose Child? The Fiction of Paule Marshall." *CLA Journal* 26, no. 1 (September, 1980): 1-15. Cook maintains that Marshall's primary theme is not the race problem or the importance of history in the lives of African Americans. He believes that Marshall's dominant theme is sexual politics.

Kapai, Leela. "Dominant Themes and Technique in Paule Marshall's Fiction." *CLA Journal* 16, no. 1 (September, 1972): 49-59. Kapai writes that Marshall's dominant themes are an identity crisis, the race problem, the importance of tradition for African Americans, and the need to share in order to achieve meaningful relationships. Her technique blends the best of the past tradition with recent innovations.

Spillers, Hortense J. "*Chosen Place, Timeless People*: Some Figurations on the New World." In *Conjuring: Black Women, Fiction, and Literary Tradition*, edited by Marjorie Pryse and Hortense J. Spillers. Bloomington: Indiana University Press, 1985. Spillers, using reader-response theory, suggests that Merle Kinbona, the principal character in "Merle" and *The Chosen Place, the Timeless People*, may be confusing to many readers. Spillers additionally posits that Merle is both the history of her island and the shaper of that history.

Mary Young

THE REST OF LIFE
Three Novellas

Author: Mary Gordon (1949-   )
Type of work: Novellas
First published: 1993

Form and Content

"Immaculate Man," the first of the three novellas in this collection, is a monologue by the unnamed female protagonist, a forty-eight-year-old social worker and divorced mother of two teenagers. Set in the early 1990's in New York state, Manhattan, and Paris, the story focuses on the protagonist's unexpected relationship with Father Clement [Frank] Buckley, the last active priest of the now-disbanded Paracletist order whose motherhouse has been turned into a battered women's shelter that Buckley keeps in repair and directs. The protagonist meets the boyishly handsome forty-five-year-old priest when she is called in as a consultant for his diocese's organization of the shelter. Clement, she observes, is a guileless man, both a poor judge of character and highly intuitive about human suffering.

An Illinois-born daughter of lackadaisical Congregationalists, the narrator initially has no guilt about their hidden relationship and little knowledge of what the Catholic church represents to priests of her and earlier generations. She is not a believer, but she assumes that worship should entail comprehensible rites that banish the dark mysteries to which Clement is devoted. Moreover, she equates the love of light with women's sexuality and, conversely, the love of dark entrances into mystery with men's desires to enter women's bodies.

Their relationship begins three months after she starts commuting from Manhattan to the shelter, where, one day, she becomes ill. It is then, in a former cell decorated with "I am the Resurrection and the Life," that they make love. The narrator feels that Clement has brought her back to faith, not in God, but in sexuality. Because he has never made love, touched a woman, or looked at pornography, she knows that his delight with her middle-aged body is rare. She also knows that he chose her when he found himself without a priestly order or work, and she understands why they will never marry. As the protagonist gradually learns from Father Boniface Lally, Clement's Paracletist mentor and best friend, their marriage would strip Clement of everything he has loved since age thirteen. Moreover, Clement's harshness with her son and daughter would rupture her and her children's loving, healthily chaotic relationship. Even without marriage, however, she cannot imagine life without him. The elderly, seriously ill Boniface, who approves of their relationship, shares her feelings, and to her he confides his never-intimated sexual attraction to Clement. Her narration ends when she and Clement are in Paris, a romantic trip he insists upon paying for with the first money he has ever earned. He vows again that he will never leave her; she remains unsure.

"Living at Home," the middle novella, is a first-person narration by an unnamed,

British-born female protagonist who, since the mid-1980's, has lived with Lauro, a fifty-seven-year-old, Italian-born foreign correspondent who is compulsively interested in Third World trouble spots and revolutions. The narrator is a respected, forty-five-year-old psychiatrist who directs a London school for autistic children. An only child of German Jewish parents who left Germany for London in 1935, the narrator—previously married three times (to a medical student, a doctor, and a half-Russian charmer) and a loving mother of two almost-grown sons—has lived with Lauro for five years. A tactful, intuitive, and kind (except to his mother and family) man, he frequently leaves on self-chosen, dangerous assignments. Seemingly impervious to a fear of death except when facing routine medical work, Lauro shares the narrator's need for "entrances and exits." Still, their relationship and London flat are their oases. As does the protagonist's voice in "Immaculate Man," this woman speaks with modest candor about Lauro, who makes her feel "that he is opening up life." Similarly, she recognizes their passionate, strong relationship as the final love of her life.

As her narration unfolds, she reveals an ability to enter autistic patients' obsessively closed worlds and to help them attempt openness with safety and without shame. Paradoxically, her medical specialty in dealing with children terrorized by change and fragmentation is intimately related to her personal life. Trying to cope with her widowed mother's decline, the psychiatrist is shamed and disoriented by the changes in her mother. The narrator also reveals radical aversions to her mother's reactions after having to flee Germany and to leave London for ten years—reactions embodied in obsessive fixations on a home, fastidiousness, and objects brought from Germany. Thus, the protagonist, despite concern for her sons, leaves each marriage when her husband at the time settles into a fixed relationship with a place and objects. When she and Lauro go to Italy for his sister's wedding, the narrator recognizes in Lauro's petulance toward his mother his similar need "to be away from her [his mother] to feel he breathed air as a man."

The novella ends late at night as the pensive narrator expects Lauro to wake up. Like the children with whom she works, she and Lauro fashion their life together around no future tense, no looking back; the present is all each claims, an open, permeable claim that admits her fear of his death and their mutual appreciation of being "mated, but in the way of our age, partial."

"The Rest of Life," the final novella, is a third-person account that is interrupted by the protagonist's italicized, first-person observations; the voice-shifts usually elaborate on a verbal cue from the preceding narration. The story opens and closes in 1991 in Italy, where Paola, the seventy-eight-year-old Turin-born protagonist, has returned after more than six decades. In 1928, after the suicide of Paola's sixteen-year-old lover Leo Calvi, Paola's unnamed father, a widower and professor of entomology, had sent her away to live with relatives in America. Since then, she has mourned for the face of her father, who, despite his love, failed to protect or defend her. Yet she has sealed her mind against remembering Leo's face, blown away by his suicide. Since she had promised to join him in suicide, the fifteen-year-old Paola left Italy with youthful perceptions of wrongdoing, betrayal, and shame, none of which was ameliorated by her father or shared, not even with her late husband Joe Smaldone, a happy-spirited Sicilian American whom she met during World War II. Still, she has tried to salvage a life that, at age fifteen, she was unwilling to give up. She recognizes that refusing to commit suicide was linked to her not wanting to leave her father and knowing that the brilliant, impetuous Leo did not, as he pretended, know it all; he was as ignorant about sex and death as she. As in her youthful poem, which mistakenly had Eurydice rather than Orpheus look back, Paola had looked back at life and at her father, and Leo had died alone. It is Paola, however, whose life, like that of Orpheus, is torn apart by maenadic women, especially her vicious aunt, whom her father does not contradict in 1928. Conversely, seven decades later, when Paola's grandson Carlo wants to marry his Nigerian American supervisor, granddaughter of an Igbo chief, Paola stands up for them, introducing Katherine to Joe's prejudiced family and defying them to injure the young couple's happiness. Their thanks is the trip back to Milan and Turin, where Paola finds that the accusing names, faces, and buildings have disappeared. Only when she goes to the half-ruined tower where Leo died does she weep because no one consoled either of them, especially Leo and all young men who died when others, such as herself, lived. Finally, she understands that "the dead, being one and many, knew there was nothing to forgive." Returning to the hotel where the doorman tells her Carlo and Katherine are waiting, she responds "Si, grazie" ("yes, thank you"); something essential has been salvaged.

Analysis

For all of the novellas, Gordon has created singular female protagonists whose lives and experiences address key issues in contemporary society and relationships. Despite these characters' distinctiveness, a close scrutiny of these women—two in their mid-forties, one in her late seventies—reveals that Gordon's development of their personalities includes a number of interesting personal and professional similarities. For example, none of the three, all of whom are now divorced or widowed, wants to remarry. None has close female friends. All have children (Paola also has grandchildren); they abhor children's being damaged, shamed, or isolated, and they delight in children's buoyant gestures of well-being. All three highly intelligent protagonists have worked as professionals who attempt to restore their constituents' lives, bodies, or minds. Each has a penchant for living in the present, for avoiding histrionics, and for a certain candid modesty in her private musings. All three are preoccupied by the meaning and implications of words in their and others' lives. Each is more troubled by what she does not know than what she knows; no one pretends to more knowledge than she has. Each articulates deep uncertainties about crucial relationships in her life at the same time that she reveals an ability to structure a life for herself that incorporates uncertainties. The two protagonists in their mid-forties savor their and their lovers' sexuality. Two of the women model their lives in stark contrast to another woman's persona: For example, as the narrator of "Living at Home" explains to Lauro, everything she is or desires as an adult is "Not My Mother"; similarly, Paola, the protagonist of "The Rest of Life," forms her sense of self around "I am not her," meaning her vicious, judgmental aunt. Gordon also places at the center of each of the protagonists' lives a man (in the case of Paola, two men) who represents a fundamentally unknowable, unsharable other world: the priesthood; Third World trouble spots; a dead, loving father-exiler; and suicide. Moreover, Gordon's depictions of these four men reveal personalities that are, in varying degrees and paired combinations, brave-weak, brilliant-ignorant, fearless-superstitious, kind-harsh, articulate-inarticulate, and sensitive-insensitive. Part of the women's more subtly defined complexities are revealed in their recognition and acceptance of the men's foibles and strengths.

Gordon does weave a few details through the novellas. For example, in "Living at Home," 1935 is the year in which the protagonist's parents flee Germany; it is also the year in which the protagonist's father in "The Rest of Life" dies after being beaten by Fascist Blackshirts, whom he defied. Likewise, Turin appears in "Living at Home" and "The Rest of Life" as, respectively, Lauro's birthplace and Paola's hometown. Despite similarities within certain features of the characters and stories, Gordon's remarkable achievement is in having developed three women protagonists whose personalities, lives, and loves remain unique, unforgettable, and informative.

Context

Like Gordon's four novels, these novellas employ a feminine perspective to address key issues in women's (and girls') lives: parents, surrogate parents, and children; careers; sexuality; autonomy; relationships; and aging. Certainly, Gordon has made a more thorough exposition of adult women's sexuality in these novellas than she has in any of her novels; she also demonstrates a newfound freedom in describing women's perceptions of male bodies, sexuality, and intercourse.

Her complex protagonists, somewhat akin to those in Margaret Drabble's novels, address change—in bodies, minds, circumstances, relationships—in informative ways. Gordon's contrasting examination of elderly women is particularly acute: For example, Lauro's and the psychiatrist's mothers in "Living at Home" have built their lives around refusals to change. By contrast, at the conclusion of the final novella, when the elderly Paola feels something hopeful move within her long-frozen spirit, she is able to celebrate and reapproach things, people, life.

Perhaps Gordon's most important contribution in these novellas is her depiction of women who have come to terms with the multiplicities and partialities of contemporary lives and relationships. Gordon's three female protagonists suggest that one's ability to embrace permeable visions of what it means to be human is essential.

Sources for Further Study

Ager, Susan. "A Trinity of Novellas from Your Best Friend, or Maybe from You." *Detroit Free Press*, August 1, 1993, p. 7H. A brief but interesting review.

Gordon, Mary. *Good Boys and Dead Girls and Other Essays*. New York: Penguin Books, 1991. These essays reflect Gordon's wide-ranging interests and include commentary on various feminist issues.

Grossman, Mary Ann. "Mary Gordon Wants to Be Known as More than a 'Catholic Writer.'" *St. Paul Pioneer Press*, October 27, 1993, p. 10E. Offers helpful and candid comments about Mary Gordon and her work.

Hughes, Kathryn. Review of *The Rest of Life*. *New Statesman and Society* 7, no. 287 (January 28, 1994): 38-39. Hughes's review of Gordon's novellas is brief but nevertheless useful.

Lurie, Allison. "Love Has Its Consequences." *The New York Times Book Review*, August 8, 1993, 1, 25. Lurie's article provides a thoughtful examination of Gordon's novellas.

Messud, Claire. "Travelling Hopefully." *The Times Literary Supplement*, February 4, 1994, 21. A well-written, extremely useful review of *The Rest of Life: Three Novellas*.

Alma Bennett

REVOLUTION FROM WITHIN
A Book of Self-Esteem

Author: Gloria Steinem (1934-   )
Type of work: Social criticism
First published: 1991

Form and Content

Gloria Steinem's *Revolution from Within* locates the possibility for revolution in the psyche rather than in the ability to act decisively and independently in the world. Wherever she traveled, Steinem found that although women were acting in courageous, ambitious, and committed ways, they did not see that they were doing so. Steinem began to admit to her own feelings of self-doubt and emptiness. Through her personal experience and the personal experiences of others, Steinem located a crucial problem for contemporary women that accompanies the great expectations they hold for themselves: As they try to succeed in many roles, their self-esteem can be damaged by the ongoing expectations that they should fill those roles. After Steinem had written 250 dry, unsuccessful pages, Steinem's friend, a family therapist, read the manuscript and commented that Steinem had a self-esteem problem. Yet Steinem had been named one of the ten most confident women in the United States. The coincidence made her even more convinced that women were in serious trouble.

To rewrite her book, Steinem added autobiographical elements and invited her readers to connect her stories with their own. Her approach reflects feminist consciousness: the movement back and forth between the personal and the political. Steinem has a political purpose for addressing self-esteem; she sees it as the basis of any real democracy. By locating strength in the self-belief, she draws connections between self-esteem and the ability to demand fairness and to change the hierarchical paradigms of the family, the nation, and even the world.

Steinem structures the book by first giving a detailed account of self-esteem. She relates not only her own parable (by this she means a personal anecdote from which more far-reaching generalizations can be made) but also a history of the notion of self-esteem that goes beyond Western culture to Egypt in 2,500 B.C.E., Hinduism, and the Upanishads. She introduces early on what will be a recurring theme throughout the book: the belief that there is a crucial core self that is a powerful part of human identity, one that needs to be recognized and liberated.

Because she locates this core identity in the child, one must, as a step toward self-healing, rediscover that unique child—a waiting true self. Hence, one must journey back to what one has lost, recover what that child experienced, and re-parent oneself in order to reclaim one's most true, creative core. In the appendix is a "Meditation Guide" that can assist one in making the journey inward.

She follows with chapters that discuss education and the ways in which it undermines intellectual and interpersonal self-esteem. She advocates not only a change in institutional structures but also the revision of the very norms against which people judge experience. By giving a brief history of scientific "facts" that have been used to bolster social prejudices, she seriously calls into question modern measuring techniques that still rank individuals based on mainstream (white, male, middle-class, heterosexual) knowledge.

The book goes on to address issues such as women's bodies, love, romance, and animal rights. Throughout, Steinem returns to the theme of authenticity. Beauty is the ability to decide what is beautiful within oneself, not how well one measures up to what is considered beautiful. Pleasure and creativity are expressions of the true self. Love exists when one is loved for an authentic self. Her message finally is that there is one true inner voice, and that by trusting it, one can stretch one's abilities without sacrificing self-esteem.

Analysis

Steinem's most central issue is that of self-esteem, particularly—though not exclusively—as it concerns women. Under this umbrella term "self-esteem," however, she is able to address the range of challenges that face contemporary women. Her style is fluid, ranging from that of an informed academic, to that of an articulate social critic, to that of a close personal friend. Although she certainly believes that she knows how women might better themselves in many settings, she does not relate her knowledge or advice with either a patronizing or a condescending attitude. Her voice is consistently supportive, even consoling at times, as she encourages her readers to reconsider how they might see themselves in more positive ways. Because of this tone, the book occasionally takes on the tenor of new age psychology, but because Steinem balances this tenor with that of the scholar who has done good research on her topic, the book cannot be dismissed as formulaic self-help jargon.

Ironically, Steinem did not receive her strongest criticism because of her dubious move into pop psychology. As she herself points out in her final chapter, "One Year Later," the majority of her critics focused on the personal revelations she makes throughout the book, especially the ones that involve her love life in the chapter on romance. Because of the emphasis on the personal within the book, Steinem was accused of abandoning feminism and the politics that have driven her career. Clearly, however, Steinem was doing something quite different in bringing into her book so much personal revelation; each personal anecdote is told as a means to build toward a generalization that takes on political significance.

For example, in the chapter on romance, she does tell about a fairly recent love affair in which she herself reenacted a common fantasy within romance mythology—that of rescue. She relates this experience, however, for a political purpose—to demonstrate to her readers how romance mythology works to disempower rather than empower women. From her own particular experience, she can extrapolate about the dissembling that women do in relationships in order to secure them, the feminine disease she refers to as empathy sickness (knowing the feelings of others better than one's own), and the tendency women have to fall in love with powerful men by way of mourning for the power they need and rarely have. She also provides a thorough and convincing analysis of Emily Brontë's star-crossed lovers, Catherine and Heath-cliff, and the patriarchal, gender-polarized culture in which women yearn, like Cath-erine, to be whole but become enmeshed instead in the addictive cycle of romance. Steinem's attention to the personal fits with the feminist view that even women's intimate lives are affected by the political.

What is more problematic, however, is her unyielding belief in the possibility of retrieving a true, authentic self. It is here that she takes a very different path from those of contemporary feminist critical theorists, who see the possibility of such a true self as suspect or simply nonexistent. Feminist theory is diverse, but an overwhelming number of feminists have long been wary of any notion of an essential self that could too easily be linked with biology. Steinem tries to avoid such essentialism by locating the true self in girlhood, before a woman meets the powerful enculturating pressures of adolescence. She wants to get back to the wild child, who is untamed, spontaneous, outspoken, and sure of herself before she is culturally trained to be nice, to be a good listener, and to defer to male authority and discourse. This may be one version of the self that it would be beneficial to reenvision, but to hypothesize that such a wild child is there waiting within all women and that she is the most authentic self one has is a troubling concept, particularly for the intellectual, because it is striking in its naïveté and oversimplification.

Nevertheless, Steinem's book contains valuable material that women can consider and put to use in their own lives. She speaks to those issues that challenge women most deeply and gives women real things that they can do to better meet those challenges without sacrificing their sense of well-being and their potential.

Context

Revolution from Within appeared during a crucial year for feminism. Susan Faludi's *Backlash*, Elizabeth Fox-Genovese's *Feminism Without Illusions*, and Naomi Wolf's *The Beauty Myth* had also recently appeared in print. Women were talking again about what it means to be a feminist and what it means to be part of the feminist community. Because it came from one of the recognized leaders of the feminist movement, Steinem's book caused a certain amount of consternation for feminist social critics. Nowhere in the title is the label "feminism" or "feminist" used. Instead, it purports to be "A Book of Self-Esteem," and the revolution described involves an interior, psychic revolution, not the overthrow of oppressive sexism. It made feminists wonder whether this was a book of social criticism or a self-help book for the victim in all women.

There continues to be a division within the feminist ranks that is now even more clearly delineated by the publication of Katie Roiphe's *The Morning After*. Some people believe that feminists dwell too much on the victimization of women and, therefore, encourage women to identify themselves as passive and helpless against the far-reaching hegemony of patriarchal ideology. Others believe that, by studying and articulating ways in which women become the victims of patriarchal hierarchies, women become empowered, because they are then more conscious of those hierarchies and self-conscious of their willingness to respect them rather than question them. Steinem would certainly be disappointed by the charge that her book encourages women to identify themselves as victims. Her aim was to write both a social critique and a self-help book, and in that sense the book is a success. It increases women's awareness while it provides ways and means to resist oppression.

Furthermore, although the book's title does suggest that its focus will be on the individual, Steinem makes it clear throughout that women realize their power only by interacting with other women, that a revolution from within is not feasible without a community that can support that revolution. Steinem ends the book with "A Proposal for the Future" (written one year after the book's initial publication), in which she calls for "A national honey-comb of diverse, small, personal/political groups that are committed to each member's welfare through both inner and outer change, self-realization and social justice." Steinem realizes that dwelling on the needs of the individual and inner change at the expense of the needs of the community and outer change will have little effect in terms of remedying social injustice. Her call for action is sensible and inspirational and provides a necessary conclusion to a book that works to further women's understanding that the personal and political are so inextricably intertwined, that women must address both in order to bring about worthwhile social change.

Sources for Further Study

Estes, Clarissa Pinkola. *Women Who Run with the Wolves: Myths and Stories of the Wild Woman Archetype*. New York: Ballantine, 1992. Estes' project, like Steinem's, is to empower women, but she goes about it by privileging feminine instinctive nature and the restoration of women's vitality by means of the Wild Woman archetype.

Fox-Genovese, Elizabeth. *Feminism Without Illusions: A Critique of Individualism*. Chapel Hill: University of North Carolina Press, 1991. Fox-Genovese addresses the important discrepancy between the commitment of women to their own personal successes as individuals and their commitment to collective communities of women that seek power in hierarchical institutions.

Gilligan, Carol, Nona P. Lyons, and Trudy J. Hanmer, eds. *Making Connections: The Relational Worlds of Adolescent Girls at Emma Willard School*. Cambridge, Mass.: Harvard University Press, 1990. Gilligan and her colleagues studied pre-adolescent girls over a period of crucial years, noting the ways in which the girls came to lose confidence in their ability to know and came to denigrate their own clear-sightedness.

Roiphe, Katie. *The Morning After: Sex, Fear, and Feminism on Campus*. Boston: Little, Brown, 1993. Roiphe's controversial book critiques feminists' focus on rape and sexual harassment because it reinscribes women's need to be protected and collapses their personal, social, and psychological possibilities. She is also critical of the rigid orthodoxy that feminists around her have created.

Wolf, Naomi. *The Beauty Myth: How Images of Beauty Are Used Against Women*.

New York: Doubleday, 1991. Wolf draws an important connection between female liberation and female beauty, arguing that images of beauty are used as political weapons against women's advancement because they, in fact, prescribe behavior, not appearance.

Janet Mason Ellerby

RICH IN LOVE

Author: Josephine Humphreys (1945-   )
Type of work: Novel
Type of plot: Domestic realism
Time of plot: The mid-1980's
Locale: Mount Pleasant and Charleston, South Carolina
First published: 1987

Principal characters:
  LUCILLE ODOM, a seventeen-year-old high school senior
  WARREN ODOM, Lucille's father, a sixty-year-old retired
    demolition expert
  HELEN ODOM, Lucille's mother, who leaves the family suddenly
    and disappears
  RAE, Lucille's sister
  BILLY McQUEEN, Rae's husband
  WAYNE FROBINESS, Lucille's friend, who wants Lucille
  RHODY POOLE, Rae's black friend
  VERA OXENDINE, Warren Odom's hair stylist

Form and Content

  Rich in Love is a coming-of-age novel about a young woman growing to adulthood in the American South toward the end of the twentieth century. Rich in the sense of place—generally, the United States, and specifically, the environs of Charleston, South Carolina—the novel interweaves and expands the family relationships of the Odoms. The precipitating action of the novel is one woman's liberation of herself from marriage.

  Lucille's mother, Helen, disappears abruptly on May 10, leaving behind her Volkswagen van with the door open and ice cream melting on the seat. Lucille finds a note that her mother has left for her father, saying that she has left to start a new life. Troubled by the note's cool tone, she rewrites it before her father comes home. For days, she and her father drive all over Mount Pleasant and Charleston, searching for her mother frantically but unsuccessfully.

  Distressed by her mother's leaving, and trying desperately to keep the family together, Lucille fails to take the exams that would enable her to complete her senior year of high school. Eventually, Helen calls Warren and Lucille on the telephone so that they know she is all right, but she refuses to come home. As Warren grows accustomed to Helen's absence, he begins dating Vera Oxendine.

  Summoned by Lucille, Rae shows up with Billy McQueen, a man she had met in Washington and married in Myrtle Beach, South Carolina, on the way to Mount Pleasant. Their marriage is at least in part the result of the fact that Rae is pregnant with a child she is not sure she wants. From Rae, Lucille learns that Helen had tried to have an abortion when she was pregnant with Lucille. The abortion had been only partly successful, and one of the twins—Lucille—survived. The truth about Lucille's past unfolds just as her present is changing.

As Warren Odom and Vera Oxendine become more involved with each other and Rae and Billy pull farther apart, Lucille becomes more desperate to keep the family together. Rae's pregnancy makes her despondent, and she withdraws from Billy. Lucille, believing that she is responsible for keeping the family together, spends more and more time with Billy, who helps her study for her makeup exams. On Halloween night, dressed in costumes (although Lucille has removed her mask), Billy and Lucille make love in the study, where for weeks Billy has been working on his doctorate and Lucille has been studying for her high school makeup exams.

Eventually, Rhody leads Lucille to Helen, who has been living in the shell of a house built by Rhody's father "on a piece of no-man's land." She has been taking the bus to a job at a gift shop not far from the Odom household. Lucille and her mother have a tearful reunion, but Helen has no intention of returning to live with Warren. "Marriage was killing me," she says.

Meanwhile, Rae's pregnancy comes to term, and she gives birth to a daughter, Phoebe. The novel ends with a rearrangement of the family into new families, all of which are connected with the old. Rae, Billy, and Phoebe live together in Charleston. Warren has moved into Vera's bungalow with her. Rhody has taken an apartment with her daughter Evelyn, Wayne has moved into a college dormitory, and Lucille has joined her mother.

Analysis

The events of the plot of *Rich in Love* suggest a much grimmer story than the one Lucille tells. Describing the plot—a seventeen-year-old whose mother leaves, who is the survivor of an attempted abortion, who has two sex relationships, whose unhappily pregnant sister considers an abortion and gives birth to her baby in a toilet—may make the book sound depressing. It is, however, not depressing at all, but life-affirming.

In fact, the book is rich in sensuous details and comic effects. Lucille's narrative voice often sounds like that of a mature and poetic adult. Humphreys' central intention is celebratory as she develops Lucille's character in a situation "rich in love." Lucille is experiencing a chaotic time in her own life at a chaotic time in history—domestic history, rather than the traditional history of wars and political upheavals.

The novel as a whole is structured around parallels: The black Poole family parallels the white Odoms. Rhody Poole, who left her daughter to be reared by her mother, parallels Rae Odom McQueen, whose mother is unlikely to rear her child. Rae's pregnancy and her not wanting the baby parallels Helen's situation when she was pregnant with Lucille. These parallels reinforce the connections among the characters' lives and put their individual decisions in perspective.

During most of *Rich in Love*, Lucille is a neglected child who is looking out for her parents, but what appears to be chaos in the Odoms' lives is the result of changing mores, including changing sex-role expectations. Lucille is therefore also growing up and learning about the varieties of love in a place she loves, a place rich not only in love but also in varieties of history.

The setting of the novel is an area that is rich in history. At one point, Lucille and Billy collect Indian pottery shards from the river bank. Lucille finds a shard and gives it to Billy, who identifies it precisely as an artifact from 500 B.C.E. Fishbone Johnson's club, where Rae goes to sing, is in an old AME (African Methodist Episcopal) Church built in 1866. At nearby Fort Moultrie, bees have made a nest in a statue of Osceola. Lucille imagines that the bees have filled the statue with honey. The honey-filled statue suggests the sweetness of Lucille's view of history.

Lucille's love for the Charleston area makes her love history as it is normally defined, but she also loves history defined a little differently. "I also felt that history was a category comprising not only famous men of bygone eras, but *me, yesterday,*" she says. Lucille's own "yesterday" takes on a complicated significance for her when Rae explains that Lucille is a twin whose sibling was aborted. She begins to distrust the past.

Lucille loves her hometown and the people closest to her. To be rich in love is to be sensitive to the things of this world. *Rich in Love* is therefore rich in comic and sensuous details. One example will show how details reflect the larger patterns of the novel. In a tender love scene, Billy and Lucille explore each other's scars, emotional and physical. Under his hair Billy hides a scar on his forehead that he got after falling off bleachers at a baseball game. Lucille pretends that she cannot see the scar, even when he points it out. Similarly, Billy claims not to be able to see the thin scar that was left when Lucille's harelip was repaired. This parallel brings the characters together emotionally; being sympathetically attentive to physical details is an aspect of the intimacy of love.

Lucille tries to hold on to the past, as does Warren when he tries to remember his life before Helen. That remembering, that history, gives Warren a firm enough sense of his own identity to go on developing. Something similar happens to Lucille, who learns how to face the future by understanding her own past.

In the jargon of social psychology, the Odoms are a dysfunctional or, as Lucille says, a "defunct" family, but *Rich in Love* affirms that there is more than one way for a family to function. In the end, all of the Odoms find new ways to get the security and assurance that the traditional family of four (as Lucille says) used to provide.

Context

When Helen telephones after she has left, Lucille wants to know, ". . . is it something feminist . . . or is it something real?" The light-hearted tone of the question captures the spirit of Humphreys' treatment of women's issues, which is not to say that the novel is antifeminist. Lucille's voice *is* a woman's point of view.

The major events in the novel are precipitated by changes in women's roles: Helen can no longer define herself as a wife and mother. Rae is not prepared to be defined that way either; nothing in her life suggests domesticity. Lucille can no longer rely on her mother as a nurturer. All of the women in the novel are unwilling to submerge their identities in their husbands' identities or in marriage. The "traditional family," as represented by the Odoms before Helen's departure, is replaced quite satisfactorily in *Rich in Love* by a new and more flexible definition of family.

Many incidents in the novel reflect changing attitudes toward sexuality and gender. No one in the novel, male or female, has to do anything. No one is bound by gender stereotypes. Neither the males nor the females are expected to be self-sacrificing. Lucille is learning a lesson in independence from her mother. Helen Odom loves Warren, Rae, Rhody, and Lucille, but she must also love herself.

Lucille has sexual intercourse with two different males without becoming a victim or an outcast. *Rich in Love* deals openly and unaffectedly with birth control. Women in the novel assume responsibility for contraception. As practiced by Lucille (and less effectively by Rae), it is a matter-of-fact choice. By the same token, Humphreys recognizes the complexity of human interaction. Finally, contraception allows Lucille to experiment with sex and learn about love in the process.

A hundred years ago in a typical novel, a character similar to Lucille might have gotten pregnant and married Wayne. Rae and Billy's marriage might have been melodramatically destroyed by Lucille's flirtation with Billy. Humphreys' novel, however, has a happy and at the same time "realistic" ending—which may, ironically, distress some readers who disapprove of Lucille's behavior. Rather than propose one answer for all women, *Rich in Love* portrays a variety of legitimate options. Rae, Billy, and Phoebe stay together, but their lives will be different from the Odoms' family life.

Changes in women's roles also mean changes in men's roles. Billy's love for Rae and his tenderness toward Lucille are presented appealingly. Humphreys has Lucille portray both Rae and Billy sympathetically, each struggling with the desire for freedom and the desire to embrace marriage as the natural outcome of love between a man and a woman.

Sources for Further Study

Henley, Ann. " 'Space for Herself': Nadine Gordimer's *A Sport of Nature* and Josephine Humphreys' *Rich in Love.*" *Frontiers: A Journal of Women's Studies* 13, no. 1 (1992): 81-89. Henley argues that "for a woman, 'being' is made possible not by belonging to but by being freed from place." Lucille, like Helen, must be freed from the Odom household to find her own identity.

Humphreys, Josephine. "Continuity and Separation: An Interview with Josephine Humphreys." Interview by Rosemary Magee. *Southern Review* 27, no. 4 (Autumn, 1991): 792-802. In this interview conducted in May, 1990, Humphreys talks about her approach to writing. She refers several times to *Rich in Love* as well as to her other novels.

——————. "My Real Invisible Self." In *A World Unsuspected: Portraits of Southern Childhood*, edited by Alex Harris. Chapel Hill: University of North Carolina Press, 1987. Humphreys contributes a section to this anthology of childhood reminiscences by eleven Southern writers.

Malone, Michael. "Rich in Words." *The Nation*, October 10, 1987, 388-389. Review-

ing *Rich in Love*, Malone compares the novel at some length with Humphreys'
earlier novel, *Dreams of Sleep*, and praises *Rich in Love* for Lucille's "wry wit, and
fine comic timing."

Seaquist, Carla. "Someone Who Cares." *Belles Lettres: A Review of Books by Women*
3, no. 5 (May/June, 1988): 5. This review, written in a slangy style for a feminist
audience, describes Lucille's narration as a "feisty female voice."

Summer, Bob. "Josephine Humphreys." *Publisher's Weekly* (September 4, 1987):
49-50. Published before *Rich in Love*, this article includes biographical information
about Humphreys.

Wickenden, Dorothy. "What Lucille Knew." *The New Republic* (October 19, 1987):
45-46. This review praises Humphreys' handling of her characters' inner lives "with
subtlety, originality and deadpan humor," but balances that praise with criticism of
the "mannered sentimentality and . . . pat psychology" of the ending of the novel.

Thomas Lisk

THE RISING OF THE MOON

Author: Lady Augusta Gregory (1852-1932)
Type of work: Drama
Type of plot: Sketch
Time of plot: The late nineteenth century
Locale: Ireland
First produced: 1907, at Abbey Theatre, Dublin, Ireland
First published: 1905

Principal characters:
THE SERGEANT, an officer in the Royal Irish Constabulary
THE MAN, a fugitive disguised as a ballad-singer
POLICEMAN B. and POLICEMAN X., two minor characters who
    constitute the search party

Form and Content

In theme, structure, and dialogue, *The Rising of the Moon* is typical of the series of brief, one-act plays which were presented as curtain-raisers in the Abbey Theatre in Dublin during its celebrated early years, which date from its foundation in 1904 to the attainment of Irish independence and the establishment of the Irish Free State in 1922. A large number of these plays, and almost all those that may be considered artistically successful within their obviously prescribed format, were written by Lady Augusta Gregory. The years in question are celebrated for having inaugurated a new kind of dramaturgy in English, for the discovery of a new generation of Irish playwrights (most notably John Millington Synge), and for making a significant contribution to cultural consciousness and cultural self-respect in Ireland at that time. Lady Gregory made artistic as well as practical contributions to these events, though her managerial skills and moral support meant more to the Abbey Theatre's survival than her dramatic works.

Although *The Rising of the Moon* is not in the first rank of the theater's plays, it does focus attention on the wider world that the theater was addressing and on the Abbey Theatre's sense of its own importance. The play's sketchiness, while dramatically limiting, underscores the representation of political activism as an area of stark choices and difficult compromises. Rather than having a plot as such, *The Rising of the Moon* derives its dramatic impact from a rhetorical conflict which represents mind-sets and forms of discourse in opposition. Although, strictly speaking, the generalized revolutionary sentiments which the Man expresses date from the years before the Abbey Theatre came into being, they denote an idealized sense of risk and suffering which the Man is willing to undertake for the common good. The Sergeant, on the other hand, appears in the service of an opposing dispensation, which seeks to criminalize the Man. The brief progress of the play clarifies and intensifies the character of this opposition between not only the two characters but also two versions of Ireland's political and cultural destiny.

The play's title is that of a well-known ballad, the second such song that the Man sings in the play. In this ballad, the rising of the moon coincides with the rising of the Irish people's hopes for revolutionary success. The lack of historical specificity, the identification of the characters through titles and common rather than proper names, and the folkloric associations of the play's title all make *The Rising of the Moon* an illuminating example of the type of generic play that Lady Gregory in effect invented. Referred to as folk plays because of the simplicity of their staging, the skeletal nature of their plot, and their recuperation of populist, if not necessarily popular, political sentiments, these plays convey a series of tableaux based on various purported truisms of the mind-set of ordinary people. In *The Rising of the Moon*, the conflict between such considerations—as freedom and responsibility, the uniform and the disguise, the Sergeant's cupidity and the Man's rhetoric, the tradition of the law and the tradition of the outlaw—may be seen as the dramatic equivalent of a genre painting. Its truth to life may be thought at odds with its vitality.

Analysis

The economic subtext of *The Rising of the Moon* provides an approach to its depiction of class realities within the Irish nationalist community and is a means of focusing on the play's unmistakable if unsophisticated ideological content. There is a price on the Man's head. That is the fact upon which the action of the play, such as it is, pivots. The amount named in the opening conversation between the policemen is a description of the value placed on the escapee by those with the power to set the market in such matters. It is also an expression of the economic status of those who are carrying out the will of such empowerment.

The police make themselves known not only by means of this financial signature but also by the fact that they are to be differentiated from the escapee's jailers, without whose help, it is suggested, the Man would not have broken free. The way in which their sympathies are engaged is putatively at odds with those of their colleagues in the security forces. Moreover, their implied opposition to the Man's freedom places them in a singular position regarding the local community as a whole. This is suggested by the Man's disguise as a ballad-singer. To disguise himself as the anonymous purveyor of works that reflect and stimulate popular sentiment is to present himself as the voice of the people, a role whose undisguised nature is revealed as the play unfolds. The implication is that the police are opposed not merely to the Man's freedom in the narrow, practical, legalistic sense of the word: Their allegiance makes them the enemies of the larger freedom for which the Man is such a powerful spokesperson.

The Sergeant is the dramatic point at which such concerns converge. He is at once the policeman with the greatest degree of visibility and responsibility in the play and the one who finds himself radically susceptible to the appeal of the Man's rhetoric. This vulnerability is partly a matter of the moment, of the heightened sense of duty that the escape has created, and of the weight of official responsibility that the Sergeant has been asked to bear. The Man's words and songs inevitably prey upon the

Sergeant's situation. Yet more than the moment is at stake. The Man is able to remind the Sergeant of the time before he was a policeman, when in his youth he was as familiar with popular ballads as any other one of the plain people of Ireland.

The Man's reminders threaten to unmask the Sergeant by appealing to a level in him that has been buried beneath the uniform. It is not surprising that the Sergeant finds the Man's singing unbearable and intolerable. Not only is the subject matter of the songs seditious—or at least addressed provocatively to the law and order which the Sergeant represents—but the songs themselves also possess an emotional appeal, evoking days of youth, enthusiasm, and commitment. They appeal to a presocial version of the Sergeant, an embodiment of himself that has not been tenable since he entered the police force. The inner man, which the Man evokes, is by implication a more valid and less constrained personage, one who was at home in his community and shared the community's awareness and articulation of its most far-reaching ambitions.

Loyalty to this earlier self dictates the Sergeant's behavior at the end of the play. His furious dismissal of the constables, and of the light that they literally might shine on the proceedings, expresses that loyalty and hints at the possibility that his actions are being guided by a different light, one which as been rekindled through his contact with the Man. This possibility is established by the Man, as he goes to hide behind the barrel and quotes the key word from the first ballad he sings: "Granuaile," one of the names in which Ireland's identity was both disguised and enshrined by poem and legend. Indeed, what the Man says to the Sergeant at this point could be repeating the fact that the Man is "the friend of Granuaile" or could be a statement of the new truth that it is the Sergeant who has rediscovered his affiliation with the motherland.

Yet, Lady Gregory is careful to have the Sergeant's closing words act as a caution against taking too lofty a view of him. The economic aspect of the play is explicitly reintroduced in these final lines, revealing that the Sergeant has not undergone a permanent transformation into a patriot by making good the Man's escape; the stolid, narrow, self-interested elements of his personality are still to the fore. By questioning what he has done for the Man, and comparing it with the reward of a hundred pounds, the Sergeant raises issues of value. The Sergeant himself may be in a quandary as to how best to attach value to the events of the play. Yet his doubt is not one which the play's contemporary audience would share. Thus, *The Rising of the Moon* attains an ideological gloss on the forces that it brings into conflict by making the audience its accomplice.

Context

As in the case of many social and cultural transfers of power, women played a substantial role in enacting and supporting the artistic and political changes which took place in Ireland during the first two decades of the twentieth century. As actresses, activists, ideologues, and combatants, their roles were identical to those of their male counterparts. Lady Augusta Gregory's career may be construed as an embodiment of the changes in women's commitment during the heyday of what is loosely referred to by political and cultural historians as the national movement of Ireland. Given Lady Gregory's origins and early years, her career might be described as exemplifying the reorientation of allegiance that distinguished members of her generation undertook.

The exemplary character of Lady Gregory's public life is highlighted in particular by her contributions to the foundation and continuation of the Abbey Theatre. These contributions were not merely artistic. It could be argued that her plays were the least significant of her various donations, although to do so would be to overlook their directness and the presuppositions that govern their topicality. Although her plays were praised by W. B. Yeats, whose patroness Lady Gregory became, the poet was much more affected by and appreciative of her generosity, level-headedness, and practicality, so that her personality as typified by Yeats occupies an honored place in the poet's personal mythology.

Her various artistic accomplishments in the fields of folklore and autobiography, in addition to drama, are a tribute to her capacity to extend her sense of the responsibilities that her social background imposed upon her. They also provide an insight on the changing cultural landscape in the Ireland of Lady Gregory's day and on the fact that such shifts of emphasis may have the effect of altering conventional assumptions about the role of women in society. Lady Gregory's career as a writer roughly coincided with the rise of the women's suffrage movement in the British Isles. Though it hardly invokes that movement, its interest in representing the populace and in giving a voice to its sentiments are in themselves contributions to the extension of the cultural franchise—not only on the part of those represented and the audiences who acknowledge and accept them but also on behalf of the author herself.

Sources for Further Study

Adams, Hazard. *Lady Gregory*. Lewisburg, Pa.: Bucknell University Press, 1973. A brief, insightful guide to Lady Gregory's various writings. Contains a biographical sketch and a chapter on each of the main areas of her works, including her plays. A chronology and a brief bibliography are included.

Coxhead, Elizabeth. *Lady Gregory: A Literary Portrait*. London: Secker and Warburg, 1966. A revised and enlarged edition of a 1962 work which uses a biographical approach to concentrate on Lady Gregory's writings, a checklist of which is included. Her literary and cultural relations with other leading figures in the Irish literary revival provide a focus for the author's approach.

Gregory, Lady Augusta. *Lady Gregory: Interviews and Recollections*. Edited by E. H. Mikhail. London: Macmillan, 1977. A selection of excerpts from memoirs, newspapers, and other contemporary sources that provide a composite portrait of Lady Gregory's public life. Her celebrated home at Coole Part enters the picture, and some of her remarks in passing about the early, controversial history of the Abbey Theatre are included.

Kohfeldt, Mary Lou. *Lady Gregory: The Woman Behind the Irish Renaissance*. New York: Athenaeum, 1985. The fullest account available of Lady Gregory's life and times. Use is made of archival material to broaden the picture of Lady Gregory's youth, though the main emphasis remains on her public work on behalf of the arts in Ireland.

Kopper, E. A., Jr. "Lady Gregory's *The Rising of the Moon*." *The Explicator* 47, no. 3 (Spring, 1989): 29-31. A brief account of the play's origins and place in the Abbey Theatre repertory. Particular emphasis is placed on the work's debt to actual events of the day.

Saddlemyer, Ann, and Colin Smythe, eds. *Lady Gregory: Fifty Years After*. Totowa, N.J.: Barnes & Noble Books, 1987. A substantial collection of essays that provide a comprehensive scholarly treatment of Lady Gregory's life and times. Several essays are devoted to her plays, and this volume also includes considerable material pertinent to an evaluation of the overall cultural significance of Lady Gregory's contribution to Irish literature.

George O'Brien

THE ROAD FROM COORAIN

Author: Jill Ker Conway (1934-   )
Type of work: Autobiography
Time of work: The 1930's to the 1950's
Locale: New South Wales and Sydney, Australia; Europe; and the United States
First published: 1989

> *Principal personages:*
> JILL KER, the author as a girl and young woman
> WILLIAM INNIS KER, her father
> EVELYN MARY (ADAMES) KER, her mother
> ROBERT KER, her brother
> BARRY KER, her brother
> ANGUS WAUGH, a neighbor of the Kers
> GEOFF COGHLAN, the manager of Coorain
> MISS EVERETT, the headmistress of Abbotsleigh school
> NINA MORRIS, a friend of Jill
> PETER STONE, another friend of Jill
> MILTON OSBORNE and ROB LAURIE, her friends in the history
>   honors program
> JOHN WARD, the head of the history department at the University
>   of Sydney and Jill's academic adviser
> ALEC MERTON, an American businessman and Jill's friend

Form and Content

Jill Ker Conway was born on a sheep ranch in the grasslands of New South Wales, Australia, was educated in Sydney, came to North America to continue her graduate studies in history at Harvard, taught and was an administrator at the University of Toronto, and became president of Smith College in Northampton, Massachusetts. Her autobiography, *The Road from Coorain*, tells of the beginning of her life journey from her childhood, adolescence, and young adulthood in Australia until she departed for the United States. This thoughtful look at Conway's formative years gives insight into the position of women in Australian society during the first half of the twentieth century and her personal struggles in dealing with the expectations of women's role in this cultural milieu.

The autobiography begins with background about the Australian land and tells how Conway's parents came to Coorain, the sheep station they owned. She relates events of her life in chronological order. The first four chapters cover her childhood at Coorain through a drought that devastated the sheep ranch and claimed her father's life. In the fifth and sixth chapters, she and her family try to cope with their loss, their relocation to urban life in Sydney, and Jill Ker's preparatory school education. The last three chapters relate the turning point of Jill Ker's self-discovery as she attended the University of Sydney and broadened her horizons during a European tour. The book concludes with her departure for the United States to study at Harvard University.

The narrative of this period of her life serves as a framework for a reflective book that confronts a number of issues. Conway writes with a perceptive eye for detail and an evocative style that captures the characters of both rural and urban Australia. Within this setting, she views the position of women from two perspectives. First, she is constantly aware of opportunities for and limitations on women in Australian culture through the tension in the relationship between herself and her mother. Second, the position of women is paralleled in the subordinate provincial status of Australia to Great Britain and the cultural differences between these two lands. These analytical observations enable Conway's book to transcend the particular events of her life while at the same time endowing women's issues with a personal humane dimension.

Analysis

Jill Ker Conway's views about herself and the place of women in twentieth century culture were shaped by her family background and the circumstances of her childhood growing up on a sheep station in the grasslands of New South Wales, Australia. The first three chapters of *The Road from Coorain*, "The West," "Coorain," and "Childhood," focus on the landscape and family setting of her early life. Her mother, Evelyn Ker, was a strong, intelligent woman, a nurse whom Conway describes as a "modern feminist" with strong views on issues such as a woman's right to abortion. Her father, William Ker, was an equally independent, strong-willed man of Scottish descent. After their marriage and the birth of their two sons, Robert and Barry, in 1930, they acquired a tract of land in the Australian bush for sheep raising. In this frontier setting, men and women, although performing different tasks, had to work together in a partnership to make the sheep-ranching operation viable.

When Jill Ker was born, her brothers were six and four years of age. She grew up accustomed to the realities of frontier life on an isolated sheep station. She worked alongside her parents, and she competed and played with her brothers. After her older brothers departed for boarding school in Sydney, she often rode horses to work the sheep with her father. These early years fostered a sense of self-reliance unmarked by distinctions between what men and women could achieve.

The power of nature as a force for change became a vivid reality in the life of Jill Ker and her family. Beginning in 1940 and continuing with increasing severity for the following four years, a great drought devastated the territory where Coorain was located. Conway describes the dramatic effects of this natural disaster in the fourth chapter, "Drought." Their sheep stock was reduced to almost nothing. Most important, her father died trying to repair a pipe to provide some water for the animals. Rejecting the usual practice of widows to sell their property, her mother was fiercely determined to keep Coorain. Eventually, however, she agreed to hire a manager and move to Sydney so that Jill could be properly educated. The train ride from Coorain to Sydney marked the end of Jill Ker's childhood and the beginning of the confrontation with a different set of expectations for women in the urban post-World War II society of the 1950's.

Living in the outback, Jill Ker had been educated at home, where she read avidly and learned the hard lessons of surviving on the land. With the abrupt move to Sydney, her primary adjustment was to the social setting of formal schooling. She relates the events of her life during her preparatory education in the fifth and sixth chapters. The family's uncertain financial situation necessitated several moves in the Sydney area before she was enrolled in Abbotsleigh private school for girls, where she excelled academically in the classical British education curriculum. She had more difficulty, however, overcoming the shyness that arose from the awkwardness she felt in encountering a completely different lifestyle from that she had led at Coorain.

She also began to question expectations of her role as a woman in society. Although Abbotsleigh school stressed leadership for women, the concept was interpreted as philanthropy or volunteer work within the confines of marriage. In addition, especially after the death of her eldest brother Bob in an automobile accident, her mother became more withdrawn and dependent on her daughter's care. Jill struggled with the issue of how much of her life she should sacrifice to maintain her mother. Although the title of the sixth chapter, "Finding the Southern Cross," refers to her father's advice about looking to the stars for orientation and direction, Jill's graduation with high honors from Abbotsleigh left her without a compass on the moral dilemmas that these questions about her future raised.

The resolution of these dilemmas was postponed as Jill Ker continued her education at the University of Sydney. Although she interrupted her studies after her first semester to work for a year, when she returned to the university, she found new academic motivation in honors programs in history and English. She also broadened her horizons with new friends she made among her fellow students and her first serious romantic relationship. Her studies brought another issue into focus. As in her earlier education, the curriculum based on Western European and, particularly, Anglo-Saxon traditions excluded distinctive Australian history and culture as well as the contributions of other societies. The title of this chapter, "The Nardoo Stones," refers to the artifacts of aboriginal Australian tribes whose significance she had ignored as she walked over them daily at Coorain.

As graduation approached, insights about sexual discrimination and the suppression of native cultures converged. Although she was ranked first in her class, her application for an appointment with the Department of External Affairs was rejected because she was a female, while two of her male peers were accepted. In this personal experience of the exercise of "biological superiority," she saw analogies with the attitudes of British imperialism toward other cultures. In both cases, those of gender and ethnic prejudice, earning "freedom through merit" was almost impossible.

Jill Ker began to find the direction she wanted for her life after her graduation from the University of Sydney. Soon after commencement, she and her mother embarked on an extended tour of Europe which included not only sightseeing but also a brief stint for Jill Ker working as a model in London. The most important result of this sojourn, which forms the subject of chapter 8, "Recharting the Globe," was to give Ker a broader global perspective. Primarily, it confirmed her realization that the implicit and explicit cultural categories of British life that had been inculcated in her since childhood did not coincide with the worldview she had formed. She concluded that she would have to shape and determine her own set of cultural values.

When she returned to Sydney, she began to take concrete steps to lead her life in accordance with her talents, expectations, and cultural perspective. The final chapter, "The Right Country," relates how she laid the foundations for new directions in her life. In part, she made the decision to pursue an academic career by doing graduate work at the University of Sydney. The subject she chose for her research was not the traditional European-oriented history, but rather a study of frontier society of Australia, which was published as *Merchants and Merinos* (1960). Her application to Harvard University to continue doctoral work was based on her recognition that historical studies in the United States were on the forefront of research in the kinds of new topics, such as frontier societies and the history of women, that interested her. Her acceptance at Harvard also provided the impetus to make the decisive break from her mother. The final preparations for her departure to "the right country" allowed her to reflect on the generational differences that separated her mother's experience from her own. She was determined to use the intellectual vocation that she had chosen to understand and overcome the limitations placed on women's abilities that had broken her mother's body and spirit.

Context

In many ways, *The Road from Coorain* is part of a substantial tradition of autobiographical writing by Australian women. Conway's work, however, has several distinguishing features. First, it excels as a work of literature through the construction of dramatic narrative and a descriptive prose style that makes the setting especially vivid. As a result, this autobiographical account enables readers to relate to the universal character of Conway's experience, which has been described by Carolyn Heilbrun as "the despair of an ambitious young woman facing a constricted female destiny." Second, Conway analyzes issues concerning women that she confronted as she grew to maturity. This analytical quality helps to provide an objective evaluation of women's place in the society in which Conway was raised. *The Road from Coorain* achieves its impact in women's studies from this integration of literary and historical features.

As a historian, educator, and writer, Conway has written and edited numerous books and articles on women's intellectual history and women in education, including *The Female Experience in Eighteenth and Nineteenth Century America: A Guide to the History of American Women* (1982) and *Women Reformers and American Culture* (1987).

Sources for Further Study

Conway, Jill Ker, ed. *Written by Herself: Autobiographies of American Women; an*

Anthology. New York: Random House, 1992. Drawing on her own experience with autobiography, Conway has edited a collection of selections from the memoirs and autobiographies of American women from Jane Addams to Zora Neale Hurston.

Conway, Jill Ker, and Susan C. Borque, eds. *The Politics of Women's Education: Perspectives from Asia, Africa, and Latin America.* Ann Arbor: University of Michigan Press, 1993. Conway includes the essay "Rethinking the Impact of Women's Education."

Conway, Jill Ker, Susan C. Borque, and Joan W. Scott, eds. *Learning About Women: Gender, Politics, and Power.* Ann Arbor: University of Michigan Press, 1989. Contains Conway's essay on "Politics, Pedagogy, and Gender."

Dixson, Miriam. *The Real Matilda: Women and Identity in Australia 1788 to the Present.* Rev. ed. New York: Penguin Books, 1984. This book analyzes the circumscribed position of women in Australian society and places these attitudes in historical context.

Hooton, Joy. *Stories of Herself When Young: Autobiographies of Childhood by Australian Women.* Oxford, England: Oxford University Press, 1990. This book examines the literary tradition of autobiographical writing by Australian women. It contains an extensive bibliography of those autobiographies.

Lees, Stella, and June Senyard. *The 1950s: How Australia Became a Modern Society, and Everyone Got a House and Car.* Melbourne, Australia: Heyland House, 1987. A re-creation of popular Australian culture at the time that Jill Ker was studying at the University of Sydney.

Karen Gould

A ROOM OF ONE'S OWN

Author: Virginia Woolf (1882-1941)
Type of work: Essays
First published: 1929

Form and Content

What is now known as *A Room of One's Own* began as two essays, parts of which were read to the Arts Society at Newnham and to the Odtaa at Girton in October of 1928. These essays were later revised and extended by Woolf into a short book of six chapters which mixes fact and fiction to analyze the roles and relationships of money and gender in regard to the production of art, specifically fiction by women.

Woolf composed the original essays to deliver as speeches to groups of young college women—women who were at that time forbidden to enter England's university system because of their gender. The topic of "women and fiction" forms the continuing motif of the book, as Woolf attempts different compositions of the question before attempting to answer them: What are women like? What is fiction written by women like? What is fiction written about women like? These questions led her to connect gender and fiction with economics at a time when women had just recently received the right to vote and the right to own property. She thus further asks such questions as "Why did men drink wine and women water?" and "What effect has poverty on fiction?"

Woolf begins to answer the questions about women and fiction by inventing a fictional college called Fernham. She refers to herself as a fictional character—"I"— and stresses that she speaks as a kind of Everywoman. She finds not only that she is barred from the library because of her gender but also that women have historically been barred from writing fiction for the same reason.

By comparing the furnishings and the food served at Fernham to those of men's universities, she suggests a correlation between women's fiction and money. The necessity of money to produce art, specifically fiction, leads Woolf to the formulaic answer of the title: What a woman needs to write fiction is money (five hundred British pounds annually) and a room of her own.

The six chapters explore the connections of gender, money, and fiction through an imagined visit to the British Museum, an examination of George Trevelyan's *History of England*, a review of nineteenth century British women novelists, a comparison of the representations of women in historical works with their representation by men in literature (including a speculation about what would have happened to William Shakespeare had he been born a woman), and a final call for an androgynous approach to the production of art.

Analysis

Adopting the tone and style of a speech, Woolf's persona addresses an imagined audience of young women in college. She describes an imagined visit to a fictional women's college (Fernham) in which she is entertained at dinner by a woman whom she calls Mary Seton and is given a history of the origin of the college. Woolf's persona details the dinner in a subtly sarcastic manner: The soup is described as a weak broth, "a plain gravy soup"; the main course as a "homely trinity" of beef, greens, and potatoes; the dessert as prunes and custard, the prunes "stringy as a miser's heart."

Woolf first asks why one gender has been allowed access to the universities while the other has not. She asks repeatedly why women have been given few resources to provide for their education, while men have been funded in a comparatively lavish manner. She draws no conclusions in the text, but she implies that the difference is not based on anything except gender.

In the second chapter, Woolf imagines a visit to the British Museum, not having found a sufficient answer to her questions regarding women and fiction. This question now has reformed itself as the question regarding women and money and fiction. Woolf looks up the category "women and fiction" and expresses surprise at the tremendous number of men who have written on the topic. Some of these men had academic qualifications, but many had "no apparent qualification save that they are not women." Noting that women have not historically written books about men, she lists the numerous subject areas in which men have written about women.

She suggests that most of these writings are useless, having been written "in the red light of emotion and not in the white light of truth." This distinction of emotional writing versus "incandescent" writing foreshadows the later discussions of Shakespeare's abilities and her call for an androgynous attitude in writing. She offers a sarcastic Freudian interpretation of the misogynistic attitude she discovers in male writings throughout history, especially in her fictitious example of Professor von X's *The Mental, Moral, and Physical Inferiority of the Female Sex*. Once again, however, Woolf suggests that equality of the sexes—for example, in occupational areas—will not change the perceived differences in gender. She reformulates the question of women, money, and fiction once again, and she heads to the shelves of history books to search for a suitable answer.

In the third chapter, Woolf consults Professor Trevelyan's *History of England*. She finds that women have little recorded history in this volume. The first reference occurs about 1470 and details the socially accepted practice of wife-beating. The next reference, about two hundred years later, confirms the status of women as property of men. Woolf contrasts these images with those of the female characters in fiction written by men, from Clytemnestra, Antigone, and Cleopatra to Clarissa, Becky Sharp, and Emma Bovary. While women in history were abused and without individual rights, she observes that women in fiction were never lacking in personality and character. Furthermore, the subject matter of the entire history of England concerns the social and public realms of male influence rather than the personal or family concerns that she suggests the female writer would have recorded.

She acknowledges that a woman of Shakespeare's time could not have written the works of Shakespeare, but she argues that it would have been a matter not of gender but of opportunity. She then imagines what Shakespeare's sister—a fictitious entity she dubs Judith—would have encountered had she been as talented as her brother William. "Judith" Shakespeare follows her aspirations for the theater and fiction writing in a manner similar to that of William, yet her life and art are stifled by the men she encounters. She ultimately kills herself out of frustration. Woolf further admires the writing of nineteenth century women in the light of their limited experiences and their lack of money even to buy paper or to have a room of their own.

In chapter 4, she expands on the difficulties faced by women writers. The profession was considered improper for women, and women such as Aphra Behn, who made a living by writing, were considered immoral. She notes that many women chose to write under a pseudonym, and she notes that these women had to write under adverse conditions. She praises the forerunners of modern novelists, such as Jane Austen, the Brontës, and George Eliot, although in Charlotte Brontë she finds that gender affects the integrity of her writing. The others show little anger or emotion in their writing, more closely approximating the unemotional, incandescent quality of Shakespeare's writing. She says that these women writers are necessary to future women writers in the same way that Shakespeare, Christopher Marlowe, Geoffrey Chaucer, and earlier poets were necessary to subsequent male writers.

Chapter 5 examines how literature written by men portrays women only through the eyes of men. Similarly, the world in literature written by men is portrayed only through male eyes, focusing only on what is important to men, such as war, sports, and so forth. All writers, however, must move beyond a gender-specific focus in order to achieve the unemotional tone she admires.

Chapter 6 broadens the discussion from gender and literature to gender and philosophy. Not only in writing but also in life in general, both women and men should try to achieve an androgynous attitude, to stop thinking of the genders as distinct from each other. If one achieves this unity of the mind, one can also achieve that incandescent quality of mind evidenced by the greatest of writers, exemplified by Shakespeare.

Context

Of all the artists and writers who were part of the Bloomsbury circle of intellectuals in early twentieth century England, Virginia Woolf has proved to be the most influential and enduring, except perhaps for Maynard Keynes and his effects on economic theory. *A Room of One's Own* has become an icon of feminism, although its content often was distorted by critics as its influence grew.

The many works alluding to Woolf's title have made the work a symbolic statement of feminist philosophy. After its first publication, however, reaction was muted. Some saw it as a harsh complaint with unrealistic expectations (for example, five hundred British pounds in 1929 was roughly equivalent to an annual income of fifty thousand dollars, a fortune for that time). Others saw it as an accurate portrayal of social conventions in regard to gender. The time in history of its publication, the period between two world wars, diminished its initial impact; in fact, Woolf reiterated much of the argument in her 1938 *Three Guineas*, mixing women's equality into the context of the masculine institutions of war and government. Indisputably, the central image of *A Room of One's Own* has contributed to the understanding that gender equality has more to do with economic power than with biology.

Woolf's work is usually considered to be ardently feminist and a product of her repression based on gender. Yet Woolf was a privileged woman with access to education other than the university, and her financial status allowed her not only to publish her own works but also to publish other writers at her and her husband Leonard's Hogarth Press. The book criticizes discrimination based on wealth; it criticizes the subjugation of any group because of economic repression, whether that group is defined by gender or any other criterion.

Woolf, like Edgar Allan Poe, was much maligned following her death by suicide in 1941; her mental instabilities were emphasized far more than her insightful social and political analysis. In more recent criticism, her artistic temperament and her gender are less the focus of study than her straightforward and innovative analysis of literature and economic power.

Sources for Further Study

Bell, Quentin. *Virginia Woolf: A Biography*. London: Hogarth Press, 1972. Written by Virginia Woolf's nephew, this first complete biography of Woolf was first published in England in two volumes (here combined). It includes numerous photographs, a detailed chronology, references, and a bibliography. Bell drew on Virginia's letters and diaries; however, his work was completed before all of Woolf's letters and diaries were compiled.

DeSalvo, Louise A. *The Impact of Childhood Sexual Abuse on Her Life and Work*. Boston: Beacon Press, 1989. A detailed study of Woolf's life and personality based on her diaries, letters, and biographical sources. Although the abuse is predicated on vague diary entries about her half brother George Duckworth, this work provides a feminist analysis of Woolf's lesbianism.

Gilbert, Sandra M., and Susan Gubar. *The Madwoman in the Attic: The Woman Writer and the Nineteenth-Century Literary Imagination*. New Haven, Conn.: Yale University Press, 1979. Perhaps the most influential feminist criticism of its time, *The Madwoman in the Attic* reevaluates nineteenth century literature by women from a feminist perspective, citing Woolf as writer, feminist, and critic.

Showalter, Elaine. *A Literature of Their Own: British Women Novelists from Brontë to Lessing*. Princeton, N.J.: Princeton University Press, 1977. Alluding to Woolf's work in its title, this analysis of women writers categorizes them into female, feminine, and feminist, which are somewhat useful but arbitrary definitions. The survey of women novelists is an early example of influential feminist revision.

Woolf, Virginia. *The Diaries of Virginia Woolf*. Edited by Anne Olivier Bell. Vols. 1-5. New York: Harcourt Brace Jovanovich, 1977-1985. Though vast, these five volumes are well indexed and provide the most authoritative source for any study of Woolf or her politics and philosophy. Includes an introduction by Quentin Bell.

_____. *Women and Fiction: The Manuscript Versions of A Room of One's*

Own. Edited by S. P. Rosenbaum. Cambridge, Mass.: Oxford University Press, 1992. For any detailed study of Woolf's thoughts and the composing process of *A Room of One's Own*, this work is mandatory.

Bradley R. Bowers

RUBYFRUIT JUNGLE

Author: Rita Mae Brown (1944-   )
Type of work: Novel
Type of plot: Picaresque
Time of plot: 1950-1968
Locale: Coffee Hollow, Pennsylvania; Ft. Lauderdale and Gainesville, Florida; and New York City
First published: 1973

> *Principal characters:*
> MOLLY BOLT, the protagonist, who grows up poor, smart, and lesbian in small-town Pennsylvania
> CARRIE BOLT, Molly's adoptive mother
> CARL BOLT, Molly's adoptive father
> LEROY DENMAN, Molly's cousin, ally, admirer, and first male sexual partner
> CAROLYN SIMPSON and CONNIE PEN, Molly's high school friends
> FAYE RAIDER, Molly's roommate and lover at the University of Florida
> HOLLY, Molly's coworker in New York City
> POLINA BELLANTONI, a scholar whose bizarre sexual fantasies interfere with her and Molly's affair

Form and Content

   Rubyfruit Jungle, Rita Mae Brown's first novel, is semiautobiographical. Its heroine, Molly Bolt, is described with considerable admiration and sympathy by her creator. Molly grows from a rebellious child into a "self-actualizing lesbian"—an unprecedented validation of lesbian existence.

   Born illegitimate and adopted in infancy, Molly learns at an early age the meaning of the word "bastard." Her sense of not belonging serves as a catalyst for her subsequent determination to carve out an identity for herself independent of class, gender, and family. Young Molly defies many small-town social expectations: She fights like a boy, locks her mother in the cellar, and engages in sex play without inhibitions. By the time Molly's family moves to Florida, where she attends high school, Molly has formulated a clear goal: to escape. She has also learned that one must "play the game" in order to accomplish the goal. For this reason, she makes high grades, excels at sports, joins the right clubs, dates the right boys (and a girl or two), generally keeps her nose clean, and earns the all-important full scholarship to college. Although Molly gets off to a promising start socially and academically, the University of Florida does not turn out to be her ticket to independence and success. She and her roommate fall in love, and both are expelled when their affair becomes known. Rejected by Carrie when she tries to return home, Molly heads north to New York, where she has heard "there are so many queers . . . that one more wouldn't rock the boat."

In New York, Molly does not immediately "rock the boat," but she does need to learn who the other passengers are. She meets many people, most of whom appear to want something from her—sex, love, obedience, commitment. The lesbians she encounters are either snobbish (Chryssa), role-bound (Mighty Mo), insecure (Holly), or only temporarily on leave from heterosexuality (Polina). The straight women, however, are far worse—obsessed with men and makeup to the exclusion of all else. The men, oddly enough, are nicer. Some of them—Ralph the college student, gay sweet Calvin, James the editor—can be counted on for help, friendship, or collegiality. Older men on the make, however, such as Mr. Cohen at work, Paul the poetry scholar ("a living study in human debris"), and Professor Walgren at New York University (a "fake-hippie, middle-aged washout"), are silly or repulsive or both.

By the end of *Rubyfruit Jungle*, Molly explicitly understands what she has known intuitively all along—that she must make her way alone. In 1968, even her summa cum laude film degree opens no doors; she is offered secretarial jobs, while less-talented male classmates enter big studios on the fast track. She has little in common with her "downwardly-mobile" contemporaries in the antiwar movement. Even the newly formed women's groups suffer from middle-class bias, conformism, and homophobia, and Molly suspects that they would "trash me just the same." The novel closes with Molly—still alone, still copyediting for Mr. Cohen—vowing to make her movies even if she has to "fight until I'm fifty."

Analysis

Rubyfruit Jungle was originally published in 1973 by the feminist press Daughters, Inc. It quickly became an underground bestseller, gaining a wide alternative readership. In 1977, Bantam reissued it as a mass-market paperback; it sold an astonishing one million copies. For mainstream readers, *Rubyfruit Jungle* represented an upbeat and amusing glimpse of contemporary lesbian life, but for lesbian readers it meant far more. Molly Bolt was a psychologically healthy, outspoken, and empowered woman—a huge contrast to most earlier fictional portrayals of lesbians. For example, a lesbian reader before 1973 would probably have read Radclyffe Hall's *The Well of Loneliness* (1928), the story of unhappy Stephen Gordon, who internalizes male psychologists' labeling of lesbians as "inverts." She might have read or seen Lillian Hellman's play *The Children's Hour* (1934), which ends with a lesbian schoolmistress declaring her love and then shooting herself. If she was lucky, she had come upon Claire Morgan's *The Price of Salt* (1952), which equivocally validated its lesbian characters. Yet a lesbian was more likely to find her reading material in "adult" bookstores or bus terminals, which sold soft-porn pulp novels about lesbians, often written by men for men. Given this limited literary background, *Rubyfruit Jungle* ("a novel about being different and loving it") had an amazing positive impact. It counteracted the "dying fall" lesbian novel, in which the heroine, lonely and ostracized, is attracted only to other psychologically unstable individuals. Instead, *Ruby-*

fruit Jungle describes Molly Bolt's "enabling escape" and her "rebellion against social stigma and self-contempt." Indeed, Molly's name may symbolize her desire for flight and freedom.

Nevertheless, it would be an oversimplification to assume that *Rubyfruit Jungle* is only about escape. Molly's name evokes a second meaning as well; a molly-bolt, available in any hardware store, is a fastener that, when inserted through wood into empty space beyond, opens and anchors itself to the away side. Similarly, the fictional Molly Bolt seeks a place in the world where, through her own grit and talent, she can feel secure—"anchored." *Rubyfruit Jungle* is at root a picaresque novel, the story of a marginalized outsider who is seeking acceptance and success. Because its *picaro* is female and gay, it has often been read as a radical work. Certainly, the striking commercial profitability of *Rubyfruit Jungle* was largely the result of the risky novelty of its subject matter. The picaresque is, however, fundamentally a conservative genre; it neither questions society's basic values nor threatens to overturn its power structure. Molly may graduate summa cum laude and Phi Beta Kappa, but she is still an outsider at the novel's end. Molly "succeeds" in remaining true to her (marginalized) self, but she fails to squeeze past the powerful male gatekeepers who control access to the realm of "corporate" prosperity.

At the same time that one recognizes how *Rubyfruit Jungle* reinforces Molly Bolt's marginality and assumes an essentially conservative view of the world, one must not underestimate the degree of Molly's nonconformism. Throughout the novel, Molly repeatedly rejects society's heterosexist assumptions, especially when they are based on artificial gender roles. As a woman, she knows that traditional marriage is an inherently unequal institution in which wives are economically, politically, and socially powerless. She has seen its stultifying effect on Carrie, on Mrs. Cohen, and on her sixth-grade friend Leota. Molly also knows that men—specifically, Carl and Leroy—suffer as marriage limits their options and even their humanity. She lays blame on the institution of marriage, based as it is on artificially constructed male and female roles and on the romantic fiction of "now and forever." An important part of Molly's education in *Rubyfruit Jungle*, however, is her realization that role-playing relationships are just as bad outside marriage as in it. She sees lesbian butch-femme role-playing as nothing more than a pathetic copying of heterosexual roles: "What's the point of being a lesbian," she asks, "if a woman is going to look and act like an imitation man?" Finally, Molly also rejects fantasy role-playing. She is disgusted to learn that Polina and her lover Paul cannot experience sexual satisfaction with each other unless they go through an elaborate transgender fantasy; Polina imagines herself in a men's room while other men admire her "big juicy cock," and Paul imagines other women fondling his "voluptuous breasts." Molly's rejection of all these roles represents an extreme position, for it includes not only marriage but also gender limitations and even monogamy. She wishes only to be herself; her vision of women's sexuality as a "rubyfruit jungle" is her closest approach to a fantasy.

In short, *Rubyfruit Jungle* sends both a conservative and a radical message. Its picaresque dimension reinforces the exclusion, even the punishment, of the gender outlaw. At the same time, although Molly Bolt does not "develop" as much as does the typical *Bildungsroman* protagonist, her education leads her to an increasingly extreme rejection of heterosexual institutions.

Sources for Further Study

Abel, Elizabeth, Marianne Hirsch, and Elizabeth Langland, eds. *The Voyage In: Fictions of Female Development.* Hanover, N.H.: University Press of New England, 1983. This valuable collection of essays examines developmental novels by women writers. Rita Mae Brown and *Rubyfruit Jungle* are discussed at length in Bonnie Zimmerman's "Exiting from the Patriarchy: The Lesbian Novel of Development." Zimmerman's 1990 book *The Safe Sea of Women* expands many ideas from this essay.

Boyle, Sharon D. "Rita Mae Brown." In *Contemporary Lesbian Writers of the United States: A Bio-Bibliographical Critical Sourcebook*, edited by Sandra Pollack and Denise D. Knight. Westport, Conn.: Greenwood Press, 1993. Boyle's article profiles Rita Mae Brown's life and work, including an extended discussion of *Rubyfruit Jungle* and a useful bibliography.

Chew, Martha. "Rita Mae Brown: Feminist Theorist and Southern Novelist." *Southern Quarterly* 22 (1983): 61-80. Chew shows how Rita Mae Brown's early novels (including *Rubyfruit Jungle*) are informed by a specifically "lesbian feminist political vision," whereas her later works are "increasingly directed toward a mainstream audience."

Farwell, Marilyn R. "Toward a Definition of the Lesbian Literary Imagination." *Signs: Journal of Women in Culture and Society* 14 (Autumn, 1988): 100-118. Although Farwell's article does not refer explicitly to *Rubyfruit Jungle*, it is an extremely useful exploration of recurring themes in lesbian literature. Farwell suggests that feminist literary critics use "lesbian" as a metaphor, a "positive, utopian image of woman's creativity."

Mandrell, James. "Questions of Genre and Gender: Contemporary American Versions of the Feminine Picaresque." *Novel: A Forum on Fiction* 20, no. 2 (Winter, 1987): 149-170. Using *Rubyfruit Jungle* and two other novels as illustrations, Mandrell explores how genre can influence a woman author's "viewpoint and the ideological slant of her work." He focuses on Rita Mae Brown's use of the picaresque genre, pointing out that Molly Bolt's story "changes nothing, . . . but, rather, *acquiesces* to and *confirms* the marginality experienced by those who are not straight, white middle-class males."

Palmer, Paulina. "Contemporary Lesbian Feminist Fiction: Texts for Everywoman." In *Plotting Change: Contemporary Women's Fiction*, edited by Linda Anderson. London: Edward Arnold, 1990. Palmer sees *Rubyfruit Jungle* as representative of early lesbian feminist fiction, which "generally utilized the form of the *bildungsroman* and concentrated, somewhat narrowly, on the theme of Coming Out."

Stimpson, Catharine R. "Zero Degree Deviancy: The Lesbian Novel in English." In *Writing and Sexual Difference*, edited by Elizabeth Abel. Chicago: University of

Chicago Press, 1982. This groundbreaking article describes and distinguishes between the "dying fall" and "enabling escape" patterns of lesbian narrative, using *Rubyfruit Jungle* as a prime example of the second category.

Zimmerman, Bonnie. *The Safe Sea of Women: Lesbian Fiction, 1969-1989.* Boston: Beacon Press, 1990. This insightful book-length study of contemporary lesbian prose literature explores the interaction between fiction and community—specifically, how lesbian novels and short stories have both reflected and shaped the lesbian community. Zimmerman describes *Rubyfruit Jungle* as the quintessential "coming-out" novel, a *Bildungsroman.*

Deborah T. Meem

RUTH

Author: Mrs. Elizabeth Gaskell (1810-1865)
Type of work: Novel
Type of plot: Historical realism
Time of plot: The 1830's
Locale: England and Wales
First published: 1853

Principal characters:
> RUTH HILTON, the uneducated, dreamy, and passive central character
> MRS. MASON, Ruth's first employer
> BELLINGHAM, a spoiled, irresponsible, rich youth who seduces Ruth
> THURSTAN BENSON, a kindly minister who opens his home to Ruth
> FAITH BENSON, the minister's unmarried sister and housekeeper
> SALLY, the industrious family retainer to the Bensons
> MR. BRADSHAW, a prosperous, self-satisfied industrialist
> MRS. BRADSHAW, the cowed, quavering wife of Bradshaw
> JEMIMA BRADSHAW, their independent-minded, strong-willed daughter
> RICHARD BRADSHAW, their weak-willed, deceitful, fallen son
> LEONARD DENBIGH, Ruth's illegitimate son

Form and Content

Ruth is the second novel by Elizabeth Gaskell, the activist wife of a reformist Unitarian minister in Manchester, England. Controversial in its day, the novel straightforwardly and realistically tracks the fortunes of Ruth Hilton, who is outside the social and political establishment and is victimized by it yet ultimately triumphs over it. The novel is among the first to deal openly and deliberately with the conditions of fallen, downtrodden women in mid-nineteenth century England.

The novel opens with orphaned, impoverished, lonely Ruth employed as a seamstress in a sweatshop in an industrial town. The girls labor long hours for low pay, and the orphans among them lack any means of escape on idle Sundays. Happenstance brings Ruth to the attention of wealthy, bored, and indolent young Bellingham, who is infatuated with her beauty, of which she herself is aware but in innocence, without guile or vanity. He pursues her relentlessly, being careful not to alarm her, appearing, seemingly casually, on her free Sundays. In her solitude, she has no adviser or guidance, and she is ultimately easy prey. Her employer, Mrs. Mason, who might have offered protection or wisdom, discharges Ruth for fraternizing with him, rendering the girl homeless, resourceless, and completely at Bellingham's mercy.

The novel demurely resumes in Wales, where Bellingham has taken Ruth, who is enamored of him. She is much taken with the landscape, but, untaught and unsophisticated, she can do little to entertain him, and he grows bored and restless. Until a small child vociferously disdains her touch, she appears to be unaware of her compromised moral position. Then Bellingham falls ill and his mother arrives to transport him to London, casting Ruth off with a token pittance.

Broken, despondent, and suicidal, Ruth is rescued by crippled and compassionate Thurstan Benson, a Dissenting minister from the north of England who is on vacation. He is clearly a man of his faith—serious, godly, and meek. He summons his gruff, hearty, reliable, and aptly named sister Faith, and they, along with their devoted servant Sally, welcome Ruth into their humble home, where she gives birth to Leonard. Ruth is overcome with love for her child and has no thought of giving him up, so Faith concocts a story that Ruth is a recently widowed relative and persuades Thurstan to promulgate it in order to encourage public acceptance of Ruth and Leonard. Thurstan tutors the boy as he grows up, sheltered in a loving, trusting, godly environment.

Ruth's simplicity, goodness, and lack of affectation earn for her the affection and respect of the townspeople, including Thurstan's leading parishioner, the wealthy, powerful industrialist Bradshaw. Overcoming the private misgivings of the Bensons, he hires Ruth as a governess for his children; Ruth's pacific nature makes her an ideal friend and model for his rebellious elder daughter Jemima, who adores her.

Secure in his dominion, Bradshaw challenges the Tory hegemony in the town by fielding his own Liberal candidate for Parliament, wealthy Mr. Donne. Confronted with Donne, Ruth finds that he is actually Bellingham (he has changed his name to gain a legacy), and he eventually discovers who she is. Although Ruth knows that he is a scoundrel, she also recognizes that she will always love him. Again, he pursues her, even proposes to her, but she refuses him and forbids him access to their son. Her course is set; her life is dedicated to her son.

In the meantime, Bradshaw learns that nefarious means (voter fraud) have assured Donne's election, but he adjusts his principles and looks away. When he discerns that his son, apprenticed in the family business, has forged Benson's signature in order to embezzle, however, Bradshaw is stern and implacable, and he disinherits the youth.

Gossip from the past suddenly discloses Ruth Hilton behind the façade of Mrs. Denbigh, and the town renounces her and the Bensons, to a lesser degree, whose sin, which they acknowledge, is to have shielded her by perpetrating a falsehood. There is no appeal or clemency for any of them; Ruth's irreproachable life since her transgression amounts to naught. Once again, she is fired unfairly from her job, despite Jemima's protestations. Bradshaw's generous support of the Dissenting chapel is lost, thereby imperiling the Bensons' already precarious finances. Faithful Sally, however, produces for her employers a secret fund she has saved. Meanwhile, Ruth, who long ago tended Bellingham during his illness, rediscovers her calling as a nurse and ministers to the poor, the sick, the needy, and those whose contagion others fear. Even her paltry remuneration is of slight benefit to the Bensons, her steadfast benefactors.

Slowly, Ruth regains public confidence on the strength of her quiet mission, and amid a highly contagious typhus epidemic she willingly attends the otherwise abandoned dying Donne, who never consciously, though evidently unwittingly, recognizes her. Nevertheless, their contact again spells doom, for she is fatally infected. This time, however, not shame but virtual beatification results. Leonard is taken on to be trained by the physician in charge of the epidemic, and the novel closes with the penitent Bradshaw, mindful of all of his flaws, consoling Leonard.

Analysis

In aesthetic terms, *Ruth* succeeds or fails for readers on two broad planes. One falls along the realism/coincidence axis, and the other depends upon the plausibility and interest of the central character. Ruth is a dreamy, passive, though not lethargic girl and woman, eager to please and thoroughly self-effacing. Throughout the novel, she is frequently pictured, when indoors and pained or troubled, flinging open the windows, no matter what the weather—in fact, the worse the weather, the better for her—to lose herself, to mingle her spirit with the gusts, the downpours, the darkness, the energies of the out-of-doors. Many critics detect in the character of Ruth evidence of Gaskell's affinity with the Romantic poet Wordsworth, for whom communion with nature yields integrity, sanity, and solace. Yet Ruth is, for the most part, without the vocabulary to articulate either her pain or her satisfactions, and although she often has very revealing dreams that obviously indicate her obsessions and anxieties, she is otherwise mute and content to serve others and obliterate herself. What Ruth's character is can best be seen in her actions and interactions with others.

Although the novel is written in the third person, Gaskell keeps the focus for the most part on Ruth, so the crux of the novel hangs on whether such a selfless, self-denying soul, who is essentially morally good, is truly a sinner and fallen woman and whether she is entirely a victim in the grip of others' control. If she is a victim, the edifying import at the heart of Gaskell's novelistic project is sacrificed. The response to the heroine then would simply be pity. Yet Gaskell's purpose of swaying public opinion to acknowledge a double standard toward the sexes can only be accomplished if informed sympathy and absolution come to a Ruth who is recognized as sole engineer of her fate. She must have willingly fallen in order to be raised up and cherished by a society that was previously swift to condemn her. Otherwise, there is no moral issue.

Whether that determination of Ruth as an independent agent can occur depends largely on how each reader interprets the degree of manipulation or authenticity of various plot devices, on which hang crucial points of the narrative. There are three of these: first, that at the worst point of her despair, along comes apparently serendipitous physical salvation via Thurstan Benson; second, just when her life appears to be in order and she is on her feet, although under an assumed identity, comes Bellingham/Donne and then public scandal. Finally, at the end, when she has surpassed public ignominy and has redeemed herself for the last time as an angel of mercy, her seducer shows up yet again to torment and finally destroy her. That these occurrences are highly coincidental cannot be denied; however, Gaskell does attempt to set them up fairly, instead of leaving them to creaky orchestration, and to account for them within the bounds of credibility.

First, Benson and Ruth have already become acquainted by the time he is needed to step in to save her, so his appearance is not really extraordinary. Second, Bellingham's first reappearance in the story comes to nothing because Ruth refuses his initiatives and her life is thus unchanged. In fact, his sudden manifestation serves to exhibit her power over him now, at least to the extent that she refuses him any further effect over her. Furthermore, given the small towns in which she has lived, it is perhaps not all that surprising that disclosure might be inevitable. Moreover, she can never be fully restored to society from her public disgrace if her hidden identity conceals the expiation for her sin. Therefore, for better or worse, her mask must be torn away.

Last and most important, it is Ruth's free choice to nurse Donne in his final illness; there is no particular moral reason to do this, since she has already become sainted in her community for her good works with the sick and the destitute. Thus, her good name is finally secure. She undertakes this task at great personal risk because she is ever faithful to her love, showing her absolute goodness by reaching out to one whose role in her life has previously brought only sorrow. Nevertheless, although readers such as Charlotte Brontë protested Ruth's dying, there is a certain necessity about it. Ruth has been redeemed; her son will be provided for; and, of paramount concern, this most acquiescent and reactive of women proves that she is her own person and has been so throughout her life. Just as she chooses her death, in effect, so did she willingly and knowingly transgress with Bellingham. Her example demonstrates Gaskell's point: Women deserve fair and equal treatment because they are just and comparable people—no more and no less.

Context

The reaction to unwed motherhood in *Ruth* may make the novel seem dated to later readers. Upon its initial publication, however, the novel, though it garnered many thoughtful and positive reviews, was greeted with widespread horror, censure, and private censorship. Although unmarried mothers and illegitimate children were familiar characters in English literature by the middle of the nineteenth century—for example, men had spun tales around them in *Tom Jones*, *The Heart of Midlothian*, and *Oliver Twist*—Gaskell's *Ruth* is the first English novel to install the woman at the center of the narrative. Moreover, Gaskell uniquely, with sympathy and with an opportunity at reformation, focuses on the woman's entire life following her seduction. In fact, although *Ruth* is often compared with its nearly exact contemporary *The Scarlet Letter*, Gaskell is even more daring than Nathaniel Hawthorne in that she begins her novel before the fall—that is, before her heroine's sexuality has been awakened.

Gaskell acknowledged that she expressly chose to write about a subject that people were unwilling to discuss. She knew women who were suffering under the double standard of the day, and she set out to write a provocative, didactic novel to open the issue up, to launch awareness, colloquy, and action. Indeed, notwithstanding those who heaped calumny on the novel, there were many readers and critics who defended *Ruth* and who declared that it opened their eyes to an unfair public morality. Nevertheless, Gaskell's later fiction turned from the moralizing toward the more aesthetic, indicating, as was the case, that she had fought enough public battles. Although for many years Gaskell's audiences celebrated her quiet, provincial, episodic *Cranford* as her masterpiece, now scholars and readers are discovering the value of Gaskell's more serious-minded fiction, and *Ruth* is acquiring a respectable reputation as a realistic depiction of an unmarried woman's tragedy and triumph, and as a representative woman's appeal for equality on behalf of all of her sisters.

Sources for Further Study

Craik, W. A. *Elizabeth Gaskell and the English Provincial Novel*. London: Methuen, 1975. A sensitive, thoughtful study that sets *Ruth* within the context of nineteenth century English novels.

Easson, Angus. *Elizabeth Gaskell*. London: Routledge & Kegan Paul, 1979. Solid, comprehensive, and astute scholarship unifying Gaskell's life and times with her works. Extensive bibliography.

Lansbury, Coral. *Elizabeth Gaskell*. Boston: Twayne, 1984. A good though somewhat sketchy overview of the novels and the author.

_____. *Elizabeth Gaskell: The Novel of Social Crisis*. New York: Barnes & Noble Books, 1975. The first study to show that Gaskell's Unitarianism was crucial to her writing. Regarding *Ruth*, however, Lansbury primarily summarizes the plot.

Pollard, Arthur. *Mrs. Gaskell: Novelist and Biographer*. Cambridge, Mass.: Harvard University Press, 1965. A major Gaskell scholar views Ruth as dull and the novel as contrived and manipulative.

Rubenius, Anna. *The Woman Question in Mrs. Gaskell's Life and Works*. 1950. Reprint. New York: Russell & Russell, 1973. An early feminist interpretation of the social, political, and economic critiques in Gaskell. Sees *Ruth* as reformist concerning patriarchal sexuality, marriage, family life, and conditions of women's work for hire.

Uglow, Jennifer S. *Elizabeth Gaskell: A Habit of Stories*. New York: Farrar, Straus & Giroux, 1993. A thorough, graceful, informative work that is likely to become the definitive biography. The work contains rewarding, informed, and perceptive literary criticism.

Wright, Edgar. *Mrs. Gaskell: The Basis for Reassessment*. London: Oxford University Press, 1965. Sees *Ruth* as an argument that environment and upbringing dictate character.

Laura Dabundo

1990

SAINT MAYBE

Author: Anne Tyler (1941-   )
Type of work: Novel
Type of plot: Domestic realism
Time of plot: The 1960's to the 1980's
Locale: Baltimore, Maryland
First published: 1991

> *Principal characters:*
> IAN BEDLOE, the "Saint Maybe" of the novel's title, who rears his
>   dead brother Danny's three children
> LUCY DEAN BEDLOE, Danny's wife and Ian's sister-in-law
> AGATHA, THOMAS, and DAPHNE BEDLOE, Lucy's children and
>   Ian's wards
> THE REVEREND EMMETT, the pastor of the Church of the Second
>   Chance
> RITA DI CARLO, Ian's wife

Form and Content

Saint Maybe, through its male protagonist, Ian Bedloe, focuses on the difficulties and responsibilities of single parenting. Doug Bedloe, Ian's father, has only once in his life changed a diaper. His son Ian's life will be more complicated—a mixture of the traditional male role of breadwinner and the traditional female role of nurturer for his dead brother's three children. At the age of nineteen, Ian quits college and becomes father and mother to Agatha, Tom, and Daphne. For the next twenty years, until 1988, when he is forty-one, he finds himself locked into responsibilities that seem both of his own choosing and, at the same time, unfairly thrust upon him.

Ironically, at the outset of the novel, Ian has been unsympathetic to Lucy Dean Bedloe for not fulfilling the ideals of her roles as wife to his brother Danny and as mother of her three children. For one thing, Ian finds Lucy too attractive to be completely trustworthy. For another, she is divorced, bringing two small children into her marriage with Danny. Furthermore, after the birth of a third child only seven months into the marriage (when she has known Danny for only a few weeks), she burdens Ian with babysitting chores after school to escape from the baby and her other two children. Once, when she returns wearing a new dress, Ian concludes that the dress is a gift from a lover. When Ian tells Danny that Lucy has been unfaithful, Danny has a car accident and dies. Lucy succumbs soon afterward, the victim of an overdose of sleeping pills.

Now it is Ian, not Lucy, who will be held accountable for his actions and made to take on adult responsibilities. Overcome by guilt, Ian visits the Church of the Second Chance. The Reverend Emmett tells him to atone for his wrongdoing, face his obligations, and become responsible for his brother's children. Ian complies, drops out of college, becomes a carpenter, and parents Agatha, Tom, and Daphne. Ian's own parents are too tired, ill, and out-of-touch to take upon themselves full parental responsibility for their grandchildren.

From 1968 to 1988, Ian sacrifices his own life for the sake of his brother's children. In six of the novel's ten chapters, the third person narrative focuses on Ian's conflicts in carrying out his role. He remains deeply religious, isolates himself from others in his work, and pushes away interested women in order to dedicate his life to the children's well-being. At the same time, he dreams of release, even hiring a private detective to look for Agatha and Tom's real father (only to learn he is deceased), lying to himself about his reasons for doing so. Four other chapters (also in the third person but told from the narrative perspectives of Agatha, Thomas, Doug, and Daphne) reveal family concern for the abnormal narrowness of Ian's life. Doug wishes his son would leave the Church of the Second Chance; the children want Ian to marry. Daphne labels Ian "Saint Maybe" for the way his virtue and cowardice intertwine. At the novel's end, Ian breaks out of his self-sacrificial pattern to marry risk-taking, sensual Rita di Carlo, only to find himself caught again in the familiar pattern of family responsibility as the father of a newborn son.

Analysis

In *Saint Maybe*, Anne Tyler is concerned with the shifting roles of changing society in the twentieth century United States. Ian Bedloe finds that he must become an androgynous figure, drawing on both his male and female characteristics in order to fulfill all the demands his family and society make upon him. Far from being liberated from responsibility and obligation, Ian finds that he must do even more than his father and forefathers before him. He must learn to be mother and father, breadwinner and nurturer, anchor and sail, for Danny and Lucy's orphaned children.

His sister-in-law Lucy, however, fails to transcend her traditional, dependent female role and survive. Poverty, lack of education, and responsibility for three small children pull her down and finally defeat her (a situation Ian comes to identify with more and more as he himself struggles to fulfill the role of single parent).

Ian's parents' (Doug and Bee Bedloe's) post-World War II optimism proves to be simplistic and outmoded (as are the separate spheres of their traditional marriage). More and more, they feel forced to retreat from present realities that do not fit their upbeat, worn-out philosophy. The foreigners down the street allow Doug to escape into their happy-go-lucky student world, playing with new American technology and complex American life. With them, Doug enjoys the luxury of suspending serious concern and everyday reality—which all must face when they return home.

In Tyler's *Saint Maybe*, characters must learn to survive, cope, and face life head-on in late-twentieth century American society. Those who succeed are most often androgynous figures such as the tall, bold, resourceful Rita di Carlo, Baltimore's resident Clutter Counselor; Ian's wards, Agatha and Daphne, who are independent women who take on new roles without losing their care for others; and Ian himself, the solitary yet nurturing protagonist of the novel. They stand in contrast to other characters who retreat from life (such as Lucy, Bee, and Doug Bedloe), characters who are demoralized by not knowing all the answers, defeated by not being able to fly, and overwhelmed by having to face daily reality (as suggested by three of the novel's chapter titles).

The Baltimore of *Saint Maybe* (as in other Tyler novels) is a city in transition, part of a larger American world of constant flux and change, yet an all-too-familiar human world of disease, difficulty, and death where people such as Danny, Lucy, and Bee Bedloe (even Beastie, their dog) seem to depart willy-nilly, leaving behind orphaned children, cluttered houses, and complex messes for others to clean. Yet, for all its seriousness, Tyler's fictional world remains a comic one in which new babies are born and loved, ordinary people learn to make sacrifices and take risks, and families and communities manage to nurture (in new and strange ways). Ian finds solace in the tiny, eccentric congregation of the Church of the Second Chance; Daphne stops accompanying Ian to church but continues to help others through Saturday "Good Work" sessions; Doug proves to be ineffectual at home but shares a beer with the foreigners down the street, helping them through hair-raising yet solvable predicaments; and Agatha, Tom, and Daphne scheme to find Ian a loving companion in tribute to his sacrifices on their behalf and forgiveness for his strange religion and embarrassing ways. If Tyler's communities and families seem somewhat loose and haphazard, the force of love still remains alive in their midst (symbolized by Ezra Tull, the restaurant owner of Tyler's 1982 *Dinner at the Homesick Restaurant*, who makes a guest appearance near the end of chapter 9, serving holiday meals to the Bedloes and other lonely, distraught people).

Anne Tyler sympathizes with each of her characters, those who fail and those who survive. Through her third-person narrative perspective, she focuses closely on five different characters (Ian is given six chapters; Agatha, Tom, Daphne, and Doug, one apiece) to convey her characters' individual lives and concerns. As her readers learn to identify with her diverse characters, those same characters learn tolerance for one another. Her protagonist Ian, especially, comes to understand his dead sister-in-law Lucy and empathize with the difficulties of her mothering role. Tyler emphasizes, however, that Ian's tolerance is hardwon—the result of constant struggle with his own guilt and his determination to make reparation for his past wrongdoings. An ordinary man, he is torn between his desire to escape his responsibilities and his determination to fulfill them, his fear of making more mistakes and his need to lead a full life. *Saint Maybe* insists on the everyday sainthood of ordinary, imperfect, struggling humanity.

Context

Throughout her novels, Anne Tyler concerns herself with family—as have a majority of American women writers from Harriet Beecher Stowe to Louisa May Alcott, Kate Chopin to Alice Walker. Tyler asks a central question in *Saint Maybe*, one that she voices again and again in her novels: What is one's obligation to one's family and what is one's obligation to oneself? While women throughout history have borne primary responsibility for the nurturance and well-being of family members, Tyler's protagonists, female as well as male, come to feel that they must make choices between their desire for domesticity, on the one hand, and their need for independence, on the other.

Sometimes Tyler's characters break from their families only to adopt new ones of their own choosing, as does Elizabeth Abbott in *The Clock Winder* (1972). At other times, they break free only to return home again, as do Sarah Leary in *The Accidental Tourist* (1985) and Charlotte Emory in *Earthly Possessions* (1977). Other protagonists must learn to bestow freedom on those within their families: Pearl Tull in *Dinner at the Homesick Restaurant* (1982), Maggie Moran in the Pulitzer Prize-winning *Breathing Lessons* (1988), and Macon Leary in *The Accidental Tourist* (1985). Some begin the journey toward freedom when they no longer believe they are needed at home: Morgan in *Morgan's Passing* (1980) and Mary Tell in *Celestial Navigation* (1974).

Ian Bedloe in *Saint Maybe* chooses domesticity to provide security for the orphaned Agatha, Tom, and Daphne, yet he desires freedom as well. When Ian breaks loose at forty-one to marry the youthful, bold Rita, he finds himself paradoxically tied once more to fatherhood and family responsibilities. Through Ian Bedloe, Tyler also focuses on her other central themes: the hardships posed by family life, the need for androgyny on the part of her fictional survivors, the influence of accident on their lives, and the artist's need for isolation versus the need for society. Drawing her characters vividly, their predicaments unflinchingly, Tyler embraces her most troubled figures with gentle affection. Her realism and compassion place her firmly within the female literary tradition.

Sources for Further Study

Carson, Barbara Harrell. "Complicate, Complicate: *Anne Tyler's Moral Imperative*," *Southern Quarterly* 31, no. 1 (Fall, 1992): 24-35. This essay argues that Tyler's novels affirm individuality while asserting life's complexity and the need for human interconnectedness. Tyler offers a female value system contradicting traditional literary equations between heroic selfhood and the simplified, isolated life.

Gullette, Margaret M. *Safe at Last in the Middle Years: The Invention of the Midlife Progress Novel.* Berkeley: University of California Press, 1988. The chapter on Tyler considers the adult dilemmas of her novels and places her fiction within a context of other late-twentieth century authors focusing on midlife problems.

Petry, Alice Hall, ed. *Critical Essays on Anne Tyler.* New York: G. K. Hall, 1992. Contains sample reviews of each of Tyler's novels through *Breathing Lessons* (1988); interviews with Tyler from 1965-1981; and critical essays on literary parallels to, and familial relationships within, her works.

Stephens, C. Ralph, ed. *The Fiction of Anne Tyler.* Jackson: University Press of Mississippi, 1990. A collection of essays from the 1989 Anne Tyler Symposium in Baltimore providing varied critical interpretations of Tyler's novels. Critics explore her recurring themes and structures; her relationship to Southern and other twentieth century authors, and her sociological, psychological, and political themes.

Voelker, Joseph C. *Art and the Accidental in Anne Tyler.* Columbia: University of

Missouri Press, 1989. This first book on Tyler considers how her Southern and Quaker past affected her vision of the world, its horrors and possibilities for grace. It argues that her characters come to view the chaos of life with greater acceptance as her novels progress.

                                                                                                              Susan S. Kissel

THE SALT EATERS

Author: Toni Cade Bambara (1931-   )
Type of work: Novel
Type of plot: Fable
Time of plot: The 1970's
Locale: Claybourne, Georgia
First published: 1980

Principal characters:
VELMA HENRY, a hardworking woman who tries to commit
    suicide
MINNIE RANSOM, the local healer, who helps Velma
SOPHIE HEYWOOD, or M'Dear, Velma's godmother
NADEEN and BUSTER, a couple who observe the healing of Velma
DR. MEADOWS, one of the visiting physicians
AHIRO, a Korean masseuse from Arkansas
OBIE, Velma's husband
PALMA, Velma's sister
CAMPBELL, a journalist
TINA/KHUFU, or ancient mother, who reminds the community of
    older values
FRED, a bus driver who comes to Claybourne

Form and Content

Claybourne, Georgia, is located between the healing salt marshes and a threatening nuclear power plant. Balancing these two extremes is the healing of Velma Henry, a worker in the plant and a central figure in the community. After trying too hard to balance the world on her own shoulders, Velma attempted suicide.

The plot and present of the novel lasts only the time it takes for Minnie Ransom to initiate Velma's self-healing, but time and space expand concentrically as the fable of Claybourne revises and updates that of the Garden of Eden. This fable reminds the reader that Adam's name means "clay" and that clay is a marriage of earth and water. Even the salt water of tears can hold human "dust" together to provide clay for the "Potter's wheel," the unifying symbol of the novel.

Claybourne itself is the potter's wheel that remolds and recenters individual lives, a united African American community dissolving differences in the shared grief and hopes of its "salt of the earth" members. Community centers unite the otherwise divided efforts of its citizens in healing confrontations that reveal their essential fellowship. The Infirmary offers both modern medicine and spiritual healing. While the larger society favors practical sciences, The Academy of the Seven Arts teaches only arts—performance, martial, medical, scientific, spiritual, fine, and human— reminding people that learning is the art of living. It is attended by ordinary people who earn no credit but become "change agents" who can transform the world.

Balance is the key connecting the opposing viewpoints within and among the centers. The masseuse Ahiro balances the education of the mind with that of the body. The Academy's political Brotherhood is balanced by The Seven Sisters, who represent the nurturing gifts of nature. In the Avocado Pit Cafe, the Sisters balance the table of six nuclear plant engineers, while the communal activists Jan and Ruby are balanced by the outside observers Donaldson and Campbell.

Outsiders who need balancing benefit when they wander through Claybourne. Fred, the overburdened bus driver, finds his own way to the Infirmary, while Dr. Meadows must leave there to wander the streets and rediscover his "country" self. This seemingly chaotic journey through time and space is centered by Velma's healing and Claybourne's spring festival, a communal healing that draws on African and Christian tradition and reminds people of rebirth and resurrection.

Velma's "eccentric" circle elongates as it is expressed in her others—in family, community, and, by extension, the larger "off-centered" families of modern society. Historically, she relives the civil protests of the 1960's noting gender inequalities and betrayals within and of the black community. Her personal past is recalled in all of its violence and pain by the wise Sophie, whose dead son Smitty was Velma's first love, in order to place the past in the larger contexts that give it meaning and make the pain bearable. Because her personal present of accumulating job and family responsibilities and disappointments has become too much to bear, Velma must be healed by communal support and put back in touch with her own spiritual strengths, as symbolized by the African Mud Mothers. The conflicts of yesterday are resolved in the necessities of today so that healthy choices can be made for possible futures, which are also explored.

Analysis

Thrust out of their own Garden of Eden in Africa, African Americans yet constitute a definable community planted in contemporary America. Here the spirit is accessible and suffering can be balanced with communal love. If people are in danger of turning into pillars of salt from too much looking backward, they are also the salt of the earth and have already survived and transformed that past.

When the rains come to Claybourne, one cannot be sure it is not acid rain or nuclear fallout. Clouds are gray tricksters, and the world outside has been dumping its garbage on its devalued members for centuries. Water brings life, however, and Claybourne's artists will take the wet mud after the storm and its healers will draw on whatever powers make themselves available, because its people still want to live. This balance of hope over fear is essential for human survival.

As she circles back through time and space, as she teaches one to sit still and be centered in one's own traditions, Toni Cade Bambara reveals the pattern of the circles, the common center/garden from which all people originated. If on the surface the circles conflict and shatter, a wider perspective promises the turning of the wheel, which reestablishes balance. A community centered in its own traditions and balancing the diversity of its members can provide healing for those members who are suffering from the violence of the moment, from the unbalancing influence of fragmented values and traditions.

Bambara's language empowers the reader by giving equal weight to spiritual and visible realities and allows him or her to wander freely through time and space, because the human mind is not buried in the present moment. Her linguistic humor includes multilevel puns that reveal the incongruity of appearances. The reader is always conscious, for example, of the immodesty of Velma's hospital gown and the unprofessional attire of Minnie Ransom. The name of the café reminds one of nature's own incongruities: The avocado pit is simply too big. Sometimes the story itself seems too big. Can one's mind stretch as far as necessity demands without breaking? Another pun on this alphabet soup in which people find themselves may be meant by Campbell's name, because he explains the encompassing unity of apparently contradictory realities.

Bambara's humor and her jazz and colloquial rhythms unite the African American community, while symbolism centers the individual on the potter's wheel to be transformed as necessary. Claybourne is there to rework the clay, to recenter readers in their traditions, to heal them when they become too eccentric to survive. When one is threatened by necessity or devalued by the apparent other, one shrinks from fear into an ever-diminishing protective circle. If one is discovered in time, before one no longer exists, then a healing community can soften and stretch that ball of clay again, recenter and remold it.

Bambara stretches and shapes her story with the same skill, finding the fragment of "white plaster"—the inflexible piece of white ideology in the rich terra-cotta of her people's clay—which has thrown them off center. Undetected these fragments defeat the potter's art, and the result may very well be a "crackpot." She also takes the reader back to the Mud Mothers, because there the clay is still enriched with the water of life.

Bambara shares her African perspective with Chinua Achebe. In *Things Fall Apart*, distraught by Western influences on his Ibo culture, Achebe's protagonist knows that when in need he must return to his mother's tribe to find balance. There he will be taught what he needs to keep "things" together, including himself. All people must be artists, reshaping their lives as needed. No face a brother or sister wears, no ritual or ceremony that seems strange, is excluded from the whole story. When one must live in the same place with people who practice "abominations," one must look through the appearance to understand, to accept their apparent differences while rejecting the ideological fragment of plaster that would throw one off balance.

Context

Bambara's own history as an activist is reflected in the gender inequalities and political activism shown in Claybourne's citizens. Her "ecofeminist" consciousness is equally apparent in the juxtaposition of the nuclear power plant and a projected dystopian future of radioactive mutants. Yet she has chosen to write a fable of hope rather than one of fear.

In order to accomplish this, Bambara writes from the perspective of the Mothers, from the African Mud Mothers to the Mother Earth ceremony celebrated in Claybourne's Spring Festival. Introducing ancient goddess values into a contemporary setting is part of the feminist revisionist tradition, which challenges Western patriarchal and rational definitions of reality. Goddess definitions return people to nature and the human comedy of rebirth and resurrection rather than the human tragedy of individual responsibility and death. The comic mode is communal; everyone is part of a community that is responsible for its members. People survive by healing one another and by tending the garden given them by nature.

People perform tasks by using their minds, but associative thinking proves to be more useful than rational counting of things. While people may recount their trials, this telling is only part of the tale. When people make connections, they better understand the past and the present; they can draw on one another and the world around them for the energy and knowledge they need.

The whole story is simple; it is also true and beautiful and maybe even humorous. One can recognize its different faces if it has managed to survive "detractors and perverters"; if it has been buried among the "ancients," then one may have to dig it out. One cannot go home to one's mother's village, as still can happen in Africa, but one can go home to one's mother's stories. Because they know their children need them, mothers are telling those stories, hoping to bring their children back to the safe circles before they spin out of control, reminding them that the road can curve back to the supporting community. Bambara is such a talespinner, and the spiraling circles of this novel carry her readers far enough back to recapture the hope of beginnings that promise to carry them forward from this, the "Last Quarter," into a future that is simultaneously diverse and unified because it is centered and yet open to change.

Sources for Further Study

Bambara, Toni Cade. "Searching for the Mother Tongue." Interview by Kalamu ya Salaam. *First World* 2, no. 4 (1980): 48-53. Bambara discusses her linguistic techniques, which explore how words gain meaning and power and replace linear structure with jazz and cyclical patterns.

DeWeaver, Jacqueline. *Mythmaking and Metaphor in Black Women's Fiction*. New York: St. Martin's Press, 1991. Provides a contemporary context for the dependence on African myth which permeates and enriches this novel.

Holloway, Karla F. C. "Revision and (Re)membrance: A Theory of Literary Structures in Literature by African American Women Writers." *Black American Literature Forum* 24, no. 4 (Winter, 1990): 617-631. Although Bambara is not mentioned in this article, the theory applies to *The Salt Eaters* in its attention to the multiple and oral voices of the "other," which inform the layers of meaning among these women writers.

Hull, Gloria T. "What It Is I Think She's Doing Anyhow." In *Conjuring*, edited by Marjorie Pryse and Hortense Spillers. Bloomington: Indiana University Press, 1985. Offers a key to the intersecting circles of Claybourne as microcosms of the necessary centering in tradition which makes possible the larger unifying circle of the human community. Discusses Bambara's symbol of the potter's wheel, which structurally unifies the novel.

Johnson, Charles. *Being and Race: Black Writing Since 1970.* Bloomington: Indiana University Press, 1988. In his discussion "The Women," Johnson briefly acknowledges the comic tone and colloquial diction of *The Salt Eaters.*

Jones, Gayl. *Liberating Voices: Oral Tradition in African American Literature.* Cambridge, Mass.: Harvard University Press, 1991. Explores in the works of Bambara and others uses of oral tradition such as the spiritual and folk language, as well as a shared female interest in health and wholeness.

Reckley, Ralph, Sr. *Twentieth Century Black American Women in Print.* Edited by Lola E. Jones. Acton, Mass.: Copley, 1991. Discusses Bambara's use of dislocation from time and space, enabling characters to operate in more than three dimensions, and her thematic concern for the displaced black woman and divided community.

Russell, Sandi. *Render Me My Story: African American Women Writers from Slavery to the Present.* New York: St. Martin's Press, 1990. Discusses Bambara's use of musical rhythms in her writing and the many voices in *The Salt Eaters* through which she seeks to unite a fragmented community.

Sternburg, Janet, ed. *The Writer on Her Work.* New York: W. W. Norton, 1980. Bambara discusses the genesis of *The Salt Eaters* from an earlier short story, its unifying themes, and the significance of the title.

Tate, Claudia, ed. *Black Women Writers at Work.* New York: Continuum, 1983. Bambara discusses her goal of telling the truth of ordinary people and her exploration of patterns for survival in *The Salt Eaters.*

Thelma J. Shinn

THE SECOND SEX

Author: Simone de Beauvoir (1908-1986)
Type of work: Social criticism
First published: Le Deuxième sexe, 1949 (English translation, 1953)

Form and Content

The "serious, all-inclusive, and uninhibited work on woman," as its translator, Howard M. Parshley, calls *The Second Sex*, consists of 1,071 pages in the Gallimard/Folio edition of the original and comprises two separate volumes.

The first volume, *Facts and Myths*, comprises three parts. The first part, "Destiny," is given over to biological data, psychoanalytic perspective, and the perspective of historical materialism (Marxist socialism): Biology does not answer the question "Why is woman the Other, the second?"; psychoanalytic research also does not, but defines woman in the context of sexuality instead of that of existential consciousness; Marxism properly stresses woman's economic instead of her physiological situation but does not provide the existentialist infrastructure that discloses the unity of *human life* (*une vie*, a life, male or female). Part 2 traces woman's situation in "History" from primitive to modern society, from nomadic existence to the women's suffrage movement. Part 3, "Myths," establishes the unilaterally male primacy of sexual myths and the manifestation of myths that develop male fears and ideals relative to woman, as exemplified in the writings of Henri de Montherlant, for whom woman is "the bread of disgust"; D. H. Lawrence, who asserts "phallic pride"; Paul Claudel, whose Catholicism views woman as fulfilling herself through subservience, ultimately as the "servant of the Lord"; and André Breton, who idealizes woman, as Dante idealized Beatrice and as Petrarch idealized Laura, and identifies woman abstractly as "Poetry." Stendhal is appended as an exemplar of one for whom woman is human; he is a "Romanticist of reality" whose sensual love of women is always informed by his experience of women as subjects, not objects, and who berated those women who looked upon themselves as objects.

The second volume, *Woman's Life Today*, consists of four parts dealing, respectively, with "The Formative Years," "Situation," "Justifications," and, under the heading "Toward Liberation," the independent woman.

"The Formative Years" traces the restraints and demands that are imposed upon woman in childhood and girlhood, the "anatomic destiny" of woman after sexual initiation, and, along with the misunderstanding that lesbianism is an inauthentic attitude, the traditional misinformation that sets it apart as unnatural.

"Situation" investigates the placement of woman as wife, as mother, in family and social life, as prostitute and hetaira, and in maturity and old age. At every turn woman, according to Beauvoir, is enlaced in repetition that results in her clinging to routine and is disempowered by male authority to the end that she herself participates in her alienation from lucidity and develops her unfamiliarity with plausibility.

"Justifications" recounts the ways in which woman compensates for her Otherness, for her being relegated to inferiority in a world of male primacy or male orientation. The categories of compensation are narcissism; self-surrender in love, which amounts to accepting her enslavement to a man as an expression of freedom to do so and to attempting transcendence of her situation as "inessential object" by total acceptance of it; and mysticism, a turning toward God.

"Toward Liberation" summarizes in graphic detail the modes of independence open to woman—abjuration of femininity through chastity, homosexuality, or viragoism, in opposition to the emphasis of femininity in coquetry, flirtation, and masochistic or aggressive love. Beauvoir insists that man is a sexual human being and that woman, as a total individual, can be equal to the male only if she too is a sexual human being, retaining her femaleness and having the same access as the male to personal satisfaction. If woman is to know the same freedom as man, her economic independence must be achieved through Marxist socialism and her sexual independence must be provided by man's willingness to yield his traditional primacy and its concomitant control of the situation of woman.

Analysis

The French Revolution's ideal of "Liberty, Equality, and Fraternity" is the standard against which Beauvoir measures the status, or situation, of woman both during and before the twentieth century. At almost every juncture, she finds that the revolutionary ideal refers to men, not to women. She concludes that the reference can best be extended to women in a world that adheres to the principles of Marxist socialism and to the tenets of existentialist freedom. It is in the context of existentialism that she analyzes the Otherness, the secondness, of woman. To her concept of woman as the Other she gives the name "alterity" (*alterité*), derived from the Latin word *alter*, which means both "other" and "second."

In the existentialism propounded by Beauvoir and Jean-Paul Sartre, the self is subject (I exist, I feel) and anyone or anything exterior to the self is object (someone or something that I may use or that I find to stand in my way). All objects constitute the Other. Beauvoir's thesis is that man sees himself collectively as subject and that woman, historically seen by man as object, must first recognize that she has been conditioned to see herself as the Other and then strive, as a free individual, both to assert herself as subject and to win recognition as subject from man. Those subjects existing in freedom (*liberté*) who see each other as subjects (as equals) live in confraternity. The very last statement of *The Second Sex* is this: ". . . it is necessary . . . that, beyond their natural differentiations, men and women affirm their brotherhood (*fraternité*) unequivocally."

The obstacle to fraternal affirmation is alterity, a persistent form of prejudicial objectification. The concept is explained in chapter 9, "Dreams, Fears, Idols," which is the last chapter of part 3, "Myths." Beauvoir claims that men see themselves as subject-heroes and define woman only in her relation to man. This renders the categories of male and female asymmetrical, as the unilateralism of sexual myths makes clear. Woman is elevated as a divine presence (Athena, the Virgin Mary, and so forth) and yet degraded as a power of evil (Eve, Pandora, Delilah). In neither case is she seen for what, in fact, she is—a free individual on an existential par with man. It is as though men justify their contempt for women by simultaneously idealizing them. Man thereby sustains his need of woman as servant and scapegoat by projecting his self-idealization onto woman as ideal being, the source of life, the healing presence, mother.

The applicability of this concept to other forms of prejudice can be readily inferred. Ethnic prejudice, for example, will justify scornful objectification of a race by conceding a very positive trait as characteristic of that race. Whites, for example, would insist that, while blacks were inferior in intelligence, they were superior in athletics; anti-Semites would, like Adolf Hitler, concede the superior intelligence of Jews as long as the Jews' alleged pecuniary bent were acknowledged. Woman, accordingly, is alternately placed upon a pedestal and consigned to a pit, but is never accorded the same level of human activity as man.

Man is not painted in *The Second Sex* as a tyrannic villain, and woman is not depicted as an inherently helpless victim. The cogency of the essay comes from its fairness and its even-tempered observations. Woman is shown as being a participant in her own subordination by reason of her acquiescence and her inauthentic acceptance of secondary status. Authenticity, the quality that Beauvoir finds Stendhal to have admired in women and reflected in his female characters, is responsible freedom. It is the awareness that, as an existent, one is free to choose and determine the course of one's existence, and it entails one's acceptance of full responsibility for one's choice. Beauvoir says matter-of-factly that women have not been in the habit of cultivating existential awareness and are consequently frustrated by discontents that they cannot fathom but from which they seek indirect and inconclusive escape. In effect, Beauvoir discloses to women their situation as secondary human beings and urges upon them, as prerequisite to authentic choice, an honest awareness of their alterity. Even if a woman chooses to remain the passive Other in relation to men, her choice, made in awareness, is an authentic action for which she accepts active responsibility. A commitment to oppose alterity is not more authentic, since any choice made in awareness is authentic, but it is the better part of action and more in keeping with Beauvoir's existentialist notions about the nature of human life.

Context

The Second Sex was received with shock in Catholic France but had no lack of buyers. Margaret Crosland notes in her biography of Simone de Beauvoir that twenty thousand copies of the first volume were sold within a week of its publication. She adds that the Catholic church banned the book and that writers such as Albert Camus and François Mauriac belittled it. The English-speaking world received it more approvingly in the Parshley translation. Beauvoir was likened in England to Mary Wollstonecraft; still, she received harsh criticism from women who were unwilling to participate in the feminist movement. Beauvoir was surprised at the shock her book had generated and bemused at being identified as a feminist. Her aim in using the abstraction "woman" was not universal feminist protest or demand but each woman's relation of "her self" to the abstraction as a point of departure toward individual self-determination.

Julia Kristeva, in "Le Temps des femmes" (1979; "Women's Time," 1981), identifies the first phase of the twentieth century women's movement as "the struggle of suffragists and of existential feminists." Beauvoir would belong to this phase, not as a suffragist but as an existentialist. According to Kristeva, two post-1968 phases reject and supersede the directions of the early movement. Jane Heath, in her essay on Beauvoir, suggests that "Simone de Beauvoir spoke predominantly the discourse of repression" and "allowed the man in her to speak." Toril Moi takes the measure of later twentieth century rejections and disfavorings of Beauvoir's writings by the feminist whose essays appear in Elaine Marks's collection *Critical Essays on Simone de Beauvoir* (1987); Moi believes that the hostility toward Beauvoir is the outgrowth of a sense of critical superiority to a predecessor whose sense of equality with the male should have developed into militant opposition to the male and whose writing is insufficiently complex.

In the history of the twentieth century feminist movement, Beauvoir's place in the vanguard is assured, even by hostile latter-day critics: The sheer quantity of books and articles about her since the 1970's ensures that attention will be paid to this important pioneer, whose conclusions relative to the "second sex" are given substance in her fiction, definition in other of her existentialist essays, and self-examination in her volumes of autobiography.

Sources for Further Study

Appignanesi, Lisa. *Simone de Beauvoir*. New York: Penguin Books, 1988. Chapter 4, "The Ethics of Existentialism," and chapter 5, "Being a Woman," constitute an essay that is pertinently ancillary to a reading of *The Second Sex*. The emphasis is on Beauvoir's "portrayal of the independent woman."

Bair, Deirdre. *Simone de Beauvoir: A Biography*. New York: Summit Books, 1990. The most informative of the biographies of Beauvoir. Chapters 26 and 28, "The High Priestess of Existentialism" and "A Book About Women," respectively, are essential to a study of *The Second Sex*.

Bieber, Konrad. *Simone de Beauvoir*. Boston: Twayne, 1979. Scorned by feminists of the 1980's and 1990's for its male obtuseness, this introductory study nevertheless contains much valuable information and includes a nineteen-page outline of *The Second Sex*. Bieber's attention to Beauvoir's slips and errors is undercut by his presenting the time setting of her short story "Monologue" as "Christmas night" when it is actually New Year's Eve.

Crosland, Margaret. *Simone de Beauvoir: The Woman and Her Work*. London: Heinemann, 1992. A searching retrospective of Beauvoir's life and career. Crosland shows how Beauvoir's commitment to feminism in the late 1960's and early 1970's had developed in coincidence with feminism's catching up to *The Second Sex*.

Evans, Mary. *Simone de Beauvoir: A Feminist Mandarin*. New York: Tavistock, 1985.

Places Beauvoir securely within the context of feminism and appraises *The Second Sex* as an exceptionally influential feminist text.

Heath, Jane. *Simone de Beauvoir*. New York: Harvester Wheatsheaf, 1989. Focuses "not on 'Simone de Beauvoir—Feminist', but on the feminine in her texts." Heath uses *The Second Sex* as a point of departure for studying Beauvoir's fictional and autobiographical works.

Moi, Toril. *Feminist Theory and Simone de Beauvoir*. Oxford, England: Basil Blackwell, 1990. A concise investigation into the critical reception and critical implications of Beauvoir's work.

Winegarten, Renée. *Simone de Beauvoir: A Critical View*. Oxford, England: Berg, 1988. A rather severe rightist assessment of Beauvoir as shrewish, domineering, naïve, and irrational in her personal and political positions. Toril Moi offers a fair corrective to Winegarten, whose anti-Marxist reading of the Marxist Beauvoir offers a challenging approach to an understanding of Beauvoir's ideological arena.

Roy Arthur Swanson

SEDUCTION AND BETRAYAL
Women and Literature

Author: Elizabeth Hardwick (1916-   )
Type of work: Literary criticism
First published: 1974

Form and Content

A collection of essays that originally appeared in the influential *New York Review of Books*, a journal that Hardwick helped to found in 1963, *Seduction and Betrayal: Women and Literature* focuses on both women's lives in literature and literature in the lives of women. As a woman critic writing about other women, both real and fictional, Hardwick provides interesting pieces of literary, biographical, and social criticism from a viewpoint that, at the time of their original appearance, was clearly in the minority.

Beginning with an extended discussion of the role of literature in the lives of the three Brontë sisters, Anne, Charlotte, and Emily, Hardwick makes her main foray into the lives of fictional women with substantial essays on three plays by the Norwegian dramatist Henrik Ibsen: *A Doll's House* (1879), *Hedda Gabler* (1890), and *Rosemersholm* (1886). This section is followed by a series of essays on three twentieth century women—Zelda Fitzgerald, Sylvia Plath, and Virginia Woolf—after which Hardwick turns to the Romantic period and the early nineteenth century. Her discussions of Dorothy Wordsworth (the sister of the poet William Wordsworth) and Jane Carlyle (the wife of the great man of letters Thomas Carlyle), which together constitute a section of her book that has been entitled "Amateurs," is followed by the volume's title essay, which is the most wide-ranging and speculative piece in the book. About the essay "Seduction and Betrayal" Hardwick tells the reader, in a prefatory note, that it was presented as a lecture at Vassar College in 1972, and the setting of its original presentation (a college audience consisting, presumably, mostly of women) may account for the rather pointed formulation of its thesis, which is that although seduction may be very damaging to the victim, the seducer's activity is fundamentally comic. The female perspective is clearly present here, since most men would be likely to regard their efforts at seduction as serious business indeed.

Hardwick shows much empathy toward the subjects of her essays, especially those women who had to overcome great obstacles in order to become published writers. There is a particular appreciation for the situation of the woman writer whose husband is also a literary artist. This sympathetic understanding no doubt has its roots in Hardwick's own situation as the wife of the poet Robert Lowell, whose stature often seemed to eclipse her work. Hardwick, who in addition to two volumes of essays and numerous short stories also produced three novels, clearly knew by experience how difficult it can be for a woman to find time and space in which to do her intellectual work.

There is also, however, clear evidence of Hardwick's ability to be truly critical of the subjects of her essays, be they men or women. There is no glossing over the fact that Thomas Carlyle's domestic behavior bordered on abuse or that William Wordsworth took advantage of his sister's work. Her censure is at its strongest, however, when she speaks about such Ibsen characters as Hedda Gabler, in whom she finds no redeeming qualities, and Rebecca West, the female protagonist of *Rosmersholm*. Hardwick is able to admire many of Ibsen's women without finding it necessary to admire those traits in them which lead to the destruction of both themselves and others.

Analysis

Hardwick's interest in the public and private lives of women manifests itself throughout *Seduction and Betrayal*, as does her special understanding of the many difficulties that have to be overcome by the successful woman writer. Most of these difficulties have to do with the position of women in the family and in society under the rule of patriarchy. In her first essay, "The Brontës," Hardwick discusses how Anne, Charlotte, and Emily Brontë developed their literary talents and careers in the face of particular challenges: poverty, illness, and lack of love.

The lives of Ibsen's women figures are of interest to Hardwick, much as if these characters had been creatures of flesh and blood. Willingly suspending her knowledge that Ibsen's women are not real human beings, she submits them to the kind of careful psychological analysis that might have been appropriate in a biographical essay. Hardwick also goes beyond the Ibsen characters themselves to the real people who inspired them, noting, for example, the connection between Ibsen's young German friend Emilie Bardach and the siren Hilde Wangel in *The Master Builder* (1892).

Hardwick's discussion of the character Nora Helmer in *A Doll's House* is an excellent example of how a consideration of both the literary figure and the human model behind her can be helpful. After offering a close, clear, concise, and insightful reading of the play, Hardwick poses the question of how the impressions of Nora which are given in the first act can be reconciled with the picture of Nora which is presented in the final act of the drama. The problem is, says Hardwick, that Nora seems to have developed too far and too fast. Hardwick points out, however, that the woman who served as the model for Nora in real life was well known to Ibsen as a resourceful and intelligent person, and she holds that Nora Helmer should therefore be regarded as someone who, from the very beginning, is a highly capable person. When the interpreter shifts the accent from Nora's development to the way in which she is forced to hide her true abilities, both Nora's character and Ibsen's drama come across as being highly unified.

Hardwick's reading of *Hedda Gabler* rivals that of *A Doll's House* in importance. Hardwick feels a need to censure Hedda, but she is also aware of the role that this bored and unmotivated protagonist has played in the cultural development that has taken place since the publication of the drama. Hedda, says Hardwick, is much more of a cultural prophecy than is Nora, because numerous literary characters created after Ibsen created her are her spiritual descendants.

The third and final section on Ibsen is devoted to a discussion of the love triangle in the play *Rosmersholm*. Its female protagonist, Rebecca West, is a strong woman who, unfortunately, is lacking in scruples. In the end, however, her destructive bent turns self-destructive, and her suicide, says Hardwick, is a logical consequence of the way she has chosen to live.

Hardwick continues her meditations on the theme of self-destruction in the next segment of her book, "Victims and Victors." Zelda Fitzgerald, Sylvia Plath, and Virginia Woolf were all tormented human beings whose sufferings, it seems, were prerequisites to their work. These are heroic women, and their defeats add to their heroism. In her discussion of Virginia Woolf, Hardwick also devotes considerable attention to the sexual experimentation of the members of the Bloomsbury group, the group of intellectuals among whom Woolf lived and worked.

As a contrast to the specifically modern tribulations of Fitzgerald, Plath, and Woolf, Hardwick details the life situations of Dorothy Wordsworth and Jane Carlyle, who essentially sacrificed their lives and possible careers for, respectively, a brother and a husband. Hardwick regards Dorothy Wordsworth as utterly dependent on others because there was no other way open to her, whereas Jane Carlyle's ironic and ambivalent bent makes her a very interesting representative of the Victorian wife.

Hardwick rounds off her volume with her essay "Seduction and Betrayal," which is largely a study of illicit sex in literature. She concludes that since innocence no longer has any social value, seduction has lost its tragic potential and sex has become useless as literary material.

Context

Seduction and Betrayal was Hardwick's second volume of essays. The first, *A View of My Own: Essays in Literature and Society* (1962), whose title alluded to Virginia Woolf's well-known feminist statement *A Room of One's Own* (1929), signaled that Hardwick was consciously placing her work in a feminist tradition of writing. Many of the essays that were collected in *Seduction and Betrayal*, particularly those that discuss Ibsen's women characters, touch on the image of women which is presented in literature. They are thus in line with much other feminist criticism that came forth in the 1960's and the early 1970's, although Hardwick is not as critical of Ibsen as some of her sister feminists were of the male authors about whom they were writing. Other essays in the volume, which are exercises in literary biography and social criticism at least as much as they are specifically *literary* criticism, show a much more acute awareness of the way women have suffered in patriarchal society. These essays are representative of a trend in women's studies which gathered momentum around the year 1975, when feminist scholars and critics developed a perspective that was centered on women, focusing their writing almost exclusively on women's literature and women's experiences in life. Hardwick's work is clearly in the vanguard of this movement and may even have had a hand in shaping it.

Hardwick has received high praise for her polished style of writing, her sensibility, and her wit. Addressing such women's concerns as how women have had to balance their relationships with men against their concern for their own work, how women, owing to their biology, have been vulnerable, and how they have had to cope with a socially limited set of options in life, she touches on themes of universal interest. Because these essays originally appeared in the pages of *The New York Review of Books*, a journal that Hardwick helped to found and edit, they reached an important segment of the American public and affected the cultural and political climate in the country.

Elizabeth Hardwick's other works include the novels *The Ghostly Lover* (1945), *The Simple Truth* (1955), and *Sleepless Nights* (1979), as well as many short stories and essays. A third volume of essays is *Bartleby in Manhattan and Other Essays* (1983).

Sources for Further Study

Friedan, Betty. *The Feminine Mystique*. New York: W. W. Norton, 1963. An exploration of the ways in which women's behavior is controlled through social norms, Friedan's book was a harbinger of the American women's movement in the latter part of the twentieth century. A classic of its kind.

Gilbert, Sandra M., and Susan Gubar. *The Madwoman in the Attic: The Woman Writer and the Nineteenth-Century Literary Imagination*. New Haven, Conn.: Yale University Press, 1979. A collection of readings of major woman writers of the nineteenth century, the volume also presents a controversial theory of female creativity. The authors maintain that male writers have traditionally looked to their sexuality as a source of imagery for explanations of their creativity, and they propose that this has put women literary artists at a disadvantage. Therefore, Gilbert and Gubar claim, women writers should explain their own creativity with reference to the female body. The scope of *The Madwoman in the Attic* is formidable. The book is, however, also highly readable.

Millett, Kate. *Sexual Politics*. Garden City, N.Y.: Doubleday, 1970. A pioneering work in feminist literary criticism, Millett's book first defines the nature of the power relationship between the sexes and then demonstrates how this relationship is enacted in works by such male authors as D. H. Lawrence, Henry Miller, Norman Mailer, and Jean Genet. A highly political work, Millett's book has been criticized for being one sided. It is, however, both powerfully argued and readable. It has a good index.

Moi, Toril. *Sexual-Textual Politics: Feminist Literary Theory*. London: Methuen, 1985. Emphasizing the Anglo-American and French traditions of feminist literary theory, Moi offers a brief and readable introduction to the field from a leftist perspective. Of particular value is Moi's discussion of the French feminist theorists Hélène Cixous, Luce Irigaray, and Julia Kristeva. Her section on Anglo-American feminist criticism gives useful summaries of the work of Betty Friedan, Kate Millett, Sandra Gilbert, and Susan Gubar, as well as Elaine Showalter. *Sexual-Textual Politics* contains an index, a bibliography, and suggestions for further reading.

Showalter, Elaine. *A Literature of Their Own: British Women Novelists from Brontë to Lessing*. Princeton, N.J.: Princeton University Press, 1977. Although some feminists believe that Showalter is not sufficiently critical of patriarchal power, Showalter's book is useful. It contains both an index and a useful bibliography

Jan Sjåvik

SELECTED POEMS

Author: Gwendolyn Brooks (1917-   )
Type of work: Poetry
First published: 1963

Form and Content

The first section of Gwendolyn Brooks's *Selected Poems* is devoted to an investigation of the world that the poet has chosen to represent: "A Street in Bronzeville." The street is dominated by women, as the presence of such figures as the mother, a hunchback girl, and Sadie and Maud indicates. The first poem in the sequence, "Kitchenette Building," is a central one because it asks what the fate of a dream would be in this world. Would it penetrate the "onion fumes" of garbage and "fried potatoes"? The speaker wonders if it might be possible, but at the end of the poem she recognizes that ordinary needs such as "lukewarm water" would keep any dream from taking hold. This is a world of limitations in which any higher aspirations must be put aside for immediate needs. The immediate needs that drive out the dream are chosen by both male and female, since these needs involve "feeding a wife" and "satisfying a man."

The next section includes two very different poems on the men of this society. The first, "The Sundays of Satin-Legs Smith," is an ironic portrait of a dandy and ladies' man. His careful dressing and scenting of his body are more elaborate than those of any woman. His treatment of women is, however, arbitrary; he admits of no "compromise." Everything must be done according to his desires; there is no commitment to any woman, since he has a different prostitute each week.

In contrast, "Negro Hero," based on Dorrie Miller, a black sailor in World War II, portrays a man who fights for equality in order to save "a part of their democracy." He had to "kick their law into their teeth in order to save them." The actions are not conventionally heroic but come from a desire to make the stated claims of the country be taken seriously and put into practice.

"Gay Chaps at the Bar" is a sequence of twelve sonnets on the war experiences of a number of black Americans. They demonstrated their courage during the war and in fighting prejudice they experienced in the military. Like the negro hero, they had to remind their oppressors of their own ideals and laws.

The central section of the volume, "Annie Allen," is an extended portrait of a representative black American woman. It is divided into four sections. The two most important poems in the first section, "Notes from the Girlhood and the Childhood," are "The Ballad of Late Annie" and "Don't Be Afraid of No." In the first poem, Annie makes clear her independent position: "Be I to fetch and carry?/ Get a broom to whish the doors/ Or get a man to marry?" Such conventional choices would diminish her as a person.

The next section, "The Anniad," is a mock-heroic celebration of Annie. She is a dreamer whose life will not be complete without a man. When the man does come into her life, however, he goes off to war, and he finds a mistress upon his return. At the end of the poem, she has only her memories to sustain herself. There is an "Appendix to The Anniad." Its three poems define her as later seeking some solace in her loss and, in the last poem, asking her mother "where is happiness."

The next group is a series of short poems, "The Womanhood." It contains fifteen separate poems that deal with social issues and motherhood. The following section, "The Bean Eaters," contains a variety of short poems. It includes an elegy for the poet's father, David Anderson Brooks, and two poems on the Emmett Till murder. The title poem and "We Real Cool" are very different but are, perhaps, Brooks's most anthologized poems.

The last section in the book, "New Poems," is primarily devoted to short portraits. The most interesting of these are the poems on Langston Hughes and Robert Frost. The other poems, "A Catch of Sly Fish," deal with typical characters in the Bronzeville world.

Analysis

Brooks's poems deal with the people and experiences of the streets of a black area she calls Bronzeville. Therefore, it is natural that she uses the words that such people would use on the street, although she does set them in a context of regular meters. Brooks does not use free verse very often in her poems; meter and rhyme seem to be necessary to create the hypnotic spell that many of her poems have. In such long poems as "The Sundays of Satin-Legs Smith" and "The Anniad," the meter is insistent and takes on the aspects of a chant. This hypnotic effect is reinforced by her use of couplets and short poetic lines. Brooks also uses such traditional literary genres as the elegy and the mock-heroic as well as such technical devices as the couplet, rhyme royal, elegy and various types of sonnet. These traditional aspects of poetic technique are, however, brought together with folk elements such as black speech patterns and jazz and blues rhythms as well as ballads. Both traditional and folk elements combine to create a compelling social vision.

The speakers and situations in Brooks's poems are primarily African American. She wishes, above all, to show the everyday lives and struggles of black people rather than present ideals that are distant from or foreign to their experience. She also attempts to portray the largest range of experience possible. This can be seen most fully in longer poems such as "The Sundays of Satin-Legs Smith" and "The Anniad," which deal with the ordinary lives of representative figures. Annie's life moves from her early years to middle age, and a number of later poems deal with the problems of old age.

The portrayal of women in this society is central to Brooks's rendition of African American society. They are the ones who remain while the men go off to war or seek someone younger or more attractive. Their endurance and resilience in the midst of oppression and limitations are a persistent theme throughout the poems.

Brooks is consistently antiwar and, for the most part, antiheroic. "Gay Chaps at the Bar" shows most clearly the failure of wartime to bring people from different races together, even if they are fighting for the same cause. The heroic is not a realizable

2012 Masterplots II

stance in Brooks's world of immediate necessities. To survive in a world of prejudice and hatred is the best one can hope for. "Of De Witt Williams on His Way to Lincoln Cemetery" contains a good example of the antiheroic in its refrain: "He was nothing but a/ Plain black boy." His world is the pool hall, the dance hall, and Forty-seventh Street. He lived fully in a world that had no place for heroism but did enable him to find joy.

Brooks counterpoints the lives of the old and the young in the section called "The Bean Eaters." The title deals with an elderly couple who "eat beans mostly. . . ." They are orderly in the way they put their clothes and things away. Their primary activity is "remembering" amid the "twinges" of age in "the rented back room." In contrast, the pool players at the Golden Shovel of "We Real Cool" live their life intensely and briefly. They think they are killing time: "We/ Jazz June," but at the end of the poem time catches them: "We/ die soon."

Brooks does express a clear social manifesto in "The Womanhood" section. In "First Fight, Then Fiddle," art must come after the social struggle. "Be deaf to music and to beauty blind./ Win war.'" In its directness and simplicity, the style reflects the necessity of abandoning all adornment until victory is achieved. Brooks does not specify the specific social victory to be achieved, but the book consistently portrays the condition of black people as oppressive and in need of immediate change.

The portraits in the last section of the book show another aspect of Brooks's art. She manages to convey character with a few sharp images. For example, Robert Frost has "common blood," but it is "glowing." Langston Hughes seems to be made up of wedded contraries; he has "Muscular tears" and is both "Helmsman" and "hatchet. . . ."

Context

Gwendolyn Brooks's *Selected Poems* was published in 1963, a number of years before women's literature and feminist criticism became prominent. Her portrayal of women characters and speakers does, however, represent a clear feminist perspective.

Brooks consistently celebrates those women who live and take chances. For example, Sadie, in "Sadie and Maud," "was one of the livingest chits/ In all the land." She had two children without being married and lived every minute. In contrast, "Maud" was safe and went to college, only to end up as "a thin brown mouse." "She is living all alone/ In this old house." Annie Allen may depend too much on dreams, but she does realize the value of saying no. She can reject the conventional traps that society places before women and live. So, too, "Cousin Vit" refuses the confinements of a ritual funeral as she goes "Back to the bars she knew and the repose/ In love-rooms and the things in people's eyes." There seems to be an injunction to live in Brooks's poems, especially those about women.

Another area of women's experience that Brooks explores is that of the mother. In the section "The Children of the Poor," Brooks traces the experience of mothers from a period in which they do not have any children through child rearing to death. The second section asks, "what shall I give my children?" For poor mothers, there is a gap between the desire and the ability to provide for their children. "And plenitude of plan shall not suffice/ Nor grief nor love shall be enough alone. . . ."

A similar view is expressed in the early poem "The Mother," in which a mother is mourning the loss of the children she has aborted. She acknowledges her "crime" but also declares her love for those she has willed not to be. "Believe me, I loved you all./ Believe me, I knew you, though faintly, I loved you/ All."

"A Bronzeville Mother Loiters in Mississippi. Meanwhile, A Mississippi Mother Burns Bacon" is told through the point of view of a white mother whose husband has just been acquitted of the murder of the "Dark Villain," Emmett Till, a young black boy from Chicago. This mother is trying to come to terms with the events that led to the lynching of Till; her burning of the bacon suggests an inner disturbance. Her meditation on the events, however, ends with a hatred not for the boy who has been killed, but for her husband. The kiss he gives her is not of love but of death. "But his mouth would not go away and neither would the/ Decapitated exclamation points in the Other Woman's eyes." The Other Woman is the mother of Emmett Till, and her presence increases the guilt of the Mississippi mother.

Sources for Further Study

Kent, George F. *A Life of Gwendolyn Brooks*. Lexington: University Press of Kentucky, 1990. This work, the best full-length biography of Gwendolyn Brooks, reveals the close relationship between her life and her art.

Melhem, D. H. *Gwendolyn Brooks: Poetry and the Heroic Voice*. Lexington: University Press of Kentucky, 1987. Melhem begins with a very brief life of Brooks and then examines in detail the poetry up until the mid-1980's. Melhem is especially good at discussing the technical aspects of Brooks's poetry and at connecting her work with the poetic tradition.

Miller, R. Baxter. *Langston Hughes and Gwendolyn Brooks: A Reference Guide*. Boston: G. K. Hall, 1978. Somewhat outdated, but still a valuable research tool for a study of Brooks's work.

Mootry, Maria K., and Gary Smith, eds. *A Life Distilled: Gwendolyn Brooks, Her Poetry and Fiction*. Urbana: University of Illinois Press, 1987. An excellent collection of essays on a wide range of subjects dealing with Brooks's art. The essays that discuss the aesthetic aspects of Brooks's poetry are especially valuable.

Shaw, Harry B. *Gwendolyn Brooks*. Boston: Twayne, 1980. A life-and-works study of Brooks in the Twayne authors series. Shaw focuses primarily on the social aspects of Brooks's poetry and fiction.

James Sullivan

SELECTED POEMS OF MARINA TSVETAYEVA

Author: Marina Tsvetayeva (1892-1941)
Type of work: Poetry
First published: 1971; rev. ed., 1981

Form and Content

Marina Tsvetayeva is one of the four great Russian poets of the twentieth century. The other three, all Tsvetayeva's contemporaries—Boris Pasternak, Osip Mandelstam, and Anna Akhmatova—are better known in the West, not least because of the almost insurmountable difficulties of translating Tsvetayeva's peculiar poetic genius. Her poetry is difficult not because it is obscure or esoteric—on the contrary, it is passionate and direct speech—but because much of its expressiveness relies on verbal association, on sound compressed, contracted, and then released with tremendous energy. Although she was established and acknowledged as a major talent by the time she left Russia in 1922, Tsvetayeva never easily fit into any school or movement.

Selected Poems of Marina Tsvetayeva is a small volume intended to give the English-speaking reader some sense of Tsvetayeva's life's work. Poet and novelist Elaine Feinstein has based her versions on literal, nonpoetic translations done by Russian-speaking scholars and translators, and out of an enormous body of work (Tsvetayeva wrote more than two thousand lyric poems) has chosen mostly shorter lyrics and arranged them in chronological order. Although Tsvetayeva's precocious adolescent verses, first published in 1908, own praise and recognition even during the literary boom of Russia's prewar years, Feinstein begins with her more mature work of 1915 and 1916. Moving from old themes (her own singularity, her own isolation, her obstinate refusal to abandon the child's sometimes startling view of the world) into new ones (passionate physical attraction and passionate physical separation from the beloved, states which in her world paradoxically and necessarily support one another), Tsvetayeva gradually moves into longer forms. Most often, she explores two states of being—love and poetry. Feinstein includes the poet's famous cycles in praise of Symbolist poet Aleksandr Blok and of Anna Akhmatova as well as several of her best-known long poems of the mid-1920's—"Poem of the Mountain," "Poem of the End," "An Attempt at Jealousy"—which trace the course of an intense love affair.

During the 1920's, Tsvetayeva also began writing prose essays and experimenting with even longer forms: narrative poems based on folklore or recent history. Feinstein includes excerpts from only one of these, *Ratcatcher*, which is a reworking of the medieval German legend of the Pied Piper. She ends with a few poems from the 1930's, when Tsvetayeva was turning more and more to prose, and when the ferocious, exuberant energy of her earlier work was turning into a stark inner severity. The last poems in the book are from a cycle dedicated to Czechoslovakia, where Tsvetayeva had spent her earlier and relatively happier years of emigration.

This selection ends with the year 1939. Tsvetayeva did not live much longer: After following her husband and daughter back to the Soviet Union that same year and seeing them disappear into Stalinist prison camps, she and her son joined writers in wartime evacuation. Ostracized and destitute, she hanged herself in the town of Elabuga in 1941.

Analysis

As with any poet, it is difficult to separate form from content, and in Tsvetayeva's case such an attempt at separation would be not only difficult but also ill-advised: Her distorted or elliptical syntax, her verbal inventiveness, her startling punctuation, her magnetic, almost hypnotic incantations—all of these embody the very way she thought. Tsvetayeva is known for her technical brilliance, her virtuoso use of a whole array of poetic devices, but for her these were never (as they were for some of her contemporaries) ends in themselves.

The lyrics in this selection span more than twenty years, and during those twenty years Tsvetayeva's voice changes several times. Yet there are always certain constants. First, her voice is always an assertion, a defining and re-defining of the self. Even in the longer poems there is always the impression of direct speech; the speaker urges, reproaches, praises, harangues. Early in her career, Tsvetayeva declared that her poetry was a lyric diary, "a poetry of proper names." She later qualified that statement in a letter of 1923: "The choice of words is first of all the choice and purging of emotions. Not all emotions are equally valid, believe me; here, too, work is required." Therefore, Tsvetayeva's poetry of proper names is not confessional poetry as such. Instead, it is mythmaking—the transformation of emotion and experience into a different reality.

The different reality—a transcendent, spiritual reality versus the reality of everyday life—was just one of a whole set of varied but opposing notions that runs throughout Tsvetayeva's work. Flesh/spirit, art/conventional morality, chastity/promiscuity, male/female—these and other paradoxes of human existence shape Tsvetayeva's self and world. What is peculiar to Tsvetayeva is that these antitheses never resolve (or dissolve) into a synthesis, and one-half of the pair never entirely triumphs; they continue to exist as paradoxical complements. In a sense, Tsvetayeva is defining herself (and her characters) by refusing to define, to exclude: The resulting "I" of the poem, whether it be a version of Tsvetayeva herself or a gypsy woman or Lilith or Helen of Troy, is an intact, contradictory whole—unlike the ironically self-conscious split selves that abound in twentieth century modernist poetry.

Her antitheses took many forms, from the "I-unlike-all-others" of her early poetry to the subtler "I-unlike-Akhmatova" of her homage to that poet (in a style reminiscent of Akhmatova's own) to the androgynous woman warrior, the Tsar-Maiden of the long poem of the same name. Feinstein did not include this poem because of its length, but there are many other examples of reversals in the nature of relationships: The female character is the stronger, brasher, more reckless. Even when the voice is not explicitly female, it may speak in defense of characters such as Shakespeare's Ophelia and Gertrude, the Bible's Lilith, mythology's Phaedra and Helen. These women, traditionally objects of either pity or fear, may be tragic and self-destructive, but they are neither helpless victims nor vicious viragos.

The reversal of the expected, the overturning of cliché, lies at the heart of Tsvetayeva's worldview and of her poetics. In Russian, word order is far more flexible than it is in English, and Russian syntax allows for startling reversals of logical sequence; Tsvetayeva may distort not only syntax but also the logical sequence of imagery, as in the beginning of "An Attempt at Jealousy," where the image of an oar precedes the metaphor to which it belongs.

Tsvetayeva's whole literary generation was extraordinarily word conscious, coining new words and rediscovering old ones. Tsvetayeva did the same things, varying the voices she used, varying their diction, sometimes combining folk dialect and street slang with Church Slavonic, the language of the Russian Orthodox Church, sometimes reverting to a more severely classical mode. Yet Tsvetayeva's coinings and word play (unlike those of many of her contemporaries) were never purely musical or alliterative; she sought the hidden relationships between phonetics and semantics— that is, between sound and meaning. This is what she does in poems such as "Poem of the Mountain," organized around *gorá* (mountain) and *góre* (sorrow), or "Wires," based on the play between *provodá* (here, telegraph wires) and *próvody* (saying farewells, seeing someone off). The sound itself leads to the meaning.

She often wrote in standard meters and stanzas, but much of her jagged, forceful, and decidedly "unladylike" rhythm comes from her use of ellipses (dropping the verb, which Russian grammar permits because the noun endings change according to their grammatical function), idiosyncratic punctuation (especially dashes), and a preference for metrical feet made up of several stressed syllables in a row In *Ratcatcher*, for example, there is one four-line stanza consisting solely of four one-syllable words.

For all Tsvetayeva's verbal and metrical complexity, however, she never leaves sense behind. She combines familiar, recognizable forms to reinvent Russian, not to invent some new esoteric language. Her poems are urgent, direct communication in which device is always subordinate to desire.

Context

The grand nineteenth century Russian literary tradition, be it in poetry or prose, did not include women. Russian literature had no Jane Austens, George Eliots, or Emily Dickinsons. It was not a matter of ignoring major talents: They simply did not exist, and even the minor talents were few and far between. Except for sentimental album-verse for domestic consumption, and diaries and personal correspondence (which might eventually become a memoir), Russian women did not write. Social upheaval and cultural change in the last decades of the century finally gave women entry into places hitherto closed: universities, laboratories, political parties, and —this time as participants, not hostesses—literary circles.

Marina Tsvetayeva, like other women artists emerging from the Silver Age of Russian culture, was faced with the stereotypes of the breathless, high-strung "lady writer." More important, she was faced with a great void. There were sympathetic and perceptive portraits of women in the Russian tradition, but there were no portraits by them, no direct expression of a female point of view.

Tsvetayeva went beyond theme and imagery to establish a point of view that was independent of male point of view rather than a reaction to it. She rewrote the whole of female mythology. Her voice begins and ends in isolation, demanding, asserting, lamenting, rejoicing openly and unironically, her points of departure being her own self and the sound of the words. Yet it would be wrong to consider her a feminist in any political sense; she was allergic to causes (except lost ones) and was adamantly apolitical and nonideological. She was capable of openly taking up with a whole series of lovers—male and female alike—while maintaining a fiercely traditional loyalty to her husband, following him first into exile in the West and later back into Stalinist Russia. She once remarked: "There is no female question in art—there are female answers to human questions, like Sappho, Joan of Arc, St. Theresa, Bettina Brentano."

In life, Tsvetayeva's own collisions with those human questions were disastrous. Simon Karlinsky has noted that while neglect, exile, persecution, and suicide were the fates of many Russian poets after the Revolution, only Tsvetayeva experienced them all. In poetry, however, her female answers produced one of the finest bodies of work in Russian literature, one that was openly acknowledged in her native country only some forty years after her death but has influenced Russian poets tremendously.

Sources for Further Study

Heldt, Barbara. *Terrible Perfection: Women and Russian Literature*. Bloomington: Indiana University Press, 1987. Heldt first gives an overview of women as characters in Russian fiction and poetry, and then looks at some women writers, including Tsvetayeva, in detail.

Karlinsky, Simon. *Marina Tsvetayeva: The Woman, Her World, and Her Poetry*. Cambridge, England: Cambridge University Press, 1985. A study intended for the general reader, emphasizing the cultural and historical factors affecting the poet.

Schweitzer, Victoria. *Tsvetayeva*. Translated by Robert Chandler and H. T. Willetts. New York: Farrar, Straus and Giroux, 1992. A definitive, meticulously researched literary biography by a leading Tsvetayeva scholar. It includes copious biographical notes on the people, both famous and obscure, surrounding Tsvetayeva.

Taubman, Jane. *A Life Through Poetry: Marina Tsvetayeva's Lyric Diary*. Columbus, Ohio: Slavica, 1989. A sympathetic and insightful treatment of Tsvetayeva's lyrics. Taubman uses biography to illuminate the art but never confuses the two.

Tsvetayeva, Marina. *Art in the Light of Conscience*. Edited and translated by Angela Livingstone. Cambridge, Mass.: Harvard University Press, 1992. Eight essays on poets and poetry written between 1922 and 1932. They range from close analysis of a translation to comparisons of individual poets, types of poets and types of minds—all written with the same energy and laconic expressiveness that is the essence of Tsvetayeva's poetry.

Jane Ann Miller

SELECTED STORIES

Author: Nadine Gordimer (1923-   )
Type of work: Short Stories
First published: 1975

Form and Content

Selected Stories includes an introduction by Gordimer and thirty-one stories written between 1943 and 1973, selected by Gordimer from her five previously published short-story collections: *The Soft Voice of the Serpent* (1951), *Six Feet of the Country* (1956), *Friday's Footprint* (1960), *Not for Publication* (1965), and *Livingstone's Companions* (1972). *Selected Stories* presents from five to eight stories from each previously published collection, always including the title story. Arranged chronologically, this collection provides a historical perspective, since more than half of the stories have political themes dealing with the difficulties of living under apartheid in South Africa. Reading *Selected Stories* provides insight into the social and political climate surrounding Gordimer as she wrote.

The stories present thirty-one separate fictional glimpses into people's lives. Not directly addressed, apartheid is revealed through the characters who are living under the system. Gordimer chronicles sometimes moments, sometimes years in the lives of whites and blacks, old and young, males and females, in various locations. Character is portrayed through either home and family, social connections, or political views. Almost half of the stories deal with husband-and-wife relationships, and of the remaining stories, eleven have female protagonists. Women's position in society and in the home and women's political views are evident throughout the collection.

The women characters are diverse as are their positions in society and their political views. In the initiation stories, for example, many of the female protagonists are young and are from the privileged white population. Yet "Good Climate, Friendly Inhabitants" and "Friday's Footprint" center on working middle-aged women, and the protagonist of "Enemies" is a seventy-one-year-old woman who once was a baroness. Other stories in the book—"A Chip of Glass Ruby," "Ah, Woe Is Me," "Happy Event," and "Something for the Time Being"—have Indian or black women as protagonists or as foils for the protagonists. A few stories are apolitical, but most are either overtly political or include political details as a concomitant part of the characters' lives. The middle-aged Indian woman—Mrs. Bamjee—in "A Chip of Glass Ruby" is arrested for her political activity, as is the young white Joyce McCoy in "The Smell of Death and Flowers"; in the former story, political activity has long become a way of life, while it is a new experience for Joyce McCoy. In contrast to the activism of these women, the young black wife in "Something for the Time Being" wishes that her husband would stop his political activities.

Yet *Selected Stories* does not deal exclusively with women or couples; several stories have male protagonists, and these, like Gordimer's women characters, are diverse: Carl Church, the London foreign correspondent in "Livingstone's Companions"; Mr. Van As, in "The Last Kiss," who is nearly seventy, an Afrikaner who once was a cartage contractor in a gold mining area of the Transvaal; Manie Swemmer, a middle-aged working man with Scottish ancestors in "Abroad"; Praise Basetse, in "Not for Publication," a young beggar taken from the streets of Johannesburg to be educated. *Selected Stories* presents characters in their daily activities, sometimes living as they choose, but often as they believe they must because of the dictates of society or politics.

Analysis

Gordimer's characters are often marred by personal weaknesses or political oppression. Most stories have external narrators who treat the characters with irony or sympathy or both, as if the flaws that merit criticism are also somehow out of the characters' control. Arrests and deaths, repression and confusion are typical in these stories. Some characters are caught in the trap of political oppression; others, in social stereotypes. Several stories juxtapose white and black characters, illustrating the different types of damage that the social and political systems engender.

The difficulties of living under apartheid are obvious in stories such as "Ah, Woe Is Me," in which Sarah works as a servant for the narrator; neither the hard work of Sarah nor the useless good intentions of the narrator are enough to help Sarah's family. Sarah never questions the justness of her plight but only wants her children to recognize their position in society and do the best they can within it. Segregated living conditions and lack of quality schools in the location force Sarah to live separately from her children for long periods. The story revolves, though, around the view of the narrator, who is wholly ineffectual in dealing with the misfortunes of Sarah's family. "Ah, Woe Is Me" is one of seven stories in the collection which are narrated in the first person. The voice of the woman of privilege telling the story of Sarah provides an ironic tension, an apparent concern amid hopelessness. A similar type of ineffectuality is noted in "Six Feet of the Country" and "Africa Emergent," two other stories with political themes narrated by white characters. "Africa Emergent" is notable in that the narrating architect not only recognizes his limitations in aiding his black acquaintances but also sees how the political system encourages mistrust between people.

Most of Gordimer's white characters are scarred by South African society. Some members of the leisure class live empty lives, following social rituals that mandate against individuality. Seventeen-year-old Kathy Hack of "A Company of Laughing Faces" learns through her mother's tutelage that being grown up means following the crowd. The external narrator describes Kathy's young social circle unfavorably— artificial, boring, and sexist. Kathy is to fit in by wearing "small tight shorts . . . [as] equipment rather than [as] clothes." At the dances, the boys "rove in predatory search," seeking a partner from the "pool" of girls. Water imagery permeates this story in which Kathy is taken to a sea resort to mingle with people her own age. The story ends with a drowning, a stark warning to all the individuals drowning in society. If Kathy does not heed the warning but instead follows the mundane social rituals, she could become like the narrator of another story in the collection—"Rain-Queen"— who learns at nineteen the ease of hypocrisy.

Two stories in the collection which are told dramatically—as if a camera and a microphone pick up the sight and sound with little interpretive input from a narrator— are "No Place Like" and "The Train from Rhodesia." The stories follow female protagonists for only a fraction of a day—just long enough for a change of plane or a stop at a train station. Yet through telling details, Gordimer reveals their inner conflicts. In "No Place Like," a woman on a brief stopover in an African airport refuses to continue on the path of her routine journey. The repetition of the need for the shiny plastic boarding card and the repeated call to Gate B emphasize society's restrictions, the plastic card necessary for passage and Gate B the symbol for chan- neled movement. The protagonist can no longer follow such regimentation. In "The Train from Rhodesia," the young wife has an epiphany while traveling with her new husband; she found life empty and thought that marriage would fill the gap. Seeing her husband cheerfully treat a black vendor with disdain awakens her to the knowl- edge that this marriage is not the answer to her emptiness. Both stories suggest through details that these women's lives are unfulfilled. In "No Place Like," regimen- tation seems to be at fault; in "The Train from Rhodesia," the privileged life is shown to be empty. The point of view of each story provides only suggestions of the causes of the all-too-clear dissatisfactions. Whether physical or psychological, dissatisfac- tion with life reigns in *Selected Stories*.

Context

Gordimer's fiction highlights the dangers of repressive cultures, whether racist or sexist. Yet she downplays her position as a woman writer; in her introduction to *Selected Stories*, she writes, "All writers are androgynous beings." Her view on feminism in South Africa is also subdued. The politics of the country precludes feminism as a primary issue; the vast differences between the lives of white and black women in South Africa make a sense of community between the two quite difficult to achieve.

Through the use of character foils, "Happy Event" from *Selected Stories* helps to clarify this position. Ella Plaistow goes to a nursing home to have an abortion, freeing herself and her husband for their planned six-month European holiday; Lena, her maid, is sentenced to six months of hard labor after a dead newborn found in the veld proves to her child. In Gordimer's story, Ella has no sympathy for Lena despite the indirect plea for help Lena sends, wrapping the infant in the blue nightgown given to her by Ella because Ella could no longer bear to wear the gown herself, associating it with her abortion.

Although downplaying her role as a woman writer, Gordimer deals frankly with women's issues such as abortion. Much of Gordimer's fiction is narrated from the woman's perspective, and woman's plight is not neglected. Many of her short stories and several of her novels, in the *Bildungsroman* tradition, focus on young women who are freeing themselves of parental authority, establishing their sexual lives, or com-

mitting themselves to political action. Other issues in Gordimer's fiction of special
concern to women are the sexism that results from a patriarchal culture and the
difficulty of reconciling one's responsibility to children and to oneself.

In 1991, Gordimer won the Nobel Prize in Literature in recognition of the quality
of her large body of writing. Her short stories and novels, if read chronologically,
provide not only an artist's vision of twentieth century South Africa but also the
history of an artist's growth. Gordimer has created many worlds, narrating them from
the perspectives of men and women, the privileged and the oppressed, the blind and
the insightful. Her different perspectives provide insights into the complexity of social
and political problems, including, but not exclusive to, those of women.

Sources for Further Study

Clingman, Stephen. *The Novels of Nadine Gordimer: History from the Inside*. Boston:
    Allen & Unwin, 1986. Places Gordimer's novels in the context of South African
    history. The subtitle emphasizes that Gordimer's treatment of history is that of one
    who is living in the midst of the events. Includes a thorough bibliography of works
    by and about Gordimer, on South African history, and on South African literature.

Eckstein, Barbara. "Pleasure and Joy: Political Activism in Nadine Gordimer's Short
    Stories." *World Literature Today* 59, no. 3 (Summer, 1985): 343-346. Suggests that
    Gordimer's stories are more complex and ambiguous than is sometimes assumed.

Gerver, Elisabeth. "Women Revolutionaries in the Novels of Nadine Gordimer and
    Doris Lessing." *World Literature Written in English* 17 (1978): 38-50. Argues that
    Gordimer's women revolutionary characters gain strength and complexity in later
    novels (1953-1974). Connects the women revolutionary characters to critical real-
    ism.

Haugh, Robert F. *Nadine Gordimer*. New York: Twayne, 1974. Deals with thirty-five
    stories and the first five novels. Prefers the stories to the novels. Includes a
    chronology of Gordimer to 1973 and a selected bibliography that has been super-
    seded by Clingman's.

Smith, Rowland, ed. *Critical Essays on Nadine Gordimer*. Boston: G. K. Hall, 1990.
    The introduction details positive and negative criticism of Gordimer's works.
    Sixteen essays originally published between 1954 and 1988 show the development
    of Gordimer criticism and deal with short stories and eight novels. Essays by Sheila
    Roberts and Dorothy Driver concentrate on Gordimer's treatment of women.
    Indexed.

Trump, Martin. "The Short Fiction of Nadine Gordimer." *Research in African Litera-
    ture* 17, no. 5 (1986): 341-369. Deals with short stories from the 1940's into the
    1980's. Categorizes many into three groups: initiation stories of young women,
    satiric stories of affluent whites, and stories of physical or moral conflict caused by
    South African apartheid. Traces the link between the political oppression of blacks
    and the social oppression of women. Provides a context for the political stories by
    dealing with Gordimer's position in South Africa.

Visel, Robin. "Othering the Self: Nadine Gordimer's Colonial Heroines." *Ariel: A*

Review of International English Literature 19, no. 4 (1988): 33-42. Addresses Gordimer's complex treatment of the white female South African who identifies her struggle for greater independence with the political struggles of blacks—the white female who identifies the black other within herself.

Marion Boyle Petrillo

SELECTED STORIES OF MARY E. WILKINS FREEMAN

Author: Mary E. Wilkins Freeman (1852-1930)
Type of work: Short stories
First published: 1983

Form and Content

These selected stories are from two of Freeman's most popular and critically acclaimed collections, *A Humble Romance* (1887) and *A New England Nun* (1891). The stories focus on small-town New England life and the struggles of working-class people. Most of Freeman's protagonists are women; they are usually older, often widowed or unmarried, but still vigorous and self-supporting. Both male and female characters vacillate between wanting solitude and freedom, and needing community and support.

Freeman's characters display heroism within their economically and geographically circumscribed existences. Strong-willed to the point of stubbornness, they support traditional values of pride, honesty, frugality, and industriousness. Martha Patch, in "An Honest Soul," works herself to exhaustion to ensure that she has correctly pieced her neighbors' scraps into their respective quilts. Harriet and Charlotte Shattuck of "A Mistaken Charity" live frugally in order to avoid the poorhouse; other women—Aurelia Flower of "A Gatherer of Simples," Jenny Wrayne of "Christmas Jenny," and Betsey Dole of "A Poetess"—also live simply, supporting themselves by means of their own work.

Freeman's women often defy social convention. Hetty Fifield of "A Church Mouse" persists in living inside the church and working as sexton. Sarah Penn, in "The Revolt of 'Mother,'" moves the contents of her cramped house into the spacious barn her recalcitrant husband has built instead of the new house she wanted. In "A Village Singer," Candace Whitcomb refuses to accept the congregation's decision to replace her as soprano soloist and speaks passionately against old-age discrimination.

Courtship plots frequently appear, but they receive nontraditional treatment. Louisa Ellis of "A New England Nun" has waited fifteen years for her fiancé's return; when he finally arrives, she realizes that she prefers living on her own. In "A Patient Waiter," Fidelia Almy has waited for her beloved's letter over the course of forty years; she dies without getting the letter but remains pathetically hopeful to the end. Similarly, "Two Old Lovers" and "A Conflict Ended" both deal with long-term courtships. "Up Primrose Hill" has two courtship plots: In one, Maria Primrose rejected Abel Rice years before; in the other, Abel's nephew Frank Rice and Annie Joy counterbalance the mistake of the older generation when they decide to marry.

Friendships between women are the central focus in "On the Walpole Road," "A Gala Dress," and "Sister Liddy." Only two of the stories have male protagonists: "A Solitary" and "A Village Lear." In all the stories, Freeman's careful use of natural detail—plant and animal life, the weather, the landscape—creates vivid settings. Her use of New England dialect also contributes to the stories' regional authenticity.

The stories are simple and to the point, without extraneous exposition. Dialogue between characters is usually brief, but Freeman's laconic New Englanders manage to convey much meaning despite their taciturnity. The stories' endings are often ironic; several conclude with the death of the central character. Although they are understated, Freeman's stories contain a psychological depth and literary richness that transcend the confines of their surface details.

Analysis

Freeman uses an omniscient narrator throughout these stories, and the tone is both wryly ironic and sympathetic to the plights of the characters. Freeman's use of irony undercuts the pathos of her plots; her wry sense of humor saves the stories from becoming too sentimentalized.

Her characters are often outcasts from society who are nevertheless productive, upstanding individuals. Christmas Jenny, who lives alone in the mountains above the village, is the object of unkind village gossip, yet she spends her meager income on rehabilitating injured animals and in caring for an adopted deaf-mute boy. Aurelia Flower also adopts a young girl; she proves her love for the child despite the grandmother's bias against her profession as a "yarb-woman." Nicholas Gunn misanthropically rejects all visitors until he realizes Stephen Forster's need for shelter and companionship.

Many of her women characters are artists, either traditionally or nontraditionally defined—singers, herbalists, quilters, seamstresses, even "A Poetess." Not only do they support themselves with their art, but they also find fulfillment through these activities. Characters' names reveal their occupations or personalities: Martha Patch is a quilter, Fidelia Almy has a faithful soul, and Aurelia Flower is an herbalist with a heart of gold.

Freeman's symbols come from the natural world and ordinary objects. In "A New England Nun," Louisa Ellis' dog Caesar represents her pent-up, misunderstood passion. Martha Patch's lack of a front window (and the perspective it would afford) shows how circumscribed her life is until her neighbors reach out to help her, offering to put a window in for her. Aurelia Flower restores her neighbors' health with her herbal preparations, just as she restores her adopted child to a loving home. The black silk dress that Elizabeth and Emily share in "A Gala Dress" and then give to Matilda Jennings represents sisterhood, not only the biological bond the sisters share, but also the generosity and friendship they extend to their neighbor.

Elderly persons are recurrent character types in the stories, and they reveal Freeman's concern with old-age discrimination and the value of the elderly. Older couples still go courting, work outdoors, take care of their own homes, and are—or would like to be—fully contributing members of society. Too often, however, they are ignored or devalued, as is Barney Swan in "A Village Lear." In "On the Walpole Road," the seventy-year-old Mrs. Green is a role model and source of wisdom to the younger woman, Almira. Harriet and Charlotte Shattuck reject the "Mistaken Charity" of their neighbors when they escape from the poorhouse to return to their dilapidated cottage outside the village; although they live there meagerly, they are nevertheless independent and beholden to no one.

Freeman does not avoid presenting the more negative aspects of small-town life in her fiction; the pernicious effects of idle gossip appear in several of the stories. The church, a central institution in her small New England towns, is just as often the source of censure and hypocrisy as of comfort and support to its parishioners. Recurrent details reveal the area's poverty: the villagers' meager resources, the small yields of their assiduously tended gardens, the frugality they must practice in order to survive, and the frequent mention of the poorhouse as another central village institution. Although poverty is usually material, it can also be spiritual—as is Nicholas Gunn's until he takes in Stephen Forster. Similarly, the hypocritical Christians of "A Village Singer" and "A Mistaken Charity" do not realize until too late the ill effects of their well-intentioned interventions in their neighbors' lives.

Some characters seek solitude as the alternative to repressive village life. Although characters such as Christmas Jenny and Nicholas Gunn seem to prefer their hermit-like status, others enjoy living alone but also value the community around them. Martha Patch is grateful for her neighbors' aid when she has nearly starved to death; Aurelia Flower discovers the joys of motherhood without being married. Louisa Ellis, in Joe Dagget's absence, has elevated her solitude almost to an art form, in which simple sewing and the distillation of herbal preparations bring her more pleasure than does human interaction.

Finally, echoes of Puritanism recur in Freeman's stories and are seen as a literary legacy from Nathaniel Hawthorne. Her characters struggle with issues of conscience and against their own (and others') strong wills. In "Conflict Ended," Marcus Woodman steadfastly refuses to enter the Congregational church, because of a ten-year-old dispute. Adoniram Penn of "The Revolt of 'Mother'" rejects his wife's requests for a new house and only realizes the value of his family when Sarah Penn forces the issue by moving into the barn. The church officials' investigation of Jenny Wrayne's home is described as a witch-hunt in "A Christmas Jenny." Like Hawthorne's short stories, Freeman's are masterpieces of psychological depth which make use of their locale's history and unique character while conveying themes that endure beyond their temporal and spatial boundaries.

Context

Freeman is most often associated with a group of late nineteenth century writers known as Local Colorists, who realistically portrayed specific regions of the United States. Like her contemporary Sarah Orne Jewett, Freeman wrote about rural New England; unlike most of Jewett's work, which idealizes small-town life, Freeman's fiction shows the restrictions as well as the benefits of close-knit communities.

Freeman's critical reputation derives not only from her skillful, realistic regional depictions, but also from the universality of her themes and the stark precision of her style. She received the Howells Medal for Fiction from the American Academy of Arts and Letters in 1926; later that same year, she was one of the first women elected to membership in the National Institute of Arts and Letters.

Freeman's fiction continues to appeal to audiences. She portrays women's concerns and their interior lives with psychological depth and complexity. Far from succumbing to the limitations imposed on them, her women characters take subtle yet significant actions to assert their independence and challenge the authorities who would otherwise continue to oppress them. One of Freeman's many accomplishments in her fiction is the creation of characters who are neither glamorous nor adventurous, but who are admirable for the courage, boldness, and assertiveness they display in their everyday lives. In their own small ways, Freeman's characters are revolutionaries: They express feminist sensibilities that, while lacking political support, result in more equitable social and economic conditions for themselves and for others.

Like many women writers, Freeman expresses the tension between the constraint of living (and writing) according to accepted social codes and the freedom of rebelling against those norms. Her women characters reject conventionality in quiet or private but nevertheless powerful ways: by rejecting marriage, supporting themselves, and living happy, fulfilling lives outside marriage or motherhood. She realistically presents women's economic conditions in poverty-stricken rural New England, but she never makes her characters pitiable. Instead, these women triumph over adversity; this is Freeman's enduring legacy.

Sources for Further Study

Foster, Edward. *Mary E. Wilkins Freeman*. New York: Hendricks House, 1956. Foster's biography of Freeman provides extensive coverage of her life and her work. Much of Foster's biographical information comes from interviews with people who knew Freeman personally. Chapters 4 and 5 deal with *A Humble Romance* and *A New England Nun*, respectively. Contains an extensive bibliography and an index.

Glasser, Leah Blatt. "Legacy Profile: Mary E. Wilkins Freeman." *Legacy* 4, no. 1 (1987): 37-45. Glasser summarizes the life and work of Freeman, and discusses Freeman's long-term friendship with Mary Wales, with whom she lived for twenty years before she married Charles Freeman.

Pryse, Marjorie. Introduction and afterword to *Selected Stories of Mary E. Wilkins Freeman*. New York: W. W. Norton, 1983. Pryse edited and selected the stories in this collection. The introduction gives general background on Freeman's life and art, placing her in the context of other New England and Local Color writers; the afterword provides critical summaries of the stories.

―――――――. "An Uncloistered 'New England Nun.'" *Studies in Short Fiction* 20 (1983): 289-295. Pryse reevaluates "A New England Nun," viewing Louisa Ellis' decision to remain solitary from a positive perspective. Within the context of her small-town existence, Louisa is heroic, wise, and ambitious—not narrow or passive, as previous critics have viewed her.

Reichardt, Mary R. "Mary Wilkins Freeman: One Hundred Years of Criticism." *Legacy* 4, no. 2 (1987): 31-44. Gives an overview of criticism on Freeman, identifying five main areas of early criticism. Summarizes feminist criticism on Freeman. Contains a bibliography.

Toth, Susan Allen. "Defiant Light: A Positive View of Mary Wilkins Freeman." *New England Quarterly* 46 (1973): 82-93. Toth emends the critical commonplace that Freeman's work focuses on weak, infirm characters and the decline of New England village life by discussing instead the vitality of Freeman's characters as they struggle against and within their local community.

Westbrook, Perry D. *Acres of Flint: Writers of Rural New England, 1870-1900.* Washington, D.C.: Scarecrow Press, 1951. Westbrook discusses more than a dozen New England writers of the late nineteenth century and devotes an entire chapter to Freeman. Westbrook focuses on Freeman's treatments of rural life, conscience, and will; he also compares her treatment of Puritan themes to Nathaniel Hawthorne's.

——————. *Mary Wilkins Freeman.* Boston: Twayne, 1967. Although chapters 2 and 3 deal specifically with *A Humble Romance* and *A New England Nun*, this study covers the range of Freeman's work and provides biographical background. Westbrook judges some of the stories in *A Humble Romance* to be superior to those in the latter collection. Includes an annotated bibliography of sources and an index.

Ann A. Merrill

SELECTED STORIES OF SYLVIA TOWNSEND WARNER

Author: Sylvia Townsend Warner (1893-1978)
Type of work: Short stories
First published: 1988

Form and Content

This selection by Sylvia Townsend Warner's literary executors of forty-five of her short stories is taken from a period of forty-five years of her work, from 1932 to 1977. It represents only a small fraction of Warner's output of short stories, which runs to fifteen volumes. At least one story is included from each of her volumes, starting with *The Salutation* (1932) and concluding with the posthumously published *One Thing Leading to Another* (1984).

According to William Maxwell—who was Warner's editor at the *The New Yorker*, where many of her stories were first published—and Susanna Pinney, who jointly edited this selection, the stories are arranged thematically rather than chronologically. Pride of place is given to Warner's finest story, "A Love Match," which was awarded the Katherine Mansfield Menton Prize in 1968. This story and the five that follow ("Winter in the Air," "Idenborough," "The Foregone Conclusion," "An Act of Reparation," and "Lay a Garland on My Hearse") all deal, in very different ways, with romantic relationships between men and women.

Thematic groupings are apparent in many of the remaining stories, which are notable for their diversity. There is a group of four stories ("Absolom, My Son," "Boors Carousing," "On Living for Others," and "Plutarco Roo") that have artists, composers, and writers as their protagonists. "Shadwell" and "Property of a Lady" both feature old women who have been neglected and forgotten in some way; the eccentric Finch family, featuring the hilarious Mrs. Finch ("As a conversationalist Mrs. Finch was considered hard to follow. Not that she was obscure: she was clear as the cuckoo; but like the cuckoo it was hard to follow her, for one could never be sure into what tree she had flown"), appears in two stories.

Although most of the stories are set in England, two exceptions are "The Apprentice," which is set in Poland during the Nazi Occupation, and "A Red Carnation," which is set in Spain during the Spanish Civil War. These are the only two stories that might properly be called political, although two adjacent stories ("The Level-Crossing" and "A Speaker from London") are also set in World War II and deal with close relationships between people which are disrupted by war.

Three stories are included from *Scenes of Childhood* (1981), a collection of sketches published posthumously describing Warner's upper-middle-class Edwardian upbringing. In these stories, she introduces an assortment of odd characters ranging from her parents to great aunts, nannies, and retired majors. "I can always appease my craving for the improbable," she wrote, "by recording with perfect truth my own childhood." The volume concludes with a selection of seven stories from *Kingdoms of Elfin* (1977), a collection of fantasies about fairy kingdoms which were written in the last phase of Warner's creative life. Some reviewers believed that these stories were among her finest work, but others saw them as a trivial indulgence on Warner's part. The fairy kingdoms she describes are not mythical or otherworldly; they closely parallel human institutions and present Warner with many opportunities for satire on religious superstitions and social snobbery of all kinds.

Analysis

Perhaps what the reader notices most consistently about Warner's stories is their quiet, subtly mocking humor. Warner's usually omniscient narrators possess an ironic detachment from their subjects, but the humor that results is never malicious. Warner rarely creates a character whom one dislikes intensely, although one may pity many of them who live lonely or otherwise circumscribed lives. Warner certainly knows her characters well; she knows what they think and the context in which they think, and only rarely does she strike a false note. These are characters who for the most part hold their emotions in check—as is proper for stories featuring so many middle-class English characters—but their inner lives carry subterranean force.

Warner also seems to relish creating the most authentic settings, as one can see in the infinite care with which the physical details and the atmosphere of the interior of an English church are evoked ("The Fifth of November") or in the way that every small element that goes into the making of a nosegay is carefully described ("The Nosegay"). Social settings are evoked with equal care. "A Love Match," for example, is a realistic portrayal of English village life and the changes it undergoes between the two world wars.

Warner's stories exhibit such a range of characters and plots that it would be a distortion to claim that she possesses any special concern with the lot of women. Women in her stories may sometimes be timid and long-suffering and lead restricted lives, but they can just as often be assertive, capable, and even overbearing. Warner's stories are told as often from the male point of view as from the female. The kind of female experience depicted in "A Widow's Quilt," however, is not untypical. Emma, who is married to dull, respectable, but self-involved Everard (the kind of boring husband who turns up with some frequency in Warner's fiction), is fascinated by a widow's quilt she sees in a museum. Told that they are made when a husband dies, she starts to make one herself. Fed up with the demands of looking after Everard, she finds in the quilt her "one assertion of a life of her own" and looks forward to the day when she will be able to sleep under it. Yet there is an ironic twist in this tale—a frequent device of Warner's. Running out of thread one day, Emma goes out in bad weather. On her return she has a heart attack and dies. Everard, of course, lives on. This quirk of fate is close to what Thomas Hardy, who was an early influence on Warner, called "time's laughingstocks." In Warner's universe, people often decline to die in the correct order or at the correct time—a device that gives punch to another story in this collection, "Their Quiet Lives."

Another story that shows a woman breaking free from the restrictions of an unsatisfying marriage is "But at the Stroke of Midnight." It is an ambitious although not entirely successful story in which the protagonist, according to Warner, "achieve[s] total innocence . . . only by going mad." Lucy Ridpath creates a new life for herself in London and for a while seems to have found a mysterious, almost spiritual power. As the title of the story suggests, however, her rebirth does not last, and the story ends with her death by drowning.

"A Love Match" is remarkable for its sympathetic portrayal of an incestuous relationship between a brother and sister. Justin Tizzard returns on leave to England after fighting in the Battle of the Somme in World War I. He stays with his sister Celia, whose fiancé was killed in the same battle. At night, Celia is horrified when she hears Justin, asleep in the adjoining room, babbling constantly, reliving the horrors of the war. On the third night, his cry awakens her, and without knowing what she is doing, she goes to his bed to comfort him. The combination of his distress and her compassion drives them to the physical act of love.

Five years after the war, they move to the small town of Hallowby, where they become respectable, rather dull citizens. Behind closed doors they delight in their success in hiding their secret. The years pass. Then, during an air raid in World War II, Hallowby is bombed. Rescue workers enter a bombed house and find that slates from the roof have fallen on the bed, crushing the bodies of Celia and Justin, who are still wrapped in each other's arms. One villager suggests that Justin must have gone into the bedroom to comfort her. The others concur, and the coroner accepts this hypothesis as truth.

Warner commented that the story was "a victory for incest and sanity," and throughout she brings out the naturalness of the relationship between Celia and Justin. They do not indulge in horrified soul-searching, but accept in a matter-of-fact way what to them seems right and inevitable. Warner emphasizes the ease with which they communicate with each other; having been brought up together with the same standards, and sharing the same memories, they feel no need to impress each other. It might perhaps be relevant to point out that Warner's own relationship with Valentine Ackland, which would have been regarded by many as illicit, may account at least in part for her unusual approach to her theme. Certainly, the love between Justin and Celia is a genuine and happy love, which none of the couples in the five stories that follow (or for that matter none of the characters in any other story in the book) enjoys.

John Updike once commented that Warner's stories "tend to convince us in process and baffle us in conclusion; they are not rounded with meaning but lift jaggedly toward new, unseen developments." This effect is in part achieved by sudden and unexpected switches in point of view. The reader is led in one direction and then is pulled rapidly in another. "Absolom, My Son," for example, focuses mostly on the frustrations of a writer, but the final scene leaves the reader contemplating not the inner life of the writer but that of his secretary. A similar device is used in "Fifth of November." Just when the reader is contemplating the shift in how Ellie, a middle-aged woman, perceives her ailing mother, the final paragraphs introduce a completely new character, the vicar of the church where Ellie has gone to pray, and the story ends with his reflections on his own attempt to engage her in conversation. As happens so often in Warner's stories, such seemingly inconsequential thoughts suggest something larger—the unseen delicate fabric of human intercourse, its small miscues and regrets that occupy the mind for a moment and then are gone.

Context

Like her own character Matthew Bateman, the writer in "Absolom, My Son," Warner was well known without ever being popular, despite the small and loyal following that she developed as a result of her *New Yorker* stories. Her influence, whether as novelist, poet, or short-story writer, has therefore been negligible, but it is doubtful whether this would have distressed her. She was not in her work a crusader for causes, and her comments about the nineteenth century novelist Elizabeth Gaskell might serve equally well to describe her own work: "She attacked no abuses, she preached no remedies, she supplied no answers, she barely questioned. She presented her characters and told their story."

On one occasion, however, Warner did comment on the place of women writers in society. That was in 1959, when she gave a Royal Society of Arts lecture on "Women as Writers." In that address, Warner made some tart observations about the alarm with which a woman writer is regarded in a patriarchal society, and she illustrated her comments with a number of historical examples that have since become a standard part of feminist arguments. Warner thought that to succeed as writers women must be "obstinate and sly," but she also remarked that it was easier for a woman to attain what she regarded as the writer's greatest virtue, self-effacement, in the sense that the reader does not feel the presence of the writer at all—a comment that does not apply to her own stories.

Sources for Further Study

Harmon, Claire. *Sylvia Townsend Warner: A Biography*. London: Chatto & Windus, 1989. A carefully researched, full-length biography that makes use of many unpublished sources, including Warner's diaries, which extended over a period of fifty years. Includes a complete bibliography of works by Warner.

Maxwell, William, ed. *Letters: Sylvia Townsend Warner*. London: Chatto & Windus, 1982. Includes hundreds of letters, covering the period from 1921 to 1978, many of them exhibiting the same literary qualities that illuminate Warner's stories. Warner offers a number of comments on her work, but unfortunately there is no subject index with which to locate them, although there is an index of recipients.

Mulford, Wendy. *This Narrow Place: Sylvia Townsend Warner and Valentine Ackland: Life, Letters, and Politics, 1930-1951*. London: Pandora Press, 1988. Focuses on the middle years of Warner's relationship with her lifelong friend Valentine Ackland, the period when they were most politically active. The emphasis is on Warner, the more successful writer, and on her novels rather than her poems or short stories.

Bryan Aubrey

SELECTED STORIES OF XIAO HONG

Author: Xiao Hong (Zhang Naiying, 1911-1942)
Type of work: Short stories
First published: 1982

Form and Content

Xiao Hong was one of the best writers in modern Chinese literature. Her short stories, which are related to her novels in theme, characterization, and style, are essential to understanding both Xiao Hong as a Chinese woman writer and her creative development. This collection contains nine of her most representative short stories arranged in chronological order.

"The Death of Wang Asao" was Xiao Hong's first attempt at fiction and was a collaboration with her common-law husband Xiao Jun. It actually appeared in their self-bound anthology of short stories and essays, *Trudging*, in 1933. The story is lyrical as well as class-conscious. It portrays the tragic death of Wang Asao under the cruelty of Landlord Zhang. Wang Asao has three children, but they all die. She adopts the homeless waif Little Huan as her daughter. Her husband, Big Brother Wang, is docked a year's pay by Landlord Zhang because the horse he is using to work for the landlord breaks its leg. He is driven crazy by anger and burns to death in a haystack fire set at the order of Landlord Zhang. Then the pregnant Wang Asao is kicked by Landlord Zhang and dies in childbirth. The story ends with Little Huan, again homeless, rolling on the ground and bawling like a baby. Despite their sympathy for the dead, the other farmhands never come to see the cause of their deaths, and they even praise Landlord Zhang for his compassion.

"The Bridge" (1936) shows Xiao Hong's unmistakable feminine style. Through poetic fluidity and musical refrains, Xiao Hong recaptures the tragic fate of a Chinese woman who is called by her husband's name, Huang Liang, adding the diminutive "zi." Huang Liangzi is married to a poor man and bears a child on the eastern side of the bridge, but she has to nurse a rich man's child on the western side of the bridge. The callings from the both sides torture her, split her personality, and confuse her mind. In the end, her own child falls from the bridge into the ditch and drowns. By using expressionistic images, the author subtly questions the inequality between the rich and poor without didacticism.

"Hands" (1936) is Xiao Hong's best-known story. The story reminds the reader of Jane Eyre's tough experience at boarding school. Its heroine, Wang Yaming, who comes from a family of dyers with blackened hands, is not rebellious, however, but all-forgiving and self-effacing. Although she is treated as a laughingstock by the headmistress as well as her classmates, is forced to sleep in the hallway, and is forbidden to join the morning drill, she accepts her fate bravely. By caricaturing Wang Yaming, the author skillfully satirizes elitist cruelty as well as the slavish mentality of its victims.

"On the Oxcart" (1937) is also one of Xiao Hong's best stories. The first-person narrator functions as a sympathetic listener. Through Aunt Wuyun's sad but touching tale, told in an oxcart on a peaceful ride in the country, the story indicts the evils of war, which not only make men desert their wives but also turn them into deserters who are fated to be executed.

"The Family Outsider" (1937) is an autobiographical tale. Although the seven-year-old narrator is the spoiled insider of the family, she forms an intimate tie with the family black sheep, Second Uncle Yu. Her honest voice constantly seduces the reader back to his or her own childhood.

"Flight from Danger" (1939) portrays a sham revolutionary called He Nansheng, who encourages his students and colleagues to resist the Japanese invasion while he himself flees with his family. The story shows the influence of Lu Xun and Lao She in probing the diseased psychology of its protagonist. The story was later developed into the comic novel *Mabole*.

"Vague Expectation" (1939) captures the maid Li Ma's love longings for Liu Lizhi, a bodyguard who joins the army to fight for the nation. It is the only tale in the collection that has an optimistic ending: In Li Ma's dream, Liu Lizhi wins the war and returns to marry her.

"North China," first published in a Hong Kong newspaper in 1941, is another story that studies the psychology of the Chinese during a national crisis. When Master Geng was young, he was enlightened and had even secretly joined Sun Yat-sen's Revolutionary Party; when his son Da Shaoye leaves home to fight the Japanese, however, he refuses to support him. Yet the son's departure makes his father start thinking. When the father finally becomes obsessed with fighting the Japanese by unceasingly writing to his lost son, his obsession is regarded by his wife and others as madness. He is shut in a garden shelter and is eventually asphyxiated by smoke from the burning charcoal.

"Spring in a Small Town" (1961) is an affectionate story about Jade, a girl who is killed by a feudal marriage. Like many young ladies, Jade loves to dress up and even dares to try fashionable high heels. When she is asked by her mother to marry a man she does not love, however, she dares not say no, and when she falls in love, she is unable to articulate her feelings. Jade pines away and eventually dies (although the man she loved does not even understand why). Apart from challenging feudal customs in this story, Xiao Hong is also concerned with the courage it takes for a woman to break her muteness and assert herself.

Analysis

Xiao Hong's short stories cover three major subjects: victimized Chinese women, class conflict, and anti-Japanese warfare. In six out of the nine stories, women are the protagonists. Xiao Hong's literary women, in the feudalistic context, have three major images: the unmitigated victim, the loving mother, and the mute daughter. Wang Asao's death during childbirth evokes pity because she was a loving mother who took in the little waif and cradled Big Brother Wang's bones when he was persecuted by the landlord and lost the sympathy of his fellow villagers. Huang Liangzi is also portrayed as a sacrificing mother whose love for children could even bridge the class gap momentarily. The helpless Wang Yaming has the responsibility to take care of her younger brothers and sisters as well as to pass on to them the lessons she has learned at school. These twin images of women help raise the unmitigated victim to the pedestal of a noble mother. The muted daughters in the stories show a progressive transformation. Jade dies tragically because of her muteness. Li Ma begins to fantasize her love with Jin Lizhi. Aunt Wuyun becomes a story weaver. The narrator in nearly all the stories is Xiao Hong herself. By orally weaving stories and by writing, a woman starts to assert herself gently.

Class consciousness pervades Xiao Hong's stories. Xiao Hong was born into a wealthy landlord family. She witnessed her father's cruelty toward the peasants. In "Wang Asao," peasants are helpless insects in the palm of Landlord Zhang. Yet Xiao Hong also portrays them as "class equals" who address one another as brothers and sisters. It is their blindness to the cause of their poverty rather than poverty itself that reduces them to unmitigated victims. In "The Bridge," Huang Liangzi's efforts to bridge the gap between the poor child and the rich child are destined to fail; the rich child is corrupted by his family, while the poor child attempts to cross the bridge to the world of the rich without any real footing. The red bridge only creates the illusion. In the story "Hands," Xiao Hong employs the laboring people's blackened but vital hands to lash at the elite education that is represented by the headmistress' "bloodless, fossil-like" hands. This elite education does not allow the poor or "the special" to disrupt its uniformity.

Xiao Hong's stories were written at a time of national crisis. From 1933 to 1940, she fled from the Japanese occupation of Manchuria to Shanghai, Chongqing, and finally to Hong Kong. Although she was physically weak, Xiao Hong used her pen to engage in the anti-Japanese war. Her first novel, *The Field of Life and Death* (1935), bears an anti-Japanese theme. "On the Oxcart" exposes the suffering inflicted on the peasants by the war. "Vague Expectations" reveals Xiao Hong's optimism about the outcome of the war: The Chinese had to win because losing "doesn't make any sense!" Xiao Hong was inclined, however, to deal with the problems of the Chinese rather than the atrocities of the Japanese aggressors. In "Flight from Danger," she probes the distorted minds of the sham revolutionaries. In "North China," she captures Master Geng's transformation in attitude from lack of support to obsession about anti-Japanese warfare. Master Geng is ridiculed because his anti-Japanese obsession is useless in front of the Japanese but exposes himself and others to danger. He is killed by those who do not appreciate his obsession, as well as by the obsession itself. Xiao Hong's satirical thrust is often double-edged.

Context

Unlike Chinese feminist writer Ding Ling, Xiao Hong seldom addresses gender issues. Although her autobiographical novels *Tales of Hulan River* and *Market Streets* reveal a feminist consciousness, her short stories mainly deal with the suffering of the victimized in society and the Chinese mentality during national crisis. Perhaps because of this broad perspective, in 1936 Lu Xun remarked that Xiao Hong "is the most promising of our women writers, and shows possibilities of becoming as much in advance of Miss Ting Ling as the latter was in succeeding Miss Bing Xin." Xiao Hong's special contribution to women's literature is her writing style. Her writing has two prominent features. First is her artistic use of autobiographical materials. Unlike her contemporaries, Xiao Hong was never obsessed with modern solipsism. In her writing, the narrator serves as an objective witness and a natural voice of history. She resists conventional characterization. Her characters, including the narrator, merge with place, rituals, customs, and everyday happenings. Although Xiao Hong was influenced by Agnes Smedley's autobiographical art in *The Daughter of Earth* and Upton Sinclair's social realistic representation in *The Jungle*, her writing remains distinctively Chinese. The second feature of her writing is a distinctively female style. Although Xiao Hong also wrote about class oppression and war, her style was different from those of the male writers of her time. Her style, as is shown in the story "Bridge" in this collection, is fluid and vocal, a style that anticipates that of the Brazilian woman writer Clarice Lispector.

Sources for Further Study

Chow, Rey. *Women and Chinese Modernity: The Politics of Reading Between West and East*. Minneapolis: University of Minnesota Press, 1991. A critical book that examines writing by male and female authors of the May Fourth period and after. The part concerning Xiao Hong analyzes the story "Hands" and its narrative techniques.

Gerstlacher, Anna, et al., eds. *Women and Literature in China*. Bochum, Germany: Studienverlag Brockmeyer, 1983. A collection of essays on Chinese women writers. Howard Goldblatt's "Life as Art: Xiao Hong and Autobiography" gives an informative analysis of Xiao Hong's use of autobiography in her *Market Street: A Chinese Woman in Harbin*.

Goldblatt, Howard. *Hsiao Hung*. Boston: Twayne, 1976. A comprehensive study of Xiao Hong's life and works. Includes a chronology and a selected bibliography.

Hsiao, Hung. *The Field of Life and Death and Tales of Hulan River*. Translated by Howard Goldblatt. Bloomington: Indiana University Press, 1979. Contains the two best novels by Xiao Hong. "Wang Asao" can be read as a prelude to *The Field of Life and Death*, and "The Family Outsider" was the basis for chapter 6 in *Tales of Hulan River*. Includes a good introduction by the translator.

Smedley, Agnes. *Battle Hymn of China*. New York: Alfred A. Knopf, 1943. The author recalls that Lu Xun personally recommended Xiao Hong's novel *The Field of Life and Death* to her "as one of the most powerful modern novels written by a Chinese woman."

Snow, Edgar, ed. *Living China: Modern Chinese Short Stories*. London: George G. Harrap, 1936. Appendix A is Nym Wales's article "The Modern Chinese Literary Movement," which discusses Xiao Hong and other modern Chinese writers and includes Lu Xun's comments on Xiao Hong.

Qingyun Wu

SENSE AND SENSIBILITY

Author: Jane Austen (1775-1817)
Type of work: Novel
Type of plot: Social realism
Time of plot: The early nineteenth century
Locale: Devonshire, England
First published: 1811

Principal characters:
  MRS. HENRY DASHWOOD, the widowed mother of Elinor,
    Marianne, and Margaret
  ELINOR DASHWOOD, a young woman of great sense and
    sensibility who is in love with the reticent Edward Ferrars
  MARIANNE DASHWOOD, Elinor's sister, who yearns for the
    intense but wayward John Willoughby
  EDWARD FERRARS, the modest and eldest son of a wealthy mother
  ROBERT FERRARS, Edward's pretentious younger brother and his
    mother's favorite
  JOHN WILLOUGHBY, a handsome and dashing rake
  COLONEL BRANDON, a young man in love with Marianne
  MRS. JENNINGS, a woman who befriends the Dashwoods
  LUCY STEELE, Edward Ferrars' fiancée

Form and Content

  Sense and Sensibility is Jane Austen's first published novel. It grew out of the sketch "Elinor and Marianne," which was written in the 1790's and was revised several times before its publication in 1811. The novel is written in the form of a comedy of manners, and in it the author satirizes the lifestyle of her characters with much humor and irony. Although it has a happy ending, *Sense and Sensibility* contains Jane Austen's usual hardheadedness, which makes her fiction powerfully realistic and timeless.

  The plot centers on Mrs. Henry Dashwood and her three daughters. Not much is said of Margaret, the youngest daughter. Elinor's and Marianne's trials as eligible young ladies are the focus of the story. Their mother, Mrs. Dashwood, has been left without much of an income, for her husband Henry has had only a life interest in his estate, which means that his wife must vacate it in favor of the new heir, her stepson, John Dashwood. On his deathbed, Henry Dashwood has made his son John promise to provide for Henry's wife and three daughters. Unfortunately, John's avaricious and insensitive wife, Fanny, convinces him that he has very little obligation to Mrs. Dashwood and her daughters, and that they can do well on their very small income. Consequently, Mrs. Dashwood has little choice but to accept the kind offer from a relative of a cottage in Devonshire, to which she moves with her three daughters.

It is difficult for Elinor to leave her family home, since she has fallen in love with the circumspect Edward Ferrars. He is a peculiar suitor, subdued and tentative, but Elinor appreciates his mild manner and modesty, and she is willing to have their courtship proceed at an even, if extremely slow, pace. Elinor understands that Edward's mother will probably oppose his marrying Elinor because Elinor does not have the great wealth or position that Edward's mother seeks in a bride for her son. To Marianne, this is provoking. Why should Elinor be content with such a hesitant lover? Why should she make excuses for Edward when Marianne attacks his want of spontaneity? To Marianne, he seems neither intense nor determined enough to seek Elinor's hand. She cannot understand why Edward is not forthright and why Elinor does not lose patience with him. Elinor finds, however, that Edward's quiet, sober demeanor is attractive; it indicates his seriousness and steadiness. She seems to sense that he feels more than he can say and that he is deliberately checking himself for reasons he cannot disclose or that he is behaving in accordance with his shy and retiring nature.

Marianne adapts quickly to Devonshire, where she begins to receive the attentions of the flamboyant John Willoughby. He seems to be everything that Edward Ferrars is not. Willoughby is Marianne's constant, entertaining companion, solicitous of her every mood. They become inseparable, and their friends and neighbors assume they are to be married, even though no engagement is announced, but Willoughby abruptly leaves Marianne and the Dashwood household, saying nothing about when he will return and leaving Marianne upset.

Marianne has spurned Elinor's advice to be prudent. Elinor believes that Marianne should not give her heart to Willoughby until he has made an outright declaration of his intentions. Marianne, however, accuses Elinor of coldness and criticizes the behavior of their new friend, Colonel Brandon, who has fallen in love with her, but who represents precisely the sort of staid manner that Marianne rejects. Colonel Brandon is several years older than Marianne, and, like Edward Ferrars, he seems to be entirely too cautious.

Elinor tries to caution Marianne even as she suffers anguish over the puzzling behavior of the uneasy Edward Ferrars, for he has not visited her at the Dashwoods' new cottage. Because of his long absence, Elinor begins to doubt his intention to marry her, even though she is still convinced that he loves her. Elinor receives another blow when Lucy Steele confides to her that she is secretly engaged to Edward. Lucy shares her news with Elinor in a taunting fashion designed to inflict the maximum amount of damage on Elinor's hopes. Neither woman, however, openly acknowledges that this is what Lucy is doing. Refusing to be provoked by Lucy, who suspects Edward of an attachment to Elinor, Elinor calmly, if painfully, negotiates the hazards of both Marianne's and her own affair, hiding her heartache from her sister and the rest of the family.

The lives of both Elinor and Marianne seem devastated when Willoughby drops Marianne and marries a wealthy woman, and when Edward's secret engagement to Lucy is revealed to his mother by Lucy's sister. All seems spoiled as Marianne falls victim to a dreadful fever and seems to be about to succumb to a wasting disease. She rallies, however, and gradually gathers strength by realizing how foolish she has been to ignore the obvious signs of Willoughby's perfidy and Elinor's patient, wise counsel. Still, Elinor's own lives seems to be blighted when a servant announces the marriage of Edward and Lucy. This turns out to be a false alarm, however, for Edward appears to make an even more startling announcement. Lucy has married his younger brother Robert, leaving Edward free to marry Elinor.

Marianne slowly recovers, bolstered by Elinor's report that Willoughby has visited to confess that he did actually love Marianne but foolishly abandoned her because he could not overcome a life of dissipated habits. She now realizes that she could never have been happy with him, and she accepts the suit of Colonel Brandon, who has acted as her family's benefactor throughout their long ordeal.

Analysis

The plot of *Sense and Sensibility* is a conventional one for its time. It raises a conflict in love that is typical of the comedy of manners, and it resolves the anxieties of its heroines in a pleasing, if unremarkable, way. It is clear from the outset that the novel will focus on the education of Marianne's sensibility. She must learn through suffering that the decorum of polite society, which she despises, has been designed to channel and discipline human feeling. To Marianne, this decorum seems cold. She rejects it in the figure of Colonel Brandon, although she eventually learns that his own sobriety is largely the result of his earlier disappointment in love. Elinor is the key to Marianne's reformation, for she shows that to behave with decorum is not tantamount to behaving in a cold and unimaginative manner. She feels things as strongly as Marianne does, but Elinor realizes that simply giving vent to feeling destroys sense. In other words, the emotions and the intellect must be kept in exquisite balance. Thus, *Sense and Sensibility* is a comedy of manners not merely because it contains many amusing scenes but also because it is centered on a plot that resolves itself through an understanding of societal manners and how they have been developed to ensure a happy ending for human lives.

Although *Sense and Sensibility* lacks the full maturity of Jane Austen's later novels, its prose style, wit, and characterization reflect her genius for precision and balance. Although Elinor, for example, is the sensible sister, she is neither humorless nor callous. She loves Edward Ferrars very much, yet she realizes that her position is fragile and that his own is precarious. Elinor must bide her time, learn what she can from Lucy Steele, and hope that her judgment of Edward has not been wrong. Above all, Elinor is interesting because her assessment of human character is so shrewd, yet she does not presume to think that she can know all the factors that have gone into Edward's perplexing behavior.

Marianne, however, believes that she should be forthright, that Elinor's demeanor is altogether too placid and her behavior too oblique. She mistakes her sister's self-control for complacency. She does not guess how much Elinor has been hurt by Edward's failure to propose marriage. Marianne takes Willoughby to be a character much like herself, and she will not countenance the idea that he might be playing with her. The irony is that she rejects Colonel Brandon, although his own history is one of disappointed love, and he is in the best position to understand how devastating Willoughby's rejection of Marianne will be.

Elinor and Marianne, representing such different sensibilities, should be at odds. That they are not is largely because of the way in which Jane Austen has handled Elinor, who quickly realizes that it would be folly to interfere actively in the concerns of her headstrong younger sister. Instead, Elinor commits herself to carefully watching Marianne and offering her point of view only when Marianne is disposed to accept it or calls for it in conversation. This characterization of Elinor is crucial to the novel, for it allows Marianne room to analyze her faults without Elinor's having attacked her.

No analysis of a Jane Austen novel would be complete without some discussion of her extraordinary style. There is, for example, the famous scene between John Dashwood and his wife Fanny. John is discussing his promise to his father to look after his stepmother and her daughters. He is trying to settle on a sum that would make them comfortable. Each figure he proposes is whittled down by his wife, who insinuates that John should not overreact to his father's deathbed request, that his father could not have meant John to give so much of his own fortune away, and that John should remember that his own children might very well miss the amount he is proposing to settle on Mrs. Dashwood, Elinor, Marianne, and Margaret. Soon enough, Fanny has reduced the figure to nothing. Yet this process of depriving the Dashwoods of their due is done in the most rational tone, as if Fanny is speaking not from avariciousness but from prudence. Her husband John responds to her in the most mild and thoughtful way, as though she has done no more than help him in managing his responsibilities rather than, as is the case, totally abandoning them. There is no better example of the way in which Jane Austen uses irony, so that the characters say one thing but mean another, imagining they are behaving decently when in fact they are behaving like beasts. Moreover, the whole scene is managed without any authorial intervention. These characters convict themselves.

Context

Jane Austen is the first great female English novelist and has been acknowledged as such in countless articles and books. An avid reader, she built on the tradition created by Samuel Richardson (1689-1761), whose novels *Pamela* (1740) and *Clarissa* (1747-1748) focus on female characters with their own distinct problems and sensibilities, and also on the work of earlier female novelists such as Fanny Burney (1752-1840), who perfected the novel of manners. Jane Austen went beyond these authors, however, in giving her female characters a new level of maturity and self-awareness. They are sharper and shrewder, more prone to criticize society even as they uphold its basic values.

Jane Austen's style has been the model for countless writers, male and female. In recent years, her complex vision of society has been increasingly appreciated. Her earliest critics thought of her as modest, a miniaturist of society who did not deal with the large issues that concern male novelists such as Sir Walter Scott (1771-1832), William Thackeray (1811-1863), or Charles Dickens (1812-1870). This view, however, has been challenged by later critics, many of them female, who see her as being much more actively involved with broader social issues—even if the social contexts of her novels seem narrow. Her recent biographers have abetted this critical trend, showing how acute Austen could be on the issues of her day and how political her sensibility and style actually are.

Sources for Further Study
Fergus, Jan. *Jane Austen and the Didactic Novel: "Northanger Abbey," "Sense and Sensibility," and "Pride and Prejudice."* Totowa, N.J.: Barnes & Noble Books, 1983. Very good on Austen's style and in situating her early novels in the tradition of eighteenth and early nineteenth century English fiction.

Honan, Park. *Jane Austen: Her Life.* London: Weidenfeld & Nicholson, 1987. Considered the standard biography, Honan's work carefully explains the context of Austen's novels, including a detailed discussion of the development of *Sense and Sensibility* through several drafts.

Ruoff, Gene W. *Jane Austen's Sense and Sensibility.* New York: St. Martin's Press, 1992. Chapters on the historical and cultural context, critical reception of the text, theoretical perspectives, and a detailed interpretation of the novel, including a section on "women's lives and men's stories." A selected bibliography and index make this an especially useful and up-to-date study.

Southam, B. C., ed. *Jane Austen: "Sense and Sensibility," "Pride and Prejudice," and "Mansfield Park," a Casebook.* London: Macmillan, 1976. Collects the most important criticism on Austen's early novels.

Tanner, Tony. Introduction to *Sense and Sensibility.* Baltimore, Md.: Penguin Books, 1969. Tanner offers an important introduction to the novel, as well as valuable notes.

Carl Rollyson

SERIOUS MONEY
A City Comedy

Author: Caryl Churchill (1938-   )
Type of work: Drama
Type of plot: Comedy
Time of plot: The late 1980's
Locale: London and New York
First produced: 1987, at the Royal Court Theatre, London, England
First published: 1987

Principal characters:
SCILLA TODD, a futures exchange dealer
JAKE TODD, Scilla's brother and her conduit for insider
    information to a worldwide network
"ZAC" ZACKERMAN, an American banker
GREVILLE TODD, the father of Jake and Scilla, a stockbroker
MARYLOU BAINES, an American arbitrageur
JACINTA CONDOR, a Peruvian businesswoman
BILLY CORMAN, a corporate raider
DUCKETT, the chair of Albion, a company which Corman is
    trying to buy

Form and Content

Churchill subtitles *Serious Money* "a city comedy" and introduces the play with a scene from Thomas Shadwell's 1692 play *The Volunteers: Or, The Stockjobbers.* Thus, she deliberately places her play in the tradition of satiric city comedies such as Ben Jonson's *Volpone*, dating back to the early seventeenth century.

The scene from Shadwell's play depicts Hackwell, Mrs. Hackwell, and two jobbers debating the usefulness of various patents, with Hackwell repeating his assertion that the only use of any patent is "to turn the penny." This sets up Churchill's major assertion—that money and greed are the only motivation in this world of jobbers and dealers.

Although Churchill lists twenty characters in her *dramatis personae*, in a real sense the major character of *Serious Money* is "the City," an international financial center inside the old city of London. The first scene following the Shadwell introduction shows three different dealing rooms in the City that clearly illustrate the effects of the "Big Bang," a change in the mode of operations for British stockbrokers that introduced an open computerized trading system and replaced the upper class "old boy" network. The rooms, each dominated by one of the Todds, presents a realistic picture of the traders, based on Churchill's extensive research, yet the style of presentation uses the Brechtian alienation effect, presenting familiar situations in a way that renders them strange.

The world of the City revolves around deals, and the plot of the play concerns Billy Corman's attempt to take over the symbolically named Albion (England). The banker "Zac" Zackerman is responsible for orchestrating the deal; he also comments on the situation, providing a history of changes in the financial world that Britain is just beginning to feel and noting that "the British empire was a cartel" but that those days are past.

A short hunt scene shows the upper class to be out of touch with reality and Zac unable to function in their world—something that no longer matters. Frosby, a jobber of Greville Todd's generation, ends this scene with a monologue lamenting stock market change and his own worthlessness, then decides to revenge himself by telling the regulatory DTI about Jake's insider dealings.

In the following scene, Zac informs Marylou Baines of Jake's death, but the news has little effect on business or the takeover bid. Scilla, who, in a flashback, discusses Jake's problems with him, is certain that he is no suicide, and she begins confronting his contacts—at first hoping to discover his murderer, but, after learning about his wealth, shifting to a search for it.

The takeover bid involves Jacinta Condor and Nigel Abjibala, who prove that representatives of the Third World are as single-mindedly greedy as their British and American counterparts; a "white knight," Ms. Biddulph, intent on "saving" Albion for her own reasons; and an intervention by Gleason, a cabinet minister, who persuades Corman to drop his takeover bid on the eve of the election to help the image of the conservative government. The loose ends of the plot are resolved in Brechtian fashion at the end by Zac's long monologue and each character's one-line summary of his or her fate. (For example, Scilla is "named by Business Week as Wall Street's rising star," and Jacinta "marries Zac next week and they honeymoon in Shanghai. [Good business to be done in China now.]") The finale is a song celebrating the reelection of the conservative government for "five more glorious years."

Analysis

Churchill's central intent in *Serious Money* is to satirize the world of the City, which may be seen as a microcosm of capitalistic society in the late twentieth century. She is concerned about the emphasis on the egoistic needs of the individual, which are satisfied at the expense of the common good. In this world, choices are made as a response to fear and greed. The considerable energy and intelligence of the traders is misplaced; they strive for personal success, but even when they achieve it, they are as much oppressed by the system as are its more obvious victims.

Churchill's use of verse dialogue conveys this, the rigid form restricting the actors, channeling their energy in the same way that the market restricts and channels the traders. The use of prose interludes (for example, Frosby's confession to the audience that, as he is about to get his revenge on Jake, he is frightened; Jake's admission to Scilla that he is in trouble with the DTI) heighten the effect of the verse. More than one critic credits the verse with augmenting the driving pace of the play, which is suitable for representing the hectic life of the City.

Churchill wants the audience to observe this world but not to sympathize with it or with the characters in it. To accomplish this distancing, she turns to a variety of devices associated with the alienation effect of German playwright Bertolt Brecht. Her characters are two-dimensional and neither demonstrate nor elicit empathy. They do not listen to one another; dialogue often overlaps, and in the hunt scene, aristocrats repeat phrases that have no meaning in the current context.

This effect is strongest in the reaction to Jake's death. His contacts are concerned about what he might have revealed, but they see his death as no obstacle to continuing business as usual, taking the same risks that have led to Jake's death. Scilla's concern that Jake has been murdered seems at first to indicate that she has some feeling for her brother, but as soon as she learns about his "serious money," greed becomes her sole motivation.

The structure of the play is episodic, and it uses a number of flashbacks. The most startling of these involve Jake's appearance after his death has been announced. A number of long presentational speeches, with the actor addressing the audience directly, also interrupt the narrative flow. Examples include Zac's speech on the changes in the financial world; Frosby's angry lament on the changes, which have shut him out of the game; and Scilla's explanation of trading futures. All these speeches provide helpful exposition, but they also interrupt the pace of the play and force the audience to listen to complex information delivered from different points of view.

The world of high-stakes finance is in itself a strange world for an ordinary theater audience. Churchill and her colleagues at the Royal Court Theatre thoroughly familiarized themselves with this world during the workshop period set up by director Max Stafford-Clark—visiting the markets, observing proceedings on the floor, then visiting embassies of countries whose commodities were being sold. When the workshop ended, Churchill continued her research, reading the daily news stories about takeovers and insider scandals that followed the Big Bang. She re-creates the world quite accurately, but the effect of the fast pace and the specialized language is often to alienate the spectator, who has not participated in this immersion. (By contrast, the traders who flocked to see the play enjoyed the re-creation of their world, even if they did not understand the satire.)

The dialogue of the play is filled with images of war and trading. These can be threatening or quite funny. The most humorous use of this imagery occurs in the love scene between Zac and Jacinta and is crucial in "making strange" this potentially ordinary scene. Jacinta compares her attraction to Zac to her attraction to Eurobonds; he finds her as fascinating as a changing interest rate. Yet even matters of love and sex yield to the real business of the financial world, for when Zac and Jacinta can finally fit a romantic interlude into their hectic schedules, they are so tired that they decide to sleep instead.

Churchill follows Brecht in using music to underscore her satire. Rock songs end each act; act 1 has a song celebrating the glory of futures (with appropriately scatological lyrics), while the song at the end of act 2 is ecstatic at the prospect of "five more glorious years" of "promiscuous" money-making, following the reelection of

2044 *Masterplots II*

the conservative government.

Churchill would not be happier, however, with the election of a labour government or a return to the "good old days" before the Big Bang. The older generation may have had more "class," more surface civility, but they were no less greedy, no less brutal to the human community at large. There is no sign of hope in this play. Men—and women—repeat the same mistakes on an ever-larger scale, even in the Third World. Only a restructuring—perhaps the development of a new social, moral, and political order—might change this. Yet this is not a change that Churchill sees coming soon.

Context

While feminists acknowledge Churchill's importance as a major dramatist, they have often been uneasy about what some have seen as her ambivalent attitude toward feminism. It is not difficult to see the reason for this. Churchill does not write from a simple position, and her female characters are not necessarily positive.

In *Serious Money*, many of the characters are women, and they have "made it." Marylou Baines controls much of the action and runs for president of the United States. Scilla Todd becomes "Wall Street's rising star." Jacinta Condor gains tremendous financial advantage. Yet their success comes at a huge price: Marylou betrays her colleagues; Scilla forgets her brother's cause; Jacinta betrays her country and its needy people. The women have become indistinguishable from the men in power. They know that the financial world is sexist, but they all accept the humiliation that is part of their initiation into this world. They adapt to the male model, and when they lead, they are as ruthless as the men. It is no coincidence that the ultimate insult among the traders, "You trade like a cunt," is accepted and used by both men and women.

The behavior of her women characters reinforces Churchill's insistence on feminism and socialism as necessarily inseparable. To escape the general oppression of the City, the system must be changed. Putting women in power positions in the old system is not enough.

However ambivalent some feminists may be about Churchill's feminism, she is widely recognized for her important contributions to socialist feminism and to the feminist theater since the 1970's. The broad appeal of *Serious Money*, which reached a wide spectrum of people, including the traders she was satirizing, assures that Churchill will be a force to be reckoned with in British theater—a strong female voice.

Sources for Further Study

Churchill, Caryl. "The Common Imagination and the Individual Voice." Interview by Geraldine Cousin. *New Theatre Quarterly* 4, no. 13 (1988): 3-16. An interview in which Churchill discusses her feminism, her use of collaborative workshops, the Joint Stock Company, and the writing of *Serious Money*, noting that most of the play was written in prose before she turned to poetry.

Cousin, Geraldine. *Churchill: The Playwright*. London: Methuen Drama, 1989. Contains information of Churchill's use of the workshop process, an analysis of her plays, and a summary chapter that attempts to connect shared themes in her work.

A section of *Serious Money* discusses the workshop at the Royal Court Theatre from which Churchill got the impetus to write the play. Illustrations include a photograph from the original Royal Court Theatre production of *Serious Money*.

Fitzsimmons, Linda. *File on Churchill*. London: Methuen Drama, 1989. Contains a general introduction and a brief chronology. A comprehensive listing of plays includes unperformed ones plus a selection of reviews and Churchill's comments on her work—excerpts from interviews on *Serious Money* among them. The bibliography lists selected play collections, essays, interviews, and secondary sources.

Kritzer, Amelia Howe. *The Plays of Caryl Churchill: Theatre of Empowerment*. New York: St. Martin's Press, 1991. Written from a feminist perspective, this book opens with an overview of theories of theater and drama and of feminist and socialist criticism in relation to Churchill's drama. The chapter "Labour and Capital" analyzes *Top Girls*, *Fen*, and *Serious Money* as characteristic of Churchill's concern about the socioeconomic effects of Margaret Thatcher's government and its policies.

Muller, Klaus Peter. "A Serious City Comedy: Fe-/Male History and Value Judgments in Caryl Churchill's *Serious Money*." *Modern Drama* 33 (September, 1990): 347-362. An analysis of *Serious Money* as a "city comedy," this article provides a history of the genre and its relationship to comedy and satire, then places the play in this context, analyzing Churchill's use of the traditional form and detailing how she goes beyond it.

Randall, Phyllis R., ed. *Caryl Churchill: A Casebook*. New York: Garland, 1988. This casebook features a variety of essays. The essay on *Serious Money* reflects on the popularity of the play's first production. Includes an annotated bibliography of secondary sources.

Elsie Galbreath Haley

SEVEN GOTHIC TALES

Author: Isak Dinesen (Baroness Karen Blixen-Finecke, 1885-1962)
Type of work: Short stories
First published: 1934

Form and Content

Karen Blixen had been working on the stories that make up *Seven Gothic Tales* for ten years before she tried to get them published in English under the masculine name Isak Dinesen. After being turned down by three publishers, she sent the manuscript to American writer Dorothy Canfield Fisher, who liked it so much that she urged a publisher friend of hers to publish it, even though no one really believed that it would make any money. When the book appeared in January of 1933, however, it was not only enthusiastically received by critics but also was chosen as a main selection of the Book-of-the-Month-Club and eagerly snapped up by readers.

The title of the collection is in some ways a misnomer, for there are many more tales here than seven; Dinesen, like the medieval and romantic storytellers from whom she draws her inspiration, often makes use of the insert tale; thus, her stories contain tales within tales within tales. Dinesen's plots are often so complex that they are difficult to describe briefly, but since plot is so important in the gothic romance in general and in Dinesen's stories in particular, a short summary of some of the stories is necessary to give some idea of their thematic implications.

The first story in the American edition of *Seven Gothic Tales*, "The Deluge at Norderney," has been called one of Dinesen's most characteristic tales because it contains so many of her typical themes and motifs. The story takes place in 1835 when a great storm strikes a summer resort on the coast of Denmark. A famous cardinal, Hamilcar von Sehestedt, is trapped in a farmhouse with three others awaiting rescue: the eccentric Miss Malin Nat-og-Dag; her companion, the young Countess Calypso; and a young man. In the tradition of Boccaccio's *Decameron*, the four tell stories while they wait. Discovering a spiritual union as a result of their stories, the two young people are joined in marriage by the cardinal, who then reveals that he is not the cardinal but Kasperson, the cardinal's secretary, a former actor. Miss Malin "marries" him in a spiritual union just before the water reaches them.

"The Old Chevalier" is a story told by a Danish nobleman, Baron von Brackel, about his adventure one wintry night in Paris in 1874 when his mistress tries to poison him. Escaping into the night, he encounters a young girl and takes her to his apartment. Although their lovemaking is idyllic, on awakening the Baron asks what he must pay for the experience. When the girl asks for twenty francs, the ideal of the night before becomes the cold reality of daylight. "The Monkey" is a supernatural story in which the prioress of a secular convent tries to get her young nephew, Boris, who has been involved in a homosexual scandal in his regiment, married to Athena, the gigantic daughter of a count. The young woman refuses to marry Boris until, following her to her room one night, he forces her to kiss him—an attack that takes on all the implications of a rape in the light of the following day. The climactic scene occurs when the prioress' pet monkey jumps on her and tears off her cap, revealing that she is the monkey disguised as the prioress, whereas the monkey is really the true prioress of the cloister.

"Supper at Elsinore" focuses on two sisters who, after the disappearance of their brother, remain unmarried. When the ghost of the brother appears when they are in their fifties and tells them of his adventurous life as a pirate who has had five different wives, they must confront the ghostliness of their own lives. "The Dreamers" is about the greatest opera singer of all time, Pellegrina Leoni, who loses her voice in a theater fire and takes up a life of wandering under various disguises. Three men tell stories of their encounters with three beautiful women, only to discover that all three were Pellegrina. Pursued by the men, Pellegrina jumps over a precipice and dies.

Analysis

The word "gothic" in the title does not refer primarily to the medieval gothic tradition, but to its Romantic revival in the late eighteenth and early nineteenth centuries, specifically identified in the imagination of Isak Dinesen with Horace Walpole, the author of the gothic novel *The Castle of Otranto*, and Lord Byron, the great Romantic poet. Seeing this period as the "last great phase of aristocratic culture," Dinesen has said that she set her tales in the past because it was a finished world, a world that she could easily recompound in her own imagination and one in which her readers would not be tempted to look for realism. As is typical of the gothic romance form, the characters in these stories are less realistic individuals than they are representatives of basic human desires and fears.

Indeed, it is the romance form of Dinesen's stories that has always drawn readers to them, not the romance associated with the cheap gothic thriller of the romantic melodrama, but the romance of the nineteenth century decadence of Charles Baudelaire and Joris-Karl Huysmans. Dinesen has often been compared with Scheherazade, the mother of all storytellers in *The Arabian Nights*, because of her fantastic plots and inset stories; but she has also been compared to Henry James for her psychological insight and her careful use of language.

Isak Dinesen is not a feminist writer in any contemporary sense of the word, for the women in her stories are not individuals coping with isolation and attempting integration into a social world that has excluded them. In fact, most of the women in Dinesen's stories fall into either one or the other of the most common and most maligned stereotypes that have plagued women throughout history; they are either masculine ideals of feminine beauty and innocence or masculine scapegoats representing female viciousness and evil—devil or angel, maiden or witch. The strongest women in Dinesen's stories are giantesses, such as Athena in "The Monkey," or murderesses, such as the mistress in "The Old Chevalier." In fact, in the latter story, Dinesen suggests that there is some relationship between the murderousness of the mistress and the facts that she is highly intelligent, that she competes with men, and that she is an "emancipated woman."

Dinesen's stories are not about time-bound social issues, but about timeless universal desires. The one-night relationship of Baron von Brackel and the young woman he meets on the street in "The Old Chevalier" represents a basic human yearning for the actualization of the ideal. "The Monkey" is an allegorical tale about the split between human spirituality and physicality. The sisters' desire for their brother in "Supper at Elsinore" is not a realistic treatment of incest, but a romantic and symbolic embodiment of narcissism and idealism.

Dinesen's stories can only be understood in terms of the Kantian philosophic foundation that underlies and informs them. Her aesthetic point of view affirms that art is more real than everyday reality, that identity is never absolute but always shifting, that life is like a marionette theater in which people live in plots determined by God, and that the quest for the ideal is the inevitable heroic gesture that must end in inevitable tragicomic conclusion. What readers looking for realism have criticized as Dinesen's focus on aristocratic decadence and sexual perversion is but the means by which Dinesen explores basic human desire.

It is for these philosophic reasons that Dinesen's stories are often about fiction making and storytelling. In following her fantastic stories within stories, the reader becomes increasingly cut off from ordinary reality, entering into a world of pure creation and imagination. Dinesen's gothic tales are the stuff that dreams are made on—not dreams that allow escape from reality, but those that plunge one deeper into the very heart of darkness that is the human psyche.

Context

Isak Dinesen's impact on women's literature does not result from the themes or characters of her stories in *Seven Gothic Tales*, but from her position as a role model for the modern woman who is making it on her own. The image of strong individualism she communicates in *Out of Africa* (1937), in which she tells her own story of her life on the dark continent running her own coffee plantation and then later returning to Denmark to make an international reputation for herself as an author, has been the source of inspiration for many women.

Isak Dinesen is probably the most influential champion in the twentieth century of the primitive power of story. In one of her tales, a cardinal tells a penitent, "Stories have been told as long as speech has existed, and sans stories the human race would have perished, as it would have perished without water." Because of the fantastic, romantic nature of her stories and the elegant, aristocratic stature of Dinesen herself, she has become almost an iconic image of the archetypal storyteller—a wise elfin creature, more than a little witchlike, who has the magical ability to create self-sustaining worlds that, even as they strike the reader with their strangeness, evoke some deep sense of recognition of the mysteries that lie at the heart of human existence.

Sources for Further Study
Green, Howard. "Isak Dinesen." In *Isak Dinesen, Storyteller*, edited by Aage Jorgen-

sen. Århus, Denmark: Akademisk Boghandel, 1972. Argues that Dinesen's stories create a world whose unfamiliar atmosphere appeals to the most primitive human need for story. Beneath the mask of timelessness, however, there is a modern combination of irony and deliberate obscurity.

Hannah, Donald. *"Isak Dinesen" and Karen Blixen: The Mask and the Reality.* London: Putnam, 1971. Particularly valuable in charting the development of Dinesen's aesthetic—especially her emphasis on the nature of story and her mask-like impersonality. The second half of the book focuses on the general characteristics of her stories and analyzes several of the most important.

Henriksen, Aage. "The Empty Space Between Art and Church." In *Out of Denmark*, edited by Bodil Warmberg. Copenhagen: Danish Cultural Institute, 1985. Henriksen says that the underlying principle of Dinesen's tales is the transformation of reality into a dream and that all of her stories are based on the complicated nature of human love.

Johannesson, Eric O. *The World of Isak Dinesen.* Seattle: University of Washington Press, 1961. An extended analysis of Dinesen's art, focusing primarily on the pervasive theme of the art of storytelling. Johannesson discusses Dinesen's treatment of characters as marionettes, her focus on epiphanies, her use of the oral tradition, her metaphoric style, and her theatricality and humor.

Langbaum, Robert. *The Gayety of Vision: A Study of Isak Dinesen's Art.* New York: Random House, 1964. The most thorough and profound study of Dinesen's imaginative vision. Langbaum shows how her fiction deals with a psychology deeper than that of the novel, a psychology on the level of myth. Argues that "The Roads Around Pisa" is central to understanding Dinesen's art, especially her insistence that one does not get at truth except by artifice and tradition. Claims that "The Deluge at Norderney" is Dinesen's supreme achievement in tragicomedy, combining the greatest number of her characteristic themes.

Thurman, Judith. *Isak Dinesen: The Life of a Storyteller.* New York: St. Martin's Press, 1982. The most detailed and factual biography of Dinesen, the first to make use of many letters and unpublished documents in Dinesen's archives. Contains helpful comments on the sources of the tales and the history of their creation.

Walter, Eugene. "Isak Dinesen." In *Isak Dinesen, Storyteller*, edited by Aage Jorgensen. Århus, Denmark: Akademisk Boghandel, 1972. An interview originally published in *The Paris Review* in which Dinesen recounts how she began writing, tells of her joy in humor, and startles her interviewer by saying she is three thousand years old and has dined with Socrates.

Whissen, Thomas R. *Isak Dinesen's Aesthetics.* Port Washington, N.Y.: Kennikat Press, 1973. A discussion of Dinesen's aesthetic theory, this book is ordered according to the process of artistic creation: from inspiration, through embodiment, to reception. Whissen discusses the importance to Dinesen's aesthetic of the notions of masquerade, pride, and loneliness and the devices of romance, tragedy, and comedy.

Charles E. May

A SEVERED HEAD

Author: Iris Murdoch (1919-   )
Type of work: Novel
Type of plot: Farce
Time of plot: The late 1950's
Locale: London
First published: 1961

> *Principal characters:*
> MARTIN LYNCH-GIBBON, a morose and reclusive cynic
> ANTONIA LYNCH-GIBBON, his wife, a society woman of
>   well-connected family
> GEORGIE HANDS, Martin's mistress, a lecturer at the London
>   School of Economics
> PALMER ANDERSON, Martin's best friend, a psychiatrist who is
>   currently "treating" Antonia
> HONOR KLEIN, Palmer Anderson's half sister
> ALEXANDER LYNCH-GIBBON, Martin's older brother, a sculptor

Form and Content

Events contradict the story that Martin tells in *A Severed Head*, while the plot's old fashioned comic turns have him stumbling from one revelation to another. Martin not only mistakes the motives of the people dear to him but also mistakes his own. His love of wife and mistress that he parades so proudly at the start of the novel is eventually exposed as love for mother and child substitutes. As his assumptions are shattered, Martin gradually loses control of himself; he drinks more and more, becoming violent, sick, and irrational. Yet he begins to listen to his submerged psyche, which leads him to have a different perception of the world. The fact that Martin cannot understand the women he loves gives the novel a distinctive feminist twist. Feminist critics have observed that authors often use male narrators to give their narratives a sense of authority. Martin's authority, however, is in question from the second chapter on, and this irony exposes some stock cultural assumptions about women and erotic experience as he loses first Antonia, and then Georgie.

Stylistically, the novel is pure Murdoch, involving a realistic and detailed attention to appearances, clothes, weather, and interiors, combined with characters who seem to be driven by dark forces beyond their control. At the beginning of the novel, Martin, full of smug self-satisfaction, returns home from a visit to his mistress, Georgie Hands. His wife soon returns from what he thought was a "session" with psychiatrist Palmer Anderson to announce that she wants a divorce so that she can marry Palmer. She and Palmer, however, want an understanding with Martin so that they can continue to maintain their long friendship—essentially, so that they do not have to feel guilty. In some way, this request renders Martin powerless, and he assumes the role of an understanding, forgiving husband, but he is now suddenly ambivalent about his mistress.

Martin first meets Honor Klein when he does Palmer the favor of picking her up at the train station, and although he conceives an instant dislike for her, he senses some of her power. Meanwhile, Martin dutifully abets the relationship between his wife and best friend, even to the extent of bringing them wine in bed. One night, while quite drunk and storing some wine at Palmer's request, Martin is discovered in Palmer's wine cellar by Honor. She goads him about Palmer and Antonia upstairs, and he responds by forcing her to the floor and beating her about the head. Later, when he recovers from his drinking bout, Martin writes a letter of apology, then realizes he is desperately, painfully, in love with Honor. When he tries to call her, he learns that she has returned to Cambridge; transfixed with emotion, he follows her. When he arrives at her house in Cambridge to declare his love, he finds Honor in bed with her half brother, Palmer.

Now that Martin knows Palmer's guilty secret, he is restored to power. Antonia, sensing a change in Palmer, returns to Martin, who is still hopelessly in love with Honor. Palmer pursues Antonia, and when he tries to force her to return, Martin punches him, again gaining power. Martin is soon confronted with another confession: Antonia has had a long-standing love affair with his brother, Alexander, and now intends to live with him. This revelation finally opens Martin's eyes, and he sees that his whole life has been based on self-delusion.

Matters come to a head when Martin waits at the airport watching Palmer and Honor leave for America, and finds that they are taking Georgie Hands, who has become Palmer's patient, with them. Martin returns to his flat to brood, and in a final reversal of plot, Honor shows up and announces that Palmer and Georgie have gone to America without her. Although she promises nothing, she offers Martin a chance to pursue his love. Martin has suffered great pain, but he begins to understand himself. Humbly, he accepts her offer. He has grown up.

Analysis

Murdoch's primary concern in many of her novels is the problem of living a moral life, which may be seen as a progressive discarding of the false "good" in favor of truth. Eros, or sexual love, is closely connected to this idea of moral change, and the power of transformed sexual energy is used as a major motif in *A Severed Head*. The novel has certain echoes of Restoration comedy in being overplotted, dazzling, witty, and in the way it illustrates that love is war and power play.

The theme of severed heads is brought out in Alexander's sculpted busts, the decapitated appearance of Honor when she leans out of Martin's car window, and Honor's keynote speech, which alludes to her sibling incest: ". . . because of what you saw, I am a terrible object of fascination for you. I am a severed head such as primitive tribes and old alchemists used to use. . . . And who knows but that long acquaintance with a severed head might lead to strange knowledge." This carefully worked out theme links knowledge with a kind of power, especially the secret knowledge that comes of indulging in forbidden acts such as incest. The plot is driven by Martin's increasing knowledge, and most of the revelations involve incestuous or symbolically incestuous relationships. Martin's need to keep a child-mistress whom he can dominate, Palmer and Honor's affair, and Martin and Antonia's marriage, with its overtones of mother-son dependence, are all variations on this theme. Even the affair of Antonia and Alexander has semi-incestuous overtones, for Antonia has sex with both her husband and her brother-in-law during the eleven years of her marriage.

One of the most frequently recurring patterns in the structure of Murdoch's early novels is that of the self-deceived male protagonist who undergoes a series of painful learning experiences that force him to confront other people's reality. Initially, Martin sees other people only as extensions of his own wishes, a tendency hilariously brought out as he travels to Cambridge to throw himself at the feet of his beloved, Honor. He knows very little about her but speculates that she is probably unattached and perhaps a virgin. When he finds that she is engaged in an incestuous affair with Palmer, Martin begins to understand the separate reality of others. More important, the balance of power between the men shifts, and shortly afterward Martin is able to knock Palmer to the floor, something he has wanted to do from the beginning. Once again, knowledge is power. Honor fits neatly into the pantheon of Murdoch's "power figures, " even though they are usually men. Sometimes Jewish, often refugees, these figures are demonic in their effect on others. Murdoch once referred to these figures as "alien gods." Honor possesses an eerie power and authority that derive at least in part from her exotic appearance and her skill with the samurai sword. As one who has spent much time among primitive tribes, she is associated in Martin's mind with the "dark gods." Although Murdoch uses the motif of powerful gods, she is not suggesting faith in the supernatural as a path to consolation. She simply uses the associations of mystery and power to endow the very human Honor Klein with the gift of transcending reality as it is usually understood. Honor speaks to the deepest submerged desires of other characters' minds.

In fact, one of Murdoch's most distinctive traits as a novelist might be called "transcendent realism." Her novels open with all the realistic conventions of character, setting, and plot, but shortly something fantastic or outrageous will happen that appears to be alien to the premise of the novel. The central character transcends the real in order to attain a transrational truth. For Murdoch, the intrusion of the unexpected is a testament to the richness of reality.

Context

Iris Murdoch's novels have not attracted much attention from female critics, perhaps because she has never written about areas of women's experience that do not overlap with men's. A fictional masculine perspective permeates all of her novels, but in the case of first-person narrators such as Martin, it is always the perspective of a corrupted male psyche who wields words with power but does not truly grasp reality. Goodness, another major theme in Murdoch's works, then becomes linked with femaleness. Murdoch's typical male protagonists are also usually childless, professional, failed in their major enthusiasms (history, in Martin's case), and involved in careers that parody their intellectual needs.

It remains to the women in her fiction to play the role of undermining these unreliable narrators. Many of her male narrators use misogynist generalizations in order to score points, but it is women who force the heroes to perceive the truth. Murdoch is clearly preoccupied by the unequal power relationships that exist between men and women and the way in which power is wielded in words. Part of the reason Murdoch's male narrators fail to see truth is that they talk too much. This suggests that the connections between the male hero, articulateness, and power are presented with considerable deliberate irony on the author's part.

A Severed Head was adapted successfully as a stage play in a collaboration between Murdoch and J. B. Priestley. The play had a tryout in Bristol, England, in 1963, ran successfully for two and a half years in London, and was released as a movie by Columbia Pictures in 1971. The novel was cut for the stage and screen version, and Georgie's abortion and ensuing despair were omitted. The theme of childless sterility, which is important in the book as a symbol of the characters' sterile lives, is significantly altered.

Sources for Further Study

Baldanza, Frank. *Iris Murdoch*. New York: Twayne, 1974. Baldanza's book remains a standard in Murdoch studies. It offers an overview of her first fifteen novels, focusing attention on Murdoch's development as an artist and changing thematic emphasis. A brief biography citing formative events in the novelist's life is included. The chapter on *A Severed Head* is a careful, detailed analysis that illuminates the novel.

Bove, Cheryl K. *Understanding Iris Murdoch*. Columbia: University of South Carolina Press, 1993. This volume, part of the series Understanding Contemporary British Literature, is intended as a guide for students and advanced nonacademic readers, to help clarify the special demands that influential contemporary literature makes. The book provides instruction in how to read Murdoch, explaining material, themes, language, point of view, structure, and symbolism.

Conradi, Peter J. *Iris Murdoch: The Saint and the Artist*. New York: St. Martin's Press, 1986. This book is an important discussion of Murdoch's work in the form of an extended essay. Conradi groups the novels chronologically into three distinct periods of Murdoch's development. There is an excellent chapter entitled "Eros in *A Severed Head* and *Bruno's Dream*."

Johnson, Deborah. *Iris Murdoch*. Bloomington: Indiana University Press, 1987. The series Key Women Writers looks at women who have established positions in the mainstream of literary tradition and explores the ways in which such writers can mesh with feminist theory. Johnson's book succeeds in finding much that speaks to feminists in Murdoch's novels, especially in the depiction of power struggles that make up life in a competitive society. The world as Murdoch shows it is one in

Masterplots II

which the old social and ethical systems no longer work, which view lends itself to
feminist analysis.
Sage, Lorna. *Women in the House of Fiction: Post-War Women Novelists*. New York:
Routledge, 1992. This is a close examination of the ways in which women writers
deal with realism and literary modernism. Sage, like Iris Murdoch, does not believe
in a special kind of "feminine" writing; she believes that women writers have
reinvented realism in a kind of "matriarchal realism." She considers Murdoch a
writer who has co-opted realism for her own purposes, particularly the concept of
traditional marriage, which Murdoch has sabotaged.

Sheila Golburgh Johnson

SEX AND DESTINY
The Politics of Human Fertility

Author: Germaine Greer (1939-   )
Type of work: Social criticism
First published: 1984

Form and Content

In *Sex and Destiny: The Politics of Human Fertility*, Germaine Greer, the author of *The Female Eunuch*, challenges the right of Western industrialized societies to impose fertility control on the rest of the world. Greer considers the social meaning of fertility and sterility, the history of contraception and eugenics, shifts in family and kinship structures, and the development of the concept of a "population explosion" (which she takes to be a figment of the imagination of racists and statisticians). Her long, dense chapters brim with statistics, quotations, anecdotes, and cross-cultural examples, all related in her characteristic witty and impassioned style.

Much of the book is a warning against the ethnocentric projection of the values of one culture onto the people of another. People who live in industrialized consumer economies (where children hamper adult live) value fertility differently from those who live in subsistence cultures (where children provide entertainment, labor, status, security of aging parents, and existential meaning). The industrialized West has too often assumed that its own values (individualism, pleasure, privacy, and the accumulation of consumer goods) are universal. Greer documents many poorly conceived "foreign aid" programs of sterilization and family planning that have been based on the unfounded assumption that everyone in every culture wishes to live in a small nuclear family. She believes that "foreign aid" that is actually intended to aid would more profitably be based on asking client populations what their own desires are. She suggests that in many cases those desires might be for healthier children, not fewer children.

Greer accuses the industrialized West of cultural arrogance that manifests itself as a failure to recognize the value of age-old strategies for maintaining population homeostasis—that is, the balance of population with resources available for its support. Such strategies include the promotion of virginity, delayed marriage, long periods of sexual abstinence after the birth of a child, induced abortion, infanticide, the cessation of sexual activity after a certain age, coitus interruptus, and any form of sexual activity that does not lead to conception. Family planning programs sponsored by industrialized market economies have, not surprisingly, tried to replace these cheap, low-tech methods with profitable, high-tech contraceptive products, such as condoms, intrauterine devices (IUDs), hormones, and surgical procedures. In so doing, they have often overridden the preferences of their client populations and super-imposed new health problems on the old. For example, unmonitored IUD use results in a high rate of infections and other serious complications. Sloppy dosing of birth control pills, injections, or implants increases the risk of cancer in women and of birth defects in their children who are accidentally exposed to dangerous levels of sex hormones in utero.

Although some of these family planning projects may simply be wrong-headed, Greer also sees racism and classism at work. From the birth of the eugenic fantasy of racial improvement through selective breeding, fertility control has been largely a matter of the rich, pale-skinned peoples of the world trying to reduce the numbers of poorer and browner ones. Greer maintains that this sort of pressure is partly a form of competition between cultures and partly an attempt to consolidate profitable markets. Industrialized nations enlarge their markets by forcing a shift from what Greer sees as the thrifty and efficient extended family systems of the past to the consumerist nuclear family of modern capitalism. In the lonely isolation of the individualistic nuclear family—which Greer often refers to as "the copulating couple"—the only gratifications that are left involve self-pleasuring and conspicuous consumption. The notion that controlling the fertility of poor populations is "for their own good" or for the good of a planet on the brink of suicidal overpopulation is, according to Greer, simply whitewash.

Analysis

Greer's first book, *The Female Eunuch* (1971), was an outcry against the suppression and misrepresentation of female sexuality. The enormous impact of that work raised the prospect that whatever came from the pen of its author could be filed under the heading "feminist theory." Contrary to those expectations, *Sex and Destiny* is not about the power imbalance between men and women. Instead, it concerns the power imbalance in another dominance relationship, the one between the "developed," largely Eurocaucasian, industrialized market economies and the "developing," largely equatorial, postcolonial Third World.

Greer takes a respectful position with regard to the practices of traditional nonindustrial societies. She repeatedly illustrates ways in which customs that seem bizarre and negative to the urbanized West were beneficial to the survival of groups that practiced them. For example, ritual sexual abstinence during the growing season had the effect of slowing the birth rate to a level that could be accommodated by available food supplies. Greer's understanding acceptance is not, however, limited to relatively neutral practices such as customs regulating when and where sexual intercourse is allowed. She also speaks, with utilitarian respect of clitoridectomy, infanticide, Islamic *purdah*, patriarchal kinship systems, and menstrual seclusion. These practices, although legitimately "traditional," have long been instrumental in the oppression of women. For this reason, some readers who expected a straightforward feminist message from Greer have been disappointed and even betrayed. Others have complained of the logical inconsistency of a cultural relativism that accepted and positively valued the practices of all cultures except, irrationally, one's own. Of her own culture, Greer has not much good to say. She diagnoses it as being anti-child, immoderately greedy, and pleasure-mad.

Greer's reputation as author of *The Female Eunuch* and apostle of the sexual revolution also predisposed readers to look for a message supporting sexual liberation. Instead, they find a serious examination of the merits of chastity, along with a critique of what Greer calls the modern "sex religion," the "new opiate of the people." This new religion is founded on the elevation of genital pleasure above all other values, and its ritual practice is the pursuit of the perfect orgasm. Greer demonstrates that this primacy of genital sensation is purely local to modern society and, by centering on the pleasure principle, draws off energy from motivation for political action. She also shows it to be directly supportive of capitalist consumption patterns in its focus on immediate gratification instead of on the well-being of a kinship line across the generations. Furthermore, the genital orgasm preoccupation does not nourish the diffuse, whole-body sensuality that is natural to women and infants. Instead, it exerts pressure toward remaking female sexuality into the image of male sexuality: goal directed and genitally centered.

Aside from the debate generated by *Sex and Destiny*'s refusal to stand on a predictable feminist and sexual liberationist platform, the book also takes its place in the controversy between those who claim that humanity is in the midst of overwhelming population growth leading to imminent collapse and those who claim that the human crisis is not caused by overgrowth of population but by uneven distribution of the goods needed to support that population—in other words, by poverty. Greer numbers herself among the second group. She dismisses overpopulation as a "myth," a "theoretical catastrophe" created by statisticians to rationalize the quasi-genocidal fertility control imposed on poor nations by rich ones. She supports her position with evidence that famine and the cheapening of human life existed even before population entered its present phase of precipitous growth. Greer accepts the theoretical possibility that the human population may outstrip the earth's capacity to feed it, but she insists that the planet has not yet reached that point. The human misery that is evident in many nonindustrialized nations, she argues, is a product of the poverty of the many and the extravagant overconsumption of the few.

Although *Sex and Destiny* takes the issue of fertility control as its subject, Greer's larger concern is the transformation of human beings into machines of consumption in the service of economic systems. This concern is consistent with her earlier work in *The Female Eunuch*. The isolation of individuals into nuclear families, the disruption of extended families, the recruitment of indigenous peoples into consumer society, the diminishment of the rewards of parenthood—Greer sees all these superficially unrelated processes as parts of a larger process: the victory of consumerism over the art of living.

Context

Critical response to *Sex and Destiny* was largely negative. The book's unexpected exaltation of the joys of traditional motherhood and of the traditional male-dominated family caused some disconcerted readers to see it as a sort of puritanical backlash against the sexual liberalism of its author's youth. Its apparent tolerance of infanticide, Indian bride-burning, and clitoridectomy was difficult to reconcile with its use of morality as an argument against sterilization. Academic readers questioned the soundness of its scholarship and pointed to a number of inaccuracies and inconsistencies. For example, Greer attacks the concept of "culling" when it is imposed by bureaucratized sterilization programs, but she apparently applauds it when it is carried out by traditional mothers and midwives who kill handicapped newborns.

In spite of the flaws and controversial positions in *Sex and Destiny*, or possibly because of them, the book and its author continue to serve as a monument to the multifaceted heterodoxy of feminism. Feminist thought is not a monolithic doctrine, and mavericks such as Greer have continued to expand the horizon of what is "thinkable." In particular, this book, notwithstanding the storms of dispute that attended its publication, helped to open the narrow focus of Western feminism to include respectful consideration of the needs of postcolonial, nonindustrialized nations. It also contributed to the feminist challenge of the validity, for women, of a sexual revolution that seemed in many ways to be designed expressly for the convenience of men.

Greer's writings have continued to span a surprising variety of forms and issues relating to literature, families, gender, and the worlds of women. Her other works include, in addition to *The Female Eunuch*, *Darling Say You Love Me* (as Rose Blight, 1969), *The Revolting Garden* (1979), *The Obstacle Race: The Fortunes of Women Painters and Their Work* (1979), *Shakespeare* (1986), *The Madwoman's Underclothes: Essays and Occasional Writings 1968-1985* (1986), *Daddy, We Hardly Knew You* (1989), *The Change* (1992), and *Kissing the Rod: An Anthology of Seventeenth-Century Women's Verse* (1989), edited jointly with Jeslyn Medoff, Melinda Sansone, and Susan Hastings.

Sources for Further Study

Behuniak-Long, Susan. "Feminism and Reproductive Technology." *Choice* 29 (October, 1991): 243-251. A bibliographic essay that lists and briefly describes scores of books that engage issues of reproductive technology from a feminist viewpoint.

Boserup, Ester. *Woman's Role in Economic Development*. New York: St. Martin's Press, 1970. A classic study of the shifting patterns of women's lives as traditional village societies are transformed by modern industrialization.

Cole, H. S. D., et al., eds. *Models of Doom: A Critique of "The Limits to Growth."* New York: Universe Books, 1973. Criticizes the methods and alarming conclusions of *The Limits to Growth*.

Ehrenreich, Barbara, and Deirdre English. *For Her Own Good: One Hundred Fifty Years of the Experts' Advice to Women*. Garden City, N.Y.: Anchor Press, 1978. Examines the ascendancy of the psychomedical experts who have assumed power over women's reproductive lives: scientists, doctors, psychotherapists, home economists, and child-rearing specialists.

Greer, Germaine. *The Female Eunuch*. New York: McGraw-Hill, 1971. This study of sexist representations of women shows the continuity of Greer's basic anticonsumerist message.

Meadows, Donella H., et al. *The Limits to Growth: A Report for the Club of Rome's Project on the Predicament of Mankind.* 2d ed. New York: Universe Books, 1974. Based on a ground-breaking computer model of current trends in population, agricultural and industrial production, natural resources, and pollution, the authors present the argument (which Greer opposes in *Sex and Destiny*) that a crisis of population and overconsumption of resources is imminent.

Donna Glee Williams

SEXING THE CHERRY

Author: Jeanette Winterson (1959-   )
Type of work: Novel
Type of plot: Fable
Time of plot: 1630-1666 and the late twentieth century
Locale: England
First published: 1989

> *Principal characters:*
> JORDAN, a young man in Renaissance England
> THE DOG-WOMAN, the independent giantess who adopted Jordan
>   as an infant
> JOHN TRADESCANT, the Royal Gardener to the king and an
>   explorer
> FORTUNATA, the youngest of the Twelve Dancing Princesses and
>   the object of Jordan's affections
> DOG-WOMAN'S NEIGHBOR, a filthy woman with occult powers
> PREACHER SCROGGS and NEIGHBOR FIREBRACE, opportunists who
>   join the Puritan uprising
> NICOLAS JORDAN, modern counterpart to Jordan, who gives up a
>   career in the Navy to join an ecological protest
> A CHEMIST, the unnamed modern recipient of Dog-Woman's
>   prodigious outrage and Fortunata's charisma

Form and Content

The title *Sexing the Cherry* refers to determining the gender of a grafted cherry tree. New to the seventeenth century, the art of grafting fruit trees is practiced by the protagonist, Jordan, during his apprenticeship to the Renaissance figure John Tradescant. Metaphorically minded, Jordan seeks to fuse himself with spirits of self-possessed women to form a hardier, more complete self. The form of the novel is itself a graft of perspectives, with its alternating narrations of a mother and her adopted son, which in turn contain the fabulous tales of others, especially women, who overcome obstacles by living fearlessly in new ways.

Indeed, Jordan, in his journey to find himself, becomes a collector of exotic experiments in living, as well as the man who brings the first pineapple to England. On one occasion, disguising himself as a woman in hopes of finding the elusive dancer Fortunata, Jordan lives among kept prostitutes who escape their fortress nightly on an underground river. On another occasion, he accompanies a word cleaner as she mops up, from her balloon, the clusters of spent phrases hovering above the town. He dreams of a town of cunning debtors who tear down and move their homes nightly to escape their creditors. He is struck by the power and melancholy of the myth of Artemis, who reminds him of his mother, and he causes a riot in a city attempting to recover from plagues of love. He is most enamored of the drifting city whose inhabitants have given up gravity. The unmoored town, beloved by the Twelve Dancing Princesses, glides by several times, embodying Jordan's sense of shifting time and space.

The Dog-Woman, in contrast, never goes far from London and keeps a linear sense of time. Through her, the reader watches Jordan grow from the infant found among the bulrushes to the young man she knows must leave her. Through her, the reader witnesses the swelling uprising of Cromwell and the Puritans. She attends the trial of King Charles I and his subsequent beheading but lives to see Cromwell's corpse unearthed and his followers dismembered, and she wreaks her own Old Testament vengeance on enough Puritans to obtain 119 eyeballs and 2,000 teeth. A revealing narrator but a protective mother, the Dog-Woman does not want to hold her son back with the knowledge of her own humiliating experience of romantic love or by letting him know how much she will miss him, and he is hurt by this.

After the climax of Jordan's own story, after he has found Fortunata and she has sent him on with a kiss, the narration takes a leap of three hundred years and is taken up by clearly recognizable descendants of the original narrators. The young Nicolas Jordan has the same boat-building obsession that his namesake possesses, and he is inspired by a painting of the first pineapple being presented to Charles II. The young, unnamed antecedent to the Dog-Woman outgrows her prepubescent girth, however, and takes on the more svelte but no less avenging profile of Artemis, and Nicolas is as taken by a glimpse of her as Jordan was with Fortunata. In both centuries, the women fight alone against the pollution and greed of their times as the men who would be heroes look to them for love.

Analysis

Like the journeys concealing journeys Jordan wishes to record, the narratives contain narratives and the meditations meditations in *Sexing the Cherry*, and, in the tradition of all fables, their true meanings seem viscerally obvious while remaining literally elusive. In outline a kind of picaresque search for an idealized, heterosexual love, the novel ultimately questions the possibility of such a union and seems to posit instead self-realization as a rather melancholy bonding with a community of self-made, parentless individuals.

Nowhere in its many tales is there an example of a happy traditional marriage. It is as if by this time in human history it is already too late for men and women to be together. By the time Jordan finds Fortunata on her island, she is past hoping to belong to someone else; she has learned to dance alone, and she recounts for him the myth of Artemis as if to argue that this has always been the way for strong women. The stories of the Twelve Dancing Princesses reiterate this point. In this feminist revision of the traditional fairy tale, the princesses create their own happy endings by escaping marriage to live alone or with other women. Their tales read like a catalog of the ways in which men are unworthy; men are unloving, unfaithful, untrusting, unattractive, distracted, depressed, intolerant, and simply pale in comparison to the women with whom three of the princesses are in love. When the novel leaps to the late twentieth century, the strong female is still unmarried and alone, passionately involved in her own work, not hating men, just wishing they would try harder.

Against this emerging litany of bad male behavior, which includes the antics of Puritans Preacher Scroggs and Neighbour Firebrace, the god Orion, and the polluting captains of industry, stands the sweet, poetic soul of the male protagonist. Jordan, who loves his Rabelaisian freak of a mother, employs great compassion and a philosophic diction in his consideration of all things and exhibits an especially high regard for women. From his earliest memory of slowly being engulfed in a fog to his finally running into himself in the smoke of burning London, Jordan is a guileless seeker of the sense of existence, whose narration captures the sympathy of the reader and helps exonerate his gender. He only wants the women he loves to ask him to stay; that they never do lends the story a tragic cast.

Educated and metaphysically minded, Jordan tests the accepted notions of his time against his gathered experiences. Discussing the nature of time itself, he notes the difference between an outward perception of linear progression and the inward sense of moving freely between memory and precognition. Indeed, Jordan himself seems to move beyond his time when he describes matter as empty space and light, and when he uses peculiarly modern phrases such as "out-of-body"' and "superconductivity." For all his precocious understanding, however, by novel's end he is more certain about the shifting nature of reality than he is about the proper stance toward love.

Inside his story is that of his mother. Uneducated and of limited experience, the Dog-Woman reaches more pragmatic and more definitive conclusions. Her language is more medieval and is infused with biblical allusion. Describing being in love as "that cruelty which takes us straight to the gates of Paradise only to remind us they are closed for ever," she resigns herself to knowing only the loyal love of her dogs and her boy. She intuitively rejects the inflexibility and narrowness of the Puritan doctrine, but she considers grafting an unnatural practice that goes against the Bible, and she refuses to believe that the earth is anything but flat. Her practicality and self-acceptance efface her fantastic girth, but it is her exceptional dimension that ultimately makes her the model of the self-sufficient woman. Men persecute her at their peril; their muskets are impotent against her.

Throughout the novel, women are granted special powers that level the playing field for them in their dealings with societies defined by men. The size of the Dog-Woman, the sorcery of the crone, the hunting skills of Artemis, the intellectual prowess of the chemist, the lightness of Fortunata, and the individual cunning of each of Fortunata's sisters give these women the edge that allows them to make their own decisions. Given the chance to live as they will, they seem to be smarting from the ways men act and not ready at novel's end to let them do more than help them achieve their goals.

Context

Given her huge proportions and seventeenth century lifetime, Jeanette Winterson's

Dog-Woman is clearly following in Gargantua's footsteps. Unlike the sixteenth century French satirist Rabelais' King in *Gargantua and Pantagruel*, she has the more modest appetite of a peasant woman, and she uses her girth to fight for social justice as she personalizes it. Hers is a caricature informed by a twentieth century sensibility that empowers the woman who is scorned because her figure fails to conform to the standards of attractiveness set by male society. Although she can wreak havoc on those who cross her, she cannot make them love her romantically, so she still suffers in the ways that women conventionally have in literature. After all, it is her son who does the adventuring after love, while she stays at home, the abandoned mother, longing for his return.

It is in the revision of the fairy tale in the stories of the Twelve Dancing Princesses that Winterson's women defy their restricted choices and refuse to accept the marriages that have been arranged for them. She also has Fortunata give Artemis' side of the story regarding the death of Orion; to hear her retell it, it was a tale not of love and accidental death but of rape and revenge. In choosing to alter the archetypes, Winterson, like Angela Carter in *Strangers and Saints* and *The Company of Wolves*, has targeted the very source of the fearsome instruction that is aimed at clipping female wings. It is a testament to these writers' literary skill that the new versions of old stories read like recast emotional truths rather than rhetorical diatribes.

Winterson's first book, *Oranges Are Not the Only Fruit*, was an autobiographical lesbian coming-out story in the tradition of Rita Mae Brown's *Rubyfruit Jungle*, tinged with a macabre religiosity reminiscent of Flannery O'Connor. Having established her sexual preference in the first person, Winterson began using the device of switching back and forth between male and female narrators, first in *The Passion* and then in *Sexing the Cherry*, as if these were two sides of herself. Virginia Woolf used a similar technique in *Orlando*, where the hero/heroine changes gender as he/she lives across centuries. Both women use gender juxtaposition to point out the inequities that women suffer solely because of their sex and use the gender switch to consider women sexually, although Winterson is not shy about having women pursue women. Hers is an inclusive vision, more focused on the nature of love and self-fulfillment than on political realities, and although it is gender-blended, ultimately, like the titular cherry, it is female.

Sources for Further Study

Brown, Rosellen. Review of *Sexing the Cherry*. *Women's Review of Books* 12 (September, 1990): 9. A critical review of *Sexing the Cherry* from a feminist perspective. Thorough and accessible, it both praises Winterson and takes her to task.

Gerrard, Nicci. *Into the Mainstream: How Feminism Has Changed Women's Writing*. London: Pandora Press, 1989. An overview of the milieu of women's writing that brings in the opinions of women writers, literary agents, and editors and puts Jeanette Winterson's early work into a comprehensible context.

Gorra, Michael. Review of *Sexing the Cherry*. *The New York Times Book Review*, April 29, 1990, p. 24. A somewhat defensive but nevertheless insightfully critical review that considers *Sexing the Cherry* a fashionable historical pastiche with a unique emotional intensity.

Hunt, Sally, ed. *New Lesbian Criticism, Literary and Cultural Readings*. London: Simon & Schuster, 1992. The essay on Jeanette Winterson discusses *Oranges Are Not the Only Fruit* as a "cross-over" text into the dominant culture that lost its radical lesbian content when it was made into a television movie.

Innes, Charlotte. Review of *Sexing the Cherry*. *The Nation* 251, no. 2 (July 9, 1990): 64-65. A substantive review of *Sexing the Cherry*, locating the work within the genre of lesbian fiction and clearly elucidating its complex reality.

Krist, Gary. Review of *Sexing the Cherry*. *Hudson Review* 43, no. 4 (Winter, 1991): 695-707. An in-depth review of *Sexing the Cherry* from a male perspective. While judging the work to be unfair to men, Krist finds much in it to admire.

Susan Chainey

SEXUAL POLITICS

Author: Kate Millett (1934-   )
Type of work: Social criticism
First published: 1970

Form and Content

Sexual Politics is a study of the political aspects of sex. It is divided into three parts: "Sexual Politics," "Historical Background," and "The Literary Reflection." In part 1, Millett gives examples of the ways in which power and domination are defined in contemporary literary descriptions of sexual activity. She analyzes the work of Henry Miller, Norman Mailer, and Jean Genet. A good example of Millett's style and point of view in this section is her treatment of Norman Mailer's novel *An American Dream*, in which "female sexuality is depersonalized to the point of being a matter of class or a matter of nature." Mailer's hero, Stephen Rojack, has anal intercourse with a German maid, Ruta, who has the "invaluable 'knowledge of a city rat.'" The word "invaluable" is Millett's, and she uses it to emphasize the ideology of sex that she finds deplorable in Mailer's writing. To combat Mailer's domination of women through his use of language, she responds with a dismissive and sarcastic style: "How evil resides in her [Ruta's] bowels or why Ruta has a greater share of it that [*sic*] her master may appear difficult to explain, but many uncanny things are possible with our author." Mailer is only one example that proves that "sex is a status category"—as Millett puts it in "Theory of Sexual Politics," the second chapter of part 1.

In part 2, Millett describes the development of sex roles in the nineteenth and twentieth centuries, the efforts of women to achieve equal status with men, and the male "patriarchal" reaction aimed at thwarting revolutionary change and women's liberation. Mary Wollstonecraft's *A Vindication of the Rights of Woman* (1792) is discussed as the "first document asserting the full humanity of women and insisting upon its recognition." The book was written in the milieu of the French Revolution, and its ideas were taken up by men and women who focused on educational reform and the establishment of schools in the 1830's, which mark the proper beginning of "The Woman's Movement." Millett surveys the political organizations, the suffrage movement, and the nature of employment in this period of the "sexual revolution." She also analyzes the polemical writings for and against women's rights, focusing on the debate between John Stuart Mill (1806-1873) and John Ruskin (1819-1900), and on the writings of Karl Marx (1818-1883) and Friedrich Engels (1820-1895)—the latter providing the "most comprehensive account of patriarchal history and economy." These philosophers and social critics are compared with literary figures such as Thomas Hardy, whose novel *Jude the Obscure* (1894) is about the trials of two male and female figures rebelling against the patriarchal institutions of their times. The last chapter of part 2, "The Counterrevolution," attempts to explain why many of the advances in women's rights were reversed or undermined. Her theory is essentially intellectual and psychological: "Only the outer surface of society has been changed;

underneath the essential system was preserved undisturbed. Should it receive new sources of support, new ratification, new ideological justifications, it could be mobilized anew." Hence, she concentrates on Sigmund Freud (1856-1939), whose theories of female sexuality were used to sponsor conservative and antifeminist arguments and actions.

In part 3, Millett conducts a spirited analysis of the content of literary works by D. H. Lawrence, Henry Miller, Norman Mailer, and Jean Genet. Each of these authors—all were thought to be daring and revolutionary—is severely chastised for promulgating a climate of opinion hostile to feminism and female liberation. She discovers that their characters, themes, and plots frustrate the possibility of revolutionary change in sexual roles and assure the continuation of a patriarchal way of life.

Analysis

Millett began writing *Sexual Politics* as a doctoral dissertation under the guidance of Steven Marcus, a distinguished critic and professor at Columbia University. In books such as *The Other Victorians: A Study of Sexuality and Pornography in Mid-Nineteenth Century England*, Marcus combines a sensitive understanding of historical trends and literary works to create a highly nuanced and sophisticated brand of cultural criticism. The structure of *Sexual Politics* shows that Millett employs Marcus' method to write a polemical and political form of history and criticism. She is not merely concerned with political and literary arguments in their historical context; she is determined to advance the argument for sexual revolution and the liberation of women. Her critique is radical in that she is calling for change and measuring the writers she studies against her criteria regarding what constitutes positive reform. She is, in other words, avowedly ideological. She is asking whether a specific work has the right politics—does it demean or honor women's rights?

By adopting an ideological position and pursuing it with verve, Millett is able to write with extraordinary energy and humor. She is not awed by the august writers she analyzes, because it is not their greatness per se that she confronts but rather their positions on the sexual issues that interest her and that she has defined to her satisfaction. She is thus her own authority on the subject, and as such she can face her formidable male subjects on the same level. It is an unusual stance for a historian or literary critic to assume, especially one who has been academically trained. Usually it is the creative writer turned critic who adopts such a commanding voice.

A good example of Millett's stance is her treatment of D. H. Lawrence's novel *The Rainbow*. Lawrence has often been admired for creating strong women, but Millett sees in his creation of Ursula a stereotype of the castrating female: "Her vehicle of destruction is moonlight, for Lawrence is addicted to the notion of the moon as a female symbol, once beneficent, but lately malefic and a considerable public danger." This is classic Millett, deflating with humor what she regards as Lawrence's pretentious symbolism and his factitious use of women to support it. To say "Lawrence is addicted" is to reduce his literary work to the level of a personal compulsion, a neurosis, and to deprive him of his authority. By calling attention to such characters and scenes, Millett is probing the peculiarity of male creations; she is implicitly asking why women have to be presented in this way. Her criticism is disconcerting because it will not take the author's creation as a given; instead, she investigates the roots of such scenes in the author's own attitudes toward women, thus making the author's literature seem tendentious.

No part of *Sexual Politics* created a greater stir when it was first published than the section on Henry Miller. Miller had been regarded as the apostle of sexual liberation, a heroic figure because he had been censored and banned in the United States. In one sentence, Millett stands the heretofore conventional view of Miller on its head: "Actually, Miller is a compendium of American sexual neuroses, and his value lies not in freeing us from such afflictions, but in having had the honesty to express and dramatize them." He is given a tribute of sorts, but hardly the kind he had been accorded by others, who hailed his freedom from bourgeois restraints and the leftover Victorianism inhibiting his contemporaries from treating sexual matters as frankly and as robustly as he did. Millett does not deny his appeal: "There is a culturally cathartic release in Miller's writing, but it is really a result of the fact that he first gave voice to the unutterable." The women in Miller's fiction are barely seen as human beings, Millett argues: "Miller confronts nothing more challenging than the undifferentiated genital that exists in masturbatory revery [*sic*]."

Millett reserves some of her angriest and funniest prose for Norman Mailer—perhaps because he is closer to her generation (he was born in 1923) and has been so outspoken about male prerogatives. As she puts it, "his critical and political prose is based on a set of values so blatantly and comically chauvinist, as to constitute a new aesthetic." His theory, says Millett, is that "men have 'more rights and more powers' because life takes more out of them, leaves them 'used more.'" One passage in her chapter on Mailer constitutes the apotheosis of her attack on the male author's infantile quest for power and domination:

> As he settles into patriarchal middle age, Mailer's obsession with machismo brings to mind a certain curio sold in Coney Island and called a Peter Meter; a quaint bit of folk art, stamped out in the shape of a ruler with printed inches and appropriate epithets to equate excellence with size. Mailer operates on this scale on an abstract or metaphoric plane. His characters, male and female, labor under simpler delusions. Guinevere [in *Barbary Shore*] is indefatigable on the subject of her lover's "whangs"; D. J. [in *Why Are We in Vietnam?*] is paralyzed with the usual fear that someone else has a bigger one.

By situating Mailer so snugly in the context of popular, pornographic culture, she deprives him of his claims to literary and male superiority. She comes close to saying that in Mailer's "new aesthetic," literature is male—no matter how ridiculous that notion seems.

Jean Genet, the last major male literary figure Millett engages, seems to represent the antithesis of Mailer, because Genet's homosexuality is something that Mailer cannot abide. Yet Millett finds the same disturbing pattern in Genet: "Masculine is superior strength, feminine is inferior weakness." The only exception to this generalization, she admits, is the intelligence and moral courage he reserves for his homosexual queens and for himself.

It is hard not to conclude from Millett's relentless polemic that male authors are virtually incapable of creating full-fledged and free female characters. Why this is so, she argues, can be understood by examining the springs of their own psychology and the society that has produced them.

Context

It is difficult to exaggerate the impact of *Sexual Politics* on literary and cultural criticism, and on the women's movement in the 1970's and afterward. It was a best-seller, a controversial work both praised and attacked, and a text used in many college courses in literature and women's studies. Although female critics before Millett raised similar issues, none of them were as bold, as inflammatory, or amusing. Even readers who opposed her ideas could no longer regard writers such as Miller and Mailer in the old way. Woman as a category in literature deserving special attention was given new meaning, and exhilarated students and scholars took up the polemics of *Sexual Politics*, refining the book's conclusions and modifying and expanding its theses. The phrase "sexual politics" became part of the vocabulary of the time.

Sexual Politics has maintained its special place in women's studies. It is universally acknowledged as a pioneering work. Feminist scholars have serious reservations about Millett's book and have deplored the crudeness of some of its techniques—chiefly a penchant for ignoring the style and structure of literary works in favor of a content analysis that implies that a writer's work is merely the sum of his or her ideas and opinions. Millett lacks subtlety, these scholars conclude, and she exaggerates the originality of her own position by ignoring the foundations in women's literature and criticism on which her own work is built. Even Millett's harshest critics, however, pay tribute to her vivid style, which continues to energize readers and to pose important questions. She set an agenda for women's studies which has by no means been exhausted.

Sources for Further Study

Belsey, Catherine, and Jane Moore, eds. *The Feminist Reader: Essays in Gender and the Politics of Literary Criticism.* New York: Basil Blackwell, 1989. The introduction links Millett's work with Germaine Greer's *The Female Eunuch* and Eva Figes' *Patriarchal Attitudes*, witty, eloquent, and wide-ranging polemics reflective of the 1960's, when the existing authorities were challenged by the politics of liberation.

Gornick, Vivian. *Essays in Feminism.* New York: Harper & Row, 1978. In "Why Do These Men Hate Women," Gornick discusses Mailer's response in *The Prisoner of Sex* to *Sexual Politics*. While praising his eloquent defense of Miller and Lawrence against Millett's "distorting polemic," she finds that other aspects of his argument confirm Millett's conclusions.

Humm, Maggie. *Feminist Criticism: Women as Contemporary Critics.* New York: St. Martin's Press, 1986. Discusses Millett as a pioneer in feminist criticism and her indebtedness to Simone de Beauvoir. Provides a close reading of the style, structure, and ideology of *Sexual Politics*.

Mailer, Norman. *The Prisoner of Sex*. Boston: Little, Brown, 1971. Mailer's rebuttal to Millett, which takes the form of a keen literary analysis of two of Millett's targets: D. H. Lawrence and Henry Miller. Mailer demonstrates that Millett rips quotations out of context and literally rewrites many of the scenes she purports to describe.

Miller, Nancy K. *Getting Personal: Feminist Occasions and the Other Autobiographical Acts*. New York: Routledge, 1991. Recognizes Millett as a pioneering feminist scholar who takes on the "massively male precincts of literary history."

Moi, Toril. *Sexual/Textual Politics: Feminist Literary Theory*. New York: Methuen, 1985. Contains a chapter on *Sexual Politics* as a feminist classic. Discusses the response of feminist critics to the book, particularly their rehabilitation of Freud and their reservations about Millett's treatment of him.

Carl Rollyson

THE SHAWL

Author: Cynthia Ozick (1928-   )
Type of work: Novella and short story
First published: 1989

Form and Content

The short story and the novella that constitute *The Shawl* were published separately in *The New Yorker*. Taken together, they present a powerful narrative about one woman's attempt to maintain sanity in the face of the tragedy of the Holocaust. In "The Shawl," a rhetorically minimalist short story, Rosa and her niece Stella walk, with Rosa's silent infant Magda wrapped into the shawl around Rosa's chest, the long cold roads to the death camp. Although Rosa's breasts are dry, the infant finds nourishment in the shawl itself, sucking it instead of screaming. Rosa is certain that her niece resents Magda's warmth and security inside the shawl; through richly suggestive images, she suggests that Stella is capable of murder or cannibalism. One day, Stella takes the shawl, causing the baby to wail. Rosa must watch in silence as a camp guard lifts the baby up on his shoulders and hurls it into the electric fence.

The novella begins after Rosa has moved from New York to Miami in order to avoid prosecution for demolishing her antique store; she was frustrated because she was unable to explain to her customers the haunting images of the Holocaust. Rosa lives as if she is still imprisoned in a concentration camp, weaving imagery of the Holocaust throughout her descriptions of Miami.

Because of the heat and her self-pity, Rosa mostly stays in her room in a retirement hotel, composing letters. She writes to Stella in crude English, pacifying her with endearments although she sees her as a "bloodsucker." She writes to Magda in a refined literary Polish, usually imagining her daughter as a doctor or a professor, addressing herself as the mother of such a distinguished daughter. At other times, she laments her stolen past, probing Magda's paternity, religion, the ghetto, motherhood, and Stella's character. In this way, the book allows the reader to see Rosa's divided self.

When Rosa finally goes to the laundromat, Simon Persky speaks to her. She imagines that he is like the other idealistic Jewish refugees and retirees she sees all over Miami, weighted down with regret for the real life they left behind. Although she identifies with their regret, she believes that she has nothing in common with them. Persky persists in making Rosa's acquaintance; through his kind acts, he begins to penetrate her shell.

Most of the story takes place after Rosa returns to the hotel and discovers that a pair of underpants is missing from her laundry. Driven by paranoia, Rosa hunts for them that night on the streets and beaches of Miami. The darkened, surreal landscape reveals to Rosa the darkness of her own mind. When she returns to the hotel, Persky is waiting. She makes an offer of friendship, allowing Persky to open the package that she believes holds the shawl of her dead daughter. They discover instead a manuscript from a "social pathologist" who wants to study Rosa as a "survivor." Rosa has a violent outburst that eventually subsides the next morning when Magda appears to Rosa. The narrative ends as Rosa's vision of Magda fades.

Analysis

Cynthia Ozick's central intention in *The Shawl* is to blur the line between life and death in order to imply the continuity of life. She conveys this impression by presenting motherhood as equally biological and spiritual. As Rosa goes from being a mother to being a survivor and a madwoman, she faces conflicts that call into doubt the integrity of her past choices. Knowing that Magda is always near her in spirit, Rosa remains deeply self-righteous about those choices.

Ozick's intention becomes clear only when the two stories are considered together. Taken alone, "The Shawl" leaves the reader with nothing except the unfillable emptiness of its aftermath. One watches as the body of Magda is replaced in Rosa's head by humming steel voices. After reading "Rosa," however, one learns that for Rosa motherhood has not ended with Magda's death; Magda has materialized as a phantasm, appearing to Rosa in many forms. Without the history of "The Shawl" as context, it takes the reader of "Rosa" much longer to discover that Magda exists only in Rosa's imagination. Examined together, the two stories emphasize the continuity of life through the spiritual bonds offered by motherhood.

By calling herself a "madwoman," Rosa links herself with a tradition in which angry or grieving women were silenced by being institutionalized as "mad." In the case of Rosa, that tradition's truthfulness is undercut by the sarcasm with which the narrator says that she is mad; she is as much a "scavenger" as a "madwoman." Persky does not view Rosa as truly mad. For him, there is "a bad way of describing, also a good way." When she says she does not like to lie, he tells her everyone must lie to get along.

By staging *The Shawl* as a Holocaust drama, Ozick raises the question of mother-hood and madness to a feverish pitch. During the Holocaust, women were doubly victimized, their bodies the objects of physical and sexual violence. Rosa tries to console herself by imagining for Magda a legitimate paternity, but it is clear from the narrative that Rosa was raped—probably repeatedly—by German soldiers. Unable to internalize the sexual violence resulting in a child, Rosa must deny the death; if she does not, her persecutors have not only marginalized her but also have erased her altogether.

Motherhood is the only state that can achieve the purity of belief—or denial—necessary for birth or rebirth. Ozick's two stories show how necessary that denial can be when one has lost everything. Rosa is typical of Holocaust survivors—she has lost her entire family (except Stella) —yet if the unimaginable horror of losing everything can be made worse, it was made so when she witnessed the murder of her own child. She lost her past and her future.

Rosa kept her baby's shawl as a relic and a talisman. It was a true piece of her past, linking her in a personal way to the witnessing. Others in the post-Holocaust era

depersonalize the Holocaust: through assimilation, like Stella; through psychologiz-
ing, like the "social pathologist" Dr. Tree; or through misdirected energy, like the old
socialists around Miami.

Ozick is hopeful about the continuity of life. As unimaginable as her loss seems,
Rosa chooses life over death. She might have identified herself as the child's mother
when Magda was exposed in the camp, ensuring her own death, but she stuffed the
shawl into her mouth instead. Similarly, at the end of "Rosa," she chooses the
liveliness of Persky's company over the phantasm of Magda. Still, Magda does not
disappear for good. Ozick's message is clear: Grieving takes many forms; denial is
one such form. Yet life goes on. The instinct for self-preservation is stronger even than
that of motherhood.

Ozick's style is to write what she calls "liturgical" fiction, which is rich with
character, irony, and poetry. In the sparse tragedy of "The Shawl," the short sentences,
concise syntax, and lugubrious and rhythmic repetition of such stinging words as
"cold, cold, the coldness of hell" not only move the story along quickly and efficiently
but also provide an immediacy that is direct and unrelenting. One does not know
where one is going, but one is not surprised at the urgency, inevitability, and fragmentation of the imprisonment when one gets there.

In "Rosa," much of the reader's information comes through letters written by Rosa
or sent to her by Stella or Dr. Tree. Ozick uses the writing-within-the-writing technique not only to convey the different voices of the characters and the different selves
of Rosa but also to show how much Rosa lives in her mind. Even the shawl becomes
Magda only in Rosa's mind. Not until she searches for the lost underpants—which
represent reality in all its commonness—does Rosa begin to recognize the need to
regain meaning in life.

Context

Like Ozick's previous stories, *The Shawl* provides a Jewish woman's perspective
on social and historical issues. While Ozick often presents the universal human
condition through the eyes of women, she claims to be a "social" writer, exploring
connections between people rather than their differences. Her "classical feminism"
denies any separate psychology on the basis of sex. She writes about the ordinary as
women experience it. Perennial issues of the intrinsic worth of all human beings, the
conflict between traditions, and the contest between the imaginary and the rational are
central in her work. Her skillful attention to these issues won her a Guggenheim
Fellowship in 1982 and caused her to be elected a member of the American Academy
and Institute of Arts and Letters.

In choosing to place these universal questions into the life of a female Holocaust
survivor, Ozick makes her contribution to the genre of women's Holocaust fiction, of
which the most famous contemporary examples are Norma Rosen's *Touching Evil*
(1969) and Susan Schaeffer's *Anya* (1974). Such fictions represent the double victimization that women are forced to endure during times of war and intensifies it to the
most sinister proportions. *The Shawl* shows survival to be the strongest instinct of all,

denying the hopelessness of many male fictionalizations of the Holocaust, such as Tadeusz Borowski's *This Way for the Gas, Ladies and Gentlemen* (1959) and other works that present the Holocaust as the final chapter in human history.

Ozick is a self-consciously Jewish woman writer, and her achievement in *The Shawl* is to make the survival of motherhood emblematic of the survival of a race. The shawl itself is the symbol that bridges two worlds. In the religious sense, the shawl is a special garment worn only by men to inspire awe and reverence during prayer. In the secular world, it is always worn by women. Ozick makes sacred the shawl by making it the living garment used by Rosa to resurrect her daughter.

The stories in *The Shawl* were included in *Best American Short Stories* (1981 and 1984) and won first prize in the annual *O. Henry Prize Stories Collection*. In *The Shawl*, Ozick begins with the most unimaginable setting in order to convey powerfully that it is often the ordinary rather than the idiosyncratic that makes survival worthwhile. The deeply imagistic use of the shawl gives meaning to the ordinary. In *The Shawl*, Ozick combines the complexity of the best moral fiction with the tightly wound prose of this century's great realists. Ozick's luminous symbols, her characters' penetrating wit, and her focused prose challenge readers to examine for themselves the most grievous act of this century against the most enduring bond known to humankind.

Sources for Further Study

Bloom, Harold, ed. *Modern Critical Views: Cynthia Ozick*. New York: Chelsea House, 1986. This volume of essays gathers together a representative selection of the best criticism so far available of Ozick's fiction, arranged by subject in chronological order of its original publication.

Klingenstein, Susanne. "Destructive Intimacy: The Shoah Between Mother and Daughter in Fictions by Cynthia Ozick, Norma Rosen, and Rebecca Goldstein." *Studies in American Jewish Literature* 11, no. 2 (Fall, 1992). This article defends the joint publication of the two stories in *The Shawl*.

Lowin, Joseph. *Cynthia Ozick*. Boston: Twayne, 1988. This useful book, organized thematically, provides a close reading of all of Ozick's writings up to 1988.

——————. "Cynthia Ozick, Rewriting Herself: The Road from 'The Shawl' to 'Rosa.'" In *Since Flannery O'Connor: Essays on the Contemporary Short Story*, edited by Loren Logsdon and Charles W. Mayer. Macomb: Western Illinois University Press, 1987. Lowin sees *The Shawl* as the summit of her art as a "rewriter."

Pifer, Ellen. "Cynthia Ozick: Invention and Orthodoxy." In *Contemporary American Women Writers: Narrative Strategies*, edited by Catherine Rainwater and William J. Scheick. Lexington: University Press of Kentucky, 1985. This essay places Ozick's fiction within the development of postmodernist or antirealist literature, with a moral bent. Includes a primary bibliography of all writings up to 1984.

Holli G. Levitsky

SHE HAD SOME HORSES

Author: Joy Harjo (1951-   )
Type of work: Poetry
First published: 1983

Form and Content

She Had Some Horses springs directly from Joy Harjo's experience as an American Indian and as a woman. The joining of these two perspectives moves her poetry from the present in which her personae speak to a temporal space that, at times, seems to span millennia and to articulate experiences in a universal voice. In particular, Harjo conjoins the deep losses suffered by contemporary American Indians—who essentially have been removed from their cultural roots and lands—with those reductions and infringements that women, whether American Indian or of other origins, experience in their daily lives. Thus the equation of gender and ethnicity serves as an underpinning to the powerful statement that the poems in this book combine to make. Harjo's writing is intensely personal: A persona's voice will often speak simultaneously to itself—working through a loss, a disappointment, or a terror—and to the reader, as if such sharing of intimacy somehow has the power to touch, sensitize, and change any who might chance to overhear.

Harjo's writing articulates sorrow, alienation, and anger, emotions that infuse and shape a poem's tone and style as well as provide insight into the writer's sense of self, racial identity, and outsider status. Although the poems' visual and emotional landscapes are often bleak, they also offer hope, particularly at the conclusion of the book's final poem, "I Give You Back."

The form of the poems also contributes to the sometimes angry, sometimes lonely, but always intense quality of the collection. Written with open lines and free and varied structure, a poem's arrangement on the page echoes the fragmentation, the angry punctuation of emotion in the face of loss and alienation, and the confusion evident in the words and rhythms. Harjo believes that poetry is meant to be heard, not read; however, the incantatory nature of a piece such as the title poem, "She Has Some Horses," takes on both an auditory and a visual chanting rhythm because the lines are arranged so densely on the page.

Analysis

The four sections of *She Had Some Horses*—"Survivors," "What I Should Have Said," "She Had Some Horses," and "I Give You Back"—are arranged so that each succeeding one informs and evokes the others. This structure allows Harjo to build upon key words and phrases, central motifs, and visceral images whose individual power is amplified because of the resonances shared with other poems in the book. Harjo's focus often revolves around wild nature, colors, animals, seasons, weather, a blighted urban landscape—the elements that provide the recurring images and controlling tone of these poems. Harjo uses these motifs to reflect the driving moods, needs, and sorrows of her self-identification as American Indian as well as of the displacement of those contemporary Indians painfully lost in urban landscapes or out of step with their own culture. These poems not only reflect Harjo's personal battles with alienation, sorrow, loneliness, and betrayal but also explore these issues as they are reflected in the lives of others, people who have been victims in circumstances similar to those that have oppressed her, her people, and the cultures of all American Indians.

Noni Daylight is a typical Harjo persona, through whom Harjo can examine the disjuncture between the traditions of the persona's tribal past, the unfulfilled rooted-ness implied by that past, and the impossible difficulties facing American Indians who move within the dominant Anglo culture of the American cityscape. Like the unnamed voices of poems such as "Anchorage," "Remember," and "Drowning Horses," Noni Daylight struggles with her fears, isolated in an Anglo city. She watches trains rumble through town in "Kansas City" in "Heartbeat," she chooses self-destructive behavior and flight by frequenting Albuquerque bars, taking drugs, and finally driving all night waiting for a cleansing "fierce anger/ that will free her." Finally, in "She Remembers the Future," Noni addresses her "otherself," evidently looking for an answer that will provide the connection to the world she has been tracking, an answer that will be more than the impulse to violence that apparently has been Noni's frequent response. Noni wants "to know/ that we're alive/ we are alive."

In many of Harjo's poems, the past of an American Indian culture—even the contemporary one left behind in the move to a big city—interweaves with the alienating landscapes of urban life. In such inhospitable settings as those of "What Music," "Backwards," or "For Alva Benson, and for Those Who Have Learned to Speak," Harjo alludes to what has been left behind in her speaker's attempt to assimilate into the white culture: life amid the wild landscapes of the Southwest, a region which contains the speaker's roots in American Indian tradition and the tribal environment of the pueblo or reservation. This analogy is particularly strong in her repeated references to wild horses, to the power of the untamed, the emotional and ethnic mustang that she invokes in such poems as "Call It Fear," "Ice Horses," or "Vision." Harjo enriches this primal identification with a sacred wild world that remains outside the Anglo urban wasteland by invoking other animal icons: the bears in "White Bear" and "Leaving" and the hawk in "Connection."

Many of Harjo's most powerful pieces situate themselves in the urban landscape, the locus of white culture and the void into which so many American Indians disappear. The alienation and anger expressed in this poetry circles back to the speakers' homelands in an attempt to connect or reconnect with their roots. It is in this setting that Harjo exhorts the listener in "Remember," saying, "Remember that you are all people and that all people/ are you." These sentiments, expressed so often in her poems, underscore the bitterness and alienation of the American Indian swallowed by the dominant Anglo culture in a world that apparently refuses to concern itself with learning about and respecting Indian history and traditions.

The book's final poem, "I Give You Back," deals directly with the fears Harjo explores in the book's other poems. No longer seeing fear as embodying the most important part of herself, the poem's persona disclaims any tie with her terror of white oppression, including rape, displacement, the murder of children, and the countless other ways that the dominant culture has brutalized the speaker and her people. As a capstone poem to this volume, "I Give You Back" claims ownership of such tyrannies as fears of joy, love, hatred, a mixed racial background, and one's own anger. Claiming herself back from fear, the persona understands the crippling nature of her terror while simultaneously embracing it as an integral part of her self. As the final poem in this collection, "I Give You Back" addresses the issues that Harjo's other poems have explored: the displacement, despair, and psychic immobility of the Indian people, whose stories her poems have brought to life. *She Had Some Horses* ends on a cathartic note, refusing to break under the tyranny of a culture that has done its best to obliterate all that is important to the people about whom Harjo writes.

Context

Harjo has said that she particularly identifies herself and her writing with the female, with the pains, sorrows, and victories of women. "The Woman Hanging from the Thirteenth Floor Window" provides the most passionate and disturbing example of her commitment to examining painful subjects explicitly through a woman's eyes: suicide, fear, and detachment in an East Chicago slum. This woman also serves as an emblem for the American Indian trapped in the white city and forced to a brink, perhaps pushed out onto that sill by an uncaring Anglo culture—ironically, in a high rise built by American Indian construction workers. Harjo has said that this poem is informed by her experience at the Chicago Indian Center. Mirroring contemporary American Indian alienation in Anglo culture, this poem ends inconclusively. Harjo does not show the woman jumping or retreating inside: Both possibilities remain, leaving the unnamed woman alone, isolated and immobilized in a city that is not her own. Although this and many of Harjo's poems speak expressly to the pain of women, they also reflect a larger suffering, that of the dispossessed American Indian of either gender, as in "Night Out" or "The Friday Before the Long Weekend."

Joy Harjo's contribution to American women's literature is particularly important because of the explicit focus of her work on the point of view of American Indian women. Almost any of her poems can be read as commentary on the outsider status not only of the Indians but of women as well, as in "Anchorage," "What Music," or "Two Horses." Harjo's poetry embodies a female sensibility and sensuality in her references to the moon; horses and other animals; wild nature; a wet, bloody fecundity; carnality; childbirth; and mothering. Harjo defines her feminism as an empowerment of women that allows them to see their warrior within. In her writing, she attempts to give women back to themselves, in the same way that she reclaims her Indian heritage. She also strives to see language anew, making it truly representative of a woman's way of seeing, and to speak honestly and openly about experiences that are particularly female.

She Had Some Horses should be classified among the important feminist books of the early 1980's; like Leslie Marmon Silko, Louise Erdrich, Paula Gunn Allen, and Linda Hogan, Harjo focuses specifically on the Native American woman's ways of being—whether as lover, griever, mother, or wise woman. The movement of the poems traces a healing process that shifts from the book's initial "Survivors" section, which offers portraits of culturally and emotionally damaged or incomplete women; through the gradually more affirming glimpses of potential healing offered in the sections "What I Should Have Said" and "She Had Some Horses"; to the strong assertion of womanly and cultural self-ownership and pride of the book's concluding section, "I Give You Back."

Sources for Further Study

Ballassi, William, John F. Crawford, and Annie O. Eysturoy, eds. *This Is About Vision: Interviews with Southwestern Writers*. Albuquerque: University of New Mexico Press, 1990. Contains an interview with Harjo that examines her treatment of diversity; her role as a teacher, a feminist, and a challenger of the literary canon; and the importance of music in her life and to her writing.

Bruchac, Joseph. "The Arms of Another Sky: Joy Harjo." In *The Sacred Hoop: Recovering the Feminine in American Indian Traditions*, edited by Paula Gunn Allen. Boston: Beacon Press, 1986. An extensive treatment of the style, structure, and subject matter of Harjo's poetry.

Harjo, Joy. Interview by Stephanie Izarek Smith. *Poets and Writers Magazine* 21, no. 4 (1993): 22-27. Examines Harjo's background, her role as a poet, her feminism, and her work.

——————. "A *MELUS* Interview with Joy Harjo." Interview by Helen Jaskoski. *MELUS: The Journal of the Society for the Study of the Multi-Ethnic Literature of the United States* 16, no. 1 (1989-1990): 5-13. Harjo discusses poets who have had an influence on her own work, her vision of what her poetry is meant to accomplish, and the concept of the woman warrior.

——————. "Ordinary Spirit." In *I Tell You Now: Autobiographical Essays by Native American Writers*, edited by Brian Swann and Arnold Krupat. Lincoln: University of Nebraska Press, 1987. Harjo's essay is a useful introduction to her life.

——————. "The Story of All Our Survival: An Interview with Joy Harjo." Interview by Joseph Bruchac. In *Survival This Way: Interviews with American Indian Poets*, edited by Bruchac. Tucson: University of Arizona Press, 1987. Harjo discusses *She Had Some Horses*, her roots, and her role as a female American Indian writer.

Pearlman, Mickey, ed. *Listen to Their Voices: Twenty Interviews with Women Who Write*. New York: W. W. Norton, 1992. The interview with Harjo explores her role as a teacher of creative writing, her own writing, and its sources in her life's experience.

Melissa E. Barth

SHILOH AND OTHER STORIES

Author: Bobbie Ann Mason (1940-   )
Type of work: Short stories
First published: 1982

Form and Content

The sixteen short stories that constitute Bobbie Ann Mason's first published collection, *Shiloh and Other Stories*, recount the lives of women in the fictional small town of Hopewell, Kentucky, who have a common desire for personal understanding. With the exception of "Nancy Culpepper" and "Lying Doggo," Mason's stories deal with different female protagonists, but each story addresses the same general theme: Every woman must find comfort in understanding herself as an individual; when she becomes the emotional appendage of a male, all of her individuality is lost.

Nancy Culpepper, the protagonist of the stories "Nancy Culpepper" and "Lying Doggo," is a typical Mason protagonist. In the first story, much of Nancy's time is spent trying to save her grandmother's photographs and trying to identify a woman in an old portrait who she believes is a distant relative also named Nancy Culpepper. She is hoping to find some connection with her familial past. Although Nancy is disappointed when she discovers that the woman in question is not Nancy Culpepper, she realizes that she has been actively searching for her own identity.

In the second story in which she appears, Nancy Culpepper is confronted with standing up against her husband's decision to put their old dog, Grover, to sleep. This stand is more than a mere attempt to save an old dog's life; Nancy needs to be and will be heard.

Mason's other female protagonists all go beyond married lives for their identities. In the collection's title story, Norma Jean Moffitt finds little emotional satisfaction in being the wife of injured and unemployed trucker Larry Moffitt. While Larry sits home making string art and dreaming of building his wife a log cabin, Norma Jean works at body building and takes continuing education classes, seeking a place of her own.

In "The Retreat" and "The Ocean," Mason's protagonists accompany their husbands on excursions in search of something that is missing in their lives. Georgeann Pickett accompanies her husband, the Reverend Shelby Pickett, on a religious retreat where she attends workshops on making a successful Christian marriage, hoping to find meaning in hers. Instead, she finds she must confront the fundamentalist view that there is no reason for unhappiness in marriage or with one's husband. Similarly, in "The Ocean," Imogene Crittendon takes a trip in a fancy camper with her husband Bill to see the Atlantic Ocean. The story ends with Bill standing looking out into the ocean and remembering his days in the Navy. Imogene finds no satisfaction in looking at the water and hearing stories about her husband's past. Instead, she finds symbolic relief from her husband's ramblings in a shady place of her own.

In "The Rookers," Mary Lou Skaggs finds a respite from running errands for her husband in her periodic games of Rook with women of similar interests and concerns. In "Still Life with Watermelon," Louise Milsap, whose husband ran away with his mistress, finds herself by making paintings of watermelons, hoping that an eccentric local bachelor will purchase her works. In a more direct manner, the first person narrator of "Residents and Transients" takes a lover while her husband is in Louisville. Her dissatisfaction goes beyond her husband's being away. She does not want to leave the rural area where she feels at home.

Other stories demonstrate women's need to belong. In "Drawing Names" and "Old Things," mothers argue with daughters about the proper thing to do. "Drawing Names" is about a family Christmas gathering to which Carolyn Sission, the story's divorced protagonist, invites her lover, Kent Ballard. For numerous reasons Kent is unable to make the trip. Kent's failure to appear speaks of male/female relationships in general: Women cannot depend upon men and must be able to depend upon themselves.

The remaining stories—"Detroit Skyline," "Offerings," "The Climber," "Graveyard Day," "The New Wave Format," and "Third Monday"—continue discussing Mason's theme of women's search for ways of finding themselves or at least of finding ways of getting their mates to recognize their special needs.

Analysis

Bobbie Ann Mason's *Shiloh and Other Stories* moved a scholar with a dissertation on Vladimir Nabokov and a study on women sleuths in literature into the forefront of American short-story writers. Shortly after its appearance in 1982, *Shiloh and Other Stories* won for Mason the PEN Hemingway Award for First Fiction and became a finalist for the National Book Critics Circle Award, the American Book Award, and the PEN Faulkner Award. In addition to receiving critical acclaim, the collection enjoyed popular success, and various works from it have appeared in anthologies as examples of well-crafted short stories.

The strength of this thematically interlaced collection stems from the stories' universality and Mason's ability to create characters who easily could live next door. Mason's fictional Hopewell is the quintessential rural American community. Its people and its problems are those experienced daily by thousands of real small-town citizens. The characters who populate this little corner of the world are nothing more than common folk, but their lives reflect the pathos found in traditional literary tragedies.

The stories' brevity and self-containment demonstrate Edgar Allan Poe's pronouncement on the characteristics of a good short story. Although thematically intertwined, these stories operate as individual vignettes or slices of life, demonstrating Mason's ability to make form fit function. The *Shiloh* stories do not rely upon a collective dynamic for their strength. Each story tells of specific people at specific moments in time.

Mason's Hopewell, Kentucky, is reminiscent of William Faulkner's Yoknapatawpha County, Mississippi; Sherwood Anderson's Winesburg, Ohio; Ernest Hemingway's Michigan; Eudora Welty's Mississippi; and Flannery O'Connor's Georgia and Tennessee. Like these earlier writers, Mason has created an identifiable place into which she thrusts her characters, therefore making them more plausible than characters who come from nowhere specific.

Mason's choice of the short story as the vehicle for telling the history of Hopewell and its inhabitants is an applicable one. She is not attempting to tell the history of the town in an extended narrative. Instead, she relates numerous individual moments that make up the greater chronology of Hopewell and the individuals about whom she writes. The impact of the *Shiloh* stories would have been negated if they had gone beyond their moments in time.

The tension needed for a literary work to succeed is not lost in these brief stories. Mason is able to expand this tension by showing that it is not limited to the life of a single individual. Like Sherwood Anderson's stories about Winesburg, Ohio, Mason's *Shiloh* stories examine moments in the lives of various individuals. As do Anderson's stories, Mason's short pieces create a collective history of a small community that is suffering from a social virus; in this case, the fact that women have no real identities of their own.

The finely wrought short stories in Mason's *Shiloh and Other Stories* are psychological case studies of women who are searching for themselves. These works place Bobbie Ann Mason safely in the company of writers who have become masters of both psychology and literary style.

Context

Bobbie Ann Mason's *Shiloh and Other Stories* continues the tradition in which women writers tell the stories of women who are looking for individual identities, a tradition perfected by such earlier writers as Kate Chopin, Willa Cather, Eudora Welty, and Harper Lee. Like her literary precursors, Mason chooses to tell women's stories through female protagonists and narrators. This technique has proved to be a successful vehicle for telling women's stories in the works of other disparate contemporary women writers such as Lee Smith, Alice Walker, Amy Tan, and Rita Mae Brown.

Feminist critics have long been concerned with the dearth of women writers who have come to the forefront of American literature and with men writers' attempts to tell women's stories. In *Shiloh and Other Stories* and in her later works, Mason takes important steps toward allaying these concerns. In each story, Mason provides a complete depiction of the momentary fragments that produce the lives that her female protagonists have been forced to live.

In none of her stories does Mason moralize or offer clear-cut answers to complex problems. Her intention is to inform rather than pontificate. Mason is able to draw her reader into her fictional world by creating believable characters who live in believable settings. The reader's concern turns from the progression of a fictional narrative to commiseration with an individual who is experiencing intense challenges to a once-stable relationship or to her attempts to come to terms with herself.

In the canon of works by women about women, Mason's short stories stand out in their portrayal of women who decide to make their own decisions about their lives. Often this individualism goes against the social grain, yet Mason's protagonists are willing to stand up to any stigma that may be cast upon them. They must live their own lives unencumbered by outside interference. Her works join the growing list of high-quality works that speak directly to the need of women to have lives and identities of their own without the fear of being branded as radical. Mason's works exemplify the new works that are being considered for canonization, works that, in the past, would have been overlooked because they were written by women, not because of any artistic weakness.

Sources for Further Study

Arnold, Edwin T. "Falling Apart and Staying Together: Bobbie Ann Mason and Leon Driskell Explore the State of the Modern Family." *Appalachian Journal* 12, (Winter, 1985): 135-141. This article attempts to show how a male and a female writer approach the theme of family differently by comparing Mason's *Shiloh* stories with the works of another Kentucky writer, Leon Driskell. This article is especially valuable to the investigator who wishes to study Mason as a feminist writer.

Giannone, Richard. "Bobbie Ann Mason and the Recovery of Mystery." *Studies in Short Fiction* 27 (Fall, 1990): 553-566. In a focused analysis of Mason's characters, Giannone is concerned with the reaction of Mason's characters to the situations in which they find themselves. In most cases, the characters find themselves without clear answers at the end of their stories.

Ryan, Maureen. "Stopping Places: Bobbie Ann Mason's Short Stories." In *Women Writers of the Contemporary South*, edited by Peggy Whitman Prenshaw. Jackson: University Press of Mississippi, 1984. The thrust of this article is to show how the women characters in the *Shiloh* stories try to find a place for themselves in a contemporary world of ever-changing moral expectations and social roles for women. To underscore her argument, Ryan shows how Mason's stories have moved the literary depiction of the South from the Old South plantations into the contemporary world of malls and beauty parlors.

White, Leslie. "The Function of Popular Culture in Bobbie Ann Mason's *Shiloh and Other Stories* and *In Country*." *The Southern Quarterly* 26 (Summer, 1988): 69-79. This article is good for its discussion of Mason's use of popular culture to depict the commonness of her characters. In *Shiloh and Other Stories* and in her Vietnam novel *In Country* (1985), Mason follows her characters through their daily lives, which are governed by the encroachment of various aspects of popular culture.

Wilhelm, Albert E. "Private Rituals: Coping with Change in the Fiction of Bobbie Ann Mason." *Midwest Quarterly* 28 (Winter, 1987): 271-282. Wilhelm provides an interesting and informative look at Mason's presentation of the private means her characters employ to deal with the changes that occur in their lives.

Thomas B. Frazier

SHIP OF FOOLS

Author: Katherine Anne Porter (1890-1980)
Type of work: Novel
Type of plot: Fable
Time of plot: August 22-September 17, 1931
Locale: On the German ship *Vera* between Veracruz, Mexico, and Bremerhaven, Germany
First published: 1962

Principal characters:
   JENNY BROWN and DAVID SCOTT, young American painters in a
      tortured relationship
   DR. SCHUMANN, the ship's doctor
   LA CONDESA, a dissolute noblewoman being deported from Cuba
      to Tenerife
   SIEGFRIED RIEBER and LIZZIE SPÖCKENKIEKER, two people
      involved in the ladies garment trade who are carrying on a
      courtship
   PROFESSOR and MRS. HUTTEN, a couple returning to Germany
      with their seasick bulldog, Bébé
   WILHELM FREYTAG, a man returning to Germany to fetch his
      Jewish wife, Mary, and her mother
   KARL and GRETA BAUMGARTNER, a couple traveling with their
      eight-year-old son, Hans
   MRS. RITTERSDORF, a woman who records her acid opinions in a
      diary
   MR. and MRS. LUTZ, a couple returning to Switzerland with their
      eighteen-year-old daughter, Elsa
   WILLIAM DENNY, an American chemical engineer
   MARY TREADWELL, a bitter American divorcée
   JULIUS LÖWENTHAL, a Jewish maker and seller of Catholic
      religious objects
   ARNE HANSEN, a large, strong, slow Swede
   KARL GLOCKEN, a hunchback who once owned a tobacco stand
   CAPTAIN THIELE, a stern, autocratic, and extremely
      class-conscious "Junker"
   RIC and RAC, six-year-old twins, a brother and sister with the
      Spanish troupe
   THE SPANISH TROUPE, a group of singers and dancers

Form and Content
   The phrase "ship of fools," as Porter mentions in a brief introductory note, is a
translation of the title of Sebastian Brant's moral allegory *Das Narrenschiff* (1494).

As Brant's work does, Porter's work reflects on the many follies of human beings. Unlike the characters portrayed in Brant's work, however, the passengers on Porter's ship are not static homilies. They reflect on their own lives and interact with one another.

Described by one critic as a "wave," *Ship of Fools* begins slowly, developing a large number of characters, crests somewhere after its mid-point with a series of mini-climaxes, and rolls quietly to a denouement that solves no one's problems. Part 1, "Embarcation" which constitutes less than a fifth of the book, introduces the passengers in Veracruz, as they prepare to board, and follows them onto the ship, offering the reader initial, sometimes misleading glimpses of all the major characters. Part 2, "High Sea," constitutes more than half of the book, and Part 3, "The Harbors," in which many of the apparently meaningful crises and decisions are resolved, constitutes less than a third of the work.

The development of characters and drama is achieved through two overarching devices: the slow building of individual and family portraits and the juxtaposition of alien elements. Either one or both of these processes may lead to a decisive moment in the life of an individual or family. Thus, Löwenthal is in a cabin with the anti-Semitic Rieber, Elsa the wallflower with the unconventional Jenny, the overbearing Mrs. Rittersdorf with the timid Mrs. Schmitt, and the fastidious and romantic Mrs. Treadwell with the crude and uninhibited Lizzie. The Huttens' crisis is precipitated by Ric and Rac, who throw Bébé overboard; Denny's obsession with Pastora leads him by mistake to Mrs. Treadwell's door, and she reacts with rage that she has stored up against her philandering ex-husband; Freytag's longing for his wife Mary is eased by his flirting with Jenny, and this precipitates the last of Jenny's confrontations with David; Hansen—obsessed by Amparo and resentful of Lizzie and Rieber's cavorting—puts an unexpected end to their affair by breaking a bottle over Rieber's head; the doctor is captivated and turned aside from his customary phlegmatic routine by La Condesa; the class-conscious Captain is humiliated at his own table by the despised Spanish troupe; and Elsa is attracted and humiliated by one of the young Spanish dancers.

Each critical moment passes, the passengers are deposited at their respective ports, and life apparently goes on—except, of course, that the Nazis will soon be affecting many of them in ways they could not imagine.

Analysis

Ship of Fools has been called a novel and has been castigated for lacking the plan and coherence of a novel. It has also been called an allegory and a moral fable (apologue). Begun during the rise of Nazism in Germany and published seventeen years after the end of World War II, the work eludes classification as a universal, allegorical comment only because it is so apparently specific to the evils that were gestating in Germany in 1931. With the exception of the uninvolved Dr. Schumann and the children, hardly a German whose mind is revealed to the reader by the omniscient narrator is not a virulent bigot.

Porter's conscious reference to Brant's allegory is, nevertheless, a clear indicator of what she had in mind. Friendly critics have defended her work by referring to earlier literary metaphors such as Ahab and the white whale in *Moby Dick*. Even more apt—and contemporary—comparisons may be made to novels by Günter Grass and the prose and stage works of Friedrich Dürrenmatt and Max Frisch, in which recognizable human traits mingle with allegory, satire, parody, the grotesque, and postwar cynicism in a text that may be taken either as specific to Germany in the 1940's and/or to the succeeding competition of the Cold War, or as a far more universal and pessimistic comment on the human condition and social institutions. On Porter's ship, the inept and the intolerant encounter the indecorous, the immoral, and the amoral.

The omniscient author allows the reader access to the thoughts of these semi-allegorical figures, where one encounters the recognizable hopes and fears of the young or the disappointed side by side with intolerance, indifference, hatred, bigotry, religious megalomania, and lust. Minds into which the reader is allowed no access are those of the pimps, prostitutes, and thieves of the Spanish troupe—sometimes called gypsies by others or themselves, who are singly or as a group responsible for many of the personal crises experienced by the other passengers. Even the young minds of Ric and Rac are closed to the reader, as they plan their ruinous mischief, suffer barbarous punishment by their parents for unknowingly thwarting a planned theft, and—apparently—explore each other sexually while hidden in a lifeboat. The thoughts of the Spanish troupe need not be elucidated, because the Spanish are the embodiment of the illegality and illicit desire that bedevil the social order and the libidos of the others and serve, therefore, to increase the fears that may fuel sexual and social repression.

The crises of individual passengers represent delayed and futile reactions to lifetimes of habit. During the latter half of the "High Sea" section, the reader is continually confronted by actions that are unexpected, uncharacteristic, or inappropriate, and that lead one to the conclusion that the characters are completely unable to change their own lives or psyches.

Shortly after Mrs. Hutten has, for the first time, had the audacity to contradict an opinion of her husband's in public, the couple discover that Bébé is missing and extend the anger and defensiveness over Mrs. Hutten's rebelliousness to blaming each other for leaving the cabin door open. In the relief and anxiety following the dog's rescue from the sea, they are overwhelmed by an unaccustomed, life-affirming, and passionate sexual union, which returns them to their original condition. He is the husband, and she is the subservient wife. The enigmatic self-sacrifice of the pathetic steerage passenger in saving the dog and losing his own life vanishes swiftly from their minds and only slightly less swiftly from the minds of the other passengers.

The other false apotheoses are similarly abortive. Elsa's infatuation ends crushingly when the object of her desire asks her to dance and she does not know how. Denny's lust leads him mistakenly to Mary Treadwell, who beats the helpless drunk with the heel of her gold sandal, providing him with a physical climax he could not have foreseen and shaking her tenuous hold on her thoughts of the cultivated and sedate life ahead of her in Paris. Freytag excuses his attempt to seduce Jenny as not serious until he actually fails, providing the feuding lovers with a last opportunity to make inconclusive war and peace. Baumgartner resorts to the goose-step he abhors to lead a parade of children to the festival given by the Spanish troupe, is joined by no adults, and finishes in disgrace with his wife, while his son is puzzled at the abrupt ending of the only activity that he has enjoyed on board and by the coupling that later reunites his parents and reestablishes the status quo. Hansen's clogged emotions are vented but not permanently altered by his attack on Rieber. Löwenthal, who has endured exile at a table for one and Rieber's calculated abuse, openly derides only Freytag, who is sent to Löwenthal's table when his Jewish connection is discovered, and the Spaniard who attempts unsuccessfully to sell him a ticket to the so-called festival. He calls her a whore in Yiddish, and she calls him a filthy pig in Romany—languages representative of two of the groups that will be targeted by the Nazi regime. Schumann, showing an interesting similarity to the aging hero of Thomas Mann's *Death in Venice* (1912), is attracted to beauty and dissolution but is finally unable to act on his feelings.

These and other expressions of futile rebellion against the routine regime of life are concluded in the final section as different passengers disembark at different ports to continue no happier and no wiser than before. It is this inconclusion, criticized by some as a novelistic fault, that is actually Porter's harsh conclusion.

Context

A major subtext of *Ship of Fools* is provided by Porter's grim presentation of the role of women of all social levels and all ages. The women of the Spanish troupe are constrained to turn over their earnings to their lovers/pimps. If they are careful, they may be able to skim some of the money and build secret funds for creating new lives as performers or shopkeepers, like those they have so deftly robbed. Mrs. Schmitt's personality is submerged under considerations of whether her dead husband Otto would approve of what she is doing at any moment. Mrs. Rittersdorf terrorizes Mrs. Schmitt and fills the pages of her diary with supercilious comments on others of whom she does not approve but whom she will not confront. Mrs. Hutten flees from her moment of rebellion to the safety of marital thralldom. Jenny flutters like a butterfly in a net but repeatedly returns to David and his quest for both love and dominance. Lizzie Spöckenkieker defines herself only in terms of which man wishes or has wished to marry her. La Condesa is so addicted to masculine admiration that she turns a blind eye to the satirical comments of her Cuban student entourage. The desperate and dependent futility of these lives invites both compassion and indignation. Racial and ethnic bigotry outlived the Nazi era as did sexual bigotry. None of what Porter says is yet beside the point.

Sources for Further Study

Bloom, Harold, ed. *Katherine Anne Porter*. New York: Chelsea House, 1986. Harold Moss's essay on the novel repeats the complaint that it has no novelistic tying up of loose ends. Robert B. Heilmann's essay on style compares Porter to Jane Austen and George Eliot, highlighting techniques such as the use of series of nouns and participles, but claims that Porter evinces no trademark mannerisms. Joan Givner examines the Porter triangle of villain/victim/not-so-innocent hero or heroine and notes the consistency of Porter's description of evil characters.

DeMouy, Jane Krause. *Katherine Anne Porter's Women: The Eye of Her Fiction.* Austin: University of Texas Press, 1983. DeMouy categorizes Porter's women in three types: the Venus figures, the traditional mother and wife figures, and the unfeminine, androgynous figures. Like many other critics, DeMouy seizes upon the vignette witnessed by Jenny Brown—a man and woman locked in mortal combat— as an explication of Porter's pessimism about the possibility of love and her latter-day feeling that men, too, are victims.

Liberman, M. M. *Katherine Anne Porter's Fiction.* Detroit: Wayne State University Press, 1971. The first chapter makes a spirited defense of Porter's novel, analyzing some of the more common criticisms and making a case for *Ship of Fools* as an apologue.

Mooney, Harry John, Jr. *The Fiction and Criticism of Katherine Anne Porter.* Rev. ed. Pittsburgh: University of Pittsburgh Press, 1962. Typical of some critical interpretations, this analysis uses some of the strengths of Porter's short stories to reflect on shortcomings of the novel and echoes other opinions that the novel's greatest fault is the absence of any possibility of human nobility.

Unrue, Darlene Harbour. *Truth and Vision in Katherine Anne Porter's Fiction.* Athens: University of Georgia Press, 1985. The chapter on *Ship of Fools* uses analyses of Porter's other work to reflect upon and illuminate the novel, mentioning or discussing the quest theme, the relationship of earlier characters to characters in the novel, and the themes of isolation, love and lust, parental dominance, racism, sexism, and classism, noting particularly Dr. Schumann's enlightened perceptions of evil and death.

Wescott, Glenway. *Images of Truth: Remembrances and Criticism.* New York: Harper & Row, 1962. The strength of the chapter on Porter is not so much the literary interpretation as the personal glimpses of Porter herself during much of her career, including the time that led up to *Ship of Fools*.

James L. Hodge

SHROUD FOR A NIGHTINGALE

Author: P. D. James (1920-   )
Type of work: Novel
Type of plot: Detective
Time of plot: January, 1971
Locale: Heatheringfield, England
First published: 1971

Principal characters:
    ADAM DALGLIESH, the chief superintendent of New Scotland Yard
    CHARLES MASTERSON, Dalgliesh's handsome subordinate
    MARY TAYLOR, the matron of Nightingale House, John
        Carpendar Hospital's nurse training school
    SISTER ETHEL BRUMFETT, the second-in-command at
        Nightingale House
    SISTER HILDA ROLFE, a discontented senior nurse
    SISTER MAVIS GEARING, the third senior nurse
    DR. STEPHEN COURTNEY-BRIGGS, the senior consultant surgeon
    HEATHER PEARCE, an unpopular student nurse who dies horribly
    JOSEPHINE FALLON, an older nursing student
    MADELEINE GOODALE, an efficient, sensible student nurse
    JULIA PARDOE, an attractive student who juggles Rolfe's and
        Masterson's attentions
    MORAG SMITH, a maid

Form and Content

A classic whodunit, *Shroud for a Nightingale* traces an investigation by Chief Superintendent Adam Dalgliesh into the sudden deaths of two students in the virtually all-female world of Nightingale House, the nurses' training school at the John Carpendar Hospital. The book opens in bleak winter with the spectacularly public, grisly poisoning—during a training inspector's visit—of Heather Pearce, the student taking the role of the patient in a demonstration of stomach-tube feeding. In the second chapter, Jo Fallon, the nurse whom Pearce replaced at the last moment, dies quietly in bed after drinking a poisoned whiskey nightcap. The remaining six chapters of the story detail Dalgliesh's careful probing of this closed community's secrets with the help of his subordinate, Masterson, with whom he has a civil but not cordial working relationship.

Introduced into the narrative in pensive reflection over the second corpse, Dalgliesh moves swiftly to a formal interrogation of Nightingale House's inhabitants. It is primarily through his eyes that the investigation unfolds, although the story also offers selective access to the consciousness of several other characters, including Masterson, the matron (Mary Taylor), and Rolfe. As Dalgliesh and Masterson interview the variously garrulous, wary, or indifferent suspects, they discover plentiful motives among revelations of adultery, abortion, homosexuality, and blackmail. Against this backdrop, Dalgliesh becomes convinced that they are dealing with a double murder, especially after gathering further clues at lunch with the three senior nurses, Rolfe, Brumfett, and Gearing. Yet his long day's work is over only after he conducts further interviews, endures a private tea with Gearing, discovers the nicotine poison hidden in a fire bucket, and fixes the time of the first murder in a midnight chat with the school's maid. The crux of the case, his intuition tells him, is the missing library book that Pearce borrowed on Fallon's card—likewise missing.

The next-to-last chapter briefly shifts setting for both detectives' interviews with witnesses in London the following day, then brings Dalgliesh back to the grounds of Nightingale House at night for a severe blow to his head. Now equipped with the library book, however, and Masterson's information about a dying patient who recognized an ex-Nazi nurse, Dalgliesh confirms his hunch that a woman committed both murders to protect the true identity of Irmgard Grobel, a war criminal. Before daylight the next morning, the discovery of Brumfett's body precipitates Dalgliesh's confrontation with the matron, who unsuccessfully tries to convince him that Brumfett, the self-confessed killer of Pearce and Fallon, also killed herself because she was Grobel. Lacking the proof to arrest her, Dalgliesh does not see justice done until months later: On the warm August day of the epilogue, he reads and then destroys the confession that the matron left for him before her suicide.

Analysis

Like James's other mysteries, *Shroud for a Nightingale* presents murder as an ultimate disruption of the moral order and an inevitable contaminant within a community. Besides being indirectly rooted in the Holocaust killings of thirty-one Russians and Poles, the two student deaths lead relentlessly to an attempt on Dalgliesh's life, a third murder, and then a suicide. Even the investigation that is essential for restoring order occasionally seems to perpetuate the chaos and ugliness of the original crimes, as when the pathologist callously probes body orifices or the police insist on a precise reenactment of the gastric-feeding demonstration. At every point, James stresses the high price that everyone pays for both the commission and the solution of a murder. Thus, the reinstatement of "normality, sanity" at the end of Dalgliesh's inquiry never entirely compensates for the losses in human life, professional stability, and ethical certitude.

James intensifies this rather somber mood by setting her nursing school in an ornate Victorian edifice in gothically gloomy environs. Nightingale House's history matches the dark impulses that belie its medical mission: Rather than commemorating Florence, the matron tells Dalgliesh, the place is named for its nineteenth century builder, Thomas Nightingale, who so abused and tortured a servant girl that she hanged herself. Here, then, is another intrusion of past evil into the present, another dark deed in which the school is shrouded.

In *Shroud for a Nightingale*, as in her other novels, James insists that the guilty must not go unpunished, with the result that she assigns a somewhat improbable suicide to Mary Taylor. At the same time, however, she makes Dalgliesh's final victory over Taylor richly ambiguous. The matron's private confession to him in their dramatic tête-à-tête both follows her compassionate tending of the detective's head wound and invokes her blameless past before her murder of her manipulative confidante Brumfett, herself a murderess; moreover, Dalgliesh feels ambivalent enough to burn rather than reveal her final written confession. Yet it is the rapport between the matron and Dalgliesh that casts the most complex shadows on his quest for truth. From the beginning, Dalgliesh not only admires her but also identifies with her professionalism, dedication, and detachment. That he could like a woman who proves to be a murderess as well as a former accused Nazi war-criminal is daunting enough; as his virtual double, she further challenges him with her accusation that, like herself, he hides behind the rules and regulations of his professional code to avoid ordinary human conflict, using them as "convenient shields to shelter behind if the doubts become troublesome." Indeed, Dalgliesh's subsequent obsession with incriminating her seems in part an attempt to exorcise his own dark, skeptical self.

Besides complicating distinctions between guilt and innocence, law and justice, detective and criminal, the novel examines the pressures of living in a small, hierarchical institution. What immediately strikes—and appalls—Dalgliesh is the overwhelming lack of privacy that makes everyone's comings and goings common knowledge, from Fallon's whiskey-nightcap ritual to Mavis Gearing's assignations with her married lover. The only intimate relationship that escapes another's knowledge at Nightingale House is Fallon's affair with Arnold Dowson, an apprentice writer from London; all other connections, private interests, and weaknesses suffer exposure to one or several other parties long before the police arrive on the scene.

Unsurprisingly, in addition to animosities, such a tight, even claustrophobic, community also breeds a struggle for, and abuse of, power on both a personal and an institutional level. Thus, Pearce sets her own death in motion by her tendency to exert power over others through blackmail. She has no trouble manipulating her classmates, but her decision to blackmail Brumfett, whom she mistakenly identifies as Irmgard Grobel, proves to be fatal. Similarly, Brumfett kills Pearce not only to protect the matron but also to preserve her own exclusive emotional hold on the woman in charge of Nightingale House. Meanwhile, Dr. Courtney-Briggs, who extends his surgeon's power over life and death to a crushing dominance over the entire hospital staff, also seems to be prepared to blackmail the matron once he discovers her past identity. Although he is an outsider to the training school, Sergeant Masterson similarly practices an unwholesome opportunism while there, taking sexual advantage of the nurse Julia Pardoe—who herself unfeelingly manipulates Hilda Rolfe's affections— as a safe, indirect way of flouting his superior's standards of behavior. In this context, Dalgliesh becomes an exemplary figure to restore order because of his scrupulousness about exerting official authority and invading personal lives only in the service of justice.

Context

James's fourth novel featuring Adam Dalgliesh, *Shroud for a Nightingale* won an Edgar from the Mystery Writers of America, a Silver Dagger from the British Crime Writers Association, and the label of "masterpiece" from a 1974 *Times Literary Supplement* review. It marked the author's entry both into the world market and into the exclusive company of England's foremost mystery writers, all of them women: Agatha Christie, Dorothy Sayers, Josephine Tey, Margery Allingham, and Ngaio Marsh. In fact, with the publication of *Shroud for a Nightingale*, the critical consensus was that James had surpassed these predecessors by creating not one-dimensional artificial puzzles but painstakingly crafted novels—complete with complex psychological characterizations, authentic descriptions, and contemporary social issues—that can hold their own outside the mystery genre. Foremost among the skillfully evoked figures in this and her other books is, of course, her contemplative poet-detective Dalgliesh, who struggles with his own life problems while conducting his expert investigations.

The novel has the healing-institution setting that James often favors for her fiction, thanks to her own background in hospital administration and medical research. In this particular case, by making the crime scene a nurses' training school, she adds the theme of professional and romantic fulfillment for women to her usual focus on society's distaste for illness, disabilities, and death. Perhaps unexpectedly for a married author who turned to her maiden surname and ungendered initials when she first took up writing in 1962, James perpetuates some sexist stereotypes here: She makes her three senior nurses variations on the "love-starved spinster" and has Dalgliesh as well as others assume that the pretty students will drop their careers as soon as they marry. In Norma Siebenheller's words, *Shroud for a Nightingale* "abounds with old-fashioned fussy old maids and silly young girls who seem dated for a book written in the early 1970's." Equally important, the most admirable woman in the book, Mary Taylor, is ultimately disqualified as matron of Nightingale House and as a romantic interest for Dalgliesh by her connection with both Nazism and murder.

Yet James's portrait of a female community leaves no doubt about how important women can be to one another, whether in rivalry, affection, or ambition. As Carolyn Heilbrun notes, one of the book's excellences is its focus on "the love one woman can have for another, ranging from possessive passion to a marvelously comfortable camaraderie." Moreover, intelligence, competence, and compassion are evident among the female staff, alongside a just contempt for Dr. Courtney-Briggs' and other doctors' male chauvinism. Dalgliesh himself does not entirely get away with his sexist assumptions about "plain" Madeleine Goodale and "masculine" Hilda Rolfe. Surely it is no coincidence, then, that James's next novel, *An Unsuitable Job for a Woman*, was a more obviously feminist narrative introducing her other sleuth, young Cordelia Gray.

Sources for Further Study

Benstock, Bernard. "The Clinical World of P. D. James." In *Twentieth-Century Women Novelists*, edited by Thomas F. Staley. Totowa, N.J.: Barnes & Noble Books, 1982. This article's presence alongside nine other essays on such mainstream authors as Margaret Drabble, Iris Murdoch, and Doris Lessing testifies to James's status as a serious writer. Particularly interesting is Benstock's assessment of ambience (especially dwellings), interior monologues, and typical dramatis personae in James's fiction.

Gidez, Richard B. *P. D. James*. Boston: Twayne, 1986. After situating James in the classic English mystery tradition, Gidez devotes one chapter to each novel in chronological order. He concludes with an analysis of the short stories, which are rarely mentioned; a helpful overview of such Jamesian themes as "Love and Marriage," "Loneliness and Alienation," "Justice and Retribution"; and an excellent selected bibliography.

Heilbrun, Carolyn. "James, P. D." In *Twentieth-Century Crime and Mystery Writers*, edited by John M. Reilly. New York: St. Martin's Press, 1980. This entry sketches in James's distinctions as the best practitioner of the art of mystery writing in the 1960's and 1970's. In assessing James's seven novels thus far, Heilbrun notes that occasionally Dalgliesh is a more routine character than he is in the entirely satisfying *Shroud for a Nightingale*.

Hubly, Erlene. "Adam Dalgliesh: Byronic Hero." *Clues: A Journal of Detection* 3 (Fall/Winter, 1982): 40-46. According to Hubly, James's detective harks back to the tradition of the tormented Byronic hero in a godless world. Thus, it is Byronic narcissism that prevents him from loving any woman but his Aunt Jane, whom he resembles, and that draws him to Mary Taylor, his female alter ego.

Joyner, Nancy Carol. "P. D. James." In *Ten Women of Mystery*, edited by Earl F. Bargainnier. Bowling Green, Ohio: Bowling Green State University Popular Press, 1981. With a strong biographical emphasis, Joyner offers insights into James's writing habits, her affinity with Sayers and Allingham, and her eye for realistic detail.

Siebenheller, Norma. *P. D. James*. New York: Frederick Ungar, 1981. This indispensable, first full-length look at James's work makes the most of Siebenheller's consultations with the author. Besides an overall appraisal of themes, characters, and style, and a detailed analysis of each novel, Siebenheller provides a useful bibliography of selected reviews. Whereas she praises Dalgliesh's three-dimensional complexity in *Shroud for a Nightingale*, she faults the book's ending as drawn out and unlikely.

Margaret Bozenna Goscilo

THE SIGN IN SIDNEY BRUSTEIN'S WINDOW

Author: Lorraine Hansberry (1930-1965)
Type of work: Drama
Type of plot: Protest drama
Time of plot: The 1960's
Locale: Greenwich Village, New York
First produced: 1964, at Longacre Theatre, New York City, New York
First published: 1965

Principal characters:
SIDNEY BRUSTEIN, a Jewish intellectual and the publisher and
    editor of a local newspaper
IRIS PARODUS BRUSTEIN, Sidney's neurotic wife
ALTON SCALES, a close friend of Sidney and a very light-skinned
    African American
MAVIS PARODUS BRYSON, Iris' older sister, who is prejudiced
    against Jews and African Americans
DAVID RAGIN, a young homosexual playwright
GLORIA PARODUS, the youngest of the three Parodus sisters, a
    high-class call girl who hopes to get out of "the life" by
    marrying Alton Scales
WALLY O'HARA, a hypocritical friend of Sidney, a lawyer who is
    running for local office

Form and Content

When Mavis declares, in response to an argument about modern drama between Sidney and David, "I just don't know whatever happened to simple people with simple problems in literature," one irony is that Lorraine Hansberry's play itself shows complex people living in a world whose problems are complex. Ironically, much later in the play, even the apparently superficial and conventional Mavis turns out to be complex, concealing depth, feelings, and problems of her own that reveal that her statement arises not from aesthetic naïveté but from a longing for happiness in her own difficult life. While Hansberry's play is a work of social protest (key repeated words are "revolution" and "revolutionary"), criticizing the oppression of women and minorities as well as societal injustice and political corruption, it also belongs to the genre of the problem play, dealing with art, love and marriage, the family, engagement versus apathy, self-realization, and philosophies of life.

The play's seven scenes (two in the first and third acts, three in the second act) move through late spring, late summer, and fall, in accord with the timetable of the O'Hara political campaign that Sidney is persuaded to join and also suggesting the cycle of birth and death, paralleling the birth of Sidney's newspaper and its later threatened extinction from the corrupt sociopolitical establishment, the flourishing of the relationship between Sidney and Iris deteriorating to separation and imminent divorce, the increasing alienation of Sidney from his friends, Sidney's idealism yielding to disillusion with the discovery of O'Hara's deceit, and the actual death by suicide of Gloria in the Brusteins' apartment. Paradoxically, underlying this cycle is a counter cycle of death to life, as Iris' self-realization and self-assertion flower, David's experimental play achieves critical and commercial success, Mavis accomplishes the closer understanding with Sidney that she has hoped for, Sidney overcomes the bitterness of being duped and finally totally commits to political engagement (the ironic opposite of his initial credo for his newspaper), and Iris hints at a possible marital reunion made possible by Sidney's self-realization or finding of his full potential and identity. The hopefulness in the cycle is conveyed by the symbolic lighting in the play's last scene, which begins gray and bleak but at the end is brighter and warmer.

The play uses a mixture of tones and styles. Some parts are nearly pure fun, such as the "running gag" of the persistent categorization by Sidney's friends of his folk song establishment as a nightclub and his equally persistent, invariably phrased correction that is was not a nightclub. The establishment's name, The Silver Dagger, seems ill-chosen for a folk-song site (though appropriate to Sidney's sharp and sometimes injurious wit) and augurs, like the nature of the place, its failure. Often, the play's humor is mixed with a serious theme or tone, as it is when Mavis brings Iris an elegant dress and jokes about Iris' present attire that all the latter needs now for Easter is a formal pair of sneakers. Ironically, the dress that Iris at first disparages as bourgeois she later dons, symbolizing her foray into the fashionable world and her separation from Sidney and his circle. The symbolism of clothing, as expressed in Iris' conspicuous costume change, is closely connected with the play's ideas about women's concerns and how women are perceived in society. Language styles in the play vary among the characters, including modish slang, philosophical and intellectual abstraction and allusion, mild oaths, Marxist analysis, popular song lyrics, ancient Greek, and Jewish phrases.

Analysis

Tracing Sidney's beliefs, political ideology, and interrelationships is one of the play's most vivid symbolic props, which is referred to or interacted with by characters eleven times throughout the drama: the poster in the apartment window which gives the play its title. At first, Sidney is reluctant to accept the sign because he wants to remain disengaged from practical politics and focus on philosophy and the arts. When he is drawn into fervent campaigning because of his liberal ideology of righteousness and freedom from corruption or oppression, the sign represents this new intensity. When the campaign begins, surprisingly, to appear to have a chance to succeed, and when O'Hara actually wins, the sign seems to represent the triumph of innocent and uncorrupted good over wickedness. When Sidney learns about O'Hara's corruption, however, life not being as simple as a fairy tale, the sign signifies betrayal and Sidney's bitterness. Finally, when he accepts the fact of betrayal but decides to fight against the candidate he has helped to elect, even though he may lose his newspaper, the sign represents Sidney's full and courageous commitment. Before Sidney has learned some humility through his experience in politics and has actualized his full humanity, he is not wise or strong enough to refrain from saying wounding things to Iris; his growth, she notes, may make possible her return to their marriage. Sidney's transcendence of bitterness is partly shown through the play's theme of the interrelation between art and life when, with good humor, he addresses the deceitful O'Hara in the play's conclusion cunningly as the arriving "deus ex machina." The events are thus appropriately cast as a Greek tragedy with the misfortunes of Gloria's death and O'Hara's triumphant deception, suggesting that O'Hara's arrival will not solve any problems, that O'Hara's winning has been unnaturally forced, and that O'Hara's backing has been not from the crane used on the ancient Greek stage but from the corrupt political machine. Sidney's pun indicates his comic resilience and willingness to continue striving rather than yield to nihilism or cynicism.

Symbolic blocking (placement of actors and actresses on stage) is used to express the themes of the need for tolerance, sympathy, and humanitarianism in the marvelous group dining scene of act 1, scene 2 (the play's longest and most complex scene). After Iris has returned with paella from work at the restaurant (and has changed from her waitress' uniform, yet another of the clothing changes symbolic of her identity problem), a dinner develops for the nonconformist circle of Iris, Sidney, Alton Scales, and David Ragin. Tension and sarcastic remarks develop between the visiting Mavis, representing conventional middle-class values and conformity, and the diners, as Mavis stands apart, ready to return to her home. Thus, Mavis' distance from the diners on the issues of art (especially the new drama), race (her prejudice against African Americans, including her dismay at the prospect of Alton marrying her sister Gloria), and bohemianism (the Brusteins) is expressed visually as well as verbally. Mavis' deep feeling and sensitivity are revealed, however, by how wounded she is by some of the remarks as well as by her trenchant observation that intellectuals and artists ought to have enough sensitivity and humanity of their own to avoid such cruelty and callousness as they have just displayed.

After Mavis' exit, the diners, who have just displayed such solidarity, divide in internal dissension, helping to illustrate the play's theme of life's ironic reversals. Alton Scales is bothered by his own and the others' treatment of Mavis, since as an African American he above all knows the effects of the failure of humanitarianism. He has proved to be intolerant of Mavis, as he also proves to be of homosexuals in the quarrel he picks with David Ragin. Ragin has himself proved to be deficient in part of the artist's or dramatist's task through his disregard of Mavis, although Hansberry, the creator of his and Mavis' character, does not so fail. When Sidney argues with Ragin about the utility of reformist politics and reformist political drama (Ragin believes that both are pointless), the breakup of what had been an apparent communion is complete, the dinner is left unfinished, and the Brusteins are left by themselves.

Context

Though not as strong or admirable as the three main female characters—Ruth,

Beneatha, and Lena Younger—in Hansberry's most widely known play *A Raisin in the Sun* (1959), the three female characters in this later play are sympathetic and have many commendable attributes and strengths, as well as some flaws and weaknesses. Like Ruth Younger, the three Parodus sisters (Mavis, Iris, and Gloria) have had significant trouble with either husband or boyfriend. Mavis has shown understanding, perseverance, and stoicism by her behavior following the discovery of her husband's longtime infidelity with another woman. Related to the play's theme of the interrelation of art and life, Mavis reveals to Sidney that with her father's encouragement she learned and recited passages in ancient Greek from the Greek tragedies, and she demonstrates with a passage from Euripides' *Medea*. Ironically, Mavis is no Medea (the title heroine of one of the first and greatest literary works dealing with the struggle of women against male and societal oppression); Mavis, unlike Medea, has not exacted terrible revenge for a husband's betrayal.

Mavis, like her sisters Gloria and Iris, has to some extent reified the symbolism of the surname, Parodus, that their father contrived from their original surname, Parodopoulos. As Mavis explains to Sidney, Parodus refers to the chorus of Greek tragedy which is "always there, commenting, watching," but "at the edge of life—not changing anything. Just watching and being." As a prostitute, Gloria has remained on the fringes of conventional society. When Alton Scales discovers and cannot be tolerant of Gloria's way of life (again proving intolerant, although he knows better perhaps than even the homosexual David Ragin and the Jew Sidney Brustein about the pain of intolerance), Gloria is pushed back into her escapist drug habit and has thoughts about suicide. Connected to the art-life theme, Gloria is finally prompted to commit suicide by dramatist David Ragin, who expresses romantic heroine worship of prostitutes as social outsiders and callously and revoltingly requests Gloria to aid a young male friend through sexual voyeurism.

Modern society's and advertising's pressures on women to value physical appearance are clear in the emphasis on women's hair and hair-care products—a motif that appears in both of Hansberry's major plays. Like Beneatha Younger in *A Raisin in the Sun*, Iris rebels against convention and male wishes by cutting her hair short. For Beneatha, her new hairdo (short and not straightened) represents defiance and an unabashed return to her roots. Iris is weary of Sidney's repeated, oppressive, depersonalizing fantasy of her as an unsophisticated Appalachian rustic with long, flowing hair, living with Sidney in a mountain rural paradise. Her new haircut represents not only her active attempt to make her way in the entertainment world but also, ironically, her acquiescence to other corrupt, identity-robbing forces, when she settles for an acting job in a television commercial for a dishonestly promoted hair-care product. Gloria's death and Sidney's peril from the political machine are turning points for both Sidney and Iris. Iris, having finally asserted herself and her need for her own identity, will return to the marriage with Sidney, if she does so at all, as a woman who will not tolerate the male gibes of Alton Scales and Wally O'Hara that a woman's place is in the oven.

Lorraine Hansberry was a pioneering and award-winning woman playwright in the

American theater who brought a new dimension to portrayals of women and women's concerns. She moved from dramatizing women's and African Americans' concerns in *A Raisin in the Sun* to dramatizing concerns for all minorities, social levels, humanity, and art itself in *The Sign in Sidney Brustein's Window*. Her premature death undoubtedly deprived American theater of additional fine plays, but both her example and her extant plays have fostered the impressive and indelible presence of women and African Americans in modern American drama.

Sources for Further Study

Bigsby, C. W. E. *Confrontation and Commitment: A Study of Contemporary American Drama, 1959-1966*. Columbia: University of Missouri Press, 1968. Chapter 9 of this study by a British scholar is an eighteen-page survey of Hansberry's plays that has a fine sense of their context in the modern American and European theater.

Carter, Steven R. *Hansberry's Drama: Commitment Amid Complexity*. New York: Penguin Group, 1993. Carter's book has a chapter on each of the major plays, black-and-white illustrations, a general introductory chapter, and a chapter on Hansberry's legacy in drama.

Cheney, Anne. *Lorraine Hansberry*. Boston: Twayne, 1984. Part of Twayne's United States Authors Series, which consists of compact and comprehensive introductions to authors, this book has separate chapters on the major plays, black-and-white illustrations, biographical information, and a chapter on Robert Nemiroff's biographical drama about Hansberry.

Miller, Jordan Y. "Lorraine Hansberry." In *Poetry and Drama*, edited by C. W. E. Bigsby. Vol. 2 in *The Black American Writer*. Deland, Fla.: Everett Edwards, 1969. Analyzes and praise Hansberry's artistry, arguing that she merits a permanent place in American drama, especially with reference to the movement from her first to her second major play.

Nemiroff, Robert. "A Portrait: The 101 'Final' Performances of *Sidney Brustein*." In *"A Raisin in the Sun" and "The Sign in Sidney Brustein's Window": Expanded Twenty-Fifth Anniversary Edition*, by Lorraine Hansberry. Edited by Robert Nemiroff. New York: New American Library, 1987. This long introduction by Nemiroff, the ex-husband of Hansberry, contains much information on Hansberry's life and details of production during the staging of *The Sign in Sidney Brustein's Window*.

Norman Prinsky

SILAS MARNER

Author: George Eliot (Mary Ann Evans, 1819-1880)
Type of work: Novel
Type of plot: Fable
Time of plot: The early nineteenth century
Locale: Rural England
First published: 1861

> *Principal characters:*
> SILAS MARNER, a reclusive weaver in the village of Raveloe
> GODFREY CASS, the eldest son of Squire Cass, the principal
>   landowner of Raveloe
> DUNSTAN CASS, Godfrey's arrogant and cruel younger brother
> NANCY LAMMETER, the daughter of Squire Lammeter and
>   Godfrey's wife
> DOLLY WINTHROP, the wife of the wheelwright Ben Winthrop
> EPPIE, Godfrey's unacknowledged natural daughter by Molly
>   Farren and Silas' adopted child

Form and Content

Set in rural England in the early nineteenth century, *Silas Marner* covers a time span of some thirty years during which Silas undergoes a process of spiritual-emotional death and rebirth. The secondary plot revolving around Godfrey Cass is of nearly equal importance, and the intersections of the two plots create the primary energies of the novel. In both stories, moreover, suffering is created by men but redeemed by women.

Silas has grown up within the fundamentalist religious community of Lantern Yard—an ironic name, because there is more spiritual darkness than illumination there. Falsely accused by his best friend William Dane of stealing the church's meager funds, and with his guilt "proven" by the drawing of lots, Silas abandons his trust in God and humankind. He takes up residence far to the south in the village of Raveloe, where he makes an adequate living by his weaving. Silas is shunned by the villagers, however, partly because of his reclusive habits and partly because Raveloe is a closed, insular community. With no sense of purpose or human connectedness, Silas becomes a solitary miser whose accumulating hoard of gold coins is his sole comfort.

In contrast, Godfrey Cass, the eldest son of the principal landowner of Raveloe, would seem to be favored by fortune. In fact, however, he lives in dread that his secret and sordid marriage to a woman in a neighboring town will be revealed by his brother Dunstan and that his hopes of marrying Nancy Lammeter thus will be destroyed. To buy Dunstan's silence, Godfrey gives Dunstan his prize horse Wildfire to sell, but Dunstan recklessly rides the horse onto a stake, mortally wounding the animal. Passing Silas' cottage on his way home from the accident, Dunstan sees that Silas is out, enters and finds the gold, and disappears mysteriously into the night.

Silas' dismayed announcement to the community of the theft cracks his shell of solitude, but the breakthrough comes with the providential arrival of Eppie a few months later. Determined to confront Godfrey with his child, Molly trudges through the snow to Raveloe but dies of exposure a few yards from Silas' cottage. Seeking the light, Eppie crawls in. For a moment, Silas, in his extreme nearsightedness, takes her golden curls for his gold coins, miraculously restored. Yet Eppie proves to be a greater treasure than the lost gold: In becoming a father to her, Silas becomes a human being once again.

Dolly Winthrop is an invaluable mentor to Silas in his parenting. She provides maternal advice and presence as well as much-needed spiritual support for Silas. In a comparable way, Nancy—now married to Godfrey—provides an emotional and spiritual center to Godfrey's life. Though childless, they are happy in each other, and Godfrey is resigned to a background role in the life of his unacknowledged daughter.

After the passage of some sixteen years, however, the discovery of Dunstan's skeleton (and Silas' gold) in a recently drained quarry brings the novel to a climax. Godfrey confesses to Nancy that Eppie is his child, expecting a severe rebuke, but Nancy, "ripened into fuller goodness" by maturity, forgives him and agrees to adopt Eppie. Neither has counted on the strength of the affection between Silas and Eppie or is aware that Eppie intends to marry Aaron Winthrop. When Eppie chooses to remain where she is, Godfrey and Nancy sadly accept her decision. Silas' journey in the final chapter to the town of his youth proves to be a fruitless quest; Lantern Yard is gone, replaced by a factory. Thus, the door is closed on Silas' past, with his understanding of its events "dark to the last," although he now has "light enough to trusten by."

Analysis

Like most of George Eliot's novels, *Silas Marner* is set in the rural England of the author's childhood memories. Like her other novels, too, the work is meticulously realistic in many aspects of its dialogue, description, and characterization. Unlike most of her novels, however, *Silas Marner* is very short, with an almost geometrically formal structure, and its plot relies upon some rather improbable incidents. Such elements reflect the author's intent to deal with profound themes in the form of a fable.

In Silas' story, George Eliot obliquely approaches the realm of spiritual truth by depicting the restoration of faith in the heart of a very simple man. The old-fashioned rural setting is important as a frame; its cultural remoteness from the world of the reader gives it the archaic simplicity and uncontested credibility of a fable or fairy tale. Even so, George Eliot critics have never been comfortable with the implication that somehow Eppie has been given to Silas by a benevolent providence in return for his lost gold. The question of the author's stance is especially problematic in view of her own agnosticism. Although George Eliot herself as a child was an ardent, evangelical Christian, in maturity (like many Victorian intellectuals) she rejected traditional beliefs for a humanist credo.

In Godfrey's story, realism predominates, and thus the author's control of theme is more secure. Godfrey's marriage to Molly Farren is the fatal step that enmeshes him in lies and guile as he tries to evade its consequences. One must beware of condemning Godfrey, however, because the author herself does not. Rather, she sees him as a type of erring humanity—a good-hearted but weak-willed young man who desperately wants to rewrite his past and enjoy a happy future with Nancy Lammeter. The role of Dunstan as a foil to Godfrey is important: Together, they represent a classic Cain-and-Abel, bad brother-good brother contrast. This structural polarity helps to create a context of judgment in which Dunstan's viciousness makes Godfrey's wrongdoing seem less damning.

Structural patterns of this kind are in fact a key to the novel's meaning. The various parallels and contrasts between the Silas and Godfrey stories show these respective halves of the novel to be formally related, like the panels of a diptych. Both Godfrey and Silas are living out the consequences of a past wrong, in which the one was the secret wrongdoer, the other the falsely accused victim. In both stories theft is a pivotal event: Dunstan's stealing of Silas' gold complements William Dane's taking of the church money. Silas suffers unjustly but magnifies his misery by becoming a virtual hermit. Godfrey suffers the pangs of conscience while maintaining an outwardly cheerful, gregarious disposition. As the ironic consequence of denying his wife and child, Godfrey remains childless, since he and Nancy apparently cannot have children, whereas Silas, the lonely bachelor, receives Eppie into his life as a daughter. In general, the unfolding of each story suggests the influence of a power or force of destiny beyond human understanding—something rather like Nemesis in Godfrey's case, and something rather like Providence in Silas'.

If the metaphysical implications of *Silas Marner* go beyond the realm of earthly reality, the primary moral intent of the author is firmly grounded in human relationships. As is the case in her other novels, the bonds of love, sympathy, and fellow feeling are the highest good that one can truly know. As such, they are redemptive in themselves and are the basis of George Eliot's "religion of humanity." Although she doubts the existence of God, she is assured of the existence of a sublime, collective goodness. Thus, in both stories, the power of human affection, especially as shown by the women of the novel, heals psychic wounds, restores humanity, and, insofar as it can, atones for wrongdoing. In Godfrey's story, it is Nancy who serves in this role. She is a "centered" personality who counterbalances Godfrey's lack of inner strength; her love for him unites her sensitive, affectionate nature with her deep moral principles. In Silas' story, Dolly Winthrop and, later, Eppie, perform comparable functions. Dolly's good sense and warm sympathy provide Silas with a lifeline to a restored faith in humanity and God. Eppie's decision at the end to remain with Silas reflects the strength of their shared affection and affirms the bonds of feeling as the surest basis of right choice.

Context

Although she was the most influential woman writing in English until the twentieth century, George Eliot has not been thought of as a women's writer. Drawn by temperament and talent to the central issues of her times, whether political, religious, social, or artistic, she made a commanding place for herself (under her real name of Mary Ann or Marian Evans) as a writer in a male-dominated intellectual world long before she wrote her first novel. Her novels were published under the masculine pseudonym in order to avoid being thought of as "feminine," and indeed for a time they were thought to be the work of a retired clergyman.

Nevertheless, in both her life and the novels on which her reputation rests, there are women's issues of significance. Her unconventional union with fellow intellectual George Henry Lewes, prevented from being a marriage because of Lewes' inability to obtain a divorce under archaic Victorian divorce laws, scandalized her contemporaries. In her own mind, however, she was right, and eventually society came to accept them as a legitimate couple. Her novels, moreover, are generally centered on problems of choice and vocation for heroines not unlike George Eliot herself. Typically, she focuses on the tension between a woman's personhhood, with its unexpressed depth of talent or feeling, and the limited social role that is available to her.

Silas Marner has no central heroine and consequently does not deal directly with such issues. If women's concerns are not at the forefront of the plot, however, they may be seen in the form of a thematic design. Without exception, the wrongdoing that drives the plot is the work of men—William Dane's betrayal of Silas, Godfrey's disavowal of Molly and Eppie, and Dunstan's theft of Silas' gold. The center of the novel's value-structure, however, is found in the triad of female characters that consists of Nancy, Dolly, and Eppie. In various ways, they demonstrate a special kind of humanity that offsets the wrongs done around them. The novel tells the reader that there are wrongs that cannot be set right, but just as unmistakably it implies that life goes on nevertheless; wounds must be healed, wrongs forgiven, troubled spirits calmed. The nurturing acts that are the positive expressions of personhood of the female characters on *Silas Marner* thus substantiate George Eliot's deepest and most keenly felt moral vision.

Sources for Further Study

Beer, Gillian. *George Eliot*. Bloomington: Indiana University Press, 1986. A feminist approach to the novels of George Eliot that acknowledges Eliot's power to redefine issues relating to gender while remaining within the traditional canon of English literature. The chapter on *Silas Marner* focuses on Silas' weaving as a metaphor, with feminine associations, for the interconnections of circumstance that form Silas' destiny.

Ermarth, Elizabeth Deeds. *George Eliot*. Boston: Twayne, 1985. A compact biographical study that addresses various moral and philosophical aspects of Eliot's intellectual achievement. Ermarth sees the bonds of sympathy and trust in *Silas Marner* as the link between the realm of circumstance and the moral order.

Paris, Bernard J. *Experiments in Life: George Eliot's Quest for Values*. Detroit: Wayne State University Press, 1965. Has limited coverage of *Silas Marner* but includes a comprehensive and penetrating analysis of the philosophical background of George Eliot's "religion of humanity."

Swinden, Patrick. *Silas Marner: Memory and Salvation*. New York: Twayne, 1992. An excellent, brief book-length study of the novel; particularly valuable in its analysis of the historical societal contexts of Lantern Yard and Raveloe.

Uglow, Jennifer. *George Eliot*. New York: Pantheon Books, 1987. Uglow explores the connections between George Eliot's life and work, in particular the traditional female values her work affirms. The discussion of *Silas Marner* emphasizes the imagery of regeneration and rebirth as an extension of the novel's implied celebration of nurturing, maternal processes.

Wiesenfarth, Joseph. *George Eliot's Mythmaking*. Heidelberg, Germany: Winter, 1977. Wiesenfarth argues that George Eliot's fiction in general embodies a mythology of fellow feeling that includes various folk, classical, and biblical sources. The chapter on *Silas Marner* explores the novel's fairy-tale analogues and influences, and relates them to its form and themes.

Charles Duncan

SILENCES

Author: Tillie Olsen (1913-   )
Type of work: Literary criticism
First published: 1978

Form and Content

Silences seeks to explore what Tillie Olsen terms "unnatural silences"—those circumstances that thwart the creative process and lead writers to delay, interrupt, abandon, and even forgo promising careers. Part 1 moves from a general discussion of debilitating influences through an analysis of the specific factors that disproportionately silence women writers. The section ends with a long interpretive account of the life and times of Rebecca Harding Davis that makes concrete Olsen's contention that writers need a nurturing environment that affords them both a fullness of time and a totality of self if they are to prevent their work from being either compromised or abandoned altogether. Part 2, which is appropriately entitled "Acerbs, Asides, Amulets, Exhumations, Sources, Deepenings, Roundings, Expansions," serves to ground and substantiate the arguments that Olsen has made in the first section of the book. To underscore the connection between the two sections, Olsen includes cross references in part 2 that point the reader to the relevant page(s) in part 1.

As her use of internal pointers makes clear and as Olsen acknowledges in her preface, *Silences* is not an orthodox volume of literary criticism. Instead, part 1 contains a compilation of previously published essays that are reinforced by what might best be termed the liner notes contained in part 2. The structure of the book, no less than the manner in which it is presented (part 1 is peppered with footnotes, while the pages in part 2 are punctuated by curious page breaks and liberal use of white space), underscores Olsen's belief that writing is not only collaborative but also interactive. She makes no pretense of presenting a definitive analysis but rather invites readers to fill in the blank spaces that she has provided and to supplement the evidence that she cites with their own examples and experiences.

Not surprisingly, the more one studies the book, the more it begins to resemble a Möbius strip, a three-dimensional figure with a one-sided surface. Despite attempts by critics to divide neatly the various sections for analysis, the sections constantly loop back upon one another, reinforcing previously made observations and setting the stage for correlative points that follow. While there are three identifiable essays in part 1, none is complete until the reader has applied insights gained from the material in the remainder of the book that flesh out Olsen's arguments. In a sense, *Silences* constitutes something of a sourcebook, a volume of materials intended to "rededicate and encourage" writers and to "expand the too sparse evidence on the relationship between circumstances and creation."

Analysis

Perhaps because of its rather unconventional format, critics have given *Silences* mixed reviews. While some have hailed the book as a feminist manifesto, others find it wanting in organization, consistency and analysis. It may be its very open-endedness and rather quixotic organization, however, that give the book its power. The structure of the book, which is clearly untidy and fragmented, appropriately reinforces Olsen's depiction of her own (and others') career, a career defined by distraction, interruption, and spasmodic efforts rather than by meditation, continuity, and sustained periods of creativity.

Olsen identifies a broad range of constraints that hamper individual and communal expression. She is not advocating an elimination of all these constraints—she sees motherhood, for example as both a constraint and a source of fulfillment—but she suggests that all people must strive to create the conditions that foster expression and creativity without negating the importance of sustaining relationships.

Undergirding Olsen's analysis are the twin beliefs that human beings are born with curiosity and creativity and that, given the proper context, they are capable of transforming the events of their everyday lives into poignant and lasting literary works. She cites many examples to demonstrate her points and leaves the reader with a much clearer understanding of the ways in which artificial constraints have limited the understanding of humanity's cultural heritage.

Olsen's analysis is punctuated by her own humanistic values and her compassion for other people. By analyzing the reasons that past masters have fallen silent, she also offers encouragement to those who have just begun to write and to those who have interrupted their careers for whatever reasons. Taken a step further, *Silences* constitutes a mandate, a clarion call to the previously silent. Her explanations of the barriers faced by those who are married, those who have children, and those who are working one (or more) jobs are not meant to condone the silences. Instead, they encourage the silenced to appreciate the value of their private reflections and imaginings and to give them the wherewithal to transform them into concrete expressions. Olsen's hope seems to be that the formerly silenced will experience a new sense of validation and purpose by being made aware of the fact that others have faced similar circumstances and, in some instances, have overcome them.

Toward the beginning of the book, she makes a reference to the "mute inglorious Miltons," whose circumstances conspire against their creative urges. She demonstrates that there is a wealth of untapped talent by referring to the richness found in folk songs, lullabies, tales, and other forms of expression within the oral tradition. It is not, Olsen argues, for lack of talent that these creators remain unknown but for lack of circumstances and/or confidence.

The circumstances that Olsen enumerates are many. Some she exemplifies by drawing on her own life: her twenty years of child rearing and working at paying jobs that left her what she terms "stolen moments" insufficient to nurture or sustain her creative self. Others are more generalized observations that run the gamut from silences caused by censorship and repression to those self-inflicted silences that stem from denial, addiction, and the like. Still others—cultural traditions, devaluation, critical attitudes, limited spheres of activity, and artificial subject matter constraints—

are those that have traditionally silenced women or denied them the recognition that they deserve.

In cataloging the factors that contribute to silences, Olsen has done much to demystify the circumstances that make it possible for some to be prolific while others remain mute. She has also done much to explain the silences that often follow a promising first novel and the relative obscurity of authors who have published extensively and yet are virtual unknowns to the majority of the reading public. Additionally, she has forced academics and publishers alike to reevaluate the importance of out-of-print books and to introduce them to new generations of readers.

Silences not only includes references to a multitude of little-known writers but also urges women to read other women and reconsider their place within the literary canon. It also emphasizes the need for networking and supportive literary friendships. These are the same kinds of concerns that led Olsen to publish lists of overlooked and undervalued writers, most of them women, in the *Women's Studies Newsletter* in 1972 and 1973.

Despite a relaxing of some of the constraints that have limited the opportunities of both women and minorities, Olsen's message remains important. In fact, as she suggested in a 1987 interview with Mickey Pearlman, "Silences are worse now than ever before, because there are more people who have [these hopes and aspirations], . . . the will, the desire, but the circumstances are not there."

Silences is a book that bears rereading and continued study. It contains important insights not only for would-be authors but also for those who are committed to redefining the literary canon so that it reflects more accurately the life and times of the working class, minorities, and women. Even when one reads *Silences* during those proverbial "stolen moments," it provides a window that reveals a rich and diverse body of literary works that have traditionally received too little attention.

Context

To measure the impact of any individual or single work on the study of literature or women's issues invites rebuttal. In the case of Tillie Olsen, however, at least part of the impact is documentable. Not only did the publication of *Silences* result in the rediscovery of works long out of print, including Rebecca Harding Davis' *Life in the Iron Mills: Or, The Korl Woman* (1861; 1972), but it also goaded publishers and academics to reconsider works that they might have previously ignored or rejected as being outside of the mainstream.

Much of Olsen's impact is not documentable. While one can cite Alice Walker's reference in *In Search of Our Mothers' Gardens* (1983) to Olsen as one who has literally saved lives, one cannot document the number of writers (female and male) who have found a fellow traveler, a supporter, in her works and who have found in her prose the will to continue.

Despite the silences that dominate Olsen's own productive years, she has given others a fresh context in which to assess both their own aspirations and the rather homogenous reading lists that have traditionally defined the literary tradition. She has also given them the resources (in the form of quotations and reading lists) to identify and study their predecessors and to learn from them.

Sources for Further Study

Faulkner, Mara. *Protest and Possibility in the Writing of Tillie Olsen*. Charlottesville: University Press of Virginia, 1993. Following an introduction that explains her critical perspective, Faulkner advances a seamless analysis that integrates the many aspects of Olsen's writings. Throughout the book, she presents Olsen as a beacon of hope, liberation, and challenge. Insights into and drawn from *Silences* inform the entire volume, but chapter 5 ("Language and Silence") is especially pertinent to Olsen's analysis of the unnatural silences that cross generational, class, and sexual boundaries.

Howe, Florence. "Literacy and Literature." *PLMA* 89, no. 3 (May, 1974): 433-441. Howe addresses the importance of a diversified canon, citing studies and personal experiences that demonstrate the stultifying impact of male-biased reading materials on adolescents and college students. Her observations reinforce and provide a context in which to approach *Silences*.

Orr, Elaine Neil. *Tillie Olsen and a Feminist Spiritual Vision*. Jackson: University Press of Mississippi, 1987. Orr approaches Olsen's work from a theological perspective that revolves around Olsen's life-affirming vision and faith in transforming possibilities. Chapter 6, "When the Angel Gains a Voice," is the most important chapter vis-à-vis *Silences*. It advances the argument that Olsen sees creativity as an expression of the sacred or holy.

Pearlman, Mickey, and Abby H. P. Werlock. *Tillie Olsen*. Boston: Twayne, 1991. Pearlman and Werlock set out to balance what they see as a sometimes overly adulatory treatment of Olsen's work. The book contains a useful chronology that is followed by both a 1984 interview/essay and a biographical sketch. Their critique of *Silences* is weakened by a reliance on textual summary and secondary quotation, but they include both a useful bibliography and helpful footnotes.

Rose, Ellen Cronan. "Limning: Or, Why Tillie Writes." *The Hollins Critic* 13, no. 2 (April, 1976): 1-13. Rose explores what she perceives to be a disparity between the aesthetic vision that shapes Olsen's essay "Silences" as well as her fiction and the polemical tone that she perceives in "One of Twelve." She suggests that Olsen has sacrificed her vision and understanding in support of a feminist rhetoric.

Shulman, Alix Kates. "Overcoming Silences: Teaching Writing for Women." *Harvard Educational Review* 49, no. 4 (November, 1979): 527-533. Infusing her critique of *Silences* with her own experiences, Shulman concludes that the work functions as a multigenerational writers' workshop through which trusted collaborators share revelatory experiences.

C. Lynn Munro

SILENT DANCING
A Partial Remembrance of a Puerto Rican Childhood

Author: Judith Ortiz Cofer (1952-   )
Type of work: Essays and poetry
First published: 1990

Form and Content

After Judith Ortiz Cofer gave a poetry reading in 1987, a friend, Hilma Wolitzer, suggested that she take some of the images and subjects of her poems and create essays out of them. *Silent Dancing* is the result of that advice. In this memoir, she creates a unique form because in it she combines her essays with poems that share similar themes or, in some cases, retell or recast the same stories. It is unlike most other memoirs because of this blending of genres. The one-hundred-fifty-page memoir is composed of fourteen brief essays and eighteen short poems, eleven of which were previously published in the poetry collections *Terms of Survival* (1987) and *Reaching for the Mainland* (1987).

Ortiz Cofer announces her intentions for the memoir in "Preface: Journey to a Summer's Afternoon." Using Virginia Woolf, the British novelist and essayist, as a guide, Ortiz Cofer wants to "trace . . . the origins of [her] creative imagination" because she believes that reclaiming memories can "provide a writer with confidence in the power of art to discover meaning and truth in ordinary events."

The "ordinary events" that Ortiz Cofer relates to the reader are actually quite remarkable. One is never quite sure how much of the memoir is a "partial remembrance" and how much of the past is, as Ortiz Cofer readily admits, "a creation of the imagination," but the stories (or *cuentos*) are all surprising, moving, and evocative of that lost time of her childhood and adolescence.

The epigraph from Virginia Woolf that begins the book identifies the principal focus of the work: "A woman writing thinks back through her mothers." The mothers that come to life in *Silent Dancing* include Woolf herself, as literary trailblazer; Ortiz Cofer's mother and grandmothers, who model roles of behavior for women; and the "mother lands" of Puerto Rico and the United States. Ortiz Cofer must come to terms with the difficulties in each of these relationships and must come into her own womanhood, a womanhood that for her includes motherhood; her memoir is dedicated not only to her mother but also to her daughter, Tanya Cofer. The traditions are passed on, in a transformed manner, from generation to generation of women.

Analysis

The two opening chapters of *Silent Dancing* serve as a type of Scylla and Charybdis—equally hazardous alternatives—for women who are coming of age.

While the men were at work and the boys played baseball, the women and girls would congregate over coffee at Mamá's and listen to stories being told; Ortiz Cofer traces her belief in the power of storytelling to these charmed afternoons.

In the first essay, "Casa," Ortiz Cofer recounts a story that was recounted to her countless times by her grandmother, Mamá. According to the story, María la Loca, the crazy lady who wanders around the village, serves as the example of the woman who allows love to defeat her. As a young woman, María fell in love with a rich man in the village (his name changes with every retelling of the story), but he abandoned her at the alter. From that moment, so the story goes, María became crazier every day, and she ended up alone, childless, and outside the social life of the community.

The second essay centers on Mamá and her desires for some sort of private life within marriage and motherhood. After she had her eighth child, three of whom died in infancy or childbirth, Mamá turned to the "only means of birth control available to a woman of her times": she gave up the comforts of sleeping with her husband and moved to a separate room in the house so that "she could be more than a channel for other lives." María and Mamá serve as the diametrically opposed roles available to women, both of which are dangerous to the spirit: the harmful solitude that results from choosing poorly in love and the equally harmful servitude that comes from loving too many people. Ortiz Cofer does not judge any of these women or any of the choices people make, but she does emphasize the power of love to ruin lives or create difficult choices.

One of the most moving essays in the memoir, "Some of the Characters," contains a section on Salvatore, who is the superintendent in an apartment that the Ortiz family rented in Paterson, New Jersey, during the Cuban missile crisis. This essay reveals the difficulties that men can have in love. Because Salvatore is homosexual, he is ostracized from the community of men in the apartment complex and is unable to find any kind of lasting love. Because of the repression of homosexuals at that time, Sal is forced into a kind of extreme loneliness. In the same essay, Ortiz Cofer talks about her sense of distance and alienation from her often-absent father. He was confined to a ship that circled Cuba during the missile crisis, and he was not allowed to make contact with anyone off the ship. He returned from this all-male world of threats and violence a changed man, a "sullen stranger." Ortiz Cofer says that her childhood ended when her father returned because he was not the same man who had gone away; his distance from the family was unbridgeable. Ortiz Cofer links this experience with her father to her portrait of Salvatore, and the two become doubles; neither is able to be touched by the outside world, and neither is able to love with any degree of satisfaction.

Although the memoir's main preoccupation is the development or failure of relationships between people, another critical element is the function of place and of national identity. Ortiz Cofer brings into sharp focus the difficult relationship between Puerto Rico and the United States and the difficulties this relationship caused in her own family.

In the title essay, "Silent Dancing," Ortiz Cofer makes clear the rift that exists between her parents regarding national identity. Once the family moved to Paterson, New Jersey, leaving the predominantly Puerto Rican barrio became her father's greatest wish and her mother's greatest fear. Her mother wanted to keep herself "pure" by speaking Spanish only and by keeping close ties with the people of the barrio and her family in Puerto Rico; her father wanted the family to move from the barrio, to begin the process of assimilation, and to "get ahead" through schooling. Ortiz Cofer was literally transported between two worlds over and over again: She lived in Puerto Rico when her father was assigned to a cargo fleet and returned to New Jersey when he had stateside duty; while in the United States, she stayed clear of associations with fellow Puerto Ricans at her father's request, and she maintained ties of all kinds— including cuisine, folklore, and language—with her native island because of her mother's influence. As a child, she spoke Spanish "like a 'Gringa' " and spoke English with a Spanish accent; she felt like a "cultural chameleon" who learned to blend into whatever environment in which she found herself. The strains and complications of her development and her relationships mirror the sometimes strained and always complicated relationship between the United States and Puerto Rico. The memoir becomes far more than a simple personal recollection or re-creation of the past; the personal is indeed political in the case of a Puerto Rican who writes about the various forces forming her identity through childhood and adolescence.

Context

Silent Dancing rises out of the memories and recollections of one woman, but the shape of that woman's consciousness was formed by a long tradition of women who wrote about gender issues. When Ortiz Cofer admits the distance she has come from her mother's dreams for her, saying, "I liberated myself from her plans for me, got a scholarship to college, married a man who supported my need to work, to create, to travel and to experience life as an individual," she is describing a personal journey as well as the movement of a generation of women. She recognizes this debt in her preface by acknowledging the influence that Virginia Woolf's writing had on her own. Her maternal grandmother, after having eight children, recognized the importance, as Woolf phrased it, of having a room of one's own, but Ortiz Cofer, because she grew up during the social flux of the sixties and studied women's writing, knew even before she married that her own internal life needed to be a central focus for her.

In comparison to other memoirs by women, *Silent Dancing* is different because of its emphasis on class and ethnicity. Patricia Hampl's *A Romantic Education*, a beautiful memoir, presents perhaps the quintessential example of a writer within the dominant culture in America yearning for roots, for a specific ethnic identity. Hampl recognizes the romanticism of this quest and eventually accepts her membership within the relatively generic middle-class, white culture. Ortiz Cofer's memoir demonstrates the overwhelming difficulties of having a specific ethnic identity. Although her Puerto Rican culture and heritage are rich and powerful, her memoir shows the pain and confusion that result from having a divided consciousness. Because she never quite fits into the fabric of either culture, she always feels a certain distance from both cultures. She writes on the cusp between the United States and Puerto Rico, and she has established herself as one of the preeminent voices in Puerto Rican American literature.

Sources for Further Study

Hampl, Patricia. *A Romantic Education*. Boston: Houghton Mifflin, 1981. This recollection of a Minnesotan girlhood and adulthood offers interesting comparisons with Ortiz Cofer's memoir. Hampl journeys into the past and to Czechoslovakia in an attempt to forge roots. A beautiful memoir.

Hasselstrom, Linda. *Land Circle: Writings Collected from the Land*. Golden, Colo.: Fulcrum, 1991. This memoir, like *Silent Dancing*, interestingly combines poetry with essays. Hasselstrom mourns the death of her husband and describes her adventure in learning to live self-sufficiently on a cattle ranch in South Dakota.

Mohr, Nicholasa. *Nilda*. New York: Harper & Row, 1973. In her first novel, Mohr portrays life in New York's Puerto Rican barrio. This is a candid portrayal of a Puerto Rican girl as she grows from a child to a teenager, learning to deal with racism and poverty.

Rodriguez, Richard. *Hunger of Memory*. Boston: David R. Godine, 1982. Rodriguez's work offers an interesting parallel with Ortiz Cofer's. Rodriguez's memoir describes the coming-of-age of a Chicano intellectual. His work presents very poignantly the pains of losing closeness with his immediate family because of his assimilation into Anglo-American culture. Unlike Ortiz Cofer, Rodriguez writes directly about political issues such as affirmative action.

Woolf, Virginia. *A Room of One's Own*. Reprint. New York: Harcourt Brace Jovanovich, 1991. Ortiz Cofer traces her origins, in many ways, to this collection of essays. A must for anyone interested in women's writing.

Kevin Boyle

SILENT SPRING

Author: Rachel Carson (1907-1964)
Type of work: Social criticism
First published: 1962

Form and Content

Citing a letter written by Olga Owens Huckins in 1958 as her inspiration for writing, Rachel Carson begins *Silent Spring* with a warning: If humans do not stop their greed and carelessness, they will destroy the earth. Huckins told Carson of her own bitter experience of a small world made lifeless; Carson then goes on to reveal how her findings as a trained scientist led her to speak out against the reckless male-dominated society that poisons the world.

To lay the groundwork for her book and to explain the title *Silent Spring*, pioneer ecofeminist Carson begins with what she calls "a fable for tomorrow." She sketches a bountiful American community that is destroyed by a strange blight that moves like a shadow of death across the land, eventually creating a spring without bees or birds—a silent spring. This mythical community has countless counterparts around the world thanks to what Carson calls the "impetuous and heedless pace of man."

Continuing with a history of life on earth to show the natural interaction between living things, *Silent Spring* meticulously exposes the lethal contamination of air, earth, rivers, and seas. Carson draws on her research into the way in which chemicals pass from one organism to another through all the links in the food chain to illustrate the need to control products she calls not "insecticides" but "biocides." She reminds citizens of their rights to protect themselves against lethal poisons that have increased alarmingly in the twentieth century.

Each chapter addresses one aspect of the deadly contamination process, explaining in scientific terms the chemical structure and then exposing the resulting effects on the natural habitat. Carson illustrates the cost of this negligence by examining regions, cities, and individuals across America that have suffered from the dangerous interaction of chemicals with the environment. These illustrations are carefully selected to extend the work beyond a strictly scientific observation into the realm of social criticism. For example, Carson describes housewives in Michigan sweeping granules of poisonous insecticide from their porches and sidewalks, where they are reported to have looked like snow. Within a few days after the insecticide-spraying operation that caused this deadly rain, Detroiters began to report large numbers of dead and dying birds to the local Audubon Society. Throughout the book, Carson's actual scenarios parallel in a frightening fashion the mythical fable that begins the book.

Horrifyingly beautiful is a way one might describe Carson's writing. Aesthetically pleasing in its sensitive descriptions of earth and its inhabitants, this 262-page work is at the same time scientifically well-documented, listing thirty pages of notes and scholarly research. While Carson remains a critical and scrupulous scientist, she makes her most persuasive appeal through her emphasis on the value and beauty of the natural world. Her criticism of a number of entities responsible for the assaults upon the environment—the narrowly specialized scientific community, the dollar-driven chemical industry, and weak government agencies—constitutes a landmark challenge to a social system in need of a warning cry. The work paves the way for extended analysis and commentary by later twentieth century ecologists and eco-feminists.

Analysis

In her desire to put an end to the false assurances that the public is asked to accept about the safety of the environment, Carson puts forth a full complement of facts, noting that the obligation to endure gives people the right to know. In the chapter "Surface Waters and Underground Seas," the author's discussion of the amazing history of Clear Lake, California, for example, exposes the results of anglers' efforts to control a small gnat, *Chaoborus astictopus*. Carson explains that their chemical of choice, DDD, a close relative of DDT, apparently offered fewer threats to fish life. Gnat control was fairly good but needed follow-applications to be truly successful. Eventually, the biocide also wiped out the grebe population and created massive concentrations of the poison in the lake's fish, which were caught and eaten by anglers. Research proved that DDD has a strong cell-destroying capacity, especially of the cells that make up the human adrenal cortex.

In "Indiscriminately from the Skies," Carson shows what extensive damage was done when irresponsible large-scale treatment was undertaken to eradicate the gypsy moth. The Waller farm in northern Westchester County, New York, was sprayed twice although its owners specifically requested agriculture officials not to proceed. Milk samples taken from the Wallers' cows contained large amounts of DDT. Although the county Health Organization was notified, the milk was still marketed. Nearby truck farms also suffered contamination. Peas tested at fourteen to twenty parts per million of DDT; the legal minimum is seven parts per million. Nevertheless, growers, fearing heavy losses, sold produce containing illegal residues. Carson strongly criticizes this "rain of death," noting that modern poisons, though more dangerous than any known before, are used more indiscriminately.

To illustrate nature's reply to society's chemical assault, the author includes the chapter "Nature Fights Back." Sometimes, chemical application has created an increase in the very problem the spraying was designed to eliminate. In Ontario, for example, blackflies became seventeen times more abundant following spraying. In the Midwest, farmers who attempted to eradicate the Japanese beetle did so success-fully, only to find that the much more destructive corn borer was unleashed following the elimination of its natural predator. Nature, it seems, is not easily molded. Yet both nature and humans are considerably weakened by the assault.

Citing society's failure to foresee potential hazards, Carson cautions that even researchers are accustomed to look for the gross and immediate effect and to ignore all else. Thus, the population must be more concerned with the cumulative and delayed effects of absorbing small amounts of chemicals over a lifetime of exposure.

The author explains that there is "an ecology of the world within our bodies." A change in even one molecule may initiate changes in seemingly unrelated organs and tissues. In a prophetic statement, for Carson herself was soon to die from cancer, she says, "The most determined effort should be made to eliminate those carcinogens that now contaminate our food, our water supplies, and our atmosphere, because these provide the most dangerous type of contact—minute exposures repeated over and over throughout the years."

To demonstrate that society must make a conscious choice to slow and eventually eliminate the chemical poisoning of the world, in her final chapter, "The Other Road," Carson reminds the reader of Robert Frost's familiar poem "The Road Not Taken." The smooth superhighway that people are on is deceptively easy and clearly disastrous. Other roads lie before modern humans, including opportunities for biological solutions to environmental problems. Some of the most fascinating of the new techniques include those that turn the strength of a species against itself. Yet Carson scorns the very premise upon which many of these biological and chemical controls rest. She says the control of nature is a phrase "conceived in arrogance, born of the Neanderthal age of biology and philosophy, when it was supposed that nature exists for the convenience of man." It is a shame that society uses its most sophisticated technology for such a primitive goal.

The final chapter, which is perhaps the most valuable, deals with the future. In it, Carson argues for humility and an intelligent approach to human interaction with all creatures. Many of the battles with nature that she describes throughout the book have been fought and lost. Unless people revere the miracle of life instead of struggling against it, they are doomed to lose again.

Context

Winner of eight awards, *Silent Spring* is a monumental book that shocked the world with its frightening revelations about the earth's contamination. Not surprisingly, Carson's profound sense of urgency awakened and angered the traditionally male-dominated scientific community, business world, and government agencies. Some critics dismissed her as a hysterical woman and a pseudoscientist, although her work shows her to be neither. Others said that she was merely a recluse interested in preserving the wildflowers along the country's roadsides. Clearly, she had a greater goal in mind. In her book, Carson calls on readers to question the masculinist philosophy and methods of controlling nature. In its boldness, her work has served as an example for ecologists and ecofeminists the world over.

Carson accepts the responsibility for the accuracy and validity of the voluminous amount of scientific research the book represents, graciously acknowledging four women who were vital to the success of the work: her three research assistants, Jeanne Davis, Dorothy Algire, and Bette Haney Duff; and her housekeeper, Ida Sprow. *Silent Spring* artfully translates Carson's scientific expertise into general readers' terms, a feat that comes as no surprise to many critics following her earlier beautifully written book *The Sea Around Us* (1951). The publication of *Silent Spring* was greeted with waves of fear by men who knew she spoke the truth, men who stood to lose power, prestige, or money through the disclosures and warnings the work contained. Carson, ironically, battled cancer herself in the final stages of writing the book, but she did not permit her personal struggle to get in the way of her goal of presenting the facts and letting the public decide.

Aside from being a concerned woman who awakened the world to the dangers in the air, earth, and water, Rachel Carson was a gifted writer who created memorable images and finely crafted sentences. She says, "deliberately poisoning our food, then policing the result—is too reminiscent of Lewis Carroll's White Knight who thought of 'a plan to dye one's whiskers green, and always use so large a fan that they could not be seen.'" Her pioneering exposé of humanity's foolish behavior strips away those equally foolish efforts to cover up the results. The silence that humanity tried to impose upon nature was broken by this brave woman's voice.

Sources for Further Study

Anderson, Lorraine, ed. *Sisters of the Earth*. New York: Vintage Books, 1991. A collection of women's works of prose and poetry about nature that reflect many of the same issues Rachel Carson raised in *Silent Spring*. The women's voices in this volume express a caring rather than a controlling relationship with nature. Contains a thirty-seven-page annotated bibliography of selected works by women about nature.

Hynes, H. Patricia. *The Recurring Silent Spring*. New York: Pergamon Press, 1989. A work that explores the struggles Carson faced and examines the social and political ramifications of her work. This book examines the new hazards of technology that Carson alluded to in her final chapter.

Inter Press Service, comp. *Story Earth: Native Voices on the Environment*. San Francisco: Mercury House, 1993. This collection of essays gives voice to non-Western cultures and their relationship between humankind and nature. Unlike Western culture, which has sought to subdue nature, the traditional societies examined in this book view it as sacred.

Wallace, Aubrey. *Eco-Heroes: Twelve Tales of Environmental Victory*. Edited by David Gancher. San Francisco: Mercury House, 1993. A series of twelve portraits of environmental activists from around the globe. Thinking globally but acting locally, these eco-heroes have received the Goldman Environmental Prize, considered the Nobel Prize for environmentalists. The essays in this collection explore the stories behind their victories.

Carol F. Bender

SKINS AND BONES
Poems 1979-87

Author: Paula Gunn Allen (1939-   )
Type of work: Poetry
First published: 1988

Form and Content

In the twenty-four poems collected in *Skins and Bones*, Paula Gunn Allen reinter-prets the historic and mythic beliefs of indigenous North American peoples from a twentieth century feminist perspective and develops a highly distinctive woman-focused tradition. By incorporating American Indian accounts of a cosmic feminine power into her poetry, she connects the past with the present and creates a complex pattern of continuity, regeneration, and change that affirms her holistic, spirit-based worldview. Allen's ability to synthesize personal reflection and social critique with her gynecentric Indian perspective simultaneously politicizes and spiritualizes her poetry. As she combines personal expression with social commentary and revisionary myth, she underscores her belief in transformation, survival, regeneration, and change.

Divided into three parts, the poems in *Skins and Bones* encompass a wide array of interrelated personal, philosophical, and social concerns, ranging from meditations on creation and death to descriptions of late-twentieth century bicultural American Indian life. In the first section, " 'C'koy'u, Old Woman': Songs of Tradition," which consists primarily of narrative poems, Allen stages a number of confrontations between Indian and European peoples and beliefs. She employs revisionist mythmak-ing to reinterpret conventional religious and historical accounts from a woman-centered, American Indian point of view. In addition to replacing the Judeo-Christian patriarchal God with C'koy'u, a female creator figure associated with indigenous North American myths, she rewrites the stories of the biblical Eve and four native women who, like Eve, are generally depicted in historical records as traitors to their peoples: Malinche, the Mexican Indian slave whose work as a translator facilitated the Spanish conquest of the Aztecs; Molly Brant, the Iroquois leader who negotiated for peace with European colonizers; Sacagawea, the Shoshoni Indian celebrated by early twentieth century European American feminists for her role in opening the North American West for European settlers; and Pocahontas, whose conversion to Chris-tianity and marriage to an Englishman are viewed as cultural betrayals. Allen con-cludes this section with two poems concerning gender relations among contemporary mixed-blood peoples.

In part 2, " 'Heyoka, Trickster': Songs of Colonization," Allen extends her exami-nation of the cultural conflicts arising between native and Eurocentric worldviews. This section contains philosophical poems contrasting Allen's holistic belief system with the fragmentation and social disorder she attributes to twentieth century peoples' exclusive reliance on reason and rational thought, as well as several highly critical explorations of increasingly negative ways in which Westernization influences North Americans of all cultural backgrounds. By associating the poems in this section with the trickster, however, who represents chaotic, creative power and unexpected change, Allen subtly reaffirms her confidence in a cosmic pattern of perpetual transformation and renewal.

The final section, " 'Naku, Woman': Songs of Generation," unites the mythic storytelling established in the opening poems with the personal reflection and explicit social critique found in part 2. This section includes Allen's meditations on love, nature, her mother's battle with lupus, her grandmother's death, and the difficult acceptance of unexpected loss, as well as two playful revisionary accounts of Deer Woman, a bisexual Cherokee/Choctaw trickster figure who seduces men and women into abandoning their old lives.

Analysis

The opening and closing poems in *Skins and Bones* offer a useful framework for interpreting the entire volume. The first piece, "C'koy'u, Old Woman," introduces the cosmic feminine creative power informing Allen's holistic worldview. This sixteen-line poem, which could be described as a twentieth century version of traditional American Indian creation songs, provides the basis for several recurring themes: the interconnections between natural and supernatural life explored in "Arousings," "Sightings I: Muskogee Tradition," and "Sightings II"; the desire for renewal expressed in "Teaching Poetry at Votech High, Santa Fe, the Week John Lennon Was Shot," "Grandma's Dying Poem," and "Something Fragile, Broken"; and an intricate pattern of continuity and change developed in "Molly Brant, Iroquois Matron, Speaks," "Taku Skanskan," and "Myth/Telling—Dream/Showing." The final poem, "New Birth," reaffirms the forward-looking, visionary perspective underlying the entire collection. In this chantlike invocation to change, Allen uses short, flowing lines to replicate the ongoing transformative process she describes throughout *Skins and Bones*.

She acknowledges the importance of death and destruction; however, as in previous pieces such as "Teaching Poetry at Votech High" and "Grandma's Dying Poem," she combines the acceptance of loss with the reaffirmation of survival, transformation, and renewal. Similarly, in "Iroquois Sunday: Watertown, 1982" and "Taking a Visitor to See the Ruins," Allen depicts the reemergence of traditional beliefs in modern contexts.

The poems collected in the first section of *Skins and Bones* provide the most explicit illustration of Allen's feminist perspective. By associating the cosmic feminine force introduced in the opening poem with positive images of female identity, Allen uses revisionist mythmaking to construct an empowering tradition of autonomous women. As she retells the stories of Eve, Malinche, Molly Brant, Sacagawea, and Pocahontas from a feminist point of view, she provides self-affirming alternatives to patriarchal myths of feminine evil. In "Eve the Fox," for example, she replaces the well-known Genesis account of the serpent's seduction of Eve and the subsequent fall into sin with a celebration of women's sexuality and physical beauty. Similarly, in "Malinalli, La Malinche, to Cortes, Conquistador," "Pocahontas to Her English Husband, John Rolfe," "Molly Brant," and "The One Who Skins Cats," Allen uses first-person narration to rewrite the commonly accepted stories of these Indian women. Unlike conventional accounts, which generally depict these women either as traitors concerned only with personal benefit or as weak-willed, innocent victims overpowered by forces beyond their control, Allen portrays them as conscious agents of change who subversively use European colonizers to undermine patriarchal social structures. Moreover, by identifying them with culturally specific manifestations of the feminine creative power described in "C'koy'u, Old Woman," she affirms her gynecentric worldview. For example in "Malinalli" she associates Malinche with Coatlicue, an ancient Mesoamerican serpent goddess, and in "The One Who Skins Cats" she identifies Sacagawea with the Mayan female creator figure Xmucané, or "grandmother of the sun."

Allen continues her construction of a personalized gynecentric tradition in the following sections by identifying this creative feminine force with transformation and rebirth. In "Grandma's Dying Poem," for example, she simultaneously speculates on the way in which her own personality and lifestyle have been shaped by her grand-mother's and replaces stereotypical views of womanhood with accounts of strong, defiant women. In other poems, such as "Arousings," "Weed," and "What the Moon Said," she revises conventional associations of women with nature to develop affir-mative images of autonomous yet interconnected female identities.

Allen's gynecentric worldview shapes her social critique as well. In "The One Who Skins Cats" and "Horns of a Dilemma," for example, Allen contrasts her belief in the interrelatedness of all forms of existence with the fragmentation and hierarchical social structures found in patriarchal cultures. In "Molly Brant," "Coyote Jungle," and "Teaching Poetry at Votech High," she critically explores twentieth century North Americans' loss of vision and spiritual paralysis, or what she describes in the latter poem as "soul sickness." Yet in Allen's holistic worldview, vision and action must work together. Thus, in "Fantasia Revolution," she criticizes those who desire trans-formation yet become paralyzed and lost in their dreams. Rather than work for social change, the people Allen describes escape into their visions of utopian living condi-tions, abundance, and peaceful revolution.

The divers tones and styles further reinforce Allen's gynecentric, spirit-based worldview. She uses accessible language and incorporates elements of Indian oral traditions into her work, thus achieving an elegant simplicity that corresponds to the cosmic pattern of continuance and transformation she describes throughout *Skins and Bones*. She employs a variety of speaking voices, ranging from celebration to humor to lament, and utilizes a number of different poetic forms, including traditional Indian chants and healing songs, elegies, and free verse. Although Allen's tone occasionally borders on resignation, her confidence in a cosmic feminine power enables her to combine the acceptance of loss with the assurance of survival and the promise of transformation.

Context

Skins and Bones reflects Allen's ongoing attempt to redefine feminism from an American Indian perspective. As in *The Sacred Hoop: Recovering the Feminine in American Indian Traditions*, her 1986 collection of scholarly essays on American Indian literary and cultural traditions, Allen rejects standard academic accounts of native cultures as primitive and patriarchal cultures, and she underscores their sophisticated metaphysical, epistemological, and social systems. By emphasizing the central social and symbolic roles that women play in historic and mythic native cultures, she provides an important corrective to the commonly held belief in an ahistorical, worldwide patriarchal system of women's oppression and offers twentieth century European American feminists alternative models for social, psychic, and political change.

Allen's revisionist mythmaking plays a significant part in her transformation of European American feminist thinking. Like a number of other twentieth century American Indian women poets, she replaces the Judeo-Christian male god and other patriarchal myths that denigrate women's abilities with positive images of female identity. Unlike those revisionist mythmakers who rely almost exclusively on the Greco-Roman mythic tradition and thus inadvertently support conventional Western associations of womanhood with biological reproduction, however, Allen associates feminine creativity with psychic and spiritual rebirth. By so doing, she simultaneously critiques U.S. feminists' ethnocentric concepts of womanhood and provides Western readers with alternative models of female identity formation. For example, by describing the female creator C'koy'u as an old woman yet associating her with creation and birth, Allen subtly challenges the ageism that devalues elderly women's creativity and denies their ability to make positive contributions to society.

By exploring the lives of Indian and mixed-blood women, Allen expands existing representations of female identity in other ways as well. In "Dear World" and "Myth/Telling—Dream/Showing," for example, her descriptions of the destructive self-divisions experienced by mixed-blood women serves as an important reminder that although all U.S. women might be oppressed, the specific forms of oppression they experience vary cross-culturally. In other poems, such as "Old Indian Ruins" and "The One Who Skins Cats," Allen draws on her personal knowledge of bicultural American Indian life to explore the various ways in which women achieve personal agency. By so doing, she provides readers with images of spiritually powerful women who kept the old beliefs yet changed them to meet present-day needs.

Sources for Further Study

Green, Rayna, ed. *That's What She Said: Contemporary Poetry and Fiction by Native American Women.* Bloomington: Indiana University Press, 1984. The introductory essay to this anthology of poetry by twentieth century American Indian women writers situates Allen's work in the context of an emerging literary tradition. This essay provides an analysis of the similarities and differences between Allen's poetic styles and those of other Indian women writers.

Hanson, Elizabeth I. *Paula Gunn Allen.* Edited by Wayne Chatterton and James H. Maguire. Boise, Idaho: Boise State University, 1990. Although this brief study of Allen's work does not include a discussion of *Skins and Bones*, it provides useful background information about Allen's life and her impact on twentieth century native literary traditions, as well as a brief summary of her creative and theoretical writings published before 1988.

Jahner, Elaine. "A Laddered, Rain-Bearing Rug: Paula Gunn Allen's Poetry." In *Women and Western American Literature*, edited by Helen Stauffer and Susan Rosowski. Troy, N.Y.: Whitson, 1982. This essay explores the ways in which Allen incorporates mythic processes and traditional American Indian beliefs into her poetry. Although this article focuses exclusively on *Coyote's Daylight Trip* (1974), it contains insightful analyses of several poetic themes and stylistic devices also found in Allen's more recent collection.

Koolish, Lynda. "The Bones of This Body Say, Dance: Self-Empowerment in Contemporary Poetry by Women of Color." In *A Gift of Tongues: Critical Challenges in Contemporary American Poetry*, edited by Marie Harris and Kathleen Aguero. Athens: University of Georgia Press, 1987. This essay analyzes the theme of self-empowerment in poetry by self-identified women of color. It briefly discusses Allen's use of myth and tribal histories to reconcile apparent opposites.

AnnLouise Keating

SLAVES OF NEW YORK

Author: Tama Janowitz (1957-   )
Type of work: Short stories
First published: 1986

Form and Content

The twenty-two stories in *Slaves of New York* offer various perspectives on the art scene of New York City. Several describe the evolution of the relationship between Eleanor, a struggling jewelry designer, and Stash, her artist boyfriend. Many of the stories share characters, with minor characters in one sometimes acting as protagonists in others. The first and last stories, "Modern Saint #271" and "Kurt and Natasha, a Relationship," are among the few that are completely independent of the others.

The stories are all vignettes, describing scenes rather than developing plots. Janowitz tells stories because they are interesting, without necessarily having a point to make. Her style is conversational, though she does indulge in some creative metaphors, as when Eleanor, narrating "Physics," spends a long paragraph comparing her "entropic life" to pizza. In "Matches," Eleanor treats a party that she gives as a metaphor for her entire life.

All the stories but the last are realistic. In "Kurt and Natasha, a Relationship," Natasha becomes involved with Kurt, hoping that he can help her in her career. Kurt, a sadist, treats Natasha terribly, sometimes chaining her to the radiator while he goes out and forcing her to cook while nearly naked, even though hot grease splashes on her skin. As she becomes more successful, she literally grows in size while he shrinks. After throwing her out, he finally admits, "I need you, therefore I am!"

In the stories involving Eleanor and Stash, Eleanor progresses from being dependent on her boyfriend to moving out after she discovers that he is seeing another woman. Even after moving out, however, she sees herself as dependent on men. In "Patterns," she meets up with Wilfredo, a bankrupt fashion designer. They go to a dinner party together, but afterward, he fails to return her calls. She stakes out his home, then resorts to consulting a psychic. At the close of the story, she buys four self-help books, including one titled *How to Make a Man Marry You in Thirty Days.*

Another recurring protagonist is Marley Mantello, a starving artist who believes that he is a genius. He wants to build the Chapel of Jesus Christ as a Woman next to the Vatican, with stations of the cross such as washing the dishes and changing diapers. When he gets rich, he tells his art dealer, he will hire John Lennon, Jimi Hendrix, Giacomo Puccini, and William Shakespeare to write an opera. The art dealer's only comment is "They're dead, Marley." Ironically, Marley finds some success in selling his art, at least to the point of having a dealer and getting a collector to invite him to breakfast. Success eludes Eleanor, however, even though she is much more in touch with reality and is willing to work for her success.

The episodes described offer insights into what the characters find important. "The Slaves in New York" introduces the characters of Stash and Eleanor, who have just moved in together. As narrator, Eleanor describes her living arrangements and those of her friends. Janowitz uses Eleanor to take various stabs at the real estate market in New York City, describing a sixth-floor walkup with no toilet as "a real find,'" renting for $1,500 a month. Most of the stories concern couples' relationships, and most are narrated by women who find themselves subservient to men.

Analysis

Slavery can take many forms. In "Case History #4: Fred," Fred takes women shopping at Tiffany's, telling them that he expects nothing in return. It is difficult to believe that he is not trying to buy them; ironically, he never consummates a purchase. In New York, control over real estate gives one control over people. Career choices also involve slavery. Artist are slaves to the whims of collectors, buyers, and art dealers, and anyone who grants a career-enhancing favor. To fall in love is to become dependent, to put control over one's happiness in the hands of another. Women, Janowitz implies, are far more likely to be slaves than slavemasters, because men take their relationships far more casually.

Artists are considered to be free spirits. Ironically, without exception the characters in this book are slaves of one sort or another. Further irony comes from the protection offered by slavery. One character owns a dog that she lets off its leash twice. On the first occasion, the dog is injured; on the second, it is killed. Characters recognize the hierarchy and strive to be owners rather than owned. Marley Mantello, for example, specifically dreams about what he will do when he is rich enough to have slaves.

Throughout these stories, women are subservient to or dependent on men. Their self-esteem is lower than that of men, even men of far less obvious merit. An example is Marley, who is sure that he is a genius even though he has difficulty selling his work. Eleanor's jewelry designs sound as creative as anything the male artists conceive, but Stash denigrates them as derivative and she believes him. Stash encourages her to make friends but becomes jealous when she does so, treating her as his property. Even as they are subjected to this type of treatment, the female characters do not always envy men. The prostitute narrator of "Modern Saint #271" ruminates about the many types of penises she has encountered and becomes "grateful I didn't have to own one of these appendages." The title of the story indicates that the narrator is one of hundreds of women in similar situations. Janowitz creates the same sense of commonality by titling two of her stories as "case histories," with numbers.

The character of Eleanor receives the most attention, serving as protagonist of many of the stories. Even though Eleanor eventually moves out of Stash's apartment, she shows little development throughout the book and almost none in any single story. After she breaks up with Stash, a voice comes into her head in "Matches," telling her to throw a party. She sees the party as a metaphor for pulling her life together. All the guests coincidentally turn out to be men; she invites dozens of her friends, wondering if any will come. She finds the party fun but traumatizing and decides that she prefers being alone and depressed. She realizes at one point that "it was hard to be almost thirty years old and so unlovable." Her situation appears to be the lot of women: to be in an unsatisfactory relationship or to be alone and depressed. Even being with Bruce Springsteen proves to be unpleasant in "You and the Boss."

It is difficult to tell at many points whether Janowitz is describing her own ephemeral surroundings or is instead satirizing the New York art scene. Some small elements are obvious satire, such as improbable flavors of ice cream (artichoke-chocolate chip) and the nonsensical but barely plausible lecture notes that Cora takes in her feminist studies classes at Yale in "Engagements." The larger elements of satire are less certain. The characters of *Slaves of New York* are shallow; the absence of depth or development of any of them leads the reader to wonder whether Janowitz is parodying the shallow world of SoHo or simply is unable to create convincing characters.

The ephemerality of the art world may be parody or a reflection of reality. Marley's desire to have dead composers write an opera may be a throwaway one-liner or an insight into the limited artistic grounding of modern artists. The many artists portrayed all create quick, bizarre pieces for shock value. Eleanor herself makes earrings and other jewelry out of plastic, which could be taken as a metaphor for the impermanence and shoddiness characterizing modern life.

As a last example of Janowitz's satire/reality, Eleanor recalls working as a model and having her hair styled to look like a bunch of grapes. She parades on a runway with other women who are also made up to look like fruit. This could be another oddity thrown in for shock value and amusement or a commentary on perceptions of women as commodities of no more worth than fruit.

Context

Slaves of New York was the first collection of stories to be a best-seller since Philip Roth's *Goodbye Columbus* (1959). In it, Janowitz offers a hip, satirical look at the New York art scene. Her take on that world is unique in that it emphasizes the role of women. Some of her female characters are heroes; all, as the title of the work implies, are in some way slaves.

The art scene as depicted is dominated by men, though one art dealer is a woman. This perhaps mirrors the larger world of work, in which men are advantaged. In Janowitz's world, men become famous and women become their girlfriends—if they are lucky. Janowitz offers some hope for women in "You and the Boss," in which she describes "you" taking the place of Bruce Springsteen's wife. By the end of the story, however, "you" leave Springsteen and are relieved, presumably because "you" have regained control over "your" life. In contrast, Eleanor struggles through many stories to find markets for her creations, while Stash, her sometime boyfriend, exerts much less effort for far greater gain. Eleanor looks to Stash for advice, assuming that he is more knowledgeable rather than simply luckier. Throughout the stories, women are subservient or in some way inferior to men. If Janowitz presents a message, it is that even in the progressive society of modern art, traditional values prevail.

Janowitz gained fame for this book largely through her own promotion. She carried her image as purveyor of pop culture to the extreme, appearing at the trendiest nightclubs and even creating a "literary video" for MTV. A film based on the book and starring Bernadette Peters as Eleanor was released in 1989.

Critics included Janowitz in the "literary brat pack" that included Jay McInerney and Brett Easton Ellis, suggesting that female writers could be just as outrageous and reflective of popular culture as their male counterparts. Indicative of her pioneering role as a female writer of this type of fiction, she was unable to publish a portion of her first novel, *American Dad* (1981), until she submitted it to *Paris Review* under the name of Tom A. Janowitz. Prior to publishing *Slaves of New York*, she had also circulated novels titled *A Cannibal in Manhattan* and *Memoirs of a Megalomaniac*. She found a publisher for a reworked version of *A Cannibal in Manhattan* in 1987 and published *The Male Cross-Dresser Support Group* in 1992. Neither book received significant critical acclaim.

Sources for Further Study
Anshaw, Carol. "Hype Springs Eternal." *The Village Voice* 31 (August 5, 1986): 46. Anshaw describes a central idea of *Slaves of New York*, that boys get to be famous and outrageous, while girls get to be girlfriends if they behave themselves. She notes the one-dimensionality of characters and sees Janowitz as standing outside the action she describes.
DePietro. Thomas. Review of *Slaves of New York*. *The Hudson Review* 39 (Autumn, 1986): 489. Describes the work as blurring the distinction between high and low culture. DePietro says that Janowitz's point in the book is unclear: The tales may be a symptom or a parody of the junk culture she describes.
Kaye, Elizabeth. "Fifteen Minutes Over SoHo." *Esquire* 110 (November, 1988): 170-176. Discusses the making of the film version of *Slaves of New York* as well as Janowitz's early life and how it affected her writing.
McInerney, Jay. "I'm Successful and You're Not." *The New York Times Book Review* 91 (July 13, 1986): 7. McInerney says that it is possible to be too hip as a writer, suggesting that Janowitz sees things at a distance. He describes her stories as static, with no development: The characters do not acquire knowledge, passion, or hope.
Prince, Dinah. "She'll Take Manhattan: Tama Janowitz's Tales for the Eighties." *New York* 19 (July 14, 1986): 36-42. A personality profile focusing on Janowitz's writing process and social world. Contains many quotations from Janowitz. Her social life and connections with Andy Warhol receive significant attention.
Sheppard, R. Z. "Downtown." *Time* 127 (June 30, 1986): 80-81. Describes Janowitz's humor as ranging from adolescent to collegiate and her intentions as satirical and sociological. Complains about the failure to follow through on promising ideas and about odd visceral connections that are difficult for the reader to make.
Sikes, Gini. "How Long Can Tama's Fifteen Minutes Last?" *Mademoiselle* 95 (April, 1989): 102-104, 276. Written just before the release of the film version of *Slaves of New York*. Predicts failure for the film and discusses how Janowitz has kept in the limelight even while failing to find critical acclaim. Describes her self-propelled publicity campaign for the book.

A. J. Sobczak

SLEEPLESS NIGHTS

Author: Elizabeth Hardwick (1916-   )
Type of work: Novel
Type of plot: Psychological realism
Time of plot: The twentieth century
Locale: New York
First published: 1979

> *Principal characters:*
> ELIZABETH, the self-conscious narrator
> ALEX, Elizabeth's intellectual friend and her first lover
> DR. Z, "the eternal husband" to Madame Mevrouw Z., "fervent romancer" to the painter, Simone, and "faithless" lover of his nurse-employee
> J., Elizabeth's childhood friend

Form and Content

Sleepless Nights is the title of Elizabeth Hardwick's novel and the recurrent image that identifies both the narrative's characteristic atmosphere and its inspirational source. It might have been titled nocturnal remembrances, a memoir of New York, for New Yorkers and New York City—in its supportive and destructive influences—constitute a major portion of the work's focus. Divided into ten short chapters, it is a first-person, confessional novel (a subcategory of the autobiographical) that, in its concern for the literary process of reconstructing life and human experience through memory, is highly self-conscious and allusive, taking as it does the act of writing from a woman's perspective and sensibility as a principal issue of the text: "But after all, 'I' am a woman."

Elizabeth, the narrator, begins her story in June of an unspecified year and, through interspersed letters written at different times and places and to different people in her past, ranges over fifty-six years, from the 1920's to 1978, emphasizing the period from 1940 (the year of her arrival in New York City from Lexington, Kentucky, to study at Columbia University) to 1973, the year of the last dated letter included in the narrative.

Sleepless Nights has a minimal amount of external action. Embodied in the complex sequence of narrated events the reader comes to understand, however, are the experiences that have shaped the writer before she begins to shape them in writing: Southern childhood in a family of eleven, with parents who paid the price of "intimacy" and adapted themselves to the disillusioned coupling of marriage; films and the imaginative freedom of reading; postadolescent loves and a surreptitious affair with an older man; university study; ill-fated love relations, a broken marriage, the gaining and losing of friends through deaths and misunderstandings; the spiritual malaise of urban social gatherings; the disorientation of change through real and imagined travels from South to North (from Kentucky to New York, from New York to Boston, from Boston to Maine, from Maine to Europe, always "carried along on a river of paragraphs and chapters, of blank verse, of little books translated from the Polish, large books from the Russian—all consumed in a sedentary sleeplessness"); and the ever-present consciousness of old age and death. All these experiences (interwoven so as to stress the theme of developing awareness) draw constant attention to the narrator's attempt to control and impose an order (and therefore meaning) on her past—in retrospect—in a way that she could not while experiencing it as life.

Recurrent in the novel from beginning to end is the narrator's awareness of the female condition. Most relevant to Elizabeth's developing consciousness as writer and woman are the numerous observations she makes of society's broken women: women in "squalid nursing homes" crocheting bedspreads; bag ladies who "sit in their rags, hugging their load of rubbish so closely it forms a part of their own bodies"; and women such as Josette, whose economic marital dependence upon Michael left her directionless at his death, and Ida, in Maine, whose "disaster" arrived in the form of Herman, a local man who one day "vanished for good," taking with him everything of use he could find in Ida's house, including, eventually, her sanity. There is also Miss Lavore, whose lonely life is redeemed by her nightly excursions to the Arthur Murray Dance Studio, where she engages changing strangers, keeping her life and theirs at a safe distance; and there is the British-accented Miss Cramer, whose earlier life of glamour and expensive possessions contrast dramatically with her lonely wait in old age for death.

The novel abounds in such illustrative perceptions of lives on the margin. Elizabeth's own experiences of men and male betrayal are epitomized by her memories of the old "gentleman in the black suit" who gave little girls chocolate ("the predator's first gift") in the darkness of the movie theater so that he could run his hands under their dresses and up their thighs, and young, intellectual, politically radical Alex Anderson, whose remembered "handsomeness" brings back images of a time of "fascinated, passionless copulation."

The longest and most symbolically revealing episode is Elizabeth's memory of bearing witness to the tragic demise of "the bizarre deity" Billie Holiday, the jazz singer whose life and relationship with her mother, Sadie, bear a striking resemblance to Elizabeth's life and relationship with her own mother. Holiday's artistic aspirations, moreover, confront Elizabeth with the isolating power of art in the life of the artist.

The novel ends as it begins, returning to the narrator's self-conscious awareness of reconstructing the emotional truths of her past through memory and the act of writing "throughout the night."

Analysis

Sleepless Nights is a highly lyrical novel written in a poetic prose that seeks to capture in its fleeting images and disconnected vignettes places, people, feelings, and occasions of personal and observed tragedy lost in time but resurrected through the

persistent power of memory. The synthesis of confessional narrative and the epistolary tradition is the principal organizational characteristic of the novel. Hardwick
intentionally juxtaposes temporal and spatial displacements as a means to approxi-
mate the authentic, "felt" process of human memory.

As a variation on the confessional narration, it is comparable to other examples of
the genre: Sylvia Plath's *The Bell Jar* (1971) or Doris Lessing's *The Golden Notebook*
(1962). In all these works, the search for identity through a probing self-analysis is
central. In accord with the conventions of the genre, there is an attempt to control the
experience of inner chaos by holding a mirror up to the self in the act of writing.
Alienation (or loss of self) and the anguish that accompanies it are the principal
sources of the emotional conflicts that compel the narrator to write, "to confess."

Hardwick's consistent deviation from narrative chronology emphasizes the complex principles of growth that are involved in the search for self-perception and
understanding. The letters to M. (eventually identified as "Mama," although quite
possibly also Hardwick's fellow writer and friend Mary McCarthy, to whom the book
is partially dedicated) gradually reveal with a minimum of explicit statement an
awareness in the narrator of some deep, shared identity between herself and her
mother, whose life she comes to see as an image of woman's limited possibilities for
control: "My mother had in many ways the nature of an exile, although her wanderings and displacements had been only in North Carolina, Tennessee, Virginia, and
Kentucky. I never knew anyone so little interested in memory, in ancestors, in records,
in sweetened back-glancing sceneries." The life of the totally unintrospective mother
is the gauge by which the narrator judges her own struggle to gain the understanding
that offers control of experience. However, the complex feelings aroused by memories
of and articulated toward her mother underscore powerfully the ambiguities involved
in feminine creativity: woman as artist versus woman as mother. Juxtaposed with the
"bizarre" story of the helpless Billie Holiday, who could be neither wife nor mother—
"not even a daughter could she easily appear to be"—is the helpless, self-sacrificing
image of Elizabeth's mother Mary, who with nine children subordinates her own
existence to "life under the dominion of nature." The narrator's tone of ambivalence
toward both is in part the result of her recognition of and personal response to
problems inherent in being a woman. Elizabeth's self-consciously "intellectual"
approach to her own experience—illustrated by the numerous literary allusions that
reverberate throughout the text—attests her refusal to be only a victim. She remembers, for example, with an imperceptible attitude of anger and contempt, reading the
story of Edmond and Jules de Goncourt's maid, Rose, and how the brothers quickly
condemned and betrayed the memory of her twenty-five years of devoted service
upon discovering that she had a "secret" life of her own apart from theirs.

The ironic texture employed throughout by Hardwick creates and sustains the
necessary narrative distance between author and narrator, narrator and reader. Like
that of Sylvia Plath in *The Bell Jar*, Hardwick's irony is often revealed in explicit
narrative statements of self-perception: Both narrators' way of seeing themselves
reflect their ways of perceiving others—especially men. Elizabeth, who is "honored"

when Alex Anderson takes her to bed and "dishonored" when she believes that she is insufficiently "imaginative" to please him, tells the reader almost simultaneously that she was "weasel-like hungry" in relation to men and, when their personal ideological contradictions surfaced, was given to "predatory chewings" on the "inauthenticity" of their actions. "Predatory" is, ironically, the word she uses on several occasions to describe the actions of men toward women, young and old.

Context

As do her two earlier novels, *Sleepless Nights* dramatizes—although from a much more personal vantage point—Hardwick's concern with the almost ineffable nature of human experience and the self-conscious awareness of "difference" which is the perspective of the female writer. As a contribution to the modern confessional novel—a genre extending back to Fyodor Dostoevski's *Notes From the Underground* (1864)—*Sleepless Nights* portrays the ways in which women struggle with modern problems such as loneliness, alienation, the difficulty of establishing meaningful and lasting relationships, and the emotional uncertainties and inner chaos that frequently accompany a consciousness of personal physical decay, economic dependence, and political marginality. Hardwick continues in this novel her exploration of the inscrutable flow of life from a perspective that is simultaneously feminine and dissident.

Essentially a writer accustomed to tackling ideas and whose preferred form is the essay as social criticism and belles-lettres, Hardwick nevertheless has been praised for her complex narrative structuring of "reminiscences" in *Sleepless Nights*, for her wit and understanding, and for the "sheer loveliness" of her sentences. Hardwick's plotless fusion of autobiography with fiction uncovers the female self as it turns toward women's experiences as a fountainhead of autonomous art. Like the theoretical articles and critical reviews that have established her presence in the ongoing feminist debate over woman as both subject and object of the literary text, *Sleepless Nights*, her most acclaimed novel, secures Hardwick's place as an important voice in that continuing discourse.

Sources for Further Study
Caplan, Brina. "The Teller as the Tale." *Georgia Review* 33, no. 4 (Winter, 1979): 933-940. An essay-review of *Sleepless Nights* which classifies it as a "novel-memoir" and compares it with Lillian Hellman's *Three* (1979). The narrative style is criticized for being too morally disengaged and fragmentary, producing the effect of an attempted "collage" that degenerates to "pastiche."

Lamont, Rosette. "The Off-Center Spatiality of Women's Discourse." In *Theory and Practice of Feminist Literary Criticism*, edited by Gabriela Mora and Karen S. Van Hooft. Ypsilanti, Mich.: Bilingual Press, 1982. Focuses on Hardwick's "fragmentary aesthetic," a style of indirect progression which has affinities with the treatment of narrative voice in Marguerite Duras' films, plays, and novels. Both writers are seen as feminist dissidents whose anarchic style reflects a rapprochement between women and their female condition of marginality.

Faust, Langdon Lynn, ed. *American Women Writers: A Critical Reference Guide from Colonial Times to the Present*. New York: Frederick Ungar, 1988. A biographical overview with brief commentary on the thematic content of principal publications.

Peters, Margaret. "Fiction Under a True Name: Elizabeth Hardwick's *Sleepless Nights*." *Chicago Review* 31, no. 2 (Autumn, 1979): 129-136. A feminist analysis of *Sleepless Nights*, emphasizing the autobiographical nature of the novel. The essay laments the oblique method of narration that distances the author from the narrating Elizabeth by "obliterating" much of Hardwick's known past. Offers comparisons between *Sleepless Nights* and Hardwick's first novel, *The Ghostly Lover* (1945).

Roland E. Bush

SLOUCHING TOWARDS BETHLEHEM

Author: Joan Didion (1934-   )
Type of work: Essays
First published: 1968

Form and Content

The first of Joan Didion's collections of essays, *Slouching Towards Bethlehem* takes its title from the last line of "The Second Coming" (1924) by Irish poet William Butler Yeats. The apocalyptic images of that poem had been, Didion says, her "points of reference" at the time she wrote the title essay in 1967. Faced with what she called a "conviction . . . that the world as I had understood it no longer existed," she went to San Francisco to learn about the emerging hippie culture in the Haight-Ashbury district: It was necessary, she wrote, "to come to terms with disorder." Most of the reviewers of this volume have read the collection as a whole in the light of the themes of social upheaval and moral decay that were raised first in this piece.

A preface to the volume contains an explanation of the genesis of the title and the motivation for several of the essays, Didion's reflections on her state of mind during the time she was writing, and descriptions of her habits as a writer during those years. The twenty essays were originally written for magazines—among them *Vogue, The Saturday Evening Post, The New York Times Magazine*, and *The American Scholar*—during the years 1965 through 1967.

The book is organized into three sections. "Life Styles in the Golden Land" contains eight essays focused on California, which are typically read either as pieces of journalism or as evidence of Didion's regionalism. The five pieces in the section titled "Personals" are often anthologized as "personal essays" in college readers and collections of modern essayists. Of the works in this volume, these are the most explicitly centered in the "I," or persona, of the writer. "Seven Places of the Mind" brings together seven essays, each centered on a geographical location: four on California; one each on Hawaii, Mexico, and Newport, Rhode Island. Neither travel pieces nor distinctly personal, these are perhaps best explained by Didion in her preface: "Since I am neither a camera eye nor much given to writing pieces which do not interest me, whatever I do write reflects, sometimes gratuitously, how I feel."

The essays in this collection represent a range of types of literary nonfiction. Some are intensely personal, offering the details of Didion's own self-doubting under titles such as "On Self-Respect" or "On Keeping a Notebook"; others address subjects such as John Wayne, Las Vegas wedding chapels, and folk singer Joan Baez's school in Carmel. Didion has published in many of the best literary periodicals, and she has become a highly respected voice in American letters.

Analysis

By the time *Slouching Towards Bethlehem* appeared, Didion had already won acclaim for her piece by the same title, published in *The Saturday Evening Post*. She was one of the most talented among what had come to be known as the New Journalists. They were practitioners of a kind of "maverick" journalism, and their work was characterized by a focus on subjects considered marginal to mainstream culture, a personal involvement by the writer in the subject, unconventional form often suggested by the subject itself, and a style that violated or transcended (depending upon the point of view) the strict laws of "objectivity" in traditional journalism by placing in the foreground the presence and perspective of the writer. Critical response to Didion's nonfiction has continued to address many of those features so highly touted in "Slouching Towards Bethlehem": her social commentary, her eye for detail, the quality of her voice, and the character or persona inhabited by her essays.

The first sentence of "Slouching Towards Bethlehem"—"The center was not holding"—takes from Yeats's poem the defining metaphor for Didion's social analysis. Danger, cataclysm, and disintegration are evoked in the opening section by an apocalyptic vision of the cultural, social, and moral conditions of the country, drawn with the broad strokes of an epic and haunting cadences in past tense. Haight-Ashbury, with its hippies, drugs, and runaways, was "where the social hemorrhaging was showing up."

Many of the stylistic devices for which Didion is best known are evident here, such as her use of anaphora in the way the sentences begin and clauses are joined, piling images in a tightening spiral of language and vision. Like a number of her other essays, "Slouching Towards Bethlehem" is constructed as a collage: bits of narrative, dialogue, and found texts organized in segments that sometimes break off abruptly and are separated only by white space, without traditional transitions, explicit connectors, or clear chronology. Some readers see the structure of "Slouching Towards Bethlehem" as disjointed, a mirror of the atomization about which Didion writes. Others see its shape as a referent more for her investigative method—accumulating experiences and impressions—than for the social chaos she encountered.

While the subjects of her essays may suggest that she is drawn to themes of social and moral disintegration, an equally important concern for Didion is an exploration of the dissonance between public stories and dreams and individual realities, often illuminated by her relentless focus on the details that do not fit the story. In "7000 Romaine, Los Angeles 38"—an essay ostensibly about the reclusive millionaire Howard Hughes—she calls this dissonance "the apparently bottomless gulf . . . between what we officially admire and secretly desire." Another essay, "Some Dreamers of the Golden Dream," is about Lucille Miller, who was accused and convicted of murdering her husband. In the details of Miller's life and trial, Didion finds a woman who seemed to have imbibed all the myths about upward mobility and the "golden dream" of suburban Southern California, and a lack of moral center that Didion suggests is somehow revealed in the geographical and cultural landscape. In "John Wayne: A Love Song," Didion explores the actor in the light of the cultural myth that had grown up around him, a myth that left no room for a man who could be defeated by a disease such as cancer.

Many of the pieces in this collection have come to be called personal essays, rooted in the strong presence of the first person at the center of the piece and in often uncomfortable revelations about Didion's life, fears, and desires. This is not to say that her other essays do not make use of the personal or the first person. "John Wayne: A Love Song" opens, for example, with memories of watching Wayne's films during the summer of 1943 and reflections on the ways in which lines from those movies have continued to have meaning for her ever since. Didion's personal revelation is not itself the focal point of this essay; it serves, instead, to illustrate a point around which the rest of the essay will develop, about the internal landscape of a generation of women and a figure who "determined forever certain of our dreams."

Differing understandings of the function of the personal in an essay have led to varying interpretations of Didion's literary nonfiction. For some, the personal voice invites analysis of her character and personality. She has been called neurotic, over sensitive, whiny, a woman of brittle nerves, extremely fragile, and consumed by a sense of loss. Indeed, much of the critical response to Didion's nonfiction labels it as autobiography, or as a means to understand the characters in her novels.

While most of the essays in *Slouching Towards Bethlehem* have to do in one way or another with California subjects, they are also about "something else," as Didion almost always asserts somewhere in each piece, and they are not comfortably catego- rized. "Notes from a Native Daughter," for example, has been read as a description of the particular flavor and character of Sacramento and the Central Valley of California, and as a nostalgic longing for the pastoral and privileged world of Didion's childhood among the landed descendants of original settlers.

Above all, in this collection Didion is a superb stylist. In the haunting rhythms of her sentences, in her startling juxtapositions, her precise effort to get the right word and the right articulation of an idea or an image, her prose is distinctive. Her voice is lyrical and intense, sometimes witty, sometimes pained. Her eye for detail creates what have been called verbal snapshots. Her driving interest in the seemingly irrele- vant or marginal, the unreported detail, is one of the most remarkable features of her essays.

Context

At the time that *Slouching Towards Bethlehem* was published, Didion was usually the only woman mentioned among the New Journalists. She is now one of the most recognized essayists in American letters, especially because the attention paid to the essay in college classrooms and literary magazines has grown in the second half of the twentieth century.

The essays in *Slouching Towards Bethlehem*, whether personal or reportage, pre- sent a woman's point of view inasmuch as Didion writes out of the particularities of what is repeatedly noted by readers and reviewers as very personal experience. Grounded in the first person, they present the voice of a woman who is not afraid to make her doubts, fears, and longings the subjects of her public musings or to include them in her investigations. Didion does not, in this volume, identify herself as being explicitly concerned with women or women's issues. Her nonfiction is rarely spoken of in terms of feminist concerns; perhaps for this reason, few reviewers and scholars have analyzed it from that critical perspective. This is less true of her fiction, largely because her main characters are all women.

In a 1970 interview, when asked specifically about the women's movement, she responded that social action "does not much engage my imagination"; in a 1979 interview she was described as "skeptical" of it. Her essay "The Women's Movement," published first in *The New York Times Book Review* (1972) and later collected in *The White Album* (1979), is an unsympathetic analysis of what was a relatively young movement at the time of her writing. Response to it by feminist critics— Catharine Stimpson most prominent among them—has taken Didion to task for, among other things, what they claim to be a superficial and inaccurate understanding of the history of the women's movement and of feminism.

Nonfiction by Didion includes the collections of essays *The White Album* (1979) and *After Henry* (1992) and the book-length works *Salvador* (1983) and *Miami* (1987). She remains foremost among American essayists, male or female, recognized for the elegance and distinctness of her style, the precision of her social critique, and the insistently strong presence of the first person in her work.

Sources for Further Study

Anderson, Chris. *Style as Argument: Contemporary American Nonfiction.* Carbon-dale: Southern Illinois University Press, 1987. Anderson closely examines the literary nonfiction of Tom Wolfe, Truman Capote, Norman Mailer, and Didion, attending particularly to the relationship between style and theme. Relying on classical and contemporary rhetorical and literary theory, Anderson claims that, despite the unique stylistic and rhetorical features of each, what these writers have in common is a self-consciousness about the limits of language. Anderson's is the only major study that engages Didion's nonfiction on its own terms rather than using it as an aid in reading her fiction or telling her biography.

Carton, Evan. "Joan Didion's Dreampolitics of the Self." *Western Humanities Review* 40 (Winter, 1986): 307-328. Carton reads the personal element in *Slouching Towards Bethlehem* as an assertion of self against the seeming disintegration of the cultural landscape which Didion appears to document. He makes his argument through an analysis of the theme and structure of the individual essays. He sees Didion's project as paradoxically related to Marxist and feminist critiques of the "natural, autonomous, decontextualized self."

Didion, Joan. "Cautionary Tales." Interview by Susan Stamberg. In *Joan Didion: Essays and Conversations*, edited by Ellen G. Friedman. Princeton, N.J.: Ontario Review Press, 1984. In an interview originally aired by National Public Radio in 1977, Didion talks about her habits and style as a writer of both fiction and nonfiction.

Felton, Sharon, ed. *The Critical Response to Joan Didion.* Westport, Conn.: Greenwood Press, 1994. Felton's introduction to this collection is the most up-to-date and far-ranging survey of the full scope of Didion's work, making thematic connections among her screenplays, fiction, and nonfiction. The volume contains reviews, selected critical response to Didion's entire canon, a chronology, and an extensive bibliography.

Henderson, Katherine Usher. *Joan Didion*. New York: Frederick Ungar, 1981. This short volume aimed at college students and the general reader, which is among the most frequently cited works of Didion criticism, devotes one chapter to each of Didion's volumes. Henderson reads Didion's fiction and nonfiction as explorations of the moral dilemmas created in the explosion of traditional American myths. She summarizes and provides publication history for each essay in *Slouching Towards Bethlehem*, but she also draws loose and misleading inferences about Didion's life from material in the essays.

Kazin, Alfred. "Joan Didion: Portrait of a Professional." *Harper's Magazine* 243 (December, 1971): 112-122. This chatty article blends stylistic analysis of Didion's sentences and her moral vision. Although Kazin is one of the most respected American literary and cultural critics, his analysis of Didion's personality may now be read as dated and patronizing.

Stimpson, Catharine. "The Case of Miss Joan Didion." *Ms.* 7 (January, 1973): 36-41. This article is useful in its description and analysis of what Stimpson calls "Didion Woman," who is either child or victim, and with whom Stimpson has lost patience. Among other things, she takes Didion to task for her ignorance about feminism in "The Women's Movement."

Laura Julier

SO FAR FROM GOD

Author: Ana Castillo (1953-   )
Type of work: Novel
Type of plot: Farce
Time of plot: The last two decades of the twentieth century
Locale: Tome, New Mexico
First published: 1993

Principal characters:
SOFÍA, called Sofi, the protagonist and mother of four daughters
ESPERANZA, Sofi's eldest daughter, a radical chicana activist and journalist
CARIDAD, Sofi's second daughter, who becomes an apprentice medicine woman
FE, Sofi's third daughter, a hardworking young woman
LA LOCA, Sofi's fourth daughter, the possessor of extraordinary powers
DOMINGO, Sofi's errant husband

Form and Content

So Far from God is a tragicomedy that details the adventures and misadventures of Sofi and her four daughters, Esperanza, Caridad, Fe, and La Loca (Hope, Charity, Faith, and the Crazy One), all of whom possess unusual traits. Set in a small desert town in New Mexico, the novel relates the rather strange occurrences in the life of Sofi, a fiercely independent and strong-willed woman who works hard to raise her daughters and continues to care for them when they return home suffering from the effects of ill-starred love affairs.

The three oldest sisters follow society's expectations by initially pursuing romantic love and marriage. In the case of Esperanza, her lover, Ruben (who renamed himself Cuauhtemoc during his chicano activist days), leaves her to marry a wealthy Anglo woman. After she accepts a job as a television reporter in Washington, D.C., she is sent to cover the Persian Gulf War; she is kidnapped and disappears for some time. The family finds out that she has been killed when the well-known figure of Mexican legend, La Llorona ("the Weeping Woman"), appears to La Loca to tell her that Esperanza is dead. The family receives the official news later.

Caridad, the second daughter, a hospital orderly, marries her high school boyfriend, Memo, after she becomes pregnant. Memo goes back to his former girlfriend, however, and Caridad has an abortion that is performed by her youngest sister, La Loca (who subsequently repeats the procedure) without their mother's knowledge. Her loving nature moves her to seek substitutes for Memo until she is bodily attacked by an evil force, a beast of legend, that almost kills her. Her mother and sisters nurse her back to life, and La Loca's powerful prayers (in something akin to a miracle) return her mutilated body to its former beauty. During her apprenticeship as a *curandera*, she joins the traditional Catholic pilgrimage to the Sangre de Cristo mountains, where she unexpectedly remains and lives as a hermit in a cave for a year. Ultimately, obsessed by a woman with whom she falls in love, Caridad dies (disappears) as she leaps off a high desert plateau with this woman.

Fe, the third daughter, has an equally strange life and also dies at a young age from cancer. Her death is the result of the chemicals she is required to use as a factory worker in a plant that subcontracts work from a Pentagon weapons contractor.

The fourth daughter, La Loca, behaves in a peculiar fashion (after her supposed death and resurrection at age three), becoming averse to human smell and the physical closeness of anyone except her mother, possessed of a special affinity to animals, a child who becomes a woman without ever leaving the confines of the area surrounding her house. In a different place, she might have been called autistic—a psychological word stripped of the mythical connotations and spiritual gifts attributed to La Loca.

While still a young woman, La Loca mysteriously contracts AIDS and dies. One by one, the other sisters die or disappear in bizarre circumstances. Nevertheless, Sofía faces her many misfortunes with strength, determination, patience, and the wisdom implied in her name. Her husband plays only a peripheral and insignificant role in her life, a background prop. In the final chapter, her daughters' untimely deaths lead Sofi to found the "prestigious" organization M.O.M.A.S. (Mothers of Martyrs and Saints), where she remains as president and a tower of strength for thirty-eight years.

Throughout the novel, the narrator immerses the reader in a tapestry of folklore, culture, legends, New Mexican recipes, and home remedies used by *curanderas*. These seemingly disparate threads are all carefully woven into the fanciful tale that runs in many directions and is full of unexpected happenings. The author also uses the narrative to explore the causes of present-day environmental problems, the callous nature of factory owners who put profits over the health and lives of workers, the dangers of cancer-producing chemicals, the critical nature of AIDS, and other contemporary social issues.

Analysis

The book's title is taken from a quote ascribed to Porfirio Diaz, president and dictator of Mexico from 1877 to 1911: "So far from God—so near the United States," a reference to the military power and territorial ambition of the country north of its border. The land and the people in the area now called New Mexico were dominated by the Spaniards in the colonial period and the United States in the postcolonial years. More than a million square miles of Mexican territory was lost by Mexico to the United States following the Mexican-American War of 1845-1848, the price exacted by the victorious Americans. As part of Mexico, the New Mexico region had had a land system of large holdings and extensive communal estates where sheep were raised. Their heritage, culture, and land have remained a source of great pride to New Mexican Hispanos and Hispanas (a long-held, self-designated term).

Castillo has used this backdrop to write an amusing farce narrating the complicated lives of a New Mexican family of women. The narrator uses the guise of a storyteller by telling her tale in the colloquial style of the oral tradition and using the voice of an uneducated woman (whose speech abounds with double negatives and convoluted phrases). The novel is written in the regional speech of the Hispano of New Mexico; English is interspersed with Spanish words and phrases and assorted Spanish anglicisms. Much of the storytelling fun is related to the meaning of Spanish words interjected by the narrator as she moves from one language to the other (code switching), a technique that the author uses quite effectively.

So Far from God, like oral history, echoes the old legends and the contemporary reality suffered by New Mexicans and Mexicans, blending the real with the unreal. An often-repeated tale told by a good storyteller loses its original, insipid details and becomes suffused with unexplained magic and fantastic occurrences to make it a more exciting story. Similarly, the novel uses this technique to raise humble circumstances and commonplace events to legendary status. In the voice of the storyteller, facts become blurred and myths are created. Old Mexican legends become part of the reality of daily life in Tome, New Mexico.

The protagonists of the novel are not meant to be serious, believable people; instead, they are comic, two-dimensional characters portraying exaggerated qualities and tendencies, and the reader has few insights into their thoughts. Fe's husband Casey (Casimiro), although an accountant, was the descendant of an old sheepherding family that had lost its landholdings in the previous fifty years. Three hundred years of sheepherding, however, seven generations of sheepherders preceding Casey, left their mark on him: He made a soft bleating sound, a whispered ba-aaa that Fe found embarrassing.

Castillo uses long chapter headings that give the reader a summary of the chapter's contents, in much the same manner that Miguel de Cervantes did in *Don Quixote de la Mancha*. In addition, the language used by the author in the titles is heavily reminiscent of the Spanish author's style: "An Account of the First Astonishing Occurrence in the Lives of a Woman Named Sofía and Her Four Fated Daughters; and the Equally Astonishing Return of Her Wayward Husband" is the first chapter heading. When the author wants to become didactic concerning the pollution of water, land, air, and people in New Mexico, she cleverly proposes it in the chapter heading: "La Loca Santa Returns to the World via Albuquerque Before her Transcendental Departure; and a Few Random Political Remarks from the Highly Opinionated Narrator." The style and language of the long headings place the reader in a certain time and place, a space where the old Spanish traditions commingle with the indigenous culture of the Americas.

Castillo brings together an amazing mixture of characters who make fun of contemporary Anglo-American cultural traits and New Mexican traditions and legends by juxtaposing them and turning the protagonists into farcical and distorted parodies of these characteristics. The novel is funnier to the Latino bilingual reader who understands the references to legends and the Spanish/English puns, but readers in general will gain deeper insights into the reality of native New Mexicans and explore a few universal "truths."

Context

A native of Chicago, Castillo is a chicana, a term with the connotation of political activism as used by Mexican Americans. Initially a poet published by small Latino presses, she later turned to fiction. In more recent years, she has been "discovered" as a Latina writer by mainstream publishers and a more general readership. Chicana critics have often defined Castillo's literary work as social protest and feminist. Her writing, however, reflects the perspective of a chicana feminist; that is, it is a feminism infused with issues of culture, ethnicity, and social justice, as well as gender-specific concerns. *So Far from God* exemplifies this tendency. The novel is not necessarily a "feminist" work; nevertheless, the narrative is written from a chicana feminist perspective. The emphasis on female protagonists to the exclusion of males, except as adjuncts to the narrative, is clear. The heroic Sofía is an exemplary mother whose qualities of independence, strength, and determination are often ascribed to males.

So Far from God is a change of pace for Castillo. Her first work of fiction, *The Mixquiahuala Letters* (1986), is an epistolary novel with a well-defined feminist focus, written in a lyrical prose. This story of the intimate friendship between two women reveals the effects of the sexual repression imposed on women by Mexican culture and the women's rebellion against this tradition. Unlike Castillo's first novel, *So Far from God* does not present the inner thoughts of women caught between two cultures with diverging viewpoints on the sexuality of women; instead, the reader perceives a multitude of issues concerning society as a whole, told by a narrator with a strong feminist perspective.

Most of Castillo's poetry has feminist themes with a deeply erotic strain. Her fiction, however, is provocative and varies thematically and in literary technique. Nevertheless, in both genres, Castillo propagates her own brand of feminism.

Castillo's first novel received the Before Columbus Foundation's American Book Award. Similarly, *So Far from God* has garnered two awards: the Carl Sandberg Literary Award in Fiction and the Mountain and Prairie Regional Booksellers Award in Fiction.

Sources for Further Study

Alarcón, Norma, et al., eds. *Chicana Critical Issues*. Berkeley, Calif.: Third Woman Press, 1993. This text focuses on issues of identity and difference and includes critical essays on chicana literature that will broaden the context for *So Far from God*. The bibliography by Lillian Castillo-Speed, "Chicana Studies: An Updated List of Materials, 1980-1991," is currently the most comprehensive in print.

Castillo, Ana. "La Macha: Toward a Beautiful Whole Self." In *Chicana Lesbians: The Girls Our Mothers Warned Us About*, edited by Carla Trujillo. Berkeley, Calif.: Third Woman Press, 1991. This philosophical essay by Castillo (written before *So Far from God*) discusses her attitude toward sexual identity, the sexual ambivalence of the two female protagonists of *The Mixquiahuala Letters*, and other topics related to her writing.

Herrera-Sobek, Maria, and Helena Maria Viramontes, eds. "Chicana Creativity and Criticism: Charting New Frontiers in American Literature." *The Americas Review* 15, nos. 3 and 4 (1987). This special double issue of the literary journal includes chicana literature and criticism. Yvonne Yarbro-Bejarano's essay "Chicana Literature, from a Chicana Feminist Perspective" discusses the relationship between chicana feminist literature and political activism in the community. This essay will give the reader of *So Far from God* a better understanding of Castillo's feminist perspective.

Horno-Delgado, Asunción, et al., eds. *Breaking Boundaries: Latina Writing and Critical Readings*. Amherst: University of Massachusetts Press, 1989. This volume contains feminist criticism of Latina writers. The authors' introduction analyzes Latina literature as an expression of cultural heritage and historical circumstances not as a search for identity. The authors also include a selected bibliography of works by and criticism of Latina writers. The article on Castillo by Norma Alarcón, "The Sardonic Powers of the Erotic in the Work of Ana Castillo," although written before the publication of *So Far from God*, gives the reader some insights into the author's work; in particular, Alarcón places the sexual ironies in Castillo's poetry and her first novel within the context of the cultural tradition of the chicana.

Limón, José E. "La Llorona, the Third Legend of Greater Mexico: Cultural Symbol, Women, and the Political Unconscious." In *Between Borders: Essays on Mexicana/Chicana History*, edited by Adelaida R. Del Castillo. Encino, Calif.: Floricanto Press, 1990. Limón's essay focuses on the three women who dominate Mexican culture: La Malinche (Hernan Cortez's interpreter and mistress), the Virgen de Guadalupe (Mexico's patron saint), and La Llorona (the Weeping Woman). This scholarly article will acquaint the reader with the complex and interrelated symbolism of the three women.

Mirandé, Alfredo, and Evangelina Enriquez. *La Chicana: The Mexican American Woman*. Chicago: University of Chicago Press, 1979. The first book published on chicanas, it gives a comprehensive historical and sociological perspective on Mexican American women. The first chapter includes an overview of legendary female figures in Mexican history, folklore, and mythology (some of whom are referred to in *So Far from God*). There is also the chapter "Images in Literature," which looks at the stereotypical images of Mexican women as portrayed by Anglo writers in the nineteenth century, followed by a discussion of contemporary chicano and chicana writers.

Irene Campos Carr

THE SOLACE OF OPEN SPACES

Author: Gretel Ehrlich (1946-   )
Type of work: Essays
First published: 1985

Form and Content

Gretel Ehrlich challenges serious myths concerning gender and its relationship to the American West in the twelve essays that constitute *The Solace of Open Spaces.* Instead of positing the West as a man's world in which men have all the power and are separated from the women's domain of home and family, Ehrlich depicts tough, capable women who are working outside the home. Most women, including Ehrlich herself, work along with the men and pull their own weight, even in the midst of personal tragedy, by adopting typically masculine qualities.

On the one hand, this book is like a typical collection of essays in that each piece is an individual unit existing independently of the others. Each essay resonates with its own artistry. Each manifests its own distinct tone, subject matter, and point of view. Each stands wonderfully on its own. On the other hand, Ehrlich also brings the essays together into a single work that clearly has a unifying story and set of thematic concerns. She mentions more than once in the preface that the book is a "narrative" and that the accumulation of essays chronicles her relationship to Wyoming, first as a place to make a documentary film on sheepherders, then as a place to mourn the death of her lover, then as a place to live and work, and finally as a place to discover and consummate another love relationship. Seen in this way, each essay relies on the others for the telling of Ehrlich's Wyoming experience, and the overall narrative transcends the concerns of the individual essays, although the essays do not create a chronological narrative by building on one another either consecutively or logically.

Instead, the essays are organized in a more unconventional narrative that Ehrlich herself describes in multiple ways in the book's preface: She says that her narrative is "written in fits and starts," is made of "digressions," and constructs a foundation made of riprap. All these descriptions suggest a structure that is inspired by the spirit of the place about which she is writing, a structure that is imitative of the choppy and chaotic Wyoming landscape and the capricious and suddenly changing Wyoming weather. The book consists of three different kinds of writing that Ehrlich weaves together, foregrounding first one and then another: an autobiography in the story of her life experiences; a natural history in her detailed observations of the landscape, the weather, and the creatures of Wyoming; and an ethnography in her story of the people who live on the land. These three kinds of writing are what make the book so digressive and so given to "fits and starts." They also suggest that Ehrlich's experiences in Wyoming were not one-dimensional. She did not simply find herself becoming attached to the landscape or the people or a particular man; she found all these experiences happening at once with more or less equal poignancy.

Analysis

Thematically, all the essays in *The Solace of Open Spaces* celebrate a tradition of viewing nature which claims that viewers are a part of the landscape they are viewing. Ehrlich, in fact, makes this relationship so strong a focus of her book that she envisions a kind of marriage between herself and Wyoming, and between other Wyoming residents and their state. This concept of marriage is endowed with a kind of sanctity and involves the way humans think about the interconnected, web-like relationship they have with everything in the universe: rocks, trees, dogs, clouds, stars, grass, snow, bugs, deer, even themselves—and, of course, other humans. Indeed, one of the most important stories weaving through these essays culminates in Ehrlich's actual marriage to a rancher, a marriage that can be seen as an echo of or an analogue for the other marriages in the book.

Because of the nature of ranch work and because animals outnumber humans in this desolate landscape, Ehrlich repeatedly suggests or implies that Wyoming residents feel close attachments—a kind of marriage—to animals. In example after example, animals are treated as friends and are invited into the human world. One sheepherder keeps warm by sleeping with the nannies; another picnics with his horse, fixing two sandwiches and a can of beer for each of them. When domestic animals are in danger, humans save their lives, and animals do the same thing for humans. When wild animals fight, show off, and make love, their lives are described as parallel to the lives of humans. Even when Ehrlich addresses the question of meat eating, she emphasizes not the butchery that would mark the animal as Other, but the ritualized harmony that can be seen in the slaughter.

A different kind of marriage occurs internally within the Wyoming residents. Whether they are male or female, most of the characters in Ehrlich's book seem to be androgynous, bringing together the stereotypical qualities of the masculine (strong, rugged, stoic, outdoorsy) with those of the feminine (patient, accepting, sensitive) and wedding them within one individual. Just as women adopt male qualities to survive in the rodeo and on the range, men move toward their opposite as well. During their rodeo events, they are "tender in their movements, as elegant as if Balanchine had been their coach." Throughout the book, Ehrlich shows that these men are not macho cowboys riding into the sunset, happily removed from the rest of society. They are not representations of toughness or conquest or power. Instead, like Ehrlich's women, who combine the masculine and the feminine, these men combine stereotypically feminine traits, traits of approachability and soft-heartedness, with their masculine characteristics.

Although thematic concerns related to marriage pervade the book both implicitly, as when Ehrlich refers to the rhythm of horse and rider as their "pas de deux," and more explicitly, as when "a good rodeo" is compared to "a good marriage," marriage rarely surfaces when Ehrlich writes about twentieth century urban society—the place she left behind when she moved to Wyoming. In moving from an urban environment to a rural Western culture, she has moved from an isolated and isolating state to a communal and married one. At one point, Ehrlich makes this point explicit when she compares the ritual in ranch life and the ritual in Indian life to the lack of ritual in mainstream America.

Throughout the book, Ehrlich demonstrates that she achieved solace not only by coming to terms with her grief but also by becoming married to the natural world. Although a reader might argue that Ehrlich's hunger for attachment to a place is sentimental and unrealistic, one must understand the seriousness of what would be at stake if Ehrlich were to look at the universe through a lens that did not focus on connection; the "barbed solitude" and the "shrill estrangement" Ehrlich sees in twentieth century urban society could lead to a greater sense of deadening separation.

Ehrlich's preoccupation with the richly layered kinds of attachment she found in Wyoming is reflected not only in her explicit statements to that effect but also in the persuasiveness of her metaphors, which attest a marriage between the human and natural worlds. For example, Ehrlich writes that the northern lights "look like talcum powder fallen from a woman's face." This typical example of her metaphoric play demonstrates how she makes radical connections between seemingly unconnected (or unconnectable) elements of creation. This use of arresting metaphors is not new: By using them, Ehrlich places herself in a tradition in which figurative language works to remove barriers almost magically and to bring together what people normally think of as separate.

Context

Although Gretel Ehrlich has written several works of fiction and poetry, *The Solace of Open Spaces*, her first collection of essays, has been her most well-received work to date. The book won an award from the American Academy of Arts and Letters, and several individual essays from it have been anthologized. *The Solace of Open Spaces* fits into a literary tradition that is often referred to as nature writing. Although this tradition is profoundly male, epitomized by the works of well-known writers such as Henry David Thoreau, John Muir, and Edward Abbey, many women have also written nonfictional accounts of their relationships with nature. In the nineteenth century, women such as Margaret Fuller and Celia Thaxter, both of whom are little known today, wrote what could be called nature writing. In the twentieth century, writers such as Mary Austin, Rachel Carson, and Annie Dillard have also, like Ehrlich, depicted themselves as women who understand both the beauties and dangers in nature and who thrive when in contact with the natural world. Ehrlich's *The Solace of Open Spaces*, though not as spiritual as Dillard's *Pilgrim at Tinker Creek* (1974), as politicized as Carson's *Silent Spring* (1962), or as overtly feminist as Austin's *The Land of Little Rain* (1903), fits solidly into this growing tradition of women writing about nature. This tradition can and probably should be looked at in conjunction with and also apart from the mainstream tradition of nature writing by men, if only to investigate the possible differences between the two.

The Solace of Open Spaces is an important book for several reasons, including the beauty of its language. Essays such as "The Solace of Open Spaces," "The Smooth Skull of Winter," and "A Storm, the Cornfield, and Elk," with their surprising images, sparse sentences, alliteration, and metaphors, read more like poetry than what is usually thought of as essayistic prose.

Since the publication of *The Solace of Open Spaces*, Gretel Ehrlich has been working on other nature essays, some of which have been collected in her second collection of essays, *Islands, The Universe, Home* (1991). Ehrlich's other books include *Geode Rock Body* (1970), *To Touch the Water* (1981), *City Tales, Wyoming Stories* (1986, coauthored with essayist Edward Hoagland), *Heart Mountain* (1988), and *Drinking Dry Clouds* (1991).

Sources for Further Study
Austin, Mary. *The Land of Little Rain*. 1903. Reprint. New York: Penguin Books, 1988. A collection of essays about Southern California's desert country which was published more than eighty years before *The Solace of Open Spaces*. Like Ehrlich, Austin concerns herself not only with the natural world but also with the people who live in a particular landscape, the communities of Piute and Shoshone Indians, Hispanic settlers, and turn-of-the-century miners.
Dillard, Annie. *Pilgrim at Tinker Creek*. New York: Harper & Row, 1974. A collection of essays that has received more critical attention than any work of nature writing by a woman. Although Dillard's essays are unquestionably more spiritual than Ehrlich's, both writers cultivate a relationship with nature that is on their own terms, not on the terms that society might have prescribed for them.
Ehrlich, Gretel. "An Interview with Gretel Ehrlich." Interview by James Wackett. *North Dakota Quarterly* 58 (Summer, 1990): 121. An interview in which Ehrlich talks about ranching, writing, rodeo, and her definition of the West. Some of the interview focuses specifically on her use of language in *The Solace of Open Spaces*.
Elbow, Peter. "The Pleasures of Voice in the Literary Essay: Explorations in the Prose of Gretel Ehrlich and Richard Selzer." In *Literary Nonfiction: Theory, Criticism, Pedagogy*. Edited by Chris Anderson. Carbondale: Southern Illinois University Press, 1989. A critical essay that explores the concept of voice in nonfiction by using examples from Ehrlich's *The Solace of Open Spaces* as well as from essayist Richard Selzer's work. Elbow closely analyzes the first two paragraphs from Ehrlich's text, arguing that their voice is rich and complex.
Hasselstrom, Linda. *Land Circle: Writings Collected from the Land*. Golden, Colo.: Fulcrum, 1991. A memoir comprising essays and poems, Hasselstrom's depiction of her experiences on a South Dakota ranch interestingly complements Ehrlich's own depiction of ranching experiences in *The Solace of Open Spaces*. Hasselstrom's book, like Ehrlich's, chronicles a woman's grieving for a loved one killed by cancer.

Cassandra Kircher

SOLSTICE

Author: Joyce Carol Oates (1938-   )
Type of work: Novel
Type of plot: Psychological realism
Time of plot: The 1980's
Locale: Bucks County, Pennsylvania
First published: 1985

Principal characters:

MONICA JENSEN, a recently divorced woman teaching English at an elite preparatory school

SHEILA TRASK, a local painter of minor renown

HAROLD BELL, Monica's former husband

MORTON FLAXMAN, Sheila's deceased husband, who had been a sculptor

KEITH RENWICK, a lawyer who takes Monica to dinner

JACKSON WINTHROP, a guest at Sheila's party who rapes Monica

JILL STARKIE, the meddlesome wife of the school's chaplain

Form and Content

Oates's relatively short sixteenth novel explores in depth the obsessive female friendship of two professional women. It occupies the time frame of an academic year, from September to May. Monica and Sheila are basically out of harmony with the comfortable, smug world of exurbanite Glenkill, though they participate in its social life. The men they meet are unpleasing and are relegated to the margins of their concern.

Monica's and Sheila's attachment grows out of their complementary yet conflicting personalities. Monica is fair, whereas Sheila is dark. Monica's passivity contrasts with Sheila's tempestuousness. Their alliance is often a power play, with each vying for control. Though infused with erotic tension, their relationship is not overtly lesbian. Both heterosexual in the past, they shy away from mutual physical contact.

The novel has four sections: "The Scar," "The Mirror-Ghoul," "Holiday," and "The Labyrinth." "The Scar" emphasizes Monica's vulnerability and preoccupation with the past, as she absent-mindedly strokes her jaw. Her isolation in the old house produces a sense of eeriness: She imagines someone calling her name, a sign of her readiness for a new relationship. Abruptly, Sheila rides into her life, mounted on a splendid horse. The spectacle hints at Sheila's rugged animal strength and authority as well as the appearance of a knightly rescuer, for from a distance Monica cannot tell if the rider is male or female. Sheila's intrusion marks the beginning of a period resembling courtship. Flattered, Monica experiences fear and exhilaration. The women regularly dine together, exchanging gifts and confidences.

With "The Mirror-Ghoul," days darken into winter and Monica feels anxiety about the passing of time. Gazing in her mirror, she sees her golden hair fading. The mirror seems to reflect her aging image and death's inevitability, an example of Oates's use of a gothic device for psychological effect. As a diversion, Sheila invents a new sexual game. The women will seek male companionship, being careful to cultivate meaningless relationships that pose no threat to their own intimacy. They invent other selves, playing at being coworkers "Sherrill Ann" and "Mary Beth," fun-loving women who drive to country roadhouses to dance, drink, and flirt with truckers and mechanics. These forays make Monica feel like a "golden girl" again, though she is uneasy. The dangerous sport ends when the men angrily accuse them of being lesbians. The women flee, with the men driving after them in enraged pursuit. Monica is terrorized. Soon afterward, Sheila unaccountably vanishes. In "Holiday," Sheila has left, it turns out, for Morocco and Monica is on her own. She visits her parents in Indiana as if to convalesce from an illness, but the atmosphere of her old home fails to comfort her. Monica's hovering parents suppose that she still suffers from the divorce, whereas she yearns for Sheila. Back in Glenkill, she marks time with aimless activities, disconsolate over Sheila, who returns in March as unexpectedly as she had left, boasting of her Arab lovers.

In "The Labyrinth," Sheila works to complete an ambitious series of paintings, "Ariadne's Thread," for her gallery showing in May. The power balance shifts subtly between the women. Monica is more in control as she skips classes and helps a grateful Sheila with household chores so that she can paint, but Monica's luck changes. When she lets a homosexual student read a revealing story before assembled faculty and students, she is rebuked, and she is eventually relieved of teaching duties for the term. At Sheila's party celebrating the completed canvases, Monica meets the man who will rape her. She falls seriously ill, lying in a delirium and haunted by her mortality. At the last, a skeletal Monica is rescued by Sheila, who rushes her to the doctor. Sheila concludes the novel with the affectionate promise that they will always be together unless one of them dies.

Analysis

Solstice begins with traditional realism, as Oates documents her characters' backgrounds, personalities, and lifestyles, but gradually the novel's structure grows fragmented, acquiring the lineaments of fable through the use of symbol and myth. There are pointed literary allusions. Most conspicuous is the reference to the cosmic image of the solstice, that time of year when the sun seems to stand still. The days of solstice, December 22 and June 22, are the shortest and longest of the year, respectively. Plot elements follow the calendar: Shortly before the winter solstice, on December 6, Monica gets an unwelcome letter from her former husband. A malefactor poisons Sheila's dog. Oates incorporates a pun on *sol* and *soul*. The approach of the solstice, with its brief dark days, disheartens Sheila, for in it she recognizes "the old, old eclipse of the soul." If the solstice brings about stasis and equilibrium, it is akin to the stillness of death. The wild oscillations in Monica and Sheila's partnership keep them off balance, but this perpetual restless movement is the essence of life.

Seasonal changes are functional. At Christmas, Sheila abruptly leaves for the warm climate of Morocco. From Monica's bereft viewpoint, Sheila withdraws like the sun in winter, leaving their companionship at a terrible standstill. With the vibrant Sheila in eclipse, Monica broods until her friend comes back, restoring life and warmth.

Sheila also needs Monica as a source of brightness. Connected to the solstice is the image of light. Sheila, as a painter, must respond to light, but Sheila's own forces are bound up with darkness. In intense light Sheila looks ravaged, while at dusk she entrances Monica with her loveliness. Not having enough light of her own—for her personality embodies the inner, chaotic forces of creativity—Sheila needs the orderly illumination that Monica provides. Sheila perceives fair-haired Monica as "a daylight personality" whose "blond aura" sheds a brightening influence and inspires her to paint light into the final Ariadne canvas.

Oates's other chief reference is to the Greek legend of Ariadne and the Labyrinth. Theseus vowed to kill the Minotaur—half bull, half man—a monster confined in a maze littered with the bones of heroes who had failed. Theseus received help from Ariadne, who, as the daughter of Helios, the Sun, was associated with the return of spring and lengthening days. Because she loved Theseus, she gave him a ball of thread with which to mark his path from labyrinthine darkness into daylight. Theseus slew the Minotaur and escaped with Ariadne; later, he deserted her. Oates makes her own use of the myth: Sheila calls her important series of paintings "Ariadne's Thread," quickly declaring that no hero is involved; this is not Theseus' achievement, but Ariadne's alone. Ariadne represents the controlling artist who holds in her hand the clue to the dangerous chaos of the maze—the creating unconscious mind—from which she emerges in triumph. As a token of the sisterhood theme, each woman offers the other the redeeming and enabling thread, their guide to empowerment and self-realization.

Oates employs a favorite motif—that of doubles—to depict two personalities forming a complementary pair. In *Solstice*, she ponders the question of art and the artist. Sheila and Monica are like alter egos, two beings grappling within a single artistic psyche, each unable to exist without the other: the chaos of the imagination against the ordering rational mind, the visual against the verbal faculties. Monica, as beholder, consumer, and critic of her friend's paintings, senses their mystery. In them, she intuits the dark turbulence, the unleashed egotism of the artist. The paintings intimidate her as she tries to understand them, for like the labyrinth they threaten to engulf her. Later, when she is more accepting, she dreams that the voluptuous paintings engulf her in sweetness.

Literature and the pictorial arts also preoccupy the two women. Monica, the English teacher, is often at a loss in an art gallery, but she respects verbal expression and loves to read. Sheila, who approves of the way visual art "assaults the eye," cares little for reading. Dismissively, she riffles through Monica's Victorian novels, which she finds too linear, too orderly.

Oates's other reinforcing literary allusions include the novel's epigraph, Emily Dickinson's poem "After great pain, a formal feeling comes," to characterize Monica's leaden, moribund psychological condition when she arrives at Glenkill. From Shakespeare's play *Cymbeline*, Oates cites the lyric—ending with an omen of death— that gives Monica her "golden girl" epithet: "Golden lads and girls all must,/ As chimney-sweepers come to dust."

Context

Although Oates at one time resisted the appellation of woman writer, she demonstrates an acute awareness of feminist issues. Before writing *Solstice*, Oates completed pseudo-gothic historical novels about women in nineteenth century America, *A Bloodsmoor Romance* (1984) and *Mysteries of Winterthurn* (1984), in which she treated patriarchal authority mockingly. In *Solstice*, she touches on feminist issues, often with irony and ambiguity.

Solstice shows that Oates is responsive to Virginia Woolf's complaint in *A Room of One's Own* (1929) that serious fiction tends to depict women in relation to men but rarely represents two women as friends. Woolf hoped that in time it might be normal to read that "Chloe likes Olivia." *Solstice* also suggests the validity of the androgynous woman, which Woolf developed in *Orlando* (1928).

Motherly and sisterly bonding, mutual support, dominance, exploitation, and female rivalry all occur in *Solstice*. Generally, Oates treats the two-friends theme without sentimentality. Yet at different times, both Monica and Sheila fulfill a maternal role toward the other. Sheila consoles Monica about her scar, after she is raped, and at the novel's close. Monica nurtures and protects Sheila when she must paint, taking over household chores and urging her to eat properly. In order to manage Sheila's practical affairs, Monica neglects other commitments, however, and becomes a victim of her own mothering instinct by sacrificing her job.

Oates has often portrayed women as victims. *Solstice* touches on the symbiotic female friendship in which the stronger woman manipulates or betrays the acquiescent weaker woman. This feature appeared in Jane Austen's *Emma* (1816), although Emma mended her ways. Doris Lessing's *The Golden Notebook* (1962) also depicted a pair of friends, one aggressive, one sensitive. Other examples of Oates's helpless women in the sister role appear in her novels *Them* (1969) and *Childwold* (1976). In Oates's story "Haunted" (1994), which is about two inseparable adolescent girls, the precocious friend who lures her indecisive "sister" to a forbidden place is ultimately murdered for her rash daring, while the weaker one, the writer, survives to tell the tale.

Unsisterly betrayal, in which a woman echoes the negative views of the patriarchy, occurs in *Solstice* when Jill Starkie supposes that Sheila will not command high fees, because she is only a woman artist. More melodramatic betrayal of woman by woman surfaced in older novels such as Samuel Richardson's *Clarissa* (1747-1748) and Charlotte Brontë's *Jane Eyre* (1847), in which women controlled other women or put them in sexual jeopardy for the benefit of their patriarchal masters. *Solstice* offers subtle hints of this conduct when Sheila lures a timorous Monica into danger at the hands of men in their bar-hopping adventures, and later when she encourages her to drive home with her future rapist, although she also phones to warn against him. On the literal level, the unpredictable Sheila can be menacing. As an emblem of the dark, vehement side of a woman's total being, however, she is a necessity. Oates would argue that female wholeness requires a woman's positive acknowledgment of her own tumultuous powers.

Sources for Further Study

Bender, Eileen T. *Artist in Residence: The Phenomenon of Joyce Carol Oates.* Bloomington: Indiana University Press, 1987. The useful commentary on *Solstice* ties the work to feminist traditions. Contains a primary and a selected secondary bibliography.

Bloom, Harold, ed. *Joyce Carol Oates: Modern Critical Views.* New York: Chelsea House, 1986. Offers only one paragraph on *Solstice*, but these twelve previously published essays consider Oates's female characters in other works.

Creighton, Joanne V. *Joyce Carol Oates: Novels of the Middle Years.* New York: Twayne, 1992. Comments throughout on the feminist outlook and gives a perceptive discussion of *Solstice*. The selected bibliography lists Oates's novels between 1987 and 1990, as well as poetry, plays, stories, and edited works. Includes a bibliography of secondary works and a chronology.

Dean, Sharon L. "Oates's *Solstice*." *The Explicator* 47 (Winter, 1989): 54-56. A brief but valuable examination of the solstice and Ariadne imagery.

Friedman, Ellen G. *Joyce Carol Oates.* New York: Frederick Ungar, 1980. Too early for *Solstice*, but a helpful introduction to Oates's work.

Lercangée, Francine. *Joyce Carol Oates: An Annotated Bibliography.* New York: Garland, 1986. Lists newspaper and magazine reviews of *Solstice*. Contains a preface and annotations by Bruce F. Michelson.

Oates, Joyce Carol. *Conversations with Joyce Carol Oates.* Edited by Lee Milazzo. Jackson: University Press of Mississippi, 1989. Published reviews and interviews from newspapers and magazines, 1969 to 1989. Contains only a brief reference to *Solstice*, but the volume provides a good survey of Oates's views on her reading and writing.

Marcelle Thiébaux

SONG OF SOLOMON

Author: Toni Morrison (1931-   )
Type of work: Novel
Type of plot: Bildungsroman
Time of plot: The early 1930's to the 1960's
Locale: Michigan and Virginia
First published: 1977

> *Principal characters:*
> MACON DEAD, an ambitious African American man
> MACON "MILKMAN" DEAD, Macon and Ruth's son, who is searching for his family's history
> RUTH FOSTER DEAD, the abused wife of Macon and the mother of Milkman, Magdalene "Lena" Dead, and First Corinthians Dead
> PILATE DEAD, Macon's sister and Milkman's aunt, who leads an unconventional life
> REBA DEAD, Pilate's daughter
> HAGAR DEAD, Reba's daughter, who has an obsessive love for Milkman
> GUITAR BAINS, Milkman's best friend

Form and Content

Song of Solomon, winner of the 1978 National Book Critics Circle Award for fiction, is an intricately woven, thematically complex novel that addresses ancestral history, class-versus-race bonds, and sexism. Milkman Dead begins searching for gold and freedom from familial ties; in the process of searching, he discovers his family history and learns about his own tribal power. Although the opening scene occurs in 1931, the characters tell stories that date back to the late nineteenth century, when Milkman's great grandfather, Solomon, flew away from a field in which he worked as a slave, leaving behind twenty-one children and an African myth of flight.

Milkman is born despite his father's efforts to make Ruth perform a home abortion. The problems in Macon and Ruth's marriage stem in part from Macon's discovery of Ruth lying naked in bed beside her father's corpse, kissing his hands. Moreover, Macon denies his wife and two daughters any respect or autonomy, using them instead as gauges of his financial success. Macon defines life as "learning to own things," and the things he owns include his family members.

When Milkman becomes a teenager, Macon tries to involve Milkman in his business of renting property in a low-income district. Macon constantly counts and rattles his keys to the properties he rents, indicating his pride in ownership. Nevertheless, it is during these years that Milkman meets Pilate, the sister from whom Macon was separated for more than twenty years; she inspires Milkman's curiosity about his family history.

Strongly connected to her own history, Pilate wears an earring that is made of a small silver box containing the original piece of paper on which her father first wrote her name. Pilate and Macon were twelve and sixteen when they witnessed their father's murder. While in hiding, fearing that the same people would kill them, they encountered a white man, whom Macon killed, and they discovered several bags of gold near a cave. Pilate and Macon argued over whether to keep the gold. They separated, and when Macon returned to the cave a couple of days later, the gold was missing. He decided that Pilate had stolen it from him.

Instead, she has carried around the bones of her father for more than twenty years. Pilate does not realize that they are her father's bones until the end of the novel. She thinks that they are the bones of the white man whom Macon killed.

After putting together pieces of stories from Pilate and Macon, Milkman travels to Virginia, where he learns that his great grandfather is the subject of folk songs sung by children and folktales told by adults. Milkman realizes his rich history, his ancestral power, and his connection to nature.

Aware of the truth, Milkman returns to Michigan. He shares his stories of the places, songs, and stories dedicated to his people. Milkman tells Pilate that the bones are her father's and takes her to Virginia to bury them on Solomon's Leap, a flat outcropping of rock that overlooks a deep valley. A participant in the search for gold, Guitar, standing in the valley, shoots and kills Pilate, thinking that he has been cheated out of his share of the gold. Empowered by his discovery of his ancestors and himself, Milkman surrenders "to the air" and leaps toward Guitar's arms.

Analysis

In many of Morrison's stories, seeking or denying one's cultural roots is a major concern. Milkman Dead, the young man who is searching for independence in *Song of Solomon*, leaves his home to find gold. Instead, he discovers the intricacies of his family's heritage, a discovery that connects him to life and, ironically, simultaneously frees him from life. Milkman begins to recognize the links between past experiences and present circumstances. Consequently, he develops an understanding of his mother's abnormal sexual behaviors and his father's obsession with owning things.

Ruth is dead inside, frightened of her husband and bored by her life. She searches for some sign of her own purpose and usefulness in life by creating elaborate arrangements to cover a watermark on her mahogany dining table. Much more alarming, she breast-feeds her son until he is old enough to walk and talk, a fact that is discovered by a town gossip who gives the boy the nickname "Milkman," which stays with him for the rest of his life.

Macon's obsession with gaining wealth and owning property is symbolized by his keys, which he counts constantly and fondles frequently in order to gain a sense of security. Macon believes that class elevation will protect him and his family from racism. He marries Ruth because she is a doctor's daughter, not because he loves her. He parades his well-dressed daughters before his lower-class tenants but rushes to guard the girls when a tenant tries to touch them. Furthermore, when Macon collects rent from these tenants, he shows little compassion for the plight of those who have limited funds. Although Morrison does not focus primarily on the class/race relationship in this novel, this concern appears to be a major theme. Rather than seeking truth or taking flight, Macon decides to live by the standards set by his capitalistic society.

Pilate refuses to do the same thing. Her only participation in society is her business of selling homemade wine, the profits from which she, Reba, and Hagar either squander or give away. Milkman says that he cannot identify the source of comfort in her home, a home of so few material comforts. Pilate's daughter, her granddaughter, her bag of bones, and her homemade earring, with which a bird flies away after she dies, seem to be her only treasures.

The flying motif of the story is based on the African myth of enslaved Africans flying back to the African continent. Whether Milkman's great grandfather died, simply left, or actually flew away from the field is undetermined. Yet the empowerment of such a myth and the oppression it suggests—an oppression so strong that it engendered such wishes or such power—attest the Africans' faith in their ability to transcend their subjugation.

The importance of ancestors and history is indicated by Morrison's emphasis on naming. The incorrect, altered, and denied names in the story create distance between the characters and their identities. When Macon's father, who is actually named Jake, registers with the Freedman's Bureau, a government organization that requires the registration of all emancipated slaves, the clerk makes errors that result in the name "Macon Dead" becoming his legal name. Macon's father begins the Dead tradition of blindly choosing the names of female children from the Bible. This is how Pilate, Reba, Hagar, and Milkman's sisters, Magdalene "Lena" Dead and First Corinthians Dead, get their names.

The names in the community are also important indications of the struggle between those in power and those in subjugation. The African Americans in the city decide to refer to the street on which the only "colored doctor" had lived as "Doctor Street," but the city's legislators order that any mail addressed to "Doctor Street" be directed to the dead letter office. In an official notice, the legislators note the street's name as "Mains Avenue and not Doctor Street." Therefore, as "a way to keep their memories alive and please the legislators as well," the African Americans refer to the street as "Not Doctor Street." In a similar way, they rename the Mercy Hospital "No Mercy Hospital," to emphasize the hospital's refusal to treat African American patients.

Context

Morrison's women in this novel are fascinating, and they are necessary to Milkman's maturity and development as well as to the fulfillment of his journey. The magnificent Pilate, juxtaposed with her brother Macon, illustrates for Milkman how far removed his parents and sisters are from natural lives. During Milkman's search in Virginia, women provide significant pieces to the puzzle of his history. An examination of Pilate, Ruth, and Hagar indicates, however, that Morrison wishes to point out that women are not allowed the freedoms that men enjoy in this society.

Milkman's mother and aunt are the two important women in his life. As the daughter of the only African American doctor in town, Ruth is bred to an upper-middle-class existence. She is presented in the novel as the underside of the ideal Southern lady image. She is totally cut off from life, benevolently imprisoned by her father, and spitefully contained by her husband, who marries her because of her class position and despises her for her inherent weakness. Ruth's life is one of uneventful waste. As critic Barbara Christian explains, her life is symbolic of the terror that awaits those women who become the emblem of a man's wealth and class position.

Unlike Ruth, Pilate exists totally outside societal structures, as is indicated by her lack of a navel. Her home, which is not even equipped with electricity, stands outside town. She sees little value in material things and sells homemade wine to provide an income for herself, her daughter, and her granddaughter. Pilate possesses admirable strength and energy, but, in order to grow and survive on her own terms, she has to move outside society.

Hagar's acceptance of European standards of beauty, such as light skin, straight hair, and thin noses, illustrates the ill effects of society's tendency to objectify women who live within it. When Milkman rejects Hagar, she concludes that her woolly hair, unfashionable clothes, and lack of makeup are the reasons. Frantically, she shops for stockings, lipsticks, and other cosmetics, hoping to transform herself into something she imagines Milkman finds acceptable.

By the end of the novel, Milkman recalls and regrets his treatment of Hagar. His experience with her and his exposure to the other women in his life lead him toward the fulfillment he enjoys as his journey closes. Morrison seems to imply that women are necessary participants in the development of males. Meanwhile, male-dominated cultures impede female development.

Sources for Further Study

Christian, Barbara. *Black Feminist Criticism: Perspectives on Black Women Writers.* New York: Pergamon Press, 1985. This compilation of criticism and commentary on literature by African American women addresses literature by Toni Morrison, Alice Walker, Gloria Naylor, and Gwendolyn Brooks. The book is composed of essays that include extensive analyses of individual works as well as examinations of common traits found in this literature. Each essay contains many explanatory notes and lists of sources.

Evans, Mari, ed. *Black Women Writers, 1950-1980.* Garden City, N.Y.: Anchor Press, 1984. This collection of essays includes a section devoted to Toni Morrison, and she contributes to this section. In the essay written by Morrison, she repeats the themes and concerns that dominate her novels.

Morrison, Toni. Interview by Claudia Tate. In *Black Women Writers at Work*, edited by Claudia Tate. New York: Continuum, 1983. This interview serves as an excellent source of information about Morrison's writing habits and techniques. Morrison discusses the beliefs and biases that shape the presentation of her ideas.

Patraka, Vivian, and Louise A. Tilly, eds. *Feminist Re-Visions: What Has Been and*

Might Be. Ann Arbor: Women's Studies Program, University of Michigan, 1983. This collection includes essays that compare narrative techniques. The critics discuss Morrison's use of naming, legend, and myth.

Pryse, Marjorie, and Hortense J. Spillers, eds. *Conjuring: Black Women, Fiction, and Literary Tradition*. Bloomington: Indiana University Press, 1985. The list of contributors to this collection of critical studies includes Claudia Tate, Gloria Hull, Bernard Bell, and others. They look at the literature of African American women, paying close attention to historical circumstances that control and limit the lives of the characters. Specifically, the contributors to this collection of essays discuss social conditions in the United States and the effects these conditions had on the writers and their works.

Jeryl J. Prescott

SONNETS FROM THE PORTUGUESE

Author: Elizabeth Barrett Browning (1806-1861)
Type of work: Poetry
First published: 1850, in *Poems*

Form and Content

Sonnets from the Portuguese chronicles the stages in the romance of poet Elizabeth Barrett Browning and her husband, poet Robert Browning. The theme of the entire sequence is announced in the first sonnet. Reading Theocritus, the speaker muses on her own life and its melancholy. While in the midst of her dismal thoughts, she is pulled from behind by the hair. She thinks it is death, but she is corrected: " 'Not Death, but Love.'" This phrase resounds throughout this entire work, which tells how love entered her life and how the beloved, as if he were truly heaven sent, turned her from darkness and the contemplation of the grave to light, love, and life.

The first stage of the relationship runs from Sonnet 1 through Sonnet 9, in which the speaker says she is not worthy to be loved. She portrays herself as old, confined, solitary, and on the verge of death, and she compares this image of herself to the beloved, who is by contrast young, vibrant, sociable, and full of the world of which he is a part. In this stage, she repeatedly asks him to leave her, although ultimately she acknowledges that they are part of each other. She knows that if he does go, she will never be the same. When God sees her tears, the beloved's tears will have blended with them.

Sonnet 10 marks the change to her acceptance of his love and her transformation. She has become aware that love dispels the darkness; she shines radiantly, with a kind of holiness. Nevertheless, her doubts continue; she asks him to love her only for the sake of love. In Sonnet 16, though, she makes the pronouncement that her "strife" is ended, saying that if he entreats her to enter into a loving relationship, she will "rise" to it, and, in Sonnet 20, she affirms life. The next five sonnets portray the union of their souls and show her as being reborn through their union. She becomes safe and happy. Sonnets 28 and 29 are breathlessly passionate love poems.

Yet the new security and confidence in love is held in balance by the insecurity of giving one's self and life over to it (Sonnets 30 to 36). In Sonnet 30, she doubts that love is real, and in the next, she asks that the beloved calm her fears. Whereas Sonnet 33 sounds a note of complete confidence in the relationship, in Sonnet 35 doubts return.

Sonnets 38 through 42 show that love has won. Homage is paid to the beloved, and the speaker now unqualifiedly opts for love and life. By the time she reaches Sonnet 42, she resolves not to let her past life impinge on her future with her beloved, who is better than she could have dreamed anyone to be. One of the most famous poems in the English language crowns the sequence—Sonnet 43, which begins, "How do I love thee?" After this most complete statement of eternal love, Sonnet 44 offers the sonnets to the beloved, just as he has given her many flowers.

Analysis

Disguised on its publication as a translation from the work of the Portuguese poet Luis Vas de Camoëns, *Sonnets from the Portuguese* consists of forty-four sonnets—fourteen-line poems of rhymed iambic pentameter. The first four lines of an Italian, or Petrarchan, sonnet make a statement that the next four lines prove. These eight lines are the "octave." There follows a "turn" in thought. The next six lines, the "sestet," prove further and conclude the statement. The Petrarchan rhyme scheme is *abba, abba, cde, cde*. Browning often writes her sestets, however, with a rhyme scheme of *cdcdcd*. She has been criticized for not adhering strictly to tradition and for not making her rhymes exact.

Nevertheless, her experiments in slant rhyme, which were previously considered technical faults, show Browning to have a more modern ear, for in the twentieth century, exact rhyme rings more and more false as the century wears on. She has been criticized also for not stopping at the ends of each quatrain or at the end of the octave, and for running the lines on past their traditional stopping points. This technique, however, which is called enjambment, delivers her sonnets from what to a modern ear is the sing-song sound of end-stopped rhyme and allows her greater fluidity of thought.

Browning has been criticized also for writing extremely personal and intense love poetry, with no mask either to protect the writer's emotions or to shield the reader from getting too close. Yet it is in this aspect that the sonnets are brilliant. This first-person point of view is actually that of the poet (the progress of the poems can be read along with the same story in Elizabeth and Robert's letters); it is also the voice of a specific woman speaking to a specific listener, and for a century and a half, readers have known who these people are: a middle-aged and ailing woman poet who has seen in her future only the same feebleness of body and spirit that she experienced earlier, and a younger man, also a poet. They tell a story that contains as much reality as romance. The romance is that her beloved has come to rescue her. The reality is that she sees herself as unrescuable. The story of the *Sonnets from the Portuguese* is the story of that middle-aged, unrescuable, and therefore unlovable (according to her) woman poet who is overwhelmed by love and by life. This is not a series of idealizing love poems, but a cycle of very real expressions of a woman who has suffered not only ill health and disappointment but also disillusionment and loss of hope.

Although the *Sonnets* are autobiographical, they are at the same time consciously crafted works written in one of the most difficult poetic forms by a major artistic voice of her time and place. The controlling idea for the entire sequence is that love is, in fact, stronger than death. She expresses this theme through certain aesthetic moves. After she has established her own melancholy, by mentioning tears and weeping, grief and heavy-heartedness, she shows that the beloved has come between her and her grave (Sonnet 7). She continues, however, to use images of grief to characterize herself, and it is in her grief and world-weariness more than anything that she claims she is unworthy of his love (Sonnet 8). She contrasts herself to him, usually using royal images to portray him, but never portraying him as concretely as she portrays herself. She shows herself to be an agent of decay: "I will not soil thy purple with my dust,/ Nor breathe my poison on thy Venice-glass" (Sonnet 9). Venetian glass was known to shatter when it came in contact with poisoned liquids.

When she speaks of the union of souls, however, the poet uses images of light and fire, flashing flames, a "golden throne" (Sonnet 12), "wings" that "break into fire" (Sonnet 22). These images gain even more brilliance because much of the imagery of the sonnets is dark, of dust and of enclosure. Yet images of light and life prevail, since love has created them. Whereas she has characterized her earlier despondency as a life that is colorless because tears have faded it, in the last sonnet she asks the beloved to "keep the colors [of the flowers] true."

Just as she compares herself to her beloved, darkness to light, and death to life, she compares past to future. She repeatedly shows that before she met him, she had lost her faith in living; she looked to God for strength to go on, but she lived in a kind of bleak despair that had no vision of a future. His love changes the entire direction of her life. She is uplifted to the point of being able to see that ever so much as the human heart thinks it wants, God gives more than one can imagine; and her beloved is more than she ever thought to pray for. She had reconciled herself to seek her future in heaven, but his love draws her back from the grave.

In Sonnet 43, many of the themes of the sequence come together. This is Browning's most famous work and one of the most famous poems in the English language. "How do I love thee? Let me count the ways" has captured the hearts of readers for almost 150 years. It is written in much more abstract terms than is the rest of the sequence, but the poems that have come before it have in a sense already defined what one reads here. For example, she has already written of souls in connections with light and ascent, so when she writes here of "the depth and breadth and height/ My soul can reach," one has already read of the expansiveness of the soul in love. She has also written over and over again about her grief and how she has thought herself destined for only the grave, so the reader should already understand about "the passions put to use/ In my old griefs." The last two lines of this sonnet pull the entire sequence together: "and, if God choose,/ I shall but love thee better after death." In the first instance, the beloved has turned her away from death to life in this world. In doing so, he has turned her away from a contemplation of heaven in an afterlife. It becomes this very love that inspires her back toward God, toward a desire for eternity. Here, however, it is not an eternity that is longed for only for the sake of its being something better than this life. It is an eternity in which temporal love has itself become eternal.

Sonnets from the Portuguese is an enduring record of the love of one individual for another and, through that love, of the restoration of hope and the enhancement of the will to live. The sequence is captivating because in it, a real female voice writes about her most private feelings of love. At first, one thinks one is hearing Shakespeare or Petrarch, but then one realizes that Browning has dropped the conventional metaphors and masks. In fact, she goes so far as hardly to create an image of the beloved at all. One hears the first-person "I," and, as much as one thinks one ought to say that it is her poetic persona, one knows that it is the voice of Elizabeth Barrett Browning.

Context

Like her female predecessors of the French and Italian Renaissance, and like Mary Wroth in the English Renaissance, in her pastoral sonnet cycle *Pamphilia to Amphilanthus* (1621), in *Sonnets from the Portuguese*, Browning inserts the female voice into the Petrarchan sonnet tradition. She assumes the stance of the silent Laura hearing Petrarch, the silent Catarina hearing Camoës, but she herself speaks of ideal love. This voice is her own, and the idealized beloved is her very real husband. Even though one hears only her voice, one can imagine the listener. In this way, Browning's sonnets border on crossing with the form her husband perfected in such poems as "My Last Duchess": the dramatic monologue, in which a specific speaker speaks to a specific listener in a specific situation. Moreover, the speaker does not stylize herself as the male Petrarchan voice stylizes himself and his beloved. She changes the tradition also by expressing concerns about her family connections.

Sonnets from the Portuguese marks Browning's breaking off from the Romantic tradition upon which her poetics rests, the style of her predecessors L. E. L. and Felicia Hemans. The masks drop away, the literary conventions transform, and Browning writes in a bold "I." Influenced by Shakespeare, John Milton, and William Wordsworth in their use of the sonnet form, she was most likely also aware of Charlotte Smith's *Elegiac Sonnets* (1787) as well as the work of the numerous other women poets of the Romantic and early Victorian eras.

In the nineteenth century, she was held in higher repute than was her husband. She had been considered, in fact, for the laureateship. Not until the twentieth century was she taken less seriously. After the widespread popularity of the play *The Barretts of Wimpole Street*, she came to be seen solely as the invalid poetess who had been perishing in her enclosed room, where she had been locked by her tyrannical father until she was rescued by the dashing Robert. She became known only for her love poetry throughout most of the twentieth century. In the 1970's, feminist critics brought back to light her social and political works, such as the verse narrative *Aurora Leigh* and "The Cry of the Children." Her poetic achievement is currently being reassessed in accord with new ways of reading women poets and in accord with contemporary assessments of writers. Her aesthetic accomplishments and her social and political themes give her a significant place in Victorian poetry.

Sources for Further Study

Cooper, Helen. *Elizabeth Barrett Browning: Woman and Artist*. Chapel Hill: University of North Carolina Press, 1988. Valuable for close readings of Browning's poems.

Falk, Alice. "Elizabeth Barrett Browning and Her Prometheuses: Self-Will and a Woman Poet." *Tulsa Studies in Women's Literature* 7, no. 1 (Spring, 1988): 69-85. Discusses Browning's translations of Aeschylus and her familiarity with and use of classical images.

Forster, Margaret. *Elizabeth Barrett Browning: A Biography*. New York: Doubleday, 1989. Shows Mary Barrett, Elizabeth's mother, to have been the shaping influence in her education. Revises the myth of Elizabeth's father as the tyrant of Wimpole Street.

Leighton, Angela. *Elizabeth Barrett Browning*. Bloomington: Indiana University Press, 1986. A feminist reevaluation of Browning's life and works that also examines the Browning myth. Discusses the poet in relation to her male predecessors.

Mermin, Dorothy. *Elizabeth Barrett Browning: The Origins of a New Poetry*. Chicago: University of Chicago Press, 1989. Mermin claims that Browning originated a female tradition in Victorian poetry. She draws heavily on Browning's earlier diary and numerous letters. Extensive notes and bibliography.

_____ . "The Female Poet and the Embarrassed Reader: Elizabeth Barrett Browning's *Sonnets from the Portuguese*." *ELH* 48, no. 2 (Summer, 1981): 351-367. Mermin makes the case for the "embarrassed reader" who is forced to be an eavesdropper; who, aware of the voice in the male sonnet tradition, hears Browning's "awkward, mawkish, and indecently personal" voice and is embarrassed.

Paul, Sarah. "Strategic Self-Centering and the Female Narrator: Elizabeth Barrett Browning's *Sonnets from the Portuguese*." *Browning Institute Studies* 17 (1989): 75-91. Sees the speaker in the *Sonnets* as covertly empowering herself. Includes an interesting discussion of reversals of gender roles.

Radley, Virginia L. *Elizabeth Barrett Browning*. New York: Twayne, 1972. Gives a short biography and studies each stage of Browning's work, including a chapter on the *Sonnets from the Portuguese*. Includes a good but dated annotated bibliography.

Stephenson, Glennis. *Elizabeth Barrett Browning and the Poetry of Love*. Ann Arbor, Mich.: UMI Research Press, 1989. Begins by discussing Browning's immediate predecessors, then examines her early ballads and lyrics, *Lady Geraldine's Courtship*, *Sonnets from the Portuguese*, *Aurora Leigh*, and *Last Poems*. Discussion of the sonnets considers how the female poet enters into a male poetic tradition, specifically examining the role of distance in the sonnet tradition and Browning's use of it as well as the replacement by Browning of predominantly visual images with predominantly "tactual" images.

Taplin, Gardner. *The Life of Elizabeth Barrett Browning*. Hamden, Conn.: Archon Books, 1970. Includes discussion of *Sonnets from the Portuguese*.

Donna G. Berliner

A SOR JUANA ANTHOLOGY

Author: Sor Juana Inés de la Cruz (1651?-1695)
Type of work: Essays and poetry
First published: 1988

Form and Content

A *Sor Juana Anthology* is a collection of some of the best poetry of Sor Juana Inés de la Cruz, along with a sample of her poetic drama and prose, selected by Mexican poet and essayist Octavio Paz and translator Alan S. Trueblood. Since her poetry is the heart of her achievement, it forms the major part of the anthology, divided to indicate general themes and type of verse: convent and court, vicarious love, music, divine love, self and the world, lighter pieces, and festive worship (*villancicos*). Sor Juana's work clearly places her among Spanish poets of the Baroque in the tradition of Luis de Góngora and Pedro Calderón de la Barca. Her lyrical poetry was praised for its ingenious use of conventional forms: decorative and exotic imagery, symbolism, hyperbole, antithesis, paradox, and references to philosophy, science, and other areas of learning. The modern reader, however, may occasionally sense an individual voice behind the conventions and appreciate glimpses of Sor Juana's struggles to express herself artistically under the constraints of being a woman in seventeenth century Mexico.

Sor Juana's poetic drama is exemplified by excerpts from *El divino Narciso* (c. 1680; *The Divine Narcissus*, 1945), a series of allegorical tableaux in which human nature reveals her quest of Christ in the form of Narcissus. As an *auto sacramental* (one-act play celebrating the Eucharist), it is considered a masterpiece.

"First Dream" (1692), Sor Juana's longest and most important poem, is included in its entirety and expresses the search for knowledge that ultimately ends in disillusionment. Using the account of a dream remembered during waking hours, Sor Juana focuses on the question of human aspiration for knowledge and understanding of the world. She demonstrates a wide range of scholarship herself, including philosophical and literary illusions, and incorporates the various images of sleep that would have been well known by her audience: contrast of night and day, sleep as death and as having dominion over human beings, and the deceptiveness of dreams.

At the end of the anthology, Sor Juana's famous justification of her pursuit of knowledge, "The Reply to Sor Philothea" (1691), is included. Upon this famous manuscript rests much of Sor Juana's reputation as a feminist. After recognizing her own overpowering desire to know and indicating how she learns not only from books but also from everyday life, she argues the case for allowing women to study. The form shows, first of all, the conventions of her time, including formulas of humility and Latin citations as well as references to Scripture. She uses scholastic argumentation and demonstrates her ability to reveal the interrelated character of fields of study. Taking information from various sources, Sor Juana compiles her argument with skill and astuteness, justifying her studies as a means of understanding Scripture better. To the criticism that she should study more sacred works, she readily agrees—although her letter reveals that she already knows much about the Bible and religious writers. Her questioning, searching mind is apparent in her careful and well-formulated argument. It is clear that she was often misunderstood—and opposed—within her convent community because of her need to study and her belief that women, like men, should be allowed full intellectual development.

Analysis

This anthology illustrates the range of poetry that Sor Juana cultivated, including occasional verse (for special occasions and poetry contests), love poetry, religious verses (especially *villancicos*), and humorous poetry. Critics have found it impossible to date most of this work since the originals have been lost and her style does not evolve. From the beginning, Sor Juana's verse shows the wit, polish, and learning expected in the Baroque period. Her work demonstrates a sense of form and proportion as well as a control of classical references and the metaphorical imagery of her time: exotic material, gems, fragrances, and creatures, often with symbolic meaning. The Baroque use of paradox, hyperbole, antithesis, repetition, and scholarly logic and argument characterize her work. In accordance with the conventions of the time, her poems are not personal revelations but rather a demonstration of poetic skill. With the forms dictated by convention, her individual talent emerges through the ingenious use of well-known images or in her particular tone or emphasis.

A number of her poems touch on conventional aspects of love, including the idealization of the beloved, the pain of separation and rejection, the feelings of distant and pure love, and the irrational effects of love. Some critics have observed that Sor Juana's perspective at times seems more masculine than feminine, that poetry addressed to a woman is often more intense than that addressed to shadowy male figures named Silvio or Fabio. One explanation notes that Sor Juana's early life lacked strong male figures; however, a more probable explanation is that the poetic tradition she was following was exclusively masculine—there was no appropriate feminine language to celebrate love. As an intellectual, she availed herself of the conventional forms.

In describing her world, Sor Juana shows great skill in portraiture with well-crafted variations to present the interplay between portrait and subject. One poem disavows a portrait of herself as flattery, reflecting the Baroque attitude toward the vanity and illusion of life. The poem ends with a conventional idea: "all efforts fail and in the end/ a body goes to dust, to shade, to nought."

Writing was a central part of Sor Juana's life and identity, and this fact is reflected in poems that identify her with her pen. Her pen expresses the pain of separation with sad, black-colored pen strokes, and words of mourning become "black tears." A frequent wordplay, made possible by the fact that *pluma* in Spanish is both pen and feather, is noted in the introductory materials, "Pluma" is a synecdoche for wing, contributing an extra dimension to the image of bold flight so important to Sor Juana. "First Dream," for example, focuses on intellectual striving, or what translator Trueblood calls "unrepentant boldness," associated with the Greek myth of Phaëthon and his failed flight in his father Helios' chariot.

Baroque poetry is characterized by its exoticism and its opulence in description. In Sor Juana's poetry, one finds references to her own land, exotic to the Europeans. One poem refers to a sorcerer's brew of "the herb-doctors of my country." In a *villancico* for the feast of the Assumption, she introduces the tocotín, a lively Aztec dance, with accompanying Nahuatl words. In others, she focuses on Africa, incorporating rhythmic African words in a refrain or presenting "two Guinean queens/ with faces of jet." The pride of her countrywomen shines forth in verses such as these: "Black is the Bride,/ the Sun scorches her face./ Though she calls herself black,/ her blackness, she shall say,/ makes her the more comely."

In other poems, Sor Juana addresses her personal situation through a direct confrontation with the price of her intellectual distinction. The most famous poses this question: "World, in hounding me what do you gain?/ How can it harm you if I choose, astutely,/ rather to stock my mind with things of beauty,/ than waste its stock on every beauty's claim?" She is also acutely aware of the role that her gender plays in the praise of her work, as well as in its criticism. In an unfinished poem, she writes of her aspirations and failures. Rationally considering the situation, she wonders if being a woman has not made European readers too quick to praise her: "Might it be the surprise of my sex/ that explains why you are willing/ to allow an unusual case/ to pass itself off as perfection?" Praised or criticized, she found herself in the difficult position of being an anomaly.

Context

Although Sor Juana is recognized today as an outstanding poet of Mexico's colonial period, her work reflects the life of an intelligent woman who was not nurtured in this endeavor by her seventeenth century environment. Not allowed to attend the university, she was essentially self-taught, and her work is the product of a searching mind which enjoyed scholarly activity. The very existence of this work is a great accomplishment.

In conflict with society's expectations of a woman of her time, Sor Juana nevertheless found a way to develop her talent. Since education was a prerogative of the Catholic church, she entered the convent of Santa Paula, of the Hieronymite Order, in 1669. Her religious duties seem to have been compatible with a very active scholastic life. Sometimes celebrated as an early feminist, Sor Juana gave voice to the idea that women did not need to remain ignorant. A *villancico* for the Saint's Day of Catherine of Alexandria (1691) uses the humorous tone of the common people in telling the story of Catherine, who "knew a lot, so they say,/ though she *was* female." Fortunately, this did not present a problem: "The makings of sainthood/ was in her, they say;/ even knowing so much/ didn't get in her way." Humor was used again in her famous poem on the double standard ("Silly, you men—so very adept/ at wrongly faulting womankind"), in which she points out that men criticize women regardless of how they act: If they spurn men, they are ungrateful; if they succumb to their advances, they are lewd.

Sor Juana's decision regarding marriage may have been influenced by the fact that she was illegitimate and had no dowry. It is clear, however, that her greatest passion was intellectual, and her choice of the convent can be seen in that light. As she argues in "The Reply to Sor Philothea," she had a vocation which could not be denied. Her explanation and defense of learning are written all the more frankly as she did not expect the letter to be published. Continued opposition within her community and as the loss of the protective support of a patron in Mexico made Sor Juana's life more difficult after the publication of "The Reply to Sor Philothea." In 1692, with the pressures of hunger riots and the resulting demands for penitential acts, she was increasingly isolated and in 1693 wrote a document of repentance herself. In the last two years of her life, she wrote nothing. Nevertheless, readers discovering her work today find a body of lyric poetry that confirms her stature as an important poet of the seventeenth century, as well as writings, including "The Reply to Sor Philothea," which are testament to a strong woman's need to understand her world and give expression to her discoveries.

Sources for Further Study

Flynn, Gerard. *Sor Juana Inés de la Cruz.* Boston: Twayne, 1971. A readable introduction to the life of Sor Juana and her work. Selections of her poetry and both secular and religious drama are reviewed, with quotations from the texts. (English translations are provided.) Includes helpful explanatory notes to each chapter and a bibliography with mainly Spanish-language sources.

Merrim, Stephanie, ed. *Feminist Perspectives on Sor Juana Inés de la Cruz.* Detroit: Wayne State University Press, 1991. Eight articles explore from a feminist perspective each of the genres in which Sor Juana wrote, also discussing her cultural climate and personal pressures. Of particular interest are the introductory essay on key issues in Sor Juana criticism and readings of "First Dream," "The Reply to Sor Philothea," and selected love poetry. Offers a brief bibliography, including English editions of her work, and a chronology.

Montross, Constance M. *Virtue or Vice? Sor Juana's Use of Thomistic Thought.* Washington, D.C.: University Press of America, 1981. Examines Sor Juana's use of Scholastic doctrine and methodology, specifically the ideas of Saint Thomas Aquinas. The author analyzes the combination of belief and questioning in "First Dream" and "The Reply to Sor Philothea." An extensive bibliography is provided, as well as the full Spanish text of "First Dream."

Paz, Octavio, ed. *Mexican Poetry: An Anthology.* Translated by Samuel Beckett. Reprint. New York: Grove Press, 1985. Complements Paz's *Sor Juana: Or, The Traps of Faith* with a discussion in the introduction of Sor Juana's place in the history of Mexican poetry. The anthology includes translations of twelve of her poems.

_____. *Sor Juana: Or, The Traps of Faith.* Translated by Margaret Sayers Peden. Cambridge, Mass.: Harvard University Press, 1988. An important biography of Sor Juana emphasizing her uniqueness as a poet and her struggle for an intellectual and creative life. Particular focus is on the key questions of why she entered a convent and why she renounced learning at the end of her life. Considers historical settings and traditions in some detail, with illustrations including portraits of Sor Juana. A helpful listing of Spanish literary terms is provided.

Royer, Fanchón. *The Tenth Muse: Sor Juana Inés de la Cruz*. Paterson, N.J.: St. Anthony Guild Press, 1952. A good introductory source. Each chapter begins with a translated quote from Sor Juana's work and presents the basic biographical facts along with interpretive commentary. The appendix contains selected poems in Spanish, as well as a short bibliography of Spanish-language sources.

Susan L. Piepke

SPEEDBOAT

Author: Renata Adler (1938-   )
Type of work: Novel
Type of plot: Picaresque
Time of plot: The 1970's
Locale: New York City
First published: 1976

>   *Principal characters:*
>   JEN FAIN, a reporter who is detached and disillusioned
>   WILL, a recently divorced lawyer and one of Jen's several lovers
>   JIM, an Atlanta lawyer and one of Jen's lovers
>   ALDO, another of Jen's lovers, a writer
>   VLAD, NED, and KATE, representative members of Jen's circle

Form and Content

Speedboat is Renata Adler's version of what nineteenth century novelist Anthony Trollope called "The Way We Live Now," though in Adler's case the "way" and the "we" are given a decidedly female spin. The speedboat of her title, though it figures in only one brief scene, or cinematic take, suggests at least two of the most salient qualities of this impressive first novel and its female narrator-protagonist: the fast pace and a seeming purposelessness. "Speedboat" is also the title of one of the novel's seven sections, each of which is further divided into numerous subsections that range in length from a single line up to, on rare occasions, two pages (half a page is the norm). The first, "Castling," sets the stage for what follows. It begins far beyond any conventional definition of *in media res.* The voice is personal yet detached, the pace not so much frenetic (a word which suggests a display of emotional intensity utterly foreign to Adler's purpose) as rapid, a succession of quick cinematic cuts between subsections and at times within them. The overall effect—helped along by the introduction of pronouns without referents, characters named but never developed and in fact rarely even sketched, and brief anecdotes of teasingly allegorical significance—is to propel the reader quickly, almost superficially, over a vaguely defined period in the life of Jen Fain. Jen appears both powerless to direct her course and yet determined to keep her narrative and her life as close to the surface as possible, where friction can be minimized.

Each of these inserted, largely self-contained narratives is a story in miniature. There is the elderly woman killed by the Doberman pinscher that had been her sole companion for many years; an essay on Evel Knievel's attempt to jump over the Grand Canyon on his motorcycle, a stunt that he intended to fail (though not quite in the way that it did); a pointed satire on the City University of New York; and the pleasure ride aboard the Italian tycoon's speedboat that leaves the American wife from Malibu with a broken back. The latter is a little allegory for the times, its blackly humorous moral carefully appended: "But violent things are always happening to the very rich, and to the poor, of course. Freak accidents befall the middle classes in their midst." Jen has already learned the lesson, scaling back her life and her narrative accordingly.

As she says, "Things have changed very much, several times, since I grew up, and, like everyone in New York except the intellectuals, I have lived several lives and still live one of them." Jen exists in a manner similar to this entirely typical sentence of hers, somewhere between deadpan and death-in-life. Against the backdrop of such events as the Watergate affair, she narrates her life and times from a shifting present, looking back when necessary to jobs and lovers she has (or has had) and countries she visits (or has visited), mainly on assignment. She rewrites grant proposals, writes political speeches (without ever indicating that she agrees or disagrees with the political positions in them), teaches part time ("by mistake"), and commutes to Washington, D.C., for meetings of the House Select Committee on Private and Institutional Corruption. Chiefly she works as a reporter. In the 1960's, she covered the Civil Rights movement and the conflict in the Mideast; now she writes articles, reviews, and a gossip column for the *Standard Evening Sun*, a tabloid. All of this information is narrated in a way that suggests a certain bewilderment on Jen's part, a strategic retreat into emotional repression. Although filled with events, people, and travel, her narrative offers little evidence that Jen's story or her life is either progressing or deepening, moving steadily and inexorably toward climax and resolution. At novel's end, she is fired from her job and learns that she is pregnant—events that Jen narrates with no more or less intensity than any others.

Analysis

Whether Jen will have the baby and whether she will tell Jim that he is the father are questions that neither Jen nor Adler try to answer. Neither are they questions about which the novel tries to interest the reader overmuch, at least directly. In this postmodern retelling of the early cliffhanger *The Perils of Pauline*, the action is not in conventional plot and/or in carefully defined moral codes. The novel's opening section, enigmatically entitled "Castling," makes that fact abundantly clear. Suggesting "casting off," "casting away," flycasting, and a chess move involving a castle (rook) and king, the word also implies a castle, city, or self under siege, a situation in which certain conventions, possibilities, and freedoms no longer apply. Yet "castling" also refers to the second or third swarm to leave a hive in season (a definition appropriate to the novel's overall structure) and, more portentously in the light of Jen's own feelings of inadequacy and her pregnancy, to what the Oxford English Dictionary calls "the offspring of an untimely birth, an abortion." Whether this particular meaning should be read in terms of Jen's being pregnant or her belonging to a post-Hemingway "lost generation" is moot. Finally, however, the anachronistic word "castling" will recall for many readers the more familiar word "quisling," or traitor. This definition is appropriate to *Speedboat* because Jen—in her "flat" style, quick cuts, and handling of all material as "found objects" and "short-lived phenomena" to be treated in terms of equivalence—betrays (that is, reveals) both herself and the group linked by age, class, and education that she represents.

Speedboat is therefore both the highly personal story of a single woman and more a broadly based look at an entire segment of contemporary society. Characteristics of that society are incorporated into a novel whose very style and structure are the narrative equivalents of the City University's open admissions policy. Jen's interest in the Broadway Junction, with its "nine crisscrossing, overlapping elevated tracks," is mirrored in the multiplicity of intersecting narrative lines, while Jen's comparison of her mind to a tenement in which only "some elevators work" offers the reader at least one way to approach a text that gives the appearance of being both overfull and disjointed. *Speedboat* is a novel in the form of an autobiography, but one in a uniquely contemporary mode—not so much developing, in terms of plot and character, as thickening by means of what one of her professors calls "synonym and contexture."

One of the most salient characteristics of *Speedboat* is the pressure experienced in every sentence as it lays claim to the reader's attention, a pressure largely missing from novels that rely on plot to maintain interest. Another is a discontinuity underscored by markers such as "Now there's this" or "And now I'm here." Riskiest of all is the leveling of experience that, while long recognized as a danger in any modern democracy, has become especially pronounced in the postindustrial period that Adler mimics and mines so effectively. For the writer, whether Adler or Jen Fain, the risk is comparable to the "pitch fatigue" experienced by one of Jen's many acquaintances, the composer who has abandoned his experiments in atonality and begun writing "tunes." Jen's and Adler's flat style is neither atonal nor melodic. Instead, it is minimalist and as such is more varied than it seems. In *Speedboat*, the matter-of-fact often slides imperceptibly into the freakish and dreamlike as a recognizable New York inches its way toward a violent, futuristic cityscape through prose which echoes that of another New York writer, Donald Barthelme: "When Dan rode his bicycle over a cliff, we all behaved in characteristic ways." Like Barthelme, Adler writes under the pressure not of a deadline but of saying things that are both "true" and "interesting," while at the same time maintaining a studied distance, an air of wised-up disbelief that characterizes both Jen and her group. "We are thirty-five," she notes, well-educated, financially well-off, "highly urban and ambitious people . . . trying to live some semblance of decent lives." Yet in this last regard, they are both unsuccessful and more especially unprepared.

Context

Winner of the Ernest Hemingway Award for the best first novel of 1976 and runner-up for the National Book Critics Circle Award for fiction, losing by a single vote to John Gardner's *October Light*. Since then, *Speedboat* has not fared nearly so well with either mainstream or feminist critics. No articles on *Speedboat* or any of Adler's work, including her novel *Pitch Dark* (1983), have appeared in scholarly journals, and the standard literary histories fail to include her except for mere mentions. A half-paragraph in the "Women's Literature" chapter of the *Harvard Guide to Contemporary American Writing* does address *Speedboat*, but it is discussed as a novel by a woman rather than as a novel about the female experience. In addition, a brief discussion of *Speedboat* as a work of literary minimalism is found in Frederick Karl's *American Fictions, 1940-1980: A Comprehensive and Critical Evaluation* (1983).

Perversely enough, one of the longest discussions of Adler's work is the one that proves most obtuse on the very issue of women's writing. Joseph Epstein's reading of Adler and Joan Didion in his condescendingly titled "The Sunshine Girls" focuses on their disjunctive style and unearned pessimism, which Epstein compares unfavorably with the "heroic" pessimism of Friedrich Nietzsche and Arthur Schopenhauer. Like *Pitch Dark*, *Speedboat* bears comparison with and is indebted to certain male literary models, especially the French New Novel, and it even comprises an odd updating of Walt Whitman's "I Hear America Singing."

Speedboat, however, is more than a novel in a contemporary mode and idiom. It is also and more specifically about the life of a contemporary woman of a certain background and situation: educated, intelligent, professional. As such, it strikes a responsive chord in much the same way that, as Jen Fain describes, a woman in the audience responds to the "maniac laughter" with which the singer used to end "Je ne suis pas folle" with some maniac laughter of her own. Were she a little more prolific, a little less postmodern, a bit more polemical and politically correct, or perhaps a bit less intent on telling all the truth but telling it "slant" (like Emily Dickinson), Adler might have received the kind of critical and especially feminist attention that her complex and uncompromising work deserves.

Sources for Further Study

Adler, Renata. *Toward a Radical Middle: Fourteen Pieces of Reporting and Criticism.* New York: Random House, 1970. The essays collected here and more especially the introduction provide valuable background for reading *Speedboat* in relation to Adler's politics, generation, and experiences as a reporter.

Epstein, Joseph. "The Sunshine Girls." *Commentary* 77 (June, 1984): 62-67. In this review of Adler's *Pitch Dark* and Joan Didion's *Democracy* (1984), Epstein surveys the two writers' careers, criticizing both for their fragmented narratives and pessimism.

Hardwick, Elizabeth. "Sense of the Present." *New York Review of Books*, November 25, 1976, 3-4, 6. Hardwick argues that *Speedboat* combines reportage, autobiography, and "deadly satire." The narrator's detachment and "disembodiment" is so severe and her alienation so predictable as to weaken "her authority as a witness."

Karl, Frederick R. *American Fictions, 1940-1980: A Comprehensive and Critical Evaluation.* New York: Harper & Row, 1983. Karl discusses *Speedboat* in his chapter on minimalist writers (Donald Barthelme, Elizabeth Hardwick, Jerzy Kosinski, Susan Sontag et al.) but not in his chapter "The Female Experience."

Kornbluth, Jesse. "The Quirky Brilliance of Renata Adler." *New York* 16 (December 12, 1983): 34-40. Although occasioned by the publication of *Pitch Dark*, Kornbluth's profile offers valuable insights into Adler's life, about whom very little is known outside New York's cultural circle.

Saltzman, Arthur M. *The Novel in the Balance*. Columbia: University of South Carolina Press, 1993. Although he faults the novel for coming down "to a series of elliptical allegories of authorial fecklessness," Saltzman praises *Speedboat* for the way it balances "maximalist evidentiary procedures and minimalist concentration."

Todd, Richard. Review of *Speedboat*. *Atlantic Monthly* 238 (October, 1976): 112-114. Argues that the atmosphere of *Speedboat* is existential but that its sensibility is not—is, in fact, free from stock response of any kind. Adler "is a spare, self-possessed writer who can do more in an aphoristic aside than many writers can do with a chapter."

Towers, Robert. Review of *Speedboat*. *The New York Times Book Review*, September 26, 1976, 6-7. Towers finds the absence of plot a problem, but he claims that the novel is redeemed by the narrator's reports of and reflections on the contemporary phenomena immediately around her. Unlike the French New Novels, *Speedboat* "is neither boring nor dehumanized."

Robert A. Morace